92% 93% 93% 94%

eText | Dynamic Study Modules | Personal inventory assessment | Study Plan

% of students who found learning tool helpful

Dynamic Study Modules help students study chapter topics effectively on their own by continuously assessing their **knowledge application** and performance in real time. These are available as graded assignments prior to class, and accessible on smartphones, tablets, and computers.

Pearson eText enhances student learning—both in and outside the classroom. Take notes, highlight, and bookmark important content. Accessible anytime, anywhere via MyLab or the app.

86%
of students would tell their instructor to keep using MyLab Management

The **MyLab Gradebook** offers an easy way for students and instructors to view course performance. Item Analysis allows instructors to quickly see trends by analyzing details like the number of students who answered correctly/incorrectly, time on task, and median time spend on a question by question basis. And because it's correlated with the AACSB Standards, instructors can track students' progress toward outcomes that the organization has deemed important in preparing students to be **leaders.**

"I was able to find myself actually learning at home rather than memorizing things for a class."
— Katherine Vicente, Student at County College of Morris

For additional details visit: www.pearson.com/mylab/management

EDITION **15**

Global Edition

Modern Management

CONCEPTS AND SKILLS

Samuel C. Certo
Emeritus Dean and Steinmetz Professor of Management

Roy E. Crummer Graduate School of Business
Rollins College

S. Trevis Certo
Jerry B. and Mary Anne Chapman Professor of Business

W. P. Carey School of Business
Arizona State University

Pearson

Harlow, England • London • New York • Boston • San Francisco • Toronto • Sydney • Dubai • Singapore • Hong Kong
Tokyo • Seoul • Taipei • New Delhi • Cape Town • Sao Paulo • Mexico City • Madrid • Amsterdam • Munich • Paris • Milan

Vice President, Business, Economics, and UK Courseware: Donna Battista
Director of Portfolio Management: Stephanie Wall
Senior Portfolio Manager: Kris Ellis-Levy
Development Editor: Nancy Lamm
Editorial Assistant: Hannah Lamarre
Content Producer, Global Edition: Nikhil Rakshit
Assistant Acquisitions Editor, Global Edition: Rosemary Iles
Senior Project Editor, Global Edition: Daniel Luiz
Manager, Media Production, Global Edition: Gargi Banerjee
Manufacturing Controller, Production, Global Edition: Caterina Pellegrino
Vice President, Product Marketing: Roxanne McCarley
Senior Product Marketer: Becky Brown
Product Marketing Assistant: Marianela Silvestri
Manager of Field Marketing, Business Publishing: Adam Goldstein
Field Marketing Manager: Nicole Price

Vice President, Production and Digital Studio, Arts and Business: Etain O'Dea
Director of Production, Business: Jeff Holcomb
Managing Producer, Business: Melissa Feimer
Content Producer: Claudia Fernandes
Operations Specialist: Carol Melville
Design Lead: Kathryn Foot
Manager, Learning Tools: Brian Surette
Content Developer, Learning Tools: Lindsey Sloan
Managing Producer, Digital Studio, Business MyLabs: Ashley Santora
Managing Producer, Digital Studio, Arts and Business: Diane Lombardo
Digital Studio Producer: Monique Lawrence
Digital Studio Producer: Alana Coles
Project Management: Thistle Hill Publishing Services
Composition: Cenveo® Publisher Services
Interior: Cenveo® Publisher Services
Cover Art: alice-photo/Shutterstock
Cover Design: Lumina Datamatics, Inc.

Microsoft and/or its respective suppliers make no representations about the suitability of the information contained in the documents and related graphics published as part of the services for any purpose. All such documents and related graphics are provided "as is" without warranty of any kind. Microsoft and/or its respective suppliers hereby disclaim all warranties and conditions with regard to this information, including all warranties and conditions of merchantability, whether express, implied or statutory, fitness for a particular purpose, title and non-infringement. In no event shall Microsoft and/or its respective suppliers be liable for any special, indirect or consequential damages or any damages whatsoever resulting from loss of use, data or profits, whether in an action of contract, negligence or other tortious action, arising out of or in connection with the use or performance of information available from the services.

The documents and related graphics contained herein could include technical inaccuracies or typographical errors. Changes are periodically added to the information herein. Microsoft and/or its respective suppliers may make improvements and/or changes in the product(s) and/or the program(s) described herein at any time. Partial screen shots may be viewed in full within the software version specified.

Microsoft® and Windows® are registered trademarks of the Microsoft Corporation in the U.S.A. and other countries. This book is not sponsored or endorsed by or affiliated with the Microsoft Corporation.

Pearson Education Limited
KAO Two
KAO Park
Harlow
CM17 9NA
United Kingdom.

and Associated Companies throughout the world

Visit us on the World Wide Web at: www.pearsonglobaleditions.com

ISBN 10: 1-292-26519-1
ISBN 13: 978-1-292-26519-3

British Library Cataloguing-in-Publication Data
A catalogue record for this book is available from the British Library.

2020 2019 2018
10 9 8 7 6 5 4 3 2 1

Typeset in Times LT Pro-Roman by Cenveo® Publisher Services

Printed and bound by Vivar, Malaysia.

Brief Contents

Contents

PART 4
Organizing

PART 5
Influencing

About the Authors

Dr. Samuel C. Certo is presently Emeritus Dean and Steinmetz Professor of Management at the Roy E. Crummer Graduate School of Business at Rollins College. Over his career, Dr. Certo has received many prestigious awards, including the Award for Innovative Teaching from the Southern Business Association, the Instructional Innovation Award granted by the Decision Sciences Institute, and the Charles A. Welsh Memorial Award for outstanding teaching. He has also received the Bornstein and Cornell Awards for teaching and global recognition of his scholarship.

Dr. Certo has also authored or co-authored several highly regarded textbooks, including *Modern Management: Concepts and Skills*, *Strategic Management: Concepts and Applications*, and *Supervision: Concepts and Applications*. His textbooks have been translated into several languages for distribution throughout the world.

His newest popular-market book, *Chasing Wisdom: Finding Everyday Leadership in Business and Life*, recommends combining business and biblical principles to build successful organizations. His podcast program emphasizing the chasing wisdom concept is available on iTunes. The number of its listeners is growing, and it now has listeners in over 200 countries.

A past chairperson of the Management Education and Development Division of the Academy of Management, he has had the honor of being presented with the group's Excellence in Leadership Award. Dr. Certo has also served as president of the Association for Business Simulation and Experiential Learning, an associate editor for *Simulation and Games*, and as a review board member of the *Academy of Management Review*. His consulting experience has been extensive and includes notable participation on boards of directors in both public and private companies.

S. Trevis Certo is the Jerry B. and Mary Anne Chapman Professor of Business in the Department of Management and Entrepreneurship in the W. P. Carey School of Business at Arizona State University. His research focuses on corporate governance, top management teams, initial public offerings (IPOs), and research methodology. Trevis's research has appeared in *Academy of Management Journal*, *Academy of Management Review*, *Strategic Management Journal*, *Journal of Management*, *Journal of Business Venturing*, *Entrepreneurship Theory and Practice*, *Journal of Management Studies*, *Business Ethics Quarterly*, *Journal of Business Ethics*, *California Management Review*, and *Business Horizons*. Trevis also serves on the editorial boards of *Academy of Management Journal* and *Strategic Management Journal*. Trevis has taught undergraduate, MBA, EMBA, and PhD courses in strategic management, research methodology, and international business at Arizona State University, Texas A&M University, Indiana University, Tulane University, and Wuhan University (China).

Letter from the Authors

Dear Colleague,

Thank you for taking the time to review our book. If you are reading this right now, you likely agree with our (perhaps biased) opinion that Management is one of the most important courses that students will take in their academic careers. Regardless of their majors, management will likely be in your students' futures. Whether your students graduate to become salesforce members, financial analysts, or supply chain specialists, they will undoubtedly work for managers. This book will help students understand how managers work. Moreover, the concepts in this text will help students prepare for their own future management positions.

It is hard to believe that this management textbook, now in its fifteenth edition, is over 35 years old. While a little younger than companies such as Apple and Microsoft, it is amazing to think that our book is older than companies like Alphabet (Google), Costco, Amazon, Lockheed Martin, and Netflix. Like these leading companies, our book has advanced over the years, relying on one constant theme: innovation. We created a product that resonated with the academic community, and we continuously innovated over the decades that followed. Specifically, over the years we have continued to integrate leading-edge research on individuals, teams, and organizations with pedagogical techniques designed to enhance students' performance, their ability to obtain employment, and ultimately their careers.

The unique approach of our book is that each chapter in our comprehensive text helps students develop a specific management skill. The content specifically focuses on how students can be more strategic and more creative, work as team members, become successful leaders, and more. We designed our chapters to build these skills (and others) to fulfill the objective of this book: To help students both obtain employment and flourish in the workplace.

The work on the pages that follow is largely the result of our interactions with the many instructors around the globe who use our book. Thank you! If we can help, please do not hesitate to email us!

Sincerely,

Samuel C. Certo   S. Trevis Certo
scerto@rollins.edu   trevis.certo@asu.edu

Preface

Build students' management confidence by helping students not only learn management concepts but also develop a target skill in each chapter.

Applying Management Concepts

Each chapter opens with a **Challenge Case** that presents a company facing a particular challenge relevant to the topic of the chapter.

CHALLENGE CASE

Diverse Employees Contribute to GE Lighting's Bright Future

Despite the common assumption that manufacturing jobs are disappearing, manufacturing companies face a hiring challenge. As experienced workers retire and technology advances, businesses need bright, hard-working employees who are comfortable with technology. GE Lighting is tapping the potential of the "millennial generation," workers born between 1982 and 2000. According to general manager Ron Wilson, the share of millennials among his manufacturing engineers and managers has doubled. The company is smoothing the way by preparing these employees to succeed. Its two-year leadership training program gives operations employees challenging assignments and brings them into contact with senior management. At the level of factory floor workers, the company partners with local com-

Tony Dejak/AP Images

CHALLENGE CASE SUMMARY

This chapter emphasizes what management is and what managers do. As a manager, James Quincey is engaged in processes that help Coca-Cola reach organizational goals. Quincey, as CEO of a major corporation, must focus on how the company can deliver top quality at a competitive price and develop new products that will keep the company abreast of the latest consumer trends. He cannot possibly develop, make, and sell all the products; rather, he leads the efforts within his group, keeping them aligned with the company's goals.

Quincey engages in planning, organizing, influencing, and controlling the work of the people at Coca-Cola. He uses human resources, as well as money, raw materials, and machinery (capital equipment). These efforts succeed when his group is both effective (successful in achieving goals) and efficient (minimizes the use of resources).

Quincey has risen in the ranks at Coca-Cola because he has demonstrated that he has management skill—the ability to carry out the process of reaching organizational goals by working with and through people and other organizational resources. According to the classic understanding, management skill is the combination of three different kinds of skills: technical, human, and conceptual skills. In this understanding of management, technical skills were especially important for Quincey when he first took on lower-management jobs. As he rose through Coca-Cola's hierarchy, Quincey depended less on the use of technical skills and more on the use of conceptual

and building cooperation, are important at all levels of management.

More recently, management skills have been viewed in terms of the activities carried out by managers. Quincey and other managers typically perform task-related, people-related, and change-related activities. Task-related activities require skills in short-term planning, clarifying objectives, and monitoring performance. People-related activities require skills in encouraging employees, providing recognition for accomplishments, developing skills in others, consulting others when making decisions, and empowering employees to solve problems. Change-related activities require skills in monitoring the organization's environment, proposing new ideas, encouraging innovation, and taking necessary risks.

The Challenge Case described how John Quincey has progressed through his career in management and the challenges of being a top manager. A career is a sequence of work-related positions over the course of a person's life. Also, in his progression to the top position at Coke, he has embodied the six management employability skills. He has demonstrated his expertise in communication, critical thinking, creativity, collaboration, knowledge application, and ethics and social responsibility. We have not yet seen the end of Quincey's career, but his path so far illustrates how a hardworking, goal-oriented person can develop skills by successfully taking on challenging positions that offer opportunities to learn more about a company's products, customers, and

At the end of each chapter is the **Challenge Case Summary**, where students read about how the company manager(s) used the concepts presented in the chapter to address the challenge.

Tips for Managing Around the Globe, Steps for Success, and **Practical Challenge** callouts highlight practical applications of management concepts.

TIPS FOR MANAGING AROUND THE GLOBE

Making the Most of International Experience

People assume that international experience will open up opportunities for managers. Certainly, if employees and customers live in different countries, familiarity with those cultures should be a big plus. For example, Andrew Gamertsfelder credited his marketing internships in Brazil with helping him land a job working for Stryker Orthopaedics in Brazil after he graduated from the University of Pittsburgh. And when the staffing firm Robert Half surveyed chief financial officers in the United States almost 70 per cent said international e for accounting and fina

However, researchers at the IE Business School in Spain conducted a study that raises questions about the value of international experience. Reviewing the careers of chief executive officers at large corporations, the researchers found that the longer the managers had worked overseas, the longer they took to reach the top jobs. Apparently, executives should balance overseas experience against staying in contact with decision makers at headquarters. To do this, exec

STEPS FOR SUCCESS

Developing Human Skills

At SAS America, Thomas Lynch's management career had stalled. Lynch, who specializes in sales support, had an excellent record of helping customers solve problems, but he was not getting key assignments or promotions. He brought the issue to his superiors, who pointed to his human skills: Although he was a great problem solver and well liked, he came across as lacking ambition. With coaching and practice, Lynch learned to pick opportunities to offer his expertise.

As Lyn important.

looking for the ability to set priorities, a positive attitude, and the ability to function well as part of a team. Here are some ways to build human skills:[27]

- Ask colleagues what you do well and what behaviors they would like to see improve.
- Learn to control your emotions. Notice what triggers a reaction, and practice ways to be calm in those situations.
- Get expert advice—seek help from a career coach,

PRACTICAL CHALLENGE: ATTAINING GOALS

Lawrence Jones Motivates Employees at UKFast

To understand how some managers influence goal attainment, consider UKFast's CEO and founder Lawrence Jones. UKFast a business-to-business hosting company, was founded in 1999, and since then Jones has used his creative leadership and passion to inspire others and attain the organization's goals—to create a global presence and build on its estimated worth of $315 million. He feels that motivation is one of the biggest assets a business can use to increase productivity and compete globally.

Jones likes a hands-on approach. He takes an active role in guiding his senior management and focuses on ensuring that UKFast and its customers

grow side-by-side. Managers are trained to keep employees geared for more by looking at three factors—competition, environment, and development. Jones encourages his employees to look to competition as a driver and a goal-setter. According to reports,[16] Jones has instilled a healthy appetite for competition in an informal way by initiating annual internal competitions among the company's technical engineers and by announcing the top 10 customer services delivered every week. The winners are treated to a big reward. While goals are attained, Jones feels the best part is that most of the employees enjoy the challenge itself.

Each chapter references assignable exercises in MyLab Management like **Watch It! Videos** about real companies to provide even more opportunities for students to apply the concepts they are learning to real-world situations.

somewhat effective despite being inefficient if demand for the finished goods is so high that the manager can get an extremely high price per unit sold and thus absorb inefficiency costs. Thus, a manager can be effective without being efficient, and vice versa. To maximize organizational success, however, both effectiveness and efficiency are essential.

MyLab Management Watch It

If your instructor has assigned this activity, go to www.pearson.com/mylab/management to complete the video exercise.

As an example of achieving efficiency and effectiveness, consider Telstra Corporation, Australia's largest telecommunication company. Like its counterparts the world over, Telstra faces the challenges of a changing industry in which mobile phones are fast becoming more popular than the landline business on which Telstra built its fortunes. To survive, Telstra is scrambling to create a nimble management team and prune the bureaucracy that slows down decision making and internal operations. In a recent reorganization of his executive team, Telstra CEO David Thodey created four groups—customer sales and support, product and marketing innovation, operations, and corporate support—all focused on effectiveness: getting more competitive while also attracting and retaining customers.[19]

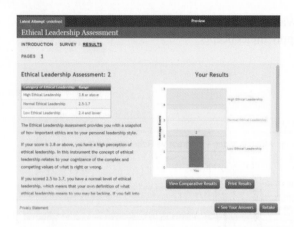

Developing Management Skills

Target Skill and **Skill and Your Career** at the opening of each chapter focus on managerial skills that employers most value in job candidates. Students can develop these skills by completing specially designed, innovative learning activities, which appear both in the text and through MyLab Management.

Personal Inventory Assessments, assignable in MyLab Management, are recommended by the authors in every chapter. These assessments provide immediate results to develop professionalism and awareness of oneself and others, giving students the skills necessary for their future career.

TARGET SKILL

Management Skill: the ability to work with people and other organizational resources to accomplish organizational goals

---

MyLab Management Assessing Your Management Skill
If your instructor has assigned this activity, go to www.pearson.com/mylab/management to complete the exercise related to the Challenge Case.

Assessing Your Management Skills is an assignment in MyLab Management with an average of 15 questions that asks the students to indicate how they would advise senior management to respond to situations in the Case Challenge and Case Challenge Summary. Students receive instant feedback on their responses. Results flow to the gradebook.

Management Skills Exercises

Management Skills Exercises provide additional discussion questions to dig into the Challenge Case and a second, short case to help students better understand how concepts apply to companies and their challenges.

MyLab Management
Discussion Questions

Go to www.pearson.com/mylab/management to complete the problems marked with this icon ✪.

✪ Cases

Coke's New CEO Battles a Changing Market

"Coke's New CEO Battles a Changing Market" and its related Challenge Case Summary were written to help you understand the management concepts contained in this chapter. Answer the following discussion questions about the introductory case to explore how fundamental management concepts can be applied to a company such as Coca-Cola.

Three **Experiential Exercises** are featured at the end of each chapter. The first type helps students use active learning, frequently in groups, to develop knowledge and skills specific to chapter content. The second, **You and Your Career**, is an exercise that asks students to reflect on chapter content to help them better understand how to manage their careers. The third type, **Building Your Management Skills Portfolio** activities, use real company examples and data points to help students demonstrate the management knowledge and skill acquired in that chapter.

Experiential Exercises

Managing Diversity

Directions. Read the following scenario and then perform the listed activities. Your instructor may wish you to perform the activities as an individual or within groups. Follow all of your instructor's directions carefully.

This chapter looks at the different challenges managers face in managing a diverse workforce. A much-neglected and oft-overlooked group are the baby boomers. In many societies, the over-55 generation represents a large percentage of the population. The increase in their numbers has come at a time when some countries have seen a fall in the number of young people entering the job market.

Identify five traits of this group of potential workers. These individuals are approaching or have reached the last decade or so of their working lives. Provide suggestions as to how a manager might supervise them. Try to be precise in your suggestions so that you could help someone be a more effective manager.

You and Your Career

Diversity in the workplace is important. It ensures that fresh ideas and ways of looking at problems and opportunities abound. However, a few firms may not value diversity as much, preferring a much more homogeneous staff. Assume you interviewed for a job for an open position at a company that you were very interested in. A week after the interview, however, you receive an e-mail letting you know that you were not selected. Coincidentally, you discover from a friend of yours who works at the company that it didn't hire you because of your race, gender, age (etc.; choose the most fitting for your circumstances).

Also assume that you filed a lawsuit and won. The judge has ruled that the company must hire you and was assessed a small fine. Would you accept the position now with the company? Why or why not?

Building Your Management Skills Portfolio

Your Management Skills Portfolio is a collection of activities specially designed to demonstrate your management knowledge and skill. Be sure to save your work. Taking your printed portfolio on an employment interview could be helpful in obtaining a job.
The portfolio activity for this chapter is Assessing Diversity at TECO Energy. Read the following about TECO Energy and answer the questions that follow.

TECO Energy is an energy company headquartered in Tampa, Florida. TECO Energy's five business units include (1) Tampa Electric, a regulated electric utility serving more than 635,000 customers in West Central Florida; (2) Peoples Gas System, Florida's largest natural gas distribution utility; (3) TECO Coal, a producer of conventional coal and synthetic fuel; (4) TECO Transport, a river and ocean waterborne transportation provider; and (5) TECO Guatemala, owner of two power plants in Guatemala. (You can learn more about the company by visiting www.tecoenergy.com.) Over the years, TECO management has focused on

---

creating a diverse workforce. Management recently reported the results of a diversity study aimed at monitoring its diversity efforts by ascertaining the present characteristics of its workforce. Part of the results of that study appears in Exhibits 1, 2, and 3.

Exhibit 1   Gender of Workforce

Company	Female	Male
TECO Energy (corporate)	62%	38%
Tampa Electric	25%	75%
Peoples Gas	28%	72%
TECO Transport	10%	90%
TECO Coal	4%	96%
TECO Guatemala (corporate)	29%	71%
TECO Guatemala	12%	88%
Total number of employees	970	4,122

Exhibit 2   Race/Ethnicity of Workforce

Company	Black	White	Hispanic	Other
TECO Energy (corporate)	6%	84%	10%	0%
Tampa Electric	14%	73%	11%	2%
Peoples Gas	14%	70%	15%	1%
TECO Transport	12%	85%	2%	1%
TECO Coal	0%	100%	0%	0%
TECO Guatemala (corporate)	0%	43%	43%	14%
TECO Guatemala*				
Total number of employees	522	3,993	399	178

* U.S. ethnicity codes not applicable to TECO Guatemala.

Exhibit 3   Leadership by Gender and Race

Company	Female	Male	Black	White	Hispanic	Other
TECO Energy (corporate)	56%	44%	4%	87%	9%	0%
Tampa Electric	30%	70%	9%	77%	11%	3%
Peoples Gas	28%	72%	6%	80%	14%	0%
TECO Transport	20%	80%	6%	91%	2%	1%
TECO Coal	9%	91%	0%	100%	0%	0%
TECO Guatemala (corporate)	29%	71%	0%	43%	43%	14%
TECO Guatemala*	11%	89%	N/A	N/A	N/A	N/A
Total number of employees	28%	72%	7%	79%	10%	4%

* U.S. ethnicity codes not applicable to TECO Guatemala.

Questions

4-10 List five major points that Exhibits 1, 2, and 3 tell management about TECO's workforce.

a. _____

b. _____

c. _____

d. _____

e. _____

4-11 How does management at TECO determine whether the present level of workforce diversity is appropriate for the company?

_____

4-12 Assume that TECO management performs a similar study in five years. Name three new dimensions of diversity that you would like the study to explore. Explain why you would like each dimension studied.

Dimension 1: _____

Why study this dimension?

_____

Dimension 2: _____

Why study this dimension?

_____

Dimension 3: _____

Why study this dimension?

_____

MyLab Management
Writing Assignments

If your instructor has assigned this activity, go to www.pearson.com/mylab/management for the following assisted-graded writing assignments:

Assisted-Grading Questions

4-13 Pinpoint five ways that discrimination might negatively affect an organization.

4-14 List five ways that you would promote diversity in an organization. How would you control your efforts to make sure they were successful?

What's New to This Edition

NEW! Management Skill and Your Career

Helps students understand the relationship between each chapter's Target Skill and future employability.

UPDATED! Reorganized Table of Contents

Reflects the changing importance placed on Entrepreneurship and Creativity and Innovation due to research on what companies are seeking in applicants.

- **Management and Entrepreneurship** chapter (formally Appendix 2) is now Chapter 2.
- **Creativity and Innovation** chapter (formally Appendix 3) is now Chapter 6.

NEW! Employability & Employability Skills

Consistent with our traditional pragmatic focus on concepts and skills, a new theme has been added on what it means to be employable and developing related skills.

NEW! Chapter-Opening Challenge Cases & Chapter-Ending Challenge Case Summaries

Half of the Challenge Cases and Challenge Case Summaries are new to this edition, including new cases on Netflix, Walt Disney Company, and Domino's Pizza.

NEW! Chapter-Ending Cases

Half of the Chapter-Ending Cases are new to this edition, including a new case on Fox News and CNN.

NEW! Experiential Exercises

Half of the chapter-ending experiential exercises are new to this edition. Exercises focus on topics like conducting feasibility studies, managing Generation Z, and understanding cultures in other countries.

NEW! Chapter Highlights: Tips for Managing Around the Globe, Steps for Success, and Practical Challenge.

Half of the highlights are new to this edition. New features focus on topics like P&G's Integrity Statement, interviewing recruits at Home Depot, and China's efforts to implement sustainable agricultural practices.

NEW AND UPDATED! Research Updates

Each chapter topic was thoroughly reviewed for timeliness of cited research, with endnotes being modified as necessary. Topics now include, for example, employability, self-managed teams, organization development, and workplace bullying.

Chapter-by-Chapter Changes

Introduction to Modern Management

Chapter 1: Introducing Modern Management: Concepts and Skills

- Updated with new Highlight: Management Skill and Your Career
- New chapter coverage on employability skills and highlights about top-paid executives
- New Challenge Case discusses Coca-Cola's new CEO, James Quincey

- New end-of-chapter case features Doze Mattresses and the challenges of managing a start-up business
- New Experiential Exercise related to conceptual skills
- New You and Your Career activity delves into managing older generations of workers

Chapter 2: Management and Entrepreneurship: Handling Start-Ups and New Ventures

- New Chapter Placement: Moved to front of book to emphasize entrepreneurship early in course
- New Highlight: Entrepreneurship Skill and Your Career
- New Challenge Case, Professor Becomes Restaurateur, focuses on start-ups
- New Experiential Exercise focuses on conducting a feasibility study
- New You and Your Career looks at hiring decisions
- New Building Your Management Skills Portfolio activity discusses the entrepreneurship process

Modern Management Challenges

Chapter 3: Society, Ethics, and Sustainability

- New Highlight: Social Responsibility Skill and Your Career
- New chapter coverage on tracking sustainability goals
- New Challenge Case addresses how IKEA builds on its commitment to the environment
- New Tips for Managing Around the Globe focuses on China's efforts to implement more sustainable agricultural practices
- New Steps for Success is about P&G's integrity statement
- New end-of-chapter case on whistle-blowing at Wells Fargo

Chapter 4: Management and Diversity

- New Highlight: Diversity Skill and Your Career
- New chapter coverage on EEOC and related case settlements
- New Tips for Managing Around the Globe that looks at Deloitte UK
- New Steps for Success discusses Generation Z
- New Practical Challenge examines Pinterest's hiring goals for a more diverse workforce
- New Challenge Case discusses how diverse employees contribute to GE Lighting's bright future
- New end-of-chapter case on Fox News and CNN's racial discrimination lawsuits
- New Experiential Exercise explores difficulty of managing older generations of workers
- New You and Your Career emphasizes discrimination

Chapter 5: Managing in the Global Arena

- New Highlight: Global Management Skill and Your Career
- New chapter coverage of foreign investment in the United States, U.S. investment abroad, non-verbal gestures and different cultures, and the United Kingdom exiting the European Union
- New Challenge Case discusses the phenomenal growth of KFC in China
- New Experiential Exercise considers understanding other cultures
- New You and Your Career examines moving a firm to China.
- New Building Your Management Skills Portfolio addresses challenges of working abroad

Chapter 6: Creativity and Innovation

- New Chapter Placement: Moved to front of book to emphasize this topic earlier in course
- New Highlight: Creativity and Innovation Skill and Your Career
- New Challenge Case: Olde Peninsula Brings Brewpub Innovation to Kalamazoo
- New end-of-chapter case focuses on autonomous vehicles
- New Experiential Exercise uses student experiences in their principles of management course to gain insight about how creativity and innovation can have an impact on the effectiveness of training environments
- New You and Your Career emphasizes creative ways to enhance résumés

Planning

Chapter 7: Plans and Planning Tools

- New Highlight: Planning Skill and Your Career
- New Steps for Success feature reviews tips for creating a budget
- New end-of-chapter case showcases how Gillette is battling Dollar Shave Club

Chapter 8: Making Decisions

- New Highlight: Decision-Making Skill and Your Career
- New Building Your Management Skills Portfolio examines the decision making in solving a garment manufacturer's problem

Chapter 9: Strategic Planning: Strategies, Tactics, and Competitive Dynamics

- New Highlight: Strategic Planning Skill and Your Career
- New Tips for Managing Around the Globe explores Ryanair's cost leadership strategy
- New end-of-chapter case focuses on strategic planning at Dyson
- New Experiential Exercise focuses on applying the PESTLE framework to Lush
- New Building Your Management Skills Portfolio activity examines strategic issues at House of Fraser

Organizing

Chapter 10: Fundamentals of Organizing

- New Highlight: Organizing Skill and Your Career
- New Tips for Managing Around the Globe shows how a French law bans work e-mail after hours
- New You and Your Career explores working in a flat versus tall organization structure
- New Building Your Management Skills Portfolio examines coordination and span of management

Chapter 11: Responsibility, Authority, and Delegation

- New Highlight: Responsibility and Delegation Skill and Your Career
- New Challenge Case examines Hy-Vee Supermarkets and manager autonomy
- New Steps for Success provides tips for delegating tasks
- New end-of-chapter case reviews Warby Parker permitting employees to choose their own projects
- New Experiential Exercise discusses centralization versus decentralization at Dairy Queen
- New You and Your Career emphasizes job descriptions
- New Building Your Management Skills Portfolio illustrates delegation at Etsy

Chapter 12: Human Resource Management

- New Highlight: Human Resource Management Skill and Your Career
- New Challenge Case discusses Netflix revamping its human resource function
- New Steps for Success gives tips for being an effective interviewer
- New Practical Challenge illustrates Organizational Politics in South Africa
- New end-of-chapter case looks at Disney using social media to recruit employees
- New Building Your Management Skills Portfolio illustrates conducting a human resource audit at Gold Star Chili

Chapter 13: Changing Organizations: Stress, Conflict, and Virtuality

- New Highlight: Organizational Change Skill and Your Career
- New chapter coverage of IBM and Yahoo! moving from virtual work arrangements back to traditional office settings
- New Tips for Managing Around the Globe: King Huen Ma and Sincere Company
- New Experiential Exercise discusses change agents in a campus organization
- New You and Your Career focuses on stress reduction

- New Building Your Management Skills Portfolio emphasizes helping employees through a major change at work

Influencing

Chapter 14: Influencing and Communication

- New Highlight: Communication Skill and Your Career
- New Practical Challenge: PepsiCo's Pilot Project
- New Tips for Managing Around the Globe: Cross-Cultural Communication
- New Steps for Success: Crafting an Elevator Speech
- New end-of-chapter case: Houston Zoo Improves Internal Communication
- New You and Your Career discusses the use of mobile devices across different generations
- New Building Your Management Skills Portfolio examines Abu Dhabi Health Services Company

Chapter 15: Leadership

- New Highlight: Leadership Skill and Your Career
- New Challenge Case: Bain & Company's CEO, Bob Bechek, Leads the Team
- New Tips for Managing Around the Globe: Adapting Your Leadership Style in Other Cultures
- New Steps for Success: Tips for Establishing a Coaching Program
- New Experiential Exercise explores leaders consulting with employees when making decisions
- New Building Your Management Skills Portfolio discusses Don Blankenship, former president of the Upper Big Branch Mine, losing 29 miners in an industrial accident

Chapter 16: Motivation

- New Highlight: Motivation Skill and Your Career
- New Challenge Case focuses on how Disney motivates employees
- New Tips for Managing Around the Globe: Motivating Employees from Other Cultures
- New Steps for Success: Tips for Disciplining Employees Effectively

Chapter 17: Groups and Teams

- New Highlight: Team Skill and Your Career
- New chapter coverage on collaboration and effective work teams
- New You and Your Career exercise focusing on cross-functional teams

Chapter 18: Building Organization Culture

- New Highlight: Organization Culture Skill and Your Career
- New Tips for Managing Around the Globe: P&G's Worldwide Business Conduct Manual
- New Steps for Success: Tips on Writing a Values Statement
- New You and Your Career feature focusing on an ideal organization culture

Controlling

Chapter 19: Controlling, Information, and Technology

- New Highlight: Controlling Skill and Your Career
- New Challenge Case highlighting how Domino's uses technology
- New end-of-chapter case emphasizes how Metail helps buyers try on clothes with virtual models
- New Experiential Exercise illustrates controlling instructional programs in organizations by having students reflect on personal experiences in their principles of management courses
- New You and Your Career emphasizes the role of information and technology in career building

Chapter 20: Production and Control

- New Highlight: Production Skill and Your Career
- New Practical Challenge: Alelion Energy Systems chooses Gothenburg for its battery plant
- New Challenge Case on Tesla increasing production while improving quality
- New end-of-chapter case examines just-in-time production at DAF Trucks
- New Experiential Exercise illustrates calculating a break-even point
- New You and Your Career explores production versus service environments
- New Building Management Skills Portfolio focuses on material controls in a manufacturing setting

Appendix 1

Managing: History and Current Thinking

- New Highlight: Comprehensive Management Skill and Your Career
- New Challenge Case focuses on Alan Mulally emphasizing innovation at Ford Motor Company
- New Practical Challenge highlight discusses how Bank of America redesigned work areas
- New Steps for Success highlights tips for better understanding employees
- New Tips for Managing Around the Globe describes crowdfunding at IBM
- New end-of-appendix case focuses on managing UPS in an Internet economy

MyLab Management

Reach every student by pairing this text with MyLab Management

MyLab is the teaching and learning platform that empowers you to reach *every* student. By combining trusted author content with digital tools and a flexible platform, MyLab personalizes the learning experience and improves results for each student. Learn more about MyLab Management at www.pearson.com/mylab/management.

- **Deliver trusted content:** You deserve teaching materials that meet your own high standards for your course. That's why we partner with highly respected authors to develop interactive content and course-specific resources that you can trust—and that keep your students engaged.
- **Empower each learner:** Each student learns at a different pace. Personalized learning pinpoints the precise areas where each student needs practice, giving all students the support they need—when and where they need it—to be successful.
  - **The Study Plan** gives students personalized recommendations, practice opportunities, and learning aids to help them stay on track.
- **Teach your course your way:** Your course is unique. Whether you'd like to build your own assignments, teach multiple sections, or set prerequisites, MyLab gives you the flexibility to easily create your course to fit your needs.
  - Choose from a library of **Personal Inventory Assessments** to promote self-reflection and engagement in students, helping them better understand management concepts.
- **Improve student results**: When you teach with MyLab, student performance improves. That's why instructors have chosen MyLab for over 15 years, touching the lives of over 50 million students.

Instructor Teaching Resources

This program comes with the following teaching resources:

Supplements available to instructors at www.pearsonglobaleditions.com	Features of the Supplement
Instructor's Resource Manual authored by Julie Boyles from Portland State University	• Chapter-by-chapter summaries • Chapter outlines with teaching notes • Additional individual assignments and group exercises • Case discussion notes • Solutions to all questions and exercises in the book
Test Bank authored by Carol Heeter from Ivy Tech Community College	1,890 multiple-choice, true/false, and essay questions with these annotations: • Learning Objective • AACSB learning standard (Written and Oral Communication; Ethical Understanding and Reasoning; Analytical Thinking; Information Technology; Interpersonal Relations and Teamwork; Diverse and Multicultural Work Environments; Reflective Thinking; Application of Knowledge) • Difficulty level (Easy, Moderate, Challenging) • Classification (Critical Thinking, Concept, Application, Analytical, or Synthesis)
TestGen® Computerized Test Bank	TestGen allows instructors to: • Customize, save, and generate classroom tests • Edit, add, or delete questions from the Test Bank • Analyze test results • Organize a database of tests and student results
PowerPoint Presentation authored by Rusty Juban from Southeastern Louisiana University	Presents basic outlines and key points from each chapter Slides meet accessibility standards for students with disabilities. Features include but are not limited to: • Keyboard and Screen Reader access • Alternative text for images • High color contrast between background and foreground colors

Acknowledgments

We are grateful beyond words for the continued acceptance of *Modern Management* by management instructors in both the United States and other countries. It has also been translated into several foreign languages, such as Portuguese and Spanish, and adopted for use in professional management training programs.

Over the years we have received personal satisfaction from the continued and growing popularity of *Modern Management*. Much of the credit for this popularity rightfully belongs to our colleagues who have supplied many of the key ideas for refinement and development. We would like to extend our warmest personal gratitude to these professionals for their dedication and commitment to making *Modern Management* what it is today.

The colleagues whose ideas contributed to this edition and all editions include:

Don Aleksy, Illinois Valley College

Michael Alleruzzo, Saint Joseph's University

Barry Axe, Florida Atlantic University

Karen Barr, Penn State University

Dan Baugher, Pace University

Dan S. Benson, Kutztown University of Pennsylvania

Gene Blackmun III, Rio Hondo College

Wayne Blue, Allegany College of Maryland

Elise A. Brazier, Northeast Texas Community College

Patricia M. Buhler, SPHR, Goldey-Beacom College, Wilmington, Delaware

Michael Carrell, Morehead State University

Tony Cioffi, Business Division, Lorain County Community College

Christy Corey, University of New Orleans

Helen Davis, Jefferson Community College–Downtown Louisville

E. Gordon DeMeritt, Shepherd University

Fred J. Dorn, University of Mississippi

Lon Doty, San Jose State University

Megan Endres, Eastern Michigan University

Joyce Ezrow, Anne Arundel Community College

Ronald A. Feinberg, Business, Accounting & Paralegal Studies, Suffolk Community College

William Brent Felstead, College of the Desert

Robert Freeland, Columbia Southern University

Theresa Freihoefer, Central Oregon Community College

Dwight D. Frink, University of Mississippi

Omid E. Furutan, University of La Verne

George Gannage, West Central Technical College

Wayne Gawlik, Joliet Junior College

Ashley Geisewite, Southwest Tennessee Community College

Adelina Gnanlet, California State University

Joseph Goldman, University of Minnesota

Scott D. Graffin, Terry College of Business, University of Georgia

Reginald Hall, Tarleton State University

Jamey R. Halleck, Marshall University

Robert W. Halliman, Austin Peay State University

LeaAnna Harrah, Marion Technical College

Heidi Helgren, Delta College

Jo Ann Hunter, Community College of Allegheny County

Steven E. Huntley, Florida Community College at Jacksonville

Robert E. Kemper, Northern Arizona University

Toni Carol Kind, Binghamton University

Dennis L. Kovach, Community College of Allegheny County

Loren Kuzuhara, University of Wisconsin

Gosia Langa, University of Maryland

Theresa Lant, New York University

Maurice Manner, Marymount College

Jon Matthews, Central Carolina Community College

Michelle Meyer, Joliet Junior College

Angela Miles, North Carolina A&T State University

Marcia Miller, George Mason University

Robert Morris, Florida State College of Jacksonville

Jennifer Morton, Ivy Tech Community College

Rhonda Palladi, Georgia State University

Donald Petkus, Indiana University

James I. Phillips, Northeastern State University

Scott A. Quatro, Covenant College

Richard Ratliff, Shari Tarnutzer, and their colleagues, Utah State University

Paul Robillard, Bristol Community College

Tim Rogers, Ozarks Technical College

Gisela Salas, Webster University, Barry University, St. Leo University, University of the Rockies

James Salvucci, Business Management, Curry College, Milton, Massachusetts

Duanne Schecter, Muskegon Community College

Johnny Shull, Central Carolina Community College

Denise M. Simmons, Northern Virginia Community College

Joe Simon, Casper College

Randi L. Sims, Nova Southern University

Gregory Sinclair, San Francisco State University

L. Allen Slade, Covenant College

Anthony W. Slone, Elizabethtown Community & Technical College

M. Smas, Kent State University

Miles Smayling, Minnesota State University, Mankato

Casey R. Smith, Shawnee State University

Charles I. Stubbart, Southern Illinois University Carbondale

Dr. Peter Szende, Boston University

Tom Tao, Lehigh University

Paul Thacker, Macomb Community College

Don Tobias, Cornell University

Larry Waldorf, Boise State University

Gloria Walker, Florida Community College at Jacksonville

Cindy W. Walter, Antelope Valley College

Bob Waris, University of Missouri Kansas City

We would also like to give special recognition to Steven Stovall, Associate Professor of Management at Wilmington College and holder of the Ralph J. Stolle Chair of Entrepreneurship. Professor Stovall made significant contributions to this edition of *Modern Management* by ensuring that published content was pragmatic and timely, and represented real-world management challenges. We are extremely grateful for Professor Stovall's impact on this new edition.

In addition, we would like to thank Carol Heeter, Julie Boyles, and Rusty Juban for updating all of the supplements to the highest quality. They worked tirelessly to provide instructional aids, and we thank them for their time and efforts. We would also like to acknowledge Kim Norbuta and the MyLab team—Nancy Lamm, Gordon Schmidt, Pam DeLotell, Amit Shah, Steven Stovall, Jennifer Lynn, Maureen Steddin, Susan Gall, and Emilia Westney—who did a terrific job of bringing the textbook's content to life with practical and relevant MyLab online exercises.

Lee A. Graf, Professor Emeritus, Illinois State University, continues to deserve special recognition for his contributions to *Modern Management* over the years. During the early years of this project, Dr. Graf made countless significant contributions that still have an impact on the character and nature of this present edition. Lee is a respected colleague, but more important, a close personal friend.

Members of our Pearson family also deserve personal and sincere recognition. Our book team has been nothing but the best: Stephanie Wall, Director of Portfolio Management; Kris Ellis-Levy, Senior Portfolio Manager; Nancy Lamm, Development Editor; Claudia Fernandes, Content Producer; Hannah Lamarre, Editorial Assistant; Becky Brown, Senior Product Marketer; Nicole Price, Field Marketing Manager; Angela Urquhart and Andrea Archer, Project Managers; and the Media and Sales Teams. Needless to say, without our Pearson colleagues, there would be no *Modern Management*.

Sam Certo would like to give special thanks to his colleagues at the Roy E. Crummer Graduate School of Business, Rollins College. Their interest and encouragement over the years have undeniably contributed to generating the personal commitment and dedication to professionalism necessary to complete and maintain projects like *Modern Management*. Thank you.

From a more personal viewpoint, Sam Certo would like to acknowledge his family. My family has always been there to encourage me in handling the difficult challenges that inevitably arise in publishing and maintaining a text of this magnitude. Thanks to my wife, Mimi, for always allowing me to lean on her during difficult times. She is my special source of strength and my moral compass. My children and grandchildren have no idea that the care and interest they show in "pop" is so inspirational.

Working over the years with my son, Trevis, on this project has been a special blessing. I like to think of *Modern Management* as a vehicle that helps to build and strengthen our father-son bond. I take great satisfaction in seeing the caring person that he has become and our professional relationship that fosters and builds upon our father-son relationship.

Emphatically, I acknowledge God's gifts that influence my life and enable me to pursue projects like *Modern Management*.

Trevis Certo would like to thank his colleagues at Arizona State University for their continued support. He would also like to thank Melissa, Skylar, Lexie, and Landon for humbling him every day.

Samuel C. Certo

S. Trevis Certo

Global Edition Acknowledgments

Pearson would like to thank the following people for their work on the Global Edition:

Contributors

Diane Sutherland
Jon Sutherland

Reviewers

Dr. Lindos Daou, Holy Spirit University of Kaslik
Khaled Haque
Vimala Venugopal, Taylor's University

Introducing Modern Management: Concepts and Skills

TARGET SKILL

 Management Skill: the ability to work with people and other organizational resources to accomplish organizational goals

MANAGEMENT SKILL AND YOUR CAREER

Management skill will be of great value to you in enhancing your career. For example, this skill can help you to focus systematically on engaging organizational resources to meet profit goals. Profit making will contribute to organizational success, build your image as a competent manager, make you valuable to your organization, and support promotions as you build your career.

OBJECTIVES

To help build my *management skill*, when studying this chapter, I will attempt to acquire:

1-1 An understanding of a manager's task

1-2 Knowledge about the management process and organizational resources

1-3 An understanding of management skill as the key to management success

1-4 Insights concerning what management careers are and how they evolve

---

MyLab Management Chapter Warm Up

If your instructor has assigned this activity, go to www.pearson.com/mylab/management to complete the chapter warm up.

CHALLENGE CASE

Coke's New CEO Battles a Changing Market

This chapter focuses on a number of introductory management topics, but one key concept is that of management employability skills (communication, critical thinking, creativity, collaboration, knowledge application, and ethics and social responsibility). The new CEO of Coca-Cola is a great example of all six of these management employability skills. Coca-Cola is a brand that has been around for over 130 years. The iconic logo script, contoured shape of the bottle, and bubbly taste have made Coke one of the most recognizable brands in the world. The beverage giant has enjoyed a worldwide popularity envied by most consumer companies. However, the last 10 years have been tough on Coke and on the carbonated beverage industry in general. Bottled water has supplanted soda as the most commonly purchased drink in the United States, and cities have begun taxing carbonated beverages heavily in hopes of raising funds and curbing obesity and diabetes.

In this current turbulent climate, James Quincey took the reins as CEO of the soda giant in 2017. Beginning his career with Coke in 1996, he oversaw operations in Latin America and Europe and worked his way up to chief operating officer, learning along the way the employability skill of knowledge application. Each position he filled in his career with the company taught him something new that he could utilize in subsequent positions. The former CEO, Muhtar Kent, had held the position for 8 years and groomed Quincey to take over the helm upon his departure.

Quincey has a number of challenges ahead of him requiring critical thinking skills. Currently the firm's soda sales account for 70 percent of global revenue.[1] And though that number is impressive, it is also a daunting figure because sales of carbonated beverages are steeply declining. In addition, the company is downsizing its number of employees as it tries to enter new beverage markets. These are major trials for the 52-year-old Quincey. The critical thinking skills needed to tackle these issues showcase Quincey's ability to use purposeful, goal-directed thinking to define and solve these problems.

"We are moving quickly to structure our organization for faster growth and to ensure we can respond to the fast-changing needs of our consumers," Quincey said.[2] The restructuring has meant cutting 1,200 jobs at the corporate office on top of the nearly 100,000 jobs lost as Coke has

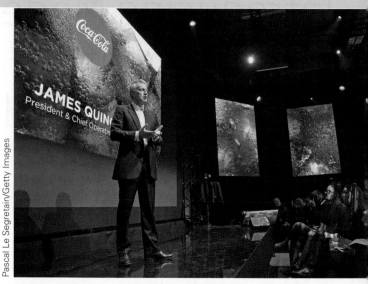

James Quincey, new CEO of The Coca-Cola Company, will need his broad-based knowledge to face current competitive challenges.

Pascal Le Segretain/Getty Images

sold off bottling operations since 2012. This is important as the company refocuses its efforts on products such as sports drinks, tea, plant-based beverages, bottled water, and flavored water—a major departure from the tried-and-true carbonated namesake of the firm.

Quincey understands that if Coke is to continue to compete with Pepsi and Dr. Pepper Snapple, he has to create new revenue streams while significantly cutting costs. This means making tough decisions about reducing staff and taking risks with the introduction of new products. As consumers seek out healthier options, the beverages of 20 years ago are no longer the top sellers. People want less sugar and fewer calories, and they want to feel good about what they are consuming. This embodies the employability skill of ethics and social responsibility. Coke's voluntary decision to manufacture a beverage that helps contribute to the reduction of diabetes and the number of obese consumers demonstrates the company's commitment to implementing strong ethical and socially responsible choices. It will be crucial for Quincey to communicate with his team about this trend. This is a critical management employability skill that is highly desirable by organizations, and Quincey's ability to convey the information effectively to his associates will be critical for Coke's success.

Coke, under Quincey, is entering a new era where deliberate management initiatives will maintain the strong market position the company has enjoyed. However, changes to a company built on a single carbonated beverage product are a necessity. In addition, Quincey is effectively demonstrating the six management employability skills that are discussed in this chapter. According to Quincey, "The brand Coca-Cola will always be the heart and soul of The Coca-Cola Company, but the company has outgrown its core brand. The company needs to be bigger than our core brand. We've been very clear that for us to drive sustainable, profitable growth of our brands, we also need to encourage and enable our consumers to control added sugar consumption."[3]

THE MODERN MANAGEMENT CHALLENGE

The Challenge Case illustrates a few of the ways that James Quincey will need his personal management skills at Coke. After studying chapter concepts, read the Challenge Case Summary at the end of the chapter to help you to relate chapter content to developing management skills to inspire innovation.

A Manager's Task

Managers influence all phases of modern organizations. Plant managers run manufacturing operations that produce the clothes we wear, the food we eat, and the automobiles we drive. Sales managers maintain a sales force that markets goods. Personnel managers provide organizations with a competent and productive workforce. The "jobs available" section in the classified advertisements of any major newspaper describes many different types of management activities and confirms the importance of management.

1-1   An understanding of a manager's task

Managers are also important because they serve a very special purpose in our lives. They are the catalysts for new and exciting products of all kinds that keep our economy and standard of living moving forward. One such new product of today is the Transportable Exam Station (TES), which brings the doctor to you. Other such products include Apple's new head-mounted iPhone, Microsoft's new tablet called Surface, and Chevrolet's new electric car called Volt.

In addition to understanding the significance to managers and society of managerial work and its related benefits, prospective managers need to know what the management task entails. The sections that follow introduce the basics of the management task through discussions of the roles and definitions of management, the management process as it pertains to management functions and organizational goal attainment, and the need to manage organizational resources effectively and efficiently.

Our society could neither exist as we know it today nor improve without a steady stream of managers to guide its organizations. Peter Drucker emphasized this point when he stated that effective management is probably the main resource of developed countries and the most needed resource of developing ones.[4] In short, all societies desperately need good managers.

Management is important to society as a whole as well as vital to many individuals who earn their livings as managers. Government statistics show that management positions have increased from approximately 10 to 18 percent of all jobs since 1950. Managers come from varying backgrounds and have diverse educational specialties. Many people who originally train to be accountants, teachers, financiers, or even writers eventually make their livelihoods as managers. Although in the short term, the demand for managers varies somewhat, in the long term, managerial positions can yield high salaries, status, interesting work, personal growth, and feelings of accomplishment.

The Associated Press has recently ranked total compensation paid to top managers in the United States. Based on the 2016 ranking, **Table 1.1** shows the names of the 10 most highly paid chief executives, the company they worked for, and how much they earned.

An inspection of the list of highest-paid executives in Table 1.1 reveals that the overwhelming majority of the top-paid executives are men. Based on the results of a recent survey at the *Wall Street Journal*, **Figure 1.1** illustrates a broad salary gap between men and women. Whereas women and men make up roughly the same proportion of the workforce, men hold a disproportionate number of higher-paying jobs according to the figure.

In addition, a notable study by the American Association of University Women indicated that the discrepancy between the pay of men versus the pay of women is a national phenomenon

TABLE 1.1   **The 10 Highest-Compensated CEOs, 2016**

Ranking	CEO Name	Company Name	Paid ($ millions)
1	Dara Khosrowshahi	Expedia	94.6
2	Leslie Moonves	CBS	56.4
3	Philippe Dauman	Viacom	54.1
4	Leonard Schleifer	Regeneron Pharmaceuticals	47.5
5	Robert Iger	Walt Disney	43.5
6	Sandeep Mathrani	General Growth Properties	39.2
7	Brian Roberts	Comcast	36.2
8	Marissa Mayer	Yahoo	36
9	David Cote	Honeywell International	33.8
10	Marc Benioff	Salesforce.com	33.4

Source: "Top 10 Highest-Paid CEOs," The Associated Press, May 25, 2016.

and is not isolated to a particular state or region.[5] As a general trend, however, the gap has narrowed since the 1970s due largely to women's progress in education and workforce participation and to men's wages rising at a slower rate.[6]

Concerns that certain managers are paid *too* much have been raised. For example, consider the notable criticism in recent years regarding the high salary paid to Robert R. Nardelli, former CEO of Home Depot.[7] Disapproval of the excessive compensation paid to Nardelli surfaced in the popular press as well as in statements by stockholders. An article in the *Wall Street Journal*, for example, questioned whether Nardelli was worth the amount he received.[8] Nardelli had been paid $63.5 million during a five-year period at Home Depot, while company shares lost 6 percent of their value. In the end, as with any manager, Nardelli's compensation should have been determined by how much value he added to the company. The more value he added, the more compensation he deserved. As a result of the growing criticism about Nardelli's compensation and Nardelli's resistance to modify his compensation level, he was fired.

Some evidence suggests that societal concern about management compensation goes well beyond one manager at one company.[9] A recent Senate Commerce Committee meeting, for example, focused on trying to justify lavish pay programs for managers at companies such as Tyco International and American Airlines when the companies were in financial trouble and laying off employees. Senators seemed unified in questioning the logic that justifies the average CEO salary being more than 400 times higher than a production worker's wages. This Senate Commerce Committee meeting should be an important signal that managers who do not exercise judicious self-control about their salaries may face future legislative control.

Figure 1.1

The salary gap between genders

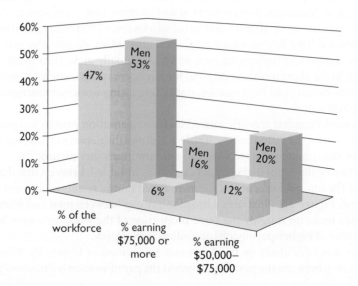

The Role of Management

Essentially, the role of managers is to guide organizations toward goal accomplishment. All organizations exist for certain purposes or goals, and managers are responsible for combining and using organizational resources to ensure that their organizations achieve their purposes. Management moves an organization toward its purposes or goals by assigning activities for organization members to perform. If the activities are designed effectively, the production of each individual worker will contribute to the attainment of organizational goals. Management strives to encourage individual activity that will lead to reaching organizational goals and to discourage individual activity that will hinder the accomplishment of those goals. Because the process of management emphasizes the achievement of goals, managers must keep organizational goals in mind at all times.[10]

This manager works with people and other resources to achieve the organization's goals.

Defining Management

Students of management should be aware that the term *management* can be (and often is) used in different ways. For instance, it can refer simply to the process that managers follow in order to accomplish organizational goals. It can also refer to a body of knowledge; in this context, management is a cumulative body of information that furnishes insights on how to manage. The term *management* can also refer to the individuals who guide and direct organizations or to a career devoted to the task of guiding and directing organizations. An understanding of the various uses and related definitions of the term will help you avoid miscommunication during management-related discussions.

As used most commonly in this text, **management** is the process of reaching organizational goals by working with and through people and other organizational resources. A comparison of this definition with the definitions offered by several contemporary management thinkers indicates broad agreement that management encompasses the following three main characteristics:

1. It is a process or series of continuing and related activities.
2. It involves and concentrates on reaching organizational goals.
3. It reaches these goals by working with and through people and other organizational resources.

A discussion of each of these characteristics follows.

The Management Process: Management Functions

The four basic **management functions**—activities that make up the management process—are described in the following sections.

Planning   Planning involves choosing tasks that must be performed to attain organizational goals, outlining how the tasks must be performed, and indicating when they should be performed. Planning activity focuses on attaining goals. Through their plans, managers outline exactly what organizations must do to be successful. Planning is essential to getting the "right" things done.[11] Planning is concerned with organizational success in the near future (short term) as well as in the more distant future (long term).[12]

Organizing   Organizing can be thought of as assigning the tasks developed under the planning function to various individuals or groups within the organization. Thus, organizing creates a mechanism to put plans into action. People within the organization are given work assignments that contribute to the company's goals. Tasks are organized so that the output of individuals contributes to the success of departments, which in turn contributes to the success of divisions, which ultimately contributes to the success of the organization. Organizing includes determining tasks and groupings of work.[13] Organizing should not be rigid; it should be adaptable and flexible to meet challenges as circumstances change.[14]

Figure 1.2

Classic mistakes commonly made by managers in carrying out various management functions

Planning
Not establishing objectives for all important organizational areas
Making plans that are too risky
Not exploring enough viable alternatives for reaching objectives

Organizing
Not establishing departments appropriately
Not emphasizing coordination of organization members
Establishing inappropriate spans of management

Influencing
Not taking the time to communicate properly with organization members
Establishing improper communication networks
Being a manager but not a leader

Controlling
Not monitoring progress in carrying out plans
Not establishing appropriate performance standards
Not measuring performance to see where improvements might be made

Influencing   Influencing is another of the basic functions within the management process. This function—also commonly referred to as *motivating, leading, directing,* or *actuating*—is concerned primarily with the people within organizations.[15] Influencing can be defined as guiding the activities of organization members in appropriate directions. An appropriate direction is any direction that helps the organization move toward goal attainment. The ultimate purpose of influencing is to increase productivity. Human-oriented work situations usually generate higher levels of production over the long term than do task-oriented work situations because people find the latter type less satisfying.

Controlling   Controlling is the management function through which managers:

1. Gather information that measures recent performance within the organization.
2. Compare present performance to preestablished performance standards.
3. From this comparison, determine whether the organization should be modified to meet preestablished standards.

Controlling is an ongoing process. Managers continually gather information, make their comparisons, and then try to find new ways of improving production through organizational modification.

History shows that managers commonly make mistakes when planning, organizing, influencing, and controlling. **Figure 1.2** shows a number of such mistakes managers make related to each function. Studying this text carefully should help managers avoid making such mistakes.

Management Process and Organizational Resources

1-2   Knowledge about the management process and organizational resources

Although we have discussed the four functions of management individually, planning, organizing, influencing, and controlling are integrally related and therefore cannot be separated in practice. **Figure 1.3** illustrates this interrelationship and also indicates that managers use these activities solely for reaching organizational goals. Basically, these functions are interrelated because the performance of one depends on the performance of the others. For example, organizing is based on well-thought-out plans developed during the planning process, and influencing systems must be tailored to reflect both these plans and the organizational design used to implement them. The fourth function, controlling, involves possible modifications to existing plans, organizational structure, or the motivation system used to develop a more successful effort.

To be effective, a manager must understand how the four management functions are practiced, not simply how they are defined and related. Thomas J. Peters and Robert H. Waterman, Jr., studied

Figure 1.3
Relationships among the four functions of management used to attain organizational goals

numerous organizations—including Frito-Lay and Maytag—for several years to determine what management characteristics best describe excellently run companies. In their book *In Search of Excellence*, Peters and Waterman suggest that planning, organizing, influencing, and controlling should be characterized by a bias for action; a closeness to the customer; autonomy and entrepreneurship; productivity through people; a hands-on, value-driven orientation; "sticking to the knitting"; a simple organizational form with a lean staff; and simultaneous loose–tight properties.

This brief introduction to the four management functions will be developed further in Parts 3 through 6 of this text.

Management and Organizational Resources

Management must always be aware of the status and use of **organizational resources**. These resources, composed of all assets available for activation during the production process, are of four basic types:

1. Human
2. Monetary
3. Raw materials
4. Capital

As **Figure 1.4** shows, organizational resources are combined, used, and transformed into finished products during the production process.

Human resources are the people who work for an organization. The skills they possess and their knowledge of the work system are invaluable to managers. Monetary resources are the

PRACTICAL CHALLENGE: ATTAINING GOALS

Lawrence Jones Motivates Employees at UKFast

To understand how some managers influence goal attainment, consider UKFast's CEO and founder Lawrence Jones. UKFast a business-to-business hosting company, was founded in 1999, and since then Jones has used his creative leadership and passion to inspire others and attain the organization's goals—to create a global presence and build on its estimated worth of $315 million. He feels that motivation is one of the biggest assets a business can use to increase productivity and compete globally.

Jones likes a hands-on approach. He takes an active role in guiding his senior management and focuses on ensuring that UKFast and its customers grow side-by-side. Managers are trained to keep employees geared for more by looking at three factors—competition, environment, and development. Jones encourages his employees to look to competition as a driver and a goal-setter. According to reports,[16] Jones has instilled a healthy appetite for competition in an informal way by initiating annual internal competitions among the company's technical engineers and by announcing the top 10 customer services delivered every week. The winners are treated to a big reward. While goals are attained, Jones feels the best part is that most of the employees enjoy the challenge itself.

Figure 1.4

Transformation of organizational resources into finished products through the production process

amounts of money that managers use to purchase goods and services for the organization. Raw materials are the ingredients used directly in the manufacturing of products. For example, rubber is a raw material that Goodyear would purchase with its monetary resources and use directly in manufacturing tires. Capital resources are the machines used during the manufacturing process. Modern machines, or equipment, can be a major factor in maintaining desired production levels. Worn-out or antiquated machinery can make it impossible for an organization to keep pace with competitors.

Managerial Effectiveness

As managers use their resources, they must strive to be both effective and efficient. **Managerial effectiveness** refers to management's use of organizational resources in meeting organizational goals. If organizations are using their resources to attain their goals, the managers are declared effective. In reality, however, managerial effectiveness can be measured by degrees. The closer an organization comes to achieving its goals, the more effective its managers are considered. Thus, managerial effectiveness exists on a continuum ranging from *ineffective* to *effective*.

Managerial Efficiency

Managerial efficiency is the proportion of total organizational resources that contribute to productivity during the manufacturing process.[17] The higher this proportion, the more efficient is the manager. The more resources wasted or unused during the production process, the more inefficient is the manager. In this situation, *organizational resources* refer not only to raw materials that are used in manufacturing goods or services but also to related human effort.[18] Like management effectiveness, management efficiency is best described as being on a continuum ranging from inefficient to efficient. *Inefficient* means that a small proportion of total resources contributes to productivity during the manufacturing process; *efficient* means that a large proportion of resources contributes to productivity.

As **Figure 1.5** shows, the concepts of managerial effectiveness and efficiency are obviously related. A manager could be relatively ineffective—with the consequence that the organization is making little progress toward goal attainment—primarily because of major inefficiencies or poor utilization of resources during the production process. In contrast, a manager could be

Figure 1.5

Various combinations of managerial effectiveness and managerial efficiency somewhat effective despite being inefficient if demand for the finished goods is so high that the manager can get an extremely high price per unit sold and thus absorb inefficiency costs. Thus, a manager can be effective without being efficient, and vice versa. To maximize organizational success, however, both effectiveness and efficiency are essential.

MyLab Management Watch It

If your instructor has assigned this activity, go to www.pearson.com/mylab/management to complete the video exercise.

As an example of achieving efficiency and effectiveness, consider Telstra Corporation, Australia's largest telecommunication company. Like its counterparts the world over, Telstra faces the challenges of a changing industry in which mobile phones are fast becoming more popular than the landline business on which Telstra built its fortunes. To survive, Telstra is scrambling to create a nimble management team and prune the bureaucracy that slows down decision making and internal operations. In a recent reorganization of his executive team, Telstra CEO David Thodey created four groups—customer sales and support, product and marketing innovation, operations, and corporate support—all focused on effectiveness: getting more competitive while also attracting and retaining customers.[19]

The Universality of Management

Management principles are universal: That is, they apply to all types of organizations (businesses, churches, sororities, athletic teams, hospitals, etc.) and organizational levels.[20] Naturally, managers' jobs vary somewhat from one type of organization to another because each organizational type requires the use of specialized knowledge, exists in unique working and political environments, and uses different technology. However, job similarities are found across organizations because the basic management activities—planning, organizing, influencing, and controlling—are common to all organizations.

The Theory of Characteristics   Henri Fayol, one of the earliest management writers, stated that all managers should possess certain characteristics, such as positive physical and mental qualities and special knowledge related to the specific operation.[21] B. C. Forbes emphasized the importance of certain, more personal qualities, inferring that enthusiasm, earnestness of purpose, confidence, and faith in their own worthiness are primary characteristics of successful managers. Forbes described Henry Ford as follows:

> A Forbes article described the characteristics of a successful business leader by describing Henry Ford. According to the article, every successful business starts with an individual like Ford who is enthusiastic, believes in the organization's purpose, is self-confident, and believes in the high value of what the organization aims to accomplish. Like any business leader, Henry Ford certainly faced many difficulties and high challenges in building the Ford Motor Company. It can be argued that only Henry Ford's enthusiastic and continued support of his company saved both him and his company from certain failure.[22]

Fayol and Forbes can describe desirable characteristics of successful managers only because of the universality concept: The basic ingredients of successful management are applicable to all organizations.

Management Skill: The Key to Management Success

Thus far, the introduction to the study of management has focused on discussing concepts such as the importance of management, the task of management, and the universality of management. This section continues the introduction to management by defining management skill and presenting both classic and more contemporary views of management skills thought to ensure management success.

1-3 An understanding of management skill as the key to management success

Defining Management Skill

No introduction to the field of management would be complete without a discussion of management skill. **Management skill** is the ability to carry out the process of reaching organizational goals by working with and through people and other organizational resources. Learning about management skill and focusing on developing it are of critical importance because possessing such skill is generally considered the prerequisite for management success.[23] Because management skills are so critical to the success of an organization, companies commonly focus on possible steps that can be taken to improve the skills of their managers.

Management Skill: A Classic View

Robert L. Katz has written perhaps the most widely accepted early article about management skill.[24] Katz states that managers' ability to perform is a result of their managerial skills. A manager with the necessary management skills will probably perform well and be relatively successful. One without the necessary skills will probably perform poorly and be relatively unsuccessful.

As an example illustrating how companies need to develop their managers' skills, consider the importance of preparing managers for working with people of other cultures. An increasingly global business world requires that managers who travel be aware of and grasp cultural differences in their dealings with coworkers, clients, and the public. Professionals at New York–based Dean Foster Associates, an intercultural consulting firm, provide cross-cultural training that helps businesspeople prepare for work overseas. For example, for a client heading to Japan, Foster conducted a five-hour session that included a traditional Japanese meal; coaching on Japanese dining etiquette; and information on business customs, socializing, and developing the proper mind-set for working outside one's native country.[25]

Katz indicates that three types of skills are important for successful management performance: technical, human, and conceptual skills.

- **Technical skills** involve the ability to apply specialized knowledge and expertise to work-related techniques and procedures. Examples of these skills are engineering, computer programming, and accounting. Technical skills are mostly related to working with "things"—processes or physical objects.
- **Human skills** build cooperation within the team being led. They involve working with attitudes and communication, individual and group interests—in short, working with people.
- **Conceptual skills** involve the ability to see the organization as a whole. A manager with conceptual skills is able to understand how various functions of the organization complement one another, how the organization relates to its environment, and how changes in one part of the organization affect the rest of the organization.

As one moves from lower-level management to upper-level management, conceptual skills become more important and technical skills less important (see **Figure 1.6**). The supportive rationale is that as managers advance in an organization, they become less involved with the actual production activity or technical areas, and more involved with guiding the organization as a whole. Human skills, however, are extremely important to managers at top, middle, and lower (or supervisory) levels.[26] The common denominator of all management levels, after all, is people.

Figure 1.6

As a manager moves from the supervisory to the top-management level, conceptual skills become more important than technical skills, but human skills remain equally important

STEPS FOR SUCCESS

Developing Human Skills

At SAS America, Thomas Lynch's management career had stalled. Lynch, who specializes in sales support, had an excellent record of helping customers solve problems, but he was not getting key assignments or promotions. He brought the issue to his superiors, who pointed to his human skills: Although he was a great problem solver and well liked, he came across as lacking ambition. With coaching and practice, Lynch learned to pick opportunities to offer his expertise.

As Lynch discovered, many human skills are important. For example, employers say they are looking for the ability to set priorities, a positive attitude, and the ability to function well as part of a team. Here are some ways to build human skills:[27]

- Ask colleagues what you do well and what behaviors they would like to see improve.
- Learn to control your emotions. Notice what triggers a reaction, and practice ways to be calm in those situations.
- Get expert advice—seek help from a career coach, leadership programs at work, and books on emotional intelligence.

Management Skill: A Contemporary View

More current thought regarding management skills is essentially an expansion of the classic view of what skills managers need to be successful. This expansion is achieved logically through two steps:

1. Defining the major activities that managers typically perform
2. Listing the skills needed to carry out these activities successfully

The major activities that modern managers typically perform are of three basic types.[28]

1. **Task-related activities** are management efforts aimed at carrying out critical management-related duties in organizations. Such activities include short-term planning, clarifying objectives of jobs in the organization, and monitoring operations and performance.
2. **People-related activities** are management efforts aimed at managing people in organizations. Such activities include providing support and encouragement to others, providing recognition for achievements and contributions, developing the skills and confidence of organization members, consulting when making decisions, and empowering others to solve problems.
3. **Change-related activities** are management efforts aimed at modifying organizational components. Such activities include monitoring the organization's external environment, proposing new strategies and visions, encouraging innovative thinking, and taking risks to promote needed change.

Reflecting on management employability skills helps to us gain insight about what skills managers need to carry out these management activities. **Management employability skills** refer to a person's ability to gain and maintain a career as a manager.[29] These skills and their definitions are listed in **Figure 1.7**.[30] This figure pinpoints six such skills, ranging from knowledge application to social responsibility. Keep in mind that Figure 1.7 is not intended as a list of *all* skills managers need to be successful but as an important list containing many of the necessary skills. One might argue, for example, that skills such as building efficient operations or increasing cooperation among organization members are critical management skills and should have prominence in Figure 1.7.

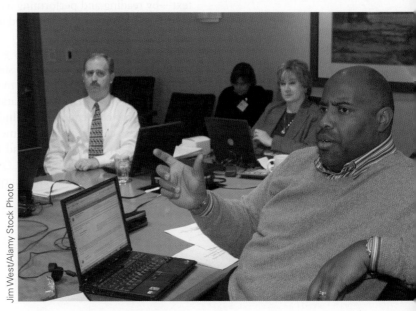

Managers are involved in daily activities that include planning, organizing, influencing, and controlling company resources in order to achieve organizational goals.

Jim West/Alamy Stock Photo

Figure 1.7

Skills managers need to perform their tasks

Communication
Effectively sharing meaning with others.

Critical Thinking
Assessing situations to identify and solve problems.

Creativity
Generating new ideas that contribute to organizational success.

Collaboration
Understanding and working within the dynamics of a group.

Personal Ethics
Dealing with people, problems, and situations with honesty and integrity.

Adaptability
Working independently or as part of a team.

Socially Responsible
Contributing to the welfare of the community.

Management Skill: A Focus of This Book

The preceding sections discussed both classic and contemporary views of management skills in modern organizations. A number of critical management skills were presented and related to top, middle, and supervisory management positions.

One common criticism of such management skill discussions is that, although understanding such rationales about skills is important, skill categories—such as technical skill, human skill, and conceptual skill—are often too broad to be practical. Many management scholars believe that these broad skill categories should contain several, more narrowly focused skills that represent the more practical and essential abilities for successfully practicing management.[31] These more narrowly focused skills should not be seen as valuable in themselves but as "specialized tools" that help managers meet important challenges and successfully carry out the management functions of planning, organizing, influencing, and controlling.

Table 1.2 summarizes the management functions and challenges covered in this text and the corresponding management skills that help address them. You will find as you study this text—by reading and performing its learning activities—that its focus on skill development is quite thorough and systematic, and focuses on helping you to develop a broad array of valuable management skills.

Because management skill is generally a prerequisite for management success, aspiring managers should strive to develop such skill. When doing so, however, managers should keep in mind that the value of individual management skills tends to vary from manager to manager, depending on the specific organizational situations faced. For example, managers facing serious manufacturing challenges might find that the ability to encourage innovative thinking aimed at meeting these challenges is their most important skill. On the other hand, managers facing a disinterested workforce might find that the ability to recognize and reward positive performance is their most valuable skill. Overall, managers should spend time defining the most formidable tasks that they face and sharpening the skills that will help them to carry out these tasks successfully.

TABLE 1.2   **Management Functions and Challenges Covered in This Text and Corresponding Management Skills Emphasized to Help Address Them**

Introduction to Modern Management

Chapter 1—Management Skill: The ability to work with people and other organizational resources to accomplish organizational goals.

Chapter 2—Entrepreneurship Skill: Involves the identification, evaluation, and exploitation of opportunities.

Modern Management Challenges

Chapter 3—Social Responsibility Skill: The ability to take action that protects and improves both the welfare of society and the interests of the organization.

Chapter 4—Diversity Skill: The ability to establish and maintain an organizational workforce that represents a combination of assorted human characteristics appropriate for achieving organizational success.

Chapter 5—Global Management Skill: The ability to manage global factors as components of organizational operations.

Chapter 6—Creativity and Innovation Skill: The ability to generate original ideas or new perspectives on existing ideas and to take steps to implement these new ideas.

Planning

Chapter 7—Planning Skill: The ability to take action to determine the objectives of the organization as well as what is necessary to accomplish these objectives.

Chapter 8—Decision-Making Skill: The ability to choose alternatives that increase the likelihood of accomplishing objectives.

Chapter 9—Strategic Planning Skill: The ability to engage in long-range planning that focuses on the organization as a whole.

Organizing

Chapter 10—Organizing Skill: The ability to establish orderly uses for resources within the management system.

Chapter 11—Responsibility and Delegation Skill: The ability to understand one's obligation to perform assigned activities and to enlist the help of others to complete those activities.

Chapter 12—Human Resources Management Skill: The ability to take actions that increase the contributions of individuals within the organization.

Chapter 13—Organizational Change Skill: The ability to modify an organization in order to enhance its contribution to reaching company goals.

Influencing

Chapter 14—Communication Skill: The ability to share information with other individuals.

Chapter 15—Leadership Skill: The ability to direct the behavior of others toward the accomplishment of objectives.

Chapter 16—Motivation Skill: The ability to create organizational situations in which individuals performing organizational activities are simultaneously satisfying personal needs and helping the organization attain its goals.

Chapter 17—Team Skill: The ability to manage a collection of people so that they influence one another toward the accomplishment of an organizational objective or objectives.

Chapter 18—Organization Culture Skill: The ability to establish a set of shared values among organization members regarding the functioning and existence of their organization to enhance the probability of organizational success.

Controlling

Chapter 19—Controlling Skill: The ability to use information and technology to ensure that an event occurs as it was planned to occur.

Chapter 20—Production Skill: The ability to transform organizational resources into products.

Appendix 1—Comprehensive Management Skill: The ability to collectively apply concepts from various major management approaches to perform a manager's job.

Management Careers

Thus far, this chapter has focused on outlining the importance of management to society, presenting a definition of management and the management process, and explaining the universality of management. Individuals commonly study such topics because they are interested in pursuing a management career. This section presents information that will help you preview your own management career. It also describes some of the issues you may face in attempting to manage the careers of others within an organization. The specific focus is on career definition, career and life stages and performance, and career promotion.

1-4   Insights concerning what management careers are and how they evolve

A Definition of Career

A **career** is a sequence of work-related positions occupied by a person over the course of a lifetime.[32] As the definition implies, a career is cumulative in nature: As people accumulate successful experiences in one position, they generally develop abilities and attitudes that qualify them to hold more advanced positions. In general, management positions at one level tend to be stepping-stones to management positions at the next-higher level. In building a career, an individual should be focused on developing the skills necessary to qualify for the next planned job and not simply taking a job with the highest salary.[33]

Career Stages, Life Stages, and Performance

Careers are generally viewed as evolving through a series of stages.[34] These evolutionary stages—exploration, establishment, maintenance, and decline—are shown in **Figure 1.8**, which highlights the performance levels and age ranges commonly associated with each stage. Note that the levels and ranges in the figure indicate what has been more traditional at each stage, not what is inevitable. According to the Census Bureau, the proportion of men in the U.S. population age 65 and older who participated in the labor force in 2008 reached 17.8 percent. This participation rate was the highest since 1985. The proportion of women in this age group was 9.1 percent, the highest since 1975.[35] As more workers beyond age 65 exist in the workforce, more careers will be maintained beyond the traditional benchmark of age 65, as depicted in Figure 1.8.

Exploration Stage
The first stage in career evolution is the **exploration stage**, which occurs at the beginning of a career and is characterized by self-analysis and the exploration of different types of available jobs. Individuals at this stage are generally about 15 to 25 years old and are involved in some type of formal training, such as college or vocational education. They often pursue part-time employment to gain a richer understanding of what a career in a particular organization or industry might be like. Typical jobs held during this stage include cooking at Burger King, stocking at a Federated Department Store, and working as an office assistant at a Nationwide Insurance office.

Establishment Stage
The second stage in career evolution is the **establishment stage**, during which individuals about 25 to 45 years old start to become more productive, or higher performers (as Figure 1.8 indicates by the upturn in the dotted line and its continuance as a solid line). Employment sought during this stage is guided by what was learned during the exploration stage. In addition, the jobs sought are usually full-time jobs. Individuals at this stage commonly move to different jobs within the same company, to different companies, or even to different industries.

Figure 1.8

The relationships among career stages, life stages, and performance

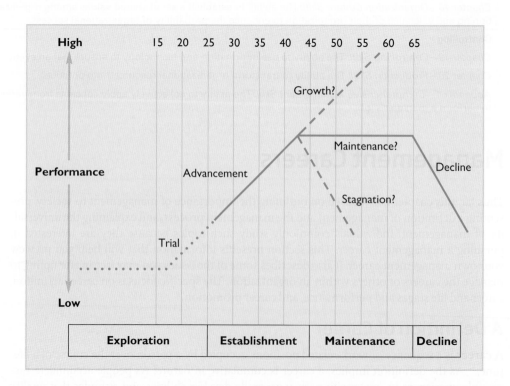

Maintenance Stage The third stage in career evolution is the **maintenance stage**. In this stage, individuals who are 45 to 65 years old show either increased performance (career growth), stabilized performance (career maintenance), or decreased performance (career stagnation).

From the organization's viewpoint, it is better for managers to experience career growth than maintenance or stagnation. For this reason, some companies such as IBM, Monsanto, and Brooklyn Union Gas have attempted to eliminate **career plateauing**—defined as a period of little or no apparent progress in a career.[36]

Decline Stage The last stage in career evolution is the **decline stage**, which involves people about 65 years old whose productivity is declining. These individuals are either close to retirement, semi-retired, or fully retired. People in the decline stage may find it difficult to maintain prior performance levels, perhaps because they have lost interest in their careers or have failed to keep their job skills up to date.

As Americans live longer and stay healthier into late middle age, many of them choose to become part-time workers in businesses, such as Publix supermarkets and McDonald's or in volunteer groups, such as the March of Dimes and the American Heart Association. Some retired executives put their career experience to good social use by working with the government-sponsored organization Service Corps of Retired Executives (SCORE) to offer management advice and consultation to small businesses trying to gain a foothold in their market.

Promoting Your Own Career

Both practicing managers and management scholars agree that careful formulation and implementation of appropriate tactics can enhance the success of a management career.[37] Planning your career path—the sequence of jobs that you will fill in the course of your working life—is the first step to take in promoting your career. For some people, a career path entails ascending the hierarchy of a particular organization. Others plan a career path within a particular profession or series of professions. Everyone needs to recognize, however, that career planning is an ongoing process, beginning with the career's early phases and continuing throughout the career.

In promoting your own career, you must be proactive and see yourself as a business that you are responsible for developing. You should not view your plan as limiting your options. First consider both your strengths and your liabilities and assess what you need from a career. Then explore all the avenues of opportunity open to you, both inside and outside the organization. Set your career goals, continually revise and update these goals as your career progresses, and take the steps necessary to accomplish these goals.

TIPS FOR MANAGING AROUND THE GLOBE

Making the Most of International Experience

People assume that international experience will open up opportunities for managers. Certainly, if employees and customers live in different countries, familiarity with those cultures should be a big plus. For example, Andrew Gamertsfelder credited his marketing internships in Brazil with helping him land a job working for Stryker Orthopaedics in Brazil after he graduated from the University of Pittsburgh. And when the staffing firm Robert Half surveyed chief financial officers in the United States, almost 70 percent said international experience would be important for accounting and finance employees in future years.

However, researchers at the IE Business School in Spain conducted a study that raises questions about the value of international experience. Reviewing the careers of chief executive officers at large corporations, the researchers found that the longer the managers had worked overseas, the longer they took to reach the top jobs. Apparently, executives should balance overseas experience against staying in contact with decision makers at headquarters. To do this, executives should take shorter assignments, participate in cross-border teamwork, and make a point of staying in touch with colleagues back home.[38]

TABLE 1.3   **Manager and Employee Roles in Enhancing Employee Career Development**

Dimension	Professional Employee	Manager
Responsibility	Assumes responsibility for individual career development	Assumes responsibility for employee development
Information	Obtains career information through self-evaluation and data collection: What do I enjoy doing? Where do I want to go?	Provides information by holding up a mirror of reality: How manager views the employee How others view the employee How "things work around here"
Planning	Develops an individual plan to reach objectives	Helps employee assess plan
Follow-through	Invites management support through high performance on the current job by understanding the scope of the job and taking appropriate initiative	Provides coaching and relevant information on opportunities

Another important tactic in promoting your own career is to work for managers who carry out realistic and constructive roles in the career development of their employees.[39] **Table 1.3** outlines what career development responsibility, information, planning, and follow-through generally include. It also outlines the complementary career development role for a professional employee.

To enhance your career success, you must learn to be *proactive* rather than *reactive*.[40] That is, you must take specific actions to demonstrate your abilities and accomplishments. You must also have a clear idea of the next several positions you should seek, the skills you need to acquire to function appropriately in those positions, and plans for acquiring those skills. Finally, you need to think about the ultimate position you want and the sequence of positions you must hold in order to gain the skills and attitudes necessary to qualify for that position.

Special Career Issues

In today's business world, countless special issues significantly affect how careers actually develop. Two issues that have had a significant impact on career development in recent years are the following:

1. Women managers
2. Dual-career couples

The following sections discuss each of these factors.

Women Managers   Women in their roles as managers must meet the same challenges in their work environments as men. Because they have joined the ranks of management more recently in large numbers, however, women often lack the social contacts that are so important in the development of a management career. Another problem for women is that, traditionally, they have been expected to manage families and households while simultaneously handling the pressures and competition of paid employment. Finally, women are more likely than men to encounter sexual harassment in the workplace.

Some management theorists believe that women may have an enormous advantage over men in future management situations.[41] They predict that networks of relationships will replace rigid organizational structures and that star workers will be replaced by teams made up of workers at all levels who are empowered to make decisions. Detailed rules and procedures will be replaced by a flexible system that calls for judgments based on key values and a constant search for new ways to get the job done. Strengths often attributed to women—emphasizing interrelationships, listening, and motivating others—will be the dominant virtues in the corporation of the future.

Despite this optimism, however, some reports indicate that the proportion of men to women in management ranks seems to have changed little in the last 10 years.[42] This stabilized proportion can probably be explained by a number of factors. For example, perhaps women are not opting to move into management positions at a greater pace than men because of trade-offs they have to make, such as not having or delaying the birth of a baby. In addition, women often indicate that it's more difficult for them to move into management positions than men because of the lack of female mentors and role models in the corporate world. **Table 1.4** lists seven steps that management can take to help ready employees with potential for advancement in an organization.[43]

Dual-Career Couples

With an increasing number of dual-career couples, organizations who want to attract and retain the best performers have found it necessary to consider how dual-career couples affect the workforce. Those in dual-career relationships even have a Facebook community devoted to their concerns.[44] The traditional scenario in which a woman takes a supporting role in the development of her spouse's career is being replaced by one of equal work and shared responsibilities of spouses. This arrangement requires a certain amount of flexibility on the part of the couple as well as the organizations for which they work. Today, burning issues such as whose career takes precedence if a spouse is offered a transfer to another city and who takes the ultimate responsibility for family concerns point to the fact that dual-career relationships involve trade-offs and that it is difficult to "have it all."

Kris Tripplaar/Tripplaar Kristoffer/SIPA/Newscom

DuPont CEO Ellen Kullman, an engineer, most likely faced challenges in her managerial roles because employers and employees sometimes see women managers as a novelty.

TABLE 1.4   **Seven Steps Management Can Take to Encourage the Advancement of Employees with Potential in Organizations**

1. *Make sure that people with potential know the top three strategic goals for the company.* Knowing these goals will help people focus their efforts on important issues. As a result, they'll be better able to make a meaningful contribution to goal attainment and become more likely candidates for promotion.

2. *Make sure that people with potential have a worthwhile understanding of career planning.* Having a vision for their careers and a career planning tool at their disposal will likely enhance the advancement of these individuals in an organization.

3. *Teach people with potential how to better manage their time.* The most effective managers are obsessed with using their time in the most valuable way possible. Helping people with potential know where their time is being invested and how to make a better investment should better ready them for promotion.

4. *Assign outstanding mentors to people with potential in the organization.* Mentors are important in readying individuals for promotion. Assigning outstanding leaders in an organization to people with potential should accelerate the process of readying these individuals for promotion.

5. *Have career discussions with people who have potential as managers.* Career discussions involving both managers and people with the potential to be managers should be held regularly. Helping these individuals to continually focus on their careers and their potential for upward mobility should help them to keep progressing toward management positions.

6. *Provide opportunities for organization members with potential to make contributions to the community.* In today's environment, managers must be aware of and contribute to the community in which the organization exists. Experience within the community should help ready these organization members for management positions.

7. *Encourage people with potential to take the initiative in obtaining management positions.* These individuals must be proactive in building the skills necessary to become a manager or be promoted to the next level of management. They should set career goals, outline a plan to achieve those goals, and then move forward with their plans.

How Dual-Career Couples Cope   Studies of dual-career couples reveal that many cope with their career difficulties in one of the following ways.[45] The couple might develop a commitment to both spouses' careers so that when a decision is made, the right of each spouse to pursue a career is taken into consideration. Both spouses are flexible about handling home- and job-oriented issues. They work out coping mechanisms, such as negotiating child care or scheduling shared activities in advance, to better manage their work and their family responsibilities. Often, dual-career couples find that they must limit their social lives and their volunteer responsibilities in order to slow their lives to a manageable pace. Finally, many couples find that they must take steps to consciously facilitate their mutual career advancement. An organization that wants to retain an employee may find that it needs to assist that employee's spouse in his or her career development as well.

CHALLENGE CASE SUMMARY

This chapter emphasizes what management is and what managers do. As a manager, James Quincey is engaged in processes that help Coca-Cola reach organizational goals. Quincey, as CEO of a major corporation, must focus on how the company can deliver top quality at a competitive price and develop new products that will keep the company abreast of the latest consumer trends. He cannot possibly develop, make, and sell all the products; rather, he leads the efforts within his group, keeping them aligned with the company's goals.

Quincey engages in planning, organizing, influencing, and controlling the work of the people at Coca-Cola. He uses human resources, as well as money, raw materials, and machinery (capital equipment). These efforts succeed when his group is both effective (successful in achieving goals) and efficient (minimizes the use of resources).

Quincey has risen in the ranks at Coca-Cola because he has demonstrated that he has management skill—the ability to carry out the process of reaching organizational goals by working with and through people and other organizational resources. According to the classic understanding, management skill is the combination of three different kinds of skills: technical, human, and conceptual skills. In this understanding of management, technical skills were especially important for Quincey when he first took on lower-management jobs. As he rose through Coca-Cola's hierarchy, Quincey depended less on the use of technical skills and more on the use of conceptual skills. However, human skills, such as communicating

and building cooperation, are important at all levels of management.

More recently, management skills have been viewed in terms of the activities carried out by managers. Quincey and other managers typically perform task-related, people-related, and change-related activities. Task-related activities require skills in short-term planning, clarifying objectives, and monitoring performance. People-related activities require skills in encouraging employees, providing recognition for accomplishments, developing skills in others, consulting others when making decisions, and empowering employees to solve problems. Change-related activities require skills in monitoring the organization's environment, proposing new ideas, encouraging innovation, and taking necessary risks.

The Challenge Case described how John Quincey has progressed through his career in management and the challenges of being a top manager. A career is a sequence of work-related positions over the course of a person's life. Also, in his progression to the top position at Coke, he has embodied the six management employability skills. He has demonstrated his expertise in communication, critical thinking, creativity, collaboration, knowledge application, and ethics and social responsibility. We have not yet seen the end of Quincey's career, but his path so far illustrates how a hardworking, goal-oriented person can develop skills by successfully taking on challenging positions that offer opportunities to learn more about a company's products, customers, and functions.

MyLab Management Assessing Your Management Skill

If your instructor has assigned this activity, go to www.pearson.com/mylab/management to complete the exercise related to the Challenge Case.

DEVELOPING MANAGEMENT SKILL

This section is specially designed to help you develop management skills. An individual's management skill is based on an understanding of the concepts and the ability to apply those concepts. The following activities will help to enhance your management skills in various organizational situations.

Class Preparation and Personal Study

To help you to prepare for class, perform the activities outlined in this section. Performing these activities will help you enhance your classroom performance significantly.

Reflecting on Target Skill

On page 31, this chapter opens by presenting a target management skill along with a list of related objectives outlining knowledge and understanding that you should aim to acquire related to this skill. Review this target skill and the list of objectives to make sure that you've acquired all pertinent information within the chapter. If you do not feel that you've reached a particular objective(s), study related chapter coverage until you do.

Know Key Terms

Understanding the following key terms is critical to your preparing for class. Define each of these terms. Refer to the page(s) referenced after a term to check your definition or to gain further insight regarding the term.

management   35
management functions   35
organizational resources   37
managerial effectiveness   38
managerial efficiency   38
management skill   40
technical skills   40
human skills   40
conceptual skills   40
task-related activities   41
people-related activities   41
change-related activities   41
management employability skills   41
career   43
exploration stage   44
establishment stage   44

maintenance stage   45
career plateauing   45
decline stage   45

Know How Management Concepts Relate

This section comprises activities that will further sharpen your understanding of management concepts. Answer essay questions as completely as possible.

1-1 How can influencing ensure that managers are as efficient as possible?

1-2 What do task-related activities mean to you? Suggest examples of task-related activities that are regularly undertaken by managers and are essential skills to perform.

1-3 Discuss your personal philosophy for promoting the careers of women managers within an organization. Why do you hold this philosophy? Explain any challenges that you foresee in implementing this philosophy within a modern organization. How will you overcome these challenges?

MyLab Management Personal
Inventory Assessments

Go to www.pearson.com/mylab/management to complete the Personal Inventory Assessment related to this chapter.

 PERSONAL
INVENTORY
ASSESSMENT

Management Skills Exercises

Learning activities in this section are aimed at helping you develop management skills.

> ## MyLab Management
> ### Discussion Questions
> Go to www.pearson.com/mylab/management to complete the problems marked with this icon ⊗.

⊗ Cases

Coke's New CEO Battles a Changing Market

"Coke's New CEO Battles a Changing Market" and its related Challenge Case Summary were written to help you understand the management concepts contained in this chapter. Answer the following discussion questions about the introductory case to explore how fundamental management concepts can be applied to a company such as Coca-Cola.

1-4 How would you describe the significance of James Quincey's work as a manager? Who benefits from his abilities and efforts?

1-5 In terms of the contemporary view of management skill, which activities and skills do you see Quincey using in his role as CEO of Coke? How do you think he acquired those skills?

1-6 Explain how Quincey has demonstrated the six management employability skills. Which employability skills are most important for becoming a CEO? Explain your answer.

College Students Revolutionize the Mattress Industry

Read the case and answer the questions that follow. Studying this case will help you better understand how concepts relating to the four functions of management can be applied in a company such as Doze Beds.

Many college students dream of one day starting a business such as opening a thriving restaurant or a high-tech start-up, or even selling the best chocolate chip cookie ever. However, two students, Brendan Rice and Russell Suskind, decided they wanted to start a mattress company. Rice, who graduated from the University of Wisconsin and loves extreme sports, and Suskind, a graduate of Syracuse University who enjoys hockey, started Doze Beds with just $10,000. And their company is changing the way consumers purchase mattresses.

Rice and Suskind teamed up when they were introduced at Venture for America: a two-year fellowship where recent college grads hone their entrepreneurial skills in cities where jobs desperately need to be created. As students, both men discovered how difficult and confusing mattress buying could be with so many options, styles, and prices.

They wanted something simpler and Doze Beds was born. The company operates on the principle that if a firm offers a basic product at a reasonable price, makes delivery a cinch, and has a transparent return policy, it will be successful.

Doze sells a 10-inch memory gel foam mattress that is ordered online, packed in a small FedEx box, and sent right to the customer's door. Without a brick-and-mortar retail store, Doze Beds avoids substantial overhead costs and the consumer enjoys buying direct from the manufacturer without heavy markups. Doze Beds has a very liberal return policy for those who decide they don't like the bed that they have purchased: They receive a full refund, and the company helps the customer find a needy venue to donate the bed. The founders of the company as well as other employees visit college campuses and music festivals all over the country to show off their product. "We find that when people are able to feel the product and interact with the brand, they are much more likely to purchase," Suskind said.[46]

Like the founders of any start-up, Rice and Suskind have had to handle the difficult challenge of taking a business from a vague concept to a tangible, smooth-running enterprise. Rice got his start at helping other young entrepreneurs while he was at the University of Wisconsin working in a business incubator. He spent most of his time on "trying to support students that had business ideas and wanted to launch their own company."[47] He found it energizing that other students were pursuing their dreams and bringing their business ideas to fruition. His affiliation with these budding entrepreneurs drove home the realization that he could start a business, too.

When Rice met Suskind at the Venture for America fellowship, the mattress business was at the forefront of their thoughts. Both had dealt with the exhausting endeavor of visiting mattress stores, being confused by the hundreds of choices, and finally having to figure out how to strap the mattress to the top of their car! They knew there had to be a better way, and that's when they developed their idea to build an online business that would involve a simple, fairly priced mattress. Because it does not have springs or any other rigid structure, it can be folded into a tight package and mailed directly to the consumer in a small box. The reviews from customers have been outstanding, and many echo Rice's sentiments when he says, "I can't wait to jump into my bed at the end of every day."[48]

Questions

1-7 In starting their business, how have Rice and Suskind used the four functions of management?

1-8 Discuss the use of organizational resources (human, monetary, raw materials, and capital) in a start-up like Doze Beds. What challenges would an entrepreneur face with each one?

1-9 Which of Katz's managerial skills (technical, human, and conceptual) do Rice and Suskind use most often? Why?

Experiential Exercises

Developing Your Conceptual Skills

Directions. Read the following scenario and then perform the listed activities. Your instructor may want you to perform the activities as an individual or within groups. Follow all of your instructor's directions carefully.

Assume you're the president of a small, regional restaurant specializing in Tex-Mex cuisine that was founded in 2007. There are six locations in the Columbus, Ohio, area, and each is doing reasonably well financially. Fortunately, the last few years have shown incredible growth, and the sixth location opened six months ago.

Now you have an opportunity before you. A rival chain of similar size is closing its doors. All of its locations are within the same geographic region as all of yours: central Ohio. Because the owner of this rival chain is anxious to be rid of the assets of his company, he has approached you about buying all six of his stores. You have the finances to make the acquisition, but you will need to borrow funds to remodel and revamp these existing structures.

Apply conceptual skills to answer these questions. If you were to buy this rival chain, what would you do with these new locations? Convert them to your brand of Tex-Mex, or open them as something different? Develop three alternatives you could do with this rival chain's stores.

You and Your Career

Upon graduation, you may find yourself in a managerial position right away. Though it is not common, it does happen for some recent graduates. One challenge you may experience is that you will be managing a team where every member is older than you. What steps can you take to ease your transition into a managerial role, especially in light of your age and inexperience? What is the best way to establish yourself as the manager of the team and earn the team's respect?

Building Your Management Skills Portfolio

Your management skills portfolio is a collection of activities specially designed to demonstrate your management knowledge and skill. Be sure to save your work. You can use this material when you are preparing for an interview.

The portfolio activity for this chapter is managing the tourist information and experience booth at a local airport.

The government is keen for local and regional airports in your country to open a tourist information and assistance booth as the first tourism-related contact point for visitors. Visitors may be international visitors or residents of your own country or region traveling on internal flights. You have been appointed as manager of the booth at your local airport with eight employees. You start the job in two weeks. There will be a wide variety of brochures, and information will be available through apps and mobile sites that are being developed. You will have to act as a liaison and booking agent for many local attractions and businesses. The primary tasks are to improve the experience for visitors and to increase tourism spending per head. The booth will be funded for one year, after which it will have to cover its own costs through booking fees.

Fill out the following form to indicate issues related to each of the management functions when you start your job as manager at the airport.

Planning Issues to Inspect

Example: The booth must be manned to cover all incoming flights.

1-10 _____

1-11 _____

1-12 _____

1-13 _____

1-14 _____

Organizing Issues to Inspect

1-15 _____

1-16 _____

1-17 _____

1-18 _____

1-19 _____

Influencing Issues to Inspect

1-20 _____

1-21 _____

1-22 _____

1-23 _____

1-24 _____

Controlling Issues to Inspect

1-25 _____

1-26 _____

1-27 _____

1-28 _____

1-29 _____

Assume that you have to ensure that an English speaker is available to cover the suggested 18-hours-a-day opening times. Explain how that change affects your organizing, influencing, and controlling activities.

_____

_____

_____

_____

_____

_____

_____

_____

_____

MyLab Management
Writing Assignments

If your instructor has assigned this activity, go to www.pearson.com/mylab/management for the following assisted-graded writing assignments:

Assisted-Grading Questions

1-30 Explain the relationships among the four functions of management.

1-31 List and define five skills that you think you'll need as CEO of a company. Why will these skills be important in your CEO position?

Endnotes

1. Jennifer Maloney, "Coke's New CEO James Quincey to Staff: Make Mistakes," *Wall Street Journal*, May 10, 2017 (online edition).
2. John Kell, "What Coca-Cola's Leadership Changes Tell Us about the Future of the Company," *Fortune*, March 23, 2017, http://fortune.com/2017/03/23/coke-new-ceo-leadership/.
3. Jay Moye, "Quincey at CAGNY: 'We Are Going to Be a Total Beverage Company,'" February 23, 2017, http://www.coca-colacompany.com/stories/quincey-at-cagny-we-are-going-to-be-a-total-beverage-company.
4. For an interesting discussion of how the World Bank is launching a pilot program to address the scarcity of well-trained managers in developing and transitional countries, see "Improving Management in Developing Countries," *Finance & Development* 40, no. 2 (June 2003): 5.
5. *The Simple Truth about the Gender Pay Gap*. Rep. American Association of University Women, 2011, http://www.aauw.org/learn/research/simpleTruth.cfm.
6. Kevin Miller, "The Simple Truth about the Gender Pay Gap," *American Association of University Women* (Spring 2017): 4.
7. "Shareholders Win One at Home Depot: An Arrogant CEO's Exorbitant Pay Had No Relation to Sagging Stock Price," *Knight Ridder Tribune Business News*, January 15, 2007, 1.
8. Alan Murray, "A Gathering Consensus on CEO Pay," *Wall Street Journal*, March 15, 2006, A2.
9. Jerry W. Markham, "The Politics of Executive Pay: Ideology, Not 'Social Justice,' Fuels Calls for Restraints on Executive Compensation," *Regulation* (March 22, 2011): 38–43.
10. John R. Schermerhorn, Jr., *Management* (New York: John Wiley, 2005), 19.
11. Jacqueline McLean, "Making Things Happen," *The British Journal of Administrative Management* (October/November 2006): 16.
12. Gary Hamel and C. K. Prahalad, "Seeing the Future First," *Fortune* (September 5, 1994): 64–70; Paul J. Di Stefano, "Strategic Planning—

Both Short Term and Long Term," *Rough Notes* 149, no. 8 (August 2006): 26.
13. T. L. Stanley, "Management: A Journey in Progress," *Supervision* 67, no. 12 (December 2006): 15–18.
14. Jared Sandberg, "Office Democracies: How Many Bosses Can One Person Have?" *Wall Street Journal*, November 22, 2005, B1.
15. In early management literature, the term *motivating* was commonly used to signify this people-oriented management function. The term *influencing* is used consistently throughout this text because it is broader and permits more flexibility in discussing people-oriented issues. Later in the text, motivating is discussed as a major part of influencing.
16. "Motivating Your Team: Top Tips," Bdaily Business News, January 21, 2015, https://bdaily.co.uk/advice/21-01-2015/motivating-your-team-top-tips/; Philip Beresford, "Britain's Top 100 Entrepreneurs 2014: No. 11—Lawrence Jones, UKFast," *Management Today*, October 26, 2014; Sirena Bergman, "How to Build a More Efficient Office," *The Guardian*, December 9, 2014; Shelina Begum, "MEN Business of the Year 2014: Winners' Stories," *Manchester Evening News*, November 14, 2014; Alison Coleman, "Let's Work Together," *Director Magazine*, March 2014, http://www.director.co.uk/MAGAZINE/2012/11_November/Lets%20get%20together_66_03.html.
17. For an interesting discussion of measuring operational efficiency in the airline industry, see Wann-Yih Wu and Ying-Kai Liao, "A Balanced Score Card Envelopment Approach to Assess Airlines' Performance," *Industrial Management* (2014): 123–143.
18. William Wiggenhorn, "Motorola U: When Training Becomes an Education," *Harvard Business Review* (July/August 1990): 71–83.
19. Mitchell Bingemann, "Telstra Rings in New Era with More Management Changes," *The Australian*, March 30, 2010, http://www.theaustralian.com; Almar Latour and Lyndal McFarland, "If You Don't Deliver Numbers You Aren't Doing Your Job," *Wall Street Journal*, March 15, 2010, http://online.wsj.com.
20. Wyatt Wells, "Concept of the Corporation," *Business History Review* 81, no. 1 (Spring 2007): 142.
21. Henri Fayol, *General and Industrial Management* (London: Sir Isaac Pitman & Sons, 1949).
22. B. C. Forbes, *Forbes* (March 15, 1976): 128.
23. Les Worrall and Cary Cooper, "Management Skills Development: A Perspective on Current Issues and Setting the Future Agenda," *Leadership & Organization Development Journal* 22, no. 1 (2001): 34–39.
24. Robert L. Katz, "Skills of an Effective Administrator," *Harvard Business Review* (January/February 1955): 33–41.
25. Tanya Mohn, "Going Global, Stateside," *New York Times*, March 8, 2010, http://www.nytimes.com.
26. For an interesting discussion of tools for human skill in encouraging food-handling safety, see Ungku Fatimah Abidin, Ungku Zainal, Susan W. Arendt, and Catherine H. Strohbehn, "Exploring the Culture of Food Safety: The Role of Organizational Influencers in Motivating Employees' Safe Food-Handling Practices," *Journal of Quality Assurance in Hospitality & Tourism* 14, no. 4 (2013): 321.
27. Dennis Nishi, "'Soft Skills' Can Help You Get Ahead," *Wall Street Journal*, May 18, 2013, http://online.wsj.com; Millennial Branding, "Millennial Branding and American Express Release New Study on Gen Y Workplace Expectations," news release, September 3, 2013, http://millennialbranding.com; Sue Shellenbarger, "Shaking Off a Shy Reputation at Work," *Wall Street Journal*, January 14, 2014, http://online.wsj.com; Dan Schawbel, "Develop Your Soft Skills for Workplace Success," *Fast Track* (Intuit blog), April 12, 2013, http://quickbase.intuit.com.
28. Gary Yukl, Angela Gordon, and Tom Taber, "A Hierarchical Taxonomy of Leadership Behavior: Integrating a Half Century of Behavior Research," *Journal of Leadership & Organizational Studies* 9, no. 1 (Summer 2002): 15–32.
29. Ruth Bridgstock, "The Graduate Attributes We've Overlooked: Enhancing Graduate Employability through Career Management Skills," *Higher Education Research & Development Journal* 28, no 1 (March 31, 2009): 31–44.
30. http://www.conferenceboard.ca/topics/education/learning-tools/employability-skills.aspx
31. Tim O. Peterson and David D. Van Fleet, "The Ongoing Legacy of R. L. Katz: An Updated Typology of Management Skills," *Management Decision* 42, no. 10 (2004): 1297–1308.
32. Don Hellriegel and John W. Slocum, Jr., *Organizational Behavior*, 13th ed. (Mason, OH: Thomson South-Western, 2010), 6.

33. Perri Capell, "Why Increased Pay Isn't Always Best Reason to Accept Another Job," *Wall Street Journal*, December 19, 2006, B8.

34. For a study exploring the role of burnout in career plateauing, see Zakaria Sorizehi, Abbas Samadi, Rohallah Sohrabi, and Nasser Kamalipoor, "Studying the Relationship between Plateauing in Career Progression Path with Personnel Burnout," *Interdisciplinary Journal of Contemporary Research in Business* 5, no. 3 (2013): 627–638.

35. Patrick J. Purcell, "Older Workers: Employment and Retirement Trends," *Monthly Labor Review* 123, no. 10 (October 2000): 19–30.

36. John W. Slocum, Jr., William L. Cron, and Linda C. Yows, "Whose Career Is Likely to Plateau?" *Business Horizons* (March/April 1987): 31–38.

37. Robert N. Lussier, *Management Fundamentals: Concepts, Applications, Skill Development* (Mason, OH: South-Western, 2012).

38. Cecilia Capuzzi Simon, "The World Is Their Workplace," *New York Times*, February 3, 2013, Business Insights: Global, http://bi.galegroup.com; Ken Tysiac, "Can You Succeed in Finance without International Experience?" *Journal of Accountancy*, July 19, 2013, http://www.journalofaccountancy.com; Ken Favaro, "Is There Really Such Thing as a 'Global CEO'?" *Fortune*, April 16, 2013, http://management.fortune.cnn.com; Burak Koyuncu, "Can International Experience Harm Careers?," *Diversity Executive*, May 16, 2012, http://diversity-executive.com.

39. Paul H. Thompson, Robin Zenger Baker, and Norman Smallwood, "Improving Personal Development by Applying the Four-Stage Career Model," *Organizational Dynamics* (Autumn 1986): 49–62.

40. Kenneth Labich, "Take Control of Your Career," *Fortune* (November 18, 1991): 87–90; Buck Blessing, "Career Planning: Five Fatal Assumptions," *Training and Development Journal* (September 1986): 49–51.

41. Thomas J. Peters, Jr., "The Best New Managers Will Listen, Motivate, Support," *Working Woman* (September 1990): 142–143, 216–217.

42. Ann Pomeroy, "Peak Performances," *HR Magazine* 52, no. 4 (April 2007): 48–53.

43. Adapted from Jan Torrisi-Mokwa, "The Seven Questions Firm Leaders Need to Ask to Advance Professional Women More Effectively," *CPA Practice Management Forum* 2, no. 12 (December 2006): 13–14.

44. Facebook, http://www.facebook.com, accessed March 25, 2010. For an interesting discussion of the challenges of dual-career versus single-career couples, see David F. Elloy and Catherine R. Smith, "Patterns of Stress, Work-Family Conflict, Role Conflict, Role Ambiguity, and Overload Among Dual-Career and Single-Career Couples: An Australian Study," *Cross-Cultural Management* 10, no. 1 (2003): 55.

45. Sharon Meers and Joanna Strober, *Getting to 50/50: How Working Couples Can Have It All by Sharing It All* (New York: Bantam, 2000). For additional information about dual-career couples relocating abroad, see Mandy E. G. van der Velde, Paul G. W. Jansen, P. Matthijs Bal, and Kim J. P. M. van Erp, "Dual-Earner Couples' Willingness to Relocate Abroad: The Reciprocal Influence of Both Partners' Career Role Salience and Partner Role Salience," *European Journal of Work and Organizational Psychology* 26, no. 2 (2017): 195–207.

46. Amanda Quick, "After Rebrand, 'Life Is Better in Bed' for Doze," June 17, 2016. Published by Tech.Co. https://tech.co/doze-rebrand-life-better-in-bed-2016-06.

47. Benjamin Seidman, "Tuck Wakes Up the Mattress Industry," Michipreneur, November 17, 2015, http://www.michipreneur.com/tuck-wakes-up-the-mattress-industry/.

48. Ibid.

2

Management and Entrepreneurship: Handling Start-Ups and New Ventures

TARGET SKILL

 Entrepreneurship Skill: involves the identification, evaluation, and exploitation of opportunities

ENTREPRENEURSHIP SKILL AND YOUR CAREER

Entrepreneurship skill will be of great value to you in enhancing your career. This skill can help you identify and exploit new market opportunities. The ability to identify and exploit opportunities will contribute to organizational success, build your image as a competent manager, make you valuable to your organization, and support promotions as you build your career.

OBJECTIVES

To help build my *entrepreneurship skill*, when studying this chapter, I will attempt to acquire:

2-1 An understanding of the three stages of entrepreneurship

2-2 An overall appreciation for the opportunity concept and an understanding of the primary types of entrepreneurial opportunities

2-3 An understanding of how to identify opportunities

2-4 Insights regarding the key components of opportunity evaluation

2-5 An appreciation for the role of opportunity exploitation in the entrepreneurship process

2-6 Insights regarding the various types of financing available to entrepreneurs

2-7 An appreciation for how existing organizations use corporate entrepreneurship

2-8 An understanding of and appreciation for the role of social entrepreneurship in society

---

MyLab Management Chapter Warm Up

If your instructor has assigned this activity, go to www.pearson.com/mylab/management to complete the chapter warm up.

CHALLENGE CASE

Professor Becomes Restaurateur

Wilmington College professor Steven Austin Stovall took his course on entrepreneurship one step further by creating a business plan alongside his students for a restaurant in the small Ohio town of Wilmington, a town of 12,000 people. A seventh-generation Texan, Stovall moved to Ohio to become a management professor at Wilmington College in 2002. Along the way, he provided consulting to the restaurant industry and learned what worked and what didn't. "Some restaurants have some fantastic ideas," he said, "but don't understand all the business aspects. Others understand the business, but can't go beyond copying what everyone else does."

In 2012, Stovall taught the college's only section of entrepreneurship to 20 students. During that class, students crafted business plans for their fictitious businesses in order to earn credit for the course, but Stovall did every step with the students. When they were conducting feasibility analyses, he conducted one, too. When they were thinking about marketing, so was he. By the end of the semester, he had written a business plan for a new entrepreneurial venture. He put the finishing touches on his business plan, he realized that he had a viable idea for a restaurant—he called it Austin's Casual Eatery, after his middle name as well as the vibrant college town in the heart of Texas. He wanted something different than what already existed, which was several chain restaurants and many competitors offering overly processed dishes or frozen ones that were simply heated up when the customer ordered one of them.

In August 2013, Austin's Casual Eatery, a 150-seat restaurant with a full-service bar, opened. After months of work turning the 140-year-old building into a modern restaurant, Stovall discovered that owning a restaurant is a lot different than consulting with one. "We thought we were prepared," he admitted, "but we weren't." The first night the store opened, a line of people went around the block, all of them waiting impatiently for a table at the newest restaurant in town. "We ran out of food on the first day," he said. "We literally only had half the menu available by 5 p.m." But the half that did remain wasn't quite what customers were wanting.

It was a learning experience for Stovall. His forecasting and food preparation were not meeting the demands of the market. After the first week, Stovall closed early one night and met with his team. "I told them we need to rethink this business. We had to ask ourselves why some things were selling beyond imagination and others weren't moving at all." Originally, Austin's opened as a tapas restaurant: small

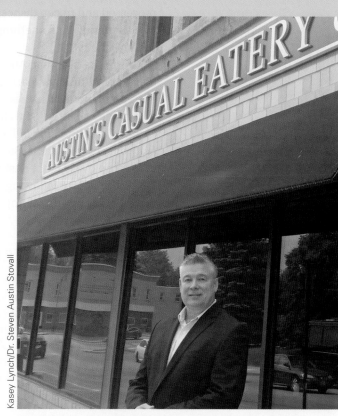

Kasey Lynch/Dr. Steven Austin Stovall

Dr. Steven Austin Stovall standing outside his 150-seat namesake restaurant in Wilmington, Ohio, faced several challenges in seeing his dream become a reality.

plates of a wide variety of food offerings that are meant to be shared. "People liked our food and the outstanding customer service, but they weren't really willing to share their order with others at the table!" So the tapas idea was gone after that first week, and Stovall and his team developed a menu of 35 appetizer and entrée items that would change seasonally. Collaboration is important for an entrepreneurial venture because when the business is small, relying on the team provides more ideas than the owner can possibly provide on his or her own. Every three months, Stovall and his general manager would sit down and determine what the top 10 selling items for the previous quarter were. Those top 10 items would remain, and 25 new menu items would appear that would feature that season's freshest offerings. A typical menu might include crab cakes, chicken empanadas, stuffed bell peppers, and a variety of handmade desserts.[1]

"As we researched and developed new menu items," said Stovall referring to his collaboration with the general manager, "our mantra became, 'ok, if our grandmothers read the list of ingredients for this dish, would they be able to pronounce and recognize each of those ingredients?'

If they wouldn't, that menu idea was gone." This philosophy of offering "real food" became the driving force of operating the business. Certainly, Stovall could have utilized more pre-processed and frozen dishes that would have been less costly to make, but his clientele was clamoring for something different than what was already available in the local restaurant market.

After the first year, Austin's Casual Eatery made close to $1 million in revenue. With a team of 32 full- and part-time staff members, Stovall's lessons in management and entrepreneurship were discovered through trial and error. "It was the mistakes we made that made us better," Stovall offered. "I'm glad we made big mistakes early so we could correct them and I'm glad we were small enough to be able to do so quickly." After several years of operations, Stovall continues to collaborate with the general manager and other employees in the restaurant to change the menu every three months and has developed a loyal following. One thing almost every customer mentions is that he or she enjoys ordering and tasting "real food."

THE ENTREPRENEURSHIP CHALLENGE

The Challenge Case illustrates the different entrepreneurship challenges that Steven Austin Stovall and Austin's Casual Eatery had to overcome. The remaining material in this chapter explains entrepreneurship concepts and helps develop the corresponding entrepreneurship skill you will need to meet such challenges throughout your career. After studying the chapter concepts, read the Challenge Case Summary at the end of the chapter to help you relate chapter content to meeting entrepreneurship challenges at Austin's Casual Eatery.

Fundamentals of Entrepreneurship

2-1 An understanding of the three stages of entrepreneurship

Entrepreneurship can be defined in a variety of ways. Most people believe that entrepreneurship entails an individual starting a new business to make money, but the meaning of the term is actually much broader. For our purposes, **entrepreneurship** refers to the identification, evaluation, and exploitation of opportunities.[2] **Figure 2.1** illustrates this process. Opportunities, in a general sense, are appropriate or favorable occasions.[3] In the entrepreneurship sense, however, the definition of *opportunity* is slightly different. Specifically, an **entrepreneurial opportunity** is an occasion to bring into existence new products and services that allow outputs to be sold at a price greater than their cost of production.[4] In other words, entrepreneurial opportunities exist when individuals are able to sell new products and services at a price that produces a profit.

Although *entrepreneurship* has a wide-ranging definition, the process still involves starting new businesses. Understanding entrepreneurship is important; one survey reports that, on average, 550,000 people start new businesses in the United States each month.[5] Other studies suggest that somewhere between 20 and 50 percent of all individuals engage in entrepreneurial behaviors.[6] Despite these new businesses, evidence also suggests that entrepreneurs find it difficult to keep their businesses going. Research reports, for example, that approximately 20 percent of new businesses do not make it past the first two years, 40 percent do not make it past four years, and 50 percent do not make it past six years.[8] **Table 2.1** displays the results of studies examining the failure rates of some new businesses. Note, however, that research also suggests that new

Figure 2.1

Stages of the entrepreneurship process

TABLE 2.1   A Summary of Entrepreneurial Failure Rates[7]

Operation	Failure Rate
New Restaurants	Approximately 51% of new restaurants fail within the first 5 years.
New Businesses	Approximately 60% of new businesses fail within the first 6 years.
New Chemical Plants	Approximately 80% of new chemical plants fail within the first 10 years.

businesses may improve the productivity of existing businesses because existing businesses improve processes to compete with new rivals entering the competitive arena.[9]

Consistent with our framework, an **entrepreneur** is an individual who identifies, evaluates, and exploits opportunities. Many associate the term *entrepreneur* with one individual starting a new business, but research suggests that approximately 75 percent of new organizations are started by entrepreneurial teams.[10] In other words, many entrepreneurs work with other people when identifying, evaluating, and exploiting entrepreneurial opportunities. Research also suggests that organizations started by entrepreneurial teams tend to perform better than those started by individual entrepreneurs working by themselves.[11] Many attribute this "team advantage" to the combination of diverse skills, experiences, and relationships of the entrepreneurial team members.[12] In addition, as new organizations develop, they require leaders with new skills. Consequently, assembling a team makes it easier for entrepreneurs to add team members with these new skills as the venture expands.[13]

It is clear that entrepreneurship represents an important piece of society. Taken together, then, these high business formation rates and high failure rates suggest that understanding the fundamentals of entrepreneurship is important. In the following sections, we highlight the primary issues that pertain to identifying, evaluating, and exploiting entrepreneurial opportunities.

Types of Opportunities

In his classic formulation of entrepreneurial opportunities, Schumpeter described five different types.[14] First, opportunities arise from the creation of new products or services. When a new type of medical device is created, for example, an opportunity exists in the form of convincing doctors to use the new device in their practices. The invention of the heart stent became an entrepreneurial opportunity for companies like Boston Scientific and Abbott Laboratories. Stents help doctors open a patient's arteries and keep them open, which in some cases enables the patient to avoid open-heart surgery altogether. Today, an estimated 1 million Americans per year undergo the stent procedure.[15]

Second, opportunities arise from the discovery of new geographical markets in which new customers will appreciate the new product or service. As an example, suppose an individual has the exclusive rights to produce and distribute within the United States action figures based on a popular movie. After saturating the domestic market, the individual might begin to distribute the action figures in China. This scenario would represent an opportunity arising from the discovery of a new geographical market.

Third, opportunities may arise from the creation or discovery of new raw materials or after discovering alternative uses for existing raw materials. For example, ethanol, which can be produced from corn, represents a new use for corn. Although farmers typically sell corn to the manufacturers of food products, ethanol provides farmers with another use for the corn they grow.

Fourth, opportunities may emerge from the discovery of new methods of production. According to Schumpeter, new methods of production allow entrepreneurs to produce goods or services at lower costs, which allows the entrepreneurs to satisfy the needs of customers more effectively. Finally, opportunities may arise from new methods of organizing. The emergence of the Internet provides an example of such an opportunity. Specifically, the Internet allows entrepreneurs to reach consumers without the need of brick-and-mortar retail locations.[16] For example, the Internet allows Netflix to offer customers a new way to rent DVDs and video games. Instead of driving to a retail outlet like Blockbuster, Netflix users order their DVDs and video games online.

In sum, five different types of opportunities arise from the creation of new products or services, the discovery of new geographic markets, the discovery of new raw materials, the discovery of new methods of production, and the discovery of new methods of organizing. **Table 2.2** summarizes and provides examples of each of these different types of opportunities. In the following sections, we describe in detail how entrepreneurs identify, evaluate, and exploit these opportunities.

2-2   An overall appreciation for the opportunity concept and an understanding of the primary types of entrepreneurial opportunities

TABLE 2.2   **Types of Opportunities**

Operation	Example
New Product or Service	Airbnb developing a new way for consumers to find lodging
New Geographic Markets	Citibank providing services in China
New Raw Materials or New Uses for Raw Materials	Under Armour using microfiber-based materials to make sports apparel
New Method of Production	Tyson Chicken raising chickens without antibiotics
New Method of Organizing	Uber developing a new way for consumers to travel

Opportunity Identification

2-3   An understanding of how to identify opportunities

Although an opportunity may exist, entrepreneurs will not be able to take advantage of it unless they are first able to identify the opportunity. Research suggests, though, that opportunities do not appear in a standard form and that individuals differ in their abilities to identify opportunities.[17] It makes sense that these differences in discernment are a good thing: If all individuals were equally able to identify opportunities, then they might all rush to exploit the same opportunities.

Which factors help determine whether individuals are able to identify opportunities? In the remainder of this section, we describe five such factors: entrepreneurial alertness, information asymmetry, social networks, cross-cultural experience, and the ability to establish means–ends relationships.

First, individuals vary in terms of **entrepreneurial alertness**, which refers to an individual's ability to notice and be sensitive to new information about objects, incidents, and patterns of behavior in the environment.[18] When individuals have high levels of entrepreneurial alertness, they are likely to identify potential entrepreneurial opportunities. In contrast, when individuals have low levels of entrepreneurial alertness, they are likely to dismiss or ignore new information and overlook potential opportunities.

Entrepreneurial alertness helped Pennsylvania farmers Amos and Jacob Miller identify a valuable opportunity. Years ago, from conversations with their customers, 32-year-old Amos and his dad, Jacob, spotted a trend in the making: Americans' interest in nutrient-dense food was growing. As a result, the Millers began expanding their farm's product line to include such foods—for example, grass-fed beef, milk-fed pork, and fermented vegetables. At a time when it's become more difficult to make a living from farming, Miller Farm revenues have topped $1.8 million. The key: recognizing a trend and acting on it.[19]

Second, individuals vary in terms of the information to which they have access, which is known as **information asymmetry**. This variation in information involves both new information and old information, and no two people share all of this information at the same time.[20] Two individuals, for example, may have access to new market information regarding a potential entrepreneurial opportunity; however, only one of these individuals has access to additional information suggesting that other people are already moving to exploit this opportunity. As such, only one of these individuals will correctly identify this opportunity.

Third, individuals vary in terms of their **social networks**, which represent individuals' patterns of social relationships. Some individuals have extended social networks (i.e., many social relationships), whereas other individuals have narrow social networks (i.e., few social relationships). Research suggests that individuals with extended networks are more likely to identify potential entrepreneurial opportunities than are those with narrow social networks.[21] Moreover, the *type* of social network may influence opportunity identification. An individual with entrepreneurial family members, for example, may be better able to identify opportunities than an individual with family members who are not entrepreneurial.[22]

Wenn/WENN Ltd/Alamy Stock Photo

One of *Inc.* magazine's "Most Impressive Women Entrepreneurs of 2016," Christine Hunsicker of Gwynnie Bee founded a plus-size clothing subscription service.

Figure 2.2
Determinants of opportunity
identification

Fourth, individuals vary in terms of their **cross-cultural experience**, which refers to experience living in a foreign country. Recent research indicates that cross-cultural experience is positively associated with opportunity identification. As individuals gain cross-cultural experience, they have access to different types of existing products, services, and customer problems associated with new cultures. This experience in turn helps them to identify new opportunities.[23]

Finally, individuals vary in terms of their abilities to assess means–ends relationships. In this context, the ability to assess means–ends relationships refers to understanding how to turn a new technology into a product or service that will be desired by consumers. For example, individuals may have access to technology but be unable to understand the potential commercial applications associated with the technology. When individuals are unable to see these associations, they are unable to identify the opportunity. In an effort to help establish these means–ends relationships, several universities are working with individuals and researchers to identify the commercial applications associated with new technologies.[24]

Taken together, these different factors influence opportunity identification. **Figure 2.2** summarizes these different factors.

Opportunity Evaluation

In the previous section, we discussed opportunity identification, which is the first step of the entrepreneurship process. In this section, we discuss the second stage of this process: opportunity evaluation. Opportunity evaluation occurs when an entrepreneur decides whether he or she has just a good idea or a viable opportunity that will provide the desired outcomes.[25] The evaluation step is "where the rubber meets the road," and it often presents a challenge. When evaluating opportunities, entrepreneurs must be honest with themselves.[26] If they are not, they may purposely ignore or accidentally overlook important factors that will limit the potential success of the opportunity.

To evaluate ideas, entrepreneurs will often engage in **feasibility analysis**, which is analysis that helps entrepreneurs understand whether an idea is practical.[27] In such an analysis, entrepreneurs study customer demands, the structure of the industry, and the entrepreneur's ability to provide the new product or service. Although entrepreneurs have many ideas, not all of them are feasible; this analysis helps them to understand whether they will be able to secure the resources required to make their ideas a reality.

Even if an idea is feasible, opportunities are associated with some risk. One of the central factors that entrepreneurs examine in the evaluation stage is the opportunity's **entrepreneurial risk**, which is the likelihood and magnitude of the opportunity's downside loss. In this context, **downside loss** refers to the resources (i.e., money, relationships, etc.) that the entrepreneur

2-4   Insights regarding the key components of opportunity evaluation

STEPS FOR SUCCESS

Testing Business Ideas

Entrepreneurs can reduce the risks of starting a business by testing their ideas before pursuing a full-scale business. Joe Demin, for example, thought the hammocks he saw in Thailand were excellent, and he wanted to sell them in the United States. But before he quit his job, he tried selling a few of the hammocks at craft fairs in his hometown. The experience helped him develop a workable plan for his new business, Yellow Leaf Hammocks.

Experienced entrepreneurs offer the following tips for testing business concepts:[28]

- Identify a group of people you expect to be interested, and send them an e-mail describing the product and/or concept. Ask them to let you know whether it appeals to them.
- Offer samples of a new product and invite reactions.
- Set up a booth at a trade show. Pay attention to visitors' questions and their reactions to your product and marketing materials.

could lose if the opportunity does not succeed. All else being equal, entrepreneurs are more likely to pursue opportunities with low levels of entrepreneurial risk and less likely to pursue opportunities with high levels of entrepreneurial risk.

Research suggests that two factors may adversely influence the accuracy of an entrepreneur's risk perceptions.[29] First, an entrepreneur's belief in the law of small numbers decreases the risk that he or she perceives with an opportunity. The **law of small numbers** refers to individuals relying on small samples of information to guide their decisions. Because small samples are more likely to provide encouraging information (i.e., the success stories of other entrepreneurs) and less likely to provide discouraging information (i.e., stories of the failures of other entrepreneurs), small samples of information tend to be biased positively. Such beliefs tend to be common among entrepreneurs because most entrepreneurs do not have access to large amounts of information.[30] As such, the extent to which individuals (perhaps subconsciously) believe in the accuracy of the law of small numbers helps determine whether they are likely to obtain biased information and thus associate low levels of risk with their ideas.

Second, the control that an entrepreneur feels with respect to the opportunity's outcome may influence perceptions of the idea's risk. **Illusion of control** exists when entrepreneurs overestimate the extent to which they can control the outcome of an opportunity.[31] The outcomes of some opportunities rely more on luck than on entrepreneurial skill. In these situations, believing that one can control the outcomes is unwise.

Taking these two factors together, when entrepreneurs evaluate opportunities, they need to pay careful attention to entrepreneurial risk—and savvy entrepreneurs work to reduce risk before investing substantial amounts of capital.[32] It is important that entrepreneurs do not fall victim to a belief in the law of small numbers or the illusion of control when evaluating opportunities because these two factors may negatively influence the accuracy of risk perceptions. In the following section, we discuss the final stage of the entrepreneurship process: opportunity exploitation.

Opportunity Exploitation

2-5 An appreciation for the role of opportunity exploitation in the entrepreneurship process

The third step in the entrepreneurship process involves exploiting an opportunity. **Exploitation** refers to the activities and investments that are committed to gain returns from the new product or service arising from the opportunity.[33] Simply stated, exploitation occurs when an entrepreneur (or group of entrepreneurs) decides that an opportunity is worth pursuing. When an entrepreneur decides that customers would highly value a new product, exploitation entails all of those activities (i.e., marketing, production, etc.) needed to sell the new product to consumers.

Entrepreneur Bryan Green successfully exploited an opportunity he identified. Unlike many Americans, Green has always enjoyed exercising. Realizing that Americans, in general, are out of shape was the opportunity and the impetus Green needed to launch Advantage Fitness Products, a company that designs, supplies, and services fitness facilities worldwide. Green designs home gyms for celebrities as well as for professional teams like the San Francisco 49ers and the New York Mets. Green says that once he exploited his opportunity, the keys to his success were to "stay flexible and execute flawlessly."[34]

MyLab Management Watch It

If your instructor has assigned this activity, go to www.pearson .com/mylab/management to complete the video exercise.

Mandoga Media/Alamy Stock Photo

Several factors can help entrepreneurs decide whether they should exploit an opportunity.[35] First, entrepreneurs are more likely to exploit an opportunity when they believe that customers will value their new product or service. When customers value a new product or service, they provide market demand. This market demand in turn helps entrepreneurs earn the resources (i.e., profits) necessary to support the opportunity exploitation.

Second, entrepreneurs are more likely to exploit an opportunity when they perceive that they have the support of important stakeholders. Stakeholders are groups such as employees, suppliers, investors, and other suppliers of capital (i.e., banks) who directly or indirectly influence organizational performance. When entrepreneurs perceive that these groups will provide support, entrepreneurs are more likely to exploit the opportunity. This tendency makes sense intuitively because these stakeholders will help ensure the success of the entrepreneur pursuing the opportunity. Conversely, it will likely prove difficult for entrepreneurs to succeed if they do not have the support of important stakeholders.

Finally, entrepreneurs are more likely to exploit opportunities when they perceive that their management team is capable. Qualified management teams bring resources (i.e., ability, knowledge, information) to the opportunity that are likely to enhance the prospects of the opportunity.[36] In contrast, when entrepreneurs feel that their management teams are incapable, they are less likely to exploit the opportunity because they will not feel that they have access to the necessary resources to ensure high levels of organizational success.

In sum, several factors influence an entrepreneur's ability to exploit opportunities. **Figure 2.3** summarizes these factors.

Facebook founder Mark Zuckerberg is one of the most successful entrepreneurs of the twenty-first century. Other people had developed ideas for social networks, but Zuckerberg outdid them in exploiting the opportunity.

Figure 2.3
Factors influencing opportunity exploitation

Financing Exploitation

2-6 Insights regarding the various types of financing available to entrepreneurs

When entrepreneurs decide that an opportunity is worth exploiting, they often lack the capital (i.e., money) needed to exploit the opportunity. Although some entrepreneurs fund their operations with their own money or with credit cards, most entrepreneurs require at least some external money to fund their operations. In this section, we review three primary sources of external capital for entrepreneurs: angel investors, venture capitalists, and bank financing.

Angel investors are wealthy individuals who provide capital to new companies.[37] Angel investors may include an entrepreneur's family and friends, but angel investors are also private individuals who did not know the entrepreneur prior to funding the opportunity. Angel investors have existed for centuries—in fact, in 1903, five angel investors helped Henry Ford launch his auto company with a total of $41,500. Within 15 years, those angels' investments were worth a whopping $145 million![38] Today, approximately 140,000 angel investors provide about $9 billion in capital to nearly 25,000 new ventures each year.[39]

Venture capitalists are firms that raise money from investors and then use this money to make investments in new firms. Many prominent companies such as Intel and Microsoft received investments from venture capitalists in their early days. The companies then used these funds to help acquire the resources (i.e., employees, equipment, etc.) that eventually made them the companies they are today. Although the use of venture capital in the United States peaked at about $100 billion during the dot-com frenzy of 1998 to 2000, the venture capital industry today totals nearly $70 billion.[40]

It is important to note that both angel investors and venture capitalists provide money to entrepreneurs and in return receive a portion of the firm's equity. In other words, in return for their investment (money) in the entrepreneur's firm, the entrepreneur gives them partial ownership of the firm. As such, when the entrepreneur's firm does well and increases in value, the investors' investments also increase in value. When the entrepreneur's firm does poorly and decreases in value, the investors' investments also decrease in value.

Although similar, angel investors and venture capitalists differ in a number of significant ways. In contrast to angel investors, venture capitalists make fewer investments, but those investments are often larger than the investments made by angel investors. In fact, the average investment of venture capitalists is approximately $4 million, whereas the average investment of angel investors is about $75,000.[41] In addition, venture capitalists typically focus on a small number of industries, whereas angel investors tend not to focus on particular industries. Finally, venture capitalists typically invest in firms after they've passed the initial, start-up stage. In other words, angel investors typically provide the initial financing to start-up ventures, and venture capitalists provide additional capital as the new venture becomes established.

In sum, angel investors and venture capitalists are sources that entrepreneurs may use to fund new ventures. While different, research suggests that angel investors and venture capitalists have an impact on innovation rates in equivalent ways within entrepreneurial firms.[42] Whether an entrepreneur obtains funding from an angel investor or from a venture capitalist, however, it is important to note that such relationships present specific challenges that entrepreneurs must manage.[43]

Bank financing occurs when an entrepreneur obtains financing from a financial institution in the form of a loan. It is important to note that, unlike angel investors or venture capitalists, banks are not investors. Instead, banks make loans to entrepreneurs and in return expect repayment of the loans with interest. Banks are not concerned with the long-term potential for returns. Instead, they are more interested in ensuring that the entrepreneur's opportunity survives long enough to ensure loan repayment. In other words, investors typically seek risk, but banks are likely to minimize risk.

Corporate Entrepreneurship

2-7 An appreciation for how existing organizations use corporate entrepreneurship

Until now, we have focused on entrepreneurial opportunities pursued by individuals or teams of individuals. It is important to note, though, that existing corporations can also identify, evaluate, and exploit opportunities. **Corporate entrepreneurship** is the process in which an individual or group of individuals in an existing corporation creates a new organization or instigates renewal or innovation within that corporation.[44] Although corporate

PRACTICAL CHALLENGE: RAISING FUNDS

Bohemian Guitars Tests the Waters of Crowdfunding

While venture capitalists grab headlines, many entrepreneurs get by with their own resources plus funds from their social networks. Now crowdfunding may expand those networks. The idea started with Kickstarter and similar websites seeking donations. Entrepreneurs using these networks hope that people will be willing to invest in a business they like in exchange for a share of the profits. However, the Securities and Exchange Commission (SEC) regulates investments and wants to ensure that crowdfunding does not defraud anyone. The SEC has thus been developing rules allowing companies to raise up to $1 million a year from crowdfunding.

Meanwhile, a few states have permitted crowdfunding on a local scale and by state residents. One company taking advantage of this opportunity is Bohemian Guitars. The Georgia start-up, which makes guitars from oilcans, could not get a bank loan but raised more than $100,000 from crowdfunding. Entrepreneurs considering this tactic must publicize the business actively in order to gain a large number of backers. They also need to communicate with their many investors to maintain enthusiasm about the business.[45]

entrepreneurship often involves establishing new organizations, these new organizations leverage the parent corporation's assets, market position, or other resources.[46] When corporate entrepreneurship results in new companies, these new companies often continue to work closely with the parent company.

It is important to recognize that corporate entrepreneurship does not necessarily require creating a new organization. Corporate entrepreneurship, for example, also involves creating new products, services, or technologies. At 3M, engineers can spend as much as 15 percent of their time on projects of their own design. The company believes that this flexibility provides the motivation that engineers need to innovate successfully, possibly leading to new products or services—or new organizations altogether.[47]

Corporate entrepreneurship can be classified into four general types.[48] First, **sustained regeneration** occurs when firms develop new cultures, processes, or structures to support new product innovations in current markets as well as introduce existing products into new markets. Sustained regeneration is the most frequently used type of corporate entrepreneurship.

Second, **organizational rejuvenation** involves improving a firm's ability to execute strategies and focuses on new processes instead of new products. GE, for instance, successfully rejuvenated itself by changing policies and procedures within the company to support innovation.

Third, **strategic renewal** occurs when a firm attempts to alter its own competitive strategy. Unlike introducing a new product or service, strategic renewal occurs when the firm tries to offer a brand-new competitive strategy. Of course, it remains quite difficult for a firm to change strategies. Walmart, for example, is facing tremendous difficulties in trying to alter its strategy to focus on more affluent customers.[49]

Fourth, **domain definition** occurs when a firm proactively seeks to create a product market position that competitors have not recognized. When pursuing domain definition, firms hope to become the first entrant in a market segment. In such situations, firms will enjoy the benefits of having no competitors. Amazon.com, for example, was one of the first companies to realize the potential of selling books online. It is important to note, though, that first movers do not always succeed. Apple's Newton, for example, was the first personal digital assistant (PDA), but this product no longer exists. Moreover, Apple's iPod was not the first digital music player on the market, but today the iPod dominates the marketplace.

In sum, there are several general types of corporate entrepreneurship. Despite its importance, not every organization can support corporate entrepreneurship. The success of corporate entrepreneurship efforts depends on many factors, including an organization's culture, practices, and even tolerance level for uncertainty.[50]

Social Entrepreneurship

2-8 An understanding of and appreciation for the role of social entrepreneurship in society

The discussion of entrepreneurship so far in this chapter has involved individuals or corporations that pursue entrepreneurial opportunities for the purposes of generating sales and profits, which we call **commercial entrepreneurship**. In recent years, researchers have begun to examine entrepreneurship in a social context. **Social entrepreneurship** involves the recognition, evaluation, and exploitation of opportunities that create social value as opposed to personal or shareholder wealth.[51] In this context, **social value** refers to the basic, long-standing needs of society and has little to do with profits. Basic, long-standing needs might include providing water, food, and shelter to individuals in need. "Social value" might also refer to more specific needs such as providing playground equipment to needy school districts or Seeing Eye dogs for those who are blind. Recent reports suggest that the growth in nonprofit organizations has increased at a faster pace than the growth of new businesses.[52]

Muhammad Yunus, an economist turned social entrepreneur, launched one of the world's most successful nonprofits: Grameen Bank, a microfinance organization. Yunus launched Grameen when he realized that small loans can make a huge difference in the life of an entrepreneur in an underdeveloped country. Grameen Bank advances microloans—and relatively low interest rates—because it is more interested in improving lives than in making money. The winner of the 2006 Nobel Peace Prize, Yunus has also received the Presidential Medal of Freedom, the highest civilian honor in the United States, which is awarded to those whose work has changed the world.[53]

Muhammad Yunus launched Grameen Bank to make loans to entrepreneurs in underdeveloped countries.

Baumanntoo B/SIPA/Newscom

How Do Commercial and Social Entrepreneurship Differ?

Although the two concepts have some similarities, substantive differences distinguish commercial entrepreneurship from social entrepreneurship. In the remainder of this section, we detail three differences with respect to mission, resources, and performance measurement.

Perhaps the most fundamental difference between commercial and social entrepreneurship involves the entrepreneur's mission or purpose. The purpose of commercial entrepreneurship is to create profits, whereas the purpose of social entrepreneurship is to create value for the public. Despite this difference in focus, it is important to note that social entrepreneurs cannot totally ignore issues surrounding sales and costs. If social entrepreneurs did ignore such important concepts, they likely would not have the money needed to continue their pursuit of social value. Even though the goal of social entrepreneurship does not involve profits, social entrepreneurs still need to monitor profit-oriented measures, including revenues and costs. In this sense, then, profits remain somewhat important, but social value dominates the goal structure of social entrepreneurs.[54]

A second primary distinction between commercial and social entrepreneurship involves the availability of resources such as funding and employees. Unlike commercial entrepreneurs, social entrepreneurs face many difficulties attracting capital from angel investors, venture capitalists, and banks. Instead, most social entrepreneurs rely on donations as sources of funding. Also, social entrepreneurs frequently face difficulties in hiring and compensating employees. Because social entrepreneurs often do not have the capital necessary to pay attractive salaries, they usually must focus on hiring people who share the organization's purpose. Such people tend to be willing to work

TIPS FOR MANAGING AROUND THE GLOBE

Taking a Global View of Opportunities: One Earth Designs

Social entrepreneurship opens up tremendous opportunities globally because so many unmet needs exist all over the world. Creative thinkers with a passion to do good can apply their talents by traveling and observing what people struggle with. Scot Frank was a Massachusetts Institute of Technology (MIT) student doing an internship in China when he discovered that rural residents of the Himalayan plateau cook and heat their homes with wood and dung. These fuels not only add to air pollution but also create dangerous fumes indoors. Frank decided to apply his engineering skills to improve their cooking methods.

Back home, Frank worked with other MIT students to design a lightweight, low-maintenance, solar-powered cooker. Its shining panels, which look like a satellite dish, concentrate the sun's rays to create a hot center for cooking. The cooker can also be used for heating and for converting heat to electricity. Frank partnered with Catlin Powers—a Harvard graduate student in environmental health who was investigating the air-quality problems in the same region—to start a business called One Earth Designs. The company has so far sold thousands of cookers, has expanded into 18 countries, and is developing a model suitable for disaster relief.[55]

for low salaries. In fact, many social entrepreneurs rely on volunteers to help their organizations fulfill their missions.

Commercial and social entrepreneurship also differ in terms of performance measures. Commercial entrepreneurs focus on quantitative measures such as profits, shareholder wealth, revenues, and costs. In contrast, social entrepreneurs focus on performance measures that are not related to money. For example, although a soup kitchen needs to monitor costs, its primary performance measure would be the number of meals served. In addition, a free meal may improve the emotional state of someone who is homeless, an outcome that is difficult to quantify.

Success Factors in Social Entrepreneurship

Although the topic of social entrepreneurship is fairly new from a research perspective, some studies have looked at the factors that influence the performance of social entrepreneurs.[56] In the remainder of this section, we discuss three factors that influence the performance of social entrepreneurs: their networks of relationships, their capital bases, and the public's acceptance of the new venture.

Previously in this chapter, we described the importance of entrepreneurs' social networks. These networks are also important for social entrepreneurs. Large networks provide social entrepreneurs with potential sources of capital to fund their social missions. In addition, large social networks can help social entrepreneurs identify potential employees and volunteers. In sum, large social networks improve the success of social entrepreneurs.

Similar to commercial entrepreneurship, an organization's capital base is important for social entrepreneurs. In fact, capital is perhaps even more important for social entrepreneurs because they do not have access to the venture capital and bank financing available to commercial entrepreneurs. Consequently, the capital raised through donations and other funding sources is extremely important for the success of social entrepreneurs.

Finally, the acceptance of a particular social entrepreneur's social values influences the success of his or her organization. When a large segment of society supports a social entrepreneur's cause, the social entrepreneur is likely to obtain the funds and employees or volunteers needed for success. In contrast, when only a small segment of society supports the social entrepreneur's cause, it is more difficult for the entrepreneur to obtain the necessary resources. For example, the National Association of Parents of the Visually Impaired Children in Israel faced difficulties raising the necessary resources because so few members of society found the organization worthy of support.[57]

CHALLENGE CASE SUMMARY

The Challenge Case describes how Steven Austin Stovall developed a restaurant called Austin's Casual Eatery. The story of Stovall's restaurant provides an example of how entrepreneurs can fine-tune their business or even change it in drastic ways after responding to market demands. Stovall noticed that a tapas restaurant in a small Ohio town was not a viable form for the business, so he changed the direction of the company immediately to ensure the viability of his entrepreneurial venture. Being able to identify an opportunity and respond to it properly is very important for a successful entrepreneur.

According to Schumpeter's classic formulation of opportunities, Austin's Casual Eatery has done well because it seized the opportunity of creating new products in a market where similar offerings did not exist. The company's reputation for excellent quality and superb customer service has driven demand for the restaurant's menu items and has created nearly $1 million in revenue.

In starting Austin's Casual Eatery, Stovall proceeded through the three steps of the entrepreneurial process. He identified an opportunity when he realized that the local restaurant market was primarily serving overly processed and frozen foods rather than made-from-scratch menu items. Next, he evaluated the opportunity after he understood what was required to open a restaurant. A full evaluation likely included figuring out if the restaurant was practical, gathering specific information on what others in the industry were doing, and deciding whether his restaurant could compete with restaurants already established in the local area. Finally, he exploited the opportunity by renovating an old building, training staff, ordering food, and opening the doors to the public.

As Stovall proceeded through these undertakings, he needed to understand the entrepreneurial risk associated with opening a tapas restaurant in a small midwestern town. If customers didn't fully embrace the tapas concept of sharing dishes and Stovall continued to operate in this manner, he likely would have been unsuccessful. Therefore, after just one week in business, he completely changed his concept from that of a tapas restaurant to one that served more traditional dishes. However, to ensure diversification from his competitors, he created a system where the menu would change every three months, keeping only those 10 items that sold the best during the prior quarter.

When Stovall met with this team to discuss the original failure of the tapas concept, he engaged in collaboration, which is one of the six management employability skills. Collaboration is the ability to work actively with others in accomplishing a task. The task was to determine what concept could replace the tapas idea. Once the direction of the restaurant was determined as a traditional restaurant with a seasonal menu, Stovall collaborated with the general manager and anyone else on the team who had ideas for a menu offering as the seasons change.

An entrepreneur must be able to adapt and change according to market pressures. As Stovall discovered the challenges of managing a large restaurant, he made those changes that ensured the company's survival. Obviously, he also took on significant risk by starting a restaurant in the first place. It is expensive, and it is an industry replete with failures. He also risked the business by changing the concept so quickly after opening from a tapas restaurant to one that offers appetizers and entrées. Overall, though, it appears that those risks were exactly the ones that needed to be taken to keep the restaurant prosperous.

MyLab Management Assessing Your Management Skill

If your instructor has assigned this activity, go to www.pearson.com/mylab/management to complete the exercise related to the Challenge Case.

DEVELOPING ENTREPRENEURSHIP SKILL

This section is specially designed to help you develop entrepreneurship skills. An individual's entrepreneurship skill is based on an understanding of the concepts and the ability to apply those concepts. The following activities will help to enhance your entrepreneurship skills in various organizational situations.

Class Preparation and Personal Study

To help you prepare for class, perform the activities outlined in this section. Performing these activities will help you enhance your classroom performance significantly.

Reflecting on Target Skill

On page 54, this chapter opens by presenting a target management skill along with a list of related objectives outlining knowledge and understanding that you should aim to acquire related to that skill. Review this target skill and the list of objectives to make sure that you've acquired all pertinent information within the chapter. If you do not feel that you've reached a particular objective(s), study related chapter coverage until you do.

Know Key Terms

Understanding the following key terms is critical to your understanding of chapter material. Define each of these terms. Refer to the page(s) referenced after a term to check your definition or to gain further insight regarding the term.

entrepreneurship **56**
entrepreneurial opportunity **56**
entrepreneur **57**
entrepreneurial alertness **58**
information asymmetry **58**
social network **58**
cross-cultural experience **59**
feasibility analysis **59**
entrepreneurial risk **59**
downside loss **59**
law of small numbers **60**
illusion of control **60**
exploitation **60**
angel investors **62**
venture capitalists **62**
bank financing **62**
corporate entrepreneurship **62**
sustained regeneration **63**

organizational rejuvenation **63**
strategic renewal **63**
domain definition **63**
commercial entrepreneurship **64**
social entrepreneurship **64**
social value **64**

Know How Management Concepts Relate

This section comprises activities that will further sharpen your understanding of management concepts. Answer these essay questions as completely as possible.

2-1 Describe the differences between opportunity identification and opportunity exploitation.

2-2 Describe the main components of social entrepreneurship, and describe how social entrepreneurship differs from commercial entrepreneurship.

2-3 Describe the different types of corporate entrepreneurship and provide examples of each.

Management Skills Exercises

Learning activities in this section are aimed at helping you to develop entrepreneurship skills.

MyLab Management
Discussion Questions

Go to www.pearson.com/mylab/management to complete the problems marked with this icon ⭐.

⭐ Cases

Professor Becomes Restaurateur

"Professor Becomes Restaurateur" and its related Challenge Case Summary were written to help you understand the management concepts contained in this chapter. Answer the following discussion questions about the introductory case to explore how fundamental management concepts can be applied to a company such as Austin's Casual Eatery.

2-4   Discuss the opportunities that Steven Austin Stovall observed in the local restaurant market. How did he evaluate and exploit those opportunities?

2-5   How risky was Stovall's move to change the entire concept of the restaurant just one week after opening? What could have gone wrong?

2-6   Describe Stovall's entrepreneurial alertness. How did it help or hurt his business?

2-7   Which management employability skill or skills did Stovall demonstrate in this case?

How Part-Time Work Became a $40 Million Business Called Drybar

Read the case and answer the questions that follow. Studying this case will help you better understand how concepts relating to entrepreneurship can be applied in a company such as Drybar.

After her children were born, Alli Webb wanted to work part time. She decided to apply her training and experience as a hairstylist to offer services in clients' homes. Her additional background in publicity would help her build the business by word of mouth. Webb also identified an opportunity: She would focus on providing only "blowouts," washing and blow-drying the client's hair. This method delivers a great look at a lower cost—and at a lower price for the client—than having hair dyed, cut, or permed. People loved the idea, and soon Webb had more jobs than she could handle on her own, although she now admits that the earnings barely covered her costs.

Still, Webb persevered; the toughest management challenge was finding enough money to keep up with the growth in demand. Her first step in expansion was to form a corporation, Drybar Holdings, and open a shop in Brentwood, an upscale part of Los Angeles. Webb and her husband tapped into their own savings and approached Webb's brother, Michael Landau, about investing $250,000. They determined that, for the idea to succeed, the salon would need to attract at least 20 to 30 customers per day. In fact, within the first few hours of opening, the salon was booked solid for six weeks. Landau was on board, and additional family and friends later invested a total of $1 million in the business. The company's continued success then attracted $2.5 million from angel investors and later $21 million from a private-equity firm. With that funding, Drybar has grown to 32 salons, $40 million in annual revenues, and 2,000 employees, including stylists—a departure from most salons, where stylists are independent contractors. On average, each salon provides 60 to 100 blowouts every day, with many repeat customers who have discovered what an affordable luxury a 40-minute, $40 blowout can be. The high number of blowouts helps make each shop more profitable than a traditional hair salon would be.

Now that Drybar is a big company, Webb's role has changed. Whereas she first built her business on her skill as a stylist, she now uses that knowledge to establish and monitor standards for her employees. She also established detailed requirements for the design of each salon and the ways stylists should interact with their customers. One feature of a Drybar blowout, for example, involves clients sitting so that they face away from the mirrors. When the blow-drying is done, the stylist whirls the client's chair around so that the client has the thrill of seeing the finished hairdo in all its glory. Webb also led the creation of a line of Drybar hair care products, using feedback from her stylists to guide the products' development. Managing the business has affected Drybar's other founders as well. Webb, her husband (who used his advertising experience to become the company's creative director), and her brother (who applied his business experience from Yahoo! and leadership of a marketing firm to the role of Drybar CEO) could not run a multimillion-dollar business on their own. Drybar therefore hired John Heffner, whose experience in consumer goods includes a position as president of OPI Products, a maker of nail care products, to be Drybar's new CEO.

However, Drybar's success has led to a new kind of risk: Others see the intense demand for the blowout procedure, so competitors, including chains such as Blo and DreamDry, are entering the market. Webb's strategy is to continue focusing on high-quality service to maintain the advantage of being the first to enter the business.[58]

Questions

2-8   What kind of opportunity did Alli Webb identify? How did entrepreneurial alertness, information asymmetry, and social networks shape her success?

2-9 What kinds of entrepreneurial risks has Webb faced? How will greater competition affect the level of risk?

2-10 What role has financing played in Drybar's success? What other sources of financing could Webb and her management team consider?

Experiential Exercises

Conducting a Feasibility Analysis

Directions. Read the following scenario and then perform the listed activities. Your instructor may want you to perform the activities as an individual or within groups. Follow all of your instructor's directions carefully.

A friend of yours who attends your university has come to you with an idea she's been thinking about. She wants to open a new hair salon or barbershop on campus that would cater exclusively to students, faculty, and staff. She wants your opinion about the viability of this proposal. Prepare a short, one- to two-page feasibility analysis where you answer the following questions: Is there a demand on campus for this business? Is there any competition? What qualifications would your friend need to be successful?

You and Your Career

Which type of person makes a better employee? Which is more attractive: a candidate with a traditional résumé of moving from job to job or one who has entrepreneurial experience? Assume a hiring manager has two candidates to choose between. The position is in sales for a leading consumer products company. One candidate has five years of experience at a competing firm in sales. The other has five years of experience as an entrepreneur for a small company that sold refurbished laptops and computers. Other than this difference, both have identical backgrounds and education. Develop a list of pros and cons for each candidate with regard to their merits for filling the open position.

Building Your Management Skills Portfolio

Your Management Skills Portfolio is a collection of activities specially designed to demonstrate your management knowledge and skill. Be sure to save your work. Taking your printed portfolio to an employment interview could be helpful in obtaining a job.

The portfolio activity for this chapter is Serving Up Drinks at KFC. Study the information given here and complete the exercises that follow.

Top managers at KFC have contacted you to help them enhance their business. In particular, executives at KFC worry that the company's focus on food means that it is not making as much profit as it could if it increased sales of drinks.

Given the success of companies such as Starbucks, some of KFC's competitors, such as McDonald's, are changing their menus to compete more effectively with Starbucks. McDonald's claims that its new line of espresso drinks represents the most significant menu change for the

company since it started serving breakfast in the 1970s. Sonic has also started selling coffee-based beverages in addition to the many shakes and fruit slushes already on the menu.

KFC would like you to identify, evaluate, and form methods of exploitation for the company regarding selling drinks. Answer the following questions pertaining to the entrepreneurship process.

2-11 Identify a specific opportunity in the marketplace regarding drinks. It could be a new drink, a new line of drinks, a new type of retail outlet, or another type of opportunity.

_____

_____

_____

2-12 Evaluate this opportunity using feasibility analysis. In particular, focus on how customers might respond to the new opportunity, indicate how industry competitors are already exploiting this opportunity, and describe KFC's ability to exploit this opportunity.

_____

_____

_____

2-13 What specific steps should KFC take to exploit this opportunity? Does the company have enough money to follow your suggestion(s) easily, or should the company pursue financing options?

_____

_____

_____

MyLab Management
Writing Assignments

If your instructor has assigned this activity, go to www.pearson.com/mylab/management for the following assisted-graded writing assignments:

Assisted-Grading Questions

2-14 Describe the main components of entrepreneurship.

2-15 Distinguish among the different types of opportunities.

Endnotes

1. Audrey Ingram, "Local Professor to Open Downtown Restaurant," *Wilmington News Journal*, July 18, 2013, A1.
2. Scott Shane and S. Venkataraman, "The Promise of Entrepreneurship as a Field of Research," *Journal of Management* 25, no. 1 (2000): 217–226.
3. *Webster's College Dictionary* (New York: Random House, 1996).
4. Scott Shane, "Prior Knowledge and the Discovery of Entrepreneurial Opportunities," *Organization Science* 11, no. 4 (2000): 448–469. See also

J. C. Short, D. J. Ketchen, C. L. Shook, and R. D. Ireland, "The Concept of 'Opportunity' in Entrepreneurship Research: Past Accomplishments and Future Challenges," *Journal of Management* 36 (2010): 40–65; "Characteristics of an Entrepreneur," http://www.scribd.com/doc/18197794, accessed May 10, 2012.

5. Robert Fairlie, E. J. Reedy, Arnobio Morelix, and Joshual Russell, "Kaufman Index Startup Activity," Ewing Marion Kauffman Foundation (2016), http://www.kauffman.org/kauffman-index/reports/~/media/a146c78b9b254cbe8b9cb2e507ce5537.ashx, accessed April 17, 2017.

6. Scott Shane and S. Venkataraman, "The Promise of Entrepreneurship as a Field of Research," *Journal of Management* 25, no. 1 (2000): 217–226.

7. Based on data from Matthew Hayward, Dean Shepherd, and Dale Griffin, "A Hubris Theory of Entrepreneurship," *Management Science* 52, no. 2 (2006): 160–172; H. G. Parsa, John Self, David Njite, and Tiffany King, "Why Restaurants Fail," *Cornell Hotel and Restaurant Administration Quarterly* 46, no. 3 (2005): 304–322; Scott A. Shane, "Failure Is a Constant in Entrepreneurship," *New York Times*, July 17, 2009, http://boss.blogs.nytimes.com.

8. Bureau of Labor Statistics, "Entrepreneurship and the U.S. Economy," https://www.bls.gov/bdm/entrepreneurship/bdm_chart3.htm, accessed April 17, 2017.

9. M. Fritsch and J. Changoluisa, "New Business Formation and the Productivity of Manufacturing Incumbents: Effects and Mechanisms," *Journal of Business Venturing* 32 (2017): 237–259.

10. A. C. Cooper and C. M. Daily, "Entrepreneurial Teams," in D. L. Sexton and R. W. Smilor, eds., *Entrepreneurship* (Chicago: Upstart Publishing Company, 2000), 127–150.

11. G. N. Chandler and S. H. Hanks, "An Examination of the Substitutability of the Founders' Human and Financial Capital in Emerging Business Ventures," *Journal of Business Venturing* 13 (1998): 353–369.

12. D. Ucbasaran, A. Lockett, M. Wright, and P. Westhead, "Entrepreneurial Founder Teams: Factors Associated with Member Entry and Exit," *Entrepreneurship Theory & Practice* (2003): 107–128.

13. C. M. Beckman, M. D. Burton, and C. O'Reilly, "Early Teams: The Impact of Team Demography on VC Financing and Going Public," *Journal of Business Venturing* 22 (2007): 147–173.

14. This discussion is based on J. Schumpeter, *Capitalism, Socialism, and Democracy* (New York: Harper & Row, 1934).

15. Joanne Silberner and Renee Montagne, "Coronary Stent Procedures Very Common," National Public Radio, transcript, http://www.npr.org, accessed February 12, 2010; A. Weintraub, "Heart Trouble," *BusinessWeek* (October 29, 2007): 54.

16. Jonathan Eckhardt and Scott Shane, "Opportunities and Entrepreneurship," *Journal of Management* 29, no. 3 (2003): 333–349.

17. Scott Shane, "Prior Knowledge and the Discovery of Entrepreneurial Opportunities," *Organization Science* 11, no. 4 (2000): 448–469; S. Venkataraman, "The Distinctive Domain of Entrepreneurship Research: An Editor's Perspective," in J. Katz and R. Brockhaus, eds., *Advances in Entrepreneurship, Firm Emergence, and Growth* (Greenwich, CT: JAI Press, 1999).

18. Alexander Ardichvili, Richard Cardozo, and Sourav Ray, "A Theory of Entrepreneurial Identification and Development," *Journal of Business Venturing* 18 (2003): 105–123; J. Tang, K. M. Kacmar, and L. Busenitz, "Entrepreneurial Alertness in the Pursuit of New Opportunities," *Journal of Business Venturing* 27, no. 1 (2012): 77–94.

19. David E. Gumpert, "An Amish Entrepreneur's Old-Fashioned Approach," *BusinessWeek*, http://www.businessweek.com, accessed April 20, 2010.

20. Alexander Ardichvili, Richard Cardozo, and Sourav Ray, "A Theory of Entrepreneurial Identification and Development," *Journal of Business Venturing* 18 (2003): 105–123; Scott Shane and S. Venkataraman, "The Promise of Entrepreneurship as a Field of Research," *Journal of Management* 25, no. 1 (2000): 217–226.

21. G. Hills, G. T. Lumpkin, and R. P. Singh, "Opportunity Recognition: Perceptions and Behaviors of Entrepreneurs," *Frontiers of Entrepreneurship Research* (Wellesley, MA: Babson College, 1997), 203–218. For a more detailed discussion of opportunity recognition, see J. Pierre-Andre and I. P. Vaghely, "Are Opportunities Recognized or Constructed? An Information Perspective on Entrepreneurial Opportunity Identification," *Journal of Business Venturing* 25, no. 1 (2010): 73–86.

22. Alexander Ardichvili, Richard Cardozo, and Sourav Ray, "A Theory of Entrepreneurial Identification and Development," *Journal of Business Venturing* 18 (2003): 105–123.

23. P. Vandor and N. Franke, "See Paris and . . . Found a Business? The Impact of Cross-Cultural Experience on Opportunity Recognition Capabilities," *Journal of Business Venturing* 31 (2016): 388–407.

24. Scott Shane, "Selling University Technology: Patterns from MIT," *Management Science* 48, no. 1 (2002): 122–137.

25. Andrew Corbett, "Experiential Learning within the Process of Opportunity Identification and Exploitation," *Entrepreneurship Theory & Practice* (2005): 473–491.

26. M. Csikszentmihalyi, *Creativity* (New York: HarperCollins, 1996). For more on how information exposure influences how entrepreneurs evaluate opportunities, see E. Autio, L. Dahlander, and L. Frederiksen, "Information Exposure, Opportunity Evaluation, and Entrepreneurial Action: An Investigation of an Online User Community," *Academy of Management Journal* 56 (2013): 1348–1371.

27. For more information on feasibility analysis, see R. G. Wyckham and W. C. Wedley, "Factors Related to Venture Feasibility Analysis and Business Plan Preparation," *Journal of Small Business Management* 28 (1990): 48–59.

28. Sarah E. Needleman, "Before Launching a Venture, Sample the Waters," *Wall Street Journal*, February 8, 2014, http://online.wsj.com; "The Experts: What's the Best Way to Test a New Business Idea?" *Wall Street Journal*, April 29, 2013, http://online.wsj.com; Janine Popick, "Got New Ideas? Test Them at a Trade Show," *Inc.*, November 4, 2013, http://www.inc.com.

29. This section based on H. T. Keh, M. D. Foo, and B. C. Lim, "Opportunity Evaluation under Risky Conditions: The Cognitive Processes of Entrepreneurs," *Entrepreneurship Theory & Practice* (2002): 125–148.

30. For an exception, see L. W. Busenitz and J. B. Barney, "Differences between Entrepreneurs and Managers in Large Organizations: Biases and Heuristics in Strategic Decision Making," *Journal of Business Venturing* 12, no. 1 (1997): 9–30.

31. E. J. Langer, "The Illusion of Control," *Journal of Personality and Social Psychology* 32, no. 2 (1975): 311–328.

32. Clark G. Gilbert and Matthew J. Eyring, "Beating the Odds When You Launch a New Venture," *Harvard Business Review*, http://hbr.org, accessed May 2010.

33. Young Rok Choi and Dean Shepherd, "Entrepreneurs' Decisions to Exploit Opportunities," *Journal of Management* 30, no. 3 (2004): 377–395.

34. Kara Ohngren, "Business Spotlight: Advantage Fitness Products," *Entrepreneur*, http://blog.entrepreneur.com, accessed February 26, 2010.

35. This discussion is based on Young Rok Choi and Dean Shepherd, "Entrepreneurs' Decisions to Exploit Opportunities," *Journal of Management* 30, no. 3 (2004): 377–395.

36. For a review of top management teams, see S. T. Certo, R. H. Lester, C. M. Dalton, and D. R. Dalton, "Top Management Team Demographics, Strategy, and Financial Performance: A Meta-Analytic Review," *Journal of Management Studies* 43 (2006): 813–839.

37. Stephen G. Morrissette, "A Profile of Angel Investors," *Journal of Private Equity* 10, no. 3 (2007): 52–66.

38. R. J. Gaston, *Finding Private Venture Capital for Your Firm: A Complete Guide* (New York: John Wiley, 1989).

39. "Angel Investor," definition, http://www.investorwords.com, last modified 2010, accessed May 4, 2010; "Finding Venture Capital or Angel Investors," About.com, Small Business Information, November 9, 2009, http://sbinformation.about.com; University of New Hampshire Center for Venture Research, "Angel Investor Market Declines in First Half of 2009," press release, http://wsbe.unh.edu, accessed October 27, 2009.

40. KPMG Enterprise, "Venture Pulse Q4 2016: Global Analysis of Venture Funding," https://assets.kpmg.com/content/dam/kpmg/xx/pdf/2017/01/venture-pulse-q4-2016-report.pdf, accessed April 19, 2017.

41. Stephen G. Morrissette, "A Profile of Angel Investors," *Journal of Private Equity* 10, no. 3 (2007): 52–66.

42. S. Dutta and T. B. Folta, A comparison of the effects of angels and venture capitalists on innovation and value creation *Journal of Business Venturing* 31 (2016): 39–54.

43. William Kerr, "Venture Financing and Entrepreneurial Success," *Harvard Business Review*, http://blogs.hbr.org, accessed May 12, 2010.

44. P. Sharma and J. J. Chrisman, "Toward a Reconciliation of the Definitional Issues in the Field of Corporate Entrepreneurship," *Entrepreneurship Theory & Practice* 23, no. 3 (1999): 11–27; R. Fini, R. Grimaldi, G. L. Marzocchi, and M. Sobrero, "The Determinants of Corporate Entrepreneurial Intention within Small and Newly Established Firms," *Entrepreneurship Theory & Practice* 36, no. 2 (2012): 387, 414.

45. Andrew Ackerman, "SEC Moves Ahead with 'Crowdfunding' Proposal," *Wall Street Journal*, October 23, 2013, http://online.wsj.com; Ruth Simon and Angus Loten, "'Crowdfunding' Gets State-Level Test Run," *Wall Street Journal*, December 4, 2013, http://online.wsj .com; Caitlin Huston, "How to Prepare for Crowdfunding," *Wall Street Journal*, February 3, 2014, http://online.wsj.com.

46. R. C. Wolcott and M. J. Lippitz, "The Four Models of Corporate Entrepreneurship," *MIT Sloan Management Review* (2007): 75–82.

47. Ibid.

48. The discussion of these forms of corporate entrepreneurship is based on J. G. Covin and M. P. Miles, "Corporate Entrepreneurship and the Pursuit of Competitive Advantage," *Entrepreneurship Theory & Practice* 23, no. 3 (1999): 47–63; D. F. Kuratko, J. S. Hornsby, and J. G. Covin, "Diagnosing a Firm's Internal Environment for Corporate Entrepreneurship," *Business Horizons* 57, no. 1 (2013): 37–47.

49. M. Troy, "Wal-Mart Tries on Fashionable New Look," *DSN Retailing Today* 45, no. 7 (April 10, 2006): 3–4.

50. Claran Heavey, Zeki Simsek, Frank Roche, and Aidan Kelly, "Decision Comprehensiveness and Corporate Entrepreneurship: The Moderating Role of Managerial Uncertainty Preferences and Environmental Dynamism," *Journal of Management Studies* 46, no. 8 (August 2009): 1289–1314.

51. J. Austin, H. Stevenson, and J. Wei-Skillern, "Social and Commercial Entrepreneurship: Same, Different, or Both?," *Entrepreneurship Theory & Practice* (2006): 1–22.

52. Ibid.

53. A. Daniels, "Respecting Your Business's Ethics Policy," *Entrepreneur*, November 2002, http://www.entrepreneur.com/article/56740; Grameen Bank, "Professor Yunus Receives Presidential Medal of Freedom," http://www.grameen-info.org, accessed May 5, 2010.

54. A. M. Peredo and M. McLean, "Social Entrepreneurship: A Critical Review of the Concept," *Journal of World Business* 41 (2006): 56–65. See also S. Estrin, T. Mickiewicz, and U. Stephan, "Human Capital in Social and Commercial Entrepreneurship," *Journal of Business Venturing* 31 (2016): 449–467.

55. Rob Matheson, "Cooking Up Innovation," MIT News Office, June 23, 2013, http://web.mit.edu; One Earth Designs, "About," http:// www.oneearthdesigns.com, accessed February 27, 2014; Katie Hammer, "Removing Indoor Pollution," *Harvard Gazette*, August 21, 2013, http://news.harvard.edu/gazette; Liyan Chen, "B Lab Announced 'Best for the World' Company List," *Inc.*, April 17, 2013, http://www.inc.com; Unreasonable Institute, "Our Network: All Fellows, Scot Frank, Fellow 2011," http://unreasonableinstitute.org, accessed February 27, 2014; Randall Lane, "30 under 30: Social Entrepreneurs," *Forbes*, December 17, 2012, http://www.forbes.com.

56. M. Sharir and M. Lerner, "Gauging the Success of Social Ventures Initiated by Individual Social Entrepreneurs," *Journal of World Business* 41 (2006): 6–20.

57. Ibid.

58. Caitlin Huston, "Hair Chain Drybar Finds Niche in Affordable Luxury," *Wall Street Journal*, November 21, 2013, http://online.wsj.com; Meghan Casserly, "Drybar: How One Woman and a Hair Dryer Became a $20 Million Operation," *Forbes*, November 1, 2012, http:// www.forbes.com; Kate Rockwood, "Most Creative People 2013: 35 Alli Webb, Founder, Drybar," *Fast Company*, June 2013, http://www .fastcompany.com; Drybar, "About Us: Meet Alli Webb and the Team at Drybar," http://www.thedrybar.com, accessed February 27, 2014.

3

Society, Ethics, and Sustainability

TARGET SKILL

Social Responsibility Skill: the ability to take action that protects and improves both the welfare of society and the interests of the organization

SOCIAL RESPONSIBILITY SKILL AND YOUR CAREER

Social responsibility skill can be of great value to you in enhancing your management career. For example, this skill can help you build loyal customers within the community that you serve. Enhanced customer loyalty will contribute to organizational success, build your image as a competent manager, make you valuable to your organization, and support promotions as you build your career.

OBJECTIVES

To help build my *social responsibility skill*, when studying this chapter, I will attempt to acquire:

3-1 A thorough understanding of the term *social responsibility*

3-2 Insights about the social responsiveness of an organization

3-3 Insights for meeting social audit challenges

3-4 Thoughts on how to meet philanthropy challenges

3-5 Ways for building sustainable organizations

3-6 An appreciation for the role that ethics plays in management

---

MyLab Management Chapter Warm Up

If your instructor has assigned this activity, go to www.pearson.com/mylab/management to complete the chapter warm up.

CHALLENGE CASE

IKEA Builds on Its Commitment to the Environment

College students furnishing apartments, young couples setting up housekeeping, and working adults trying to stretch their earnings flock to IKEA for furniture and household goods. Most customers visit IKEA stores and select items packed in flat cartons for easy assembly at home, although a growing number purchase from the retailer's website. IKEA's main attraction is the array of beautifully designed items that are tailored to fit smaller spaces and are priced affordably.

IKEA's managers see the company as much more than a furniture store, however. They have a vision: "to create a better everyday life for the many people." Creating a better everyday life includes enabling people to buy items that make their surroundings beautiful and functional. It also includes taking responsibility for the company's impact on the larger world.

IKEA expresses that commitment in its management decisions. One of those decisions was the appointment of Steve Howard as IKEA Group's chief sustainability officer. Howard is responsible for reducing IKEA's negative impact on the environment and increasing the ways the company cares for the environment. For example, the company constantly looks for ways to reduce packaging, both the size of cartons and the amount of materials used in packaging. These changes lower shipping costs by reducing the paper, wood, and fossil fuels used in transportation. Better planning of distribution, such as shipping items directly to stores instead of to regional warehouses, also lowers the use of transportation resources. IKEA is also cutting its use of energy in factories and stores. By constructing energy-efficient buildings and installing solar panels and efficient lighting, the company is pursuing a goal of producing as much energy from renewable sources as it consumes from all sources by 2020.

Under Howard's leadership, IKEA extends its concern about the environment to relationships with its suppliers. The company has established a supplier code of conduct in which, for example, it forbids child labor. Employees also help suppliers reduce their use of energy, water, pesticides, and other resources—changes that help the suppliers become more efficient.

IKEA's managers see the company's role as a corporate citizen extending beyond environmental issues. Acting on the belief that the company has "a responsibility to help build a better future and have a positive impact," the

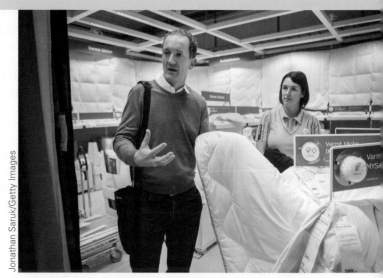

Steve Howard, IKEA Group's chief sustainability officer, is responsible for reducing IKEA's negative impact on the environment and increasing the ways the company cares for the environment.

company established the IKEA Foundation, which partners with organizations such as the World Wildlife Fund (WWF) to promote sustainable forestry and the United Nations High Commissioner for Refugees (UNHCR; also known as the UN Refugee Agency) to provide relief to displaced persons.

IKEA's experience in innovative design allows the company to give helpful advice about challenges such as how to house refugees or provide lighting where electricity is unavailable (for instance, it can provide solar-powered lamps). All of these efforts relate to the management employability skill of ethics and social responsibility. Howard and other managers at IKEA are using appropriate guiding principles to influence the way individuals and the organization behave within the society in which IKEA operates.

Can a business thrive by pursuing goals beyond profits? IKEA's commitment to social responsibility encourages innovation that gives the company a competitive edge. When IKEA saves money by using resources wisely (efficient lighting alone saves more than $20 million a year), it passes on some of the savings to consumers, thereby cementing its position as an affordable place to shop. Helping suppliers save money strengthens those business relationships. IKEA has enjoyed growing revenues, market share, and profits even in regions struggling with economic stagnation. No wonder Howard calls sustainability the "future of business."[1]

THE SOCIAL RESPONSIBILITY CHALLENGE

The Challenge Case illustrates social responsibility, sustainability, and ethics issues related to managing IKEA. The remaining material in this chapter explains social responsibility concepts and helps develop the corresponding social responsibility skill you will need to meet such challenges throughout your career. After studying chapter concepts, read the Challenge Case Summary at the end of the chapter to help you relate chapter content to meeting social responsibility challenges at IKEA.

Managers strive to accomplish organizational goals. The way in which managers accomplish those goals, however, is extremely important. Contemporary management theory emphasizes that managers, in accomplishing goals, should be good corporate citizens. A manager who is a **good corporate citizen** is committed to building an organization's local community and environment as a vital part of managing. This chapter focuses on how managers can be good corporate citizens by upholding the principles of corporate social responsibility. Discussion begins by covering the fundamentals of social responsibility, the target skill for this chapter.

Fundamentals of Social Responsibility

3-1 A thorough understanding of the term *social responsibility*

The term *social responsibility*, also referred to in the management literature as *corporate social responsibility*, means different things to different people. For the purposes of this chapter, however, **social responsibility** is the managerial obligation to take action that protects and improves both the welfare of society as a whole and the interests of the organization. According to the concept of social responsibility, a manager must strive to achieve societal as well as organizational goals.[2] This obligation is important for managers worldwide, including those in emerging economies.[3]

Michael E. Campbell is the top manager at Arch Chemicals.[4] Campbell has thoroughly explained how his company focuses on social responsibility through its production of water sanitization products. According to Campbell, water supplies are undergoing extreme swings in developed and underdeveloped countries around the globe due to violent storms and floods. Campbell believes that water shortages are increasing and in the near future will affect more than 450 million people. Also, according to Campbell, even when water is available, it is not unusual to find water sources that are too contaminated for people to drink without the risk of serious illness. Following the spirit of the social responsibility concept, Campbell emphasized that by considering both human need and, someday at least, profits, companies in the chemical industry are beginning to develop a wide range of technologies that can help secure safe drinking water for the world's poor.

The amount of attention given to the area of social responsibility by both management and society has increased in recent years and probably will continue to increase.[5] The following sections present the fundamentals of businesses' social responsibility by discussing these topics:

1. Areas of social responsibility
2. Varying opinions on social responsibility
3. Conclusions about the performance of social responsibility activities by business

Areas of Social Responsibility

The areas in which business can act to protect and improve the welfare of society are numerous and diverse. Perhaps the most publicized of these areas are urban affairs, consumer affairs, community volunteerism, and employment practices. The one area that is arguably receiving the most attention currently is the area of ecology conservation, popularly called "going green."[6] An international effort sponsored by the United Nations is currently under way and growing to get large companies to start thinking seriously about ecosystems and how to maintain them. And companies are responding. For example, the Coca-Cola Company is exploring ways to maintain its bottling operation in India without using underground water; the Mohawk Home Company is developing a new line of bathroom rugs with all-natural fibers;[7] and Kellogg's is developing environmentally sensitive products, such as its organic Rice Krispies.[8] Pressure groups are also springing up to persuade companies to "go green." One such group, The Center for Health, Environment, and Justice, was founded and is led by grassroots leader Lois Gibbs.

Varying Opinions on Social Responsibility

Although numerous businesses are already involved in social responsibility activities, much controversy remains about whether such involvement is necessary or even appropriate. The following two sections present some arguments for and against businesses performing social responsibility activities.[9]

Arguments for Business Performing Social Responsibility Activities

Probably the best-known argument for the performance of social responsibility activities by business begins with the premise that business, as a whole, is a subset of society, one that exerts a significant impact on the way society exists. Because business is such an influential member of society, the argument continues, it has the responsibility to help maintain and improve the overall welfare of society.[10] If society already puts this responsibility on its individual members, why should its corporate members be exempt?

In addition, some people argue that business should perform social responsibility activities because profitability and growth go hand in hand with responsible treatment of employees, customers, and the community. This argument says, essentially, that performing social responsibility activities is a means of earning greater organizational profit.

Researchers continue to study the relationship between social responsibility and revenue growth.[11] However, empirical studies have not yet demonstrated a definitive relationship between social responsibility and profitability. In fact, several companies that have been acknowledged leaders in social commitment—including Control Data Corporation, Atlantic Richfield, Dayton-Hudson, Levi Strauss, and Polaroid—have simultaneously experienced serious financial difficulties.[12] No direct relationship between social responsibility activities and these financial difficulties was shown, however.

Arguments against Business Performing Social Responsibility Activities   The best-known argument against business performing social responsibility activities was advanced by Milton Friedman, one of America's most distinguished economists. Friedman argued that making business managers responsible simultaneously to business owners for reaching profit objectives and to society for enhancing societal welfare sets up a conflict of interest that could potentially cause the demise of business as it is known today. According to Friedman, this demise will almost certainly occur if business is continually forced to perform socially responsible actions that directly conflict with private organizational objectives.[13]

Friedman also argued that to require business managers to pursue socially responsible objectives may, in fact, be unethical because doing so compels managers to spend money on some individuals that rightfully belongs to other individuals. Following Friedman's argument, a corporate executive is an employee of a business and is directly responsible to owners of that business. Overall, this responsibility is to conduct business in ways desired by the owners. Usually, owners desire to maximize profit while following the basic rules of society, which reflect both laws and ethical customs. When managers reduce profit, they are spending owners' money. When managers raise prices of products, they are spending customers' money.[14]

An example that Friedman might have used to illustrate his argument is the Control Data Corporation. Former chairperson William Norris involved Control Data in many socially responsible programs that cost the company millions of dollars—from building plants in the inner city and employing a minority workforce to researching farming on the Alaskan tundra. When Control Data began to incur net losses of millions of dollars in the mid-1980s, critics blamed Norris's "do-gooder" mentality. Eventually, a new chairperson was installed to restructure the company and return it to profitability.[15]

TABLE 3.1   **Primary Functions of Several Federal Agencies That Enforce Social Responsibility Legislation**

Federal Agency	Primary Agency Functions
Equal Employment Opportunity Commission (EEOC)	Investigates and conciliates employment discrimination complaints that are based on race, sex, or creed.
Office of Federal Contract Compliance Programs	Ensures that employers holding federal contracts grant equal employment opportunity to people regardless of their race or sex.
Environmental Protection Agency (EPA)	Formulates and enforces environmental standards in areas such as water, air, and noise pollution.
Consumer Product Safety Commission	Strives to reduce consumer misunderstanding of manufacturers' product design, labeling, and so on by promoting clarity of these messages.
Occupational Safety and Health Administration (OSHA)	Regulates safety and health conditions in nongovernment workplaces.
National Highway Traffic Safety Administration (NHTSA)	Attempts to reduce traffic accidents through the regulation of transportation-related manufacturers and products.
Mining Enforcement and Safety Administration	Attempts to improve safety conditions for mine workers by enforcing all mine safety and equipment standards.

Conclusions about the Performance of Social Responsibility Activities by Business

The preceding sections presented several major arguments for and against businesses performing social responsibility activities. Regardless of which argument or combination of arguments particular managers embrace, they generally should make a concerted effort to do the following:

1. Perform all legally required social responsibility activities.
2. Consider voluntarily performing social responsibility activities beyond those legally required.
3. Inform all relevant individuals of the extent to which the organization will become involved in performing social responsibility activities.

Performing Required Social Responsibility Activities   Federal legislation requires that businesses perform certain social responsibility activities. In fact, several government agencies have been established expressly to enforce such business-related legislation (see **Table 3.1**). The Environmental Protection Agency (EPA), for instance, has the authority to require businesses to adhere to certain socially responsible environmental standards. Examples of specific legislation requiring the performance of social responsibility activities are the Equal Pay Act of 1963, the Equal Employment Opportunity Act of 1972, the Highway Safety Act of 1978, and the Clean Air Act Amendments of 1990.

Voluntarily Performing Social Responsibility Activities   Adherence to legislated social responsibilities is the minimum standard of social responsibility performance that business managers must achieve. Managers must ask themselves, however, how far beyond the minimum they should go.

Determining how far to go is a simple process to describe, yet it is difficult and complicated to implement. It entails assessing the positive and negative outcomes of performing social responsibility activities over both the short and the long terms, and then performing only those activities that maximize management system success while making a desirable contribution to the welfare of society.

Events at the Sara Lee Bakery plant in New Hampton, Iowa, illustrate how company management can voluntarily take action to protect employees' health. Many employees at the plant began to develop carpal tunnel syndrome, a debilitating wrist disorder caused by repeated hand motions. Instead of simply having its employees go through physical therapy—and, as the principal employer in the town, watching the morale of the town drop—Sara Lee thoroughly investigated the problem. Managers took suggestions from factory workers and had their engineers design tools to alleviate the problem. The result was a virtual elimination of carpal tunnel syndrome at the plant within a short time.[16]

Communicating the Degree of Social Responsibility Involvement

Determining the extent to which a business should perform social responsibility activities beyond legal requirements is a subjective process. Despite this subjectivity, however, managers should have a well-defined position in this vital area and should inform all organization members of that position.[17] Taking these steps will ensure that managers and organization members behave consistently to support the position and that societal expectations of what a particular organization can achieve in this area are realistic.

Nike, the world-famous athletic gear manufacturer, felt so strongly that its corporate philosophy on social responsibility issues should be clearly formulated and communicated that the company created a new position, vice president of corporate and social responsibility. Maria Eitel, a former public relations executive at Microsoft, was hired to fill that position and is now responsible for clearly communicating Nike's thoughts on social responsibility both inside and outside the organization.[18]

Overall, managers are facing increasing pressure from stakeholders to be socially responsible. Action that is consistent with socially responsible ideals is commendable, so managers should support social responsibility activities in their organizations. They must clearly communicate to stakeholders, however, that such activities will not take the place of profit maximization but complement it.[19]

Allen Eyestone/ZUMA Press Inc/Alamy Stock Photo

Home Depot employees in the Team Depot program provide disaster relief. This effort communicates the company's concern for the community, and it is well aligned with Home Depot's business mission of providing supplies to disaster-stricken areas.

Social Responsiveness

The previous section discussed social responsibility, a business's obligation to take action that protects and improves the welfare of society along with the business's own interests. This section defines and discusses **social responsiveness**, the degree of effectiveness and efficiency an organization displays in pursuing its social responsibility activities.[20] The greater the degree of effectiveness and efficiency, the more socially responsive the organization is said to be. The next two sections address the following issues:

3-2 Insights about the social responsiveness of an organization

1. Determining whether a social responsibility exists
2. Social responsiveness and decision making

Determining Whether a Social Responsibility Exists

One challenge facing managers who are attempting to be socially responsive is to determine which specific social obligations are implied by their business situation. Managers in the tobacco industry, for example, are probably socially obligated to contribute to public health by pushing for the development of innovative tobacco products that do less harm to people's health than present products do, but they are not socially obligated to help reclaim shorelines contaminated by oil spills.

Clearly, management has an obligation to be socially responsible toward its stakeholders. A **stakeholder** is any individual or group that is directly or indirectly affected by an organization's

TABLE 3.2 **Stakeholders of a Typical Modern Organization and Examples of Social Obligations That Managers Owe to Them**

Stakeholder	Social Obligations Owed
Stockholders/owners of the organization	To increase the value of the organization
Suppliers of materials	To deal with them fairly
Banks and other lenders	To repay debts
Government agencies	To abide by laws
Employees and unions	To provide a safe working environment and to negotiate fairly with union representatives
Consumers	To provide safe products
Competitors	To compete fairly and to refrain from restraints of trade
Local communities and society at large	To avoid business practices that harm the environment

decisions.[21] Managers of successful organizations typically have many different stakeholders to consider: stockholders, or owners of the organization; suppliers; lenders; government agencies; employees and unions; consumers; competitors; and local communities as well as society at large. **Table 3.2** lists these stakeholders and gives a corresponding example of how a manager is socially obligated to each of them.

Social Responsiveness and Decision Making

The socially responsive organization that is both effective and efficient meets its social responsibilities without wasting organizational resources in the process. Determining exactly which social responsibilities an organization should pursue and then deciding how to pursue them are the two most critical decisions for an organization to make in order to maintain a high level of social responsiveness within an organization.

Figure 3.1 is a flowchart that managers can use as a general guideline for making social responsibility decisions that enhance the social responsiveness of their organizations. This figure implies that for managers to achieve and maintain a high level of social responsiveness within their organization, they must pursue only those responsibilities their organization possesses and has a right to undertake. Once managers decide to meet a specific social responsibility, they must determine the best way to undertake activities related to meeting this obligation. That is, managers must decide whether their organization should undertake the activities on its own or acquire the help of outsiders with more expertise in the area.

TIPS FOR MANAGING AROUND THE GLOBE

China Focuses on Agricultural (Ag) Sustainability

In 2017, China, the largest farming sector in the world, announced that a greater focus on sustainability in agricultural processes would be a central focus of the government. Though the country often cites the need for "green" ag practices, this year marks the first time that it is at the forefront of governmental policy. This is substantial for a country that previously ignored the environmental impact of a wide variety of industries, including farming and manufacturing.

This new policy makes sense. China continues to grow and is now the world's fourth largest consumer of organic food. The government desires to reduce the need for imports by fostering organically produced food within the country. It is doing this through reduced taxes in rural areas as well as the establishment of innovation centers throughout agricultural sectors. China also intends to educate farmers on water conservation, such as utilizing drip irrigation and developing crops that are drought resistant. The idea is to grow sustainable products to feed a rapidly growing population so that the Chinese people can rely less on foreign countries for organic food.[22]

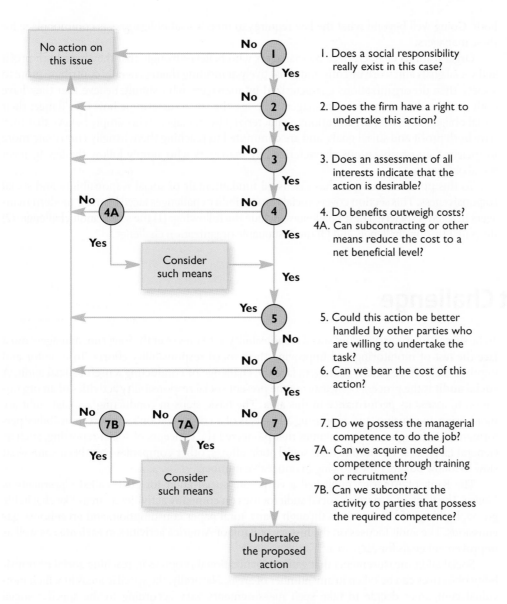

Figure 3.1

Flowchart of social responsibility decision making that generally will enhance the social responsiveness of an organization

1. Does a social responsibility really exist in this case?

2. Does the firm have a right to undertake this action?

3. Does an assessment of all interests indicate that the action is desirable?

4. Do benefits outweigh costs?
4A. Can subcontracting or other means reduce the cost to a net beneficial level?

5. Could this action be better handled by other parties who are willing to undertake the task?
6. Can we bear the cost of this action?

7. Do we possess the managerial competence to do the job?
7A. Can we acquire needed competence through training or recruitment?
7B. Can we subcontract the activity to parties that possess the required competence?

Approaches to Meeting Social Responsibilities

Various managerial approaches to meeting social obligations are another determinant of an organization's level of social responsiveness. A desirable and socially responsive approach to meeting social obligations does the following:[23]

1. Incorporates social goals into the annual planning process.
2. Seeks comparative industry norms for social programs.
3. Presents reports to organization members, the board of directors, and stockholders on social responsibility progress.
4. Experiments with different approaches for measuring social performance.
5. Attempts to measure the cost of social programs as well as the return on social program investments.

Normally, different managers approach meeting social responsibilities differently. Some approach meeting such responsibilities as a *requirement*. These managers view their primary responsibility as making a profit and, as a result, do only what is required by law to meet social responsibilities. Next, some managers approach meeting social responsibilities by recognizing that they have both profit and social goals, and pursue them in mostly an obligatory fashion. These managers only occasionally go beyond what is required by law to meet social obligations. Still other managers approach meeting social responsibilities by believing strongly that they have both profit and social goals, and respond by working proactively and intently on reaching both. Going well beyond what the law requires to meet social obligations is commonplace for these managers.

Organizations characterized by managers who believe strongly that they have both profit and social goals and work intently and proactively at meeting them generally contribute more to society than do organizations characterized by managers who simply believe that they have both profit and social goals, or managers who use the law to determine how they'll meet their social obligations. Also, organizations characterized by managers who simply believe that they have both profit and social goals, and are committed to reaching them usually contribute more to society than organizations characterized by managers who simply follow the law to meet social obligations.

To this point, this chapter has discussed fundamentals of social responsibility and social responsiveness. This section covers social responsibility challenges faced by most modern managers in today's society. These challenges include the following: (1) the social audit challenge, (2) the philanthropy challenge, and (3) the sustainable organization challenge.

The Social Audit Challenge

3-3   Insights for meeting social audit challenges

To be successful in carrying out social responsibility activities over the long run, managers must face the test of monitoring and improving their social responsibility efforts. To monitor and improve their efforts, many managers face the challenge of conducting a useful social audit. A **social audit** is the process of measuring the present social responsibility activities of an organization to assess its performance in this area. The basic steps in conducting a social audit are monitoring, measuring, and appraising all aspects of an organization's social responsibility performance. Although some companies that pioneered the concepts of social reporting, such as General Electric, still continue their social audit efforts, other companies have been somewhat slow to follow but are now growing in noticeable number.

The Bank of America published a corporate social audit for 2010 called *Opportunity in Motion*. The Bank of America's social audit focuses on company activities in areas like charitable giving, building of communities through loans, total paper consumption, and greenhouse gas emissions. The audit focuses on the history of Bank of America activities in each area as well as improvement goals for each area.[24]

As part of its social audit, Starbucks measures its progress in terms of maintaining a responsible buying area—one that maintains safe working conditions and protects worker rights.

Social audit measurements that gauge organizational progress in reaching social responsibility objectives can be taken in any number of areas. Naturally, the specific areas in which individual companies decide to take such measurements vary according to the specific social responsibility objectives to be met. Starbucks, a roaster, marketer, and retailer of specialty coffee in more than 50 countries, is well known for both setting responsible social goals and taking measurements to determine progress in reaching those goals. The *Starbucks Global Responsibility Report: Goals and Progress 2010* gives us an excellent example of areas the company measures in conducting its social audit. A few of these areas are highlighted below:[25]

1. **Environmental Area**—Starbucks is committed to minimizing its environmental footprint and inspiring others to do the same. **Environmental footprint** is a measure of the usage of environmental resources. The greater the amount of resources consumed by an organization, the greater the organization's footprint. Here social audit measurements could focus on Starbucks closely monitoring recycling and waste procedures. In addition, measurements could focus on charting energy usage to see if energy is being

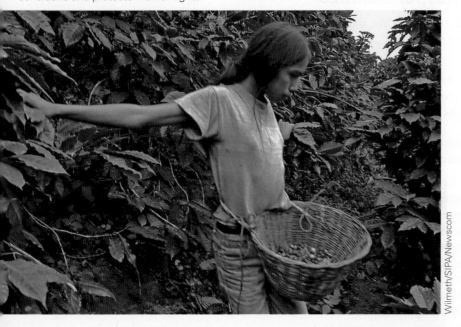

Wilmeth/SIPA/Newscom

used responsibly. Starbucks could also make sure that company buildings are constructed in a socially responsible fashion. Such buildings, for example, would include dimensions that enable water conservation as well as energy conservation.

2. **Community Area**—Starbucks is committed to building better neighborhoods, cities, and countries where it operates. In this area, the company focuses on helping to promote community service, creating jobs, and supporting youth activities by issuing grants that enable youth activities in communities. These grants are called Starbucks Youth Action Grants. Social audit measurement in this area could include following up on grants being awarded to see if the awards are having the planned impact on society.

3. **Responsible Buying Area**—Starbucks is committed to furnishing customers with products that are produced by suppliers who are also committed to socially responsible activities. As a result, Starbucks buys from suppliers who furnish safe and humane working conditions for employees. In addition, the company buys from suppliers who protect worker rights and comply with child labor laws. Measurements in this area could involve site visits to suppliers' locations to see if working conditions are consistent with Starbucks's values.

4. **Wellness Area**—Starbucks is dedicated to supporting policies and efforts to improve the health of individuals in communities in which it operates. The company is also committed to offering food and beverages that support the wellness of customers. As an example, Starbucks offers its customers low-fat apple bran muffins and drinks like the Iced Skinny Latte, which has only 60 calories and zero fat. Social audit measurements in this area could focus on determining if adequate and appropriate policies are being supported as well as finding out if enough health-conscious products are being offered to customers.

The Philanthropy Challenge

One popularly used component of social responsibility is **philanthropy**, which promotes the welfare of others through generous monetary donations to social causes. As an example of philanthropic giving, more and more managers are donating to an organization called The First Tee. The First Tee is a national, not-for-profit organization based in St. Augustine, Florida, and is the official charity of the PGA Tour. The goal of The First Tee is to build character among youth through the game of golf. Experiences in the program emphasize building core values like honesty, integrity, and respect for other youth. The First Tee has over 750 program locations around the world.

3-4 Thoughts on how to meet philanthropy challenges

Overall, philanthropy aims to increase the well-being of people. Improving human welfare through philanthropy by businesses commonly includes donations geared toward supporting the arts, education, world peace, and disaster relief. Modern managers commonly must meet the challenge of designing and implementing an efficient and effective philanthropy focus.

When making philanthropic gifts, it is generally recommended that managers donate to causes that in some way benefit the organization as well as society.[26] Managers should thus strive to make such gifts in societal areas that afford the organization a competitive advantage in the marketplace. Consider the following examples of companies making philanthropic donations to enhance their competitive advantage:

1. ExxonMobil makes donations to develop infrastructure in underdeveloped countries. This infrastructure development improves the well-being of citizens of the countries along with helping the company to be more competitive by doing its business more effectively and efficiently within the countries.

2. Apple Computer commonly donates computers and other products to schools to help young people to become more computer proficient. Although such donations help human welfare, they also help students and teachers alike to become more computer sophisticated and better enabled to buy Apple products in the future.

3. American Express donates to secondary schools in underdeveloped countries to provide travel industry career training for students about to enter the labor market. This training improves the welfare of the students and also helps the company become more competitive by building expertise within the countries to provide travelers with mechanisms to use charge cards. Travelers are one of the main sources of revenue for American Express credit cards.

Critics often demean businesses because they view the philanthropic donations made to enhance competitive advantage as self-serving and not genuinely made to promote the well-being of others. Such criticism, however, is generally considered unfounded. Remember that the manager's fundamental social responsibility is to stakeholders like employees, customers, and investors. Making donations to causes that do not somehow protect and enhance the continuity of the organization would be socially irresponsible because such donations would not support the well-being of the organization's stakeholders.

The Sustainable Organization Challenge

3-5 Ways for building sustainable organizations

To be successful in building and operating socially sensitive organizations over the long run, modern managers must face the challenge of crafting sustainable organizations. This section discusses the sustainable organization challenge as a test that modern managers must commonly succeed at in order for organizations to be good corporate citizens.

In recent decades, there has been an undeniably growing interest in sustainability.[27] This interest focuses on topics like how organizations can better conserve natural resources, reduce organizational waste, recycle used resources, and preserve the environment by protecting threatened plant and animal species.[28] The following sections define sustainability, define a sustainable organization, discuss why managers should build sustainable organizations, and outline steps that managers can use to help build sustainable organizations.

Defining Sustainability

Traditionally, the term *sustainability* has been used within management literature to describe the ability of a company to maintain a steady and improving stream of earnings. More recently, however, the term is often used in a much different way. In this section, which reflects this newer, different use of the term, **sustainability** is the degree to which a person or entity can meet its present needs without compromising the ability of other people or entities to meet needs.[29]

To illustrate the meaning of sustainability, assume that as part of its normal production process, an entity rids itself of contaminated waste by dumping it into a river. If this dumping renders the river toxic and unusable for fishing or recreation, the entity would be considered unsustainable. On the other hand, if the entity purifies the waste before dumping it to protect the cleanliness of the river, the entity would be considered sustainable. Overall, the more an entity increases its ability to meet present needs without compromising the ability of others to meet their needs in the future, the more sustainable the entity is.

Defining a Sustainable Organization

Building upon the earlier definition of sustainability, a **sustainable organization** is an organization that has the ability to meet its present needs without compromising the ability of future generations to meet their needs. In building a sustainable organization, management should strive to make the organization sustainable in three areas: the economy, the environment, and society. In terms of the economy, the sustainable organization engages in certain behaviors such as minimizing waste by not overproducing goods and generating a fair profit for stakeholders. Regarding the environment, the sustainable organization engages in certain behaviors that are akin to protecting natural resources like air, water, and land. In terms of society, the sustainable organization engages in certain behaviors such as maintaining the well-being and protection of the communities in which it does business.[30]

For example, consider recent events at PepsiCo, with its billion-dollar portfolio of food and beverage brands. After measuring the carbon footprint of its Tropicana orange juice brand, managers discovered that more than one-third of Tropicana's carbon emissions—the single largest source—came from the use of fertilizers during the growing process. As a result, Tropicana partnered with two manufacturers of low-carbon fertilizers and one of its orange growers, SMR Farms in Bradenton, Florida, to conduct long-term tests of the fertilizers and identify an alternative to reduce Tropicana's carbon emissions. The study will last at least five years, to match the maturity cycle of orange trees, and its findings could affect global best practices in agriculture. Adopting behaviors that protect the world's natural resources will help PepsiCo achieve its sustainability goals.[31]

Managers have historically focused on the yardstick of profit, or the *bottom line*, as the primary gauge for evaluating organizational performance. As noted in the previous section, more recently, managers are evaluating organizational performance by examining three sustainability gauges: the economy (which includes profit), the environment, and society. All three sustainability gauges for organizational performance considered collectively are commonly referred to as the **triple bottom-line**.[32]

The term *triple bottom-line* emphasizes that managers should focus on building organizations that are sustainable in economic, environmental, and societal activities. Essentially, the overall degree of sustainability achieved by any organization is judged by collective accomplishments in all three of these areas. If any one area is lacking in sustainability, the organization as a whole is lacking in sustainability. Being able to answer yes to questions like the following would indicate that an organization is operating in a manner that is consistent with the triple bottom-line standard:

Is the organization providing a fair return to its stakeholders? (economic area)

Is the organization protecting or improving the natural environment through its work methods? (environmental area)

Is the organization protecting or improving the overall quality of life in the communities in which it does business? (societal area)

MyLab Management Watch It

If your instructor has assigned this activity, go to www.pearson.com/mylab/management to complete the video exercise.

Why Sustainability?

Some people ask if building sustainable organizations is worthwhile. Management theorists and practicing managers alike present many sound reasons why managers should build sustainable organizations. The following sections discuss a few such reasons.

Increased Profit
Perhaps the most often used reason why managers should build sustainable organizations is that increased sustainability commonly results in more profitable organizations. History shows that sustainability doesn't have to be a burden on profit.[33] According to Brian Walker, the CEO of Herman Miller, achieving a position of leadership in sustainability can boost product demand. Walker found that customers are reluctant to buy from a company simply because of a worthwhile history of sustainability and probably won't pay a premium for its products.[34] However, a sustainable company is the type of company with which modern-day customers like to do business.[35]

Increased Productivity
Another reason commonly given to explain why managers should strive to build sustainable organizations relates to employee productivity.[36] Many management theorists and practitioners claim that increased labor productivity is commonly the most immediate payoff of sustainability. According to this line of reasoning, a sustainable organization builds its workplace to include features like temperature control, clean air, noise control, and appropriate lighting. Workers in such workplaces have been shown to be as much as 16 percent more productive than workers in workplaces without these features.

Increased Innovation
A third reason commonly given to explain why managers should pursue sustainability is that such a pursuit often serves as a catalyst for innovation.[37] Management researchers are now finding that a by-product of pursuing sustainability is a flood of valuable organizational and technological innovations that help organizations become more successful.[38]

To illustrate, consider recent events at Sam's Club, a discount retail division of Wal-Mart that specializes in the sale of products like jewelry, clothes, and food. Management at Sam's Club decided to pursue increasing sustainability by decreasing energy costs. One solution to decreasing energy costs was quite an innovation, a new milk jug. According to Doug McMillon, CEO of Sam's Club, the new jug increased the shelf life of milk in stores. Because of this greater shelf life, the new jug actually helped to reduce energy costs by eliminating the need for more than 10,000 milk truck deliveries to various stores. This milk jug innovation at Sam's Club was an outcome of the effort to increase sustainability and resulted in making the organization not only more sustainable but also more successful.

Steps for Achieving Sustainability

The actual steps that managers take to increase organizational sustainability can vary drastically from organization to organization. For example, to increase sustainability, a chemical company might take steps to reduce hazardous waste, a shoe manufacturer might take steps to reduce energy consumption, and a food products company might take steps to buy food products only from suppliers who grow food using approved fertilizers.

Overall, to have a successful sustainability effort, a manager must understand the unique characteristics of the particular organization and the industry within which that organization exists. Based on this understanding, management must tailor sustainability activities and processes that best meet the needs of the individual organization.

Despite the fact that many of management's steps to achieve sustainability can vary significantly from organization to organization, there are some steps that a manager can take to help build a sustainable organization regardless of the organization. These steps include the following:

Setting sustainability goals. Management should set goals that clearly indicate what the organization is attempting to accomplish in the area of sustainability. Such goals provide organization members with clear targets on which they can focus their sustainability efforts. Such targets also provide a vehicle that management can use to ensure that organization members have a unified, collective impact on organizational sustainability.

Consider the following sustainability goal set by Marks & Spencer, one of the largest retailers in the United Kingdom: becoming the first major retailer to ensure that six key raw materials—palm oil, soya, cocoa, beef, leather, and coffee—come from sustainable sources that do not contribute to deforestation, one of the biggest causes of climate change.

Marks & Spencer's sustainability goal is a clear indication that the company will enhance its own sustainability by supporting suppliers who are focused on enhancing their own sustainability. In essence, Marks & Spencer's sustainability goal is to help eliminate deforestation by doing business with suppliers with the same goal. By establishing this goal and making sure that all organization members understand it, Marks & Spencer is guiding its buyers to do business with only those suppliers who will help make Marks & Spencer a more sustainable organization.

PRACTICAL CHALLENGE: ACHIEVING SUSTAINABILITY

Free Recycled Water in Abu Dhabi

The Middle East knows that water, an essential commodity, cannot be wasted. In the UAE, it was the Abu Dhabi Sewerage Services Company (ADSSC) that has successfully demonstrated an effective and sustainable process for wastewater management. Following a successful pilot in Al Ain, the first city in the UAE to utilize 100 percent of its 650,000 cubic meters of recycled water, a similar program is being rolled out in Abu Dhabi. Though Abu Dhabi recycles all of its 850,000 cubic meters of wastewater every day, around 40 percent of it is wasted due to a lack of infrastructure. The ADSSC is undertaking an extensive expansion of its collection network, including a Strategic Tunnel Enhancement Program (STEP). Part of the project is 45 kilometers of link sewers to connect the existing systems to the new deep tunnel—by 2030, this will be able to cope with 1.7 million cubic meters per day.[39]

Hiring organization members who can help the organization become more sustainable. A primary feature in accomplishing any worthwhile activity in an organization is having talented people who can perform that activity. If an organization does not have people with the appropriate talents to accomplish the activity, individuals who possess the necessary talent should be recruited and hired. Such recruiting and hiring will normally increase the probability that the activity is performed successfully.

Following the reasoning given above, hiring appropriately talented people can also be a primary decision to ensure that necessary sustainability activities are successfully performed in organizations. For example, many organizations have sustainability projects that focus on improving the use of energy and materials through new building construction or remodeling. Such projects typically explore topics like energy efficiency, materials selection, water savings, and indoor environmental quality. The U.S. Green Building Business Council runs a program called **LEED (Leadership in Energy and Environmental Design)**, an ecology-oriented certification program that rates the ecology impact of buildings of all types. Hiring individuals who understand the LEED program could help ensure that sustainability-oriented construction or remodeling projects will be performed successfully in the organization.

As another example, Weis Markets, a regional grocery store chain headquartered in Pennsylvania, made a special hire to help with the company's sustainability efforts.[40] The company hired Patti Olenick, a sustainability specialist from the Pennsylvania Department of Environmental Protection. Olenick has extensive experience in waste management, recycling, and composting. She was hired to help the company develop a more systematic and coordinated approach to Weis Market sustainability programs.

Rewarding employees who contribute to an organization's sustainability goals. In all organizations, managers must encourage appropriate behavior, behavior that contributes to the accomplishment of organizational goals. In the sustainability area, managers should reward organization members who contribute to the accomplishment of sustainability goals. The purpose of the reward is to recognize organization members for what they've accomplished in the area of sustainability and to increase the probability that such organization members will continue to make contributions toward accomplishing organizational sustainability goals in the future.

The Colorado Department of Health and Public Environment provides an excellent illustration of how management can use rewards to encourage organization members to contribute to the attainment of sustainability goals. Management has designed and implemented an awards program that gives employees who excel in pursuing sustainability activities a cash award at a banquet held at the Denver Museum of Nature and Science. All employees are encouraged to nominate individuals who have implemented a new sustainability program, have demonstrated innovation in sustainability solutions, or have displayed leadership in protecting the environment.

Tracking progress in reaching sustainability goals. As stated previously, setting sustainability goals is a critical component of an organization's sustainability effort. Such goals set clear targets on which all organization members can focus. However, simply setting such goals is not enough. Managers must also track an organization's progress in reaching such goals. Knowing if an organization is on schedule, behind schedule, or ahead of schedule in reaching sustainability goals is critical to ensuring that the organization ultimately reaches those goals. If an organization is not on track for reaching sustainability goals, adjustments should be made to get the organization back on track.

DuPont is a science-based company that focuses on creating solutions that contribute to a better, safer, and healthier life. Well-known products offered by DuPont include a material used to coat cooking utensils called Teflon, a component of bulletproof vests called Kevlar, and a solid surface material for making kitchen countertops called Corian. In late 1999, DuPont established an energy goal for 2010 of holding energy consumption at its 1990 level.[41]

Through a sustainability focus, DuPont has set the goal of improving the livelihoods of at least three million farmers and their rural communities by the end of 2020. Because DuPont management knows that "what you count gets done," the company keeps track of how many farmers it affects. Through 2015, the company has directly reached more than 1.2 million farmers to help them strengthen their agricultural systems and improve productivity. As an example of this help, the Rice Farm Schools Program in India—a collaboration between DuPont Pioneer, Crop Protection, and the Uttar Pradesh Department of Agriculture—will provide more than half a million small farmers with practical expertise and training, from seed planting to harvest, while demonstrating the value of hybrid seeds.[42]

Managers and Ethics

3-6 An appreciation for the role that ethics plays in management

The study of ethics in management can be approached from many different directions. Perhaps the most practical approach is to view ethics as catalyzing managers to take socially responsible actions. The movement to include the study of ethics as a critical part of management education began in the 1970s, grew significantly in the 1980s, and is expected to continue growing in the twenty-first century. John Shad, chair of the Securities and Exchange Commission (SEC) during the 1980s, when Wall Street was shaken by a number of insider trading scandals, recently pledged a $20 million trust fund to the Harvard Business School to create a curriculum in business ethics for MBA students. Television producer Norman Lear gave $1 million to underwrite the Business Enterprise Trust, which will give national awards to companies and "whistle blowers ... who demonstrate courage, creativity, and social vision in the business world."[43]

The following sections define *ethics*, explain why ethical considerations are a vital part of management practices, discuss a workable code of business ethics, and present some suggestions for creating an ethical workplace.

A Definition of Ethics

The famous missionary physician and humanitarian Albert Schweitzer defined *ethics* as "our concern for good behavior. We feel an obligation to consider not only our own personal well-being, but also that of other human beings." This meaning is similar to the precept of the Golden Rule: Do unto others as you would have them do unto you.[44]

In business, **ethics** can be defined as the capacity to reflect on values in the corporate decision-making process, to determine how these values and decisions affect various stakeholder groups, and to establish how managers can use these observations in day-to-day company management.[45] Ethical managers strive for success within the confines of sound management practices, which are characterized by fairness and justice.[46] Interestingly, using ethics as a major guide when making and evaluating business decisions is popular not only in the United States but also in the very different societies of India and Russia.[47]

Why Ethics Is a Vital Part of Management Practices

John F. Akers, former board chair of IBM, has said that it makes good business sense for managers to be ethical. Unless they are ethical, he believes, companies cannot be competitive in either national or international markets. According to Akers, a manager should not talk about ethics without talking about competitiveness. Companies cannot be competitive if they are built on cultures wherein people stab one another in the back, try to take advantage of one another, and try to steal from one another and if they are based on dishonesty. Certainly, Akers would not deny that managers should be ethical to be morally correct. He would also add, however, that managers should be ethical as a strategy for being competitive with rival firms.[48]

Although ethical management practices may not be linked to specific indicators of financial profitability, conflict is not inevitable between ethical practices and making a profit. Overall, the essence of competitiveness presumes underlying values of truthfulness and fair dealing. The employment of ethical business practices can enhance overall corporate health in three important areas: productivity, stakeholder relations, and government regulation.

Productivity   The employees of a corporation constitute one major stakeholder group that is affected by management practices. When management is determined to act ethically toward stakeholders, then employees will be positively affected. For example, a corporation may decide that business ethics requires it to make a special effort to

Company charity events, like this Mercedes-Benz Corporate Run in Miami, Florida, enhance the company's positive public image.

RosaIreneBetancourt 13/Alamy Stock Photo

ensure the health and welfare of its employees. To this end, many corporations have established employee advisory programs (EAPs) to help employees with family, work, financial or legal problems, and with mental illness or chemical dependency. These programs have even enhanced productivity in some corporations. For instance, Control Data Corporation found that its EAP reduced health costs and sick-leave usage significantly.[49]

Stakeholder Relations   The second area in which ethical management practices can enhance corporate health is by positively affecting outside stakeholders such as suppliers and customers. A positive public image can attract customers who view such an image as desirable. For example, Johnson & Johnson, the world's largest maker of health-care products, is guided by "Our Credo," which was announced more than 60 years ago by General Robert Wood Johnson to the company's employees, stockholders, and members of its community. The credo stresses the idea that Johnson & Johnson sees its primary focus as being of meaningful service to doctors, nurses, patients, and mothers and fathers of all who use their products. The credo also stresses that the company constantly focuses on reducing costs in order to provide products at reasonable costs.

Government Regulation   The third area in which ethical management practices can enhance corporate health is in minimizing government regulation. Where companies are believed to be acting unethically, the public is more likely to put pressure on legislators and other government officials to regulate those businesses or to enforce existing regulations. For example, in 2010, thinking that smokeless tobacco may be a cancer-causing product, a federal government subcommittee on health held hearings to explore the impact of smokeless tobacco on the nation's youth and its use in major league baseball.[50]

A Code of Ethics

A **code of ethics** is a formal statement that acts as a guide for the ethics of how people within a particular organization should act and make decisions. Ninety percent of *Fortune* 500 firms and almost half of all other firms have ethics codes. Many organizations that do not already have an ethics code are giving serious consideration to developing one.

Codes of ethics commonly address issues such as conflict of interest, competitors, privacy of information, gift giving, and giving and receiving political contributions or business. A code of ethics developed by Nissan of Japan, for example, barred all Nissan employees from accepting almost all gifts or entertainment from, or offering them to, business partners and government officials.[51] The new code was drafted by Nissan president Yoshikazu Hanawa and sent to 300 major suppliers.[52]

According to a recent survey, the development and distribution of a code of ethics is perceived as an effective and efficient means of encouraging ethical practices *within* organizations.[53] **Figure 3.2** contains highlights of the code of ethics that Publix Super Markets uses to encourage ethical behavior for financial managers within the company.

Managers cannot assume merely because they have developed and distributed a code of ethics that organization members have all the guidelines they need to determine what is ethical and to act accordingly. It is impossible for one code to cover all ethical and unethical conduct within an organization. Managers should thus view codes of ethics as tools that must be evaluated and refined periodically so that they will be comprehensive and usable guidelines for making ethical business decisions efficiently and effectively.[54]

Creating an Ethical Workplace

Managers commonly strive to encourage ethical practices, not only to be morally correct but also to gain whatever business advantage lies in projecting an ethical image to consumers and employees.[55] Creating, distributing, and continually improving a company's code of ethics is one common step managers can take to establish an ethical workplace.

Another step many companies are taking to create an ethical workplace is to appoint a chief ethics officer. The chief ethics officer has the job of ensuring that organizational ethics and values are integrated into daily decisions at all organizational levels. Such officers recommend,

Figure 3.2

Highlights of the Code of Ethics for financial managers at Publix Super Markets[56]

> Publix Super Markets, Inc. is committed to the highest standards of business and ethical conduct. This includes conducting business in accordance with the spirit and letter of applicable laws and regulations. In particular, Publix's financial managers are vested with a higher level of responsibility over the financial affairs of Publix. Financial managers must fulfill this responsibility by adhering to a high ethical standard. This Code provides principles to which Publix's financial managers are expected to adhere and advocate. Publix financial managers will:
>
> 1. Act with honesty and integrity, avoiding actual or apparent conflicts between his or her personal interests and the interests of Publix, including receiving improper personal benefits as a result of his or her position.
>
> 2. Manage financial transactions and reporting systems and procedures so that business transactions are properly authorized and completely, timely and accurately recorded on Publix's books and records in accordance with generally accepted accounting principles and established company financial policies.
>
> 3. Perform responsibilities with a view to causing periodic reports and other documents filed with the SEC and other public communications to contain information that is full, fair, accurate, complete, timely and not misleading…

help implement, and reinforce strategies aimed at integrating appropriate conduct throughout all phases of company operations. **Figure 3.3** lists a few characteristics that a person should have to be a successful chief ethics officer.

Another way to promote ethics in the workplace is to furnish organization members with appropriate training. General Dynamics, McDonnell Douglas, Chemical Bank, and American Can Company are examples of corporations that conduct training programs aimed at encouraging ethical practices within their organizations.[57] Such programs do not attempt to teach managers what is moral or ethical but instead give them criteria they can use to help determine how ethical a certain action might be. According to the Markkula Center for Applied Ethics at Santa Clara University, managers can feel confident that a potential action will be considered ethical by the general public if it is consistent with one or more of the following ethical standards:[58]

1. **The Utilitarian Standard** is a guideline that indicates that behavior can generally be considered ethical if it provides the most good for or does the least harm to the greatest number of people. Corporate activity that meets this standard produces the greatest good for and the least harm to all company stakeholders, including employees and customers.
2. **The Rights Standard** is a guideline that says that behavior is generally considered ethical if it respects and promotes the rights of others. This guideline indicates that in order to be ethical, corporate behavior must respect the dignity of human nature. Under this standard, for example, corporate action that reflects unfair labor practices like paying abnormally low wages or using child labor would be considered unethical.
3. **The Virtue Standard** is a guideline that determines behavior to be ethical if it reflects high moral values. Behavior that is consistent with this standard is action that reflects virtues like honesty, fairness, and compassion. Examples of business behavior that reflect this standard would include honesty in advertising about the worthwhile features of a product or paying suppliers a fair price for their goods no matter how much bargaining power is held over them.

Overall, managers must take responsibility for creating and sustaining conditions in which people are likely to behave ethically and for minimizing conditions in which people might be

Figure 3.3

Skills needed to be a successful chief ethics officer[59]

> 1. The ability to be objective
> 2. The ability to understand the structure of an organization
> 3. The ability to know and maneuver within an organization's culture
> 4. The ability to communicate clearly and concisely
> 5. The ability to deal with conflict
> 6. The ability to keep matters confidential

STEPS FOR SUCCESS

Creating an Ethical Work Environment

Procter & Gamble's Integrity Statement for Suppliers

Procter & Gamble (P&G) is one of the largest consumer products companies in the world. Based in Cincinnati, Ohio, the firm produces everything from deodorant and soap to paper towels and detergent. A company this large often has thousands of suppliers, and P&G holds them to a high standard. Suppliers are required to follow a set of guidelines, some of which include topics such as the following:[60]

- **Child Labor.** No business partner may utilize workers younger than 15. No one under 18 years of age may engage in hazardous work.

- **Forced Labor and Human Trafficking.** Employment must be voluntary and freely chosen. External business partners are forbidden from utilizing prison labor, trafficked individuals, or slave labor.
- **Discrimination.** Suppliers cannot discriminate based on race, color, gender, age, national origin, religion, sexual orientation, gender identity and expression, marital status, citizenship, disability, veteran status, or medical condition.
- **Environmental Sustainability.** It is expected that business partners will abide by all applicable environmental laws and that they will share P&G's commitment to environmental stewardship.

tempted to behave unethically. Two practices that commonly inspire unethical behavior in organizations are giving unusually high rewards for good performance and giving unusually severe punishments for poor performance. By eliminating such factors, managers can reduce any pressure on employees to perform unethically in organizations.

Following the Law: Sarbanes–Oxley Reform Standards

Around the turn of the most recent century, Enron Corporation was an American energy and commodities company headquartered in Houston, Texas. Enron employed about 20,000 people and claimed revenue of about $101 billion in 2000. Because of the company's claimed phenomenal performance in the areas of electricity, natural gas, and paper, *Fortune* magazine named Enron "America's Most Innovative Company" for six consecutive years.

To the dismay of Enron stakeholders and society in general, outrageous management practices were uncovered that seemed aimed at unjustifiably maximizing the personal wealth of top managers to the detriment of the well-being of other organizational stakeholders.[61] As an example, Enron management used inaccurate accounting reports to deceive employees, shareholders, legal authorities, the media, and the general public. These reports grossly overstated the condition of company performance, thereby allowing top managers to justify their inflated salaries. Upon learning of the deception, some employees were outraged, and others experienced financial disaster because they'd invested in what turned out to be worthless company stock and company retirement programs. Needless to say, managers involved in such deceitful practices were prosecuted to the full extent of the law.

Amid public outcries over such practices, the Sarbanes–Oxley Act of 2002 was passed to try to prevent such deception by publicly owned companies. The general thrust of this legislation focuses on promoting ethical conduct.[62] Areas covered include maintaining generally accepted accounting practices, evaluating executive compensation, monitoring fundamental business strategies, understanding and mitigating major risks, and ensuring a company structure and processes that enhance integrity and reputation.

Managers who do not follow the stipulations of the Sarbanes–Oxley Act face significant jail time. Infractions such as engaging in securities fraud, impeding a financial investigation by regulators, and committing mail fraud can result in up to 25 years of imprisonment. The Sarbanes–Oxley Act and related infraction penalties create hope that grossly unethical behavior will be significantly discouraged in the future.

The Sarbanes–Oxley Act seems to support whistle-blowing as a vehicle for both discouraging deceptive management practices and encouraging ethical management practices. **Whistle-blowing** is the act of an employee reporting suspected misconduct or corruption believed to exist within the organization. A **whistle-blower** is the employee who reports the alleged activities. Whistle-blowers can make their reports in a number of different ways, including reporting suspected organizational wrongdoings to proper legal authorities and/or proper management authorities. The Sarbanes–Oxley Act prohibits retaliation by employers against whistle-blowers.

One of the most famous whistle-blowers of modern times is Sherron Watkins, former vice president of Enron Corporation.[63] Watkins testified to Congress that she was extremely alarmed by information she had received about Enron's finances and had warned then-chairman Kenneth Lay that investors were being duped by inflated profit statements. Watkins attempted, with no success, to persuade Lay to restate and reissue corporate financial statements after eliminating accounting misrepresentations. Enron, once the seventh-largest corporation in the United States, declared bankruptcy in December 2001. The bankruptcy cost thousands of employees their jobs and retirement pensions, and investors lost millions of dollars. Perhaps based primarily on Watkins's testimony, Lay was charged and found guilty on six criminal counts of fraud. Lay died at age 64 while awaiting sentencing for his Enron conviction.[64]

Ethics abuses at major corporations and other highly publicized business missteps have highly sensitized Americans to greed and corporate corruption. Business scholars see ethics remaining a hot topic for years to come.[65]

CHALLENGE CASE SUMMARY

Social responsibility entails management's obligation to take actions that protect and improve the welfare of society in conjunction with the interests of the organization and is an important management employability skill. From the Challenge Case that opened the chapter, recall that IKEA protects and improves its communities through innovation in the conservation of resources as well as the charitable work of the IKEA Foundation. IKEA makes substantial contributions by applying its resource-saving ideas to its own products and processes and by helping its suppliers operate more sustainably. Making such investments in the welfare of society is essential to being a good business citizen. Corporations must also take steps, however, to protect their own interests while making social investments. For example, by operating more efficiently in its use of energy and packaging resources, IKEA saves money. It then passes along the savings, and the lower prices attract more customers without cutting into its profits.

IKEA should commit to benefiting society because of the vast power the company possesses for creating such benefits. It should be remembered, however, that the costs of social responsibility activities can be passed to consumers, and action should be taken only if it is financially feasible. For IKEA to invest in social responsibility activities to its own financial detriment would be socially irresponsible given the company's commitment to employees and stockholders.

IKEA can and does become involved in many different areas of social responsibility. Currently, however, the business focuses on its sustainable use of natural resources. In addition, its IKEA Foundation supports environmental concerns as well as charitable work that targets children and disaster relief. No matter how much IKEA does in pursuing social responsibility goals, it will no doubt be criticized by some people for not doing enough. At this point, IKEA's activities in the area of social responsibility appear to be highly significant.

IKEA's activities within the sphere of social responsibility could result in a short-run decrease in profits simply because of the costs of those activities. For example, constructing energy-efficient buildings, installing solar panels, and upgrading light fixtures have initial costs.

At first glance, such actions might seem unbusinesslike, but the company forecasts long-run savings and may obtain other benefits. Performing social responsibility activities could also significantly improve IKEA's public image and could be instrumental in generating increased sales.

Some social responsibility activities are legislated and therefore must be performed by businesses. Most of the legislation requiring these activities is aimed at large companies.

Examples of legislated activities include required levels of product safety and employee safety. Because IKEA is not required by law to support causes such as sustainable forestry or child welfare, whatever IKEA contributes to these causes would be strictly voluntary. In making a decision about how to support society, IKEA's managers should assess the positive and negative outcomes of such support, over both the long and the short terms, and then establish whatever support, if any, would maximize its success and offer some desirable contribution to society.

IKEA should also communicate to all organization members, as well as society, which causes it will support and why. The use of its website would greatly facilitate this communication.

In addition, IKEA should strive to maintain a relatively high degree of social responsiveness when pursuing its social responsibility activities. To do this, management should make decisions that focus on IKEA's established social responsibility areas and approach meeting those responsibilities in appropriate ways. In terms of supporting children's health and education, for example, management must first decide whether IKEA has a social responsibility to become involved through the design and application of its products or efforts in these issues. Assuming managers decide that IKEA has such a responsibility, they must then determine how to accomplish the activities necessary to meet the responsibility. For example, IKEA might employ its expertise to develop more ideas for refugee housing. Making appropriate decisions will help IKEA meet social obligations effectively and efficiently.

In terms of implementing an approach to meeting social responsibilities that will increase IKEA's social responsiveness, management should try to view the company as having both societal and economic goals. In addition, management should attempt to anticipate social problems and actively work to prevent them. Managers at IKEA should know that pursuing social responsibility objectives is a major management activity.

IKEA's managers must understand that, for the company to succeed in meeting social responsibility objectives, it must be able to meet two major challenges. The first challenge is conducting a useful social audit, which would measure IKEA's social responsibility activities in order to assess its social responsibility performance. The IKEA social audit, at a minimum, should measure and evaluate the company's activities that focus on economics, quality of life, social investment, and problem solving.

The second challenge for IKEA's management in meeting social responsibility objectives is through philanthropy.

IKEA's philanthropic efforts should strive to increase the welfare of humanity while benefiting IKEA and its future. Criticism expressing that such donations are completely self-serving should not distract IKEA's managers. They must instead keep in mind that most people would agree that IKEA's first social responsibility is to its stakeholders and that any donations that do not in some way benefit these stakeholders is socially irresponsible.

IKEA management should also continue to focus on the company's efforts to be a sustainable organization, one that meets its operational needs without compromising the ability of future generations to meet their needs. In heeding such a focus, IKEA should concentrate on activities like minimizing waste and protecting natural resources like air, water, and land. IKEA should continue to benefit from such activities through increases in profit, productivity, and innovation.

IKEA's management would want corporate decisions to be sustainable—that is, such decisions should be able to meet the company's present needs without compromising the needs of others in the future. It would be up to management to determine the steps the company must take to improve organizational sustainability. For example, the chief sustainability officer may need to hire additional staff with the expertise to help IKEA improve its sustainability.

To measure the level of sustainability at IKEA, managers could use the triple bottom-line approach. With this approach, managers would assess IKEA's activities in economic, environmental, and societal terms. For example, they would ask these questions:

Is IKEA performing profitably and providing a fair return to stakeholders? (economic)

Is IKEA reducing its carbon footprint, minimizing its energy use, or otherwise improving the natural environment through its work methods? (environmental)

Is IKEA enhancing the overall quality of life in the communities in which it does business? (societal)

Answers to these questions will help IKEA's management determine whether the company's policies are appropriate.

Assuming managers at IKEA are ethical, their decisions should reflect only the highest moral code in order to enhance the well-being of all company stakeholders. In essence, managers should act in the way that they want others to act in their dealings with IKEA. Decisions at IKEA will be ethical if they are truthful and fair to all concerned, if they build goodwill and better relationships, and if they are beneficial to all concerned. IKEA management can use the Virtue, Rights, and Utilitarian Standards to help ensure that all actions taken are ethical.

> **MyLab Management** Assessing Your Management Skill
>
> If your instructor has assigned this activity, go to www.pearson.com/mylab/management to complete the exercise related to the Challenge Case.

DEVELOPING SOCIAL RESPONSIBILITY SKILL

This section is specially designed to help you develop social responsibility skills. An individual's social responsibility skill is based on an understanding of the concepts and the ability to apply those concepts. The following activities will help to enhance your social responsibility skills in various organizational situations.

Class Preparation and Personal Study

To help you to prepare for class, perform the activities outlined in this section. Performing these activities will help you enhance your classroom performance significantly.

Reflecting on Target Skill

On page 72, this chapter opens by presenting a target management skill along with a list of related objectives outlining knowledge and understanding that you should aim to acquire related to that skill. Review this target skill and the list of objectives to make sure that you've acquired all pertinent information within the chapter. If you do not feel that you've reached a particular objective(s), study related chapter coverage until you do.

Know Key Terms

Understanding the following key terms is critical to your preparing for class. Define each of these terms. Refer to the page(s) referenced after a term to check your definition or to gain further insight regarding the term.

Know How Management Concepts Relate

This section comprises activities that will further sharpen your understanding of management concepts. Answer essay questions as completely as possible.

3-1 What's the relationship between social responsibility and ethics?

3-2 How does an organization test its monitoring of and improvements to their social responsibility in the long run? What steps should be taken to ensure this takes place?

3-3 Philanthropy aims to increase the well-being of people. Do you agree with this statement? Suggest some typical philanthropic activities by businesses.

> **MyLab Management**
> **Personal Inventory Assessments**
>
> Go to www.pearson.com/mylab/management to complete the Personal Inventory Assessment related to this chapter.
>
> **PERSONAL INVENTORY ASSESSMENT**

Management Skills Exercises

Learning activities in this section are aimed at helping you develop social responsibility skills.

MyLab Management
Discussion Questions
Go to www.pearson.com/mylab/management to complete the problems marked with this icon ✪.

✪ Cases

IKEA Builds on Its Commitment to the Environment

The Challenge Case "IKEA Builds on Its Commitment to the Environment" and its related Challenge Case Summary were written to help you understand the management concepts contained in this chapter. Answer the following discussion questions about the introductory case to explore how fundamental management concepts can be applied to a company such as IKEA.

3-4 Do you think IKEA has a responsibility to support education and safety in the communities in which it does business? Explain.

3-5 Assuming IKEA has such a responsibility as addressed in Exercise 3-4, in what instances would it be relatively easy for the company to be committed to living up to it?

3-6 Assuming IKEA has such a responsibility as addressed in Exercise 3-4, in what instances would it be relatively difficult for the company to be committed to living up to it?

Whistle-Blowing at Wells Fargo

Read the case and answer the questions that follow. Studying this case will help you better understand how concepts relating to the functions of management can be applied in a company such as Wells Fargo.

Imagine going to work for a company where you discover that something unethical or even illegal is occurring. What would you do? Would you simply quit and walk away, or would you tell your boss or perhaps the president of the company? Would you even consider going outside the firm and contacting a governmental agency about the behavior? These are difficult questions to answer until you're faced with such a situation. However, circumstances like this do occur, and recently the government has started handing down stiff penalties for companies who retaliate against those who call attention to unethical and illegal business practices.

In 2017, the largest award ever handed out to an individual through the whistle-blowing program at the Occupational Safety and Health Administration (OSHA) amounted to $5.4 million. The unnamed manager who won the award worked for Wells Fargo, a major banking and financial services company based in San Francisco. He had contacted a bank ethics hotline and notified his superiors that he suspected fraudulent business practices were being conducted at the company. At present, it has not been made public whether the concern this employee had was connected to the scandal affecting the company when hundreds of thousands of bank accounts and credit card accounts were set up on behalf of customers without their knowledge or consent.

Other employees had also apparently tried to notify corporate executives, and there may have been retaliation against some of those associates as well. In all, nearly two million fraudulent accounts were created because employees throughout the company were under pressure to reach certain sales goals. In other words, thousands of employees knowingly created false accounts in order to achieve these sales targets. The new president, Timothy Sloan, has acknowledged that terminations of a few employees may have been motivated by retaliation for speaking out. Sloan replaced John Stumpf, who left the company under pressure from the board after the scandal broke.

The employee who won the $5.4 million award unfortunately had to wait six years for the judgment because OSHA has a backlog of similar cases. Also, the complexity of this particular case delayed the ruling because investigators had to determine if the unnamed manager was actually terminated for reporting the unethical business practices and not for some other reason. Still, the manager won a record award, and it has been ruled that Wells Fargo must rehire him. Currently, there is no word on whether he has accepted a position at the company.[66]

Employees who engage in whistle-blowing against current or former employers are protected by OSHA. Each year, the agency investigates over 3,000 claims filed by whistle-blowers, and with awards like this one for a Wells Fargo employee, companies have taken notice. Firms must be very careful that they are not retaliating or discriminating against any employee who goes through the proper channels of notifying corporate executives or OSHA itself. Depending on the nature of the situation, an employee has 30 to 180 days to file a complaint with OSHA if he or she feels that retaliation or discrimination has occurred after blowing the whistle.[67] This is important because often whistle-blowers are unable to find employment in the same industry: Potential employers may be reluctant to hire a whistle-blower.

Questions

3-7 How important are whistle-blowing laws for protecting an employee who feels that something is not right? Should these laws even exist? Why or why not?

3-8 If you noticed that your current employer is doing something unethical or illegal, what steps would you take?

3-9 If you were looking to hire a highly qualified candidate, but you discovered that he or she has blown the whistle at three previous employers, would you still hire this person? Why or why not?

Experiential Exercises

The Environmental Impact Team

Directions. Read the following scenario and perform the listed activities. Your instructor may want you to perform the activities as an individual or within groups. Follow all of your instructor's directions carefully.

You are the head of a major British newspaper, *Guardian Unlimited*, and have just completed a social audit of your organization's business activities. Your company produces a progressive, enlightened newspaper and a website that regularly cover social responsibility topics. You conducted the social audit to make sure your company measures up to the high standards your editors expect of other companies. In the past, your company has won several social responsibility awards in areas such as encouraging diversity, innovations in social reporting, and employee giving to social responsibility causes.

Based on the results of your audit, you have set a new social responsibility goal for your newspaper for the upcoming three-year period. This goal is simple: to persuade your readers to have a positive impact on the environment.

You have established a group called the Environmental Impact Team to help you outline how your new goal will be accomplished. You are presently meeting with this team for the first time. Lead your group in outlining plans, organization features, an influence system, and a control mechanism, all aimed at achieving this new goal.

You and Your Career

The preceding information implies that managers should communicate to other organization members the extent to which the organization will be involved in performing social responsibility activities. Could the lack of such communication hinder your career success as a manager? Explain. If you were the president of the school in which you are taking this management class, what would you say to professors and students regarding the overall position on social responsibility that *you* would like the school to embrace? What specific activities should be pursued that correspond to this position?

Building Your Management Skills Portfolio

Your Management Skills Portfolio is a collection of activities specially designed to demonstrate your management knowledge and skill. Be sure to save your work. Taking your printed portfolio to an employment interview could be helpful in obtaining a job.

The portfolio activity for this chapter is identifying corporate social responsibilities. Read the following about CVS Health and answer the questions that follow.

CVS Health is a pharmacy retail company with nearly 10,000 locations, 158,000 employees, and about $180 billion in revenue. Based in Woonsocket, Rhode Island, the firm is dedicated to being a good corporate citizen. Recently,

CVS Health released its *Prescription for a Better World* report where it describes its efforts with corporate social responsibility. This report identifies ways CVS is currently meeting its corporate social responsibility objectives and offers insight into future goals.

Some of the recent activities have been quite impressive. In Virginia, CVS Health established the MinuteClinic that serves 60,000 veterans in a partnership with the U.S. Department of Veterans Affairs. The pilot program was so successful that the company has expanded it to Phoenix, Arizona, too. In the retail stores, CVS has begun increasing the number of healthier food and beverage options that line the shelves. Through its Pharmacists Teach program, the company has reached nearly 200,000 students about the dangers of prescription drug abuse.[68]

Now the management team at CVS Health has come to you with the hope that you can help them expand their corporate social responsibility activities. Answer the following questions as you think about how you could improve CVS Health's corporate social responsibility program.

Planning Issues to Inspect

Category: Social Responsibilities

Provide three reasons why corporate social responsibility is important for a retailer like CVS Health.

3-10 _____

_____

3-11 _____

_____

3-12 _____

_____

List three corporate social responsibility activities CVS Health could engage in with regard to marketing.

3-13 _____

_____

3-14 _____

_____

3-15 _____

_____

List three corporate social responsibility activities CVS Health could institute with regard to the employees of the company.

3-16 _____

_____

3-17 _____

_____

3-18 _____

_____

List three corporate social responsibility activities CVS Health could put into effect with regard to its suppliers.

3-19 _____

_____

3-20 _____

_____

3-21 _____

_____

List three corporate social responsibility activities CVS Health could start with regard to the communities that it serves.

3-22 _____

_____

3-23 _____

_____

3-24 _____

_____

MyLab Management
Writing Assignments

If your instructor has assigned this activity, go to www.pearson.com/mylab/management for the following assisted-graded writing assignments:

Assisted-Grading Questions

3-25 Now that you have studied the arguments "for" and "against" as presented in the chapter, what is your personal position about businesses performing social responsibility activities?

3-26 How can society help businesses meet social obligations?

Endnotes

1. Emily Chasan, "How IKEA Protects the Environment and Sofa Margins," *Wall Street Journal*, January 28, 2014, http://blogs.wsj.com; Rahim Kanani, "Why IKEA Thinks This Mega-Trend Will Define the Next 30 Years of Business," *Forbes*, February 7, 2014, http://www.forbes.com; Jens Hansegard, "UN Refugee Agency Needs to Think Like a Business, Says IKEA Foundation," *Wall Street Journal*, February 5, 2014, http://online.wsj.com; Shawn McCarthy, "IKEA Brings Build-It-Yourself Environmental Plan to Canada," *Toronto Globe and Mail*, November 14, 2013, http://www.theglobeandmail.com; Cathy Proctor, "IKEA's Colorado Store Doubles Down on Solar Power," *Denver Business Journal*, January 23, 2014, http://www.bizjournals.com/denver; Jens Hansegard and Niclas Rolander, "IKEA Chief Says Focus to Remain on Stores," *Wall Street Journal*, January 28, 2014, http://online.wsj.com; IKEA, "IKEA Foundation," http://www.ikea.com, accessed February 10, 2014; IKEA, "People and the Environment," http://www.ikea.com, accessed February 10, 2014.

2. For a good discussion of many factors involved in the modern meanings of social responsibility, see Frank Vanclay and Ana M. Esteves, *New Directions in Social Impact Assessment: Conceptual and Methodological Advances* (Cheltenham: Edward Elgar, 2011). "The Definition of Social Responsibility" is adapted from Keith Davis and Robert L. Blomstrom, *Business and Society: Environment and Responsibility*, 3rd ed. (New York: McGraw-Hill, 1975), 6. For illustrations of how social responsibility fits into the working lives of

modern managers, see Gerard I. J. M. Zwetsloot, "From Management Systems to Corporate Social Responsibility," *Journal of Business Ethics* 44 (2003): 201–208; Christine Hemingway and Patrick Maclagan, "Managers' Personal Values as Drivers of Corporate Social Responsibility," *Journal of Business Ethics* 50 (2004): 33.

3. Bindu Arya and Gaiyan Zhang, "Institutional Reforms and Investor Reactions to CSR Announcements: Evidence from an Emerging Economy," *Journal of Management Studies* 46, no. 7 (May 14, 2009): 1089–1112.

4. Patricia L. Short, "Keeping It Clean," *Chemical & Engineering News* 85, no. 17 (April 23, 2007): 13.

5. Matteo Tonello, "The Business Case for Corporate Social Responsibility," *The Harvard Law School Forum on Corporate Governance and Financial Regulation*, The President and Fellows of Harvard College, June 26, 2011, http://blogs.law.harvard.edu/corpgov/2011/06/26/the-business-case-for-corporate–social-responsibility/, accessed March 27, 2012.

6. Virginia Gewin, "Industry Lured by the Gains of Going Green," *Nature* (July 14, 2005): 173.

7. "Mohawk Going Green in Bath Rugs," *Home Textiles Today* 28, no. 7 (February 26, 2007): 12.

8. Kate Arthur, "Going Green: Simple Changes Make Vast Improvements on the Environment," *Knight Ridder Tribune Business News* [Washington edition], March 2, 2007, 1.

9. For extended discussion of arguments for and against social responsibility, see William C. Frederick, Keith Davis, and James E. Post, *Business and Society: Corporate Strategy, Public Policy, Ethics*, 6th ed. (New York: McGraw-Hill, 1988), 36–43.

10. For discussion in favor of corporate social responsibility, see Jane Fuller, "Banking on a Good Reputation: Companies Should Look at Corporate Social Responsibility on a Cost–Benefit Approach, Not by Whatever Campaign Is in the News," *Financial Times* (2003): 6.

11. For discussions of the relationship between corporate social performance and financial performance, see John Peloza and Jingzhi Shang, "How Can Corporate Social Responsibility Activities Create Value for Stakeholders? A Systematic Review," *Journal of the Academy of Marketing Science* 39, no. 1 (2011): 117–135; Baruch Lev, Christine Petrovits, and Suresh Radhakrishnan, "Is Doing Good for You? How Corporate Charitable Contributions Enhance Revenue Growth," *Strategic Management Journal* 31, no. 2 (September 2009): 182–200.

12. J. B. McGuire, A. Sundgren, and T. Schneeweis, "Corporate Social Responsibility and Firm Financial Performance," *Academy of Management Journal* (December 1988): 854–872; Julian Birkinshaw, Nicolai J. Foss, and Siegwart Lindenberg "Combining Purpose with Profits" *MIT Sloan Management Review* 55, no. 3 (Spring 2014): 49–56.

13. For Friedman's view, see "Freedom and Philanthropy: An Interview with Milton Friedman," *Business and Society Review* (Fall 1989): 11–18.

14. Milton Friedman, "Does Business Have Social Responsibility?" *Bank Administration* (April 1971): 13–14.

15. Eric J. Savitz, "The Vision Thing: Control Data Abandons It for the Bottom Line," *Barron's* (May 7, 1990): 10–11, 22.

16. Joan E. Rigdon, "The Wrist Watch: How a Plant Handles Occupational Hazard with Common Sense," *Wall Street Journal*, September 28, 1992, 1.

17. For insights regarding SC Johnson Wax's position on social responsibility involvement, see Reva A. Holmes, "At SC Johnson Wax Philanthropy Is an Investment," *Management Accounting* (August 1994): 42–45.

18. Bill Richards, "Nike Hires an Executive from Microsoft for New Post Focusing on Labor Policies," *Wall Street Journal*, January 15, 1998, B14.

19. Geoffrey B. Sprinkle and Laureen A. Maines, "The Benefits and Costs of Social Responsibility," *Business Horizons* 53 (2010): 445–453.

20. Samuel C. Certo and J. Paul Peter, *The Strategic Management Process*, 3rd ed. (Chicago: Irwin, 1995), 219; Marianne M. Jennings, "Manager's Journal: Trendy Causes Are No Substitute for Ethics," *Wall Street Journal*, December 1, 1997, A22.

21. Carlo Wolff, "Living with the New Amenity," *Lodging Hospitality* (December 1994): 66–68; for an article demonstrating the importance of stakeholders' opinions in social responsibility, see David Wheeler, Barry Colbert, and Edward Freeman, "Focusing on Value: Reconciling Corporate Social Responsibility, Sustainability and a Stakeholder Approach in a Network World," *Journal of General Management* 28 (2003): 1.

22. Andrew Amelinckx, Modern Farmer, February 9, 2017, http://modernfarmer.com/2017/02/china-moves-implement-sustainable-ag-practices-good-everybody/.

23. S. Prakash Sethi, "Dimensions of Corporate Social Performance: An Analytical Framework," *California Management Review* (Spring 1975): 58–64.

24. To view the 2013 Bank of America Corporate Social Responsibility Report, visit http://newsroom.bankofamerica.com/press-release/community-development/bank-america-releases-corporate-social-responsibility-report.

25. For additional information about Starbucks's activities in these and other areas having an impact on society, see https://www.starbucks.com/responsibility, accessed April 4, 2017.

26. Michael E. Porter and Mark R. Kramer, "The Competitive Advantage of Corporate Philanthropy," *Harvard Business Review* (December 2002): 56–68. For discussion of the role of employees in promoting philanthropy in businesses, see Alan R. Muller, Michael D. Pfarrer, and Laura M. Little, "A Theory of Collective Empathy in Corporate Philanthropy Decisions," *Academy of Management Review* 39, no. 1 (January 1, 2014): 1–21.

27. David A. Lubin and Daniel C. Esty, "The Sustainability Imperative," *Harvard Business Review* 88, no. 5 (May 1, 2010). For a review of sustainability management research, see Amanda Williams, Steve Kennedy, Felix Philipp, and Gail Whiteman, "Systems thinking: A review of sustainability management research," *Journal of Cleaner Production*, 148, no. 1 (April 2017): 866–881.

28. Jeffrey Pfeffer, "Building Sustainable Organizations: The Human Factor," *Academy of Management Perspective* (February 2010): 34–45.

29. United Nations, *Report of the World Commission on Environment and Development*, United Nations General Assembly Resolution 42/187, December 1987. For a different viewpoint on the importance of sustainability, see John A. Vucetich and Michael P. Nelson, "Sustainability: Virtuous or Vulgar?," *BioScience* 60, no. 7 (July/August 2010).

30. Vince Luchsinger, "Strategy Issues in Business Sustainability," *Business Renaissance Quarterly* 4, no. 3 (Fall 2009): 163–174.

31. "PepsiCo Launches Groundbreaking Pilot Program to Reduce Carbon Footprint of Tropicana," *CSRWire*, May 18, 2010, http://www.csrwire.com.

32. Mark Hollingworth, "Building 360 Organizational Sustainability," *Ivey Business Journal Online* (November/December 2009).

33. Ram Nidumolu, C. K. Prahalad, and M. R. Rangaswami, "Why Sustainability Is Now the Key Driver of Innovation," *Harvard Business Review* (September 2009): 1.

34. Josette Akresh-Gonzales, "Herman Miller CEO Brian Walker on Meeting Sustainability Goals—With Customer Help," *Harvard Business Review* (December 2009): 1. For an interesting outline of Bicardi Limited's proactive position on sustainability, see "Bacardi Limited Charts Bold Course in Building a Sustainable Future," *PR Newswire Europe Including UK Disclose* (February 4, 2014).

35. Michael S. Hopkins, "What Executives Don't Get about Sustainability (and Further Notes on the Profit Motive)," *MIT Sloan Management Review* 51, no. 1 (Fall 2009): 40.

36. Michael S. Hopkins, "8 Reasons Sustainability Will Change Management," *MIT Sloan Management Review* 51, no. 1 (Fall 2009): 27–30.

37. Daniel C. Esty and Andrew S. Winston, *Green to Gold: How Smart Companies Use Environmental Strategy to Innovate, Create Value, and Build Competitive Advantage* (New Haven, CT: Yale University Press, 2006).

38. Ram Nidumolu, C. K. Prahalad, and M. R. Rangaswami, "Why Sustainability Is Now the Key Driver of Innovation," *Harvard Business Review* (September, 2009): 56–64.

39. "Strategic Tunnel Enhancement Programme (STEP), Abu Dhabi—Water Technology," https://www.water-technology.net/projects/strategic-tunnel-enhancement-program-abu-dhabi/; Engineers Australia, "Technical Talk—Strategic Tunnel Enhancement Programme (STEP)," https://www.engineersaustralia.org.au/Event/technical-talk-strategic-tunnel-enhancement-programme-step; Binsal Abdul Kader, "Abu Dhabi to Recycle 100% of Waste Water within 3 Years," GulfNews.com, October 12, 2014, https://gulfnews.com/news/uae/environment/abu-dhabi-to-recycle-100-of-waste-water-within-3-years-1.1397536.

40. "Weis Markets Adds Sustainability Specialist," *Ecology, Environment & Conservation Business* (May 8, 2010): 93.

41. DuPont Company, "2008 Sustainability Report," 4. For ideas on how taking sustainability steps makes good business sense, see Michael S. Hopkins, "How SAP Made the Business Case for Sustainability," *MIT Sloan Management Review* 52, no. 1(Fall 2010): 69–72.

42. DuPont 2015 Sustainability Progress Report, http://foodsecurity.dupont.com/about-us/food-security-goals/, accessed April 4, 2017.

43. For an interesting discussion of the ethical dilemma of fairly allocating an individual's time between work and personal life, see Paul B. Hoffmann, "Balancing Professional and Personal Priorities," *Healthcare Executive* (May/June 1994): 42.

44. Archie B. Carroll, "In Search of the Moral Manager," *Business Horizons* (March/April 1987): 7–15. For a study linking the relationship between ethics and sustainability, see Lam D. Nguyen, Bahaudin G. Mujtaba, Chat N. Tran, and Quan H. M. Tran, "Sustainable Growth and Ethics: A Study of Business Ethics in Vietnam Between Business Students and Working Adults," *The South East Asian Journal of Management* 7, no. 1 (April 2013): 41–56.

45. For an article outlining the relationship between ethics and management, see Elliott Jaques, "Ethics for Management," *Management Communication Quarterly* 17 (2003): 136.

46. Sundeep Waslekar, "Good Citizens and Reap Rewards," *Asian Business* (January 1994): 52. See also Genine Babakian, "Who Will Control Russian Advertising?," *Adweek* [Eastern Edition] (August 1, 1994): 16.

47. Natalie M. Green, "Creating an Ethical Workplace," *Employment Relations Today* 24, no. 2 (Summer 1997): 33–44.

48. "Helping Workers Helps Bottom Line," *Employee Benefit Plan Review* (July 1990).

49. Sandy Lutz, "Psych Hospitals Fight for Survival," *Modern Healthcare* (May 8, 1995): 62–65.

50. http://legislative.cancer.gov/hearings/research.

51. James B. Treece, "Nissan Rattles Japan with Tough Ethics Code," *Automotive News* (May 4, 1998): 1, 49. To see Nissan's ethics code, go to http://www.annualreportowl.com/Nissan/2013/Annual%20Report?s=nissan+ethics+code.

52. Richard A. Spinell, "Lessons from the Salomon Scandal," *America* (December 28, 1991): 476–477; Touche Ross, *Ethics in American Business* (New York: Touche Ross & Co., January 1988). For a view on developing a code of ethics for the workplace, see O. C. Ferrell, "An Assessment of the Proposed Academy of Marketing Science Code of Ethics for Marketing Educators," *Journal of Business Ethics* 19, no. 2 (April 1999): 225–228.

53. For additional insights on how and why to create an ethical workplace, see Curt Smith, "The Ethical Workplace," *Association Management* 52, no. 6 (June 2000): 70–73.

54. For an interesting study of ethics codes, see Lawrence Chonko, Thomas Wotruba, and Terry Loe, "Ethics Code Familiarity and Usefulness: Views on Idealist and Relativist Managers under Varying Conditions of Turbulence," *Journal of Business Ethics* 42 (2003): 237.

55. Alan L. Otten, "Ethics on the Job: Companies Alert Employees to Potential Dilemmas," *Wall Street Journal*, July 14, 1986, 25.

56. Based upon: http://www.socinfo.com/d2F5a.2c.d.html#1st page.

57. Gene R. Laczniak, "Framework for Analyzing Marketing Ethics," *Journal of Macromarketing* (Spring 1983): 7–18. See also Patricia Haddock and Marilyn Manning, "Ethically Speaking," *Sky* (March 1990): 128–131.

58. http://www.scu.edu/ethics/practicing/decision/framework.html.

59. For more discussion of such skills, see: www.eoa.org.

60. "Sustainability Guidelines for External Business Partners," https://www.pgsupplier.com/en/pg-values/sustainability.shtml.

61. Standard & Poor's details Enron's deception and its impact on the company's rating in a letter to the House committee, *PR News* (March 20, 2002).

62. "Special Report: SEC Follows Up on Sarbanes–Oxley Reform Standards," *Directors & Trustees Digest* 62, no. 3 (March 2003): 1.

63. John Schwartz, "Playing Know and Tell," *New York Times*, June 9, 2002, 4.2.

64. The Associated Press, "Enron Ruling to Stand," *New York Times*, November 22, 2006, 6.

65. Stephen M. Paskoff, "Ten Ethics Trends for 2010," *Workforce Management*, December 2009, http://www.workforce.com.

66. Stacy Cowley, "Whistle-blower Wins $5 million and a Job Back," *New York Times*, April 4, 2017, B1.

67. Gerald Calvasina, Richard Calvasina, and Eugene Calvasina, *Journal of Legal, Ethical & Regulatory Issues* 19, no. 1 (2016): 56–64.

68. "CVS Health Corporate Social Responsibility Activities Address Important National and Local Health Care Issues and Contribute to Economic Growth," https://www.cvshealth.com/newsroom/press-releases/cvs-health-corporate-social-responsibility-activities-address-important.

Management and Diversity

TARGET SKILL

Diversity Skill: the ability to establish and maintain an organizational workforce that represents a combination of assorted human characteristics appropriate for achieving organizational success

DIVERSITY SKILL AND YOUR CAREER

Diversity skill can be of great value to you in enhancing your management career. For example, this skill can help you build a more creative workforce. Enhanced workforce creativity will contribute to organizational success, build your image as a competent manager, make you valuable to your organization, and support promotions as you build your career.

OBJECTIVES

To help build my *diversity skill*, when studying this chapter, I will attempt to acquire:

4-1 A definition of diversity

4-2 An understanding of the advantages of diversity in organizations

4-3 An awareness of the challenges facing managers within a diverse workforce

4-4 An understanding of the strategies for promoting diversity in organizations

4-5 Insights into how managers promote diversity

MyLab Management Chapter Warm Up

If your instructor has assigned this activity, go to www.pearson.com/mylab/management to complete the chapter warm up.

CHALLENGE CASE

Diverse Employees Contribute to GE Lighting's Bright Future

Despite the common assumption that manufacturing jobs are disappearing, manufacturing companies face a hiring challenge. As experienced workers retire and technology advances, businesses need bright, hard-working employees who are comfortable with technology. GE Lighting is tapping the potential of the "millennial generation," workers born between 1982 and 2000. According to general manager Ron Wilson, the share of millennials among his manufacturing engineers and managers has doubled. The company is smoothing the way by preparing these employees to succeed. Its two-year leadership training program gives operations employees challenging assignments and brings them into contact with senior management. At the level of factory floor workers, the company partners with local community colleges to prepare qualified young workers for high-tech manufacturing. This facilitates the development of the management employability skill of knowledge application, which is the ability to learn a concept and then appropriately apply that knowledge in another setting. As these new employees receive additional training, they are developing their knowledge application skill.

By recruiting a new generation of production workers, GE Lighting brings together people of different ages. But that is hardly the only measure of this company's diversity. While manufacturing has historically been dominated by men, GE Lighting's CEO, Maryrose Sylvester, is an example of a talented woman finding opportunities at General Electric. Sylvester, who earned a bachelor's degree in procurement and production management and a master's in business administration, joined GE as an intern. She worked her way up, taking management positions in high-technology and lighting industries. Now, as GE Lighting's CEO, she is responsible for a $3 billion business employing 13,000 people, including 700 at the headquarters in Cleveland, Ohio.

Sylvester earned her elevation to the CEO position by promoting technology leadership and increasing revenues. However, she appreciates the need to help people gain access to opportunities. In the 1990s, for example, she participated in launching a group called the GE Women's Network. She also endorses GE Lighting's support for the MC² STEM High School in Cleveland (STEM stands for science, technology, engineering, and mathematics). Its students learn through completing projects and internships with

General Electric president and CEO, Maryrose T. Sylvester, holds a journal taken out of the GE time capsule in Cleveland.

local companies and by spending tenth grade at GE Lighting's headquarters, where employees become mentors, tutoring and guiding them. When students master the high school's math and science classes, they comprise a pool of talent right at GE's doorstep.

These efforts are part of GE's corporate-wide diversity programs. Employees can find support and learn skills by joining affinity groups; a few are the African American Forum; the Gay, Lesbian, Bisexual, Transgender and Allies Alliance; and the Hispanic Forum. A chief diversity officer sets goals and measures results, meeting regularly with other top executives. Other diversity programs have specific goals to meet. For example, Get Skills to Work helps match up veterans with jobs where they can apply the skills they gained in the military, and STEM Camp encourages girls in junior high to explore science and technology.

GE's commitment to diversity is part of its corporate vision. GE is well known for rewarding performance and sees valuing diversity as a way to ensure that it finds and keeps the best talent, wherever it might be.

GE Lighting is at an exciting point in its hundred-plus-year history. Light-emitting diodes (LEDs) and other new technology are opening up ways for consumers and businesses to enjoy the advantages of efficient lighting, and GE is expanding production globally. To succeed, it needs the best from *all* its employees.[1]

THE DIVERSITY CHALLENGE

The Challenge Case illustrates the diversity challenge that GE Lighting's management strives to carry out. The remaining material in this chapter explains diversity concepts and helps develop the corresponding diversity skill that you will need to succeed at meeting such challenges throughout your career. After studying chapter concepts, read the Challenge Case Summary at the end of the chapter to help you relate chapter content to building diversity at GE Lighting.

Defining Diversity

Diversity refers to characteristics of individuals that shape their identities and the experiences they have in society. This chapter provides information about workforce diversity and discusses the strengths and weaknesses of a diverse workforce. Understanding diversity is essential for managers today because managing diversity will undoubtedly constitute a large portion of the management agenda well into the twenty-first century.[2]

4-1 A definition of diversity

This chapter describes some strategies for promoting social diversity in organizations. It also explains how diversity is related to the four management functions. Given the overarching nature of this topic, you will probably find yourself reflecting on diversity as you study future chapters. For example, you will reflect on diversity as you study the legal foundation for developing an inclusive workforce, affirmative action, and Equal Employment Opportunity (EEO), discussed in Chapter 12, and ideas about organizational change, discussed in Chapter 13.

The Social Implications of Diversity

Workforce diversity is not a new issue in the United States. Although not always voluntarily, people from various other regions and cultures have been immigrating to its shores since colonial times. As a result, the American population has always been a mix of races, ethnicities, religions, social classes, physical abilities, and sexual orientations.[3] These differences—along with the basic human differences of age and gender—comprise diversity. The purpose of exploring diversity issues in a management textbook is to suggest how managers might include diverse employees equally, accepting their differences and utilizing their talents.[4]

Majority and Minority Groups Managers must understand the relationship between two groups in organizations: majority groups and minority groups. **Majority group** refers to that group of people in the organization who hold most of the positions that command decision-making power, control of resources and information, and access to system rewards. **Minority group** refers to that group of people in the organization who are fewer in number than the majority group or who lack critical power, resources, acceptance, and social status. Together, the minority and majority group members form the entire social system of the organization.

However, the majority group is not always the group that is larger in number: Sometimes, in fact, the minority group is actually greater in number. For example, women are seen as a minority group in many organizations because they are underrepresented in executive positions. In most health-care organizations, for instance, women outnumber men; although men are numerical minorities in health-care organizations, they are seldom denied social status because white males hold most positions of power in the health-care system hierarchy, such as physicians and health-care administrators.

Advantages of Diversity in Organizations

Safeway gained market share by hiring more women leaders and a workforce representative of its customer base.

4-2 An understanding of the advantages of diversity in organizations

Managers are becoming more dedicated to seeking a wide range of talents from every group in American culture because they now realize that distinct advantages come from doing so.[5] For one thing, as you will see in Chapter 17, group decisions often improve the quality of decision making. For another, work groups or teams that can draw on the contributions of a multicultural membership gain the advantage of a larger pool of information and a richer array of approaches to solve work problems.[6]

Gaining and Keeping Market Share

Today, managers must understand increasingly diverse markets. Failure to discern customers' preferences can cost a company its business in the United States and abroad. Some people argue that one of the best ways to ensure that an organization is able to penetrate diverse markets is to include diverse managers among the organization's decision makers.[7]

Diversity in the managerial ranks has the additional advantage of enhancing a company's credibility with customers. Employing a manager who is the same gender or ethnic background as that of customers may imply to those customers that their day-to-day experiences will be understood. One African American female manager found that her knowledge of customers paid off when she convinced her company to change the name of a product it intended to sell at Wal-Mart. "I knew that I had shopped for household goods at Wal-Mart, whereas the CEO of this company, a white, upper-middle-class male, had not. He listened to me and we changed the name of the product."

Morrison cites a case in which a company lost an important opportunity for new business in a southwestern city's predominantly Hispanic community. The lucrative business ultimately went to a competitor that had put in charge of the project a Hispanic manager who solicited input from the Hispanic community.

Consider how Safeway gained market share through diversity. One of North America's largest food retailers, with about 1,700 grocery stores, Safeway faced increasingly stiff competition from companies such as Target and Wal-Mart. In response, Safeway initiated a program to position itself as an employer of choice. In addition, with 70 percent of its customers being women, Safeway wanted to expand its workforce diversity to be more consistent with its customer base. Safeway recognized that a diverse workforce would help the company better understand and respond to customer needs and create a competitive edge in the marketplace. With industry leadership traditionally male, Safeway's initiative supporting women leaders broke from the norm. Today, management openly credits its past diversity efforts as the foundation of the present levels of diversity and profitability.[8]

Cost Savings

Companies incur high costs in recruiting, training, relocating, and replacing employees and in providing competitive compensation packages. According to Morrison, Corning Corporation's high turnover among women and people of color was costing the company an estimated $2 to $4 million a year. Many managers who were questioned for her study felt that the personnel expenses associated with turnover—often totaling as much as two-thirds of an organization's budget—could be reduced by instituting diversity practices that would give nontraditional managers more incentive to stay. When nontraditional managers remain with an organization, nontraditional employees at lower levels feel more committed to the company.

In addition to the personnel costs, executives are distressed by the high legal fees and staggering settlements resulting from lawsuits brought by employees who feel they have been

TABLE 4.1   **Advantages of a Diverse Workforce**

Improved ability to gain and keep market share
Cost savings
Increased productivity
A more innovative workforce
Minority and women employees who are more motivated
Better quality of managers
Employees who have internalized the message that "different" does not mean "less than"
A workforce that is more resilient when faced with change

discriminated against. For example, $17.7 million in damages was awarded to a woman employed by Texaco who claimed she had been passed over for a management promotion because of her gender. Executives are finally learning that such sums would be better spent on promoting diversity.

Increased Productivity and Innovation

Many executives quoted in Morrison's study believe productivity is higher in organizations that focus on diversity. These managers find that employees who feel valued, competent, and at ease in their work setting enjoy coming to work and perform at a high level.

Morrison also cites a study by Donna Thompson and Nancy DiTomaso that concluded that a multicultural approach has a positive effect on employees' perception of equity. This in turn has a positive effect on employees' morale, goal setting, effort, and performance. The managers in Morrison's study also saw innovation as a strength of a diverse workforce. In essence, diversity becomes the spark that ignites innovation.[9]

Better Quality Management

Morrison also found that including nontraditional employees in fair competition for advancement usually improves the quality of management by providing a wider pool of talent. According to the research she cites, exposure to diverse colleagues helps managers develop breadth and openness.

The quality of management can also be improved by creating more effective personnel policies and practices that, once developed, will benefit all employees in the organization, not just minorities. According to Morrison's study, many of the programs initially developed for nontraditional managers resulted in improvements that were later successfully applied throughout the organization. For example, ideas such as adding training for mentors, upgrading techniques for developing managers, and improving processes for evaluating employees for promotion—all concepts originally intended to help nontraditional managers—were later adopted for wider use. See **Table 4.1** for more information on the advantages of a diverse workforce.

At first glance, the advantages of diversity to an organization seem undeniable. In a survey focusing on small to medium-sized enterprises, however, more managers disagreed that diversity contributes to performance than the number of managers that agreed.[10] But these findings do not dispute the overall conclusion that diversity contributes to improved organizational performance. Instead, they seem to indicate that many managers still need to be convinced of the benefits that accrue to an organization through diversity.

MyLab Management Watch It

If your instructor has assigned this activity, go to www.pearson.com/mylab/management to complete the video exercise.

Challenges That Managers Face in Working with Diverse Populations

4-3 An awareness of the challenges facing managers within a diverse workforce

As you have seen, an organization may find numerous compelling reasons to encourage diversity in its workforce. For managers to appreciate the implications of promoting diversity fully, however, they must understand some of the challenges they will face in managing a diverse workforce. Changing demographics and several issues arising from these changes are discussed in the following sections.[11]

Changing Demographics

Demographics are statistical characteristics of a population. They are also an important tool that managers can use to study workforce diversity. According to a report done for the U.S. Department of Labor by the Hudson Institute, the workforce and jobs of the twenty-first century will parallel changes in society and in the economy. This report indicates that five demographic issues will be especially important to managers in the twenty-first century:[12]

1.   The population and the workforce will grow more slowly than at any time since the 1930s.
2.   The average age of the population and the workforce will rise, and the pool of young workers entering the labor market will shrink.
3.   More women will enter the workforce.
4.   Minorities will make up a larger share of new entrants into the labor force.
5.   Immigrants will represent the largest share of the increase in the general population and in the workforce.

The changing demographics of a population over an extended period can give managers insight into future diversity management challenges. For example, **Figure 4.1** provides projections for average annual percentage changes in various races of the U.S. population. According to the projections, the black population will grow at more than twice the annual rate of change of the white population between 1995 and 2050. Through 2020, the Asian and Pacific Islander population group is projected to be the fastest-growing population segment. By 2000, the Asian population had expanded to more than 11 million, and it will double its current size by 2020 and triple its current size by 2040. The American Indian, Eskimo, and Aleut segment is projected to grow but not nearly as significantly as the Asian segment. Growth of the Hispanic

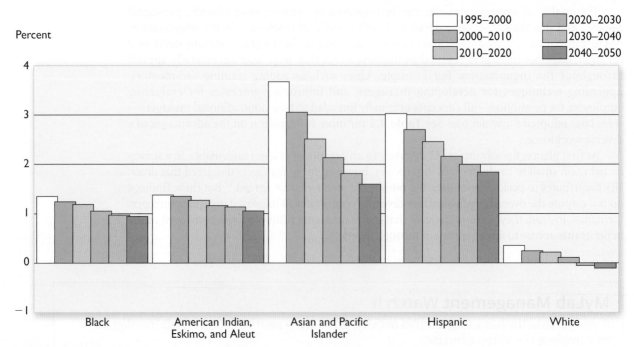

Figure 4.1   Average annual percentage changes in the U.S. population by race, 1995–2050

population will also be a major element of total population growth. Each year from now to 2050, the Hispanic segment is projected to add more people to the U.S. population than the white segment will. Such demographic trends seem to indicate that the ability to handle diversity challenges will be valuable to managers in the future.

Multigenerational Workforce

Another diversity-related challenge facing managers concerns the number of generations working in an organization. The more generations that a manager must manage, the more diverse the workforce and the more challenging the workforce is to manage.

Managers commonly manage multiple generations on a daily basis. These generations have been labeled and defined as follows:[13]

The Millennial Generation or Generation Y. People born after 1980 turned 18 to 33 years old in 2014, are 27 percent of the adult population, and are 57 percent of the non-Hispanic white population.

Generation X. People born between 1965 and 1980 turned 34 to 49 years old in 2014, are 27 percent of the adult population, and are 61 percent of the non-Hispanic white population.

The Baby Boom Generation. People born between 1946 and 1964 turned 50 to 68 years old in 2014, are 32 percent of the adult population, and are 72 percent of the non-Hispanic white population.

The Silent Generation. People born between 1928 and 1945 turned 69 to 86 years old in 2014, are 12 percent of the adult population, and are 79 percent of the non-Hispanic white population.

Managing multiple generations is challenging because each generation brings its own unique experiences, values, and issues into the workplace. For example, baby boomers are staying in the workforce longer than previous generations did and are typically more interested in wellness, having part-time jobs, and having life longevity than other generations. On the other hand, Generation X is generally interested in a balance of personal life and work, while Generation Y is interested in being part of a team, working in a collaborative environment, and engaging with social media and other technologies.[14]

The manager's job is to understand the array of generations that exist in the workplace and to shape them into an engaged, productive team. Reverse mentoring is one useful tool that managers can use to help create such a team. **Reverse mentoring** is a process that pairs a senior employee with a junior employee for the purpose of transferring work skills, such as Internet skills, from the junior employee to the more senior employee. Popularized by Jack Welch, the former CEO at General Electric Corporation, the program was credited with helping to spread Internet skills within the company and enabling the company to become better positioned for doing e-business.

Overall, in shaping this productive multigenerational work team, managers should always keep in mind the special traits of each generation and use those traits to the organization's advantage. For example, managers should keep in mind that millennials were raised on using social media. Enlisting the help of millennials in using social media to collect information quickly, make sense of it, and respond to it in real time should be helpful for quickly solving organizational problems.[15]

Ethnocentrism and Other Negative Dynamics

The changing demographics described in the Hudson Institute's report set in motion certain social dynamics that can interfere with workforce productivity. If an organization is to be successful in diversifying, it must neutralize these dynamics.

Ethnocentrism
Our natural tendency is to judge other groups less favorably than our own. This tendency is the source of **ethnocentrism**, the belief that one's own group, culture, country, or customs are superior to those of others. Two related dynamics are prejudices and stereotypes. A **prejudice** is a preconceived judgment, opinion, or assumption about an issue, behavior, or group of people.[16] A **stereotype** is a positive or negative assessment of members of

a group or their perceived attributes. One example of stereotyping in the United States involves Muslims. Many Muslims living in the United States fear that because some Muslims are high-profile terrorists, Americans might tend to stereotype all Muslims as terrorists. U.S. Muslims represent more than 6 percent of the U.S. population; they constitute a disproportionate number of college graduates, professionals, and business owners in American society; and they are responsible for only a negligible amount of crime. Many argue that stereotyping all Muslims as terrorists is drastically unfair to the U.S. Muslim population. A recent study by the Pew Forum found that, of all groups in the United States, Muslims experience the most workplace discrimination.[17]

Overall, it is important for managers to know about negative dynamics such as ethnocentrism and stereotyping so that they can monitor their own perceptions and help their employees view diverse coworkers more accurately.

Discrimination

When verbalized or acted upon, these negative dynamics can cause discomfort and stress for the judged individual. In some cases, there is outright discrimination. **Discrimination** is the act of treating an issue, person, or behavior unjustly or inequitably on the basis of stereotypes and prejudices. Consider the person with a disability who is turned down for a promotion because the boss feels that this employee is incapable of handling the frequent travel required for this particular job. The boss's prejudgment of this employee's capabilities on the basis of his or her "difference"—and implementation of the prejudgment through differential treatment—constitutes discrimination. Or consider an older worker who is turned down for a job because the manager thinks the worker is too old for the job. The actual turning down of the potential employee based on this managerial feeling could be considered age discrimination.[18]

Tokenism and Other Challenges

Discrimination occurs when stereotypes are acted upon in ways that affect hiring, pay, or promotion practices—for example, when older employees are steered into less visible job assignments, which are unlikely to provide opportunities for advancement. Other challenges facing minorities and women include the pressure to conform to the organization's culture, extreme penalties for mistakes, and tokenism. **Tokenism** refers to being one of the few members of your group in the organization.[19] "Token" employees are given either very high or very low visibility in the organization. One African American male indicated that his white female manager "discouraged" him from joining voluntary committees and task forces within the company—and at the same time, in his performance appraisal she criticized him for being "aloof" and taking a "low-profile approach."

In other cases, minorities are seen as representatives or spokespeople for all members of their group. As such, they are subject to high expectations and scrutiny from members of their

PRACTICAL CHALLENGE: SETTING DIVERSITY TARGETS

Pinterest Sets Hiring Goals for a More Diverse Workforce

In July 2015, Pinterest realized it had a major diversity problem. About 80 percent of its high-tech employees were male and most of those were either white or Asian. So the 800-employee company made diversity hiring a priority.

First, it required that every time a manager conducted interviews for a leadership role, that manager had to interview one female and one person from an underrepresented demographic. Next, Pinterest broadened the number and kinds of universities where it conducted recruiting. Third, every employee is required to receive training on bias and diversity. And

finally, the company instituted a mentoring program for black software engineers.

Each of these steps had an immediate impact on the diversity of the growing Pinterest workforce. But executives didn't stop there. They typically received many candidates simply through referrals of existing employees. So they asked employees to try and refer more women and candidates with more diverse backgrounds. After only six weeks, the number of female referrals increased by 26 percent and there were 55 times more candidates from ethnically diverse backgrounds than before.[20]

own group. One Latino male employee described how other Latinos in the company "looked up to him" for his achievements in the organization. In general, ethnocentrism, prejudices, and stereotypes inhibit people's ability to process information accurately.

Sometimes, however, people of color are the most compelling spokespersons in promoting the issue of diversity. In 1983, an African American lawyer in New York named James O'Neal founded a program called Legal Outreach to increase diversity in the legal profession. The program helps African American students in New York elementary schools prepare for careers in law. Legal Outreach's comprehensive program includes after-school academic support, workshops that teach study and life skills, college preparation courses, field trips, and more. Now nationally acclaimed, the program has succeeded in sending more than 300 students to college, two-thirds of them to some of the nation's most prestigious institutions. Eighty-five percent graduate in four years, and more than one-third go on to graduate or law school. Legal Outreach stands as a model of a pipeline diversity program for other cities to replicate.[21]

Negative Dynamics and Specific Groups

The following sections discuss these negative dynamics more fully as they pertain to women, minorities, older workers, and workers with disabilities.

Women

Rosabeth Moss Kanter has researched the pressures women managers face. In her classic study of gender dynamics in organizations, she emphasizes as one of those pressures the high expectations women have of other women.[22]

Gender Roles

Women in organizations confront **gender-role stereotypes**, or perceptions about people based on what our society believes are appropriate behaviors for men and women. Both sexes find their self-expression constrained by gender-role stereotyping. For example, women in organizations are often assumed to be good listeners, an attribution based on our societal view that women are nurturing. Although this assessment is a positive one, it is not true of all women or of any one woman all the time—hence the negative side of this stereotypical expectation of women in the workplace.

Women professionals, for instance, often remark that they are frequently sought out by colleagues who want to discuss non-work-related problems. Women managers also describe the subtle sanctions they experience from both men and women when they do not fulfill the expectations that they will be nurturing managers.

The Glass Ceiling and Sexual Harassment

A serious form of discrimination affecting women in organizations has been dubbed the *glass ceiling*.[23] The term refers to an invisible "ceiling," or barrier, to advancement.[24] This term, originally coined to describe the limits confronting women, is now also used to describe the experiences of other minorities in organizations. Although both women and men struggle to balance work and family concerns, it is still more common for women to assume the primary responsibility for household management as well as their careers, and sometimes they are denied opportunities for advancement because of this stereotype.

Sexual harassment, another form of discrimination, is defined as any unwanted sexual language, behavior, or imagery negatively affecting an employee.[25] According to the Equal Opportunity Commission, sexual harassment may include requests for sexual favors when such favors explicitly or implicitly become a term or condition of an individual's employment or education. Managers must keep in mind that, although sexual harassment more often targets women, men can also be victims of sexual harassment in the workplace or educational settings.

Minorities

Racial, ethnic, and cultural minorities also confront inhibiting stereotypes about their groups. Like women, they must deal with misunderstandings and expectations based on their ethnic or cultural origins.

Many members of ethnic or racial minority groups have been socialized to be members of two cultural groups—the dominant culture and their particular racial or ethnic culture. Ella Bell, professor of organizational behavior at Massachusetts Institute of Technology (MIT), refers to this dual membership as *biculturalism*. In her study of African American women, she terms the stress of coping with membership in two cultures simultaneously as **bicultural stress**.[26] She also indicates that **role conflict** (having to fill competing roles because of membership in two cultures) and **role overload** (having too many expectations to fulfill comfortably) are common characteristics of bicultural stress. Although these are problems for many minority groups, they are particularly intense for women of color because this group experiences negative dynamics affecting *both* minorities and women.

Internalized norms and values of one's culture of origin can lead to problems and misunderstandings in the workplace, particularly when a manager relies solely on the cultural norms of the majority group while dealing with people not of that group. According to the norms of American culture, for example, it is acceptable—even beneficial—to praise an individual publicly for a job well done. In cultures that place primary value on group harmony and collective achievement, however, this way of rewarding an employee can cause emotional discomfort because the employee may fear that, if praised publicly, she will "lose face" in her group.

Being a woman and a member of a minority group can present a double hurdle in investment banking. For this reason, leadership at Morgan Stanley initiated its Emerging Manager Program to identify and support up-and-coming asset managers, particularly women of color. The program seeks to partner with and provide capital to asset managers in underrepresented segments (such as women-owned and minority-owned businesses). The goal is to increase the number of female and minorities in asset management, thereby creating a broader pool of talent and ultimately enhancing business results.[27]

Older Workers   Older workers are a significant and valuable component of the labor force.[28] Approximately 16 million Americans over 55 years of age are employed or looking for work. Older workers are becoming an important labor force component. From 2002 to 2012, progressively fewer younger employees were available for hire because of the slow population growth between 1966 and 1985. During this same period, the pool of older workers available for hire increased faster than that of any other age segment and comprised more than 19 percent of the labor market.[29]

Anticipating this simultaneous shortage of younger workers and increase in the number of older workers in the labor market, many managers have recommended that now is the time to start recruiting older workers.[30] Successful tactics for recruiting older workers include asking for referrals from current employees, using employment agencies, contacting local senior citizens community groups, and surveying members of various churches. Advantages of hiring older workers include their willingness to work nontraditional schedules, their ability to serve as mentors, and their strong work ethic. Disadvantages of hiring older workers might include their lack of technology experience and possible increased benefit costs to the organization due to their health-care needs. Once hired, management must focus on meeting the needs of older workers. For example, management must understand issues such as job preferences and that the personal needs of older versus younger workers are normally different. As a result, management may have to take special steps to meet the needs of the two different groups of workers. However, such steps will help management retain older workers and encourage older workers to be as productive as possible.[31]

Effective managers retain their valuable older workers by recognizing and meeting their special needs.

Layland Masuda/Shutterstock

Stereotypes and Prejudices   Older workers face some specific challenges because of managers' views of older people. Stereotypes and prejudices link age with senility, incompetence, and lack of worth in the labor market. Jeffrey Sonnenfeld, an expert on senior executives and older workers, compiled research findings from several studies of older employees. He found that managers view older workers as "deadwood" and seek to "weed them out" through pension incentives, biased performance appraisals, and other methods.[32]

Sonnenfeld's compilation of research indicates that even though older managers are more cautious, less likely to take risks, and less open to change than younger managers, many are high performers. Studies that tracked individuals' careers over the long term conclude that a peak in performance occurs at about age 45 to 50, and a second peak occurs at about age 55 to 60. Performance in some fields (e.g., sales) either improves with age or does not significantly decline.

It is thus the manager's responsibility to value older workers for their contributions to the organization and to see that they are treated fairly. This task requires an understanding of and sensitivity to the physiological and psychological changes that older workers sometimes experience. Supporting older workers also requires paying attention to how performance appraisal processes, retirement incentives, training programs, blocked career paths, union insurance pensions, and affirmative action goals affect this segment of the workforce.

Workers with Disabilities   People with disabilities are subject to the same negative dynamics that plague women, minorities, and older workers. For example, one manager confessed that before he attended diversity training sessions offered through a nearby university, he felt "uncomfortable" around people who are disabled. One professional with a disability reported that she was always received warmly over the phone and told that her background was exactly what the company was looking for, but when she showed up for job interviews, she was often rebuffed and informed that her credentials were insufficient.

Many companies are rejecting such negative dynamics, however, and taking proactive steps to employ workers with disabilities. For example, Walgreens Company, the nation's largest drugstore chain, proactively pursues the hiring of workers with disabilities. The company's 670,000-square-foot distribution center in Anderson, South Carolina, which services stores throughout the southeastern United States, was designed to be adaptable to the needs of workers with disabilities. Nearly half the facility's 700 employees have a disability of some kind, such as autism, mental retardation, and hearing or vision impairments. The facility's success has prompted the company to increase its hiring of candidates with disabilities. *Careers and the Disabled* magazine named Walgreens the "Private-Sector Employer of the Year" for its commitment to hiring and promoting workers with disabilities.[33]

Strategies for Promoting Diversity in Organizations

This section looks at several approaches to diversity and strategies that managers can consider as they plan for promoting cultural diversity in their organizations. First, the six strategies for modern management offered by the Hudson Institute report focusing on the twenty-first-century workforce are explored. Then the requirements of the Equal Employment Opportunity Commission, which is legally empowered to regulate organizations to ensure that management practices enhance diversity, are discussed, along with affirmative action. Next, promoting diversity through various levels of commitment is covered. Finally, promoting diversity through pluralism is discussed.

4-4   An understanding of the strategies for promoting diversity in organizations

Promoting Diversity through Hudson Institute Strategies

According to the Hudson Institute, six major issues demand the full attention of U.S. business leaders of the twenty-first century and require them to take the following actions:[34]

1. **Stimulate balanced world growth**—The United States must pay less attention to its share of world trade and more attention to the growth of the economies of other nations of the world, including the nations in Europe, Latin America, and Asia, with which the United States competes.
2. **Accelerate productivity increases in service industries**—Prosperity will depend much more on how quickly output per worker increases in health care, education, retailing, government, and other services than on gains in manufacturing.
3. **Maintain the dynamism of an aging workforce**—As the age of the average American worker climbs toward 40, the nation must make sure that its workforce does not lose its adaptability and willingness to learn.
4. **Reconcile the conflicting needs of women, work, and families**—Despite a huge influx of women into the workforce in the last two decades, many organizational policies covering pay, fringe benefits, time away from work, pensions, welfare, and other issues do not yet reflect this new reality.

5. **Fully integrate African American and Hispanic workers into the economy**—The decline in the number of "traditional" white male workers among younger workers, the rapid pace of industrial change, and the increasing skill requirements of the emerging economy make the full utilization of minority workers a particularly urgent necessity for the future.

6. **Improve the education and skills of all workers**—Human capital (knowledge, skills, organization, and leadership) is the key to economic growth and competitiveness.

As these key strategies for modern management suggest, many of the most significant managerial challenges that lie ahead result from dramatic demographic shifts and other complex societal issues. Organizations—and ultimately their leaders and managers—will need to clarify their own social values as they confront these dynamics. *Social values*, discussed further in Chapter 9, are the relative worth society places on different ways of existence and functioning.

The six strategies outlined in the Hudson Institute report strongly imply that organizations need to become more inclusive—that is, to welcome a broader mix of employees and to develop an organizational culture that maximizes the value and potential of each worker. As with any major initiative, commitment to developing an inclusive organization begins at the top of the organizational hierarchy. However, on a day-to-day operational basis, each manager's level of commitment is a critical determinant of how well or how poorly the organization's strategies and approaches will be implemented.

Promoting Diversity through Equal Employment and Affirmative Action

The Equal Employment Opportunity Commission (EEOC) is the federal agency that enforces the laws regulating recruiting and other management practices. Chapter 12 contains a more extended discussion of the EEOC. Affirmative action programs are designed to eliminate barriers and increase opportunities for underutilized or disadvantaged individuals. These programs are positive steps toward promoting diversity and have created career opportunities for both women and minority groups.

Unquestionably, complying with EEOC legislation can help to promote diversity in organizations and, as a result, help organizations gain the many diversity-related advantages discussed earlier. On the other hand, not following the legislation can be expensive. **Table 4.2** highlights a number of recent EEOC settlements that illustrate how ignoring EEOC legislation can be expensive. Overall, managers should view the EEOC as a source of guidance on how to

TABLE 4.2   Sample EEOC Case Settlements

EEOC Wins Record Settlement for Former Texas-Based Sara Lee Factory Workers
Federal authorities announced a record $4 million settlement for former Sara Lee factory workers based on allegations that the company's Paris, Texas, plant subjected some of its black employees to a racially hostile work environment.[35]
Sheriff, County Settle with Former Deputy
A civil rights lawsuit against eastern Oregon Malheur County and Malheur County Sheriff Brian Wolfe came to an end with a settlement agreement. In brief, Brad Williams accused Wolfe of discriminatory employment practices with respect to religion, retaliation, and violation of Brad Williams's civil rights. Williams received a settlement sum of $475,000.[36]
EEOC Reaches $95K Settlement in Disability Discrimination Suit
A title insurance company based in Rockville, Maryland, has agreed to pay $95,000 to settle a case brought by the U.S. Equal Employment Opportunity Commission on behalf of a former employee who claimed she was fired after requesting a part-time schedule to accommodate treatments for her kidney disease.[37]
EEOC HIV Discrimination Settlement: Lessons for Employers
The EEOC has settled an HIV discrimination lawsuit. Gregory Packing, the manufacturer and distributor of Suncup juice products, agreed to pay $125,000 to settle charges that it illegally terminated a machine operator after learning he was HIV positive.[38]

Broad-based diversity efforts based on:
- Effective implementation of affirmative action and EEOC policies
- Organization-wide assessment and management's top-down commitment to diversity
- Managerial commitment tied to organizational rewards
- Ongoing processes of organization assessment and programs for the purpose of creating an organizational climate that is inclusive and supportive of diverse groups

Diversity efforts based on:
- Effective implementation of affirmative action and EEOC policies
- Ongoing education and training programs
- Managerial commitment tied to organizational rewards
- Minimal attention directed toward cultivating an inclusive and supportive organizational climate

Diversity efforts based on:
- Narrowly defined affirmative action and EEOC policies combined with one-shot education and/or training programs
- Inconsistent managerial commitment; rewards not tied to effective implementation of diversity programs and goal achievement
- No attention directed toward organizational climate

Diversity efforts based on:
- Compliance with and enforcement of affirmative action and EEOC policies
- No organizational supports with respect to education, training
- Inconsistent or poor managerial commitment

Diversity efforts based on:
- Compliance with affirmative action and EEOC policies
- Inconsistent enforcement and implementation (those who breach policies may not be sanctioned unless noncompliance results in legal action)
- Support of policies is not rewarded; organization relies on individual managers' interest or commitment

No diversity efforts:
- Noncompliance with affirmative action and EEOC

Figure 4.2

Organizational diversity continuum

build organizational diversity and reap its related advantages rather than as a source of punishment when EEOC legislation is not followed.

Still, organizations can do much more. For example, some employees are hostile toward affirmative action programs because they feel these programs have been misused to create **reverse discrimination**—that is, they discriminate against members of the majority group in order to help groups that are underrepresented in the organization. When management implements appropriate legal approaches but stops short of developing a truly multicultural organization, intergroup conflicts are highly likely.

Promoting Diversity through Organizational Commitment

Figure 4.2 shows the range of organizational commitment to multiculturalism. At the top of the continuum are organizations that have committed resources, planning, and time to the ongoing shaping and sustaining of a multicultural organization. At the bottom of the continuum are organizations that make no effort whatsoever to achieve diversity in their workforces. Most organizations fall somewhere between the extremes depicted in the figure.

Ignoring Differences   Some organizations make no effort to promote diversity and do not even bother to comply with affirmative action and EEOC standards. These organizations

send a clear message to their employees that the dynamics of difference are unimportant. By ignoring EEOC policies, they send their managers the even more detrimental message that it is permissible to maintain exclusionary practices.

Complying with External Policies
Some organizations base their diversity strategies solely on compliance with affirmative action and EEOC policies. They make no attempt to provide education and training for employees, nor do they use the organization's reward system to reinforce managerial commitment to diversity. Managers in some companies in this category breach company affirmative action and EEOC policies with impunity. When top management does not discipline them, the likelihood of costly legal action against the organization increases.

Enforcing External Policies
Some organizations go so far as to enforce affirmative action and EEOC policies but provide no organizational support for diversity education or training. Managerial commitment to a diverse workforce is either weak or inconsistent.

Responding Inadequately
Other organizations comply fully with affirmative action and EEOC policies but define these policies quite narrowly. Organizational systems and structures are inadequate to support real organizational change. In addition, education and training in diversity are sporadic, and managerial rewards for implementing diversity programs are inconsistent or nonexistent. Although these organizations may design some useful programs, the programs are unlikely to result in any long-term organizational change, and thus the organizational climate never becomes truly receptive to diverse groups.

Implementing Adequate Programs
Some organizations effectively implement affirmative action and EEOC policies, provide ongoing education and training programs pertaining to diversity, and tie managerial rewards to success in meeting diversity goals and addressing diversity issues. However, such companies may still make only a minimal attempt to cultivate the kind of inclusive and supportive organizational climate in which employees will feel comfortable.

Compliance with EEOC policies is one way to promote diversity.

Auremar/Fotolia

Taking Effective Action
The most effective diversity efforts are based on managerial implementation of affirmative action and EEOC policies that are developed in conjunction with an organization-wide assessment of the company's systems and structures. Such an assessment is necessary to determine how these systems and structures support or hinder diversity goals.

Generally, for such a comprehensive assessment to take place, top management must accept the idea that diversity is important to the company. Actually, support from the top is critical to all successful diversity efforts and underlies tying organizational rewards to managers' commitment to diversity. Ongoing assessment and continuing programs are also necessary to create an organizational climate that is inclusive and supportive of diverse groups.

Promoting Diversity through Pluralism

Pluralism refers to an environment in which differences are acknowledged, accepted, and seen as significant contributors to the entirety. A diverse workforce is most effective when managers are capable of guiding the organization toward achieving pluralism. Approaches or strategies to achieve effective workforce diversity have been classified into five major categories by Jean Kim of Stanford University:[39]

1. "Golden Rule" approach
2. Assimilation approach
3. "Righting-the-wrongs" approach
4. Culture-specific approach
5. Multicultural approach

Each approach is described briefly in the following sections.

TIPS FOR MANAGING AROUND THE GLOBE

Deloitte UK "Hides" College and University Degrees

The professional services firm Deloitte, with offices in the United Kingdom, has begun a new hiring strategy to promote diversity. When candidates apply for a position, the hiring manager is not privy to which university or college the candidate attended. This is known as a "blind CV" hiring strategy. CV stands for "curriculum vitae" and is another name for a résumé.

According to David Sproul, senior partner and chief executive of Deloitte UK, hiring managers receive a "contextualization" of a candidate's experience that details the person's experience and overall academic performance without giving away where the individual went to school. This ensures that those who come from a socially disadvantaged background have the same opportunity as candidates who graduated from the most prestigious universities. Only after a job offer is made is the candidate's alma mater revealed. Sproul indicates that this helps the social mobility of those who come from economically depressed areas and diversifies the types of employees Deloitte UK hires.[40]

"Golden Rule" Approach

The "Golden Rule" approach to diversity relies on the biblical dictate "Do unto others as you would have them do unto you."[41] The major strength of this approach is that it emphasizes individual morality. Its major flaw is that individuals apply the Golden Rule from their own particular frames of reference without knowing the cultural expectations, traditions, and preferences of the other person.

One African American male manager recalled a situation in which he was having difficulty scheduling a work-related event. In exasperation, he suggested scheduling the event for a Saturday. He was then reminded by a coworker that many of the company's Jewish employees go to religious services on Saturday. He was initially surprised but then somewhat embarrassed that he had simply assumed that "all people" attend "church" on Sunday.

Assimilation Approach

The assimilation approach advocates shaping organization members so that they fit in with the existing culture of the organization. This approach pressures employees who do not belong to the dominant culture to conform—at the expense of their own cultures and worldviews. The end result is a homogeneous culture that suppresses the creativity and diversity of views that could benefit the organization.

One African American woman in middle management said, "I always felt uncomfortable in very formal meetings. I tend to be very animated when I talk, which is not the norm for the company. Until I became more comfortable with myself and my style, I felt inhibited. I was tempted to try to change my style to fit in."

The multicultural approach to pluralism assumes that an entire organization must change in order to accept the diversity of its workforce.

"Righting-the-Wrongs" Approach

"Righting the wrongs" is an approach that addresses past injustices experienced by a particular group. When a group's history places its members at a disadvantage for achieving career success and mobility, policies are developed to create a more equitable set of conditions. For example, the original migration of African Americans to the United States was forced on them as slaves. Righting-the-wrongs approaches are designed to compensate for the damages African Americans have suffered because of historical inequalities.

This approach most closely parallels the affirmative action policies, which will be discussed in Chapter 12. It goes beyond affirmative action, however, because it emphasizes drawing on the unique talents of each group in the service of organizational productivity.

GaudiLab/Shutterstock

Culture-Specific Approach

The culture-specific approach teaches employees the norms and practices of another culture to prepare them to interact with people from that culture effectively. This approach is often used to help employees prepare for international assignments. The problem with this approach is that it usually fails to give employees a genuine appreciation for the culture they are about to encounter.

Stewart Black and Hal Gregersen, in their study of managers on assignment in foreign countries, found that some managers identify much more with the parent firm than with the local operation.[42] For instance, one male manager, after spending two years opening retail outlets throughout Europe, viewed Europeans as "lazy and slow to respond to directives." Obviously, his training and preparation had failed to help him adjust to the European host countries and to appreciate their peoples and cultures.

Multicultural Approach

The multicultural approach gives employees the opportunity to develop an appreciation both for differences of a culture and for variations in personal characteristics. This approach focuses on how interpersonal skills and attitudinal changes relate to organizational performance. One of its strengths is that it assumes the organization itself—as well as the individuals working within it—will be required to change in order to accommodate the diversity of the organization's workforce.

The multicultural approach is probably the most effective approach to pluralism because it advocates change on the part of management, employees, and organization systems and structures. It has the added advantage of stressing that equity demands making some efforts to "right the wrongs" so that underrepresented groups are fairly included throughout the organization.

How Managers Promote Diversity

4-5 Insights into how managers promote diversity

Managers play an essential role in bringing forth the potential capabilities of each person within their departments. This task requires competencies that are anchored in the four basic management functions of planning, organizing, influencing, and controlling. In this context, planning refers to the manager's role in developing programs to promote diversity, while organizing, influencing, and controlling take place in the implementation phases of those programs.

Planning

Recall from Chapter 1 that planning is a specific action proposed to help the organization achieve its objectives. It is an ongoing process that includes troubleshooting and continually identifying areas where improvements can be made. Planning for diversity may involve selecting diversity training programs for the organization or setting diversity goals for employees within the department.

Setting goals for the recruitment of members of underrepresented groups is a key component of diversity planning. If top management has identified Hispanics as an underrepresented group within the company, every manager throughout the company will need to collaborate with the human resources department to achieve the organizational goal of increased Hispanic representation. For example, a manager might establish goals and objectives for the increased representation of this group within five years. To achieve this five-year vision, the manager will need to set benchmark goals for each year.

Organizing

According to Chapter 1, organizing is the process of establishing orderly uses for all resources within the management system. To achieve a diverse workplace, managers have to work with human resource professionals in the areas of recruitment, hiring, and retention so that the best match is made between the company and the employees it hires. Managerial responsibilities in this area may include establishing task forces or committees to explore issues and provide ideas, carefully choosing work assignments to support the career development of all employees, and evaluating the extent to which diversity goals are being achieved.

After managers have begun hiring from a diverse pool of employees, they will need to focus on retaining them by paying attention to the many concerns of a diverse workforce. In the case of employees with families, skillfully using the organization's resources to support their needs of daycare for dependents, allowing flexible work arrangements in keeping with company policy, and assigning and reassigning work responsibilities equitably to accommodate the use of family leave are all examples of managers applying the organizing function.

Influencing

According to Chapter 1, influencing is the process of guiding the activities of organization members in appropriate directions. Integral to this management function are an effective leadership style, good communication skills, knowledge about how to motivate others, and an understanding of the organization's culture and group dynamics. In the area of diversity, influencing organization members means that managers not only must encourage and support employees to participate constructively in a diverse work environment but also must themselves engage in the career development and training processes that will give them the skills to facilitate the smooth operation of a diverse work community.

Managers are also accountable for informing their employees of breaches of organizational policy and etiquette. Let us assume that the diversity strategy selected by top management includes educating employees about organizational policies concerning diversity (e.g., making sure that employees understand what constitutes sexual harassment) as well as providing workshops for employees on specific cultural diversity issues. The manager's role in this case would be to hold employees accountable for learning about company diversity policies and complying with them. Managers could accomplish this task by consulting with staff and holding regular group meetings and one-on-one meetings when necessary. To encourage participation in diversity workshops, the manager may need to communicate to employees the importance that the organization places on this knowledge base. Alternatively, the manager might choose to tie organizational rewards to the development of diversity competencies. Examples of such rewards are giving employees public praise or recognition and providing workers with opportunities to use their diversity skills in desirable work assignments.

Controlling

Overseeing compliance with the legal stipulations of the EEOC and affirmative action is one aspect of the controlling function in the area of diversity. According to Chapter 1, controlling is the set of activities that make something happen as planned. Hence, the evaluation activities

STEPS FOR SUCCESS

Generation Z Members and Their Challenges

It's always a dangerous proposition to make broad generalizations about any demographic, but organizations have already noted some key characteristics of the newest generation to enter the workforce: Generation Z. Whether they're called postmillennials, the information generation, the iGeneration, or the homeland generation, Generation Z members are the group born after 1995 and have come right on the heels of the millennials.

You are probably a member of this generation, and you'll be shaping the workplace for many years. Researchers studying this generation have noted that Generation Z members are more ethnically diverse and technologically savvy than any previous generation. Trends in intermarriage as well as immigration have created diversity in the American population not seen before. Your generation also uses social media, mobile phones, and other technology in ways that make your life more convenient and even more customized.[43]

Managers have discovered that you're not necessarily as keen on the latest and greatest as the millennials were. Plus, you're more likely to join a midsize company rather than a highly diversified, global giant corporation. But studies show that you're much more likely to seek out training, and a flexible work schedule is more desired than one with set hours.[44]

necessary to assess diversity efforts are part of the controlling role that managers play in shaping a multicultural workforce.

Managers may find this function to be the most difficult of the four to execute. It is not easy to evaluate planned-change approaches in general, and it is particularly hard to do so in the area of diversity. The most successful diversity approaches often reveal more problems as employees begin to speak openly about their concerns. In addition, subtle attitudinal changes in one group's perception of another group are difficult to measure. What *can* be accurately measured are the outcome variables of turnover; representation of women, minorities, and other under-represented groups at all levels of the company; and legal problems stemming from inappropriate or illegal behaviors (e.g., discrimination and sexual harassment).

Managers engaged in the controlling function in the area of diversity need to monitor their units' progress continually with respect to diversity goals and standards. They must also decide what control measures to use (e.g., indicators of productivity, turnover, absenteeism, or promotion) and how to interpret the information these measures yield in light of diversity goals and standards.

For example, a manager may need to assess whether the low rate of promotions for African American men in her department is due to subtle biases against this group or group members' poor performance compared to that of others in the department. She may find that she needs to explore current organizational dynamics as well as create effective supports for this group. Such supports might include fostering greater social acceptance of African American men among other employees, learning more about the African American males' bicultural experiences in the company, making mentoring or other opportunities available to members of this group, and providing them with some specific job-related training.

Management Development and Diversity Training

Given the complex set of managerial skills needed to promote diversity, it is obvious that managers will need organizational support if the company is to achieve its diversity goals. One important component of the diversity strategy of a large number of companies is diversity training.[45] **Diversity training** is a learning process designed to raise managers' awareness and develop their competencies to deal with the issues endemic to managing a diverse workforce. Managers are recognizing more and more often that a diverse workforce is critical to the exploration of new ideas and the creation of innovation in organizations and that diversity training is a valuable tool in achieving this diversity.[46]

Basic Themes of Diversity Training
Training is the process of developing qualities in human resources that will make employees more productive and better able to contribute to organizational goal attainment. Some companies develop intensive programs for management and less intensive, more generalized programs for other employees. Such programs are discussed further in Chapter 12 and generally focus on the following five components or themes:

1. Behavioral awareness
2. Acknowledgment of biases and stereotypes
3. Focus on job performance
4. Avoidance of assumptions
5. Modification of policy and procedure manuals

Stages in Managing a Diverse Workforce
Donaldson and Scannell, authors of *Human Resource Development: The New Trainer's Guide*, have developed a four-stage model to describe how managers progress in managing a diverse workforce.[47] In the first stage, known as "unconscious incompetence," managers are unaware that some behaviors they engage in are problematic for members of other groups. In the second stage, "conscious incompetence," managers go through a learning process in which they become conscious of the behaviors that hinder their competence in their interactions with members of diverse groups.

The third stage is one of becoming "consciously competent." Managers learn how to interact with diverse groups and cultures by deliberately thinking about how to behave. In the last stage, "unconscious competence," managers have internalized these new behaviors and feel so

TABLE 4.3   **Organizational Challenges and Supports Related to Managing a Diverse Workforce**

Organizational Challenges	Organizational Supports
Employees' difficulties in coping with cultural diversity	Educational programs and training to assist employees in working through difficulties
Resistance to change	Top-down management support for diversity
Ethnocentrism	Managers who have diversity skills and competence
Lack of information and misinformation	Education and training
Prejudices, biases, and stereotypes	Awareness raising
Reasons employees are unmotivated to understand cultural differences:	Peer support
Lack of time and energy and unwillingness to assume the emotional risk necessary to explore issues of diversity	Organizational climate that supports diversity
Absence of social or concrete rewards for investing in diversity work	Open communication with manager about diversity issues
Interpersonal and intergroup conflicts arising when diversity issues are either ignored or mismanaged	Recognition for employee development of diversity skills and competencies
Work-group problems	Recognition for employee contributions to diversity goals
Lack of cohesiveness	Organizational rewards for managers' implementation of organizational diversity goals and objectives
Communication problems	
Employee stress	

comfortable relating to others different from themselves that they need to devote little conscious effort to do so. Managers who have progressed to the "unconscious competence" stage will be the most effective with respect to interacting in a diverse workforce. Effective interaction is key to carrying out the four management functions previously discussed.

Table 4.3 summarizes our discussion of the challenges facing those who manage a diverse workforce. Managers, who are generally responsible for controlling organizational goals and outcomes, are accountable for understanding these diversity challenges and recognizing the dynamics described here. In addition to treating employees fairly, they must influence other employees to cooperate with the company's diversity goals.

Understanding and Influencing Employee Responses   Managers cannot rise to the challenges of managing a diverse workforce unless they recognize that many employees have difficulties coping with diversity. Among these difficulties are natural resistance to change, ethnocentrism, and lack of information and outright misinformation about other groups, as well as prejudices, biases, and stereotypes. Some employees lack the motivation to understand and cope with cultural differences, which require time, energy, and a willingness to take some emotional risks.

Another problem is that employees often receive no social rewards (e.g., peer support and approval) or concrete rewards (e.g., financial compensation or career opportunities) for cooperating with the organization's diversity policies.

Despite all these difficulties, managers cannot afford to ignore or mismanage diversity issues because the cost of doing so is interpersonal and causes intergroup conflicts. These conflicts often affect the functioning of the work group by destroying cohesiveness and causing communications problems and employee stress.

Managers who are determined to deal effectively with their diverse workforce can usually obtain organizational support. One primary support is education and training programs designed to help employees work through their difficulties in coping with diversity. Besides recommending such programs to their employees, managers may find it helpful to enroll in available programs themselves.

Getting Top-Down Support

Another important source of support for managers dealing with diversity issues is top management. Organizations that provide top-down support are likely to exhibit the following features:

1. Managers skilled at working with a diverse workforce
2. Effective education and diversity training programs
3. An organizational climate that promotes diversity and fosters peer support for exploring diversity issues
4. Open communication between employees and managers about diversity issues
5. Recognition of employees' development of diversity skills and competencies
6. Recognition of employee contributions to diversity goals
7. Organizational rewards for managers' implementation of organizational diversity goals and objectives

CHALLENGE CASE SUMMARY

An organization such as GE Lighting that uses the diverse talents of its workforce can reap many rewards. Some experts believe that one of the best ways for a company such as GE Lighting to capture a diverse customer base is to make sure that its decision makers are a diverse group. Diversity could include people of different religions, sexes, nationalities, and generations.

Promoting a diverse group of decision makers will ensure sensitivity to diversity issues, giving GE Lighting a better chance of establishing businesses characterized by such diversity. At GE's parent company headquarters, the chief diversity officer and Corporate Diversity Council ensure that diversity goals are part of the company's strategy. Not only does this type of arrangement keep diversity on the agenda for planning and control, it also ensures top-down support for valuing diversity.

Diversity activity takes many forms at General Electric overall and at GE Lighting in particular. Its partnership with MC^2 STEM High School and support for STEM Camp encourage female, urban, and minority students to consider technology-related careers. Affinity groups and training programs help its employees gain support and learn skills for succeeding in a highly competitive business environment. Programs such as Get Skills to Work help the company recruit workers such as returning veterans who otherwise might have difficulty finding job opportunities. Learning new concepts and being able to apply them in another setting is the essence of the management employability skill of knowledge application.

The success of a company such as GE Lighting in its diversity program enhances the productivity of its diverse workforce. An organization's diversity programs helps a diverse workforce feel valued and at ease in its work setting and thereby perform better than workers who feel their organization has little respect for them as people. As a result of its required diversity training, GE Lighting can retain employees and thus lower personnel costs related to recruiting and training.

Legislation and government involvement cannot provide complete direction for creating diversity in organizations. GE Lighting's managers, including Maryrose Sylvester and others, understand that organizations should not wait for laws and government to provide guidelines for creating a diverse organization. Instead, management should re-create the company to reflect the markets in which it operates. For example, given demographics reflecting population trends, GE Lighting will probably be recruiting and hiring a greater proportion of Asian and Hispanic employees.

If an organization such as GE Lighting increases the proportion of Asian and Hispanic employees, company diversity training programs should be modified to include sensitivity toward factors relevant to the Asian and Hispanic cultures. This training should emphasize factors such as religion, values, and behavioral norms specific to these two groups. Such modification of diversity training at GE Lighting would be aimed at eliminating ethnocentrism within the company relating to these two demographic groups.

When management is committed to diversity, diversity programs are normally successful. In turn, by virtue of its financial investment in global diversity, GE Lighting demonstrates its commitment to building a world-class organization—a fact that is not lost on current and future employees. A reputation for diversity makes GE Lighting more attractive as an employer—and enables GE Lighting to attract and retain high-performing employees. In turn, top performers are typically the most successful at innovation and productivity—areas where GE Lighting needs to excel if it is to hold competitive advantage in the marketplace.

In terms of the organizational diversity continuum, GE Lighting's commitment to diversity seems broad based. This broad-based commitment is reflected in company-wide practices related to recruiting, hiring, and training a diverse workforce. The broad-based commitment is also evident in GE's selection of a woman to head its lighting business. Consistent with diversity initiatives in most organizations, GE's managers are given extensive diversity training. Managers in a company such as GE who know how to interact with people of different cultures will be the most successful in creating productive multicultural teams in organizations. Overall, diversity training for managers at GE is aimed to help them become more sensitive to other cultures and thereby more capable of using planning, organizing, influencing, and controlling skills to help the organization meet its diversity goals.

In addition to managers, nonmanagers within the organization can be a focus of specially designed diversity training.

MyLab Management Assessing Your Management Skill

If your instructor has assigned this activity, go to www.pearson.com/mylab/management to complete the exercise related to the Challenge Case.

DEVELOPING DIVERSITY SKILL

This section is specially designed to help you develop diversity skills. An individual's diversity skill is based on an understanding of the concepts and the ability to apply those concepts. The following activities will help to enhance your diversity skills in various organizational situations.

Class Preparation and Personal Study

To help you prepare for class, perform the activities outlined in this section. Performing these activities will help you enhance your classroom performance significantly.

Reflecting on Target Skill

On page 97, this chapter opens by presenting a target management skill along with a list of related objectives outlining knowledge and understanding that you should aim to acquire related to that skill. Review this target skill and the list of objectives to make sure that you've acquired all pertinent information within the chapter. If you do not feel that you've reached a particular objective(s), study related chapter coverage until you do.

Know Key Terms

Understanding the following key terms is critical to your understanding of chapter material. Define each of these terms. Refer to the page(s) referenced after a term to check your definition or to gain further insight regarding the term.

diversity   **99**

majority group   **99**

Know How Management Concepts Relate

This section comprises activities that will further sharpen your understanding of management concepts. Answer essay questions as completely as possible.

4-1 One key advantage of diversity in organizations is cost saving. Why is this the case? Give examples of cost saving.

4-2 What is meant by the term "glass ceiling"? How does it affect the prospects of some people in the workforce and impact their careers? How do you think it will be shaped in the future by organizations?

4-3 Assume you are ethnocentric. List three specific beliefs about your own culture that you might possess. Would such beliefs be a hindrance or a help in your becoming a successful manager? Explain.

MyLab Management
Personal Inventory Assessments

Go to www.pearson.com/mylab/management to complete the Personal Inventory Assessment related to this chapter.

    PERSONAL
INVENTORY
ASSESSMENT

Management Skills Exercises

Learning activities in this section are aimed at helping you develop diversity skills.

MyLab Management
Discussion Questions

Go to www.pearson.com/mylab/management to complete the problems marked with this icon ⭐.

⭐ Cases

Diverse Employees Contribute to GE Lighting's Bright Future

The Challenge Case that introduced this chapter, "Diverse Employees Contribute to GE Lighting's Bright Future," and its related Challenge Case Summary were written to help you better understand the management concepts contained in this chapter. Answer the following discussion questions about the Challenge Case to better understand how concepts relating to management and diversity can be applied in an organization such as GE Lighting.

4-4 How important is it to GE Lighting to have a diverse workforce? Discuss fully.

4-5 How would you control diversity activities at GE Lighting if you were top management?

4-6 As GE Lighting's top management, what steps would you take to increase commitment to diversity throughout the organization? Be as specific as possible.

CNN, FOX News, and the *New York Times* Face Racial Discrimination Lawsuits

Read the case and answer the questions that follow. Studying this case will help you better understand how concepts relating to the four functions of management can be applied in a company such as CNN, FOX News, and the New York Times.

The "news" is something we often take for granted. It's ubiquitous in our lives with the technological connectivity we have in today's busy world. We receive regular news feeds on our phones, and when there is a major breaking story, all the major networks preempt programming to cover the event. Even our friends post updates to the latest news story on Facebook, ensuring that we always know what is going on around us.

But when it comes to news organizations, we want them to be unbiased and present coverage in a fair and transparent manner. We want to know that the information we receive is truthful and offers the facts, not opinions or personal agendas. We also expect that those organizations are being fair and transparent behind the scenes with their human resources. That's why, in 2017, the news industry itself became the leading news story. Allegedly, CNN, Fox News, and the *New York Times* were discriminating against nonwhite employees. The shock of this sent reverberations across the industry.

CNN, which was launched in 1980, was America's first 24-hour, all-news network. It is broadcast into nearly 100 million homes and has often been at the forefront of breaking major world news stories. However, a group of 175 former and current employees have contacted attorneys about a class-action lawsuit against the cable network. According to the claimants, the headquarters are fraught with racism, with black employees being paid thousands less than their white counterparts. The allegations also include comments made by managers to black employees regarding slavery and that it's "hard to manage black people."[48]

Meanwhile at Fox News (which was started in 1996 and is also broadcast into about 100 million households), so far six people have filed similar suits against the conservative network. Headlining the list is Kelly Wright, a black reporter and news anchor who has been with the organization since 2003. Wright's suit claims that he was blocked from major programs on Fox News and that Bill Shine, Fox News co-president, regularly asked him, "[H]ow do black people react to you" or "how do you think white viewers look at you?"[49] Other complaints against Fox News include walls being constructed to keep black or dark-skinned associates from entering certain parts of the building, mocking speech patterns, and perpetuating stereotypes.

Even print media are not immune to claims of racism. The venerable *New York Times*, which was founded in 1851 and has a circulation of over half a million, is being accused of discrimination at the same time as the two news networks. The allegations at the *New York Times* are that the newspaper prefers to hire white employees and also pays the black and Latino workers less than white associates. One claimant states that the reason for the discrimination is that most of the readers of the *Times* are white; therefore, white employees are better able to connect with the readership, again, according to the lawsuit.

All three news organizations have vociferously denied all the allegations. They claim there is no merit to any of the cases, and these organizations want to be presented with evidence of the allegations from the accusers and their attorneys. If not settled out of court, these cases are likely to remain in the public eye for several years. It is possible that other former and current employees of both networks may join the lawsuits.

Questions

4-7 Assess the allegations against CNN, Fox News, and the *New York Times*. What is being claimed by those filing the lawsuits?

4-8 If these allegations are found to be true, what steps should each organization take to ensure that this does not happen again? If they are found to be false, is there anything each company can do to continue to show its commitment to diversity?

4-9 Why is it important for companies to have a diverse workforce? What impact would a homogeneous group of employees have if they were all white males, for example?

Experiential Exercises

Managing Diversity

Directions. Read the following scenario and then perform the listed activities. Your instructor may wish you to perform the activities as an individual or within groups. Follow all of your instructor's directions carefully.

This chapter looks at the different challenges managers face in managing a diverse workforce. A much-neglected and oft-overlooked group are the baby boomers. In many societies, the over-55 generation represents a large percentage of the population. The increase in their numbers has come at a time when some countries have seen a fall in the number of young people entering the job market.

Identify five traits of this group of potential workers. These individuals are approaching or have reached the last decade or so of their working lives. Provide suggestions as to how a manager might supervise them. Try to be precise in your suggestions so that you could help someone be a more effective manager.

You and Your Career

Diversity in the workplace is important. It ensures that fresh ideas and ways of looking at problems and opportunities abound. However, a few firms may not value diversity as much, preferring a much more homogeneous staff. Assume you interviewed for a job for an open position at a company that you were very interested in. A week after the interview, however, you receive an e-mail letting you know that you were not selected. Coincidentally, you discover from a friend of yours who works at the company that it didn't hire you because of your race, gender, age (etc.; choose the most fitting for your circumstances).

Also assume that you filed a lawsuit and won. The judge has ruled that the company must hire you and was assessed a small fine. Would you accept the position now with the company? Why or why not?

Building Your Management Skills Portfolio

Your Management Skills Portfolio is a collection of activities specially designed to demonstrate your management knowledge and skill. Be sure to save your work. Taking your printed portfolio to an employment interview could be helpful in obtaining a job.

The portfolio activity for this chapter is Assessing Diversity at TECO Energy. Read the following about TECO Energy and answer the questions that follow.

TECO Energy is an energy company headquartered in Tampa, Florida. TECO Energy's five business units include (1) Tampa Electric, a regulated electric utility serving more than 635,000 customers in West Central Florida; (2) Peoples Gas System, Florida's largest natural gas distribution utility; (3) TECO Coal, a producer of conventional coal and synthetic fuel; (4) TECO Transport, a river and ocean waterborne transportation provider; and (5) TECO Guatemala, owner of two power plants in Guatemala. (You can learn more about the company by visiting www.tecoenergy.com.) Over the years, TECO management has focused on creating a diverse workforce. Management recently reported the results of a diversity study aimed at monitoring its diversity efforts by ascertaining the present characteristics of its workforce. Part of the results of that study appears in Exhibits 1, 2, and 3.

Exhibit 1   Gender of Workforce

Company	Female	Male
TECO Energy (corporate)	62%	38%
Tampa Electric	25%	75%
Peoples Gas	28%	72%
TECO Transport	10%	90%
TECO Coal	4%	96%
TECO Guatemala (corporate)	29%	71%
TECO Guatemala	12%	88%
Total number of employees	970	4,122

Exhibit 2   Race/Ethnicity of Workforce

Company	Black	White	Hispanic	Other
TECO Energy (corporate)	6%	84%	10%	0%
Tampa Electric	14%	73%	11%	2%
Peoples Gas	14%	70%	15%	1%
TECO Transport	12%	85%	2%	1%
TECO Coal	0%	100%	0%	0%
TECO Guatemala (corporate)	0%	43%	43%	14%
TECO Guatemala*				
Total number of employees	522	3,993	399	178

* U.S. ethnicity codes not applicable to TECO Guatemala.

Exhibit 3   Leadership by Gender and Race

Company	Female	Male	Black	White	Hispanic	Other
TECO Energy (corporate)	56%	44%	4%	87%	9%	0%
Tampa Electric	30%	70%	9%	77%	11%	3%
Peoples Gas	28%	72%	6%	80%	14%	0%
TECO Transport	20%	80%	6%	91%	2%	1%
TECO Coal	9%	91%	0%	100%	0%	0%
TECO Guatemala (corporate)	29%	71%	0%	43%	43%	14%
TECO Guatemala*	11%	89%	N/A	N/A	N/A	N/A
Total number of employees	28%	72%	7%	79%	10%	4%

* U.S. ethnicity codes not applicable to TECO Guatemala.

Questions

4-10 List five major points that Exhibits 1, 2, and 3 tell management about TECO's workforce.

a. _____

b. _____

c. _____

d. _____

e. _____

4-11 How does management at TECO determine whether the present level of workforce diversity is appropriate for the company?

_____

_____

4-12 Assume that TECO management performs a similar study in five years. Name three new dimensions of diversity that you would like the study to explore. Explain why you would like each dimension studied.

Dimension 1: _____

Why study this dimension?

_____

_____

_____

Dimension 2: _____

Why study this dimension?

_____

_____

_____

Dimension 3: _____

Why study this dimension?

_____

_____

_____

MyLab Management
Writing Assignments

If your instructor has assigned this activity, go to www.pearson.com/mylab/management for the following assisted-graded writing assignments:

Assisted-Grading Questions

4-13 Pinpoint five ways that discrimination might negatively affect an organization.

4-14 List five ways that you would promote diversity in an organization. How would you control your efforts to make sure they were successful?

Endnotes

1. Steve Minter, "The iGeneration Comes to Manufacturing (We Hope)," *Industry Week* (December 2013): 18–23; GE Lighting, "Maryrose T. Sylvester, President and CEO, GE Lighting," GE Pressroom, http://pressroom.gelighting.com, accessed March 3, 2014; Grant Segall, "Maryrose Sylvester of GE Lighting Glows about Our City: My Cleveland," Cleveland.com, December 5, 2013, http://blog.cleveland.com; Dan Alexander, "Big Business Bets on Education, Turning Factories and Corporate Campuses into Schools," *Forbes*, December 9, 2013, http://www.forbes.com; Mariko Nobori, "Tutoring and Mentorship Brings Authentic Learning to MC² STEM High School," *Edutopia*, February 27, 2013, http://www.edutopia.org; "GE Ranked 10 in 2013 Diversity MBA 50 Out Front Companies for Diversity Leadership," *DiversityMBA*, August 21, 2013, http://diversitymbamagazine.com; General Electric Co. (GE), "Why GE," GE careers page, http://www.geconsumerandindustrial.com, accessed March 3, 2014; GE, "Empowering Employees to Be Successful," GE Citizenship, http://www.gecitizenship.com, accessed March 3, 2014; "GE Adds Jobs in Illinois, Ohio at Lighting Plants," *Bloomberg Businessweek*, August 22, 2013, http://www.businessweek.com; GE Lighting, "GE Lighting Broadens Colorado Footprint with New Site in Longmont," news release, February 18, 2014, http://pressroom.gelighting.com; "GE Lighting Celebrates 100th Anniversary," *Electrical Wholesaling* (May 2013): 24.
2. *Fortune* magazine annually publishes its "100 Best Companies to Work For" list and provides a data cut of the rankings by percentage of minority employees. For the most recent list, see "100 Best Companies to Work For 2012: Minorities," http://archive.fortune.com/magazines/fortune/best-companies/2012/minorities/.
3. "Sexual Orientation in the Workplace," Report from the British Medical Association (November 2007).
4. For an article describing the benefits of diversity management, see Mary Salomon and Joah Schork, "Turn Diversity to Your Advantage," *Research Technology Management* 46 (2003): 37.
5. Subhash C. Kundu and Archana Mor, "Workforce Diversity and Organizational Performance: A Study of IT Industry in India," *Employee Relations* 39, no. 2 (2017): 160–183.
6. For discussion of gaining the advantage of creativity through diversity, see Terri Schlichenmeyer, "Your Business Doing Well. It Could Be Better," *Washington Informer* (September 22, 2016), 34.
7. Sabina Nielsen, "Top Management Team Diversity: A Review of Theories and Methodologies," *International Journal of Management Reviews* 12, no. 3 (September 2010): 301–316.
8. Ann Pomeroy, "Cultivating Female Leaders," *HR Magazine* 52, no. 2 (February 2007): 44–51.
9. Frans Johansson, "Masters of the Multicultural," *Harvard Business Review* 83, no. 10 (October 2005): 18–19.
10. Jonathan Moules, "Benefits of Ethnic Diversity Doubted," *Financial Times* (February 20, 2007): 4.
11. For a detailed look at the potential pitfalls of diversity management, see C. Von Bergen, Barlow Soper, and Teresa Foster, "Unintended Negative Effects of Diversity Management," *Public Personnel Management* 31 (2002): 239–252.
12. William B. Johnston and Arnold E. Packer, "Executive Summary," in *Workforce 2000: Work and Workers for the Twenty-First Century* (Indianapolis: Hudson Institute, June 1987), xiii–xiv.
13. Pew Research: Social and Demographic Trends, "Millennials in Adulthood: The Generations Defined," http://pewsocialtrends.org/2014/03/07/millennials-in-adulthood/sdt-next-america-03-07-2014-0-06.
14. Jean Phillips and Stan Gully, *Organizational Behavior* (Mason, OH: South-Western, 2014), 77–78.
15. Vineet Nayar, "Handing the Keys to Gen Y," *Harvard Business Review* 91, no. 5 (May 2013): 40.
16. Roosevelt Thomas, "Affirmative Action or Affirming Diversity," *Harvard Business Review* (1990): 110.
17. "The Five Groups That Experience the Most Discrimination in the Workplace," Libel.com, http://www.libel.com, accessed October 22, 2009; Roosevelt Thomas, "Stereotyping Muslims? Know Your Facts," *Knight Ridder Tribune Business News*, June 17, 2006, 1.
18. Michele Himmelberg, "Age Discrimination Alleged," *Knight Ridder Tribune Business News*, April 14, 2007.
19. Rosabeth Moss Kanter, *Men and Women of the Corporation* (New York: Basic Books, 1977).
20. Siofra Pratt, "6 Companies Doing Their Bit to Improve Diversity and Inclusion," October 5, 2016, https://www.socialtalent.co/blog/6-companies-doing-their-bit-to-improve-diversity-inclusion.
21. American Bar Association, "Legal Outreach Is Model for Diversity Pipeline Success," press release, http://www.abanow.org, accessed February 6, 2010.
22. Rosabeth Moss Kanter, "Numbers: Minorities and Majorities," in *Men and Women of the Corporation* (New York: Basic Books, 1977), 206–244. For a closer look at the effects of gender-role stereotypes, see N. Lane and N. Piercy, "The Ethics of Discrimination: Organizational Mindsets and Female Employment Disadvantage," *Journal of Business Ethics* 44 (2003): 313.
23. Tim Hindle, "The Glass Ceiling," *The Economist* (May 5, 2009).
24. Annelies van Vianen and Agneta Fischer, "Illuminating the Glass Ceiling: The Role of Organizational Culture Preferences," *Journal of Occupational and Organizational Psychology* 75 (2002): 315.
25. Susan Webb, *Step Forward: Sexual Harassment in the Workplace* (New York: MasterMedia, 1991); Susan B. Garland, "Finally, a Corporate Tip Sheet on Sexual Harassment," *BusinessWeek* (July 13, 1998): 39. See also Maureen O'Connor, Barbara Gutek, Margaret Stockdale, Tracey Geer, and Renee Melancon, "Explaining Sexual Harassment Judgments: Looking Beyond Gender of the Rater," *Law and Human Behavior* 28 (2004): 69.
26. Ella Bell, "The Bicultural Life Experience of Career Oriented Black Women," *Journal of Organizational Behavior* 11 (November 1990): 459–478.
27. Tina Vasquez, "New Morgan Stanley Program Focuses on Diversity—Despite Tough Economic Climate," GlassHammer.com, http://www.theglasshammer.com, accessed March 31, 2010.
28. For insights on the commitment to quality of older versus younger employees, see Paul R. Jackson, "Employee commitment to quality: Its conceptualization and measurement," *The International Journal of Quality & Reliability Management* 21, no. 6/7 (2004): 714–730.
29. Department of Labor Statistics, "Civilian Labor Force by Age, Sex, Race, and Hispanic Origin—1992, 2002, and Projected 2012," February 11, 2004.
30. "Time to Start Focusing on Attracting Older Workers," *HR Focus* 81, no. 2 (February 2004): 13–14.
31. "Companies May Lose Older Workers with Shortsighted Policies," *PR Newswire*, May 29, 2007.
32. Jeffrey Sonnenfeld, "Dealing with the Aging Workforce," *Harvard Business Review* 56 (1978): 81–92.
33. Company website, "Walgreens Recognized as Private-Sector Employer of the Year for People with Disabilities," press release, http://news.walgreens.com, accessed April 15, 2010.
34. William B. Johnston and Arnold E. Packer, "Executive Summary," in *Workforce 2000: Work and Workers for the Twenty-First Century* (Indianapolis: Hudson Institute, June 1987), xii–xiv.
35. Bill Hethcock, "EEOC Wins Record Settlement for Former Texas-Based Sara Lee Factory Workers," *Dallas Business Journal*, December 21, 2015.
36. Tanya Bañuelos, "Sheriff, County Settle with Former Deputy," *The Argus Observer*, May 26, 2017.
37. Lauren Kirkwood, "EEOC Reaches $95K Settlement in Disability Discrimination Suit," *The Daily Record*, March 23, 2015.
38. Casey C. Sullivan, "EEOC HIV Discrimination Settlement: Lessons for Employers," *Free Enterprise*, March 18, 2015.
39. Jean Kim, "Issues in Workforce Diversity," Panel Presentation at the First Annual National Diversity Conference (San Francisco, May 1991).
40. Grace Lewis, "Deloitte Switches to 'Blind CV' Hiring Strategy to Boost Diversity," People Management, October 1, 2015, http://www2.cipd.co.uk/pm/peoplemanagement/b/weblog/archive/2015/10/01/deloitte-switches-to-blind-cv-hiring-strategy-to-boost-diversity.aspx.
41. *The Holy Bible*, Authorized King James Version (Nashville: Holman Bible Publishers, 1984).
42. J. Stewart Black and Hal B. Gregersen, "Serving Two Masters: Managing the Dual Allegiance of Expatriate Employees," *Sloan Management Review* (Summer 1992): 61–71.

43. Ron Ruggless, "Restaurants Look Ahead to Gen Z," *Nation's Restaurant News*, October 24, 2016: 10–13.

44. "Here Comes Gen Z!," *Managing People at Work* 4, no. 1 (January 1, 2017): 3.

45. Gwendolyn Combs, "Meeting the Leadership Challenge of a Diverse and Pluralistic Workplace: Implications of Self-Efficacy for Diversity Training," *Journal of Leadership and Organizational Studies* 8 (2002): 1.

46. Richard Lowther, "Embracing and Managing Diversity at Dell," *Strategic HR Review* 5, no. 6 (September/October 2006): 16–19.

47. Les Donaldson and Edward E. Scannell, *Human Resource Development: The New Trainer's Guide*, 2nd ed. (Reading, MA: Addison-Wesley, 1986), 8–9.

48. Max Jaeger, "Lawyers Sue Times, CNN, Fox News for Racial Discrimination," *New York Post* (online edition), April 26, 2017, http://nypost.com/2017/04/26/mainstream-media-outlets- sued-for-racial-discrimination/.

49. Josh Lowe, "Fox News Anchor Joins Lawsuit against Network Alleging Racial Discrimination," *Newsweek* (online edition), April 26, 2017, http://www.newsweek.com/fox-news-sexual-harassment-racial-discrimination-lawsuit-589846.

Managing in the Global Arena

TARGET SKILL

 Global Management Skill: the ability to manage global factors as components of organizational operations

GLOBAL MANAGEMENT SKILL AND YOUR CAREER

Global management skill will be of great value to you in enhancing your career. For example, this skill can help you to plan effectively how to reach the objectives of multinational corporations. Effective planning in multinational corporations contributes to organizational success, builds your image as a competent manager, makes you valuable to your organization, and supports promotions as you build your career.

OBJECTIVES

To help build my *global management skill,* when studying this chapter, I will attempt to acquire:

5-1 An understanding of international management

5-2 Insights on how to categorize organizations by level of international involvement

5-3 Insights about what constitutes a multinational corporation

5-4 Information about those who work in multinational corporations

5-5 Knowledge about how management functions relate to managing multinational corporations

5-6 A useful definition of transnational organizations

5-7 Ideas about special issues that can have an impact on managing in the international arena

---

MyLab Management Chapter Warm Up

If your instructor has assigned this activity, go to www.pearson.com/mylab/management to complete the chapter warm up.

CHALLENGE CASE

KFC Opens a Store a Day in China

In the United States, we are accustomed to seeing a KFC restaurant in every major city and small town. TV and Internet advertisements feature Colonel Sanders, played by different actors, who touts the company's secret recipe and that the chicken is "finger lickin' good." KFC's growth in the United States is an impressive study in itself, but the exponential expansion of the quick-service giant in China is even more noteworthy.

The first location of a KFC in China was in Tiananmen Square in 1987. The company was even able to get a foothold in the country ahead of McDonald's once the Chinese government paved the way for more Western businesses to operate in the country. Since then, the company has continued to grow. To date, there are over 5,100 locations and, on average, a new KFC opens somewhere in China every single day.

What is driving this success? The answer highlights the importance of a company recognizing that its traditional forms of growth in the United States probably wouldn't work in Asian markets. KFC has taken a unique approach with its expansion in China. First, the company has localized the menu, tailoring offerings specific to the market. In the United States, a typical KFC menu has about 30 items, but in China, guests have over 50 to choose from. One common menu item in China is *congee*—a porridge that consists of an egg, mushrooms, pickles, and pork. Other offerings include a Beijing chicken roll and a Sichuan-style spicy diced chicken.[1]

Another reason for the phenomenal growth that KFC has experienced is a strong relationship with the Chinese government. The company has faced challenges such as suppliers who provided KFC with expired processed chicken as well as raw food that was heavily laden with antibiotics. KFC's quick response to drop these suppliers and open all its locations to frequent health inspections has helped the firm succeed. KFC's willingness and eagerness to correct these problems is an example of the management employability skill of ethics and social responsibility. The guiding principle KFC is using to respond to scandals and issues ensures that the firm is recognized by customers as a company that truly wishes to provide a safe product free from dangerous effects.

KFC is owned by Yum! Brands, and the Chinese division of the parent company also owns Pizza Hut and Taco Bell, which are also seeing moderate growth in the

Sorbis/Shutterstock

KFC's exponential expansion in China is noteworthy— over 5,100 locations and growing daily!

country. From the beginning of KFC's Chinese operations, store managers realized that growth hinged on the firm's flexibility in what it offered and how it offered its products. Referring to those early days of KFC's first foray into the country, Sam Su, CEO of Yum! Brands China, said, "Although customers didn't like the food much, KFC made steady progress."[2] Part of the progress stemmed from the understanding that in Chinese culture, food is central. A bucket of chicken simply does not equate to a repeat customer. However, chicken spiced with local flavors and offered in a pleasing setting with a hostess and employees who teach children English words brings in repeat customers.

KFCs in China are about twice the size of the typical U.S. location, too. The reasons are the extensive menu and a larger seating area, where families dine together alongside business executives who are having a meeting. They also employ about twice the number of associates than does a U.S. store. Again, food preparation of more than 50 menu items requires a larger team to get the work done on a daily basis.

The lesson learned is that KFC did not try to force its distinctive American brand, store layout, and menu on a different culture. It moved slowly, discovered more about the culture, and then tailored its operations to appeal to the local customer base. Once successfully established, the chain has grown by leaps and bounds. And to epitomize the company's success, in a typical year, KFC now opens about 600 to 700 new stores in China.

THE GLOBAL MANAGEMENT CHALLENGE

The Challenge Case illustrates how KFC has grown its operations in China. The global management challenge for managers includes understanding the need to manage internationally and managing a multinational corporation and its workforce. After studying chapter concepts, read the Challenge Case Summary at the end of the chapter for added help in relating chapter content to meeting global management challenges at KFC.

Fundamentals of International Management

Most U.S. companies see great opportunities in the international marketplace today.[3] Although the U.S. population is growing slowly but steadily, the population in many other countries is exploding. For example, it has been estimated that in 1990, China, India, and Indonesia together already had more than 2 billion people, or 40 percent of the world's population.[4] Obviously, such countries offer a strong profit potential for aggressive businesspeople throughout the world.

This potential does not come without serious risk, however. Managers who attempt to manage in a global context face formidable challenges. Some of these challenges are the cultural differences among workers from different countries, different technology levels from country to country, and laws and political systems that can vary immensely from one nation to the next.

International management is simply the performance of management activities across national borders.[5] It entails reaching organizational objectives by extending management activities to include an emphasis on organizations in foreign countries.[6] The trend toward increased international management, or *globalization*, is now widely recognized. The primary question for most firms is not *whether* to globalize but *how* and *how quickly* to do so, and how to measure global progress over time.[7]

International management can take several different forms, from simply analyzing and fighting competition in foreign markets to establishing a formal partnership with a foreign company. Domino's Pizza is an example of a company that sees international opportunities and acts on them without hesitation. Domino's has been so aggressive internationally that, at present, its international sales are a significant component of company success. It's been reported that international business contributes as much as 35 percent of its annual income. The company attributes much of its success internationally to the fact that pizza is universally liked and can be easily adapted. For example, the company can go into India or Japan and simply add different toppings to cater to local tastes, whereas it's much more difficult for other restaurant chains to adapt their products to local flavors.[8]

JPMorgan Chase is an example of a bank involved in international management. JPMorgan Chase, the second-largest bank in the United States, is one of the latest financial institutions to launch a global banking business, targeting rapidly growing economies such as Brazil, China, and India. The bank sells loans and commercial banking services to multinational organizations in an effort to expand its business outside the United States and reduce its dependence on the U.S. economy.[9] Many other U.S. banks are pursuing similar international management activities.

The noteworthy trend that already exists in the United States and other countries toward developing business relationships in and with foreign countries is expected to accelerate even more in the future. As **Figure 5.1** illustrates, U.S. investment in foreign countries and investment by foreign countries in the United States have grown since 2009 and are expected to continue growing, with slowdowns or setbacks only in recessionary periods. The figure also shows that, more recently, investments by foreign countries in the United States and U.S. investments in foreign countries continue to increase at a significant pace. As an interesting

5-1 An understanding of international management

Figure 5.1

U.S. investment in foreign countries versus foreign investment in the United States[10]

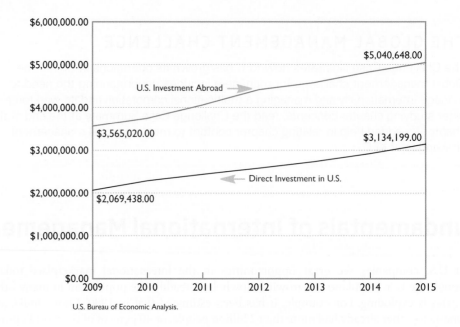

U.S. Bureau of Economic Analysis.

Figure 5.2

U.S. direct investment abroad, by country, for 2015[11]

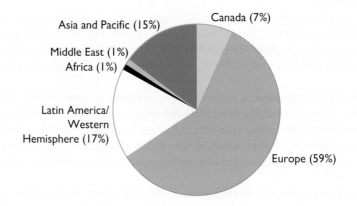

side note, **Figure 5.2** shows that, in 2015, U.S. foreign investments focused most heavily in Europe and Latin America/Western Hemisphere. This snapshot is equivalent to that of several years preceding 2015 and is expected to be equivalent to that of several years after. **Figure 5.3** shows that European countries were by far the most significant foreign investors in the United States in 2015. These data also are equivalent to that of several years preceding 2015 and are expected to be equivalent to that of several years after. Information of this nature has spurred both management educators and practicing managers to insist that knowledge of international management is necessary for a thorough understanding of the contemporary fundamentals of management.[13]

Figure 5.3

Foreign direct investment in the United States, by region, for 2015[12]

Note: Percentages do not add to 100 due to rounding.

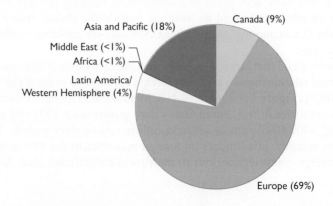

Categorizing Organizations by *Level* of International Involvement

A number of different categories have evolved to describe the extent to which organizations are involved in the international arena. These categories are domestic organizations, international organizations, multinational organizations, and transnational or global organizations. As **Figure 5.4** suggests, this categorization format describes a continuum of international involvement, with domestic organizations representing the least and transnational organizations representing the most international involvement. Although the format may not be perfect, it is useful for explaining the primary ways in which companies operate in the international realm.[14] The following sections describe these categories in more detail.

5-2   Insights on how to categorize organizations by level of international involvement

Domestic Organizations

Domestic organizations are organizations that essentially operate within a single country. These organizations normally not only acquire necessary resources within a single country but also sell their goods or services within that same country. Although domestic organizations may occasionally make an international sale or acquire some needed resource from a foreign supplier, the overwhelming bulk of their business activity takes place within the country where they are based.

Although inclusion in this category is not determined by size, most domestic organizations today are quite small. Even small business organizations, however, are following the trend and becoming increasingly involved in the international arena.

International Organizations

International organizations are organizations that are based primarily within a single country but that have continuing, meaningful international transactions—such as making sales and purchasing materials—in other countries. Nu Horizons is an example of a small company that can be classified as an international organization. This distributor of electronic goods made mainly by some 40 U.S. manufacturers has about 5,000 customers and is the fastest-growing company in Melville, New York. Nu Horizons is considered an international organization because an important part of its business is to act as the primary North American distributor of electronic components made by Japan's NIC Components Corp.[15] Nu Horizons was ultimately acquired by Arrow Electronics, in part because of its global reach.[16]

In summary, international organizations are involved more extensively in the international arena than are domestic organizations but are less involved than either multinational or transnational organizations.

Multinational Organizations: The Multinational Corporation

The *multinational organization*, commonly called the *multinational corporation (MNC)*, represents the third level of international involvement. This section of the text defines the multinational corporation, discusses the complexities involved in managing such a corporation, describes the risks associated with its operations, explores the diversity of the multinational workforce, and explains how the major management functions relate to managing the multinational corporation.

Figure 5.4   Continuum of international involvement

Multinational Corporations

5-3 Insights about what constitutes a multinational corporation

The term *multinational corporation* first appeared in American dictionaries about 1970, and it has since been defined in various ways in business publications and textbooks. For the purposes of this text, a **multinational corporation** is a company that has significant operations in more than one country. Essentially, a multinational corporation is an organization that is involved in doing business at the international level. It carries out its activities on an international scale, which disregards national boundaries, and it is guided by a common strategy from a corporation center.[17]

Neil H. Jacoby explains that companies go through six stages to reach the highest degree of multinationalization. As **Table 5.1** indicates, multinational corporations can range from slightly multinationalized organizations, which simply export products to a foreign country, to highly multinationalized organizations, which have some of their owners in other countries. According to Alfred M. Zeien, a past CEO of Gillette Company, it can take up to 25 years to build a management team with the requisite skills, experience, and abilities to shape an organization into a highly developed multinational company.[18]

In general, the larger the organization, the greater the likelihood that it participates in international operations of some sort. Companies such as General Electric, Lockheed, and DuPont, which have each accumulated more than $1 billion annually from export sales, are examples of this generalization. You will find exceptions, of course.

In some industries, even small businesses can prosper in the global marketplace. For example, BRK Electronics, a small firm in Aurora, Illinois, holds a substantial share of world sales in smoke detectors. The company has an advantage because of its reputation for high-quality smoke alarms, carbon monoxide alarms, and fire extinguishers. BRK's market share has grown through its local distributors in countries like Australia, Mexico, and New Zealand.[19] As noted earlier, an increasing number of smaller organizations such as BRK Electronics are undertaking international operations.

Complexities of Managing the Multinational Corporation

From the discussion so far, it should be clear that international management and domestic management are quite different. Classic management thought indicates that international management differs from domestic management because international management involves operating:[20]

1. Within different national sovereignties
2. Under widely disparate economic conditions
3. Among people living within different value systems and institutions
4. In places experiencing the industrial revolution at different times
5. Often over great geographical distance
6. In national markets varying greatly in population and area

Figure 5.5 shows some of the more important management implications of these six variables and some of the relationships among them. Consider, for example, the first variable. Different national sovereignties generate different legal systems. In turn, each legal system implies a unique set of rights and obligations involving property, taxation, antitrust (control of monopoly) law, corporate law, and contract law. In turn, these rights and obligations require the firm to acquire the skills necessary to assess the international legal considerations. Such skills are different from those required in a purely domestic setting.

TABLE 5.1   **Six Stages of Multinationalization**

Stage 1	Stage 2	Stage 3	Stage 4	Stage 5	Stage 6
Exports its products to foreign countries	Establishes sales organizations abroad	Licenses use of its patents and know-how to foreign firms that make and sell its products	Establishes foreign manufacturing facilities	Multinationalizes management from top to bottom	Multinationalizes ownership of corporate stock

Figure 5.5   Management implications based on six variables in international systems and the relationships among them

PRACTICAL CHALLENGE: MANAGING RISK

Risk Management: Indonesia's Industry Ministry Steps Up

Every business has to manage risks, improve workforce skills, and cut costs. Part of that process is engaging the national government to fund and support employee training and development. Southeast Asia is an incredibly competitive marketplace, particularly in the rubber, steel, and palm oil industries. Around 60 percent of Indonesian manufacturing workers have skill certification, but the establishment of eight new polytechnics by 2019 aims to increase this figure. This is in recognition of the need to have a competent and skilled workforce to ensure that Indonesian businesses are more competitive and innovative. Indonesian manufacturing accounts for over 20 percent of GDP. The risks are too high to ignore the need for investment to encourage further investment from abroad. Without initiatives such as these, Indonesia runs the risk of losing investment and potential employment opportunities and of being forced to import manufacturing goods it could have produced itself.

Risk and the Multinational Corporation

Developing a multinational corporation obviously requires a substantial investment in foreign operations. Normally, managers who make foreign investments expect such investments to accomplish the following:[21]

1. Reduce or eliminate high transportation costs
2. Allow participation in the rapid expansion of a market abroad
3. Provide foreign technical, design, and marketing skills
4. Earn higher profits

Unfortunately, many managers decide to internationalize their companies without having an accurate understanding of the risks involved in doing so.[22] For example, political complications involving the **parent company** (the company investing in the international operations) and various factions within the **host country** (the country in which the investment is made) could prevent the parent company from realizing the desirable outcomes just listed. Some companies attempt to minimize this kind of risk by adding standard clauses to their contracts stipulating that, in the event a business controversy cannot be resolved by the parties involved, they will agree to mediation by a mutually selected mediator.[23]

The likelihood of achieving desirable outcomes related to foreign investments is usually somewhat uncertain and certainly varies from country to country. Nevertheless, managers faced with making a foreign investment must assess this likelihood as accurately as possible. Obviously, an unwise decision to invest in another country can cause serious financial problems for the organization.

The Workforce of Multinational Corporations

5-4   Information about those who work in multinational corporations

As organizations become more global, their members tend to become more diverse. Managers of multinational corporations face the continual challenge of forming a competitive business team made up of people of different races who speak different languages and come from different parts of the world. The following sections explain two functions that should help managers build such teams:

1. They furnish details about and related insights into the various types of organization members generally found in multinational corporations.

2. They describe the adjustments that members of multinational organizations normally must make to become efficient and effective contributors to organization goal attainment, and they suggest how managers can facilitate these adjustments.

Types of Organization Members Found in Multinational Corporations

Workers in multinational organizations can be divided into three basic types:

- **Expatriate**—An organization member who lives and works in a country where he or she does not have citizenship[24]
- **Host-country national**—An organization member who is a citizen of the country in which the facility of a foreign-based organization is located[25]
- **Third-country national**—An organization member who is a citizen of one country and works in another country for an organization headquartered in still another country

Organizations that operate globally may employ all three types of workers. The use of host-country nationals, however, is increasing because they are normally the least expensive to employ. Such employees, for example, do not need to be relocated or undergo training in the culture, language, or tax laws of the country where the organization is doing business. Both expatriates and third-country nationals, on the other hand, would have to be relocated and normally undergo such training.

Workforce Adjustments

Working for a multinational corporation requires more difficult adjustments than working in an organization that focuses primarily on domestic activities. Probably the two most difficult challenges, which pertain to expatriates and third-country nationals rather than to host-country nationals, are adjusting to a new culture and repatriation.[26]

Adjusting to a New Culture

Upon arrival in a foreign country, many people experience confusion, anxiety, and stress related to the need to make cultural adjustments in their organizational and personal lives.[27] From a personal viewpoint, food, weather, and language may all be dramatically different, and driving may be done on the "wrong" side of the road. As an example of personal anxiety that can be caused by adjusting to a new culture, a U.S. expatriate working in São Paulo, Brazil, drove out of a parking lot by nudging his way into a terrible traffic jam. When a Brazilian woman allowed him to cut in front of her, the expatriate gave her the "OK" signal. The expatriate's "OK" sign is considered to be a vulgar gesture in the Brazilian culture.[28]

From an organizational viewpoint, workers may encounter different attitudes toward work and different perceptions of time in the workplace. To illustrate, the Japanese are renowned for their hard-driving work ethic, but Americans have a slightly more relaxed attitude toward work. On the other hand, in many U.S. companies, working past quitting time is seen as exemplary, but in Germany, someone who works late is commonly criticized.

Members of multinational corporations usually have the formidable task of adjusting to a drastically new organizational situation. Managers must help these people adjust quickly and effortlessly so that they can begin contributing to organizational goal attainment as soon as possible.[29]

Repatriation

Repatriation is the process of bringing individuals who have been working abroad back to their home country and reintegrating them into the organization's home-country operations.[30] Repatriation has its own set of adjustment problems, especially for people who have lived abroad for a long time. Some individuals become so accustomed to the advantages of an overseas lifestyle that they greatly miss it when they return home. Others idealize their homeland so much while they are abroad that they become disappointed when it fails to live

Expatriates and third-country nationals must undergo career and cultural training in the country in which the organization does business.

Roy Johnson/dbimages/Alamy Stock Photo

up to their fantasies when they return. Still others acquire foreign-based habits that are undesirable from the organization's viewpoint and are hard to break.[31]

Managers must be patient and understanding with repatriates. Some organizations provide repatriates with counseling so that they will be better prepared to handle readjustment problems. Others have found that providing employees, before they leave for foreign duty, with a written agreement specifying what their new duties and career paths will be when they return home reduces friction and facilitates the repatriate's adjustment.

The advantages of having organization members participate in an international experience in business are well known and are increasing in number. Organization members who have succeeded in the global environment are valuable assets to their organizations. One of the significant challenges to organizations is retaining these highly sought-after individuals throughout a successful repatriation process and after they complete their overseas assignments.[32]

Management Functions and Multinational Corporations

5-5 Knowledge about how management functions relate to managing multinational corporations

The sections that follow discuss the four major management functions—planning, organizing, influencing, and controlling—as they occur in multinational corporations.

Planning in Multinational Corporations

Planning was defined in Chapter 1 as determining how an organization will achieve its objectives. This definition is applicable to the management of both domestic and multinational organizations, but with some differences.

The primary difference between planning in multinational organizations and planning in domestic organizations is in the plans' components. Plans for multinational organizations include components that focus on the international arena, whereas plans for domestic organizations do not. For example, plans for multinational organizations could include the following:

1. Establishing a new salesforce in a foreign country
2. Developing new manufacturing plants in other countries through purchase or construction
3. Financing international expansion
4. Determining which countries represent the most suitable candidates for international expansion

The following sections discuss several issues, ranging from importing and exporting to the North American Free Trade Agreement (NAFTA), that can affect the way managers plan for multinational corporations.

Imports/Exports
Imports/exports planning components emphasize reaching organizational objectives by **importing** (buying goods or services from another country) or by **exporting** (selling goods or services to another country).

Organizations of all sizes import and export. On the one hand, Winebow, Inc., a relatively small company based in Montvale, New Jersey, imports and distributes wine, champagne, and other spirits in New York, New Jersey, Pennsylvania, and Washington, D.C.[33] On the other hand, extremely large and complex organizations, such as Ford Motor Company, the second-largest U.S. automaker, recently announced that it would begin exporting more automobiles manufactured at its plant in India to China and other countries as demand for its products in India begins to subside.[34]

License Agreements
A **license agreement** is a right granted by one company to another to use its brand name, technology, product specifications, and so on, in the manufacture or sale of goods and services. The company to which the license is extended pays a fee for the privilege. International planning components in this area involve reaching organizational objectives through either the purchase or the sale of licenses at the international level.

For example, in the past the Tosoh Corporation purchased a license agreement from Mobil Research and Development Corporation to commercialize Mobil's process for extracting mercury from natural gas. Tosoh, a Japanese firm, uses its subsidiaries in the United States, Japan, the Netherlands, Greece, Canada, and the United Kingdom as bases of operations from which to profit from Mobil's process.[35]

Upon entering into a license agreement, both companies should be absolutely certain that they understand the terms of the agreement. Sometimes companies end up in litigation as a means of settling disagreements regarding specifics of the contents of a license agreement. Naturally, the cost of such litigation can be high and can significantly diminish the advantages that both companies thought they would gain as a result of entering into the agreement.[36]

Interestingly, Tosoh Corporation has recently submitted process patent applications itself, perhaps a calculated step in a plan to bolster company revenue through the licensing of unique processes that it owns.[37]

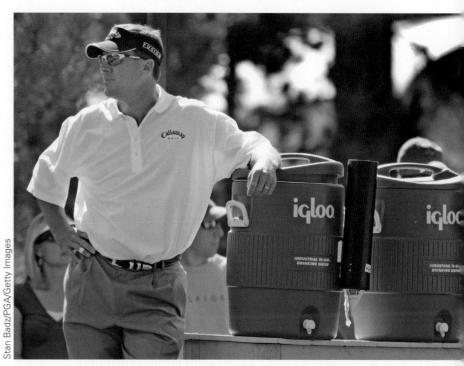

Stan Badz/PGA/Getty Images

Texas-based company Igloo entered into a license agreement with Taiwan's First Designs Global (FDG). FDG has the right to use the Igloo brand on products it makes, and Igloo has the benefit of FDG's manufacturing expertise and presence in Asia.

Direct Investing   **Direct investing** uses the assets of one company to purchase the operating assets (e.g., factories) of another company. International planning in this area emphasizes reaching organizational objectives through the purchase of the operating assets of another company in a foreign country.

For example, Japanese firms have a rich and continuing tradition in making direct investments in the United States. In fact, many people believe that a new wave of direct Japanese investment in the United States is coming. Several large Japanese companies have announced plans to expand their U.S. production facilities. These planned direct investments are focused on building competitive clout for Japanese companies in core industries such as automobiles, semiconductors, electronics, and office products. Lower manufacturing wages and lower land costs in the United States than in Japan are key attractions for Japanese firms. For example, because the cost of building a factory was 30 percent cheaper in the United States than in Japan, Ricoh Company decided to spend $30 million to start making thermal paper products near Atlanta, Georgia. One of the largest Japanese direct investments in the United States was Toyota Motor Company's $900 million expansion of its Georgetown, Kentucky, plant. The lower costs associated with expanding and operating the Georgetown plant were the key reason Toyota decided to make this investment.[38]

Joint Ventures   An **international joint venture** is a partnership formed between a company in one country and a company in another country for the purpose of pursuing some mutually desirable business undertaking.[39] International planning components that include joint ventures emphasize the attainment of organizational objectives through partnerships with foreign companies. For example, joint ventures between car manufacturers are becoming more and more common as companies strive for greater economies of scale and higher standards in product quality and delivery.

Planning and International Market Agreements   To plan properly, managers of a multinational corporation—or of any other organization participating in the international arena—must understand numerous complex and interrelated factors present within the organization's international environment. Managers should have a practical grasp of international environmental factors such as the economic and cultural conditions and the laws and political circumstances in the foreign countries within which their companies operate.

One international environmental factor that affects strategic planning has lately received significant attention: An **international market agreement** is an arrangement among a cluster of countries that facilitates a high level of trade among these countries. In planning, managers must consider existing international market agreements as they relate to the countries in which their organizations operate. If an organization is located in a country that is party to an international market agreement, the organization's plan should include steps for taking maximum advantage of that agreement. On the other hand, if an organization is located in a country that is *not* party to an international market agreement, the organization's plan must include steps for competing with organizations located in nations that are parties to such an agreement. The most notable international market agreements are discussed here.

The European Union (EU)

The **European Union (EU)** is an international market agreement, established in 1994, that is dedicated to facilitating trade among member nations. To that end, the nations in the EU have agreed to eliminate tariffs among themselves and work toward meaningful deregulation in areas such as banking, insurance, telecommunications, and airlines. More recently, the nations have tried to develop a set of standardized accounting principles to help facilitate business transactions among members.[40] Long-term members of the EU initially included Denmark, the United Kingdom, Portugal, the Netherlands, Belgium, Spain, Ireland, Luxembourg, France, Germany, Italy, and Greece. As indicated by the United Kingdom's recent request to withdraw from EU membership, however, the future of the EU may seem somewhat tenuous.[41] **Figure 5.6** identifies countries that are presently members of the EU.

North American Free Trade Agreement (NAFTA)

The **North American Free Trade Agreement (NAFTA)** is an international market agreement aimed at facilitating trade among member nations. Current NAFTA members include the United States, Canada, and Mexico.[42] To facilitate trade, these countries have agreed to actions such as phasing out tariffs on U.S. farm exports to Mexico, opening up Mexico to American trucking, and safeguarding North American pharmaceutical patents in Mexico.

Figure 5.6

Members of the European Union—2017

Source: http://europa.eu/about-eu/countries/index_en.htm

NAFTA has had a significant impact since its implementation in January 1994. Figures show that, since the agreement went into effect, U.S. exports to Mexico have increased 30 percent, and Mexican exports to the United States have increased 15 percent. Trade between the United States and Canada has also exploded since NAFTA took effect.

At this point, however, the future of NAFTA is debatable. Trade among NAFTA countries has had both pros and cons. Pros include the reduction or elimination of taxes on imported goods from NAFTA countries. Cons include farmers in Mexico being overwhelmed by the ease of importing American agricultural products.[43]

Asian-Pacific Economic Cooperation (APEC) APEC was established in 1989 to further the economic growth and prosperity of the Asia-Pacific community. Since its beginning, APEC has worked to reduce tariffs and other trade barriers across the Asia-Pacific region. APEC is based on the concept that free and open trade creates greater opportunities for international trade and related prosperity among member nations. Thus, the organization works diligently to create an environment in which goods can be transported safely and efficiently among countries. APEC has 21 members, including Canada, the People's Republic of China, Indonesia, and the United States. APEC's entire country membership is depicted in **Figure 5.7**. Comparison of APEC and EU member countries shows that EU member countries are concentrated in Europe, whereas APEC member countries are spread around the globe.

To sum up, numerous countries throughout the world are already signatories to international market agreements. In addition, the number of countries that are parties to such agreements may increase in the future.

Organizing Multinational Corporations

Organizing was defined in Chapter 1 generally as the process of establishing orderly uses for all resources within the organization. This definition applies equally to the management of domestic organizations and to the management of multinational organizations. However, two organizing topics as they relate specifically to multinational corporations bear further discussion: organization structure and the selection of managers.[44]

Figure 5.7 APEC member nations

Figure 5.8

Partial multinational organization charts based on function, product, and territory, respectively

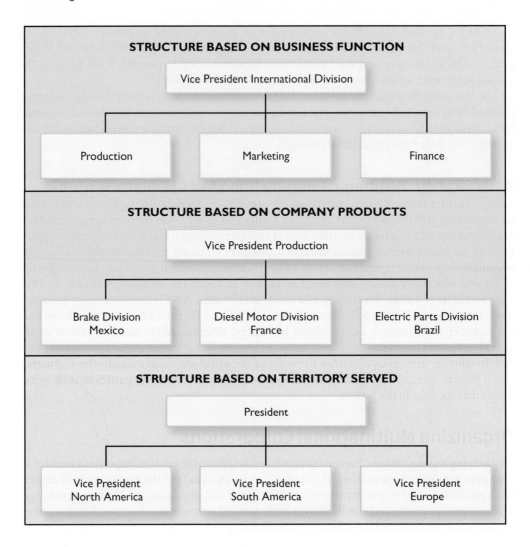

STRUCTURE BASED ON BUSINESS FUNCTION

Vice President International Division

Production | Marketing | Finance

STRUCTURE BASED ON COMPANY PRODUCTS

Vice President Production

Brake Division Mexico | Diesel Motor Division France | Electric Parts Division Brazil

STRUCTURE BASED ON TERRITORY SERVED

President

Vice President North America | Vice President South America | Vice President Europe

Organization Structure

Basically, *organization structure* is the sum of all established relationships among resources within an organization, and the *organization chart* is the graphic illustration of organization structure. **Figure 5.8** illustrates several ways in which organization charts can be designed for multinational corporations. Briefly, multinational organization charts can be set up according to the major business functions the organization performs, such as production or marketing; the major products the organization sells, such as brakes or electrical parts; or the geographic areas within which the organization does business, such as North America or Europe. The topic of organization structure is discussed in much more detail in Chapter 10.

As with domestic organizations, there is no one best way to organize a multinational corporation. Instead, managers must analyze the multinational circumstances that confront the corporation and develop an organization structure that best suits those circumstances.

Selection of Managers

For multinational organizations to thrive, they must have competent managers. One characteristic believed to be a primary determinant of how competently managers can guide multinational organizations is their attitudes toward how such organizations should operate.

Managerial Attitudes toward Foreign Operations

Over the years, management theorists have identified three basic managerial attitudes toward the operation of multinational corporations: ethnocentric, polycentric, and geocentric. The **ethnocentric attitude** reflects the belief that multinational corporations should regard home-country management practices as superior to foreign-country management practices. Managers with an ethnocentric attitude are prone to stereotype home-country management practices as sound and reasonable and foreign management practices as faulty and unreasonable. The **polycentric attitude** reflects the belief that, because foreign managers are closer to foreign organizational units, they probably understand those units better, and therefore foreign management practices should generally be viewed as more insightful than home-country management practices. Managers with a **geocentric attitude** believe that the overall quality of management recommendations, rather than the location of managers, should determine the acceptability of the management practices used to guide multinational corporations.[45]

Modern managers should continually monitor ethnocentric, polycentric, and geocentric attitudes that exist in organizations to make sure that those attitudes are consistent with the global aspirations of the organization. One example of this monitoring involves the Coca-Cola Company, in which management constantly monitors its Chinese website. The purpose of this monitoring is to examine how Coca-Cola, the number-one brand in the world, is using its website to communicate with management as well as with the public in the world's largest market, China. Management wants to make sure that the site appropriately integrates ethnocentric and polycentric views to support the Chinese segment of the company's global strategy.[46]

Advantages and Disadvantages of Each Management Attitude

It is extremely important to understand the potential advantages and disadvantages of these three attitudes within multinational corporations. The ethnocentric attitude has the advantage of keeping an organization uncomplicated, but it generally causes organizational problems because it impedes the organization from receiving feedback from its foreign operations. In some cases, the ethnocentric attitude even results in resentment toward the home country within the foreign society.

The polycentric attitude permits the tailoring of foreign organizational segments to their cultures, which can be an advantage. Unfortunately, this attitude can result in the substantial disadvantage of creating numerous foreign organizational segments that are individually run and distinctive, which makes them difficult to control.

The geocentric attitude is generally thought to be the most appropriate for managers in multinational corporations to have. This attitude promotes collaboration between foreign and home-country management and encourages the development of managerial skills regardless of the organizational segment or country in which managers operate. However, an organization characterized by the geocentric attitude generally incurs high travel and training expenses, and many decisions are made by consensus. Although the risks from such a wide distribution of power are significant, the potential payoffs—better-quality products, worldwide utilization of the best human resources, increased managerial commitment to worldwide organizational objectives, and increased profit—generally outweigh the potential harm. Overall, managers with a geocentric attitude contribute more to the long-term success of a multinational corporation than do managers with an ethnocentric or a polycentric attitude.

Influencing People in Multinational Corporations

Influencing was defined in Chapter 1 as guiding the activities of organization members in appropriate directions through communicating, leading, motivating, and managing groups. Influencing people in a multinational corporation, however, is more complex and challenging than doing so in a domestic organization.

Culture

The factor that probably contributes most to this increased complexity and challenge is culture. **Culture** is the set of characteristics of a given group of people and their environment. The components of a culture that are generally designated as important are norms, values, customs, beliefs, attitudes, habits, skills, state of technology, level of education, and religion. As a manager moves from a domestic corporation involving basically only one culture to a multinational corporation involving several cultures, the task of influencing usually becomes more difficult.

To influence employees of many cultures successfully, managers in multinational corporations should do the following:

1. **Acquire a working knowledge of the languages used in the countries that house foreign operations**—Multinational managers attempting to function without such knowledge are prone to making costly mistakes.

2. **Understand the attitudes of people in the countries that house foreign operations**—An understanding of these attitudes can help managers design business practices that are suitable for each distinct foreign situation. For example, Americans generally accept competition as a tool to encourage people to work harder. As a result, U.S. business practices that include some competitive aspects seldom create significant disruption within organizations. Such practices could cause disruption, however, if introduced into either Japan or a European country.

3. **Understand the needs that motivate people in the countries housing foreign operations**—For managers in multinational corporations to be successful at motivating employees in different countries, they must present these individuals with opportunities to satisfy their personal needs while being productive within the organization. In designing motivation strategies, multinational managers must understand that employees in different countries often have quite different personal needs. For example, the Swiss, Austrians, the Japanese, and Argentineans tend to have high security needs, whereas Danes, Swedes, and Norwegians tend to have high social needs. People in Great Britain, the United States, Canada, New Zealand, and Australia tend to have high self-actualization needs.[47] Thus, to be successful at influencing diverse employees, multinational managers must understand their employees' needs and shape organizational components such as incentive systems, job designs, and leadership styles to correspond to these needs.

Hofstede's Ideas for Describing Culture

One of the most widely accepted methods for describing values in foreign cultures was developed by Geert Hofstede.[48] According to Hofstede's research, national cultural values vary on five basic dimensions:

1. **Power Distance.** Power distance is the degree to which a society promotes an unequal distribution of power. Countries that heavily promote power distance have citizens who tend to emphasize, expect, and accept leadership that is more autocratic than democratic. According to Hofstede's research, Mexico and France are examples of countries that tend to value more autocratic leadership, whereas the United States is an example of a country that tends to value more democratic leadership.

2. **Uncertainty Avoidance.** Uncertainty avoidance is the extent to which a society feels threatened by uncertain or unpredictable situations. People in countries that are high in uncertainty avoidance prefer being in more defined and predictable situations. Based on Hofstede's research, Greece and Japan feel more threatened by uncertainty than do the United States and Canada. Correspondingly, the citizens of Greece and Japan would be less able to tolerate risk and uncertainty in their lives than would the citizens of the United States.

3. **Individualism and Collectivism.** Individualism–collectivism is the degree to which people in a society operate primarily as individuals or operate primarily within groups. People operating as individuals tend to focus on meeting their own needs, to be self-reliant, and to succeed by competing with others. On the other hand, people who operate collectively tend to build relationships with others and downplay individualism; business success is pursued through relationships and cooperation among group members. According to Hofstede's research, China and South Korea are examples of countries that emphasize collectivism, whereas Australia, Canada, and the United States are examples of countries that emphasize individualism.

4. **Masculinity and Femininity.** Masculinity–femininity is the extent to which a culture emphasizes traditional masculine or feminine values. Traditional masculine values include competitiveness, assertiveness, success, and wealth. Traditional feminine values include caring for and nurturing others, and increasing the quality of life. According to Hofstede's research, the Scandinavian countries tend to admire more traditional feminine values, whereas Japan and the United States tend to approve of more traditional masculine values.

5. **Short-Term and Long-Term Orientation.** Short-term–long-term orientation is the degree to which a culture deemphasizes short-run success in favor of long-run success. Cultures that focus more on long-run success emphasize activities like planning, educating, rewarding long-run results, and keeping a future-oriented perspective. Conversely, cultures that focus more on short-run success emphasize training to enable one to do a job now, rewarding short-term results, and maintaining a day-to-day perspective. Given Hofstede's research, Asian societies generally are among the countries most focused on long-term success. Pakistan is an example of a country that values a short-term orientation.

STEPS FOR SUCCESS

Examples of Business Etiquette in Other Cultures

American business culture is unique unto itself, with firm handshakes, direct eye contact, and plenty of personal space. However, other countries have different norms, and being aware of those differences is important for those doing business in these countries or with representatives from these countries. Here are some examples of business etiquette in other cultures:[49]

- In Finland, business meetings are brief and direct.
- In India, language in meetings is nuanced, subtle, and indirect.

- In South Korea, China, and Singapore, business men and women use formal addresses such as "Mr. Smith" or "Mrs. Smith."
- In Mexico and Italy, it is acceptable to be late to a meeting.
- In Japan, status, rank, and a person's position in a hierarchy are highly valued.
- In Norway, there are very few layers of management, with businesses preferring a flat organizational structure.

The broad appeal and acceptance of Hofstede's work over recent decades is undeniable.[50] As a general guideline, managers faced with doing business within different countries should understand the cultural values within those countries. To increase the probability of organizational success based on this understanding, management should strive to design and implement actions consistent with those values. Hofstede's research provides worthwhile insights for how managers can define values in foreign cultures and react appropriately to them. Fortunately, management scientists continue to examine Hofstede's work to refine its worth to modern managers further.[51]

Controlling Multinational Corporations

Controlling was defined in Chapter 1 as making something happen the way it was planned to happen. As in domestic corporations, control in multinational corporations requires that standards be set, performance be measured and compared to standards, and corrective actions be taken if necessary. In addition, control in areas such as labor costs, product quality, and inventory is important to organizational success regardless of whether the organization is domestic or international.

Kimberly-Clark Corporation is a U.S. multinational corporation that produces mostly paper-based consumer products. Kimberly-Clark's brand-name products include Kleenex facial tissue, KimWipes scientific cleaning wipes, and Huggies disposable diapers. One of Kimberly-Clark's challenges as a multinational corporation is controlling purchasing costs. To help meet this challenge, the company established a *global* procurement function to direct all purchasing for the company. By handling all purchasing activities in one spot rather than in many different places throughout the world, this change helps the company minimize the number of people needed in the purchasing function. This change was expected to save Kimberly-Clark as much as $500 million by 2013.[52]

Special Difficulties   Control of a multinational corporation involves certain complexities. First, to deal with the problem of different currencies, management must decide how to compare profits generated by organizational units located in different countries and therefore expressed in terms of different currencies. Another complication is that organizational units in multinational corporations are generally geographically separated. This increased distance usually makes it difficult for multinational managers to keep a close watch on operations in foreign countries.

Improving Communication   One action that successful managers take to help overcome the difficulty of monitoring geographically separated foreign units is carefully designing the communication network or information system that links the units. A significant part of this design requires all company units to acquire and install similar computer equipment in all offices, both foreign and domestic, to ensure the availability of network hookups when communication becomes necessary. Such standardization of computer equipment also facilitates communication among all foreign locations and makes equipment repair and maintenance easier (and therefore less expensive). Consistent with this need to use technology to communicate in the multinational arena, companies like Cisco Systems and Hewlett Packard Enterprise are focusing on providing managers with communication capability via data center networks established to provide communication in real time and store data regarding organizational performance.[53]

MyLab Management Watch It

If your instructor has assigned this activity, go to www.pearson.com/mylab/management to complete the video exercise.

Transnational Organizations

5-6 A useful definition of transnational organizations

A **transnational organization**, also called a *global organization*, views the entire world as its business arena.[54] Doing business wherever it makes sense is the primary goal; national borders are considered inconsequential. The transnational organization transcends any single home country, with ownership, control, and management located in many different countries. Transnational organizations represent the fourth, and maximum, level of international activity as depicted on the continuum of international involvement presented in Figure 5.4. Seeing great opportunities in the global marketplace, some MNCs have transformed themselves from home-based companies with worldwide interests into worldwide companies pursuing business activities around the globe and claiming no loyalty to any one country.

Perhaps the most commonly cited transnational organization is Nestlé.[55] Although Nestlé is headquartered in Vevey, Switzerland, its arena of daily business activity is truly the world. Nestlé has a diversified list of products that include instant coffee, cereals, pharmaceuticals, coffee creamers, diet foods, ice cream, chocolates, and a wide array of snack foods. Its acquisition of the French company Perrier catapulted Nestlé into market leadership in the mineral water industry. Nestlé has more than 210,000 employees and operates 494 factories in 71 countries worldwide, including the United States, Germany, Portugal, Brazil, France, New Zealand, Australia, Chile, and Venezuela. Of Nestlé's sales and profits, about 35 percent come from Europe, 40 percent come from North and South America, and 25 percent come from other countries. As with most transnational organizations, Nestlé has grown by acquiring companies rather than by expanding its present operations.[56]

International Management: Special Issues

5-7 Ideas about special issues that can have an impact on managing in the international arena

The preceding section of this chapter discussed planning, organizing, influencing, and controlling multinational corporations. This section focuses on two special issues that can help to ensure management success in the international arena: maintaining ethics in international management and preparing expatriates for foreign assignments.[57]

Maintaining Ethics in International Management

As discussed in Chapter 3, *ethics* is a concern for good behavior and reflects the obligation that managers consider not only their own personal well-being but also that of other human beings as they lead organizations. Having a manager define what ethical behavior is can indeed be challenging and becomes increasingly challenging as managers consider the international implications of management action. What seems ethical in a manager's home country might be unethical in a different country.

The following guidelines can help managers ensure that management action taken across national borders is truly ethical. Managers can ensure that such action is ethical by doing the following:

Respecting Core Human Rights

This guideline underscores the idea that all people deserve an opportunity to achieve economic advancement and an improved standard of living. In addition, all people have the right to be treated with respect. Much effort has been made by major sporting goods companies, including Nike and Reebok, to ensure that this guideline is followed in the business operations they conduct in other countries.[58] These companies have joined forces to crack down on child labor, establish minimum wages comparable to an individual country's standards, establish a maximum 60-hour workweek with at least one day off, and support the establishment of a mechanism for inspecting apparel factories worldwide. These companies have also committed themselves to the elimination of forced labor, harassment, abuse, and discrimination in the workplace.

Respecting Local Traditions

This guideline suggests that managers hold in high regard the customs of foreign countries in which they conduct business. In Japan, for example, people have a long-standing tradition that individuals who do business together exchange gifts. Sometimes these gifts can be expensive. For example, when U.S. managers started doing business in Japan, accepting a gift felt like accepting a bribe. As a result, many of these managers thought that the practice of gift giving might be unethical. However, as U.S. managers have come to know and respect this Japanese tradition, most have come to tolerate, and even encourage, this practice as ethical behavior in Japan. Some managers even set different limits on gift giving in Japan than they do elsewhere in the world.

Determining Right from Wrong by Examining Context

This guideline suggests that managers evaluate the specifics of the international situation confronting them when determining whether a particular management activity is ethical. Although some activities are wrong no matter where they take place, others are unethical in one setting but acceptable in another. For instance, the chemical EDB, a soil fungicide, is banned from use in the United States. In hot climates, however, it quickly becomes harmless through exposure to intense solar radiation and high soil temperatures. Thus, as long as EDB is monitored, companies may be able to use it ethically in certain parts of the world.

Most managers and management scholars agree that implementing ethical management practices across national borders enhances organizational success. Although following the guidelines just described does not guarantee that management action taken across national borders will be ethical, it should increase the probability of its ethicality.

TIPS FOR MANAGING AROUND THE GLOBE

Managing Expatriates

Managing a team of expatriates can be a challenging task. This is especially true if you're the manager who has sent a team of employees overseas to work for a year or more while you remain at home. Managing from a distance is never easy; managers can take some steps to manage expatriates effectively. Here are some questions those who are managing expatriates should ask:[59]

- What are the risks associated with the country expatriates are being assigned to?

- What are the health concerns of the expatriates, and what is the quality of the health-care system in the country?

- What weather patterns might be encountered in the country, such as hurricanes in the Caribbean?

- Will cell phones work in the country?

- Do the expatriates speak the local language?

- How will the expatriates travel within the country?

- Whom will the expatriates call if they encounter trouble?

Preparing Expatriates for Foreign Assignments

The trend of U.S. companies forming joint ventures and other strategic alliances that include foreign operations is increasing. As a result, the number of expatriates being sent from the United States to other countries is also rising.[60]

The somewhat casual approach of the past toward preparing expatriates for foreign duty is being replaced by the belief that these managers need special tools to be able to succeed in difficult foreign assignments.[61] To help expatriates adjust, home companies are providing assistance in finding homes and high-quality health care in host countries. Companies are also responding to expatriates' insistence that they need more help from home companies on career planning related to foreign assignments, career planning for spouses forced to go to the foreign assignment country, and better counseling for the personal challenges they will face during their foreign assignments.[62]

Many companies prepare their expatriates for foreign assignments by providing special training programs. Specific features of these programs vary from company to company, depending on the situation. Most of these programs, however, usually contain the following core elements:

- **Culture profiles**—Expatriates learn about the new culture in which they will be working.
- **Cultural adaptation**—Expatriates learn how to survive the difficulties of adjusting to a new culture.
- **Logistical information**—Expatriates learn basic information, such as personal safety, whom to call in an emergency, and how to write a check.
- **Application**—Expatriates learn about the specific organizational roles they will have.

Expatriates generally play a critical role in determining the success of an organization's foreign operations. The tremendous personal and professional adjustments that expatriates must make, however, can delay their effectiveness and efficiency in foreign settings. Sound training programs can lower the amount of time expatriates need to adjust and can thereby help them become productive more quickly.[63]

CHALLENGE CASE SUMMARY

As the Challenge Case showed, international management is essential to the future growth of KFC. The company's greatest expansion is occurring in China. Beginning in 1987, the company moved from just a single location to well over 5,000. It opens, on average, more than a store a day in the country. As it has grown beyond the boundaries of the United States, it has become a more multinational corporation—an organization with significant operations in more than one country. Managing such an organization is highly complex. The CEO and his team need to account for differences in economic conditions, people, levels of technology, market sizes, and laws. In doing so, the company must also account for the risks of investments in many different countries. Managers at KFC need to balance the risks against the market potential and prepare the company to manage the risks.

Careful planning is essential for a multinational company. At KFC, this function includes the company's needs for foreign purchasing, manufacturing, and distribution of food and supplies, as well as financing needs. The company also needs to identify the strengths and weaknesses that franchise owners will face in their local labor forces as well as the local demand for various kinds of fast food. It must determine what roles imports and exports will play in its food purchases, and it may need license agreements for some of its franchises, depending on local laws and customs.

There have been a few challenges for KFC in China, such as suppliers who were violating food safety standards. KFC's quick response to address these issues and find new suppliers shows that the company is demonstrating the management employability skill of ethics and social responsibility. The firm is using appropriate guiding principles to influence the way individuals and organizations behave within the society in which they operate.

A multinational company's organizational structure may be based on function, product, territory, customers, or manufacturing processes. The organizational structure of KFC is based on territories served. The company is owned by Yum! Brands, and the Yum! Brands China division is overseeing the growth throughout China. There are also Yum! Brands divisions in other parts of the world, such as Latin America, Africa, and Europe.

Influencing people in a multinational corporation such as KFC becomes increasingly complicated as the company extends its global presence. The cultures of people in the various locations where the restaurant operates differ. KFC acknowledges these differences in the different menu choices and service options it tailors for each locale. When corporate management travels to or works in other countries, managers benefit from having a working knowledge of the languages spoken and of the attitudes and needs that motivate people in each country. For example, rewards that motivate employees in Chinese KFC restaurants may be quite different from the rewards that are the most motivating in the United States.

MyLab Management Assessing Your Management Skill

If your instructor has assigned this activity, go to www.pearson.com/mylab/management to complete the exercise related to the Challenge Case.

DEVELOPING GLOBAL MANAGEMENT SKILL

This section is specially designed to help you develop global management skills. An individual's global management skill is based on an understanding of the concepts and the ability to apply those concepts. The following activities will help to enhance your global management skills in various organizational situations.

Class Preparation and Personal Study

To help you prepare for class, perform the activities outlined in this section. Performing these activities will help you enhance your classroom performance significantly.

Reflecting on Target Skill

On page 123, this chapter opens by presenting a target management skill along with a list of related objectives outlining knowledge and understanding that you should aim to acquire related to that skill. Review this target skill and the list of objectives to make sure that you've acquired all pertinent information within the chapter. If you do not feel that you've reached a particular objective(s), study related chapter coverage until you do.

Know Key Terms

Understanding the following key terms is critical to your understanding of chapter material. Define each of these terms. Refer to the page(s) referenced after a term to check your definition or to gain further insight regarding the term.

international management   **125**
domestic organizations   **127**
international organizations   **127**
multinational corporation   **128**
parent company   **130**
host country   **130**
expatriate   **131**
host-country national   **131**
third-country national   **131**
repatriation   **131**
planning   **132**
importing   **132**
exporting   **132**

Know How Management Concepts Relate

This section comprises activities that will further sharpen your understanding of management concepts. Answer essay questions as completely as possible.

5-1 Discuss three similarities and three differences between international versus transnational organizations.

5-2 List and define the three types of organization members found in multinational organizations. Discuss the contribution that each type can bring to creating the success of the organization.

5-3 In terms of international market agreements, distinguish between the European Union (EU) and the North American Free Trade Agreement (NAFTA). Are they very similar to or different from each other? Why should managers consider such agreements?

5-4 List and describe Hofstede's five dimensions of values in foreign cultures. Why do you think managers would find these useful when influencing employees?

MyLab Management
Personal Inventory Assessments

Go to www.pearson.com/mylab/management to complete the Personal Inventory Assessment related to this chapter.

Management Skills Exercises

Learning activities in this section are aimed at helping you develop global management skills.

MyLab Management
Discussion Questions

Go to www.pearson.com/mylab/management to complete the problems marked with this icon ⭐.

⭐ Cases

KFC Loves Global Growth

"KFC Opens a Store a Day in China" and its Challenge Case Summary were written to help you better understand the management concepts contained in this chapter. Answer the following discussion questions about the Challenge Case to understand how concepts relating to managing in the global arena can be applied in a company like KFC.

5-5 Do you think that at some point in your career you will become involved in international management? Explain.

5-6 Assuming that you are involved in managing a KFC in China, what challenges do you think would be the most difficult for you in improving this Chinese KFC's success? Why?

5-7 Evaluate the following statement: KFC can learn to manage its U.S. operations better by studying how successful competitive operations are managed in other countries.

Coca-Cola's Effort to Refresh the Whole World

Read the case and answer the questions that follow. Studying this case will help you better understand how concepts relating to global expansion can be applied in an organization such as the Coca-Cola Company.

People know Coca-Cola as a global brand. However, when the company entered the Indian market in the mid-1990s, it was the company's second try. Coca-Cola had operated there from 1950 until 1977, when it left with other Western firms in reaction to a law requiring foreign businesses to have Indian partners. A decade and a half later, the government relaxed restrictions on foreign companies, and the enormous population and economic growth lured Coca-Cola back. Now India has become one of the company's top 10 markets.

Coca-Cola reentered India by purchasing the brands and distribution system of an Indian soft-drink company. Despite this advantage, the return brought challenges. Employee turnover was high until Coca-Cola improved hiring and training. To build stronger business relations, it identified local sources for its materials and invested in farms selling key ingredients. It learned about its customers—for example, that young Indians are heavy users of mobile devices and that the small stores where most people shop have poor electric service and need help keeping drinks cold. The solution: company-provided, solar-powered coolers. Other problems have been more difficult to solve. Farmers are pushing back against efforts to open a new bottling plant. They also grumble that Coke is using too much water, causing shortages. Indeed, the water supply in India has decreased dramatically, although the farmers themselves may be contributing to the problem. Whatever the cause, the government is restricting water use and the locations of bottling plants.

Coca-Cola's CEO, Muhtar Kent, is well prepared to lead his company in facing these challenges. Kent has a global perspective from his childhood as the son of a Turkish diplomat. Besides living in Sweden, Iran, Poland, Thailand, and the United States, Kent lived two years in New Delhi, India, when his father was posted there. He saw India as a beautiful and exciting—but also complex and challenging—place. Later, as a manager, he learned that doing business there requires flexibility. Just as the company has been creative in adapting its distribution to the needs of India's small merchants, advertising combines corporate-wide themes with locally tailored messages. In a recent television ad, Indian movie stars present a story of young people experiencing moments of joy; Coke's "Open Happiness" theme is about a universal emotion.

Efforts such as these have helped to make Coca-Cola the world's largest beverage company. Headquartered in Atlanta, Georgia, it sells products in more than 200 countries. Along with its signature cola, the company sells more than 3,500 products, including brands such as Dasani, Minute Maid, Powerade, Sprite, and Vitaminwater.

Because of Coke's global presence, the company has a global perspective on social responsibility. It identifies the needs of the communities where it operates and the actions that will benefit both the company and those communities. For example, by extending electric power grids into Indian villages, it makes life more comfortable while making it easier for stores to sell cold soft drinks. By addressing climate change, it is also addressing drought and the disruptions to its supply of sugar beets and sugar cane that are caused by changes to regional weather patterns. The company is especially concerned about water conservation. In India, it intends to conserve water, locate plants only where there is sufficient water, and provide more support to local communities. Other efforts at sustainability include recycling of plastics and reduction of carbon emissions.

These efforts preserve Coca-Cola's standing as a respected brand and a multimillion-dollar business. The global scope is essential, as North American consumers have increasingly cut back on soda consumption. Coca-Cola's fastest growth has come from international markets, especially China and India. Today, if a consumer "opens happiness" in a bottle of Coke, he or she could be anywhere in the world.[64]

Questions

5-8 Based on the description in the case, is Coca-Cola Company a domestic, international, multinational, or transnational organization? Why?

5-9 How can an understanding of India's culture help a Coca-Cola manager succeed there?

5-10 Besides the measures described, what else can Coca-Cola do to maintain ethical conduct in the countries where it operates?

Experiential Exercises

Understanding Other Cultures

Directions. Read the following scenario and then perform the listed activities. Your instructor may want you to perform the activities as an individual or within groups. Follow all of your instructor's directions carefully.

Many growing U.S. companies find that international expansion is a key part of their business plan. There are a variety of reasons for this, such as dilution of the U.S. market, tax advantages, and cost savings.

You work for a manufacturing firm producing soy-based, sugar-free candy that is marketed as a healthy alternative for typical sweet treats. Your company has been in business for 15 years and has done very well in the United States. Now, you are looking at expanding operations internationally. Currently, you have three manufacturing facilities across the United States, with each plant consisting of approximately 400 employees. Though you could export your product, you have made the decision to build a new facility in a foreign country because you feel there may be some cost savings.

First, choose a country for your new manufacturing plant. Try to think of one where you will enjoy some cost savings in either labor or raw materials. Next, list at least 10 details you would need to know about the country, its laws, and culture. You may need to do some research on your selected country and its favorable or unfavorable business environment. Be sure also to address the quality and availability of the labor market for the part of the world you are focusing on.

You and Your Career

You have just taken a role in sales and marketing for a major international property developer. The company will be headquartered in China and will open for business in less than three months. It is hoped that Chinese nationals will be trained as soon as possible to take on many of the roles.

You know that China is a diverse and vibrant business environment; however, few of the Europeans earmarked for transfer to the new headquarters have any experience or understanding of the Far East.

You know that one of your roles will be to manage a group of Chinese trainees, so you carried out some research to help you understand the likely work ethics of Chinese workers:

- Punctuality is extremely important (it is something of a virtue)
- Hard work and determination are common as they are believed to be the key to success
- Work is results-driven (over 2,000 hours worked per year is not uncommon)
- There is a perception that hard work is superior to talent
- Perfection is much sought-after

You will need to carry out some more research on Chinese employees to understand how you can train them in the most effective way.

5-11   Based your research, is what you have found about Chinese culture important for building your career at this company? Explain.

5-12   With this new understanding of the culture, would you change the way you manage Chinese people while in China? How?

Building Your Management Skills Portfolio

Your management skills portfolio is a collection of activities specially designed to demonstrate your management knowledge and skill. Be sure to save your work. You can use this material while preparing for an interview.

The portfolio activity for this chapter is Managing a Business in India. Study this information and complete the exercises that follow.

You are a Western-educated business manager who has been working in the Middle East for the past two years. Your Dubai-based energy sector business has just bought a solar panel manufacturing plant in India. You know very little about Indian business practices, but your company's intention is not to impose Middle Eastern business norms and practices but to encourage the continuation of an Indian approach (which has proved successful so far in the Indian market). You have been given a middle-management post and have been reading as much as possible about how Indian business operates. Based on your study, you have come up with the following points about the different ways in which Middle Eastern and Indian companies function:

- Middle Eastern companies tend not to be too concerned about punctuality, whereas in India it is appreciated (but not always reciprocated)
- Middle Eastern companies prefer close, personal interaction, and eye contact in conversations, whereas distance is preferred and sustained eye contact is not the norm in India.
- Middle Eastern companies value tact and find disagreement embarrassing, whereas in India the word "no" is too negative and "maybe" suggests disagreement—both find disagreement problematic, but in different ways.
- Middle Eastern employees usually have 32 days' vacation a year, whereas in India, factory workers have 12–24 days.
- Middle Eastern companies are beginning the process of being decentralized, with some delegation, whereas Indian companies tend favor top-down decision-making.

Exercise 1: Based on the information given, list three major challenges you will face as a manager in India and the steps you will take to meet these challenges.

Challenge 1: _____

What I will do to meet Challenge 1:

_____

_____

_____

Challenge 2: _____

What I will do to meet Challenge 2:

_____

_____

_____

Challenge 3: _____

What I will do to meet Challenge 3:

_____

_____

Exercise 2: Based on the information given, to be successful in India, you will probably have to change, to some extent, the way you plan, organize, influence, and control. List the changes for each management function you may have to make.

Changes to the way I will plan in India:

_____

_____

_____

Changes to the way I will organize in India:

_____

_____

_____

Changes to the way I will influence people in India:

_____

_____

_____

Changes to the way I will control in India:

_____

_____

_____

Exercise 3: Do you think you will be successful in this job as a manager in India? Why or why not?

_____

_____

_____

Exercise 4: Overall, what did you learn from this experience?

_____

_____

_____

MyLab Management
Writing Assignments
If your instructor has assigned this activity, go to www.pearson.com/mylab/management for the following assisted-graded writing assignments:
Assisted-Grading Questions
5-13 What are the risks and rewards of operating a multinational organization?
5-14 Discuss the role of "examining context" in maintaining ethical practices in international management situations.

Endnotes

1. "Kentucky Fried China: Colonel Sander's Success in the East," InternshipsChina, http://internshipschina.com/kentucky-fried-china-colonel-sanders-success-east/.

2. David Bell and Mary L. Shelman, "KFC's Radical Approach to China," *Harvard Business Review* 89, no. 11 (November 2011): 137–142.

3. For insights regarding ethical issues related to business opportunities in China, see Davis A. Krueger, "Ethical Reflections on the Opportunities and Challenges for International Business in China," *Journal of Business Ethics* 89 (November 2009): 145.

4. "Dossier: Telecommunications in Asia, Malaysia, Thailand," *International Business Newsletter* (June 1993): 12.

5. Jean J. Boddewyn, Brian Toyne, and Zaida L Martinez, "The Meanings of International Management," *Management International Review* 44, no. 2 (Second Quarter 2004): 195–212.

6. For a summary of recent developments in international management, see Steve Werner, "Recent Developments in International Management Research: A Review of 20 Top Management Journals," *Journal of Management* 28 (2002): 277.

7. Robert N. Lussier, Robert W. Baeder, and Joel Corman, "Measuring Global Practices: Global Strategic Planning through Company Situational Analysis," *Business Horizons* 37 (September/October 1994): 56–63. For a detailed look at Hitachi Maxell, a successful internationally managed company, see Ray Moorcroft, "International Management in Action," *British Journal of Administrative Management* (March/April 2001): 12–13.

8. Annie Gasparro, "Dominos Is Growing Internationally," *Wall Street Journal* [Eastern edition], June 15, 2011.

9. Natasha Gural, "JP Morgan Goes Global with Corporate Banking," *Forbes*, http://www.forbes.com, accessed January 29, 2010.

10. U.S. Bureau of Economic Analysis.

11. U.S. Bureau of Economic Analysis.

12. U.S. Bureau of Economic Analysis.

13. Mary Zellmer-Bruhn and Cristina Gibson, "Multinational Organizations Context: Implications for Team Learning and Performance," *Academy of Management Journal* 49, no. 3 (June 2006): 501–518.

14. For additional information regarding various forms of organization based on international involvement, see Arvind Phatak, *International Dimensions of Management* (Boston: Kent, 1993).

15. "Nu Horizons Electronics," *Fortune* (June 13, 1994): 121. For an empirical study assessing the mobility of knowledge within a multinational corporation, see Anil K. Gupta and Vijay Govindarajan, "Knowledge Flows within Multinational Corporations," *Strategic Management Journal* 21, no. 4 (April 2000): 473–496.

16. "Arrow Electronics Acquires Nu Horizons Electronics," *The Street*, 2010.

17. U.S. Department of Commerce, *The Multinational Corporation: Studies on U.S. Foreign Investment* (Washington, DC: Government Printing Office).

18. Benjamin Gomes-Casseres, "Group versus Group: How Alliance Networks Compete," *Harvard Business Review* 72 (July/August 1994): 62–74. For additional information about Alfred Zeien see http://www.hbs.edu/leadership/20th-century-leaders/Pages/details.aspx?profile=alfred_m_zeien.

19. Company website, http://www.brkelectronics.com, accessed May 3, 2017.

20. This section is based on foundation material in Richard D. Robinson, *International Management* (New York: Holt, Rinehart & Winston, 1967), 3–5. For a focus on the complexity of the impact of poverty on ethical values from country to country, see Tendai Chikweche and Richard Fletcher, "Entrepreneurship and Ethics under Extreme Conditions of Poverty: Exploring the Realities," *Society and Business Review* 12, no. 1 (2017): 4–19.

21. 1971 Survey of National Foreign Trade Council, cited in Frederick D. Sturdivant, *Business and Society: A Managerial Approach* (Homewood, IL: Richard D. Irwin, 1977), 425.

22. For discussion on using banks to help mitigate this risk, see Friederike Niepmann and Tim Schmidt-Eisenlohr, "International Trade, Risk, and the Role of Banks," *Journal of International Economics* 107 (July 2017): 111–126.

23. "NCR's Standard Contract Clause," *Harvard Business Review* 72 (May/June 1994): 125; for additional information on mediation, see James C. Fruend, "Three's a Crowd—How to Resolve a Knotty Multi-Party Dispute through Mediation," *The Business Lawyer* 64, no. 2 (February 2009): 359.

24. For a discussion of family adjustments as a major factor in expatriate failure, see Sandra L. Fisher, Michael E. Wasserman, and Jennifer Palthe, "Management Practices for On-Site Consultants: Lessons Learned from the Expatriate Experience," *Consulting Psychology Journal: Practice and Research* 59, no. 1 (March 2007): 17.

25. For an interesting article discussing the work relationship between expatriates and host-country nationals, see Charles M. Vance and Yongsun Paik, "Forms of Host-Country National Learning for Enhanced MNC Absorptive Capacity," *Journal of Managerial Psychology* 20, no. 7 (2005): 590–606.

26. Jan Selmer, "Cross-Cultural Training and Expatriate Adjustment in China: Western Joint Venture Managers," *Personnel Review* 34, no. 1 (2005): 68–84.

27. For a look at the challenges facing women expatriates, see Babita Mathur-Helm, "Expatriate Women Managers: At the Crossroads of Success, Challenges and Career Goals," *Women in Management Journal* 17 (2002): 18.

28. Tim Cameron, "7 Innocent Gestures That Can Get You Killed Overseas," cracked.com, June 4, 2008.

29. "Winebow Appointed as Exclusive U.S. Importer of Ceretto," *PR Newswire* (January 30, 2013). For a discussion of the challenges associated with cross-cultural work assignments and the competencies required to meet the challenges, see Lynn S. Paine, "The China Rules," *Harvard Business Review* (June 2010); Mansour Javidan, Mary Teagarden, and David Bowen, "Managing Yourself: Making It Overseas," *Harvard Business Review* (April 2010).

30. For a review of the possible effects of repatriation, see Margaret A. Shaffer, David Harrison, A. Black Stewart, and Lori Ferandi, "The Persistent Myth of High Expatriate Failure Rates: A Reappraisal," *Journal of Applied Psychology* 9, no. 1 (January 2006): 109–135.

31. For an interesting discussion of repatriation in a Spanish context, see Ma Eugenia Sánchez Vidal, Raquel Sanz Valle, and Ma Isabel Barba Aragón, "Analysis of the Repatriation Adjustment Process in the Spanish Context," *International Journal of Manpower* 31, no. 1 (2010): 21.

32. David C. Martin and John J. Anthony, "The Repatriation and Retention of Employees: Factors Leading to Successful Programs," *International Journal of Management* 23, no. 3 (September 2006): 620–631.

33. "Winebow Appointed as Exclusive U.S. Importer of Ceretto," *PR Newswire*, January 30, 2013.

34. "Ford to Expand Exports from India as Demand Slows," *Mint* [New Delhi], November 29, 2013.

35. For a discussion of Tosoh Corporation's continued growing international footprint, see "$23.41 Billion Toluene Market—Global Forecast to 2021: Growing Petrochemical (Aromatics) Industry in

Asian Countries—Research and Markets," *PR Newswire*, January 23, 2017.

36. Leonard Berkowitz, "Supreme Court Says You Can License and Sue," *Research Technology Management* 50, no. 2 (March/April 2007): 9.

37. "Researchers Submit Patent Application, Novel Metallosilicates, Processes for Producing the Same, Nitrogen Oxide Removal Catalyst, Process for Producing the Same, and Method for Removing Nitrogen Oxide," *Journal of Transportation* (September 8, 2012): 2821.

38. Robert Neff, "The Japanese Are Back—But There's a Difference," *BusinessWeek*, Industrial/Technology Edition (October 31, 1994): 58–59.

39. For insights on adding organizational value through international joint ventures, see Iris Berdrow and Henry Lane, "International Joint Ventures: Creating Value through Successful Knowledge Management," *Journal of World Business* 38 (2003): 15; see also Lifeng Geng, "Ownership and International Joint Ventures' Level of Expatriate Managers," *Journal of American Academy of Business* 4 (2004): 75.

40. Shyam Sunder, "Uniform Financial Reporting Standards," *The CPA Journal* 77, no. 4 (April 2007): 6, 8–9.

41. European Union Issues Statement on UK Notification to Leave EU, *Targeted News Service*, March 30, 2017.

42. For an interesting article discussing how NAFTA countries settle disputes among themselves, see John H. Knox, "The 2005 Activity of the NAFTA Tribunals," *The American Journal of International Law* 100, no. 2 (April 2006): 429–442.

43. Fritz Lodge, "Trump Trade: The Future of NAFTA," *The CIPHER Brief*, December 20, 2016.

44. For an interesting discussion of organizing to go global, see Peter W. Liesch, Peter J. Buckley, Bernard L. Simonin, and Gary Knight, "Organizing the Modern Firm in the Worldwide Market for Market Transactions," *Management International Review* 52, no. 1 (February 2012): 3–21.

45. For excellent discussion of the possible impact of geocentric thought on executive staffing and multinational corporation strategies, see: Sangeetha Lakshman, C. Lakshman, and Christophe Estay, "The Relationship between MNCs' Strategies and Executive Staffing," *International Journal of Organizational Analysis* 25, no. 2 (2017).

46. Yan Tian, "Communicating with Local Publics: A Case Study of Coca-Cola's Chinese Web Site," *Corporate Communications* 11, no. 1 (2006): 13–22.

47. Geert Hofstede, "Motivation, Leadership, and Organization: Do American Theories Apply Abroad?," *Organizational Dynamics* 9 (Summer 1980): 42–63; for an investigation of the relevance of Hofstede's ideas in Jordan, see Mahmud Alkailani, Islam A. Azzam, and Abdel Baset Athamneh, "Replicating Hofstede in Jordan: Ungeneralized, Reevaluating the Jordanian Culture," *International Business Research* 5, no. 4 (April 2012): 71–80.

48. Geert Hofstede, *Geert Culture's Consequences: International Differences in Work-Related Values* (Beverly Hills, CA: Sage, 1980); Hofstede, *Geert Culture's Consequences: Comparing Values, Behaviors, Institutions, and Organizations across Nations*, 2nd ed. (London, England: Sage, 2001).

49. "How Cultural Differences Impact International Business in 2017," Hult International Business School, http://www.hult.edu/news/cultural-differences-impact-international-business/.

50. Vas Taras, Bradley L. Kirkman, and Piers Steel, "Examining the Impact of Culture's Consequences: A Three-Decade, Multilevel, Meta-Analytic Review of Hofstede's Cultural Value Dimensions," *Journal of Applied Psychology* 95, no.3 (2010): 405–439.

51. Robert J. House, Paul J. Hanges, Mansour Javidan, and Peter Dorfman, *Culture, Leadership, and Organizations: The GLOBE Study of 62 Societies* (Thousand Oaks, CA: Sage, 2004).

52. Jake Kanter, "Procurement at Kimberly-Clark Goes Global," Supply Management.com, March 23, 2010, http://www.supplymanagement.com.

53. "TMR Updates on the Data Center Networking Market," *Wireless News*, March 20, 2017.

54. For further information about developing global organizations, see Philip Harris, "European Challenge: Developing Global Organizations," *European Business Review* 14 (2002): 416; see also Jonathon Cummings, "Work Groups, Structural Diversity, and Knowledge Sharing in a Global Organization," *Management Science* 50 (2004): 352.

55. To gain a feel for the broad range of activities occurring at a transnational company such as Nestlé, study the career of Paul Grimwood: "Paul Grimwood—Chairman and CEO, Nestle USA, Nestle SA," *Boardroom Insiders Profiles* (San Francisco: Boardroom Insiders, Inc., 2016).

56. Byeong-Seon Yoon, "Who Is Threatening Our Dinner Table? The Power of Transnational Agribusiness," *Monthly Review* 58, no. 6 (November 2006): 56–64.

57. This section is mainly based on Thomas Donaldson, "Values in Tension: Ethics away from Home," *Harvard Business Review* 74, no. 5 (September/October 1996): 48–62.

58. Max Nisen, "How Nike Solved Its Sweatshop Problem," BusinessInsider.com, May 9, 2013; Layna Mosley, "Workers' Rights in Global Value Chains: Possibilities for Protection and Peril," *Journal of New Political Economy* 22, no. 2 (2017).

59. Timothy Daniel, "Travel and Risk: Remember 'The W's' to Keep Travelers Safe," *Solutions for Enterprise Security Leaders* 50, no. 6 (June 2013): 40–42.

60. Lyman Stone, "In an Age of Global Citizenship, American Expatriates Increase," thefederalist.com, May 4, 2015.

61. Stephen J. Armstrong and Yan Li, "A Study of Anglo Expatriate Managers' Learning, Knowledge Acquisition, and Adjustment in Multinational Companies in China," *Academy of Management Learning & Education* 16, no. 1 (March 1, 2017): 1–22.

62. A number of websites are now dedicated to the subject of expatriate life and provide different viewpoints through blogs, articles, reports, tips for pursuing the expatriate life, and more. Examples include Expat Exchange and Future Expats Forum.

63. For a different view of the long-term value expatriates bring to organizational performance, see Yulin Fang, Guo-Liang Frank Jiang, Shige Makino, and Paul W. Beamish, "Multinational Firm Knowledge, Use of Expatriates, and Foreign Subsidiary Performance," *Journal of Management Studies* 47, no. 1 (January 2010): 27–54.

64. Muhtar Kent, "Thinking Outside the Bottle," *McKinsey & Company Insights and Publications*, December 2013, http://www.mckinsey.com/insights; Coca-Cola Company, "Coca-Cola at a Glance," Our Company, http://www.coca-colacompany.com, accessed March 10, 2014; Jay Moye, "20 Years Later: A Look Back at Coke's Dramatic 1993 Return to India," Coca-Cola Company: Stories, December 6, 2013, http://www.coca-colacompany.com/stories; "Coca Cola Takes Earthy, Small Town Route; Gets Farhan and Deepika to Open 'Small Joys,'" *Campaign India*, February 28, 2014, http://www.campaignindia.in; Amy Kazmin, "Coke Bottles Go Unfilled in Central India," *Financial Times*, February 2, 2014, http://www.ft.com; Agence France-Presse, "Indian Authorities Threaten to Demolish Coca-Cola Plant," *Industry Week*, January 24, 2014, http://www.industryweek.com; Coral Davenport, "Industry Awakens to Threat of Climate Change," *New York Times*, January 23, 2014, http://www.nytimes.com; Siddharth Cavale, "Coke Revenue Misses Estimates as Soda Sales Slow," Reuters, February 18, 2014, http://www.reuters.com.

Creativity and Innovation

TARGET SKILL

Creativity and Innovation Skill: the ability to generate original ideas or new perspectives on existing ideas and to take steps to implement these new ideas

CREATIVITY AND INNOVATION SKILL AND YOUR CAREER

Creativity and innovation skill will be of great value to you in enhancing your career. This skill can help you generate, modify, and implement new ideas. The ability to generate, modify, and implement new ideas contributes to organizational success, builds your image as a competent manager, makes you valuable to your organization, and supports promotions as you build your career.

OBJECTIVES

To help build my *creativity and innovation skill*, when studying this chapter, I will attempt to acquire:

6-1 A definition of *creativity* and an awareness of its importance in organizations

6-2 Insights into the drivers of individual creativity

6-3 Guidelines on how to increase creativity in organizations

6-4 A definition of innovation and an understanding of the relationship between creativity and innovation

6-5 An awareness of the innovation process

6-6 An understanding of total quality as a base for spawning creative ideas

6-7 An understanding of the primary components of the quality improvement process

---

MyLab Management Chapter Warm Up

If your instructor has assigned this activity, go to www.pearson.com/mylab/management to complete the chapter warm up.

CHALLENGE CASE

Olde Peninsula Brings Brewpub Innovation to Kalamazoo

Kalamazoo, in the southwestern part of the state of Michigan, sits about equidistant from Detroit and Chicago. It's a relatively small city with 76,000 citizens.[1] Since the 1990s, however, the town has seen a rise in the number of microbreweries and brewpubs. A microbrewery is an establishment that brews its own beer but can sell only those creations to its customers; in other words, it cannot sell any other manufacturers' products, wine, or alcohol. A brewpub, on the other hand, brews its own beer, typically has a restaurant, and can also sell beer from other producers, as well as sell wine and cocktails.

The first brewpub in the city was Olde Peninsula Brewpub and Restaurant, which was founded in 1996. When it first appeared, customers were confused. "The downtown area was just beginning to become revitalized," says founder Steve Blinn. "The city was doing well at bringing office tenants to downtown, but not restaurants. We knew that if the city brought people, then they would eat!" But at the same time he was establishing Olde Peninsula, the large chain restaurants were also entering the market. Companies like Applebee's and Outback Steakhouse were gaining a foothold among customers. "Initially, we were constantly compared to these cookie-cutter places," recalls Blinn. "Around the time we started, dual-income families with busy lifestyles just wanted to go out to eat because they were too busy to cook at home."

What Blinn was attempting to do in 1996 was introduce an innovative concept that would not be like all the other restaurants in Kalamazoo. "Our motto has always been," says Blinn, "step back in time, relax and enjoy food the way it is supposed to be cooked." Before it became a marketing phenomenon, Olde Peninsula was sourcing local ingredients and letting customers know that their food was fresh, cooked to order, and could be delivered to their table just as quickly as any of the chains. And, unlike the big chains, Olde Peninsula is in a very old building—it was built in 1874. "Our competitors were opening brand new, ultra-modern buildings on developing corners in suburban neighborhoods," Blinn says. "We, on the other hand, kept the old floors, doors, ceiling, fixtures, and basically anything else we could to maintain the charm of the structure and to keep our costs of renovation down." When they first opened, customers would walk in and say, "Wow, everything looks so old," and Blinn would reply, "Perfect!"

Maciej Maksymowicz/123RF

Olde Peninsula Brewpub in Kalamazoo, Michigan is a great example of the growth of the brewpub, which is a restaurant or pub that brews beer on its premises. Steve Blinn, founder of Olde Peninsula, has developed some creative ways to lead innovation at his establishment.

Blinn graduated with a marketing degree from Western Michigan University, and his first job after college was working in sales for a local beer distributor. "I had a challenge trying to sell so-called 'aging' brands of beer like Pabst, Old Milwaukee, Beck's, and Foster's," says Blinn. Then, the owner of the distributing company decided to take a chance on craft beer like Sam Adams, Sierra Nevada, Pete's Wicked Ale, and many more. "This is when I learned about craft beer and it opened my eyes to what beer should be," remembers Blinn. As he was learning more about the art of craft beer, he and his wife, Marie, and took a trip to Chicago, where they stumbled upon a restaurant and brewery in an old part of town called Goose Island. "As soon as we entered," Blinn says, "my wife and I knew this was exactly the kind of brewpub we wanted to bring to Kalamazoo."

Certainly, Blinn was innovative in 1996 by bringing the brewpub concept to Kalamazoo, but with so many other breweries and brewpubs for customers to choose from today, he has to continue innovations and encourage creativity among his team. "About 70 percent of our income," Blinn reveals, "is from food. We have to constantly keep up with dining trends and be ahead of our competitors." Recently, the brewpub introduced flat-bread sandwiches, which consists of warm pita bread with the customer's favorite topping along with a side of beer-battered fries, pub chips, or onion rings. Some choices for flatbread sandwiches include pulled pork, turkey bacon cheddar, and house-made chicken salad. These flatbread sandwiches have been a hit for Blinn and his team. In addition to the extensive made-from-scratch menu of food, the brewpub offers a wide variety of craft beers with clever names like Rockin' Razberry Wheat, Stout Chocula, and Haymarket Cream Ale. And the brewery part of the business also stays innovative with its hot pepper–infused creations, which age the beer in a variety of hot peppers. Seasonal beers are also being crafted throughout the year.

The ever-present challenge for Blinn is to remain innovative with new food and beer offerings because it is a small single-location business competing against national chains with millions of dollars in advertising money at their disposal. According to Blinn, "When it comes to marketing, we educate our customers on what a brewpub is, but we also market our relaxing atmosphere, consistently good food, top notch service, and of course, a superb selection of beverages."[2]

THE CREATIVITY AND INNOVATION CHALLENGE

The Challenge Case discusses how Steve Blinn at Olde Peninsula Brewpub and Restaurant has used innovation to help it compete against larger, national chains. The case also points out that, although a business may be innovative initially, it must always be seeking creative and innovative offerings to remain competitive. This chapter discusses concepts to help managers such as Steve Blinn find creative ways to meet such organizational challenges. Topics covered are creativity, innovation, and total quality management as a catalyst for creativity and innovation.

Creativity

This chapter begins with a focus on *creativity*. A definition of creativity, the importance of creativity in organizations, creativity in individuals, and increasing creativity in organizations are discussed in the following sections.

6-1 A definition of *creativity* and an awareness of its importance in organizations

Defining Creativity

Creativity is the ability to generate original ideas or new perspectives on existing ideas.[3] In today's society, the term *creativity* often sparks thoughts of the arts and literature of highly original contributions such as Michelangelo's work on the figure of *David*, and Herman Melville's *Billy Budd*.

Although how best to define creativity from a management viewpoint may be somewhat controversial, creativity in organizations does indeed relate to generating original ideas or new perspectives on existing ideas.[4] Originality or newness, however, is not enough when analyzing creativity from an organizational perspective; an idea must also be useful and actionable. Overall, an idea must have a desirable impact on how organizational goals are accomplished. That is, an idea must be evaluated on whether it has a positive impact on critical organizational factors such as productivity, communication, coordination, or product quality.

Creativity in Organizations

Creativity involves seeing issues from different angles and breaking away from old rules and norms, which bind us to traditional methods of accomplishing tasks. Creativity, on the other hand, allows us to be diverse and helps us find new answers and solutions to problems, both old and new.[5]

The relationship between breaking away from old rules and norms for accomplishing tasks and meeting critical organizational challenges is obvious. For example, many managers face the daily challenge of motivating organization members and, as a result, are constantly searching for new ways to encourage employees to be more committed to their work. In addition, managers often face the challenge of dealing more effectively with competitors and thus are frequently searching for new ways to increase the quality of their products or to develop new and more competitive products. Overall, meeting the challenges of motivating organization members or dealing more effectively with competitors is necessary to ensure organizational success. Because creativity is the source of new ideas on how to meet such challenges, managers should view creativity as a vital element in ensuring the success of their organization.

Creativity in Individuals

6-2 Insights into the drivers of individual creativity

Within each individual, creativity is a function of three components. These components are expertise, creative thinking skills, and motivation. **Figure 6.1** illustrates these three components and depicts how, when they overlap, they result in creativity.

Expertise, as depicted in Figure 6.1, is everything that an individual knows and can do in the broad domain of his or her work. This knowledge pertains to work-related techniques and procedures as well as to a thorough understanding of overall work circumstances. Take, for example, a produce worker in a supermarket. Her expertise includes the basic abilities of trimming and cleaning fresh fruits and vegetables, constructing appealing displays that encourage customers to buy the produce, and building customer relations. As with all organization members, the abilities of this produce worker can be acquired through formal education, experience, and interactions with peers and other professionals.

Creative thinking is the capacity to combine existing ideas in new arrangements. Overall, creative thinking determines how flexibly and imaginatively individuals approach problems. For example, the produce worker will tend to be more creative if she feels comfortable disagreeing with people about how the produce department presently functions. Such disagreement will often result in new thoughts about how to improve the department, such as how to keep produce fresher for longer periods. In addition, she will tend to have more creative success if she keeps persevering to deal with and solve department problems, such as buying new technology to keep produce cool, rather than always looking for quick solutions. This continual attention to problems will afford the produce worker the vigilance necessary to generate creative solutions to complex organizational problems.

Motivation, as depicted in Figure 6.1, refers to an individual's need or passion to be creative. If an individual feels a need to be creative, that individual is more likely to be creative. Expertise and creative thinking are the individual's raw materials for being creative, but only motivation will determine whether that individual will actually be creative. An individual can be driven to be creative either extrinsically, through organizational rewards and punishments, or intrinsically, through personal interest and passion related to a situation.

Activision CEO Bobby Kotick is an example of an individual who is driven, both extrinsically and intrinsically, to succeed. A video game enthusiast since childhood, Kotick bought video game company Activision when it was called Mediagenic. He not only restored the company's original name but also restored its culture to one that rewards game developers for their creativity and diligence. Although Activision grows by acquiring other video game developers, it strives to nurture and preserve the unique culture of each acquired company and its talented workforce.[6]

People are usually most creative when they are motivated by personal interest, satisfaction, and the challenge of the work. Continuing with our supermarket example, the produce worker might have the expertise and critical thinking necessary to be creative, but she will probably not be creative unless she is so motivated. Generally, the produce worker will be more motivated to be creative if she is personally interested in the supermarket's problems, tends to be personally satisfied by solving these problems, and sees solving the problems as challenging.

Figure 6.1

The three components of creativity

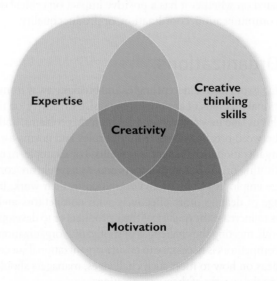

PRACTICAL CHALLENGE: ENABLING CREATIVITY

UN Development Program Backs Creative Responses to Crises

In ordinary circumstances, managers might struggle to spark employees' creativity. In a disaster, however, conditions provide more than enough motivation to spark creativity. The challenge then becomes locating resources. The United Nations Development Program (UNDP) helped meet that challenge by supporting reconstruction after the 2004 tsunami that killed 170,000 in Indonesia and the 2013 typhoon that killed thousands in the Philippines and left 4 million homeless.

Along with needing food, water, and shelter, survivors faced a huge problem: The storm had turned homes, workplaces, vehicles, and trees into mountains of debris. The UNDP paid local people to carry the trash away, sort through it, and develop creative ways to reuse it. In so doing, it created jobs and enabled the founding of new businesses. Tim Walsh—a former chemical engineer, current environmental consultant, and volunteer project manager with UNDP—sees potential everywhere. By training carpenters, UNDP enables them to salvage timber and produce lumber from uprooted trees to make furniture. Providing equipment such as a shredder, an extruder, and a blow molder allows people to recycle plastic trash to make bags, string, buckets, and more.[7]

Increasing Creativity in Organizations

As discussed, creativity is a critical ingredient for meeting challenges in organizations of all types. Accordingly, managers should conscientiously take specific actions aimed at building creativity in organizations. To encourage creativity in organizations, managers can take the steps discussed in the following sections.[8]

6-3 Guidelines on how to increase creativity in organizations

Challenge Workers   Of all the steps that managers can take to stimulate creativity, perhaps the most effective is providing organization members with an appropriate level of job-related challenge. When people feel appropriately challenged, they seem almost naturally to search for new creative ideas to help perform a job in an improved way. However, people should not be placed in jobs that are too simple or too difficult for them. If organization members have jobs that stretch their abilities too little, they can easily become bored on the job and distracted from being creative. If a job stretches worker abilities too much, workers can feel overwhelmed and are therefore not inclined to generate creative solutions to job-related problems. Managers must strive to understand both organization members and their jobs in order to ensure that workers are challenged at the level that encourages creative solutions for meeting job challenges.

Establish Worker Autonomy   People tend to be more creative in their jobs when they have some freedom to affect the process they have to use to perform their jobs. This freedom should not be provided, of course, unless organization members have a clear understanding of the work goals to be accomplished. Without such understanding, organization member creativity will lack the internal guidance needed to promote organizational success. Overall, creativity is used to the best advantage of organizations when members understand the work goals to be accomplished and can exercise some freedom in determining the best ways to accomplish those goals.

Afford Time for Accomplishing Work   Having appropriate amounts of time is commonly discussed as a critical resource for fueling creativity in organization members. Without enough time in which to perform a job appropriately, organization members might be so engaged in performing the job that generating creative solutions to job-related problems is reduced. Managers who issue unnecessarily tight deadlines to push organization members to reach greater levels of production can cause employees to feel simultaneously overly managed and helpless in terms of being creative.

Figure 6.2

A matrix comparing time pressure and the likelihood of creative thinking

Time Pressure

	Low	High
High	Creative thinking under low time pressure is more likely when people feel as if they are on an expedition. They • show creative thinking that is more oriented toward generating or exploring ideas than identifying problems. • tend to collaborate with one person rather than with a group.	Creative thinking under extreme time pressure is more likely when people feel as if they are on a mission. They • can focus on one activity for a significant part of the day because they are undisturbed or protected. • believe that they are doing important work and report feeling positively challenged by and involved in the work. • show creative thinking that is equally oriented toward identifying problems and generating or exploring ideas.
Low	Creative thinking under low time pressure is unlikely when people feel as if they are on autopilot. They • receive little encouragement from senior management to be creative. • tend to have more meetings and discussions with groups rather than with individuals. • engage in less collaborative work overall.	Creative thinking under extreme time pressure is unlikely when people feel as if they are on a treadmill. They • feel distracted. • experience a highly fragmented workday, with many different activities. • don't get the sense that the work they are doing is important. • feel more pressed for time than when they are "on a mission" even though they work the same number of hours. • tend to have more meetings and discussions with groups rather than with individuals. • experience lots of last-minute changes in their plans and schedules.

Likelihood of Creative Thinking

In the past, many managers believed that organization members usually generate their best creative ideas when operating under tight time constraints. Based on this belief, managers imposed tight deadlines as a tactic for encouraging creativity in organizations. More recent research suggests, however, that time pressures can actually affect creativity in different ways, depending on other organizational conditions.[9]

The time pressure–creativity matrix presented in **Figure 6.2** illustrates that managers can either encourage or discourage the likelihood of creative thinking in organizations, depending on how high time pressure and low time pressure are combined with various organizational factors. According to this matrix, given the condition of low time pressure, the likelihood of creativity in an organization might be low if workers feel they're *on autopilot* and get little encouragement from management to be creative. Under the same low time pressure condition, however, the likelihood of creativity in an organization might be high if people feel they're *on an expedition* and thereby are characterized by having creativity geared toward exploring ideas.

High time pressure is also examined in Figure 6.2. Given a high time pressure condition, the likelihood of creativity in an organization might be high if people feel they're *on a mission* to discover solutions to job-related problems. Under the same high time pressure condition, however, the likelihood of creativity in an organization might be low if people feel they're *on a treadmill* and commonly experience extensive last-minute changes to schedules and plans.

Establish Diverse Work Groups

Work groups that are characterized by members with a diversity of perspectives and backgrounds tend to be more creative than groups characterized by members who have similar backgrounds and perspectives. Diversity by itself, however, is simply not enough. To complement this diversity, members of a work group should be excited about accomplishing the group's work goal(s), be willing to help each other through difficult periods and setbacks, and recognize and respect the differences among the unique knowledge and perspectives that group members possess.[10]

Personally Encourage Workers   As with any other desirable behavior in organizations, managers should personally encourage organization members to be creative. Such encouragement may take many different forms and range from a verbal thank you to awarding a creative achievement certificate of appreciation, or to holding a creativity appreciation luncheon.

Because managers are extremely busy and under constant pressure to achieve results, they can be easily distracted from personally encouraging creativity. Organization members often find their work challenging and interesting and demonstrate creativity in the short run without much personal encouragement from management. To sustain creativity in organization members over the long run, however, encouragement from management is vital. Such encouragement lets organization members know that creativity is important to the organization and assures them that management values creative efforts, even those that ultimately prove to be unsuccessful.[11]

Establish Systems Support   To complement personal encouragement of creativity, organizational systems and procedures should noticeably support organization member creativity.[12] Such organizational support clearly indicates that organization member creativity is highly valued. Organizational procedures that promote information sharing and collaboration related to solving organizational problems are examples of this support. In addition, research suggests that managers who are trustworthy and provide employees with developmental feedback help increase employee creativity.[13]

The Coca-Cola Company is often cited for building organizational systems that support employee creativity. At Coca-Cola, being creative is considered an everyday activity, not an activity initiated by a new program or focused on from time to time only. Instead, creativity is a constant focus that is supported throughout the very structure of the company, including in the way organization members interact during meetings and problem-solving collaboration.[14]

Hire and Retain Creative People   As one last tactic for increasing creativity in organizations, managers can attempt to hire and retain organization members who are creative. Although this tactic may sound simple, it can be difficult to implement because identifying people who are creative can be a formidable challenge. However, retaining creative employees is particularly important given research suggesting that individuals' social structures can influence their creativity.[15] In other words, it may help to surround creative employees with other creative employees. To help managers identify creative people, **Figure 6.3** contains a list of characteristics that creative people tend to possess.

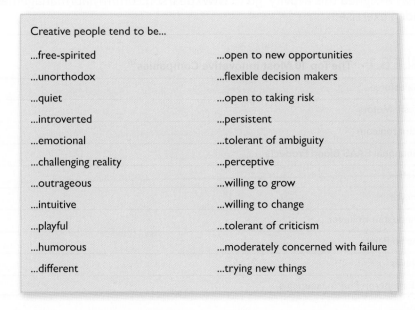

Creative people tend to be...

...free-spirited	...open to new opportunities
...unorthodox	...flexible decision makers
...quiet	...open to taking risk
...introverted	...persistent
...emotional	...tolerant of ambiguity
...challenging reality	...perceptive
...outrageous	...willing to grow
...intuitive	...willing to change
...playful	...tolerant of criticism
...humorous	...moderately concerned with failure
...different	...trying new things

Figure 6.3

Characteristics of creative people

Innovation and Creativity

6-4 A definition of innovation and an understanding of the relationship between creativity and innovation

This second major chapter section builds on the topic of creativity by discussing *innovation*. The discussion focuses on defining innovation, linking innovation and creativity, and the innovation process.

Defining Innovation

The term *innovation* can be defined in several different ways.[16] From a management viewpoint, **innovation** is the process of applying a new idea to the improvement of organizational processes, products, or services. Innovation is critical to the long-run success of virtually any organization. Used correctly, the collective intelligence of an organization has the power to spark innovation.[17] On the other hand, without innovation, organizations tend to become less competitive and less desirable to customers as well as to organization members, and organizations that do not innovate tend to fail.[18] Many management theorists believe that innovation can fuel the prosperity not only of organizations but also of nations.[19] To this end, Amazon.com reports that approximately 500 hardcover and 2,000 paperback books with the word *innovation* in their titles were published in 2016.[20]

There is no doubt, though, that innovation starts with employees. In fact, a recent long-term study of new product development in two organizations states that social networks with strong relationships and active participation in decision making help foster innovation.[21] As Arthur Levinson, chair and chief executive officer of Genentech, one of the world's leading biotechnology companies, has said, "If you want an innovative environment, hire innovative people, listen to them tell you what they want, and do it."[22] Such attitudes toward innovation help to explain why 43 percent of executives in a recent poll stated that their corporation has a chief innovation officer in place.[23]

Amazon is known as one of the world's most innovative companies because of its ability to diversify and develop in creative ways. Founded in 1994 as an online bookseller, Amazon soon expanded its product line well beyond books. Today, customers can order electronics, office supplies, toys, and a host of other merchandise—even groceries and automotive supplies—from the Amazon website. The company has also broadened and diversified its products and services. Its offerings include consumer electronics (e.g., Kindle e-readers, Fire tablets, Echo smart speakers, etc.), video and music services, extensive cloud-computing services, data storage and computing services, and more.[24] **Table 6.1** lists the top 10 most innovative companies in the world.

MyLab Management Watch It

If your instructor has assigned this activity, go to www.pearson.com/mylab/management to complete the video exercise.

TABLE 6.1   **The Top 10 Most Innovative Companies**[25]

1. Salesforce
2. Tesla Motors
3. Amazon.com
4. Shanghai RAAS Blood Products
5. Netflix
6. Incyte
7. Hindustan Unilever
8. Asian Paints
9. Naver
10. Regeneron Pharmaceuticals

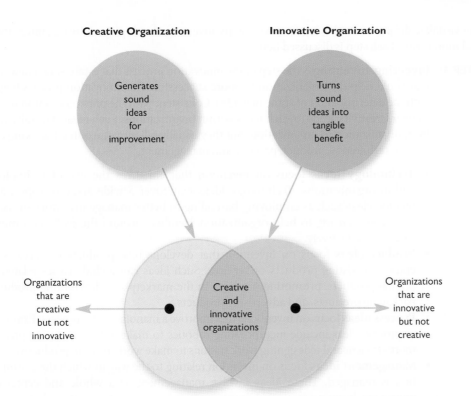

Creative Organization

Generates sound ideas for improvement

Innovative Organization

Turns sound ideas into tangible benefit

Organizations that are creative but not innovative

Creative and innovative organizations

Organizations that are innovative but not creative

Figure 6.4
Managers should strive to build organizations that are both creative and innovative

Innovation is the process of turning creative ideas into something tangible. Ford Motor Company president and CEO Mark Fields is committed to a driverless fleet of cars by 2021. Over $1 billion is being spent on research and development of these cars by Ford.

Michael Nagle/Bloomberg/Getty Images

Linking Innovation and Creativity

Confusion often exists in organizations over the relationship between innovation and creativity.[26] Basically, innovation involves turning a new idea into new or improved processes, products, or services that promote the attainment of organizational goals. The ideas on which innovation is based come from creativity in the organization. Innovation is the process of turning those ideas into something tangible that benefits the organization. An organization that is creative but not innovative has a fertile source of good ideas, but it lacks the ability to make those ideas tangible. An organization that is innovative but not creative has the ability to turn ideas into tangible benefits, but it lacks good ideas in the first place. **Figure 6.4** illustrates that organizations can be either creative or innovative and makes the point that managers should strive to build organizations that are a source of sound ideas and that are also capable of turning the ideas into tangible benefits for the organization.

The Innovation Process

Innovation process is defined as the steps managers take to implement creative ideas. In reality, the number of steps that specific implementations require is often debatable. Such steps can range from straightforward steps, such as issuing specific orders to production supervisors, to complicated steps that might include determining the potential value of an innovation under consideration. To make managing the innovation process more practical, however, managers

6-5 An awareness of the innovation process

can visualize the process as having five main steps: inventing, developing, diffusing, integrating, and monitoring. Each step is discussed here.[27]

STEP 1:   **Inventing. Inventing** is the step of the innovation process that establishes a new idea that could help the organization be more successful. The innovation process begins with the determination of some new idea. Consistent with the previous section of this chapter, creativity leads to such ideas within organizations. Such ideas naturally vary from organization to organization, but they usually fall into one of the following categories: technology, product, process, and management.[28]

- **Technology ideas** focus on invention that enhances the use of technology within organizations. Technology ideas can cover a wide array of topics and include ideas such as employing barcoding to better manage inventory or using videoconferencing to help organization members around the globe communicate more effectively.
- **Product ideas** focus on invention that develops new products or services or enhances existing products or services. Such ideas can include issues related to pricing products, promoting products in the marketplace, distributing products, packaging products, and advertising products.
- **Process ideas** focus on inventions that improve a manufacturing process. Examples of process ideas include incorporating robotics to make a manufacturing process more efficient and redesigning work stations to make workers more productive.
- **Management ideas** focus on invention relating to the way in which the organization is managed. These ideas involve management as a whole and center on improving human resource management, redesigning organizational structure, changing organizational leadership, or refining competitive strategy.

An interesting example of introducing a new product involves the distribution of television shows and movies.[29] Netflix, a company started in 1997 as a mail-order distributor of DVDs to consumers, progressed to deliver television shows and movies digitally through Internet streaming. Recently, Netflix started producing its own television shows, which are available exclusively to Netflix subscribers. This production process has shown to be a new feat for Netflix, with *House of Cards*, *Stranger Things*, and *The Crown* winning both critical acclaim and prominent awards.

STEP 2:   **Developing. Developing** is that step of the innovation process that makes a new idea practical. After being established in step 1, an idea must next be developed, or made practical as a vehicle for enhancing organizational success. Some creative ideas defy practicality and should never be pursued.[30] On the other hand, some ideas are practical and can be focused on diverse areas such as improving cell phone service to attract more customers,[31] adding attractions to a theme park to make it more competitive,[32] or better training to conquer the hurdle of getting professionals both comfortable and effective with operating newly purchased equipment.[33]

3M Company, formerly known as Minnesota Mining and Manufacturing Company, has become world famous for developing new ideas. Perhaps the most well-known 3M innovation is the Post-it Note. 3M may very well have achieved this fame through its formal, simple, and well-established company policy that helps ensure that every idea that deserves to be developed is indeed developed. This policy encourages employees to see whether managers in other parts of the company will help develop a new idea after the employee's immediate boss has rejected it.[34]

Netflix's new idea for producing a new drama illustrates step 1 of the innovation process. Step 2 of the innovation process indicates that this new idea must now become practical. In essence, management must now determine feasible methods for producing the new dramatic series. In the case of Netflix, this process includes determining where the show will be filmed, which actors will star in the show, and who will direct the actors.

STEP 3:   **Diffusing. Diffusing** is that step of the innovation process that puts a new idea to use by end users or customers. Step 3 of the innovation process takes place after an idea has been established (step 1) and developed (step 2). If the idea is for an improvement to an organizational process, organization members who would be affected by the idea would explore using the idea to test its utility and worth. If the idea is for establishing a new product, perhaps certain customers would be given a prototype to test the ultimate utility and worth of the product.

In the Netflix example, the idea for producing a new dramatic series was established, and the new series became practical in innovation process steps 1 and 2, respectively. In step 3, customers would actually be shown the first episodes of the series to determine the show's utility and worth to customers. If customer feedback was negative at this point, Netflix might wish to discontinue the idea or take additional time to improve it. If customer feedback was positive, Netflix would probably proceed to the next step of the innovation process.

STEP 4: **Integrating. Integrating** is that step of the innovation process that establishes an invention as a permanent part of the organization. If the invention focuses on a new organizational process, for example, management takes steps to make the new process standard operating procedure within the organization. If the invention focuses on a new product, management takes steps to start manufacturing and selling the new product to the marketplace. In the example of relating Netflix's new dramatic series to the innovation process, the idea for the series has been established and developed or made practical, and customers have verified the desirable value and worth of the series. Now, in step 4, Netflix management integrates the idea or makes the dramatic series an established component of the company's product line. In essence, management takes appropriate steps to allow customers to view the new show.

STEP 5: **Monitoring. Monitoring** is the step of the innovation process in which a newly implemented idea is tracked to determine if and when the idea should be improved or terminated. Management monitors newly implemented ideas to make sure that the contributions to organizational success generated by the ideas continue to accrue. As long as the implemented ideas continue to contribute to organizational success, the useful lives of those ideas will continue. When new ideas cease to make a contribution to organizational success, however, the ideas should be improved or terminated.

At this stage of the innovation process in the Netflix example, the idea for the show was established, it was made practical for use, customers endorsed the idea, and the show is now available for streaming. Now Netflix must monitor the contribution the show makes to organizational success and improve or discontinue it when the contribution becomes unacceptable. **Figure 6.5** summarizes the major steps of the innovation process discussed here and shows how the Netflix example relates to each step.

STEPS FOR SUCCESS

Inviting Inventions at a Hackathon

Among its other meanings, *hacking* can refer to clever and often rapid writing of software and modification of devices by passionate experts in computers and other technologies. Some organizations have harnessed this creative activity by hosting or sponsoring hackathons—competitive events where teams are challenged to hack their way to the best solution in the course of an evening or weekend. For example, Massachusetts Institute of Technology recently hosted a hackathon to develop ideas for improving health-care delivery. In one night, teams of doctors, computer programmers, engineers, and researchers developed ideas for sharing images and improving diagnoses.

Here are some tips for running a hackathon to promote inventing:[35]

- Define a clear mission for the event.
- Reserve a space with plenty of electrical outlets. Order generous quantities of coffee, soft drinks, and snacks.
- Involve technical and business experts as well as sponsors who will encourage and finance the hackers so that they can develop ideas with potential.
- Market the event to hackers, including students. Mention the free food and prizes as well as resources such as coaching and potential investors.

Figure 6.5   How steps of the innovation process relate to Netflix

This stage of the innovation process often includes *reverse innovation*, which involves taking a concept or a product created for a very specific use and extending it to a new, often larger audience. For example, General Electric announced that it would introduce two of its medical devices, formerly sold only in emerging markets, in the United States. The company's $1,000 handheld electrocardiogram device was originally created for physicians who practice in rural areas of India. GE's portable, PC-based ultrasound machine was created for use in rural China. By selling these products in the United States, GE will not only realize a profit but will also make health care more affordable.[36]

Catalyst for Creativity and Innovation: Total Quality Management

6-6   An understanding of total quality as a base for spawning creative ideas

As discussed earlier, creativity spawns new ideas that promote organizational success, and innovation makes those ideas a reality. Also discussed earlier was the idea that organization member expertise is normally a significant catalyst in spawning new, creative ideas.

This section presents critical insights into building expertise in total quality management (TQM) in both managers and nonmanagers in organizations. This expertise is intended as a wellspring of new, creative, quality-oriented ideas that promote organizational success. Major topics discussed are the essentials of total quality management and creative ideas based on TQM expertise.

Essentials of Total Quality Management

This section outlines the fundamental principles of total quality management. Topics include defining TQM, the importance of quality in organizations, established quality awards, and the quality improvement process.

Defining Total Quality Management
Quality is defined as how well a product does what it is supposed to do—how closely and reliably it satisfies the specifications to which it was built. Quality is presented as the degree of excellence on which products or services can be ranked on the basis of selected features.

Total quality management (TQM) is the continuous process of involving all organization members in ensuring that every activity related to the production of goods or services has an appropriate role in establishing product quality.[37] In other words, all organization members should emphasize the appropriate performance of activities throughout the company to maintain the quality of products offered by the company. Under the TQM concept, organization members work both individually and collectively to maintain the quality of the products offered to the marketplace.

Although the TQM movement actually began in the United States, its establishment, development, and growth throughout the world are largely credited to the Japanese. The Japanese believe that a TQM program should be company-wide and must include the cooperation of all people within a company. Top managers, middle managers, supervisors, and workers throughout the company must work together to ensure that all phases of company operations appropriately affect product quality. These company operations include areas such as market research, research and development, product planning, design, production, purchasing, vendor management, manufacturing, inspection, sales, after-sales customer care, financial control, personnel administration, and company training and education.

The Importance of Quality   Many managers and management theorists warn that U.S. organizations that don't produce high-quality products will soon be unable to compete in the world marketplace. A 1990 book by Armand V. Feigenbaum stated the problem succinctly:

> Quality. Remember it? American manufacturing has slumped a long way from the glory days of the 1950s and 1960s when "Made in the U.S.A." proudly stood for the best that industry could turn out. . . . While the Japanese were developing remarkably higher standards for a whole host of products, from consumer electronics to cars and machine tools, many U.S. managers were smugly dozing at the switch. Now, aside from aerospace and agriculture, there are few markets left where the U.S. carries its own weight in international trade. For American industry, the message is simple: Get Better or Get Beat.[38]

Producing high-quality products is not an end in itself. Rather, successfully offering high-quality goods and services to the marketplace typically results in three important ends for the organization: a positive company image, lower costs and higher market share, and decreased product liability costs.

POSITIVE COMPANY IMAGE

A reputation for high-quality products creates a positive image for an organization, and organizations gain many advantages from having such an image. A positive image helps a firm recruit valuable new employees, accelerate sales of its new products, and obtain needed loans from financial institutions. To summarize, high-quality products generally result in a positive company image, which in turn leads to numerous organizational benefits.[39]

LOWER COSTS AND HIGHER MARKET SHARE

Activities that support product quality also benefit the organization by yielding lower costs and greater market share. **Figure 6.6** illustrates this point. As shown in the top half of this figure, greater market share or gain in product sales is a direct result of customer perception of improved product quality. As shown in the bottom half of the figure, organizational activities that contribute to product quality result in benefits such as increased productivity, lower rework

TIPS FOR MANAGING AROUND THE GLOBE

Michelin's Quality Advantage

For a multinational company, a significant challenge is appealing to customers from different cultures. One strategy that makes sense in any language is to offer a measurably superior level of quality. That is the approach taken in the tire industry by Michelin, which has factories in 17 countries and sells 14 percent of the world's tires.

According to Pete Selleck, president of Michelin's operations in North America, Michelin offers this level of quality by stressing consistency. Tires are not a complex product, so the way to be the best is to ensure that every tire meets specifications. Michelin ensures this by giving quality control workers an unusually high degree of control over manufacturing. If they identify any defects, production stops until employees fix the problem. Production employees are also authorized to halt production if they see anything going wrong. Its commitment to quality enables Michelin to earn top ratings for its tires, and consumers are willing to pay a premium of as much as 20 percent to use Michelin tires.[40]

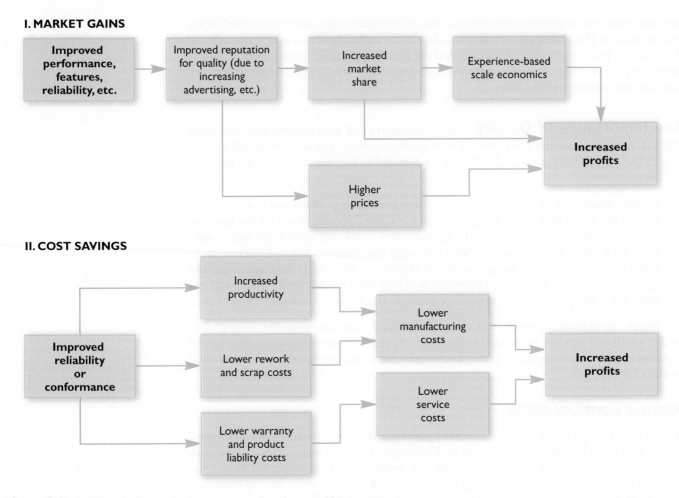

Figure 6.6   TQM typically results in greater market share and lower costs

and scrap costs, and lower warranty costs, which in turn result in lower manufacturing costs and lower costs of servicing products after they are sold. Figure 6.6 also makes the important point that both greater market share and lower costs attributed to high quality usually result in greater organizational profits.

DECREASED PRODUCT LIABILITY COSTS

Product manufacturers are increasingly facing costly legal suits over damages caused by faulty products. More and more, organizations that design and produce faulty products are being held liable in courts for damages resulting from the use of such products. To take one dramatic example, Pfizer, a company that develops mechanical heart valves, recently settled an estimated 180 lawsuits by heart-implant patients claiming that the valves used in their implants were faulty.[41] Successful TQM efforts typically result in improved products and product performance, and the typical result of improved products and product performance is lower product liability costs.

Established Quality Awards
Recognizing all these benefits of quality, U.S. companies have placed significant emphasis on manufacturing high-quality products. Several major awards have been established in the United States and abroad to acknowledge those organizations that produce exceptionally high-quality products and services. The most prestigious international award is the Deming Award, established in Japan in honor of W. Edwards Deming, who introduced Japanese firms to statistical quality control and quality improvement techniques after World War II. The most widely known award in the United States is the Malcolm Baldrige National Quality Award, which is awarded by the American Society of Quality and Control and was established in 1988.[42] As these examples suggest, quality is an increasingly important element in an organization's ability to compete in today's global marketplace.

The Quality Improvement Process

Two approaches may be taken to improve quality. The first approach, advocated by most of the quality experts, can be described as "incremental improvement"—or improving one thing at a time. Actually, many incremental improvements may be undertaken simultaneously throughout an organization; for example, in 1982 Toyota averaged instituting 5,000 improvements per day.

The second approach, advocated by Michael Hammer, consists of completely reengineering a process.[43] This approach requires starting with a clean slate in which management looks at operations and asks, "If we were to start over today, how would we do this?"

Each approach is discussed in detail in the following sections.

6-7 An understanding of the primary components of the quality improvement process

The Incremental Improvement Process

Researchers and consultants have advocated a variety of incremental approaches to achieving excellent quality in products and processes. Despite their differences, almost all of these plans have remarkable similarities. Although a specific improvement process may not precisely follow the order given in **Figure 6.**7, most such processes at least approximate it.

STEP 1: **An area of improvement is chosen, which often is called the improvement "theme"**—Either management or an improvement team may choose the theme. Examples are:

- Reduction in production cycle time
- Increase in the percentage of nondefective units produced
- Reduction in the variability of raw material going into production
- Increase in on-time deliveries
- Reduction in machine downtime
- Reduction in employee absenteeism

Many other examples are possible, of course, but these suffice to make the point that an improvement objective must be chosen. Consider a pizza company whose delivery business is lagging behind that of its competitors, chiefly because of slow deliveries. The improvement theme in this case might be a reduction in delivery time (i.e., cycle time).

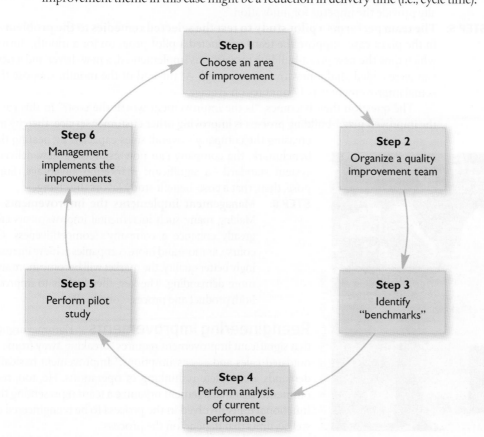

Figure 6.7

The incremental approach to improving quality

STEP 2:   **If a quality improvement team has not already been organized, one is organized**—Members of this team might include:

- One or more associates directly responsible for the work being done
- One or more customers receiving the benefits of the work
- One or more suppliers providing input into the work
- A member of management
- Perhaps one or more experts in areas relevant to solving the problem and making the improvement

For the pizza delivery company, the team might include two pizza builders, a driver, a university student customer, a local resident customer, and a store manager.

STEP 3:   **The team benchmarks the best performers—that is, identifies how much improvement is required to match the best performance**—For example, the pizza company may discover in this step that the benchmark (i.e., the fastest average time between the moment an order is taken and the moment of front-door delivery) established by a competitor is 20 minutes.

Suppose the pizza delivery company's current average delivery performance is 35 minutes. That leaves a minimum possible improvement of 15 minutes on average.

STEP 4:   **The team performs an analysis to find out how current performance can be improved to meet or beat the benchmark**—Factors to be analyzed here include potential problems related to equipment; materials; work methods; people; and the environment, such as legal constraints, physical conditions, and weather.

To return to the pizza delivery company, suppose the team discovered that the pizza-building process could be shortened by 4 minutes. Also suppose they found an average lag of 5 minutes between the time a pizza is ready and the time the delivery van picks it up. Finally, suppose the team discovered that a different oven could shorten cooking time by 7 minutes. Total potential savings in delivery time, then, would be 16 minutes—which would beat the benchmark by 1 minute.

The common phrase "Necessity is the mother of invention" serves as a reminder that, in some cases, constraints—both within and outside an organization—can actually provide the impetus for innovation.[44]

STEP 5:   **The team performs a pilot study to test the selected remedies to the problem**—In the pizza case, suppose the team conducted a pilot program for a month, during which time the new pizza-building process was implemented, a new driver and a new van were added, and a new oven was rented. At the end of the month, suppose the actual improvement was 17 minutes on average.

The question then becomes, "Is the improvement worth the cost?" In this case, the improved pizza-building process is improving other customer service, thereby increasing the company's overall sales capacity. By beating the benchmark, the company can now establish a new delivery system standard—a significant marketing advantage. Suppose, then, that a cost–benefit study favors the changes.

STEP 6:   **Management implements the improvements**—Making many such incremental improvements can greatly enhance a company's competitiveness. Of course, as more and more companies achieve increasingly better quality, the market will become more and more demanding. The key, therefore, is to improve both product and process continually.

Reengineering Improvements

Hammer argues that significant improvement requires "breaking away from . . . outdated rules and . . . assumptions." Improvement basically demands a complete rethinking of operations. He, too, recommends that management organize a team representing the functional units involved in the process to be reengineered as well as units that depend on the process.

Teams of employees who are directly responsible for how work is done are well positioned to make continuous, incremental improvements in quality.

Marco Vacca/Marka/Alamy Stock Photo

One important reason for reengineering instead of attempting incremental improvements is the need to integrate computerized production and information systems. This change is expensive and is difficult to accomplish piecemeal through an incremental approach.

Hammer outlines seven principles of reengineering:

- **Principle 1: Organize around outcomes, not tasks**—Traditionally, work has been organized around different tasks, such as sawing, typing, assembling, and supervising. This first principle of reengineering instead has one person or team perform all the steps in an identified process. The person or team would be responsible for the outcome of the total process.

- **Principle 2: Have those who use the output of the process perform the process**—For example, a production department may do its own purchasing and even its own cost accounting. This principle requires a broader range of expertise from individuals and teams as well as a greater integration of activities.

- **Principle 3: Subsume information-processing work into the real work that produces the information**—Computer technology now makes it possible for a work process to process information simultaneously. For example, scanners at checkout counters in grocery stores both process customer purchases and update accounting and inventory records at the same time.

- **Principle 4: Treat geographically dispersed resources as though they were centralized**—Hammer uses Hewlett-Packard as an example of how this principle works: Each of the company's 50 manufacturing units had its own purchasing department, which prevented the company from achieving the benefits of scale discounts. Rather than centralize purchasing, which would have reduced the responsiveness to local manufacturing needs, Hewlett-Packard introduced a corporate unit to coordinate local purchases so that scale discounts could be gained. That way, local purchasing units retain their decentralized authority and preserve their local responsiveness.

- **Principle 5: Link parallel activities instead of integrating their results**—Several processes are often required to produce products and services. Too often, though, companies segregate these processes so that the product comes together only at the final stage. Meanwhile, problems that occur in one or more processes may not become apparent until the final step, at which point it is too late to fix the problems. It is better, Hammer says, to coordinate the various processes so that problems are avoided or recognized and taken care of right away.

- **Principle 6: Put the decision point where the work is performed and build control into the process**—Even though traditional bureaucracies separate decision authority from the work, this principle suggests that the people doing the work are the ones who should make the decisions about that work. The salesperson should have the authority and responsibility to approve credit, for example. This principle saves time and allows the organization to respond more effectively and efficiently to customer needs. Some managers worry that this principle will reduce control over the process. However, control can be built into the process. In the example just cited, the criteria for credit approval can be built into a computer program so that the salesperson has guidance for every credit decision.

- **Principle 7: Capture information once and at the source**—Computerized online databases help make this principle achievable. It is now easy to collect information when it originates and then to store it and send it to those who need it.

Reengineering allows major improvements to be made all at once. Although reengineering can be an expensive way to improve quality, today's rapidly changing markets sometimes demand such a drastic response—even and especially when firms experience poor performance.[45]

Creative Ideas Based on TQM Expertise

Expertise in TQM—understanding TQM principles—can serve as a foundation for generating creative ideas in organizations. Indeed, the number of creative ideas that can be spawned by TQM expertise seems limitless. Keep in mind, however, that an idea that may seem new and creative in one organization may not be new and creative in another because it has already been considered.

Figure 6.8

Possible creative ideas for enhancing organizational success based on Crosby's thoughts about TQM

1. Dedicate the quality management function to measuring conformance to requirements and reporting any differences accurately.

2. Continually inform all employees about the progress of quality improvement and related successes.

3. Begin each management meeting with a factual and financial review of quality.

4. Create relevant policies on quality management that are clear and unambiguous.

5. Educate suppliers to ensure that they will deliver quality materials in a dependable fashion.

6. Dedicate top management to having customers receive products as promised.

7. Dedicate all managers to getting jobs done correctly the first time.

8. Develop communication systems that allow employees to inform management immediately about any observed deviations from quality.

9. Develop communications systems that allow managers to respond immediately to quality issues.

10. Establish an organizational bias toward handling quality issues immediately.

The following sections discuss several possible ideas for organizations based on the work of Philip B. Crosby and W. Edwards Deming, two internationally acclaimed quality experts.[46]

Possible Creative Ideas Based on Crosby's Work   Philip B. Crosby is known throughout the world as an expert in the area of quality and is considered a pioneer of the quality movement in the United States.[47] His work provides managers with valuable insights on how to achieve product quality. According to Crosby, organizational integrity, systems, communications, operations, and policies must all be consistent with the goal of achieving product quality before significant progress in reaching product quality can be made and maintained. Several possible creative ideas based on Crosby's work for achieving quality in organizations are listed in **Figure 6.8**.

Possible Creative Ideas Based on Deming's Work   W. Edwards Deming was originally trained as a statistician and began teaching statistical quality control in Japan shortly after World War II. He is recognized internationally as a primary contributor to Japanese quality improvement programs. Deming advocated that the way to achieve product quality is to improve continuously the design of a product and the process used to manufacture it.[48] According to Deming, management has the primary responsibility for achieving product quality. Several possible creative ideas based on Deming's work for achieving quality in organizations are listed in **Figure 6.9**.

Figure 6.9

Possible creative ideas for enhancing organizational success based on Deming's thoughts about TQM

1. Publish quality goals for all workers so they know exactly what they are expected to do.

2. Use product inspections to improve the manufacturing process and to reduce costs.

3. Choose your suppliers on the basis of how they can support your quality goals.

4. Train for maintaining quality.

5. Drive out fear of reporting mistakes.

6. Build teams (not just individuals) that focus on quality.

7. Eliminate production processes based simply on producing a quota.

8. Create production processes based upon learning how to improve the processes.

9. Build pride for maintaining quality.

10. Encourage self-development of workers as more useful players in maintaining quality.

CHALLENGE CASE SUMMARY

The Challenge Case demonstrates how Olde Peninsula Brewpub and Restaurant has been an innovative company since its inception. In essence, founder Steve Blinn must seek original ideas or ideas based on existing conditions at Olde Peninsula that will help to meet this challenge. The ideas must be not only original but also useful and actionable. That is, the ideas must help Olde Peninsula become more productive, communicate more effectively, achieve better coordination, and improve customer and employee satisfaction. Such ideas are important because they will help Olde Peninsula break away from old rules and norms about accomplishing tasks. At Olde Peninsula, the expertise, motivation level, and creative thinking skills of the organization members will be the foundation on which creative ideas will be conceived.

Information in this chapter provides insights for Blinn and his team regarding how to encourage creativity within the company. For example, developing flatbread sandwiches and hot pepper–infused beer shows that Blinn is not content with the status quo.

Blinn should focus not only on searching for creative ideas but also on innovating, or putting those ideas into action. As an example, assume that to shorten the time it takes servers to enter food orders for the kitchen, Blinn provides servers with digital tablets connected to Wi-Fi. Computerized order processing would indeed be creative—a new, useful, actionable idea. This idea is not a *product idea* (an invention that focuses on developing new products) but is rather a *process* improvement. After generating the new process idea, Blinn must develop the idea, or make it serviceable. This includes ideas for whether to develop the order-processing software in-house, hire someone to develop it, or buy existing software, along with plans for training employees how to use the system. Once the idea is made serviceable, it must be diffused. The company might train one or a few people in how to use the new system, and then those people could train and support other users. Once the new system is integrated into the organization, it must be monitored to make sure it continues to contribute to organizational success.

Blinn has learned that expertise in total quality management—in this case, developed in the course of developing new food and beer offerings—can serve as a stimulus for generating creative ideas within the company. Applying TQM requires that Blinn and his managers educate themselves and other organization members about what this commitment entails. All associates of Olde Peninsula should know that product, service quality, and adherence to specifications for the company's processes must be maintained. For every process through which the company serves customers—by greeting guests, preparing orders, keeping an adequate stock of merchandise, filling orders, and so on—there must be specifications for high-quality performance. Olde Peninsula employees should realize that TQM needs to be a continuous process that involves everyone within the company, from Blinn to the newest bus person.

Olde Peninsula has much to gain from maintaining high-quality service. High quality gives the company a positive image both inside and outside the organization. Such an image can be especially valuable when an organization is trying to recruit new and talented management. High quality can also reduce costs associated with errors and waste and help the company gain market share. Olde Peninsula's high quality can decrease liability costs; for example, good safety processes can reduce liability associated with injuries, and accurate compliance with health laws can prevent food-handling mistakes in that area.

Blinn and his managers can deliberate on continuing to improve quality either incrementally or through reengineering. Incremental involvement would focus on improving Olde Peninsula's quality slowly and over time. It could involve steps such as targeting one process at the brewpub for improvement, establishing a quality improvement team to effect desired improvements, identifying benchmarks or standards for quality, comparing current operations with the benchmarks, and performing a pilot study to see whether formulated improvement activities are effective and efficient. Improvements that deliver the desired results would become normal operating procedure. Reengineering improvement would focus on improving quality through more drastic improvement in the nearer term.

Blinn and his managers can study the work of Crosby and Deming to gain possible new ideas for implementing and maintaining the company's quality improvement process. Such ideas might include building an organization culture that has a bias for handling quality issues quickly and thoroughly, dedicating top management to having customers receive all offerings as promised, and training associates in how to improve process quality.

MyLab Management Assessing Your Management Skill

If your instructor has assigned this activity, go to www.pearson.com/mylab/management to complete the exercise related to the Challenge Case.

DEVELOPING CREATIVITY AND INNOVATION SKILL

This section is specially designed to help you develop creativity and innovation skills. An individual's creativity and innovation skill is based on an understanding of the concepts and the ability to apply those concepts. The following activities will help to enhance your creativity and innovation skills in various organizational situations.

Class Preparation and Personal Study

To help you prepare for class, perform the activities outlined in this section. Performing these activities will help you enhance your classroom performance significantly.

Reflecting on Target Skill

On page 149, this chapter opens by presenting a target management skill along with a list of related objectives outlining knowledge and understanding that you should aim to acquire related to that skill. Review this target skill and the list of objectives to make sure that you've acquired all pertinent information within the chapter. If you do not feel that you've reached a particular objective(s), study related chapter coverage until you do.

Know Key Terms

Understanding the following key terms is critical to your preparing for class. Define each of these terms. Refer to the page(s) referenced after a term to check your definition or to gain further insight regarding the term.

creativity **151**
innovation **156**
innovation process **157**
inventing **158**
developing **158**
diffusing **158**
integrating **159**
monitoring **159**
quality **160**
total quality management (TQM) **160**

Know How Management Concepts Relate

This section comprises activities that will further sharpen your understanding of management concepts. Answer essay questions as completely as possible.

6-1 Define and describe the relationships among expertise, creative thinking skills, motivation, and creativity.

6-2 Explain the differences between creativity and innovation.

6-3 Describe the five steps of the innovation process.

Management Skills Exercises

Learning activities in this section are aimed at helping you develop creativity and innovation skills.

⭐ Cases

Olde Peninsula Brings Brewpub Innovation to Kalamazoo

"Olde Peninsula Brings Brewpub Innovation to Kalamazoo" and its related Challenge Case Summary were written to help you understand the management concepts contained in this chapter. Answer the following discussion questions about the Challenge Case to explore how the concepts of creativity and innovation can be applied in a company such as Olde Peninsula Brewpub and Restaurant.

6-4 How is creativity and innovation being utilized at Olde Peninsula Brewpub and Restaurant?

6-5 Develop a new food menu offering for Olde Peninsula. Once you have your idea, explain how each of the five steps in the innovation process would be addressed.

6-6 What advice would you give to Steve Blinn about total quality management? Explain how he can ensure quality improvement at Olde Peninsula.

Ford Plans Fully Autonomous Cars by 2021

Read the case and answer the questions that follow. Studying this case will help you better understand how concepts relating to innovation can be applied in a company such as Ford.

There is a car race going on right now that you may not be aware of: Several companies are attempting to develop vehicles that drive themselves. And you may be surprised who is involved. Companies like Uber, General Motors, Mercedes, and even Google are all vying for the perfect autonomous car.[49] Ford, however, is committed to being first and to having a fleet of these driverless cars by 2021.

Ford has already built a major research facility in the heart of Silicon Valley—an area more known for software and Internet businesses than automobiles. But Ford's commitment goes beyond just a building; it is also spending over $1 billion in research and development. According to Mark Fields, president and CEO of Ford, "The next decade will be defined by automation of the automobile, and we see autonomous vehicles as having as significant an impact on society as Ford's moving assembly line did 100 years ago."[50]

The goal for Ford is to have a commercially viable autonomous car by 2021. This ambitious objective is the culmination of several innovative steps. Ford has partnered with a number of high-tech companies to achieve a fully driverless car. But this involves more than just steering the vehicle. The company is doing extensive research in the areas of 3-D mapping, radar technology, camera sensors, and advanced algorithms. Already, Ford has an autonomous test fleet of 30 Ford Fusion hybrid sedans. In 2018, it plans to have 90. Much of the testing will be in the autonomous vehicle–friendly states of Arizona, Michigan, and California.

The key to Ford's success lies in the study of innovative artificial intelligence that will ultimately power and operate these special vehicles. By partnering with technology companies, Ford is relying on the innovations of these firms to create driverless cars, while Ford is manufacturing the vehicles themselves. One such artificial intelligence company is Argo AI, which was founded by former employees of Google and Uber. Argo AI is providing expertise and research that Ford does not have. "As Ford expands to be an auto and a mobility company," says Fields, "we believe that investing in Argo AI will create significant value for our shareholders by strengthening Ford's leadership in bringing self-driving vehicles to market in the near term."[51]

So why do we need driverless cars? It all comes down to safety. Have you ever known anyone who didn't complain about other drivers? The human factor involved in driving a car means that the driver does not always signal properly, brakes too hard, drives too fast, doesn't obey traffic signals or stop signs, and so forth. And with the omnipresent concern of distracted drivers due to cell phone use, an autonomous vehicle can be much safer and protect people from serious injury and death. Ford wants to lead the way in protecting drivers of the future. Fields says, "We're dedicated to putting on the road an autonomous vehicle that can improve safety and solve social and environmental challenges for millions of people—not just those who can afford luxury vehicles."

Questions

6-7 How is Ford being innovative in its search for autonomous vehicles? Explain.

6-8 Discuss how creativity and innovation are linked at Ford.

6-9 If you were Mark Fields, CEO of Ford, what other innovations would you seek for the automobile industry in the next 20 years?

Experiential Exercises

Innovating This Course

Directions. Your introductory management course and this textbook discuss fundamental concepts necessary to understand the field of management. In other disciplines at your university, however, students often have an opportunity to practice concepts. For example, in biology, you might dissect a frog; in chemistry, you bend glass tubing; and in math, you factor quadratic equations. But when it comes to management, few companies are likely to permit college students to practice their management skills within their operations.

In a team of three to five students, think of ways an introductory management course can be innovative with hands-on practice. In other words, develop five ways this course can give you real-world experience.

You and Your Career

We hope that you have already begun maintaining a résumé that captures the new experiences, knowledge, and skills you acquire as you pursue your college degree. When you graduate, you will be competing for jobs with other college graduates across the country. Getting an interview with the company you are most interested in can be challenging. However, if your résumé can stand out from the crowd, you will have a better chance of having it read by a recruiter and possibly getting an interview. List five creative ways to get your résumé noticed among the hundreds and even thousands of other résumés that recruiters review.

Building Your Management Skills Portfolio

Your management skills portfolio is a collection of activities specially designed to demonstrate your management knowledge and skill. Be sure to save your work. You can use this material while preparing for an interview.

The portfolio activity for this chapter is about customer to customer (C2C) e-commerce in China. Study this information and complete the exercises that follow.

Alibaba dominates e-commerce C2C business in China through its highly successful auction site Taobao. Back in 2003, the U.S. giant eBay acquired EachNet for $180 million as its jumping-off point to expand into China. EachNet, founded in 1999, was the top auction site in China at the time, with a 90 percent market share. In the same year, Alibaba spent $52 million developing their own service, Taobao. Within a year, it had captured 50 percent of the market; by 2010 it had completely displaced eBay with an 80 percent market share.

Success for Alibaba was based on creating an auction site that matched the specific demands of the Chinese consumer, such as reducing auction fees and providing a workable platform for small businesses.

Develop a similar auction service that can better match the needs of your country or region compared to global sites such as eBay. Follow the five steps of the innovation process and record your answers as you go through it.

6-10   *Inventing:* Describe the main characteristics of your auction site.

_____

_____

_____

6-11   *Developing:* Describe how you can make the new service match the needs of the C2C market.

_____

_____

_____

6-12   *Diffusing:* How would you test functionality and consumer responses to the service?

_____

_____

_____

6-13   *Integrating:* How would you roll the service out across the region?

_____

_____

_____

6-14   *Monitoring:* Describe how you would monitor the service to ensure that it continued to be robust and met the needs of the users.

_____

_____

_____

MyLab Management
Writing Assignments

If your instructor has assigned this activity, go to www.pearson.com/mylab/management for the following assisted-graded writing assignments:

Assisted-Grading Questions

6-15   Describe five ways that organizations might increase creativity among their employees.

6-16   Define *total quality management (TQM)*, and describe the relationship between TQM and innovation.

Endnotes

1. "About Kazoo," http://www.kalamazoocity.org/.
2. Interview with Steve Blinn, May 23, 2017.
3. For an excellent review of research on creativity, see H. Sarooghi, D. Libaers, and A. Burkemper, "Examining the Relationship between Creativity and Innovation: A Meta-Analysis of Organizational, Cultural, and Environmental Factors," *Journal of Business Venturing* 30 (2016): 714–731.
4. Cameron M. Ford, "Creative Developments in Creativity Theory," *Academy of Management Review* 25, no. 2 (April 2000): 284–285. For an interesting look at the relationship between creativity and unethical behavior, see L. C. Vincent and M. Kouchaki, "Creative, Rare, Entitled, and Dishonest: How Commonality of Creativity in One's Group Decreases an Individual's Entitlement and Dishonesty," *Academy of Management Journal* 59 (2016): 1451–1473.
5. David K. Carson, "The Importance of Creativity in Family Therapy: A Preliminary Consideration," *Family Journal* 7, no. 4 (October 1999): 326–334.
6. Jeff Cork, "Bobby Kotick Traces His Roots, Announces Indie Game Competition," *Game Informer*, February 18, 2010, http://gameinformer.com.
7. Aurora Almendral, "Turning a Million Cubic Yards of Post-Typhoon Trash into Jobs," *Weekend Edition*, February 9, 2014, http://www.npr.org; "Yolanda Survivors Hired to Clear Mountains of Waste," *Philippine Star*, November 29, 2013, http://www.philstar.com; Pilko and Associates, "Our Global Team: Tim Walsh," http://www.pilko.com, accessed April 18, 2014.
8. This section is based on Teresa M. Amabile, "How to Kill Creativity," *Harvard Business Review* 76, no. 5 (September/October 1998): 77–89.
9. Teresa M. Amabile, Constance N. Hadley, and Steven J. Kramer, "Creativity under the Gun," *Harvard Business Review* 80, no. 8 (August 2002): 52–61. See also Markus Baer and Greg R. Oldham, "The Curvilinear Relation between Experienced Creative Time Pressure and Creativity: Moderating Effects of Openness to Experience and Support for Creativity," *Journal of Applied Psychology* 91, no. 4 (2006): 963–970.
10. To better understand how team dynamics influence research and development, see G. Chen, J. Farh, E. M. Campbell-Bush, Z. Wu, and X. Wu, "Teams as Innovation Systems: Multilevel Motivational Antecedents of Innovation in R&D Teams," *Journal of Applied Psychology* 98 (2013): 1018–1027. To better understand how employee social networks improve creativity, see G. Hirst, D. Van Knippenberg, J. Zhou, E. Quaintane, and C. Zhu, "Heard It through the Grapevine: Indirect Networks and Employee Creativity," *Journal of Applied Psychology* 100, no. 2 (2015): 567–574.
11. To understand how team leaders foster creativity, see Y. Gong, T. Kim, D. Lee, and J. Zhu, "A Multilevel Model of Team Goal Orientation, Information Exchange, and Creativity," *Academy of Management Journal* 56 (2013): 827–851.
12. For more information on the cross-level factors that foster creativity, see Giles Hirst, Daan Van Knippenberg, and Jing Zhou, "A Cross-Level Perspective on Employee Creativity: Goal Orientation, Team Learning Behavior, and Individual Creativity," *Academy of Management Journal* 52, no. 2 (2009): 280–293.
13. Jennifer M. George and Jing Zhou, "Dual Tuning in a Supportive Context: Joint Contributions of Positive Mood, Negative Mood, and Supervisory Behaviors to Employee Creativity," *Academy of Management Journal* 50, no. 3 (2007): 605–622.
14. John J. Kao, "The Art & Discipline of Business Creativity," *Strategy & Leadership* 25, no. 4 (July/August 1997): 6–11.
15. Jill E. Perry-Smith, "Social yet Creative: The Role of Social Relationships in Facilitating Individual Creativity," *Academy of Management Journal* 49, no. 1 (2006): 85–101.
16. N. Anderson, K. Potocnik, and J Zhou, "Innovation and Creativity in Organizations: A State-of-the-Science Review, Prospective Commentary, and Guiding Framework," *Journal of Management* 40 (2014): 1297–1333.
17. For an interesting discussion of how some organizations use collective intelligence to innovate effectively, see "A Billion Brains Are Better Than One," *MIT Sloan Management Review*, March 18, 2010, http://sloanreview.mit.edu.
18. James M. Higgins, *Innovate or Evaporate: Test & Improve Your Organization's IQ* (Winter Park, FL: The New Management Publishing Company, 1995). For more on the relationship between creativity and innovation, see J. E. Perry-Smith, and P. V. Mannucci, "From Creativity to innovation: The Social Network Drivers of the Four Phases of the Idea Journey," *Academy of Management Review* 42 (2017): 53–79.
19. John Kao, *Innovation Nation* (New York: Free Press, 2007).
20. These statistics are based on Amazon.com's search function.
21. Bob Kijkuit and Jan van den Ende, "With a Little Help from Our Colleagues: A Longitudinal Study of Social Networks for Innovation," *Organization Studies* 31, no. 4 (2010): 451–479.
22. Jena McGregor, "Special Report: 25 Most Innovative Companies," *BusinessWeek* (May 14, 2007): 52–60.
23. L. Kwoh, "You Call That Innovation?," *Wall Street Journal*, http://online.wsj.com/article/SB10001424052702304791704577418250902309914.html, last updated May 23, 2012.
24. Chuck Salter, "Most Innovative Companies 2010," *Fast Company*, February 17, 2010, http://www.fastcompany.com. For more information on how top executives influence innovation, see Q. Li, P. G. Maggitti, K. G. Smith, P. E. Tesluk, and R. Katila, "Top Management Attention to Innovation: The Role of Search Selection and Intensity in New Product Introductions," *Academy of Management Journal* 56 (2013): 893–916.
25. "The World's Most Innovative Companies," https://www.forbes.com/innovative-companies/list/#tab:rank, accessed August 10, 2017.
26. For more information on the link between creativity and innovation, see Bob Kijkuit and Jan van den Ende, "The Organizational Life of an Idea: Integrating Social Network, Creativity and Decision-Making Perspectives," *Journal of Management Studies* 44, no. 6 (2007): 863–882.
27. This discussion is based on D. R. Nayak and J. M. Ketteringham, *Breakthroughs* (New York: Rawson Associates, 1986). To better understand the effects of a company's geographic profile and innovation, see M. Ozer and W. Zhang, "The Effects of Geographic and Network Ties on Exploitative and Exploratory Product Innovation," *Strategic Management Journal* 36 (2015): 1105–1114.
28. James Higgins, *101 Creative Problem Solving Techniques: The Handbook of New Ideas for Business* (Winter Park, FL: The New Management Publishing Company, 1994), 9–10.
29. John C. Dvorak, "Razors with No Blades," *Forbes* (October 18, 1999): 168.
30. Claire Beale, "Strategic Thinking Will Never Rescue a Poor Creative Idea," *Campaign* (August 24, 2001): 14.
31. Tim Hanrahan, "New Cellphone Service Helps Find Friends and Place to Hang Out," *Wall Street Journal*, May 22, 2003, B1.
32. Bruce Orwall, "Universal's Anxious Summer," *Wall Street Journal*, May 22, 2003, B1.
33. Kristinha McCort, "Learning a New Definition," *Millimeter* 29, no. 11 (November 2001): 29–32.
34. Frances Horibe, "Innovation, Creativity, and Improvement," *The Canadian Manager* 28, no. 2 (Spring 2003): 20.
35. Amy Dockser Marcus, "'Hackathons' Aim to Solve Health Care's Ills," *Wall Street Journal*, April 4, 2014, http://online.wsj.com; Ibby Caputo, "Hacking to Improve Health Care," *WGBH News*, March 18, 2014, http://wgbhnews.org; Miguel Paz, "How to Organize a Successful Hackathon," *PBS Idea Lab*, June 8, 2013, http://www.pbs.org; Erin Tao, "Hackathon Planning in Less than 10 Steps," *TechCrunch*, March 31, 2012, http://techcrunch.com; Mikal E. Belicove, "Why and How to Host a Hackathon," *Entrepreneur*, January 17, 2012, http://www.entrepreneur.com.
36. Jeffrey R. Immelt, Vijay Govindarajan, and Chris Trimble, "How GE Is Disrupting Itself," *Harvard Business Review*, October 2009, http://hbr.org.
37. For more information on these three contributions, see Charles H. Fine and David H. Bridge, "Managing Quality Improvement," in M. Sepheri (ed.), *Quest for Quality: Managing the Total System* (Norcross, GA: Institute of Industrial Engineers, 1987), 66–74. See also Klaus J. Zinc, "From Total Quality Management to Corporate Sustainability Based on Stakeholder Management," *Journal of Management History* 13, no. 4 (2007): 394–401.
38. For some of Crosby's more notable books in this area, see Philip B. Crosby, *Quality Is Free* (New York: McGraw-Hill, 1979); *Quality without Tears* (New York: McGraw-Hill, 1984); *Let's Talk Quality: 96 Questions You Always Wanted to Ask Phil Crosby* (New York: McGraw-Hill, 1989); *Leading* (New York: McGraw-Hill, 1990).

39. "The Push for Quality," *BusinessWeek* (June 8, 1987): 131.

40. Travis Hessman, "Michelin's Obsession with Quality," *Industry Week*, April 25, 2013, http://www.industryweek.com; Michelin, corporate website, http://www.michelin.com/corporate, accessed April 18, 2014; "J. D. Power: Michelin and Pirelli Rank Highest," *Modern Tire Dealer*, March 27, 2014, http://www.moderntiredealer.com.

41. A. V. Feigenbaum, *Total Quality Control* (New York: McGraw-Hill, 1983).

42. For a broadening discussion of a positive image, see Susan Watkins, "A Positive Image Is Not Just the Business of Business," *Public Management* 82, no. 7 (July 2000): 8–10.

43. From Michael Schroeder, "Heart Trouble at Pfizer," *BusinessWeek* (February 26, 1990): 47–48.

44. Michael Gibbert and Philip Scranton, "Constraints as Sources of Radical Innovation? Insights from Jet Propulsion Development," *Management & Organizational History* 4, no. 4 (2009): 385–399.

45. Scott F. Latham and Michael Braun, "Managerial Risk, Innovation, and Organizational Decline," *Journal of Management* 35, no. 2 (March 2009): 258–281.

46. For a discussion of companies that have won the Malcolm Baldrige National Award, see Karen Bemowski, "1994 Baldrige Award Recipients Share Their Expertise," *Quality Progress* (February 1995): 35–40.

47. Michael Hammer, "Reengineering Work: Don't Automate, Obliterate," *Harvard Business Review* (July/August 1990): 104–112.

48. See Deming's 14 Points (January 1990 revision) from W. Edwards Deming, *Out of Crisis* (Cambridge, MA: MIT Center for Advanced Engineering Study, 1986).

49. Hadley Reynolds, "Anticipate a Bumpy Ride," *KM World*, March 2017, 4–5.

50. "Looking Further," Ford company website, http://corporate.ford.com/innovation/autonomous-2021.html.

51. Lucas Mearian, "Ford to Invest $1B in A.I. Startup toward Self-Driving Cars," *CIO*, February 11, 2017, p. 1.

Plans and Planning Tools

7

 Planning Skill: the ability to take action to determine the objectives of the organization as well as what is necessary to accomplish these objectives

PLANNING SKILL AND YOUR CAREER

Planning skill will be of great value to you in enhancing your career. This skill can help you set and achieve objectives. The ability to determine and achieve objectives contributes to organizational success, builds your image as a competent manager, makes you valuable to your organization, and supports promotions as you build your career.

OBJECTIVES

To help build my *planning skill*, when studying this chapter, I will attempt to acquire:

7-1 An understanding of the general characteristics of planning

7-2 Knowledge regarding different types of plans

7-3 Insights about the major steps of the planning process

7-4 An understanding of the relationship between planning and organizational objectives

7-5 An appreciation for the potential of a management by objectives (MBO) program

7-6 Knowledge about different types of planning tools

MyLab Management Chapter Warm Up

If your instructor has assigned this activity, go to www.pearson.com/mylab/management to complete the chapter warm up.

CHALLENGE CASE

Wal-Mart Plans to Have What You Want

Wal-Mart's executives admit that one of the company's biggest problems is running out of popular items. Customers who don't find what they want at Wal-Mart will buy somewhere else. But the problem is not as easily solvable as it might seem. Suppose Wal-Mart orders double what it expects to sell. Stores might never run out of products, but Wal-Mart would have to pay for buying and storing the extra goods. The company eventually would no longer be able to compete based on low price. Therefore, Wal-Mart's managers have become experts in planning exactly what stores will need.

Consider how Wal-Mart prepared after a recent Black Friday, the Friday after Thanksgiving, which launches the year's biggest selling season. At Wal-Mart, planning starts a year in advance. On the Monday after Black Friday, a team of employees under Steve Bratspies, executive vice president of general merchandise, reviewed what worked that Friday and how the company could do better the following year. The team identified its major problem (out-of-stock items) and its major success: one-hour price guarantees for featured items, meaning that shoppers who come to the store for a featured item will receive it at the featured price even if the store runs out of the item and provides it later.

The team determined that next year on Black Friday, Wal-Mart would carry more inventory of items expected to be hot sellers and would expand its one-hour guarantees to cover 21 items, up from 3 in the current year. Also, the planners expected stiffer competition because of the shorter holiday season (Thanksgiving would fall relatively late in the month). They decided to match competitors' Black Friday deals the entire week preceding Black Friday and to open stores the evening of Thanksgiving Day.

Although Black Friday is a big event, satisfying customers is a year-round challenge that requires plans for day-to-day activities. In particular, Wal-Mart managers plan how to minimize the costs of moving products from suppliers to warehouses, to stores, and to online shoppers. A major cost is transportation. Logistics managers have developed a sophisticated network for transportation and storage aimed at more than 95 percent of products being available when desired. Managers are beginning to apply this expertise to the stores by improving plans for staffing stores and creating better procedures for keeping shelves stocked.

Technology helps Wal-Mart meet these planning challenges. Wal-Mart uses a computer system called store-level

K2 images/Shutterstock

Wal-Mart shoppers on Black Friday benefit from the store team's plan to carry more inventory of items they expect to be hot sellers.

distribution resource planning (DRP) in which planners forecast the level of demand they expect at each store, and the system calculates the product amounts needed in each warehouse and from each supplier to meet demand in the months ahead. The DRP system also collects sales data from the stores and, if actual sales differ from the forecasted sales, it adjusts the amounts to be ordered.

Skilled planners and sophisticated planning tools are essential for Wal-Mart. The budget-conscious consumers who shop there are increasingly stressed in today's economy, so Wal-Mart and its competitors are fighting for every dollar they can earn or save.[1]

THE PLANNING CHALLENGE

The Challenge Case focuses on decisions at Wal-Mart. The case ends with the implication that sound planning is necessary to compete in an industry where businesses cannot afford to waste money. Topics in this chapter will help managers like those at Wal-Mart understand why planning is so important not only for ensuring future profitability but also for carrying out day-to-day organizational activities. The fundamentals of planning are described in this chapter, which (1) outlines the general characteristics of planning, (2) discusses steps in the planning process, (3) describes the planning subsystem, (4) elaborates on the relationship between organizational objectives and planning, (5) discusses the relationship between planning and the chief executive, and (6) summarizes the qualifications of planners and explains how planners can be evaluated.

General Characteristics of Planning

The first part of this chapter is a general introduction to planning. The sections in this part discuss the following topics:

1. Definition of planning
2. Purposes of planning
3. Advantages and potential disadvantages of planning
4. Primacy of planning

7-1 An understanding of the general characteristics of planning

Defining Planning

Planning is the process of determining how the organization can get where it wants to go and what it will do to accomplish its objectives. In more formal terms, planning is "the systematic development of action programs aimed at reaching agreed-upon business objectives by the process of analyzing, evaluating, and selecting among the opportunities which are foreseen."[2]

Planning is a critical management activity regardless of the type of organization being managed. Modern managers face the challenge of sound planning in small and relatively simple organizations as well as in large, more complex ones; they face the same challenge in nonprofit organizations such as libraries as well as in for-profit organizations such as General Motors.[3]

Purposes of Planning

Over the years, management writers have presented several different purposes of planning. For example, a classic article by C. W. Roney indicates that organizational planning has two types of purposes: protective and affirmative. The protective purpose of planning is to minimize risk by reducing the uncertainties surrounding business conditions and clarifying the consequences of related management actions. The affirmative purpose is to increase the degree of organizational success.[4]

Whole Foods Market, a leading provider of natural and organic foods, relies on the affirmative purpose in its planning. The company uses planning to ensure its success, as measured by the systematic opening of new stores. Currently, Whole Foods has approximately 500 stores in the United States, Canada, and the United Kingdom. Whole Foods's CEO, John Mackey, believes that increased company success is not an accident but a direct result of careful planning.[5]

Another purpose of planning is to establish a coordinated effort within the organization. Where planning is absent, coordination and organizational efficiency are also often absent. Still another purpose of planning is to ensure integration among an organization's various business units; otherwise, the managers of these units might seek to maximize their own objectives.[6]

The fundamental purpose of planning, however, is to help the organization reach its objectives. As Koontz and O'Donnell put it, the primary purpose of planning is "to facilitate the accomplishment of enterprise and objectives."[7] All other purposes of planning are spin-offs of this fundamental purpose.

Planning: Advantages and Potential Disadvantages

A vigorous planning program produces many benefits. First, it helps managers to be future-oriented. They are forced to look beyond their everyday problems to forecast what situations may confront them in the future.[8] Second, a sound planning program enhances decision coordination. No decision should be made today without some idea of how it will affect a decision that might have to be made tomorrow. The planning function thus pushes managers to coordinate their decisions. Third, planning emphasizes organizational objectives. Because organizational objectives are the starting points for planning, managers are continually reminded of exactly what their organization is trying to accomplish.[9]

Overall, planning is advantageous to an organization, particularly in the creation of new ventures.[10] According to an often-cited survey, as many as 65 percent of all newly started

Figure 7.1

Planning as the foundation for organizing, influencing, and controlling

businesses are not around to celebrate a fifth anniversary. This high failure rate seems primarily a consequence of inadequate planning. Successful businesses have an established plan, a formal statement that specifies the objectives the organization is attempting to achieve. Planning does not eliminate risk, of course, but it does help managers identify and deal with organizational problems before they cause havoc in the business.[11]

The downside is that if the planning function is not well executed, planning can have several disadvantages for the organization. For example, an overemphasized planning program can take up too much managerial time. Managers must strike an appropriate balance between time spent on planning and time spent on organizing, influencing, and controlling. If they don't, some activities that are extremely important to the success of the organization may be neglected.[12]

Overall, the advantages of planning definitely outweigh the disadvantages. Usually, the disadvantages of planning result from using the planning function incorrectly.

Primacy of Planning

Planning is the primary management function—the one that precedes and is the basis for the organizing, influencing, and controlling functions of managers. Only after managers have developed their plans can they determine how they want to structure their organization, place their people, and establish organizational controls. As discussed in Chapter 1, planning, organizing, influencing, and controlling are interrelated. Planning is the foundation function and the first one to be performed. Organizing, influencing, and controlling are all based on the results of planning. **Figure 7.1** shows this interrelationship.

Types of Plans

7-2   Knowledge regarding different types of plans

With the repetitiveness dimension as a guide, organizational plans are usually divided into two types: standing and single-use. A **standing plan** is used over and over again because it focuses on organizational situations that occur repeatedly. A **single-use plan** is used only once—or, at most, a few times—because it focuses on unique or rare situations within the organization. As **Figure 7.2** illustrates, standing plans can be subdivided into policies, procedures, and rules, and single-use plans can be subdivided into programs and budgets.

Standing Plans: Policies, Procedures, and Rules

A **policy** is a standing plan that furnishes broad guidelines for taking action that is consistent with reaching organizational objectives. For example, an organizational policy relating to personnel might be worded as follows: "Our organization will strive to recruit only the most talented employees." This policy statement is broad, giving managers only a general idea of what to do in the area of recruitment. However, the policy is intended to emphasize the extreme importance management attaches to hiring competent employees and to guide managers' actions accordingly.

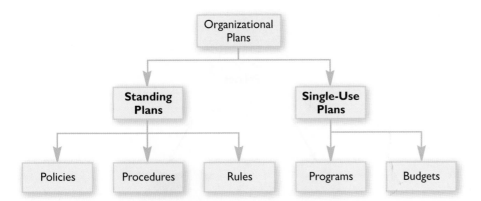

Figure 7.2
Standing plans and single-use plans

As another example of an organizational policy, consider companies' responses to studies showing that one out of every four workers in the United States is attacked, threatened, or harassed on the job during a 12-month operating period. To deal with this problem, many managers are developing weapons policies. A sample policy could be: "Management strongly discourages any employee from bringing a weapon to work." This policy would encourage managers to deal forcefully and punitively with employees who bring weapons into the workplace.[13]

As mentioned in a previous chapter, many organizations today adopt sustainability policies. For example, consider H&M, a discount retailer of men's, women's, and children's fashion apparel. H&M's sustainability policy is closely linked to its business objective, which is to offer fashion and quality at the best price. That means H&M aims to sell only merchandise that has been produced using methods that are environmentally and socially sustainable. In addition, H&M commits to "clean and efficient" transportation as well as environmentally friendly production protocols throughout its global supply chain.[14]

A **procedure** is a standing plan that outlines a series of related actions that must be taken to accomplish a particular task. In general, procedures outline more specific actions than policies do. Organizations usually have many different sets of procedures covering the various tasks to be accomplished. Managers must therefore apply the appropriate organizational procedures carefully and properly for the situations they face.[15]

As an example, Apple changed its manufacturing procedures to integrate green principles into its operations. To eliminate lead in its computer displays, Apple eliminated cathode-ray

Tips for Setting a Budget

Whether you're a multibillion-dollar international business or a college student, setting a budget is important. By using the following tips, both as a consumer and a manager, you will understand how to establish a budget:

- Be aware of how much money you make. Know the amount of income you can truly count on, not what you *hope* to make.
- Have a solid grasp on expenses. Keep track of all of the money "going out."
- Be realistic. If you're certain that you'll get an income increase this year, assume it's probably 2 to 3 percent and not 50.

- Determine a savings amount. Set aside a certain percentage or dollar figure to go into savings.
- Pay off debt. Make certain your budget includes figures to pay off any outstanding loans.
- Evaluate your budget. Check the budget each month to ensure that you stay on track.
- Rework your budget, if necessary. Unexpected expenses do occur, so if one month is particularly devastating for expenses, adjust accordingly for the following months.

Figure 7.3
A successful standing plan program with mutually supportive policies, procedures, and rules

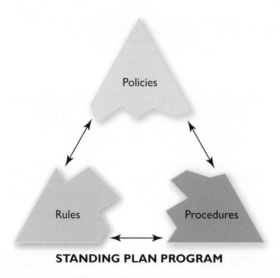

tubes from its designs. Through innovation, the company also managed to eliminate two other deadly chemicals, arsenic and mercury, from its products.[16]

A **rule** is a standing plan that designates specific required actions. In essence, a rule indicates what an organization member should or should not do and allows no room for deviation. An example of a rule that many companies are now establishing is no smoking. The concept of rules may become clearer if one thinks about the purpose and nature of the rules in games such as Scrabble and Monopoly.

Although policies, procedures, and rules are all standing plans, they differ from one another and have different purposes within the organization. As **Figure 7.3** illustrates, however, in order for the standing plans of an organization to be effective, policies, procedures, and rules must be consistent and mutually supportive.

Single-Use Plans: Programs and Budgets

A **program** is a single-use plan that is designed to carry out a special project within an organization. The project itself is not intended to exist over the entire life of the organization. Rather, it exists to achieve a purpose that, if accomplished, will contribute to the organization's long-term success.

A common example is the management development program found in many organizations. This program exists to raise managers' skill levels in one or more of the following areas: technical, conceptual, or human relations skills. Increasing managerial skills, however, is not an end in itself. Instead, the end or purpose of the program is to produce competent managers who are equipped to help the organization be successful over the long term. In fact, once managerial skills have been raised to the desired level, the management development program can be deemphasized. Skills on which modern management development programs commonly focus include understanding and using the computer as a management tool, handling international competition, and planning for a major labor shortage.[17]

A stadium costs billions of dollars to build and requires a budget that plans how funds will be obtained and spent.

A **budget** is a single-use financial plan that covers a specified length of time. It details how funds will be spent on labor, raw materials, capital goods, information systems, marketing, and so on, as well as how the funds will be obtained.[18] Although budgets are planning devices, they are also strategies for organizational control. They are discussed in more detail in Chapter 20.

Steps in the Planning Process

The planning process consists of the following six steps. It is important to note, though, that the planning process is dynamic; in other words, effective planners continuously revisit the planning process.

1. **State organizational objectives**—Because planning focuses on how the management system will reach organizational objectives, a clear statement of those objectives is necessary before planning can begin. Often planners examine important elements of the environment of their organizations, such as the overall economy or competitors, when forming objectives. In essence, objectives stipulate those areas in which organizational planning must occur.[19]

2. **List alternative ways of reaching objectives**—Once organizational objectives have been clearly stated, a manager should list as many available alternatives as possible for reaching those objectives.

3. **Develop premises on which to base each alternative**—To a large extent, the feasibility of using any one alternative to reach organizational objectives is determined by the premises, or assumptions, on which the alternative is based. For example, two alternatives a manager could generate to reach the organizational objective of increasing profit might be to (a) increase the sale of products presently being produced or (b) produce and sell a completely new product. Alternative (a) is based on the premise that the organization can gain a larger share of the existing market. Alternative (b) is based on the premise that a new product would capture a significant portion of a new market. A manager should list all the premises for each alternative.

4. **Choose the best alternative for reaching objectives**—An evaluation of alternatives must include an evaluation of the premises on which the alternatives are based. A manager usually finds that some premises are unreasonable and can therefore be excluded from further consideration. This elimination process helps the manager determine which alternative would best accomplish organizational objectives. The decision making required for this step is discussed more fully in Chapter 8.

5. **Develop plans to pursue the chosen alternative**—After an alternative has been chosen, a manager begins to develop strategic (long-range) and tactical (short-range) plans.[20] More information about strategic and tactical planning is presented in Chapter 9.

6. **Put the plans into action**—Once plans that furnish the organization with both long-range and short-range direction have been developed, they must be implemented. Obviously, the organization cannot directly benefit from the planning process until this step is performed.

Figure 7.4 shows the sequencing of the six steps of the planning process.

7-3 Insights about the major steps of the planning process

Figure 7.4
Elements of the planning process

STEP 1   State organizational objectives

STEP 2   List alternative ways of reaching objectives

STEP 3   Develop premises upon which each alternative is based

STEP 4   Choose best alternative for reaching objectives

STEP 5   Develop plans to pursue chosen alternative

STEP 6   Put the plans into action

Target Corporation is an example of a company that has made charitable giving a significant element of its strategic plan. Since its founding in 1962, Target has allocated 5 percent of company revenues—more than $3 million a week—to programs that serve the communities in which it operates. Consistent with its concern for the health and safety of its communities, Target earmarked $50,000 to aid the National Wildlife Foundation in its cleanup efforts following the explosion of the *Deepwater Horizon* oil rig in the Gulf of Mexico.[21]

Organizational Objectives: Planning's Foundation

7-4 An understanding of the relationship between planning and organizational objectives

The previous section made the point that managers start planning by stating or formulating organizational objectives. Only after they have a clear view of organizational objectives can they appropriately carry out subsequent steps of the planning process. Organizational objectives serve as the foundation on which all subsequent planning efforts are built. The following sections focus on organizational objectives, a critical component of the planning process:

1. Defining organizational objectives
2. Pinpointing areas in which organizational objectives should be established
3. Illustrating how managers work with organizational objectives
4. Discussing management by objectives, an approach to management based mainly on organizational objectives

Definition of Organizational Objectives

An **organizational objective** is the target toward which the open management system is directed. Organizational input, process, and output—topics discussed in Chapter 3—help managers reach organizational objectives (see **Figure 7.5**). Properly developed organizational objectives reflect the purpose of the organization—that is, they flow naturally from the organization's mission. The **organizational purpose** is what the organization exists to do, given a particular group of customers and customer needs. **Table 7.1** contains several statements of organizational purpose, or mission, as developed by actual companies.[22] If an organization is accomplishing its objectives, it is accomplishing its purpose and thereby justifying its reason for existence.

Organizations exist for various purposes and thus have various types of objectives. A hospital, for example, may have the primary purpose of providing high-quality medical services to the community. Therefore, its objectives are aimed at furnishing this service. The primary purpose of a business organization, in contrast, is usually to make a profit. The objectives of the business organization, therefore, concentrate on ensuring that a profit is made. Some companies, however, assume that if they focus on organizational objectives such as producing a quality product at a competitive price, profits will be inevitable.

Such is the case at Lincoln Electric Company. Although profitability is essential for all profit-oriented businesses, management at Lincoln Electric attracted attention when it seemed to diminish the role of profit in the company's organizational objectives:[23]

> The goal of the organization must be this—to make a better and better product to be sold at a lower and lower price. Profit cannot be the goal. Profit must be a by-product. This is a state of mind and a philosophy. Actually, an organization doing this job as it can be done will make large profits, which must be properly divided between user, worker, and stockholder. This takes ability and character.

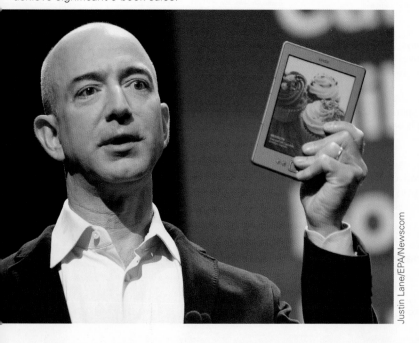

Amazon.com, Inc. seeks to be the global leader in e-commerce. Here, CEO Jeff Bezos holds a Kindle, which helped Amazon achieve significant e-book sales.

Justin Lane/EPA/Newscom

Figure 7.5
How an open management
system operates to reach
organizational objectives

In a 1956 article that has become a classic, John F. Mee suggested that organizational objectives for businesses can be summarized in three points:[24]

1. Profit is the motivating force for managers.
2. Service to customers by the provision of desired economic values (goods and services) justifies the existence of the business.
3. Managers have social responsibilities in accordance with the ethical and moral codes of the society in which the business operates.

Deciding on the objectives for an organization, then, is one of the most important actions managers take. Unrealistically high objectives are frustrating for employees, while objectives that are set too low do not encourage employees to maximize their potentials. Managers should establish performance objectives that they know from experience are within reach for employees but are not within *easy* reach.[25]

Areas for Organizational Objectives

Peter F. Drucker, one of the most influential management writers of modern times, believed that the survival of a management system is endangered when managers emphasize only the profit objective because this single-objective emphasis encourages managers to take action that will make money today but will hold little regard for how a profit will be made tomorrow.[26]

Managers should strive to develop and attain a variety of objectives in all areas where action is critical to the operation and success of the management system. Following are the eight key areas in which Drucker advised managers to set management system objectives:

1. **Market standing**—Management should set objectives indicating where it would like the company to be in relation to its competitors.
2. **Innovation**—Management should set objectives outlining its commitment to the development of new methods of operation.

TABLE 7.1   **Examples of Statements of Organizational Purpose**

Campbell Soup Company	Together we will build the world's most extraordinary food company.
Eli Lilly & Company	We provide customers "Answers That Matter" through innovative medicines, information, and exceptional customer service that enable people to live longer, healthier, and more active lives.
Nike	To bring inspiration and innovation to every athlete in the world.
Charles Schwab	Our mission is to provide the most useful and ethical financial services in the world.
Wendy's	Our mission is to deliver superior quality products and services for our customers and communities through leadership, innovation, and partnerships.

3. **Productivity**—Management should set objectives outlining the target levels of production.
4. **Physical and financial resources**—Management should set objectives regarding the use, acquisition, and maintenance of capital and monetary resources.
5. **Profitability**—Management should set objectives that specify the profit the company would like to generate.
6. **Managerial performance and development**—Management should set objectives that specify rates and levels of managerial productivity and growth.
7. **Worker performance and attitudes**—Management should set objectives that specify rates of worker productivity as well as desirable attitudes for workers to possess.
8. **Public responsibility**—Management should set objectives that indicate the company's responsibilities to its customers and society and the extent to which the company intends to live up to those responsibilities.

According to Drucker, the first five goal areas relate to tangible, impersonal characteristics of organizational operation, and most managers would not dispute their designation as key areas. Designating the last three as key areas, however, could arouse some managerial opposition because these areas are more personal and subjective. Regardless of this potential opposition, an organization should have objectives in all eight areas in order to maximize its probability of success.

Increasing shareholder value represents an additional planning consideration for many publicly traded companies. For example, global oil producer ConocoPhillips unveiled plans to sell $10 billion in assets over a two-year period. Proceeds from the sale, the company said, would be used to pay down debt and increase shareholder value.[27]

Working with Organizational Objectives

Appropriate objectives are fundamental to the success of any organization. Theodore Levitt noted that some leading U.S. industries could be facing the same financial disaster as the railroads faced years ago because their objectives were inappropriate for their organizations.[28]

Managers should approach the development, use, and modification of organizational objectives with the utmost seriousness. In general, an organization should set three types of objectives:[29]

1. **Short-term objectives**—targets to be achieved in one year or less
2. **Intermediate-term objectives**—targets to be achieved in one to five years
3. **Long-term objectives**—targets to be achieved in five to seven years

The necessity of predetermining appropriate organizational objectives has led to the development of a management guideline called the *principle of the objective*. This principle holds that before managers initiate any action, they should clearly determine, understand, and state organizational objectives.

Planning for the future often requires an organization to revisit its original objectives. For example, consider recent planning efforts at Audi. The company reached its goal of delivering 1.5 million cars more than one year ahead of schedule. To celebrate the occasion, leaders set a new goal of delivering 2 million cars. To achieve this goal, Audi wants to increase the number of models it produces from 49 to 60. These goals help to support the company's primary objective of surpassing BMW as the world's largest luxury sales manufacturer.[30]

Guidelines for Establishing Quality Objectives

The quality of goal statements, like that of all humanly developed commodities, can vary drastically. Here are some general guidelines that managers can use to increase the quality of their objectives:[31]

1. **Let the people responsible for attaining the objectives have a voice in setting them**—
   Often the people responsible for attaining the objectives know their job situation better than

managers do and can therefore help make the objectives more realistic. They will also be better motivated to achieve objectives that they have had a say in establishing. Work-related problems that these people face should be thoroughly considered when developing objectives.[32]

2. **State objectives as specifically as possible**—Precise statements minimize confusion and ensure that employees have explicit directions for what they should do.[33] Research shows that when objectives are not specific, the productivity of individuals attempting to reach those objectives tends to fluctuate significantly over time.

3. **Relate objectives to specific actions whenever necessary**—In this way, employees do not have to infer what they should do to accomplish their goals.

4. **Pinpoint expected results**—Employees should know exactly how managers will determine whether an objective has been reached.

5. **Set goals high enough that employees will have to strive to meet them but not so high that employees will give up trying to meet them**—Managers want employees to work hard but do not want them to become frustrated.[34] At the same time, however, research suggests that setting high goals may lead to unethical behavior.[35]

6. **Specify when goals are expected to be achieved**—Employees must have a time frame for accomplishing their objectives. They then can pace themselves accordingly.

7. **Set objectives only in relation to other organizational objectives**—In this way, suboptimization can be kept to a minimum.

8. **State objectives clearly and simply**—The written or spoken word should not impede communicating a goal to organization members.

Management by Objectives (MBO)

Some managers regard organizational objectives as such an important and fundamental part of management that they use a management approach based exclusively on objectives. This approach, called management by objectives (MBO), was popularized mainly through the writings of Peter Drucker. Although mostly discussed in the context of profit-oriented companies, MBO is also a valuable management tool for nonprofit organizations such as libraries and community clubs. The MBO strategy has three basic parts:[36]

7-5 An appreciation for the potential of a management by objectives (MBO) program

1. All individuals within an organization are assigned a specific set of objectives that they try to reach during a normal operating period. These objectives are mutually set and agreed upon by individuals and their managers.[37]

2. Performance reviews are conducted periodically to determine how close individuals are to attaining their objectives.

3. Rewards are given to individuals on the basis of how close they come to reaching their goals.

The MBO process consists of five steps (see **Figure 7.6**):

1. **Review organizational objectives**—The manager gains a clear understanding of the organization's overall objectives.

2. **Set worker objectives**—The manager and the worker meet to agree on worker objectives to be reached by the end of the normal operating period.

3. **Monitor progress**—At intervals during the normal operating period, the manager and the worker check to see whether the objectives are being reached.

4. **Evaluate performance**—At the end of the normal operating period, the worker's performance is judged by the extent to which the worker reached the objectives.

5. **Give rewards**—Rewards given to the worker are based on the extent to which the objectives were reached.

Factors Necessary for a Successful MBO Program

Certain key factors are essential to the success of an MBO program. First, top management must be committed to the MBO process and set appropriate objectives for the organization. All individual MBO goals will be based on these overall objectives; thus, if the overall objectives are inappropriate, individual MBO objectives will also be inappropriate, and related individual work

Figure 7.6
The MBO process

activity will be nonproductive. Second, managers and subordinates together must develop and agree on each individual's goals. If each party is to regard the individual objectives as a serious guide for action, both managers and subordinates must feel that the objectives are just and appropriate. Third, employee performance should be evaluated conscientiously against established objectives. This evaluation helps determine whether the objectives are fair and whether appropriate means are being used to attain them. Fourth, management must follow through on employee performance evaluations by rewarding employees accordingly.

If employees are to continue striving to reach their MBO program objectives, managers must reward those who do reach, or surpass, their objectives rather than those whose performance falls short of their objectives. It goes without saying that such rewards must be given fairly and honestly. Managers must be careful, though, not to conclude automatically that employees have produced at an acceptable level simply because they reached their objectives. Perhaps the objectives were set too low in the first place, and managers failed to recognize it at the time.[38]

MBO Programs: Advantages and Disadvantages

Experienced MBO managers claim that the MBO approach has two advantages. First, MBO programs continually emphasize what should be done in an organization to achieve organizational goals. Second, the MBO process secures employee commitment to attaining organizational goals. Because managers and subordinates have developed the objectives together, both parties are sincerely interested in reaching those goals.

MBO managers also admit that MBO has certain disadvantages. One is that the development of objectives can be time-consuming, leaving both managers and employees less time to do their actual work. Another is that the elaborately written goals, careful communication of goals, and detailed performance evaluations required in an MBO program increase the volume of paperwork in an organization.

On balance, however, most managers believe that the MBO's advantages outweigh its disadvantages. Therefore, they find MBO programs beneficial.[39]

MyLab Management Watch It

If your instructor has assigned this activity, go to www.pearson.com/mylab/management to complete the video exercise.

Planning Tools

7-6 Knowledge about different types of planning tools

Planning tools are techniques managers can use to help develop plans. The remainder of this chapter discusses forecasting and scheduling, two of the most important of these tools.

Forecasting

Forecasting is the process of predicting the likelihood of uncertain events or outcomes that will influence the operation of the organization.[40] Although sophisticated forecasting techniques have been developed rather recently, the concept of forecasting can be traced at least as far back in the management literature as Fayol. The importance of forecasting lies in its ability to help managers understand the future makeup of the organizational environment, which in turn helps them formulate more effective plans.[41] Despite the importance of forecasting, a survey of manufacturers suggests that forecasting is an imprecise science.[42] According to this survey, on average, sales forecasts are off by approximately 20 percent. As such, managers continue to search for more accurate forecasting tools, and some even suggest that forecasting can serve as a strategic advantage.[43] In the following sections, we describe the forecasting process, and then we list a number of tools managers might use to improve forecasts.

How Forecasting Works   William C. House, in describing the Insect Control Services Company, developed an excellent illustration of how forecasting works. In general, Insect Control Services forecasts by attempting to do the following:[44]

1. Establish relationships between industry sales and national economic and social indicators.[45]
2. Determine the impact that government restrictions on the use of chemical pesticides will have on the growth of chemical, biological, and electromagnetic energy pest-control markets.
3. Evaluate sales growth potential, profitability, resources required, and risks involved in each of its market areas (commercial, industrial, institutional, governmental, and residential).
4. Evaluate the potential for expansion of marketing efforts in geographic areas of the United States as well as in foreign countries.
5. Determine the likelihood of technological breakthroughs that would make existing product lines obsolete.

David Gordon/Alamy Stock Photo

Sales managers in Guneagal try to forecast demand for scotch whisky accurately so the company's production managers can plan how to meet the demand profitably.

Types of Forecasts   In addition to the general type of organizational forecasting done by Insect Control Services, specialized types of forecasting, such as economic, technological, social trends, and sales, are available. Although a complete organizational forecasting process should, and usually does, include all these types of forecasting, sales forecasting is considered the key organizational forecast. A *sales forecast* is a prediction of how high or low sales of the organization's products or services will be over the period of time under consideration. It is the key forecast for organizations because it serves as the fundamental guideline for planning. Only after the sales forecast has been completed can managers decide, for example, whether more salespeople should be hired, whether more money for plant expansion must be borrowed, or whether layoffs and cutbacks in certain areas are necessary. Managers must continually monitor forecasting methods to improve them and to reformulate plans based on inaccurate forecasts.[46]

Methods of Sales Forecasting   Modern managers have several different methods available for forecasting sales. The two broad types of sales forecasting methods are qualitative and quantitative. In the following section, we highlight popular qualitative methods (i.e., jury of executive opinion, salesforce estimation). We also highlight quantitative (i.e., moving average, regression, product stages) forecasting methods, which are becoming more prominent as the availability of "big data" increases.[47]

QUALITATIVE METHODS

Jury of Executive Opinion Method.   The **jury of executive opinion method** of sales forecasting is straightforward. Appropriate managers within the organization assemble to discuss

TIPS FOR MANAGING AROUND THE GLOBE

Pyramid Inspiration for Project Management in Egypt

The pyramids of Egypt were built by many thousands of skilled craftsmen, but the project management and planning tools needed to control these vast construction programs were no doubt as sophisticated as any that you can find in modern-day Egypt.

Architects are well-versed in project management, which is a vital approach for complex operations that need to be well-organized and efficient. Pyramid construction time was anything from 10 to 20 years and at an estimated cost of $650 million.

In January 2018, the German conglomerate Siemens announced a $9.4 billion project to build three combined-cycle gas-fired plants in Egypt. This was one part of a range of power station projects announced by the Egyptian government, probably the biggest and most expensive construction projects since the pyramids were built.

The pyramids are tangible proof that project management did not start with Gantt. But history also makes it clear that the most challenging aspect of project management is human resources and creating an environment in which people perform to the best of their abilities.[48]

their opinions on what will happen to sales in the future. Because these discussion sessions usually revolve around hunches or experienced guesses, the resulting forecast is a blend of informed opinions.[49]

A similar, more recently developed forecasting method, called the *Delphi method*, also gathers, evaluates, and summarizes expert opinions as the basis for a forecast, but the procedure is more formal than that for the jury of executive opinion method.[50] The basic Delphi method employs the following steps:

STEP 1: Various experts are asked to answer, independently and in writing, a series of questions about the future of sales or whatever other area is being forecasted.

STEP 2: A summary of all the answers is then prepared. No expert knows how any other expert answered the questions.

STEP 3: Copies of the summary are given to the individual experts with the request that they modify their original answers if they think it is necessary.

STEP 4: Another summary is made of these modifications, and copies again are distributed to the experts. This time, however, expert opinions that deviate significantly from the norm must be justified in writing.

STEP 5: A third summary is made of the opinions and justifications, and copies are once again distributed to the experts. Justification in writing for *all* answers is now required.

STEP 6: The forecast is generated from all the opinions and justifications that arise from step 5.

Salesforce Estimation Method.   The **salesforce estimation method** is a sales forecasting technique that predicts future sales by analyzing the opinions of salespeople as a group. Salespeople continually interact with customers, and from these interactions, they usually develop a knack for predicting future sales. As with the jury of executive opinion method, the resulting forecast normally is a blend of the informed views of the group.

The salesforce estimation method is considered to be a valuable management tool and is commonly used in business and industry throughout the world. Although the accuracy of this method is generally good, managers have found that it can be improved by taking simple steps such as providing salespeople with sufficient time to forecast and offering incentives for accurate forecasts. Some companies help their salespeople become better forecasters by training them to better interpret their interactions with customers.[51]

QUANTITATIVE METHODS

Moving Average.   The **moving average method** utilizes historical data to predict future sales levels. Specifically, forecasters compute average sales levels for *x* historical time periods; forecasters are able to choose the time periods that best fit their situations. Suppose, for example, that forecasters at Toyota are using a five-year moving average to predict future automobile sales. In 2015, they would select the five most recent years—2010 to 2014—and compute

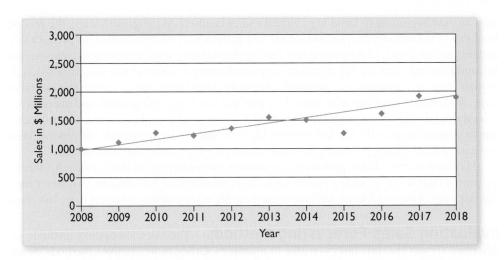

Figure 7.7
Regression analysis method

average automobile sales during that period. In 2014, they would have relied on sales data from 2009 to 2013, and in 2013, they would have relied on sales data from 2008 to 2012. Because the five-year time period changes each year to reflect the five most recent years, this method is referred to as a moving average.

Regression.   The **regression method** predicts future sales by analyzing the historical relationship between sales and time.[52] Using this information, analysts can use regression to forecast future sales. Specifically, regression provides forecasters with a trend line that best illustrates the historical relationship between sales and time. Forecasters can use this trend line to predict future sales. **Figure 7.7** illustrates an example of a trend line that can be used to forecast future sales. Managers often use statistical programs such as SPSS or SAS to conduct regression analysis.

Although the actual number of time periods included in regression varies from company to company, as a general rule, managers should include as many time periods as necessary to ensure that important sales trends do not go undetected. For example, at the Coca-Cola Company, management believes that to predict the annual sales of any one year accurately, it must chart annual sales in each of the 10 previous years.[53]

Product Stages.   The data in Figure 7.7 indicate steadily increasing sales for B. J.'s Men's Clothing over time. In the long term, however, products generally go through what is called a *product life cycle,* so the predicted increase based on the last decade of sales should probably be considered overly optimistic. A **product life cycle** is made up of the five stages through which most products and services pass. These stages are introduction, growth, maturity, saturation, and decline.[54] The **product stages method** predicts future sales by using the product life cycle to better understand the history and future of a product.

Figure 7.8 shows how the five stages of the product life cycle are related to sales volume for seven products over a period of time. In the introduction stage, when a product is brand new,

Figure 7.8
Stages of the product life cycle

sales are just beginning to build (e.g., virtual reality headset). In the growth stage, the product has been in the marketplace for some time and is becoming more accepted, so product sales continue to climb (e.g., tablet computers). During the maturity stage, competitors enter the market, and although sales are still climbing, they are climbing at a slower rate than they did in the growth stage (e.g., smartphone, personal computer). After the maturity stage is the saturation stage, when nearly everyone who wanted the product has it (e.g., refrigerators and microwaves). Sales during the saturation stage typically are due to the need to replace a worn-out product or due to population growth. The last product life cycle stage—decline—finds the product being replaced by a competing product (e.g., conventional [not high-definition] televisions).

Managers may be able to prevent some products from entering the decline stage by improving product quality or by adding innovations. Other products, such as scissors, may never reach this last stage of the product life cycle because there are no competing products to replace them.

Evaluating Sales Forecasting Methods

The sales forecasting methods just described are not the only ones available to managers. Other, more complex methods include the statistical correlation method and the computer simulation method.[55] The methods just discussed, however, do provide a basic foundation for understanding sales forecasting.

In practice, managers find that each sales forecasting method has distinct advantages and distinct disadvantages. Therefore, before deciding to use a particular sales forecasting method, a manager must carefully weigh these advantages and disadvantages as they relate to the manager's organization. The best decision may be to use a combination of methods to forecast sales rather than just one method. In fact, recent research suggests that combining quantitative and qualitative forecasting methods, as opposed to using only quantitative or only qualitative methods, results in better forecasts.[56] Whatever method or methods are finally adopted, the manager should be certain the method is logical, fits the needs of the organization, and can be adapted to changes in the environment.

One study surveyed forecasters to gauge their familiarity with using these forecasting methods.[57] The authors of the study then compared these familiarity statistics with two similar studies conducted in the 1980s and 1990s. The results of the study, which are displayed in **Table 7.2**, reveal some interesting trends. First, the results suggest the increasing popularity of quantitative forecasting methods; in fact, 100 percent of forecasters polled in the 2000s were familiar with the moving average method. In contrast, familiarity with qualitative methods—especially the jury of executive opinion method—has decreased over time.

Scheduling

Scheduling is the process of formulating a detailed listing of activities that must be accomplished to attain an objective, allocating the resources necessary to attain the objective, and setting up and following time tables for completing the objective. Scheduling is an integral part of every organizational plan. Two popular scheduling techniques are Gantt charts and the program evaluation and review technique (PERT).

Gantt Charts

The **Gantt chart**, a scheduling device developed by Henry L. Gantt, is essentially a bar graph with time on the horizontal axis and the resource to be scheduled on the vertical axis. It is used for scheduling resources, including management system inputs such as human resources and machines.

TABLE 7.2 **Familiarity with Forecasting Methods**

	1980s	1990s	2000s
Qualitative Methods			
Jury of Executive Opinion	87%	82%	74%
Salesforce Estimation	84%	85%	83%
Quantitative Methods			
Moving Average	92%	98%	100%
Regression	80%	88%	97%

Note: The numbers in this table reflect the percentage of respondents who were "familiar" or "somewhat familiar" with the corresponding forecasting method.

Figure 7.9
Completed Gantt chart

Figure 7.9 shows a completed Gantt chart for a work period titled "Workweek 28." The resources scheduled over the five workdays on this chart were the human resources Wendy Reese and Peter Thomas. During this workweek, both Reese and Thomas were supposed to produce 10 units a day. Note, however, that actual production deviated from planned production. There were days when each of the two workers produced more than 10 units as well as days when each produced fewer than 10 units. Cumulative actual production for workweek 28 shows that Reese produced 40 units and Thomas 45 units over the five days.

FEATURES

Although simple in concept and appearance, the Gantt chart has many valuable managerial uses.[58] First, managers can use it as a summary overview of how organizational resources are being employed. From this summary, they can detect facts such as which resources are consistently contributing to productivity and which are hindering it. Second, managers can use the Gantt chart to help coordinate organizational resources: The chart can show which resources are not being used during specific periods, thereby allowing managers to schedule those resources for work on other production efforts. Third, the chart can be used to establish realistic worker output standards. For example, if scheduled work is being completed too quickly, output standards should be raised so that workers are scheduled for more work per time period.

Program Evaluation and Review Technique (PERT) The main weakness of the Gantt chart is that it does not contain any information about the interrelationship of tasks

PRACTICAL CHALLENGE: MEETING DEADLINES

Philippine Banks and FATCA

To ensure that their people meet schedules, managers have to be sure that those schedules are realistic and supported by sufficient resources. When there is a punitive cost attached to allowing schedules to slip, the organization and their people need to focus.

In 2010, the U.S. government introduced legislation to discourage tax evasion. All institutions were required to report to the Internal Revenue Service (IRS) if they have American tax-paying clients. A 30-percent levy would be placed on organizations failing to report on time. Philippine banks failed to recognize that the legislation applied to them as well.

By 2015, the U.S. and Philippine governments had reached an agreement to share tax-related information on individuals and corporations. This put the onus back on the banks to ensure compliance. Two years later, over 150 financial institutions had completed their registration via the IRS portal (this included several Tier 1 banks).

Schedules had slipped; many small banks cited uncertainty about the processes and lack of clarity over the regulations. More alarmingly, many of the larger banks had not made any progress at all. Luckily for them, the IRS decided to relax many of the penalties if an institution could prove they were working on compliance but had not yet finished.[59]

to be performed. Although all tasks to be performed are listed on the chart, it is not possible to tell whether one task must be performed before another can be started. The **program evaluation and review technique (PERT)**, a technique that evolved partly from the Gantt chart, is a scheduling tool that does emphasize the interrelationship of tasks.

DEFINING PERT

PERT is a network of project activities showing both the estimates of time necessary to complete each activity and the sequence of activities that must be followed to complete the project. This scheduling tool was developed in 1958 for designing and building the Polaris submarine weapon system. The managers of this project found Gantt charts and other existing scheduling tools of little use because of the complicated nature of the Polaris project and the interdependence of the tasks to be performed.[60]

The PERT network contains two primary elements: activities and events. An **activity** is a specified set of behaviors within a project, and an **event** is the completion of major project tasks. Within the PERT network, each event is assigned corresponding activities that must be performed before the event can materialize.[61]

FEATURES

A sample PERT network designed for building a house is presented in **Figure 7.10.** Events are symbolized by boxes and activities by arrows. To illustrate, the figure indicates that after the event "Foundation complete" (represented by a box) is indeed complete, certain activities (represented by an arrow) must be performed before the event "Frame complete" (represented by another box) can commence.

Two other features of the network shown in Figure 7.10 should be pointed out. First, the left-to-right presentation of events shows how the events interrelate or the sequence in which they should be performed. Second, the numbers in parentheses above each arrow indicate the units of time necessary to complete each activity. These two features help managers ensure that only necessary work is being done on a project and that no project activities are taking too long.[62]

CRITICAL PATH

Managers need to pay close attention to the **critical path** of a PERT network—the sequence of events and activities requiring the longest period of time to complete. This path is called *critical* because a delay in completing this sequence results in a delay in completing the entire project. The critical path in Figure 7.10 is indicated by thick arrows; all other paths are indicated by thin

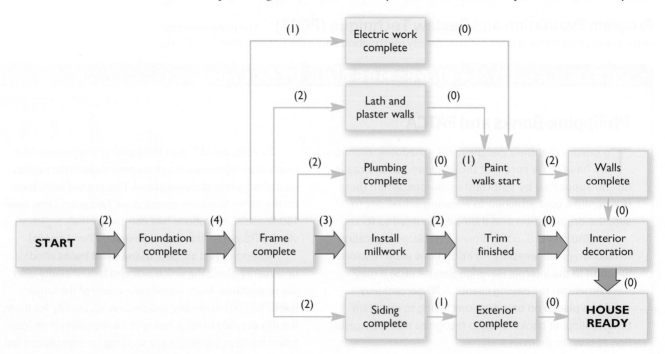

Figure 7.10   PERT network designed for building a house

arrows. Managers try to control a project by keeping it within the time designated by the critical path. The critical path helps them predict which features of a schedule are becoming unrealistic and provides insights into how those features might be eliminated or modified.[63]

STEPS IN DESIGNING A PERT NETWORK

When designing a PERT network, managers should follow four primary steps:[64]

STEP 1: List all the activities and events that must be accomplished for the project and the sequence in which these activities and events should be performed.

STEP 2: Determine how much time will be needed to complete each activity and event.

STEP 3: Design a PERT network that reflects all the information contained in steps 1 and 2.

STEP 4: Identify the critical path.

Why Plans Fail

If managers know why plans fail, they can take steps to eliminate the factors that cause failure and thereby increase the probability that their plans will be successful. A study by K. A. Ringbakk determined that plans fail when:[65]

1. Corporate planning is not integrated into the total management system.
2. There is a lack of understanding of the different steps of the planning process.
3. Managers at different levels in the organization have not properly engaged in or contributed to planning activities.
4. Responsibility for planning is incorrectly vested solely in the planning department.
5. Management expects that plans developed will be realized with little effort.
6. Too much is attempted at once in starting formal planning.
7. Management fails to operate by the plan.
8. Financial projections are confused with planning.
9. Inadequate inputs are used in planning.
10. Management fails to grasp the overall planning process.

It is important to note that failed plans do not always lead to permanent business failures. In some instances, a failing plan can be salvaged through some adjustment or a bit of fine-tuning. In such cases, a "plan B" may provide just the right fit.[66]

CHALLENGE CASE SUMMARY

It seems apparent from the facts in the Challenge Case that Wal-Mart's managers must focus heavily on planning in order for the company's low-price strategy to be successful. Such a process should help determine issues such as what inventory must be purchased to meet demand without waste, when orders should be placed, where merchandise should be stored to meet demand promptly, and how employees can efficiently move inventory onto the shelves as customers buy the items. This process should also focus on how to maintain the quality of Wal-Mart's service.

Because of the many related benefits of planning, Wal-Mart's managers should make certain that the planning process is thorough and comprehensive, one particularly notable benefit of which is the probability of increased profits. To gain the benefits of planning, however, Wal-Mart's managers must be careful that the planning function is well executed and not overemphasized.

Wal-Mart management should also keep in mind that planning is the primary management function. Thus managers should not begin to organize, influence, or control a system until planning for the system is completed.

Planning is the foundation on which all other management functions at Wal-Mart should be based.

Managers like those at Wal-Mart should use their planning process to produce a practical plan for their activities. The process of developing this plan should consist of six steps, beginning with a statement of an organizational objective to design the plan successfully and ending with guidelines for putting the new plan into action. In this case, the ultimate organizational objective involves refocusing the company to build on its historical strengths.

Planning at Wal-Mart, as at any other company, begins with a statement of organizational objectives, the targets toward which the overall organization is aiming. These targets should be consistent with the purpose of Wal-Mart, the reason the company exists. Objectives for a company such as Wal-Mart normally include profit targets, service quality targets, and social responsibility targets. Other organizational objectives would normally focus on market standing, innovation, productivity, and worker performance and attitude. Overall objectives for a company such as Wal-Mart should be of three basic types: short-term objectives to be achieved in a year or less, intermediate objectives to be achieved in one to five years, and long-term objectives to be achieved in five to seven years. In addition, Wal-Mart and similar companies would normally develop a hierarchy of objectives so that individuals at different levels of the organization know what they must do to help reach organizational targets.

Planning for Wal-Mart's activities, such as Black Friday promotions and logistics efficiency, should emphasize how to implement activities to help reach various organizational targets. Overall, Wal-Mart's planning, as it pertains to these and other business activities, should focus on enhancing the accomplishment of its short-term, intermediate-term, and long-term objectives that exist throughout the company's hierarchy of objectives.

Planning activities at a company such as Wal-Mart tend to be more valuable the greater the quality of the organizational objectives. To increase the quality of objectives at Wal-Mart, managers can take steps that allow people responsible for attaining objectives to have a voice in setting them, that state objectives as clearly and simply as possible, and that pinpoint the results expected when the objectives are achieved.

Management at Wal-Mart might be so committed to managing via organizational targets that MBO becomes the primary management approach within the company. Such an approach would involve Wal-Mart's management in monitoring the progress workers are making in reaching established objectives and in using rewards and punishments to hold workers accountable for actually reaching the objectives. An MBO program might be advantageous to Wal-Mart because it would continually emphasize what needs to be accomplished to reach organizational targets. On the other hand, an MBO program might be a disadvantage to Wal-Mart because the process itself can be time-consuming.

One of the planning tools available to Wal-Mart management is forecasting, which involves predicting future environmental events that could influence the operation of the company. Although various types of forecasting—such as economic, technological, and social trends forecasting—are available, Wal-Mart's managers would especially focus on sales forecasting because it predicts how high or low sales will be during the time period managers are considering.

To forecast sales, Wal-Mart's management could also ask its store managers for opinions on predicted sales. Although the opinions of such individuals may not be completely reliable, these people are closest to the market and ultimately make the sales. Wal-Mart might also use the jury of executive opinion method by having its executives discuss their opinions of future sales. This method would be quick and easy to use and, assuming that Wal-Mart executives have a good feel for product demand, might be as valid as any other method the company might use.

Finally, Wal-Mart's management could use the regression analysis method to analyze the relationship between sales and time. Although this method takes into account the cyclical patterns and history of sales, it also assumes the continuation of these patterns into the future without considering outside influences such as economic downturns, which could cause the patterns to change.

Because each sales forecasting method has advantages and disadvantages, managers at Wal-Mart should carefully analyze each method before deciding which method or combination of methods should be used.

Scheduling is another planning tool available to Wal-Mart management. It involves the detailed listing of activities that must be accomplished to reach an objective. For example, Wal-Mart uses schedules to plan how many employees will be needed to work in each store during specific time periods. When employees arrive at work, schedules tell individual workers which checkout line to work in or what items to restock. Sophisticated scheduling software also helps Wal-Mart plan the timing of deliveries to each of its warehouses and stores, with the goal of keeping items in stock at the lowest possible cost.

DEVELOPING PLANNING SKILL

This section is specially designed to help you develop planning skills. An individual's planning skill is based on an understanding of the concepts and the ability to apply those concepts. The following activities will help to enhance your planning skills in various organizational situations.

Class Preparation and Personal Study

To help you prepare for class, perform the activities outlined in this section. Performing these activities will help you enhance your classroom performance significantly.

Reflecting on Target Skill

On page 173, this chapter opens by presenting a target management skill along with a list of related objectives outlining knowledge and understanding that you should aim to acquire related to that skill. Review this target skill and the list of objectives to make sure that you've acquired all pertinent information within the chapter. If you do not feel that you've reached a particular objective(s), study related chapter coverage until you do.

Know Key Terms

Understanding the following key terms is critical to your preparing for class. Define each of these terms. Refer to the page(s) referenced after a term to check your definition or to gain further insight regarding the term.

Know How Management Concepts Relate

This section comprises activities that will further sharpen your understanding of management concepts. Answer these essay questions as completely as possible.

7-1 What are the two main types of single-use plans used by organizations around the world?

7-2 Managers use different types of objectives, developing, using, and modifying them according to organizational needs. Briefly explain the various objectives. Provide an example of each type for an organization of your choice.

7-3 Describe the relationship between planning and the other general functions of management (organizing, controlling, and influencing). In your opinion, which of the four functions is most important?

Management Skills Exercises

Learning activities in this section are aimed at helping you develop planning skills.

MyLab Management
Discussion Questions

Go to www.pearson.com/mylab/management to complete the problems marked with this icon ★.

★ Cases

Wal-Mart Plans to Have What You Want

The Challenge Case "Wal-Mart Plans to Have What You Want" (p. 174) was written to help you better understand the management concepts contained in this chapter. Answer the following discussion questions about the Challenge Case to better understand how principles of planning can be applied in a company like Wal-Mart.

7-4 What special challenges would Wal-Mart face in automating its planning by using a distribution resource planning (DRP) system? What steps would you take to meet these challenges?

7-5 Would you have Wal-Mart's chief executive officer or an appointed planning executive do the planning for Black Friday? Why?

7-6 List three criteria that you would use to evaluate Wal-Mart's planning for Black Friday. Explain why you chose each criterion.

Gillette Finds New Ways to Compete with Dollar Shave Club

Read the case and answer the questions that follow. Studying this case will help you better understand how concepts relating to planning can be applied in a company such as Gillette.

In 2011, the company Dollar Shave Club was launched. It had an impact on the male grooming business in ways that had not been seen in decades. For years, Gillette, which Procter & Gamble purchased in 2005, dominated the industry. Gillette was founded over one hundred years ago and paved the way for the safety razor business as men moved away from the often scary straight razor blade to one with a handle in which individual blades could be inserted and removed when dull. Dollar Shave Club, on the other hand, with its quirky ads and reliance on social media, has caused Gillette to take notice. Dollar Shave Club became a market disrupter when it revolutionized how men buy razors. Using a subscription model, the company mails razors to consumers for a monthly fee that varies between $1 and $9, depending on the level the consumer chooses.[67]

Male grooming is an activity that is not particularly noteworthy, but men spend billions of dollars each year on razors, shaving creams and gels, after-shave lotions, and facial hair trimmers. The design of the razor has remained basically unchanged in the century it has existed. But how men buy their grooming tools has changed. Before, consumers went to a store, purchased a razor, used it until it was no longer sharp, and then acquired another. When disposable blades entered the market, it made shaving even more convenient because users did not have to remove a blade from the handle and insert a new one—when the blade becomes dull on a disposable razor, the entire item, including the handle, is thrown away.

But Dollar Shave Club changed how consumers garner their grooming tools. By using a subscription model, the company can base manufacturing forecasts on the number of paid subscribers. In other words, it does not have to make and then inventory millions of razors in the hopes that they sell.

Gillette has enjoyed a dominant position in the industry. Even today, with upstarts like Dollar Shave Club, Gillette has 65 percent of the market share. But Dollar Shave Club and similar competitors have begun chipping away at that figure. Therefore, Gillette has now put into place plans to go head-to-head with Dollar Shave Club, by disrupting the subscription model that has been so successful so far.

One of the complaints some consumers have about companies like Dollar Shave Club is that the subscription model does not take into account the variability of use that occurs during any given month. Therefore, some subscribers have found themselves with too many blades being sent when they are not needed. Gillette's response is to make the process of purchasing blades even easier than the subscription model.

Gillette's new service is called Gillette on Demand, and all the consumer has to do is text the word *blades* to the company and the refill blades are mailed directly to the purchaser. As an incentive, every fourth order is free.[68] This strategy means that consumers do not have to feel locked into a subscription plan. They can just order directly from the manufacturer when they see it is time for additional blades. Gillette on Demand assures customers that the blades will arrive in two to three days after ordering. It remains to be seen if Dollar Shave Club will institute a similar ordering model for its customers.

Questions

7-7 Assess Gillette's plan for using a texting model to compete with Dollar Shave Club's subscription model. How was Gillette's move an effective strategic plan?

7-8 Would you characterize Gillette's new texting model with Gillette on Demand a standing plan or a single-use plan? Why?

7-9 If Dollar Shave Club also introduces a texting model, how should Gillette revise its plans?

Experiential Exercises

Developing Objectives for the Don Cesar

Directions. Read the following scenario and then perform the listed activities. Your instructor may want you to perform the activities as an individual or within groups. Follow all of your instructor's directions carefully.

You have just been hired as the new assistant manager at the Don Cesar Beach Resort (www.doncesar.com) in St. Petersburg, Florida. This resort, which opened in 1928, has a storied history. The manager of the resort has assigned you and your team the task of identifying new objectives for the resort. He thinks that your fresh perspective might help the organization thrive for the next 100 years. Lead your group by outlining five objectives for the resort. Use the Guidelines for Establishing Quality Objectives listed on pages 182 and 183 to better understand the quality of the five objectives your team developed. Based on these guidelines, which objective was the best? Which objective was the worst? Why?

You and Your Career

The previous section discusses the role of objectives in the planning process. Understanding the importance of objectives will help you further develop your planning skills. As you think about your academic career thus far, describe the role of your own objectives in determining your course grades. Do you have objectives regarding your course grades? Now, think about your career in the future. Do you think employers will find your planning skills attractive? Thinking longer term, how do you think your planning skills will influence your career progression?

Building Your Management Skills Portfolio

Your management skills portfolio is a collection of activities specially designed to demonstrate your management knowledge and skill. Be sure to save your work. You can use this material while preparing for an interview.

The portfolio activity for this chapter is about making an investment in a franchise in Singapore. Study this information and compete the exercises that follow.

Three investors have each put in $100,000 to establish a new business in Singapore. As they want a business that has a proven track record of success, they have asked you to select a franchise opportunity. You have decided to use the franchise and business opportunity portal and search service at singapore.franchiseasia.com to identify a short list of potential investments. Two of the investors are already active in the food-and-beverage markets, and the third has a chain of clothing retail stores. You do not have to be influenced by their current business interests, but something familiar may

encourage them to give the investment the go-ahead. The investors will take a keen interest in the business but will not have the time for hands-on management, which they will leave to you and any management team you put in place.

Your objective involves establishing a plan to invest up to $300,000 in a new franchise. After deciding on your franchise, your investors want you to work through the first five steps of the planning process: (1) State organizational objectives, (2) list alternative ways of reaching those objectives, (3) develop premises on which to base each alternative, (4) choose the best alternative for reaching objectives, and (5) develop plans to pursue the chosen alternative. In the space provided, respond to the following enquiries regarding the first five steps of the planning process.

7-10 Briefly describe the most important characteristics of your chosen franchise.

_____

_____

7-11 Develop three organizational objectives for your chosen franchise.

_____

_____

_____

7-12 Choose one of the three objectives to explore in more detail. List three alternative ways to reach this objective.

_____

_____

_____

7-13 Develop premises to evaluate each of these three alternatives.

_____

_____

_____

7-14 Based on these premises, choose the alternative that is most likely to reach the objective.

_____

_____

_____

7-15 As you think about this alternative, list the significant steps needed to implement this alternative.

_____

_____

_____

11. Kenneth R. Allen, "Creating and Executing a Business Plan," *American Agent & Broker* (July 1994): 20–21.

12. For a discussion of how improper planning might result in a competitive disadvantage, see Yolanda Sarason and Linda Tegarden, "The Erosion of the Competitive Advantage of Strategic Planning: A Configuration Theory and Resource-Based View," *Journal of Business and Management* 9 (2003): 1.

13. Jennifer A. Knight, "Loss Control Solution to Limiting Costs of Workplace Violence," *Corporate Cashflow* (July 1994): 16–17. For an interesting study that explores the emotional conflicts and confusion around corporate success and failure, see Mikita Brottman, "The Company Man: A Case on White-Collar Crime," *American Journal of Psychoanalysis* 69, no. 2 (2009): 121–135.

14. Company website, http://www.hm.com, accessed May 4, 2010.

15. Kirkland Wilcox and Richard Discenza, "The TQM Advantage," *CA Magazine* (May 1994): 37–41.

16. Company website, "A Greener Apple," http://www.apple.com, accessed May 21, 2010.

17. From "Seize the Future—Make Top Trends Pay Off Now," *Success* (March 1990): 39–45.

18. For an interesting article discussing the ethical and cultural challenges involved with budgeting, see Patricia Casey Douglas and Benson Wier, "Cultural and Ethical Effects in Budgeting Systems: A Comparison of U.S. and Chinese Managers," *Journal of Business Ethics* 60, no. 2 (2005): 159–174.

19. For a discussion of U.S. shortsightedness in planning, see Michael T. Jacobs, "A Cure for America's Corporate Short-Termism," *Planning Review* (January/February 1992): 4–9. For a discussion of the close relationship between objectives and planning, see "Mistakes to Avoid: From a Business Owner," *Business Owner* (September/October 1994): 11.

20. For an overview of strategic planning, see Bryan W. Barry, "A Beginner's Guide to Strategic Planning," *The Futurist* 32, no. 3 (April 1998): 33–36.

21. Company website, "Target Donates $50,000 to Support Oil-Spill Cleanup Efforts," May 7, 2010, http://pressroom.target.com.

22. For an excellent resource on mission statements, see Jeffrey Abrahams, *101 Mission Statements from Top Companies* (Berkeley, CA: Ten Speed Press, 2007).

23. James F. Lincoln, "Intelligent Selfishness and Manufacturing," *Bulletin* 434 (New York: Lincoln Electric Company).

24. John F. Mee, "Management Philosophy for Professional Executives," *Business Horizons* (December 1956): 7.

25. David J. Campbell and David M. Furrer, "Goal Setting and Competition as Determinants of Task Performance," *Journal of Organizational Behavior* 16, no. 4 (July 1995): 377–390.

26. Peter F. Drucker, *The Practice of Management* (New York: Harper & Bros., 1954), 62–65, 126–129. For an interesting discussion on objectives and innovation, see Barton G. Tretheway, "Everything New Is Old Again," *Marketing Management* 7, no. 1 (Spring 1998): 4–13. For a tribute to Drucker, see A. J. Vogo, "Drucker, of Course," *Across the Board* 37, no. 10 (November/December 2000): 1.

27. "ConocoPhillips to Shed Half of Lukoil Stake," Forbes.com, March 24, 2010, http://www.forbes.com.

28. Charles H. Granger, "The Hierarchy of Objectives," *Harvard Business Review* (May/June 1964): 64–74; Richard E. Kopelman, "Managing for Productivity: One-Third of the Job," *National Productivity Review* 17, no. 3 (Summer 1998): 1–2. Reprinted with the permission of American Management Association International. New York, NY. All rights reserved; see also Robert Kaplan and David Norton, "How Strategy Maps Frame an Organization's Objectives," *Financial Executive* 20 (2004): 40.

29. Geoffrey Moore, "To Succeed in the Long Term, Focus on the Middle Term," *Harvard Business Review* 85, no. 7/8 (2007): 84–91.

30. F. Geiger, "Audi to Invest $30 Billion through 2018," *Wall Street Journal*, December 27, 2013, http://online.wsj.com/news/articles/SB10001424052702303345104579283811039817926?KEYWORDS=%22new+goal%22, accessed January 21, 2014; A. Cremer, "VW's Audi, Porsche to Keep Growing after Top 2013 Sales," Reuters, January 9, 2014, http://www.reuters.com/article/2014/01/09/porsche-sales-idUSL6N0KJ1ZC20140109, accessed January 21, 2014.

31. Robert L. Mathis and John H. Jackson, *Personnel: Human Resource Management* (St. Paul, MN: West Publishing, 1985), 353–355.

MyLab Management
Writing Assignments

If your instructor has assigned this activity, go to www.pearson.com/mylab/management for the following assisted-graded writing assignments:

Assisted-Grading Questions

7-16 Summarize the primary advantages and disadvantages regarding planning. In your opinion, what is the principal advantage of planning? What is the principal disadvantage of planning?

7-17 Explain five of the primary reasons why plans fail. In your opinion, which one of these reasons is most important? Why?

Endnotes

1. Angela Moscaritolo, "How Walmart Is Gearing Up for Black Friday," *PC Magazine*, November 19, 2013, http://www.pcmag.com; Susanna Kim, "Walmart's Black Friday, Thanksgiving Plans Try to Control Crowds: Will They Work?" *ABC News*, November 20, 2013, http://abcnews.go.com; Tom Andel, "Walmart and the Logistics of Customer Service," *Material Handling & Logistics* (July 2013): 4–5; "Logistics Team Learns to Be Better, Smarter," *MMR*, December 9, 2013, Business Insights: Global, http://bi.galegroup.com; Renee Dudley, "Wal-Mart Trims Forecast as Economy Restrains Shoppers," Bloomberg, http://www.bloomberg.com; Shelly Banjo, "Shoppers Can't Shake the Blues," *Wall Street Journal*, November 14, 2013, http://online.wsj.com; Larry Smith, "Connecting the Consumer to the Factory," *Supply Chain Management Review*, May–June 2013, Business Insights: Global, http://bi.galegroup.com.

2. Harry Jones, *Preparing Company Plans: A Workbook for Effective Corporate Planning* (New York: Wiley, 1974), 3; Richard G. Meloy, "Business Planning," *The CPA Journal* 63, no. 8 (March 1998): 74–75.

3. Robert G. Reed, "Five Challenges Multiple-Line Companies Face," *Market Facts* (January/February 1990): 5–6. For an article on minimizing risk, see "Prior Planning Is Key to Averting a Crisis," *Investor Relations Business* (July 23, 2001): 8.

4. C. W. Roney, "The Two Purposes of Business Planning," *Managerial Planning* (November/December 1976): 1–6; Linda C. Simmons, "Plan. Ready. Aim," *Mortgage Banking* 56, no. 5 (February 1996): 95–96. For an interesting account of the planning function in an international setting, see Gabriel Ogunmokun, "Planning: An Exploratory Investigation of Small Business Organizations in Australia," *International Journal of Management* 15, no. 1 (March 1998): 60–71.

5. Company website, http://www.wholefoodsmarket.com, accessed May 15, 2010; Wendy Zellner, "Moving Tofu into the Mainstream," *BusinessWeek* (May 25, 1992): 94.

6. Paula Jarzabkowski and Julia Balogun, "The Practice and Process of Delivering Integration through Strategic Planning," *Journal of Management Studies* 46, no. 8 (August 2009): 1255–1288.

7. Harold Koontz and Cyril O'Donnell, *Management: A Systems and Contingency Analysis of Management Functions* (New York: McGraw-Hill, 1976), 130.

8. For an interesting discussion on how the importance of planning relates even to day-to-day operations, see Teri Lammers, "The Custom-Made Day Planner," *Inc.* (February 1992): 61–62.

9. For other benefits of planning, see Scott Ransom, "Planning Is Vital New Skill for Physician Executives," *Physician Executive* 29 (2003): 59.

10. A study on the impact of business planning on new ventures is described in Andrew Burke, Stuart Fraser, and Francis J. Greene, "The Multiple Effects of Business Planning on New Venture Performance," *Journal of Management Studies* 47, no. 3 (May 2010): 391–415.

32. Harry Levinson, "Management by Whose Objectives?," *Harvard Business Review* 81 (2003): 107. For more on the importance of employee voice in goal setting, see A. N. Li, H. Liao, S. Tangirala, and B. M. Firth, "The Content of the Message Matters: The Differential Effects of Promotive and Prohibitive Team Voice on Team Productivity and Safety Performance Gains," *Journal of Applied Psychology* (March 30, 2017).

33. E. Gonzalez-Mule, S. H. Courtright, D. DeGeest, J. Seong, and D. Hong, "Channeled Autonomy: The Joint Effects of Autonomy and Feedback on Team Performance through Organizational Goal Clarity," *Journal of Management* 42 (2016): 2018–2033.

34. R. Kanfer, M. Frese, and R. E. Johnson, "Motivation Related to Work: A Century of Progress," *Journal of Applied Psychology*, 102 (2017): 338–355.

35. D. T. Welsh and L. D. Ordonez, "The Dark Side of Consecutive High Performance Goals: Linking Goal Setting, Depletion, and Unethical Behavior," *Organizational Behavior and Human Decision Processes* 123 (2014): 79–89.

36. Robert Rodgers and John E. Hunter, "Impact of Management by Objectives on Organizational Productivity," *Journal of Applied Psychology* (1991): 322–335; Jerry L. Rostund, "Evaluating Management Objectives with the Quality Loss Function," *Quality Progress* (August 1989): 45–49; Peter Crutchley, "Management by Objectives," *Credit Management* (May 1994): 36–38; William J. Kretlow and Winford E. Holland, "Implementing Management by Objectives in Research Administration," *Journal of the Society of Research Administrators* (Summer 1988): 135–141.

37. MBO deals with objectives that are designed based on input from both managers and workers. Nonetheless, some workers may have some subconscious objectives that are not known to managers. For an interesting examination of such objectives, see Alexander D. Stajkovic, Edwin A. Locke, and Eden S. Blair, "A First Examination of the Relationships between Primed Subconscious Goals, Assigned Conscious Goals, and Task Performance," *Journal of Applied Psychology* 91, no. 5 (2006): 1172–1180.

38. Charles H. Ford, "Manage by Decisions, Not by Objectives," *Business Horizons* (February 1980): 17–18. For an interesting description of how firms in Sweden employ MBO, see Terry Ingham, "Management by Objectives—A Lesson in Commitment and Cooperation," *Managing Service Quality* 5, no. 6 (1995): 35–38.

39. For a different viewpoint on the MBO approach, see Harry Levinson, "Management by Whose Objectives?" *Harvard Business Review* (Summer 2010): 28–38.

40. P. J. H. Shoemaker and P. E. Tetlock, "Superforecasting: How to Upgrade Your Company's Judgment," *Harvard Business Review* (May 2016).

41. Charles F. Kettering, "A Glimpse at the Future," *Industry Week* (July 1, 1991): 34.

42. Joanne Tokle and Dennis Krumwiede, "An Overview of Forecasting Error among International Manufacturers," *Journal of International Business Research* 5, no. 2 (2006): 97–105.

43. T. Doering and N. C. Suresh, "Forecasting and Performance: Conceptualizing Forecasting Management Competence as a Higher-Order Construct," *Journal of Supply Chain Management* 52 (2016): 77–91.

44. William C. House, "Environmental Analysis: Key to More Effective Dynamic Planning," *Managerial Planning* (January/February 1977): 25–29. The basic components of this forecasting method, as well as those of other methods, are discussed in Chaman L. Jain, "How to Determine the Approach to Forecasting," *Journal of Business Forecasting Methods & Systems* (Summer 1995): 2, 28. For information about software applications designed to help companies in their planning and forecasting, see "Planning and Forecasting," *Financial Executive* 17, no. 3 (May 2001): 14–15.

45. For an excellent discussion of the influence of industry dynamics on forecasting, see Hao Tan and John A. Mathews, "Identification and Analysis of Industry Cycles," *Journal of Business Research* 63, no. 5 (2010): 454–462.

46. Marshall L. Fisher et al., "Making Supply Meet Demand in an Uncertain World," *Harvard Business Review* (May/June 1994): 83–89; to understand how managerial incentives influence forecast accuracy, see Q. Cheng, T. Luo, and H. Yue, "Managerial Incentives and Management Forecast Precision," *The Accounting Review* 88 (2013): 1575–1602.

47. G. George, E. C. Osinga, D. Lavie, and B. A. Scott, "Big Data and Data Science Methods for Management Research," *Academy of Management Journal* 59 (2016): 1493–1507.

48. ResearchGate, "Building the Case for Historical Project Management," https://www.researchgate.net/publication/304929486_Building_the_Case_for_Historical_Project_Management_Building_the_Case_for_Historical_Project_Management; Egypt Today, "World's 3 Largest Power Plants Are Being Built in Egypt," https://www.egypttoday.com/Article/3/41067/World%E2%80%99s-3-largest-power-plants-are-being-built-in-Egypt.

49. For a new product sales forecast model based on an analytic network process framework, see Dimitra Voulgaridou, Konstantinos Kirytopoulos, and Vrassidas Leopoulos, "An Analytic Network Process Approach to Sales Forecasting," *Operational Research* 9, no. 1 (2009): 35–53.

50. Olfa Hemler, "The Uses of Delphi Techniques in Problems of Educational Innovations," no. 8499, RAND Corporation, December 1966. For an interesting article employing the Delphi method to analyze international trends, see Michael R. Czinkota and Ilkka A. Ronkainen, "International Business and Trade in the Next Decade: Report from a Delphi Study," *Journal of International Business Studies* 28, no. 4 (Fourth Quarter 1997): 827–844.

51. James E. Cox, Jr., "Approaches for Improving Salespersons' Forecasts," *Industrial Marketing Management* 18 (November 1989): 307–311; Jack Stack, "A Passion for Forecasting," *Inc.* (November 1997): 37–38. For more information on forecasting, see Nassim N. Taleb, *The Black Swan: The Impact of the Highly Improbable* (New York: Random House, 2007).

52. For an application of time series analysis, see Lester Hunt and Yasushi Ninomiya, "Unraveling Trends and Seasonality: A Structural Time Series Analysis of Transport Oil Demand in the UK and Japan," *Energy Journal* 24 (2003): 63.

53. N. Carroll Mohn, "Forecasting Sales with Trend Models—Coca-Cola's Experience," *Journal of Business Forecasting* 8 (Fall 1989): 6–8. For an interesting article that describes the use of time series analysis in predicting the alcohol consumption of Europeans, see David E. Smith and Hans S. Solgaard, "Global Trends in European Alcoholic Drinks Consumption," *Marketing and Research Today* 26, no. 2 (May 1998): 80–85. For a historical perspective of time series analysis, see D. S. G. Pollock, "Statistical Visions in Time: A History of Time Series Analysis, 1662–1938," *Economica* 67, no. 267 (August 2000): 459–461.

54. For information on product life cycles, see George S. Day, "The Product Life Cycle: Analysis and Applications Issues," *Journal of Marketing* 45, no. 4 (1981): 60–67; to understand how life cycles may vary based on a company's industry, see E. V. Karniouchina, S. J. Carson, J. C. Short, and D. J. Ketchen, Jr., "Extending the Firm vs. Industry Debate: Does Industry Life Cycle Stage Matter?," *Strategic Management Journal* 34 (2013): 1010–1018.

55. For elaboration on these methods, see George A. Steiner, *Top Management Planning* (London: Collier-Macmillan, 1969), 223–227.

56. See also M. Seifert and A. L. Hadida, "On the Importance of Linear Model and Human Judge(s) in Combined Forecasting," *Organizational Behavior and Human Decision Processes* 120: 24–36.

57. This discussion and the accompanying table are based on Teresa M. McCarthy, Donna F. Davis, Susan L. Golicic, and John T. Mentzer, "The Evolution of Sales Forecasting Management: A 20-Year Longitudinal Study of Forecasting Practices," *Journal of Forecasting* 25 (2006): 303–324. For an alternative view of several case studies related to the worst business forecasting practices of companies and their solutions, see Lad A. Dilgard, "Worst Forecasting Practices in Corporate America and Their Solutions—Case Studies," *Journal of Business Forecasting* 28, no. 2 (2009): 4–13.

58. James Wilson, "Gantt Charts: A Centenary Appreciation," *European Journal of Operational Research* 149 (2003): 430. To better understand the sensitivity of Gantt charts, see S. A. Oke and O. E. Charles-Owaba, "A Sensitivity Analysis of an Optimal Gantt Charting Maintenance Scheduling Model," *The International Journal of Quality & Reliability Management* 23, no. 2/3 (2006): 197–229.

59. Wouter Delbaere, "FATCA Readiness of Banks in Philippines," Wolters Kluwer Financial Services, www.wolterskluwerfs.com/comment/FATCA-readiness-in-the-Philippines.pdf; ASEAN Briefing, "The Philippines Signs IGA on FATCA with the United States," July 17, 2015, https://www.aseanbriefing.com/news/2015/07/17/

the-philippines-signs-iga-on-fatca-with-the-united-states.html; Jay A. Ballesteros, "FATCA: Where Are We Now?", BusinessWorld Online, September 21, 2015, http://bworldonline.com/content. php?section=Economy&title=fatca-where-are-we-now&id=115621.

60. Willard Fazar, "The Origin of PERT," *The Controller* (December 1962). For a discussion of software packages that draw preliminary PERT and Gantt charts, see Pat Sweet, "A Planner's Best Friend?," *Accountancy* (February 1994): 56, 58. See also Curtis F. Franklin, Jr., "Project Managers Toolbox," *CIO* 11, no. 2 (October 15, 1997): 64–70. For an extension of the Gantt chart, see Harvey Maylor, "Beyond the Gantt Chart: Project Management Moving On," *European Management Journal* 19, no. 1 (February 2001): 92–100.

61. See also H. M. Soroush, "The Most Critical Path in a PERT Network," *Journal of the Operational Research Society* 45 (March 1994): 287–300.

62. For insights about using PERT, see Jose Perez, Salvador Rambaud, and Jose Velasco, "Some Indications to Correctly Use Estimations of an Expert in the PERT Methodology," *Central European Journal of Operations Research* 11 (2003): 183.

63. Avraham Shtub, "The Integration of CPM and Material Management in Project Management," *Construction Management and Economics* 6 (Winter 1988): 261–272; Michael A. Hatfield and James Noel, "The Case for Critical Path," *Cost Engineering* 40, no. 3 (March 1998): 17–18.

64. For extended discussion of these steps, see Edward K. Shelmerdine, "Planning for Project Management," *Journal of Systems Management* 40 (January 1989): 16–20.

65. Kjell A. Ringbakk, "Why Planning Fails," *European Business* (July 1970). See also William G. Gang, "Strategic Planning and Competition: A Survival Guide for Electric Utilities," *Fortnightly* (February 1, 1994): 20–23.

66. Alden M. Hayashi, "Do You Have a 'Plan B'?," *MIT Sloan Management Review*, October 1, 2009, http://sloanreview.mit.edu.

67. "Dollar Shave Club Continues to Shake Things Up," *Chain Drug Review* 38, no. 17 (November 7, 2016): 24.

68. Phil Wahba, "Gillette Is Betting on Texting to Compete with Dollar Shave Club," fortune.com, May 9, 2017.

Making Decisions

8

DECISION-MAKING SKILL AND YOUR CAREER

Decision-making skill will be of great value to you in enhancing your career. This skill can help you evaluate and choose alternatives that increase the likelihood of accomplishing your objectives. Choosing alternatives that increase the likelihood of accomplishing objectives contributes to organizational success, builds your image as a competent manager, makes you valuable to your organization, and supports promotions as you build your career.

OBJECTIVES

To help build my *decision-making skill*, when studying this chapter, I will attempt to acquire:

8-1 A fundamental understanding of the term *decision*

8-2 An understanding of each element of the rational decision-making process

8-3 An appreciation of the role of intuition in decision making

8-4 Insights regarding the various tools used to make decisions

8-5 An understanding of how groups make decisions

MyLab Management Chapter Warm Up

If your instructor has assigned this activity, go to www.pearson.com/mylab/management to complete the chapter warm up.

CHALLENGE CASE

Whole Foods Decides to Open in Detroit

Even people who love to shop at Whole Foods sometimes jokingly call the store "Whole Paycheck." Why, then, did the company recently decide to open a store in Detroit—a city that in recent decades has been known mainly for its depressed economy and plummeting population?

Although Whole Foods has a reputation for moving cautiously on expansion decisions, the Detroit store represents the first time the company chose to build in what the *Detroit Free Press* described as a "distressed urban location."

To arrive at the decision, Whole Foods's executives looked at a variety of criteria. The neighborhood to be served by the store, which includes Wayne State University and the Detroit Medical Center, has recently experienced population growth. And in nearby downtown, Quicken Loans rented office space for its Michigan staff of 3,000. Thanks to these employers, there is nearby traffic of professionals who might be attracted to an upscale store. In fact, Whole Foods sees pent-up demand in the area because supermarket chains have fled the city, forcing residents to drive to the suburbs to buy groceries.

Whole Foods also saw qualities in Detroit suggesting that its residents would embrace the new store. As the retailer's employees worked with citizens' and business development groups, they noticed practical evidence of an interest in eating well. For instance, residents have established more than 800 community gardens in Detroit's acreage of vacant lots. In addition, tens of thousands shop at Detroit's popular Eastern Market, one of the nation's largest farmers' markets. Taken together, Red Elk Banks, Whole Foods's operations chief in Michigan, says these practices represent important factors in the decision to open a Detroit store.

Complementing these practices, Whole Foods also obtained demographic information supporting the idea of a new store in Detroit. This information showed a desire for more access to organic foods. The information also showed buying power: Detroiters have been spending $200 million annually in the suburbs. By choosing a location near freeways, Whole Foods hopes to capture some of the people traveling between the city and the suburbs.

Whole Foods's president of Midwest operations, Michael Bashaw, told the *Wall Street Journal*, "We certainly expect [the Detroit store] to be profitable." Time will tell whether or not Bashaw was a good forecaster and whether the site selection illustrates keen business insight or foolish optimism.[1]

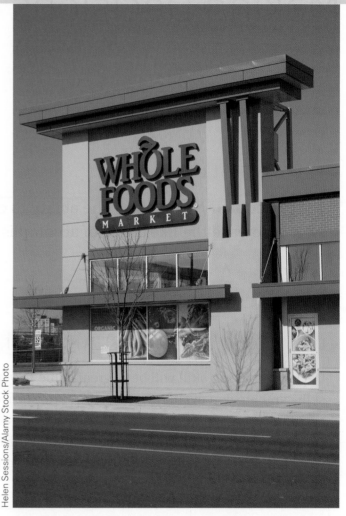

Helen Sessions/Alamy Stock Photo

Whole Foods opened a store in Detroit because research showed that the area's growing population was interested in organic food.

THE DECISION-MAKING CHALLENGE

The Challenge Case focuses on the opening of a Whole Foods store. The information in this chapter discusses specifics surrounding a decision-making situation and provides insights about the steps Whole Foods management might have taken in making this decision. This chapter discusses (1) the fundamentals of decisions, (2) the decision-making process, (3) various decision-making conditions, (4) decision-making tools, and (5) group decision making. These topics are critical to managers and other individuals who make decisions.

Fundamentals of Decisions

Definition of a Decision

A **decision** is a commitment to a course of action that serves the interests of certain individuals.[2] *Decision making* is the process of choosing the best alternative for reaching objectives. Decision making is covered in the planning section of this text, but because managers must also make decisions when performing the other three managerial functions—organizing, influencing, and controlling—the subject requires a separate chapter.

We all face different types of decision situations. A decision situation may involve simply choosing whether to spend the day studying, swimming, or golfing. More complex decisions involve choosing where to live, which job to accept, and whom to marry. The ramifications of some of these decisions are trivial, but at other times they are long-lasting.

Managers make decisions affecting the organization daily and communicate those decisions to other organization members.[3] Not all managerial decisions are of equal significance to the organization. Some affect a large number of organization members, cost a great deal of money to carry out, and have a long-term effect on the organization. Such significant decisions can have a major impact not only on the management system itself but also on the career of the manager who makes them. Other decisions are fairly insignificant, affecting only a small number of organization members, costing little to carry out, and producing only a short-term effect on the organization.

Types of Decisions

Decisions can be categorized according to how much time a manager must spend making them, what proportion of the organization must be involved in making them, or the organizational functions on which they focus. Probably the most generally accepted method of categorizing decisions, however, is based on computer language; it divides all decisions into two basic types: programmed and nonprogrammed.[4]

A **programmed decision** is routine and repetitive, and the organization typically develops specific ways to handle such decisions. A programmed decision might involve determining how products will be arranged on the shelves of a supermarket. For this kind of routine, repetitive problem, standard-arrangement decisions are typically made according to established management guidelines.

In contrast, a **nonprogrammed decision** is typically a one-shot decision that is usually less structured than programmed decisions. An example of the type of nonprogrammed decision that more and more managers must make is whether to expand operations into the "forgotten continent" of Africa.[5] Another example is deciding whether a supermarket should carry an additional type of bread. The manager making this decision must consider whether the new bread will merely stabilize bread sales by competing with existing bread carried in the store or actually increase bread sales by offering a desired brand of bread to customers who have never before bought bread in the store. These types of issues must be dealt with before the manager can finally decide whether to offer the new bread. **Table 8.1** shows traditional and modern ways of handling programmed and nonprogrammed decisions.

8-1   A fundamental understanding of the term *decision*

TABLE 8.1   **Traditional and Modern Ways of Handling Programmed and Nonprogrammed Decisions**

Types of Decisions	Decision-Making Techniques	
	Traditional	**Modern**

Programmed:
Routine, repetitive decisions
Organization develops specific processes for handling them
	1. Habit
	2. Clerical routine:
	    Standard operating procedures
	3. Organization structure:
	    Common expectations
	    A system of subgoals
	    Well-defined information channels
		1. Operations research:
		    Mathematical analysis models
		    Computer simulation
		2. Electronic data processing

Nonprogrammed:
One-shot, ill-structured, novel policy decisions
Handled by general problem-solving processes
	1. Judgment, intuition, and creativity
	2. Rules of thumb
	3. Selection and training of executives
		1. Heuristic problem-solving techniques applied to:
		    Training human decision makers
		    Constructing heuristic computer programs

Figure 8.1

Decision programming
continuum

Programmed and nonprogrammed decisions should be thought of as being at opposite ends of the decision programming continuum, as illustrated in **Figure 8.1**. As the figure indicates, however, some decisions are neither programmed nor nonprogrammed, but fall somewhere between the two. One of the key distinctions between programmed versus nonprogrammed decisions is that programmed decisions typically require less time and effort compared to nonprogrammed decisions.

The Responsibility for Making Organizational Decisions

Many different kinds of decisions must be made within an organization—such as how to manufacture a product, how to maintain the machines, how to ensure product quality, and how to establish advantageous relationships with customers. Because organizational decisions can be so varied, some type of rationale must be developed to stipulate who within the organization has the responsibility for making which decisions.

One such rationale is based primarily on two factors: the scope of the decision to be made and the levels of management. The **scope of the decision** is the proportion of the total management system that the decision will affect. The greater this proportion, the broader the scope of the decision is said to be. *Levels of management* are simply lower-level management, middle-level management, and upper-level management. The rationale for designating who makes which decisions is that the broader the scope of the decision, the higher the level of the manager responsible for making that decision. **Figure 8.2** illustrates this rationale.

To better understand the role of delegation in different contexts, consider the decisions facing sisters Heather Castagna and Holly Rand, the owners of Lubbock, Texas–based Green Queens, a recycling company. An uptick in residential business and several new commercial contracts required Castagna and Rand to make major decisions about their firm's future, including a possible location change and the need to hire additional employees. As small-business owners, Castagna and Rand are responsible for making such decisions; they cannot delegate them to others.[6]

It is important to point out that the manager who is responsible for making a particular decision can seek the advice of other managers or subordinates before settling on an alternative. In his article "Moon Shots for Management," business thinker Gary Hamel observes that senior-level

Shaw Industries Paves the Way for Good Decisions

The main challenge with programmed decisions is the initial planning of what to do in each possible situation. For international businesses, that challenge is extremely complex when managers consider all the different situations possible. Take the example of Shaw Industries, the world's largest maker of carpeting. The company, based in Dalton, Georgia, operates 10 subsidiaries in Europe, Asia, and Australia. Its 25,000 employees produce yarn, manufacture carpets and hardwood and laminate flooring, transport goods, and sell millions of dollars' worth of products.

Coordinating these activities requires a multitude of decisions about what to order and when, and how much to produce and where. To make such decisions quickly and consistently across divisions, Shaw invested in sophisticated software called enterprise resource planning (ERP). The ERP system it selected, NetSuite OneWorld, includes decision rules for activities such as inventory management, manufacturing, and purchasing, and it creates financial reports to show whether decisions need to be adjusted.[7]

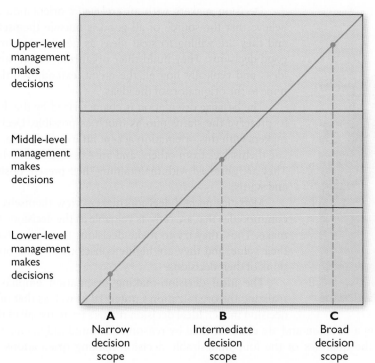

Figure 8.2
Level of managers responsible for making decisions as decision scope increases from A to B to C

decision making is often marked by "executive hubris, unstated biases, and incomplete data." Hamel suggests that employees closest to a situation are often in the best position to evaluate alternatives or weigh in on the issues that will affect the decision.[8] Consistent with this idea, some managers prefer to use groups and input from other employees to make certain decisions.

Consensus is one method a manager can use in getting a group of people to arrive at a particular decision. **Consensus** is an agreement on a decision by all the individuals involved in making that decision. It usually is reached after lengthy deliberation and discussion by members of the decision group, who may be either all managers or a mixture of managers and subordinates.[9]

The manager who asks a group to produce a consensus decision must bear in mind that groups will sometimes be unable to arrive at a decision. Lack of technical skills or poor interpersonal relations may prove insurmountable barriers to arriving at a consensus. When a group is stalemated, a manager needs to offer assistance in making the decision or simply make it herself.

Decisions arrived at through consensus have both advantages and disadvantages. One advantage of this method is that it focuses "several heads" on the decision. Another is that employees are more likely to be committed to implementing a decision if they helped make it. The main disadvantage of this method is that it often involves time-consuming discussions relating to the decision, which can be costly to the organization.

Elements of the Decision Situation

In their article, "Basic Frameworks for Decision," Charles Wilson and Marcus Alexis isolate several basic elements of the decision situation.[10] Five of these elements are defined and discussed in this section.

The Decision Makers
Decision makers, the first element of the decision situation, are the individuals or groups who actually make the choice among the alternatives. According to Ernest Dale, weak decision makers usually have one of four orientations: receptive, exploitative, hoarding, or marketing.[11]

Decision makers who have a *receptive* orientation believe that the source of all good is outside themselves, and therefore they rely heavily on suggestions from other organization members. Basically, they want others to make their decisions for them.

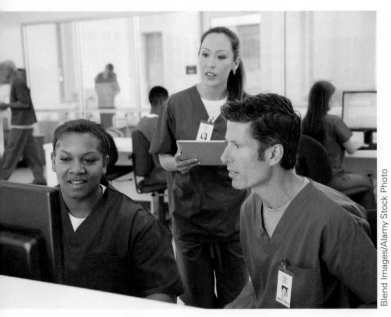

Blend Images/Alamy Stock Photo

Ideally this nursing manager emphasizes the organization's potential, uses all her talents to make decisions, and applies reason and sound judgment.

Decision makers with an *exploitative* orientation also believe that the source of all good is outside themselves, and they are willing to steal ideas as necessary to make good decisions. They build their organizations on others' ideas and typically hog all the credit, extending little or none to the originators of the ideas.

The *hoarding* orientation is characterized by the desire to preserve the status quo as much as possible. Decision makers with this orientation accept little outside help, isolate themselves from others, and are extremely self-reliant. They are obsessed with maintaining their present position and status.

Marketing-oriented decision makers view themselves as commodities that are only as valuable as the decisions they make. Thus, they try to make decisions that will enhance their value, and they are highly conscious of what others think of their decisions.

The ideal decision-making orientation emphasizes realizing the organization's potential as well as that of the decision maker. Ideal decision makers try to use all of their talents when making a decision and are characterized by reason and sound judgment. They are largely free of the qualities of the four undesirable decision-making orientations just described.[12]

For an example of an ideal decision maker, consider Jeff Brown, whose chain of ShopRite supermarkets operates in economically depressed communities in Pennsylvania and New Jersey—communities that other grocery chains view as too risky. Brown, whose company was named one of the region's top employers, entrusts his employees with the authority to make major store decisions and the freedom to learn from their mistakes without fear of reprisal. Union leaders say Brown encourages their union members—his employees—to think creatively and try new ideas. In their many years of dealing with Brown, the union claims, no case has ever gone to arbitration.[13]

Goals to Be Served   The goals that decision makers seek to attain are another element of the decision situation. In the case of managers, these goals should most often be organizational objectives. (Chapter 7 discussed the specifics of organizational objectives.)

Relevant Alternatives   The decision situation is usually composed of at least two relevant alternatives. A **relevant alternative** is one that is considered feasible for solving an existing problem and for implementation. Alternatives that will not solve an existing problem or cannot be implemented are irrelevant and should be excluded from the decision-making situation.

Ordering of Alternatives   The decision situation requires a process or mechanism for ranking alternatives from most desirable to least desirable. This process can be subjective, objective, or a combination of the two. Past experience of the decision maker is an example of a subjective process, and the rate of output per machine is an example of an objective process.

Choice of Alternatives   The last element of the decision situation is the actual choice among available alternatives. This choice establishes the decision. Typically, managers choose the alternative that maximizes long-term return for the organization.

The Rational Decision-Making Process

8-2   An understanding of each element of the rational decision-making process

A decision is a choice of one alternative from a set of available alternatives. The **rational decision-making process** comprises the steps the decision maker takes to arrive at this choice. The process a manager uses to make decisions has a significant impact on the quality of those decisions.

Figure 8.3
Model of the decision-making process

If managers use an organized and systematic process, the probability that their decisions will be sound is higher than if they use a disorganized and unsystematic process.[14]

A model of the decision-making process that is recommended for managerial use is presented in **Figure 8.3**. In order, the decision-making steps this model depicts are as follows:

1. Identify an existing problem.
2. List possible alternatives for solving the problem.
3. Select the most beneficial of these alternatives.
4. Implement the selected alternative.
5. Gather feedback to find out whether the implemented alternative is solving the identified problem.

The paragraphs that follow elaborate on each of these steps and explain their interrelationships.[15]

This model of the decision-making process is based on three primary assumptions.[16] First, the model assumes that humans are economic beings with the objective of maximizing satisfaction or return. Second, it assumes that, within the decision-making situation, all alternatives and their possible consequences are known. Its last assumption is that decision makers have some priority system to guide them in ranking the desirability of each alternative. If each of these assumptions is met, the decision made will probably be the best possible one for the organization. In real life, unfortunately, one or more of these assumptions is often not met, and therefore the decision made is less than optimal for the organization.

Identifying an Existing Problem

Decision making is essentially a problem-solving process that involves eliminating barriers to organizational goal attainment. The first step in this elimination process is identifying exactly what the problems or barriers are: Only after the barriers have been adequately identified can management take steps to eliminate them.

As a classic example of making decisions to overcome a problem, consider how Canadian brewer Molson handled a barrier to success: a free-trade agreement that threatened to open Canadian borders to U.S. beer. Although the borders were not due to open for another five years, Molson decided to deal immediately with the impending threat of increased beer competition from the United States by increasing production and sales of its other product line: specialty chemical products. Within four years, Molson's chemical sales exceeded its beer sales. Essentially, the company identified its problem—the threat of increased U.S. competition for beer sales—and dealt with it by concentrating on sales in a different division.[17]

Chester Barnard stated that organizational problems are brought to the attention of managers mainly by the following means:[18]

1. Orders issued by managers' supervisors
2. Situations relayed to managers by their subordinates
3. The normal activity of the managers themselves

Listing Alternative Solutions

Once a problem has been identified, managers should list the various possible solutions. Few organizational problems are solvable in only one way. Managers must search for the numerous available alternative solutions to most organizational problems.

Figure 8.4

Additional factors that limit a manager's number of acceptable alternatives

Before searching for solutions, however, managers should be aware of five limitations on the number of problem-solving alternatives available:[19]

1. Authority factors (e.g., a manager's superior may have told the manager that a certain alternative is not feasible)
2. Biological or human factors (e.g., human factors within the organization may be inappropriate for implementing certain alternatives)
3. Physical factors (e.g., the physical facilities of the organization may be inappropriate for certain alternatives)
4. Technological factors (e.g., the level of organizational technology may be inadequate for certain alternatives)
5. Economic factors (e.g., certain alternatives may be too costly for the organization)

Figure 8.4 presents additional factors that can limit a manager's decision alternatives. This diagram uses the term *discretionary area* to depict all the feasible alternatives available to managers. Factors that limit or rule out alternatives outside this area are legal restrictions, moral and ethical norms, formal policies and rules, and unofficial social norms.[20]

Finally, managers should be aware of the negative effects of generating too many alternatives. Intuitively, generating more alternatives would seemingly lead to more effective decision making. Research suggests, however, that having too many alternatives may actually demotivate decision makers, which harms decision making; this is known as the **paradox of choice**.[21]

To reduce the influence of the paradox of choice, individuals may reduce the number of alternatives from which they must choose to form a smaller and more manageable set of alternatives. Research indicates that there exist two types of strategies that individuals use to reduce the number of alternatives. **Inclusion** occurs when individuals choose a smaller set of the most desirable alternatives from a larger set of alternatives. **Exclusion** occurs when individuals exclude the least desirable alternatives from a larger set of alternatives. Research suggests that, compared to inclusion, exclusion results in a larger consideration set. Therefore, the risk of eliminating a potentially desirable alternative is greater using inclusion than it is using exclusion.[22]

Selecting the Most Beneficial Alternative

Decision makers can select the most beneficial solution only after they have evaluated each alternative carefully. This evaluation should consist of three steps. First, decision makers should collect as much information as possible and list, as accurately as possible, the potential effects of each alternative as if the alternative had already been chosen and implemented.[23] Second, they should assign a probability factor to each of the potential effects; that is, they should indicate how probable the occurrence of the effect would be if the alternative were implemented.[24] Third, keeping organizational goals in mind, decision makers should compare each alternative's expected effects and the respective probabilities of those effects.[25] After these steps have been completed, managers will know which alternative seems most advantageous to the organization.

Managers should be aware, however, that research suggests that past decisions often influence current choices of alternatives.[26] Consequently, managers should try to avoid the natural tendency to make the same choices repeatedly.

Implementing the Chosen Alternative

The next step is to put the chosen alternative into action. Decisions must be supported by appropriate action if they have a chance of success.

Gathering Problem-Related Feedback

After the chosen alternative has been implemented, decision makers must gather feedback to determine the effect of the implemented alternative on the identified problem. If the identified problem is not being solved, managers need to seek out and implement another alternative.

Bounded Rationality

We just described the rational decision-making process. However, Herbert Simon questioned the ability of managers to make rational decisions. In his opinion, managers are not able to make perfectly rational decisions. Instead, Simon put forth the idea that managers deal with **bounded rationality**, which refers to the fact that managers are bounded in terms of time, computational power, and knowledge when making decisions.[27] In other words, managers do not always have access to the resources required to make rational decisions. As a result of bounded rationality, Simon suggested that managers **satisfice**, which occurs when an individual makes a decision that is not optimal but is "good enough." For example, a manager may hire the first person who is acceptable according to the hiring criteria and not interview the remaining candidates. In this example, a better candidate may exist, but the manager has satisficed by selecting the first "acceptable" candidate.

PRACTICAL CHALLENGE: DECISION MAKING AND INTUITION

Tony Fernandes Is Not a Rational Thinker (Or Maybe He Is)!

With the Malaysian government committed to Malaysia Airlines (MAS), trying to compete with the national carrier should have been the antithesis of rational thinking. During a stopover in London, Malaysian-British entrepreneur Tony Fernandes saw Stelios Haji-Ioannou, founder of easyJet, on the television. He listened as Stelios explained the low-cost carrier model. Fernandes knew it would work in Southeast Asia.

Conceived as a sister airline to MAS and founded by the Malaysian government, AirAsia had repeatedly failed to produce profits. When Fernandes approached the government in 2001, the airline had been reduced to a shell company carrying a debt of $37 million. The Malaysian government had been trying to offload AirAsia for two years and jumped at the chance to sell it to Fernandes' Tune Air. For the princely sum of $0.26, Fernandes received two old air carriers and debts of over $11 million. By 2013, AirAsia was reporting a net income of $111 million.[28]

Decision Making and Intuition

8-3 An appreciation of the role of intuition in decision making

As already discussed, the rational decision-making process includes a sequence of five steps. We also noted, however, that researchers have highlighted the potential influence of bounded rationality on this process. More recent research has suggested that individuals may also rely on additional processes when making decisions. In fact, Stanovich and West suggest that individuals use two different processes when making decisions.[29] According to their framework, the rational decision-making process discussed in the previous section is known as "System 2."

Complementing this formal system of decision making, Stanovich and West suggest that individuals also rely on a less formal process based on intuition to make decisions; they refer to this process as "System 1." Consistent with their framework, System 2 is a process described as being slow, comprehensive, and deliberate, whereas System 1 is described as being fast, automatic, and intuitive. **Intuition**, in fact, refers to an individual's inborn ability to synthesize information quickly and effectively.[30] Taken together, some researchers suggest that individuals employ the more sophisticated System 2 process to monitor or override the more automatic System 1 process. Often, however, System 2 does not monitor System 1 effectively; in such cases, intuition drives decision making.

Decision-Making Heuristics and Biases

Daniel Kahneman and Amos Tversky were awarded the Nobel Prize for further examining the role of intuition in decision making. In particular, their groundbreaking research examined how individuals use **heuristics**, or simple rules of thumb, to make decisions. In addition, Kahneman and Tversky examined how these heuristics introduce bias in decision-making processes. **Bias** refers to departures from rational theory that produce suboptimal decisions. In other words, when managers rely on rules of thumb when making decisions, their decisions are often flawed. Kahneman and Tversky's work spurred a great deal of interest in the discovery and examination of a number of decision-making biases. Researchers have discovered many other decision-making biases; **Table 8.2** summarizes some of the more prominent biases examined by decision-making researchers.

Decision-Making Conditions: Risk and Uncertainty

In most instances, it is impossible for decision makers to know exactly what the future consequences of an implemented alternative will be. The word *future* is the key in discussing decision-making conditions. Because organizations and their environments are constantly changing, future consequences of implemented decisions are not perfectly predictable. In general, the two different conditions under which decisions are made are risk and uncertainty. Although many managers use them interchangeably, these two terms are in fact different.

TABLE 8.2   **Common Decision-Making Biases**[31]

Name of Bias	Brief Description
Bandwagon Effect	The tendency to believe certain outcomes will occur (i.e., the stock market will increase) because others believe the same thing
Confirmation Bias	The tendency to search for information that supports one's preconceived beliefs and to ignore information that contradicts those beliefs
Loss Aversion	Characteristic of individuals who tend to more strongly prefer avoiding losses rather than acquiring gains
Overconfidence	When assessing our ability to predict future events, the tendency to believe that our forecasts are better than they truly are
Unrealistic Optimism	Individuals' tendency to believe that they are less susceptible to risky events (i.e., earthquakes, disease transmission, etc.) than others

Frank Knight distinguished between risk and uncertainty almost a century ago.[32] According to his framework, **risk** refers to situations in which statistical probabilities can be attributed to alternative potential outcomes. For example, the probabilities associated with the potential outcomes of roulette are known to individuals in advance. In contrast, **uncertainty** refers to situations where the probability that a particular outcome will occur is not known in advance. A manager, for instance, may be unable to articulate the probability that building a new manufacturing facility will increase a firm's sales in five years.[33]

Despite this distinction between risk and uncertainty, it is important to note that objective standards are not always available when examining a situation with alternative potential outcomes. Specifically, two managers may attribute differing levels of uncertainty or risk to the same or similar decisions. For example, suppose that the managers of two competing firms—Alpha Inc. and Beta Inc.—are each considering opening new manufacturing facilities in China but are unsure whether the new plants will improve the firms' profitability. Suppose, however, that the manager of Alpha Inc. has previously opened 12 new facilities in China, but the manager of Beta Inc. has no such experience. As such, the manager of Alpha Inc. has more information about opening these plants and might be able to better estimate the risk probabilities associated with profitability versus failure compared to the manager of Beta Inc. In fact, the manager of Beta Inc. might not be able to estimate any risk probabilities but instead must view this plant with complete uncertainty.

Now that we have distinguished between risk and uncertainty, the question remains: Why do we need to distinguish between these two terms? Research suggests that individuals dislike uncertainty even more than they dislike risk.[34] Vague or unknown probabilities of success are more likely to discourage managers from undertaking actions than is risk. This negative influence of uncertainty has implications for all sorts of decisions, such as hiring new employees, introducing new products, or acquiring other firms.

MyLab Management Watch It

If your instructor has assigned this activity, go to www.pearson.com/mylab/management to complete the video exercise.

Decision-Making Tools

Most managers develop an intuition about what decisions to make—a largely subjective feeling based on years of experience in a particular organization or industry, which gives them insights into decision making for that industry or organization.[35] Although intuition is often an important factor in making a decision, managers generally emphasize more objective decision-making tools. The two most widely used tools are probability theory and decision trees.[36]

8-4 Insights regarding the various tools used to make decisions

Probability Theory

Probability theory is a decision-making tool used in risk situations—situations in which decision makers are not completely sure of the outcome of an implemented alternative.[37] Probability refers to the likelihood that an event or outcome will actually occur, which is estimated by calculating an expected value for each alternative considered. Specifically, the **expected value (EV)** for an alternative is the income (I) that the alternative would produce, multiplied by its probability of producing that income (P). In formula form, $EV = I \times P$. Decision makers generally choose and implement the alternative with the highest expected value.[38]

An example will clarify the relationship among probability, income, and expected value. A manager is trying to decide where to open a store that specializes in renting surfboards. She is considering three possible locations (A, B, and C), all of which seem feasible. For the first year of operation, the manager has projected that, under ideal conditions, her company would earn $90,000 in Location A, $75,000 in Location B, and $60,000 in Location C. After studying historical weather patterns, however, she has determined that there is only a 20 percent chance—or a 0.2 probability—of ideal conditions occurring during the first year of operation in Location A.

Figure 8.5

Expected values from locating a surfboard rental store in each of three possible locations

Alternative (locations)	Potential income	Probability of income	Expected value of alternatives
A	$90,000	.2	$18,000
B	75,000	.4	30,000
C	60,000	.8	48,000

I	x	P	=	EV

Locations B and C have a 0.4 and a 0.8 probability, respectively, of ideal conditions during the first year of operations. Expected values for each of these locations are as follows: Location A—$18,000; Location B—$30,000; Location C—$48,000. **Figure 8.5** shows the situation this decision maker faces. According to her probability analysis, she should open a store in Location C, the alternative with the highest expected value.

Decision Trees

In the previous section, probability theory was applied to a relatively simple decision situation. Some decisions, however, are more complicated and involve a series of steps. These steps are interdependent; that is, each step is influenced by the step that precedes it. A **decision tree** is a graphic decision-making tool typically used to evaluate decisions involving a series of steps.[39]

John F. Magee developed a classic illustration that outlines how decision trees can be applied to a production decision.[40] In his illustration (see **Figure 8.6**), the Stygian Chemical Company must decide whether to build a small or a large plant to manufacture a new product with an expected life of 10 years (Decision Point 1 in Figure 8.6). If the choice is to build a large plant, the

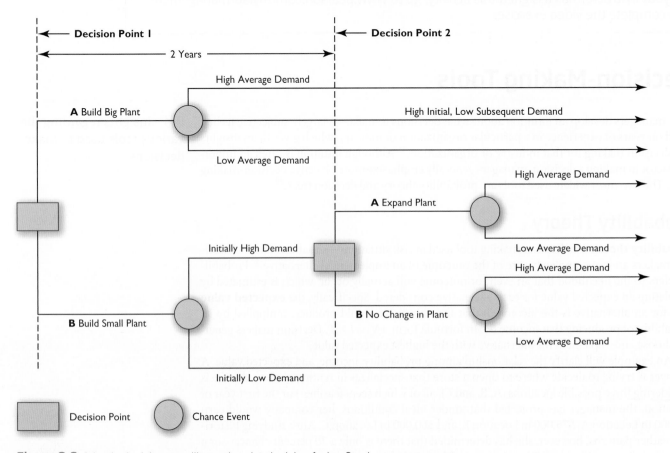

Figure 8.6 A basic decision tree illustrating the decision facing Stygian management

company could face high or low average product demand, or high initial and then low demand. If the choice is to build a small plant, however, the company could face either initially high or initially low product demand. If the small plant is built and product demand is high during an initial two-year period, management could then choose whether to expand the plant (Decision Point 2). Whether the decision is made to expand or not to expand, management could then face either high or low product demand.

Now that various possible alternatives have been presented, the financial consequence of each different course of action must be compared. To compare these consequences adequately, management must do the following:

1. Study estimates of investment amounts necessary for building a large plant, for building a small plant, and for expanding a small plant.
2. Weigh the probabilities of facing different product demand levels for various decision alternatives.
3. Consider projected income yields for each decision alternative.

Analysis of the expected values and net expected gain for each decision alternative helps management decide on an appropriate choice.[41] *Net expected gain* is defined in this situation as the expected value of an alternative minus the investment cost. For example, if building a large plant yields the higher net expected gain, Stygian management should decide to build the large plant.[42]

Group Decision Making

Earlier in this chapter, decision makers were defined as individuals or groups that actually make a decision—that is, choose a decision alternative from those available. This section focuses on groups as decision makers. The two key topics discussed here are the advantages and disadvantages of using groups to make decisions and the best processes for making group decisions.

8-5 An understanding of how groups make decisions

Advantages and Disadvantages of Using Groups to Make Decisions

Groups commonly make decisions in organizations.[43] For example, groups are often asked to decide what new product should be offered to customers, how policies for promotion should be improved, and how the organization should reach higher production goals. Groups are so often asked to make organizational decisions because certain advantages come with having a group of people rather than an individual manager make a decision. One advantage is that a group can generally think of more and better decision alternatives than an individual can: A group can draw on collective, diverse organizational experiences as the foundation for decision making, whereas an individual manager has only his or her limited experiences to draw on.[44] Another advantage is that, when a group makes a decision, the members of that group tend to support the implementation of the decision more fervently than they would if the decision had been made by an individual. This support can be of significant help to a manager in successfully implementing a decision. A third advantage of using a group rather than an individual to make a decision is that group members tend to regard the decision as their own, and this feeling of ownership makes it more likely that they will strive to implement the decision successfully rather than prematurely give in to failure.

However, having groups rather than individual managers make organizational decisions may also involve some disadvantages. Perhaps the disadvantage discussed most

There are advantages and disadvantages of using groups to make decisions.

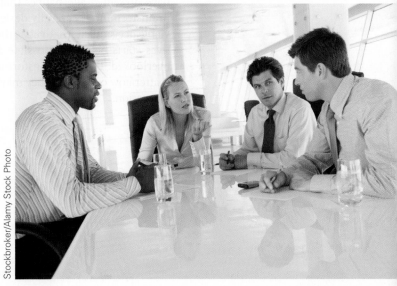

Stockbroker/Alamy Stock Photo

Facilitating Group Decisions

Managers often lead groups that are trying to arrive at a decision. To prevent a discussion from stalling and to get more creative ideas on the table, try these tips for helping groups make good decisions:[45]

- Instead of talking about whether alternatives are good or bad or whether a group member is right or wrong, talk about the pros and cons of every alternative.

- Identify the main issue, such as customer satisfaction or company strategy, and evaluate the alternatives in terms of that issue.
- Be sure to look at more than one alternative. Ask all the participants to suggest their two best choices.
- If group opinion is divided, look for a choice that all group members say they can live with. People are more likely to support implementation if they can accept the decision.

often is that it takes longer for groups to make a decision because groups must take the time to present and discuss all members' views. Another disadvantage is that group decisions cost the organization more than individual decisions do simply because group decisions take up the time of more people in the organization. Finally, group decisions can be of lower quality than individual decisions if they become contaminated by the group members' efforts to maintain friendly relationships among themselves. This phenomenon of compromising the quality of a decision to maintain relationships within a group is referred to as *groupthink* and is discussed more fully in Chapter 17, "Groups and Teams."[46]

Managers must weigh all these advantages and disadvantages of group decision making carefully, factoring in unique organizational situations, and give a group the authority to make a decision only when the advantages of doing so clearly outweigh the disadvantages.

Processes for Making Group Decisions

Making a sound group decision regarding complex organizational circumstances is a formidable challenge. Fortunately, several useful processes have been developed to assist groups in meeting this challenge. The following sections discuss three such processes: brainstorming, nominal group technique, and Delphi technique.

Brainstorming   **Brainstorming** is a group decision-making process in which negative feedback on any suggested alternative by any group member is forbidden until all members have presented alternatives that they perceive as valuable.[47] **Figure 8.7** shows this process. Brainstorming is carefully designed to encourage all group members to contribute as many viable decision alternatives as they can think of. Its premise is that, if the evaluation of alternatives starts before all possible alternatives have been offered, valuable alternatives may be overlooked. During brainstorming, group members are encouraged to state their ideas, no matter how outlandish they may seem, while an appointed group member records all ideas for discussion.[48]

Figure 8.7
The brainstorming process

Group members state ideas → Group leader records each idea where group can read it → Ideas evaluated only after all have been recorded

No comments on ideas at this stage

Armstrong International's David Armstrong discovered an intriguing method for discouraging the premature evaluation of ideas during a brainstorming session: He allows only one negative comment per group member. Before discussion begins, he hands every member one piece of M&M's candy. Once a member makes a negative comment, he or she must eat the piece of candy. Because a group member is required to have an uneaten piece of candy to make a negative comment, members are very judicious about using their sole opportunity to be negative.[49] Once everyone's ideas have been presented, the group evaluates the ideas and chooses the one that holds the most promise.

Nominal Group Technique

The **nominal group technique** is another useful process for helping groups make decisions. This process is designed to ensure that each group member has equal participation in making the group decision.[50] It involves the following steps:

STEP 1: Each group member writes down his or her ideas on the decision or problem being discussed.

STEP 2: Each member presents his or her ideas orally. The ideas are usually written on a board for all other members to see and refer to.

STEP 3: After all members present their ideas, the entire group discusses these ideas simultaneously. Discussion tends to be unstructured and spontaneous.

STEP 4: When discussion is completed, a secret ballot is taken to allow members to support their favorite ideas without apprehension. The idea receiving the most votes is adopted and implemented.

Delphi Technique

The **Delphi technique** is a third useful process for helping groups make decisions. The Delphi technique involves circulating questionnaires on a specific problem among group members, sharing the questionnaire results with them, and then continuing to recirculate and refine individual responses until a consensus regarding the problem is reached.[51] In contrast to the nominal group technique and brainstorming, the Delphi technique does not have group members meet face-to-face. The formal steps followed in the Delphi technique are the following:

STEP 1: A problem is identified.

STEP 2: Group members are asked to offer solutions to the problem by providing anonymous responses to a carefully designed questionnaire.

STEP 3: Responses of all group members are compiled and sent out to all group members.

STEP 4: Individual group members are each asked to generate a new solution to the problem after they have studied the individual responses of all other group members compiled in step 3.

Step 5: Steps 3 and 4 are repeated until a consensus solution is reached.

Evaluating Group Decision-Making Processes

All three of the processes just presented for assisting groups in reaching decisions have both advantages and disadvantages. Brainstorming offers the advantage of encouraging the expression of as many useful ideas as possible but also offers the disadvantage of wasting the group's time on ideas that are wildly impractical. The nominal group technique, with its secret ballot, offers a structure in which individuals can support or reject an idea without fear of recrimination. Its disadvantage is that group members have no way of knowing why individuals voted the way they did. The advantage of the Delphi technique is that ideas can be gathered from group members who are too geographically separated or busy to meet face-to-face. Its disadvantage is that members are unable to ask questions of one another.

As with any other management tool, managers must carefully weigh the advantages and disadvantages of these three group decision-making tools and adopt the one—or some combination of the three—that best suits their unique organizational circumstances. Most important, research suggests that if a group decision-making process becomes problematic, managers should intervene to change and/or reset the process.[52]

CHALLENGE CASE SUMMARY

When evaluating the question of whether to locate a store in Detroit, the managers at Whole Foods definitely faced a formal decision situation, a situation requiring a choice among a number of alternatives. Whole Foods's management scrutinized this decision carefully because of its significance to the organization as a whole and to the careers of the Whole Foods's managers actually making the decision. To a degree, store location decisions are programmed; retailers typically have a set of criteria they use for measuring potential demand, and they select sites that meet the standards of all the criteria. As the case illustrates, however, creative thinking also plays a role in decisions as complex as site selection.

High-level managers at Whole Foods were involved in making the costly and difficult-to-reverse decision of the selection of the location for a new store. These managers most likely sought input from employees lower in the hierarchy who had insights from marketing research and knowledge of consumers and organizations in Detroit. Managers at headquarters were interested in the insights not only from data and marketing experts but also from employees who had experience with store operations in Michigan. Probably the decision required a consensus of several decision makers.

As management at Whole Foods evaluated the decision about locating in Detroit, they were most likely aware of all the elements of the decision situation. Both the internal and external environments of Whole Foods were likely a focus of the analysis. For example, internally, did Whole Foods have the financial resources to open another store, and did it have the expertise to make the right buying decisions for Detroit shoppers? Externally, how would businesspeople in Detroit react to the opening of a Texas-based retailer? Reason and sound judgment were needed to establish management's orientation in making this decision. Also, management had to keep the retail chain's organizational objectives in mind. The new store would have to contribute to overall profits, not just be a nice gesture toward a struggling city. In arriving at the decision, management probably listed alternatives such as locating stores in other cities and other Detroit neighborhoods and compared the potential of the midtown Detroit market with those other markets.

After eliminating alternatives that were expected to be less profitable, Whole Foods's management had to evaluate all remaining locations, select one (or none), and implement the decision. Implementation involved finding a developer for the site, working with the developer on the new store's design and construction, and then negotiating a lease for the new site. In addition, it needed to hire staff to run the new store and order the merchandise to sell.

This decision-making process involved a great deal of uncertainty. Management had no guarantees that other retailers would not enter the area while it built and staffed the new store—or perhaps after Whole Foods had begun to show the way to operate profitably in Detroit. Management also did not know whether the Detroit residents who said they would like to shop at Whole Foods would actually do so. Nor could it control the direction that Detroit's economy and population would take in the years between decision making and store opening. Management *did* know, however, what has worked in the past to stop competitors and what kinds of decisions have resulted in successful store operations elsewhere in Michigan and throughout the United States. Therefore, Whole Foods could estimate the probable outcome for each proposed alternative and base its decision on the alternative with the most favorable probable outcome.

Decision makers at Whole Foods could have used some tools for making better decisions. One is probability theory, which generates an expected value for various decision alternatives. Management could then have implemented the alternative with the highest expected value. Also, because the location decision involved a series of steps related to each of several alternatives, Whole Foods could have used a decision tree to assist in picturing and evaluating each alternative. For example, if a competitor had opened a midtown Detroit store before Whole Foods finished its construction process, Whole Foods might have changed some of its decisions about staffing and stocking its store based on the competitor's actions and outcomes.

Whole Foods's management must remember, however, that business judgment is an adjunct to the effective use of any decision-making tool. The purpose of such a tool is to improve the quality of the judgment, not to replace the judgment. In other words, Whole Foods's management must not only choose alternatives based on the probability theory and decision tress but must also use good judgment in deciding what is best for the company.

In the current situation, Whole Foods's management also had to decide which individuals would be involved in making the decision to locate a store in Detroit. First, a decision of this magnitude should probably be made by a group of top leaders drawn from many different organizational areas. A group decision would almost certainly have been better than an individual decision in this case because a group would have had a broader perspective of Whole Foods and the market than any one person in the company would. Therefore, the group would have been more likely to make an appropriate decision.

Perhaps the group decision-making process used to select the location should have included methods discussed in the text. Brainstorming sessions would have ensured that all ideas for locations surfaced, whereas the nominal group technique would have compelled group members to focus

on the urgency of making the decision by requiring them to vote on whether to invest in the new site. The Delphi technique could have been used to obtain important input on the decision from experts in Michigan and at the Texas headquarters by asking them to provide their written views through a specially designed questionnaire. However, using a group to make this decision would have been time-consuming and expensive. But once the decision had been made, group members would have been committed to it, regarded it as their own, and done everything in their power to ensure that the company is successful.

MyLab Management Assessing Your Management Skill

If your instructor has assigned this activity, go to www.pearson.com/mylab/management to complete the exercise related to the Challenge Case.

DEVELOPING DECISION-MAKING SKILL

This section is specially designed to help you develop decision-making skills. An individual's decision-making skill is based on an understanding of the concepts and the ability to apply those concepts. The following activities will help to enhance your decision-making skills in various organizational situations.

Class Preparation and Personal Study

To help you prepare for class, perform the activities outlined in this section. Performing these activities will help you enhance your classroom performance significantly.

Reflecting on Target Skill

On page 199, this chapter opens by presenting a target skill along with a list of related objectives outlining knowledge and understanding that you should aim to acquire related to that skill. Review this target skill and the list of objectives to make sure that you've acquired all pertinent information within the chapter. If you do not feel that you've reached a particular objective(s), study related chapter coverage until you do.

Know Key Terms

Understanding the following key terms is critical to your preparing for class. Define each of these terms. Refer to the page(s) referenced after a term to check your definition or to gain further insight regarding the term.

Know How Management Concepts Relate

This section comprises activities that will further sharpen your understanding of management concepts. Answer these essay questions as completely as possible.

8-1 Describe the primary steps involved in the rational decision-making process.

8-2 Explain why a decision-making process has room for biases. List and describe five common decision-making biases.

8-3 Explain the limitations that managers should take into consideration when looking at problem-solving alternatives.

MyLab Management
Personal Inventory Assessment

Go to www.pearson.com/mylab/management to complete the Personal Inventory Assessment related to this chapter.

   PERSONAL INVENTORY ASSESSMENT

Management Skills Exercises

Learning activities in this section are aimed at helping you develop decision-making skills.

MyLab Management
Discussion Questions

Go to www.pearson.com/mylab/management to complete the problems marked with this icon ✪.

✪ Cases

Whole Foods Decides to Open in Detroit

The Challenge Case "Whole Foods Decides to Open in Detroit" (p. 200) and its related Challenge Case Summary were written to help you understand the management concepts contained in this chapter. Answer the following discussion questions about the Challenge Case to explore how decision-making concepts can be applied to a company such as Whole Foods.

8-4 List three alternatives that Whole Foods's management might have considered in opening a store to serve Detroit residents before selecting the mid-town site.

8-5 What information would management have needed to evaluate those three alternatives?

8-6 Do you think you would have enjoyed making the decision to open a Whole Foods store in midtown Detroit? Explain.

HP's Tough Decisions

Read the case and answer the questions that follow. Studying this case will help you better understand how concepts relating to decision making can be applied in an organization such as Hewlett-Packard.

The days of a bulky computer hard drive, keyboard, monitor, and mouse are behind us, right? Tablets, smartphones, and other devices are the way of the future, or so

it would seem. However, one company, Hewlett-Packard (HP), is betting on the continuation of traditional personal computers (PCs).

The story of HP is innovative, sometimes tumultuous, and always fascinating. With several prior high-profile CEOs such as Léo Apotheker, Carly Fiorina, and Mark Hurd, the company has ridden the waves of technology with the personal computer and crashed hard with its inability to keep up with Apple's advent of smart technology. The new CEO, Meg Whitman, is making some key decisions for the company that could affect its future. Formerly CEO of eBay, Whitman brings to the table a strong background that includes experience at Procter & Gamble and Disney. In addition, she made an unsuccessful bid for the governor's office in California. When she took over the company in September 2011, she faced a recent history of scandals, infighting, and lackadaisical attitudes. Some tough decisions had to be made.

Just a month prior to Whitman's appointment as CEO, the company had announced that it would sell off its PC business and cease production of its fledgling TouchPad tablet. The PC business was a significant part of HP's income and history. At its founding in 1939, HP offered a wide variety of scientific and technological products, and it entered the PC market in the late 1960s and early 1970s. As the company grew during the last decades of the twentieth century, it added printers and scanners to its product line. In 2011, the TouchPad was a very modest attempt to compete with Apple's iPad. The decisions to end the PC part of its business and stop producing the TouchPad caused HP's stock price to fall 20 percent (Bandler and Burke, 2012). Upon her arrival, however, Whitman reversed one of those decisions: She announced that the PC division would not be sold or folded; instead, it would be merged with the printer division. The TouchPad, though, was history.

Whitman felt that keeping the PC division was crucial. "HP needs consistency more than anything else," she said (Heichler, 2012). She argued that losing the PC business would do irreparable harm to the rest of HP's products and services. In other words, the PC is integral to HP's survival.

To achieve success, though, some changes had to be made. First, more money is being invested in research and development, something that had declined under previous CEOs. "We underinvested in innovation," Whitman said (Edwards, 2012). Second, sales across the board will have to improve. A steady decline in revenues and a dropping stock price have certainly hurt the company. And finally, HP is considering a reentry into the consumer mobile market. To compete with Apple, the company is working on a lightweight PC that has a detachable touchscreen (Edwards, 2012).

In the meantime, though, the company is struggling. Even with severe cost cuttings, margins continue to drop. After profits declined 31 percent in the second quarter of 2012, Whitman announced that 27,000 employees would be laid off, approximately 8 percent of HP's entire workforce (Worthen, 2012).

Whitman understands that HP is facing a steep uphill challenge. With confidence she states, "I've done this a number of times in my career. It's what great business leaders do" (Bandler and Burke, 2012). The company not only faces a late entry into the tablet market but is also attempting to maintain and innovate in a world where the desktop computer is becoming a nostalgic tool of business from a bygone era. But she is not discouraged. "Strategy is about the art of exclusion," she says. "If something isn't working, then you've got to do something different. The cost of inaction is far greater than the cost of making a mistake" (Heichler, 2012).[53]

Questions

8-7 What do you think about Meg Whitman's decision to keep the PC business at HP? Would you have made the same decision?

8-8 Using the rational decision-making process, evaluate Whitman's decision. In other words, what was the existing problem, what were the possible alternatives, and so on?

8-9 How would you characterize the scope of Whitman's decision? What levels of management were affected? Should Whitman have used consensus in making her choice? Why or why not?

Experiential Exercises

Decision Making as a Group

Directions. Read the following scenario and then perform the listed activities. Your instructor may want you to perform the activities as an individual or within groups. Follow all of your instructor's directions carefully.

A representative of McDonald's has contacted your group to help make an important decision. Due to the increasing hostility of the press regarding the unhealthy nature of some of the company's products, top management is concerned about the company's future. In response, some members of McDonald's management team would like the company to diversify into markets and/or industries that have nothing to do with food products. Use the nominal group technique discussed in this chapter to address this important issue for McDonald's. At the end of this exercise, you should have at least one

recommendation for McDonald's top management team. When you have finished this exercise, list the primary advantages and disadvantages of the nominal group technique. Be prepared to share your conclusions with the rest of your class.

You and Your Career

Earlier in the chapter, we discussed the importance of decision making and described a number of factors that influence decision making. Describe a scenario in which poor decision-making skills could hinder your career as a manager. What are some strategies you might employ to improve your decision-making skill? Explain. Describe two examples from your life that would help you communicate your decision-making skill to potential employers.

Building Your Management Skills Portfolio

Your management skills portfolio is a collection of activities specially designed to demonstrate your management knowledge and skill. Be sure to save your work. You can use this material while preparing for an interview.

The portfolio activity for this chapter is about making an investment in a franchise in Singapore. Study this information and complete the exercises that follow.

You are the European sales director for a major Singapore-based garment manufacturer. The family-run business has been operating for over 20 years and has worked hard to establish its reputation as one of the fastest and most flexible garment manufacturers in the region. Fast fashion is a growing trend in many markets, and switching designs and styles at short notice while remaining highly competitive requires almost instant manufacture and resupply.

You have noticed increasing competition from Vietnam, Bangladesh, India, Pakistan, and Egypt. Sales have dropped by 30 percent as retailers spread their orders to maintain reliable supply and production times. Your company's production lead time from initial samples to the end product being mass produced for shipment has slipped from 6–8 weeks to 8–12 weeks. At the same time, the average competitor has cut their production lead time to 6–10 weeks. This leaves you at a competitive disadvantage.

Using the decision-making process, determine what the garment manufacturer should do to arrest the drop in sales at crucial times of the year. For each step in the process listed below, describe what you would tell the owners.

8-10 Identify the existing problem.

_____

_____

_____

8-11 List possible options for solving the problem.

_____

_____

_____

8-12 Select the most beneficial of these options.

_____

_____

_____

8-13 Implement the selected options.

_____

_____

_____

8-14 Gather feedback to find out whether the implemented option is solving the identified problem.

_____

_____

_____

MyLab Management
Writing Assignments

If your instructor has assigned this activity, go to www.pearson.com/mylab/management for the following assisted-graded writing assignments:

Assisted-Grading Questions

8-15 Distinguish between programmed and non-programmed decisions. Use examples to support your response.

8-16 Compare the advantages and disadvantages associated with group decision making.

Endnotes

1. Case based on John Gallagher, "Whole Foods Co-CEO Vows No Half Steps at Midtown Detroit Store," *Detroit Free Press*, http://www.freep.com, accessed April 14, 2012; John Bussed, "Whole Foods' Detroit Gamble," *Wall Street Journal*, http://online.wsj.com, accessed March 8, 2012; Michael Wayland, "CEO: If Successful, Detroit Whole Foods Store Could Become Blueprint for Other Cities," *Live*, http://blog.mlive.com, accessed April 14, 2012; Jeff Karoo, "Detroit Sees Whole Foods as Proof of Progress," *Time*, http://newsfeed.time.com, accessed April 14, 2012; Whole Foods, "Welcome to the Midtown Detroit Store," Stores: Michigan, http://wholefoodsmarket.com, accessed April 30, 2012.

2. J. F. Yates and S. Oliveira, "Culture and Decision Making," *Organizational Behavior and Human Decision Processes* 136 (2016): 106–118.

3. Abraham Zaleznik, "What Makes a Leader?," *Success* (June 1989): 42–45; Daphne Main and Joyce C. Lambert, "Improving Your Decision Making," *Business and Economic Review* 44, no. 3 (April/June 1998): 9–12.

4. Mervin Kohn, *Dynamic Managing: Principles, Process, Practice* (Menlo Park, CA: Cummings, 1977), 38–62.

5. William H. Miller, "Tough Decisions on the Forgotten Continent," *Industry Week* (June 6, 1994): 40–44.

6. Walt Nett, "Family-Run Recycling Company Faces Big Decisions as It Grows," *Lubbock Avalanche-Journal*, April 18, 2010, http://www.lubbockonline.com.

7. NetSuite, "World's Largest Carpet Manufacturer Rolls Out NetSuite OneWorld to Power Global Growth in a Two-Tier ERP Model," news release, October 8, 2013, http://www.netsuite.com; NetSuite, "NetSuite: The World's #1 Cloud ERP Solution," Products Overview,

http://www.netsuite.com, accessed January 3, 2014; Shaw Industries, "Our Story: Shaw History," http://shawfloors.com/about-shaw/history, accessed January 8, 2014.

8. Gary Hamel, "Moon Shots for Management," *Harvard Business Review*, February 2009, http://hbr.org.

9. Marcia V. Wilkof, "Organizational Culture and Decision Making: A Case of Consensus Management," *R&D Management* (April 1989): 185–199.

10. Charles Wilson and Marcus Alexis, "Basic Frameworks for Decision," *Academy of Management Journal* 5 (August 1962): 151–164.

11. For a discussion of the importance of understanding decision makers in organizations, see Walter D. Barndt, Jr., "Profiling Rival Decision Makers," *Journal of Business Strategy* (January/February 1991): 8–11.

12. For an analysis of several flawed decisions made by executives as well as recommendations for avoiding decision-making pitfalls, see Sydney Finkelstein, Jo Whitehead, and Andrew Campbell, "Think Again: Why Good Leaders Make Bad Decisions," *Business Strategy Review* 20, no. 2 (Summer 2009): 62–69.

13. Maria Panaritis, "Putting Trust Where Others Don't Dare," *Philadelphia Inquirer*, March 21, 2010, http://www.philly.com.

14. "New OCC Guidelines for Appraising Management," *Issues in Bank Regulation* (Fall 1989): 20–22.

15. For an extended discussion of this model, see William B. Werther, Jr., "Productivity through People: The Decision-Making Process," *Management Decisions* (1988): 37–41.

16. These assumptions are adapted from James G. March and Herbert A. Simon, *Organizations* (New York: Wiley, 1958), 137–138.

17. William C. Symonds, "There's More Than Beer in Molson's Mug," *BusinessWeek* (February 10, 1992): 108.

18. Chester I. Barnard, *The Function of the Executive* (Cambridge, MA: Harvard University Press, 1938).

19. For further elaboration on these factors, see Robert Tannenbaum, Irving R. Weschle, and Fred Massarik, *Leadership and Organization: A Behavioral Science Approach* (New York: McGraw-Hill, 1961), 277–278.

20. For more discussion of these factors, see F. A. Shull, Jr., A. I. Delbecq, and L. L. Cummings, *Organizational Decision Making* (New York: McGraw-Hill, 1970).

21. Thomas Kidaa, Kimberly K. Morenob, and James F. Smitha, "Investment Decision Making: Do Experienced Decision Makers Fall Prey to the Paradox of Choice?," *Journal of Behavioral Finance* 11, no. 1 (2010): 21–30. See also B. Scheibehenne, Rainer Greifendeder, and Peter M. Tood, "Can There Ever Be Too Many Options? A Meta-Analytic Review of Choice Overload," *Journal of Consumer Research* (2010): 37.

22. T. Kogut, "Choosing What I Want or Keeping What I Should: The Effect of Decision Strategy on Choice Consistency," *Organizational Behavior and Human Decision Processes* 116 (2011): 129–139.

23. M. H. Bazerman and O. Sezer, "Bounded awareness: Implications for Ethical Decision Making," *Organziational Behavior and Human Decision Processes* 136 (2016): 95–105.

24. For an interesting discussion regarding the complexities involved with assigning and understanding probabilities, see B. Bilgin and L. Brenner, "Context Affects the Interpretation of Low but Not High Numerical Probabilities: A Hypothesis Testing Account of Subjective Probability," *Organizational Behavior and Human Decision Processes* 121 (2013): 118–128.

25. For a worthwhile discussion of forecasting and evaluating the outcomes of alternatives, see J. R. C. Wensley, "Effective Decision Aids in Marketing," *European Journal of Marketing* (1989): 70–79.

26. A. Arad, "Past Decisions Do Affect Future Choices: An Experimental Demonstration," *Organizational Behavior and Human Decision Processes* 121 (2013): 267–277.

27. H. A. Simon, *Models of Man: Social and Rational* (New York: Wiley, 1957). In an interesting extension of how factors in the environment may influence subconscious decision making, see K. A. Carlson, R. J. Tanner, M. G. Meloy, and J. E. Russo, "Catching Nonconscious Goals in the Act of Decision Making," *Organizational Behavior and Human Decision Processes* 123 (2014): 65–76.

28. Benjamin Zhang, "AirAsia CEO Tony Fernandes Turned a 29-Cent Investment into a Billion-Dollar Empire," *Business Insider* (India), December 29, 2014; Philip Ross, "Tony Fernandes, AirAsia CEO,

Turned Struggling Airline into World-Class Budget Carrier," *International Business Times,* February 4, 2015; https://www.scribd.com/doc/34150260/Dato-Tony-Fernandes-Biography.

29. K. E. Stanovich and R. F. West, "Individual Differences in Reasoning: Implications for the Rationality Debate," in T. Gilovich, D. Griffin, and D. Kahneman, eds., *Heuristics and Biases: The Psychology of Intuitive Judgment* (Cambridge: Cambridge University Press, 2002); Daniel Kahneman, "A Perspective on Judgment and Choice," *American Psychologist* 58, no. 9: 697–720. See also Jonathan St. B. T. Evans, "Dual-Processing Accounts of Reasoning, Judgment, and Social Cognition," *Annual Review of Psychology* 5 (2008): 255–278.

30. Eduardo Salas, Michael Rosen, and Deborah DiazGrandos, "Expertise-Based Intuition and Decision Making in Organizations," *Journal of Management* 36, no. 4 (2010): 941–973.

31. For a complete review of research involving heuristics and biases, see Thomas Gilovich, Dale Griffin, and Daniel Kahneman, *Heuristics and Biases: The Psychology of Intuitive Judgment* (Cambridge: Cambridge University Press, 2002). For information on how emotion can influence decision making, see J. M. George and E. Dane, "Affect, Emotion, and Decision Making," *Organizational Behavior and Human Decision Processes*, 136 (2016): 47–55.

32. Frank Knight, *Risk, Uncertainty, and Profit* (Boston: Houghton Mifflin, 1921).

33. Many chief executives resort to reorganization in an attempt to improve their company's performance, but research suggests that most reorganizations fail because they don't improve the quality of decision making. See Marcia W. Blenko, Michael C. Mankins, and Paul Rogers, "The Decision-Driven Organization," *Harvard Business Review,* June 2010, http://hbr.org.

34. Truman F. Bewley, "Knightian Decision Theory, Part I," *Decisions in Economics and Finance* 25, no. 2 (2002): 79–110.

35. Steven C. Harper, "What Separates Executives from Managers," *Business Horizons* (September/October 1988): 13–19; to better understand the negative influence of poor decision making, see Joseph L. Bower and Clark G. Gilbert, "How Managers' Everyday Decisions Create or Destroy Your Company's Strategy," *Harvard Business Review* 85, no. 2 (2007): 72–79.

36. The scope of this text does not permit elaboration on these three decision-making tools. However, for an excellent discussion on how they are used in decision making, see Richard M. Hodgetts, *Management: Theory, Process and Practice* (Philadelphia, PA: Saunders, 1975), 234–266.

37. For more information on probability theory and decisions, see Johannes Honekopp, "Precision of Probability Information and Prominence of Outcomes: A Description and Evaluation of Decisions Under Uncertainty," *Organizational Behavior and Human Decision Processes* 90 (2003): 124.

38. Richard C. Mosier, "Expected Value: Applying Research to Uncertainty," *Appraisal Journal* (July 1989): 293–296. See also Amartya Sen, "The Formulation of Rational Choice," *American Economic Review* 84 (May 1994): 385–390.

39. For an example of how financial analysts use decision trees to reduce risk, see Joseph J. Mezrich, "When Is a Tree a Hedge?," *Financial Analysts Journal* 50, no. 6 (November/December 1994): 75–81.

40. John F. Magee, "Decision Trees for Decision Making," *Harvard Business Review* (July/August 1964). To better understand the relationships among decision trees, firm strategy, and financial analysis, see Michael Brydon, "Evaluating Strategic Options Using Decision-Theoretic Planning," *Information and Technology Management* 7, no. 1 (2006): 35–49.

41. Rakesh Sarin and Peter Wakker, "Folding Back in Decision Tree Analysis," *Management Science* 40 (May 1994): 625–628.

42. For a different view of how organizations can incorporate a scientific approach in their decision-making processes, see "Putting the Science in Management Science?," *MIT Sloan Management Review,* March 2010, http://sloanreview.mit.edu.

43. This section is based on Samuel C. Certo, *Supervision: Quality and Diversity through Leadership* (Homewood, IL: Austen Press/Irwin, 1994), 198–202. See also D. van Knippenberg, W. P. van Ginkel, and A. C. Homan, "Diversity Mindsets and the Performance of Diverse Teams," *Organizational Behavior and Human Decision Processes* 121 (2013): 183–193.

44. Clark Wigley, "Working Smart on Tough Business Problems," *Supervisory Management* (February 1992): 1.

45. Sarah Cliffe, "Making Decisions Together (When You Don't Agree on What's Important)," *Harvard Business Review,* November 12, 2013, http://blogs.hbr.org; Will Yakowicz, "Butting Heads over a Key Decision? How to Break the Logjam," *Inc.,* November 12, 2013, http://www.inc.com; Erik Sherman, "Four Ways to Make Smarter Decisions," *Inc.,* June 17, 2013, http://www.inc.com; Margaret Heffernan, "Don't Just Go with the Majority Opinion: Here's Why," *Inc.,* April 19, 2013, http://www.inc.com.

46. Ferda Erdem, "Optimal Trust and Teamwork: From Groupthink to Teamthink," *Work Study* 52 (2003): 229. For more on group decision making in international contexts, see C. Qian, Q. Cao, and R. Takeuchi, "Top Management Team Functional Diversity and Organizational Innovation in China: The Moderating Effects of Environment," *Strategic Management Journal* 34 (2013): 110–120.

47. Joseph Alan Redman, "Nine Creative Brainstorming Techniques," *Quality Digest* (August 1992): 50–51.

48. For more information on idea generation, see Merry Baskin, "Idea Generation," *Brand Strategy* 172 (2003): 35.

49. David M. Armstrong, "Management by Storytelling," *Executive Female* (May/June 1992): 38–41.

50. Philip L. Roth, L. F. Lydia, and Fred S. Switzer, "Nominal Group Technique—An Aid for Implementing TQM," *CPA Journal* (May 1995): 68–69; Karen L. Dowling, "Asynchronous Implementation of the Nominal Group Technique: Is It Effective?," *Decision Support Systems* 29, no. 3 (October 2000): 229–248.

51. N. Delkey, *The Delphi Method: An Experimental Study of Group Opinion* (Santa Monica, CA: Rand Corporation, 1969); Gene Rowe and George Wright, "The Delphi Technique as a Forecasting Tool: Issues and Analysis," *International Journal of Forecasting* 15, no. 4 (October 1999).

52. C. M. Fisher, "An Ounce of Prevention or a Pound of Cure? Two Experiments on In-Process Interventions in Decision-Making Groups," *Organizational Behavior and Human Decision Processes* 138 (2016): 59–73.

53. James Bandler and Doris Burke, "How HP Lost Its Way," *Fortune* (2012); Cliff Edwards, "HP Crawls Back, One Giant Screen at a Time," *Bloomberg Businessweek* (2012); Elizabeth Heichler, "Whitman Plans to 'Stay the Course' at HP," *Computerworld* (2012); Ben Worthen, "H-P Shows Age with Layoffs," *Wall Street Journal* (2012).

9

Strategic Planning: Strategies, Tactics, and Competitive Dynamics

TARGET SKILL

 Strategic Planning Skill: the ability to engage in long-range planning that focuses on the organization as a whole

STRATEGIC PLANNING SKILL AND YOUR CAREER

Strategic planning skill will be of great value to you in enhancing your career. This skill can help you engage in long-range planning that focuses on the organization as a whole. This ability contributes to organizational success, builds your image as a competent manager, makes you valuable to your organization, and supports promotions as you build your career.

OBJECTIVES

To help build my *strategic planning skill,* when studying this chapter, I will attempt to acquire:

9-1 Knowledge of the definitions of strategic planning and planning

9-2 Insights regarding the main aspects of the strategic management process

9-3 Knowledge of the key components of environmental analysis

9-4 An understanding of the role of organizational direction in strategic management

9-5 An appreciation for the primary aspects of strategy formulation

9-6 Insights regarding strategy implementation

9-7 An appreciation for the importance of strategic control

9-8 Insights into what tactical planning is and how strategic and tactical planning should be coordinated

9-9 An awareness of how competitive dynamics can influence an organization's financial performance

---

MyLab Management Chapter Warm Up

If your instructor has assigned this activity, go to www.pearson.com/mylab/management to complete the chapter warm up.

CHALLENGE CASE

Facebook Positions Itself to Stay Relevant

In less than a decade, Mark Zuckerberg has transformed Facebook from a start-up social network for college students to an international corporation with more than a billion monthly active users, more than three-fourths of them outside the United States and Canada. In the company's words, its mission is "to give people the power to share and make the world more open and connected." But Facebook's success depends on more than whether its technology empowers users. People must also linger on Facebook, thereby creating an audience for advertisements.

Facebook's popularity helped transform the way people use the Internet by making the experience a social one, with user-generated content. In so doing, Facebook became a key online destination. Today, two-thirds of Internet users in the United States and even more in Europe use Facebook. But challenges remain: Success attracts other innovators, who provide competing ways of engaging people online, and users' tastes and interests change.

One of Facebook's hurdles is changing technology. In recent years, consumers have been buying powerful mobile devices and using them to stay in touch. Facebook was originally created for users who would sit down at a computer and perhaps spend an hour on a social network, playing games and buying items for the games. However, mobile users behave differently, posting a short status update or photo on Facebook and then moving on. Facebook was unprepared to offer a robust version of the site for mobile users, who then began switching to mobile-friendly services such as Snapchat (for sharing videos and messages) and Twitter (for sharing brief messages). If mobile users want to play a game, they typically download the game app and skip Facebook altogether.

Facebook reacted by hiring hundreds of software engineers to improve its software for mobile devices. It also retooled its approach for generating revenue to rely more on advertising than on games. In the early months of this approach, the company has begun to see growing numbers of mobile users and larger revenues from mobile advertising. Facebook has also begun to experiment with video ads. A Facebook news feed could be an attractive location for a video clip such as a movie trailer. If advertisers are interested, online video ads could begin competing with television, which charges about eight times as much for reaching the same-sized audience.

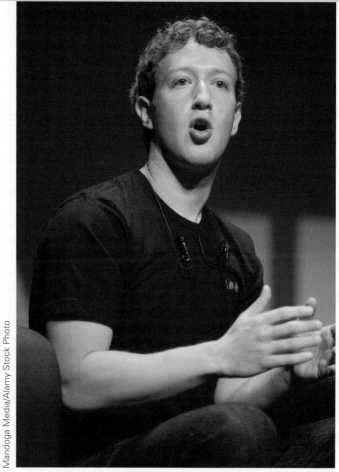

Mandoga Media/Alamy Stock Photo

Mark Zuckerberg, founder of Facebook, faces a challenge to keep the company relevant with changing technology and a younger generation of users.

Facebook also purchased Instagram, a company that developed a service for sharing photos and videos in a social network. Facebook then used Instagram's talent and brand to launch a mobile app that resembles Snapchat, a service popular with young people, the very demographic who has been spending less time on Facebook. Although Internet users may be using other social media, they do continue to find uses for Facebook, and the number of monthly visitors to the site has continued to increase. To maintain this growth, Zuckerberg must continuously monitor and evaluate Facebook's strategy.[1]

THE STRATEGIC PLANNING CHALLENGE

The Challenge Case highlights the competitive direction recently taken by Facebook. Developing a new direction of this sort is actually part of Facebook's strategic planning process. The material in this chapter explains how developing a competitive strategy is part of strategic planning and discusses the strategic planning process as a whole. Major topics included in this chapter are (1) strategic planning, (2) tactical planning, (3) comparing and coordinating strategic and tactical planning, and (4) competitive dynamics.

Strategic Planning and Strategy

9-1 Knowledge of the definitions of strategic planning and planning

If managers want to be successful strategic planners, they must understand the fundamentals of strategic planning and how to formulate strategic plans.[2] This section presents the basic principles of strategic planning. In doing so, it discusses the definitions of both *strategic planning* and *strategy* in detail.

Strategic planning is long-range planning that focuses on the organization as a whole.[3] In conducting strategic planning, managers consider the organization as a total unit and ask themselves what must be done in the long term to attain organizational goals.[4] *Long range* is usually defined as a period of time extending about three to five years into the future. Hence, in strategic planning, managers try to determine what their organization should do to be successful three to five years from now. The most successful managers tend to be those who take a comprehensive approach to strategic planning and are careful not to cut corners during the process, all the while encouraging innovative strategic thinking within their organization.[5]

Managers may have difficulty trying to decide exactly how far into the future they should extend their strategic planning. As a general rule, they should follow the **commitment principle**, which states that managers should commit funds for planning only if they can anticipate, in the foreseeable future, a return on planning expenses as a result of long-range planning analysis. Realistically, planning costs are an investment and therefore should not be incurred unless a reasonable return on that investment is anticipated.[6]

Strategy is defined as a broad and general plan developed to reach long-term objectives. Organizational strategy can, and generally does, focus on many different organizational areas, such as marketing, finance, production, research and development, and public relations. As such, it gives broad direction to an organization.[7]

Strategy is actually the end result of strategic planning. Although larger organizations tend to be more precise in developing organizational strategy than smaller organizations are, every organization should have a strategy of some sort.[8] For a strategy to be worthwhile, though, it must be consistent with organizational objectives, which in turn must be consistent with organizational purpose. **Table 9.1** illustrates this relationship between organizational objectives and strategy by presenting sample organizational objectives and strategies for three well-known business organizations.

TABLE 9.1   **Examples of Organizational Objectives and Related Strategies for Three Organizations in Different Business Areas**

Company	Type of Business	Sample Organizational Objectives	Strategy to Accomplish Objectives
Ford Motor Company	Automobile manufacturing	1. Regain market share recently lost to Honda and Toyota	1. Resize and downsize present models 2. Continue to produce subintermediate, standard, and luxury cars 3. Emphasize use of hybrid engines and fuel efficiency
Burger King	Fast food	1. Increase productivity	1. Increase people efficiency 2. Increase machine efficiency
CP Railroad	Transportation	1. Continue company growth 2. Continue company profits	1. Modernize 2. Develop valuable real estate holdings 3. Complete an appropriate railroad merger

Figure 9.1 Steps of the strategic management process

MyLab Management Watch It

If your instructor has assigned this activity, go to www.pearson.com/mylab/management to complete the video exercise.

Strategic Management Process

Strategic management is the process of ensuring that an organization possesses and benefits from the use of an appropriate organizational strategy.[9] In this definition, an appropriate strategy is the one best suited to the needs of an organization at a particular time.

The strategic management process is generally thought to consist of five sequential and continuing steps:[10]

9-2 Insights regarding the main aspects of the strategic management process

1. Environmental analysis
2. Establishment of an organizational direction
3. Strategy formulation
4. Strategy implementation
5. Strategic control

The relationships among these steps are illustrated in **Figure 9.1**.

Environmental Analysis

The first step of the strategic management process is environmental analysis. In essence, an organization can be successful only if it is appropriately matched to its environment. **Environmental analysis** is the study of the organizational environment to pinpoint environmental factors that can significantly influence organizational operations. Managers commonly perform environmental analyses to help them understand what is happening both inside and outside their organizations and to increase the probability that the organizational strategies they develop will appropriately reflect the organizational environment.

9-3 Knowledge of the key components of environmental analysis

To perform an environmental analysis efficiently and effectively, a manager must thoroughly understand how organizational environments are structured. For purposes of environmental analysis, the environment of an organization is generally divided into three distinct levels: general environment, operating environment, and internal environment.[11] **Figure 9.2** illustrates the positions of these levels relative to one another and to the organization; it also shows the important components of each level. Managers must be well aware of these three environmental levels, understand how each level affects organizational performance, and then formulate organizational strategies in response to this understanding.

Figure 9.2

The organization, the levels of its environment, and the components of those levels

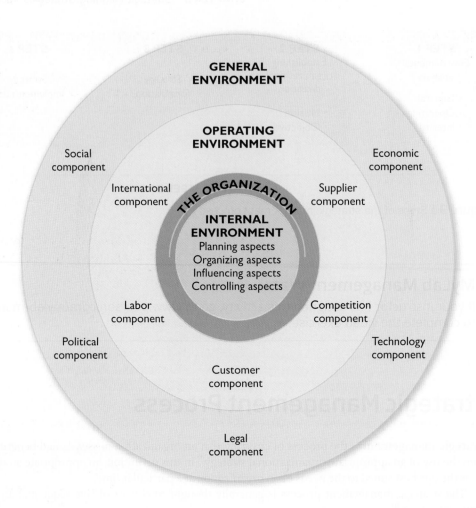

The General Environment

The level of an organization's external environment that contains components having broad, long-term implications for managing the organization is the **general environment**. The components normally considered part of the general environment are economic, social, political, legal, and technological.

The Economic Component
The economic component is what indicates how resources are being distributed and used within the environment. This component is based on **economics**, the science that focuses on understanding how people of a particular community or nation produce, distribute, and use various goods and services. Important issues to consider in an economic analysis of an environment are generally the wages paid to labor, inflation, the taxes paid by labor and businesses, the cost of materials used in the production process, and the prices at which produced goods and services are sold to customers.

These economic issues can significantly influence the environment in which a company operates and the ease or difficulty the organization experiences in attempting to reach its objectives. For example, it should be somewhat easier for an organization to sell its products at higher prices if potential consumers in the environment are earning relatively high wages and paying relatively low taxes than if these same potential customers are earning relatively low wages and have significantly fewer after-tax dollars to spend.

Organizational strategy should reflect the economic issues in the organization's environment. To continue with the preceding example, if the total amount of after-tax income that potential customers earn has significantly declined, an appropriate organizational strategy might be to lower the price of goods or services to make them more affordable. Such a strategy should be evaluated carefully, however, because it could have a serious impact on organizational profits.

The Social Component

The social component is the part of the general environment that describes the characteristics of the society in which the organization functions. Two important features of a society that are commonly studied during environmental analysis are demographics and social values.[12]

Demographics are the statistical characteristics of a population. These characteristics include changes in numbers of people and income distributions among various population segments. Such changes can influence how eagerly goods and services are received within the organization's environment and thus should be reflected in organizational strategy.

For example, the demand for retirement housing would probably increase dramatically if both the number and the income of retirees in a particular market area doubled.[13] Effective organizational strategy would include a mechanism for dealing with such a probable increase in demand within the organization's environment.

An understanding of demographics is also helpful for developing a strategy aimed at recruiting new employees to fill certain positions within an organization. Knowing that only a small number of people have a certain type of educational background, for example, would tell an organization that it should compete more intensely to attract people with this educational background. To formulate a recruitment strategy, managers need a thorough awareness of the demographics of the groups from which employees eventually will be hired. This practice, known as strategic workforce planning (SWP), helps organizations identify the workforce they need to achieve their strategic goals. Some early adopters of SWP, such as 3M, are able not only to track their workforce spending and determine how it affects revenues but also to compare their data to those of competitors. The recent global economic downturn stalled the use of SWP, however. In attempting to ride out the recession, many employers adopted a wait-and-see attitude toward workforce planning until business stabilized.[14]

Social values are the relative degrees of worth that a society places on the ways in which it exists and functions. Over time, social values can change dramatically, causing significant changes in how people live. These changes alter the organizational environment and, as a result, have an impact on organizational strategy. It is important for managers to remember that, although changes in the values of a particular society may occur slowly or quickly, they are inevitable.

Andres Rodriguez/Fotolia

In the United States, the percentage of workers under age 25 is expected to fall, while the share of older workers is expected to rise. This could affect how companies plan to grow, for example, how they plan to fill entry-level jobs.

The Political Component

The political component is that part of the general environment related to government affairs. Examples include the type of government in existence, government's attitude toward various industries, lobbying efforts by interest groups, the status of the passage of laws, and political party platforms and candidates. The recent shift of China's political leaders from ignoring to now monitoring and improving air quality illustrates how the political component of an organization's general environment can change at the international level.[15]

The Legal Component

The legal component is that part of the general environment that contains passed legislation. This component comprises the rules or laws that society's members must follow. Some examples of legislation that specifically aim at the operation of organizations are the Clean Air Act, which focuses on minimizing air pollution; the Occupational Safety and Health Act, which aims at ensuring a safe workplace; the Affordable Care Act, which provides all Americans with access to affordable health care; and the Consumer Products Safety Act, which upholds the principle that businesses must provide safe products for consumers. Over time, new laws are passed and some old laws are amended or eliminated.

TABLE 9.2   Important Aspects of the International Component of an Organization's Operating Environment

Legal Environment	Cultural Environment
Legal tradition	Customs, norms, values, beliefs
Effectiveness of legal system	Language
Treaties with foreign nations	Attitudes
Patent and trademark laws	Motivations
Laws affecting business firms	Social institutions
	Status symbols
Economic Environment	Religious beliefs
Level of economic development	
Population	**Political System**
Gross national product	Form of government
Per capita income	Political ideology
Literacy level	Stability of government
Social infrastructure	Strength of opposition parties and groups
Natural resources	Social unrest
Climate	Political strife and insurgency
Membership in regional economic blocs (EEC, LAFTA, etc.)	Government attitude toward foreign firms
Monetary and fiscal policies	Foreign policy
Nature of competition	
Currency convertibility	
Inflation	
Taxation system	
Interest rates	
Wage and salary levels	

The Technology Component   The technology component is the part of the general environment that includes new approaches to producing goods and services. These approaches can be new procedures as well as new equipment. The trend toward exploiting robots to improve productivity is an example of the technology component. The increasing use of robots in the next decade should vastly improve the efficiency of U.S. industry.

The International Component   The international component is the operating environment segment that is composed of all the factors relating to the international implications of organizational operations. Although not all organizations must deal with international issues, the number that have to do so is increasing dramatically and continuously in the twenty-first century. Factors in the international component include other countries' laws, cultures, economics, and politics.[16] Important variables within each of these four categories are presented in **Table 9.2**.

U.S.-based Hershey's recent acquisition of Chinese candy maker Shanghai Golden Monkey provides an example of the importance of the company's international component. Before the acquisition, Hershey opened a research facility in Shanghai to develop candy and snacks that would appeal to Chinese consumers. Traditionally, Hershey has avoided large acquisitions, but this deal helps it focus on its primary international market, China, where candy consumption has increased nearly 40 percent over the past five years.[17]

The Industry Environment

The level of an organization's external environment that contains components normally having relatively specific and immediate implications for managing the organization is the **industry environment**. The **Five Forces Model**, perhaps the best-known tool for industry analysis, was

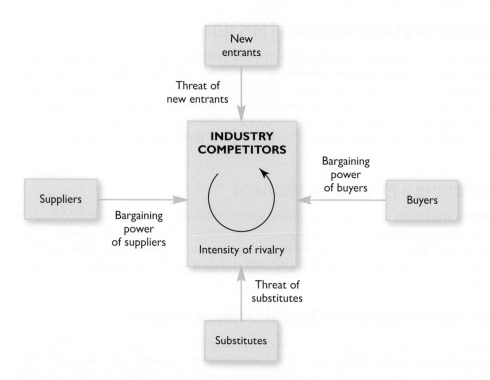

developed by internationally acclaimed strategic management expert Michael E. Porter.[18] Essentially, Porter's Model outlines the primary forces that determine competitiveness within an industry and illustrates how those forces are related.

Porter's Model is presented in **Figure 9.3**. According to the model, the attractiveness of an industry is determined by five alternative forces. First, the **threat of new entrants** refers to the ability of new firms to enter an industry; as the threat of new entrants increases, the attractiveness of the industry decreases. Second, **buyer power** refers to the power that customers have over the firms operating in an industry; as buyer power increases, the attractiveness of the industry decreases. Third, **supplier power** denotes the power that suppliers have over the firms operating in an industry. As supplier power increases, industry attractiveness decreases. Fourth, the **threat of substitute products** refers to the extent to which customers use products or services from another industry instead of the focal industry. As the threat of substitute products increases, which implies that customers have more choices, the attractiveness of the industry decreases. Finally, **intensity of rivalry** refers to the intensity of competition among the organizations in an industry. As the intensity of rivalry increases, the attractiveness of the industry decreases.

The Internal Environment

The level of an organization's environment that exists inside the organization and normally has immediate and specific implications for managing the organization is the **internal environment**. In broad terms, the internal environment includes marketing, finance, and accounting. From a more specific management viewpoint, it includes planning, organizing, influencing, and controlling within the organization.

Establishing Organizational Direction

The second step of the strategic management process is establishing organizational direction. Through an interpretation of information gathered during environmental analysis, managers can determine the direction in which the organization should move. Two important ingredients of organizational direction are organizational mission and organizational objectives.

9-4   An understanding of the role of organizational direction in strategic management

Determining Organizational Mission

The most common initial act in establishing organizational direction is determining an organizational mission. **Organizational mission** is the purpose for which—the reason why—an organization exists. In general, the firm's organizational mission reflects information such as what types of products or services it produces, who its customers tend to be, and what important values it holds. An organizational mission is a broad statement of organizational direction and is based on a thorough analysis of information generated through environmental analysis.[19]

Developing a Mission Statement

A **mission statement** is a written document developed by management, normally based on input by managers as well as nonmanagers, that describes and explains the mission of the organization.[20] The mission is expressed in writing to ensure that all organization members have easy access to it and thoroughly understand exactly what the organization is trying to accomplish.

The Importance of an Organizational Mission

An organizational mission is important to an organization because it helps increase the probability that the organization will be successful. There are several reasons why it does this. First, the existence of an organizational mission helps management direct human effort in a common direction. The mission makes explicit the major targets that the organization is trying to reach and helps managers keep these targets in mind as they make decisions. Second, an organizational mission serves as a sound rationale for allocating resources. A properly developed mission statement gives managers general but useful guidelines about how resources should be used to best accomplish organizational purpose. Third, a mission statement helps management define broad but important work areas within an organization and therefore the critical jobs that must be accomplished.[21]

The Relationship between Mission and Objectives

Organizational objectives were defined in Chapter 7 as the targets toward which the open management system is directed. Sound organizational objectives reflect and flow naturally from the purpose of the organization, which is expressed in its mission statement. As a result, useful organizational objectives must reflect and flow naturally from an organizational mission, which in turn was designed to reflect and flow naturally from the results of an environmental analysis.[22]

Strategy Formulation: Tools

9-5   An appreciation for the primary aspects of strategy formulation

After managers involved in the strategic management process have analyzed the environment and determined the proper organizational direction through the development of a mission statement and organizational objectives, they are ready to formulate strategy. **Strategy formulation** is the process of determining appropriate courses of action for achieving organizational objectives and thereby accomplishing the organizational purpose.

Managers formulate strategies that reflect environmental analysis, lead to fulfillment of the organizational mission, and result in the attainment of organizational objectives. Special tools that managers can use to assist them in formulating strategies include the following:

- Critical question analysis
- SWOT analysis
- Business portfolio analysis

These three strategy development tools are related but distinct. Managers should use the tool or combination of tools that seems most appropriate for them and their organizations.

STEPS FOR SUCCESS

Ask the Right Questions

Managers gain experience by thinking about day-to-day goals for their department or function, and business founders usually start with an idea for a product. Thinking strategically can be a struggle. If the four basic critical questions are too overwhelming for a planning session, start with these questions to get the ideas flowing:[23]

- What did our organization do worst this year? How can we correct that?

- What did our organization do best this year? How can we repeat that success?
- Why do our customers buy from us? What are their alternatives?
- What real problems do our customers face? How can we solve one of those problems better than our competitors can?
- What makes us different from our competitors?
- What is preventing us from achieving more?

Critical Question Analysis

A synthesis of the ideas of several contemporary management writers suggests that formulating an appropriate organizational strategy is a process of **critical question analysis**:[24]

- **What are the purposes and objectives of the organization?** The answer to this question will tell management where the organization should be going. As indicated earlier, an appropriate strategy reflects both organizational purpose and organizational objectives. By answering this question during the strategy formulation process, managers are likely to remember this important point and thereby minimize inconsistencies among the organization's purposes, objectives, and strategies.
- **Where is the organization presently going?** The answer to this question can tell managers whether the organization is achieving its goals and, if it is, whether the level of progress is satisfactory. Whereas the first question focuses on where the organization should be going, this one focuses on where the organization is actually going.
- **In what kind of environment does the organization now exist?** Both internal and external environments—factors inside and outside the organization—are included in this question. For example, assume that a poorly trained middle-management team and a sudden influx of competitors in a market are respective factors in the internal and external environments of an organization. Any strategy formulated, if it is to be appropriate, must deal with these factors.
- **What can be done to better achieve organizational objectives in the future?** The answer to this question will result in the strategy of the organization. The question should be answered, however, only *after* managers have had an adequate opportunity to reflect on the answers to the previous three questions. Managers cannot develop an appropriate organizational strategy unless they have a clear understanding of where the organization wants to go, where it is going, and in what environment it exists. This understanding is typically achieved through discussion, negotiation, and compromise.[25]

SWOT Analysis

SWOT analysis is a strategic development tool that matches internal organizational strengths and weaknesses with external opportunities and threats. (SWOT is an acronym for a firm's **S**trengths and **W**eaknesses and its environmental **O**pportunities and **T**hreats.) It is important to note that when using SWOT analysis, "strengths" and "weaknesses" are those of the manager's firm, and "opportunities" and "threats" exist in the firm's external environment. SWOT analysis is based on the assumption that, if managers carefully review such strengths, weaknesses, opportunities, and threats, a useful strategy for ensuring organizational success will become evident to them.[26]

Business Portfolio Analysis

Business portfolio analysis is another strategy development tool that has gained wide acceptance. **Business portfolio analysis** is an organizational strategy formulation technique that is based on the philosophy that organizations should develop strategy much as they handle investment portfolios. That is, just as sound financial investments should be supported and unsound ones discarded, sound organizational activities should be emphasized and unsound ones deemphasized. Two business portfolio tools are the BCG Growth-Share Matrix and the GE Multifactor Portfolio Matrix.

The BCG Growth-Share Matrix
The Boston Consulting Group (BCG), a leading manufacturing consulting firm, developed and popularized a portfolio analysis tool that helps managers develop organizational strategies based on market share of businesses and the growth of markets in which businesses exist.

The first step in using the BCG Growth-Share Matrix is identifying the organization's strategic business units (SBUs). A **strategic business unit** is a significant organizational segment that is analyzed to develop organizational strategy aimed at generating future business or revenue. Exactly what constitutes an SBU varies from organization to organization. In larger organizations, an SBU could be a company division, a single product, or a complete product line. In smaller organizations, it might be the entire company. Although SBUs vary drastically in form, each has the following four characteristics:[27]

a. It is a single business or collection of related businesses.
b. It has its own competitors.
c. It has a manager who is accountable for its operation.
d. It is an area that can be independently planned for within the organization.

After SBUs have been identified for a particular organization, the next step in using the BCG Matrix is to categorize each SBU within one of the following four matrix quadrants (see **Figure 9.4**):

- **Star**—An SBU that is a **star** has a large share of a high-growth market and typically needs large amounts of cash to support rapid and significant growth. Stars also generate large amounts of cash for the organization and are usually segments in which management can make additional investments and earn attractive returns.
- **Cash Cow**—An SBU that is a **cash cow** has a large share of a market that is growing only slightly. Naturally, these SBUs provide the organization with large amounts of cash, but because the market is not growing significantly, the cash is generally used to meet the financial demands of the organization in other areas, such as the expansion of a star SBU.

Figure 9.4
The BCG Growth-Share Matrix

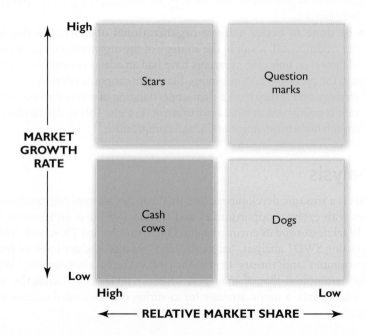

- **Question Mark**—An SBU that is a **question mark** has a small share of a high-growth market. Such SBUs are dubbed "question marks" because it is uncertain whether management should invest more cash in them to gain a larger share of the market or deemphasize or eliminate them. Management will choose the first option when it believes it can turn the question mark into a star and will choose the second when it thinks further investment would be fruitless.
- **Dog**—An SBU that is a **dog** has a relatively small share of a low-growth market. Such SBUs may barely support themselves; in some cases, they actually drain off cash resources generated by other SBUs. Examples of dogs are SBUs that produce typewriters or cash registers.

Companies such as Westinghouse and Shell Oil have successfully used the BCG Matrix in their strategic management processes; however, this technique has some potential pitfalls. For one thing, the matrix does not consider factors such as (1) various types of risk associated with product development; (2) threats that inflation and other economic conditions can create in the future; and (3) social, political, and ecological pressures. These pitfalls may be the reason for recent research results indicating that the BCG Matrix does not always help managers make good strategic decisions.[28] Managers must therefore remember to weigh such factors carefully when designing an organizational strategy based on the BCG Matrix.

The GE Multifactor Portfolio Matrix   With the help of McKinsey and Company, a leading consulting firm, the General Electric Company (GE) developed another popular portfolio analysis tool called the GE Multifactor Portfolio Matrix. This tool helps managers develop organizational strategy that is based primarily on market attractiveness and business strengths. The GE Multifactor Portfolio Matrix was intentionally designed to be more comprehensive than the BCG Growth-Share Matrix.

Basic use of the GE Multifactor Portfolio Matrix is illustrated in **Figure 9.5**. Each of the organization's businesses or SBUs is plotted on a matrix in two dimensions: industry attractiveness and business strength. Each of these two dimensions is actually a composite of a variety of factors that each firm must determine for itself given its own unique situation. As examples, industry attractiveness might be determined by factors such as the number of competitors in an industry, the rate of industry growth, and the weakness of competitors within an industry; business strength might be determined by factors such as a company's financially solid position, its good bargaining position over suppliers, and its high level of technology use.

Several circles appear in Figure 9.5, each representing a company line of business or SBU. Circle size indicates the relative market size for that line of business. The shaded portion of a circle represents the proportion of the total SBU market that a company has captured.

Figure 9.5
GE's Multifactor Portfolio Matrix

I – Invest/grow
S – Selective investment
H – Harvest/divest

Ian Dagnall/Alamy Stock Photo

Dollar Tree's strategy focuses on selling name-brand and off-brand products at lower prices than its competitors.

Specific strategies of a company are implied by where its businesses (represented by circles) fall on the matrix. Businesses falling in the cells that form a diagonal from lower left to upper right are medium-strength businesses, which should be invested in only selectively. Businesses above and to the left of this diagonal are the strongest and the ones that a company should invest in and help to grow. Businesses in the cells below and to the right of the diagonal are low in overall strength and are serious candidates for divestiture.

Portfolio models are graphic frameworks for analyzing relationships among the businesses of an organization, and they can provide useful strategy recommendations. However, no model yet devised gives managers a universally accepted approach for dealing with these issues. Thus, Portfolio models, then, should never be applied in a mechanistic fashion, and any conclusions they suggest must be carefully considered in light of sound managerial judgment and experience.

Strategy Formulation: Types

Understanding the forces that determine competitiveness within an industry should help managers develop strategies that will make their companies more competitive within the industry. Porter has developed three generic strategies to illustrate the kinds of strategies managers might develop to make their organizations more competitive.[29]

Differentiation

Differentiation, the first of Porter's strategies, focuses on making an organization more competitive by developing a product or products that customers perceive as being different from products offered by competitors. Differentiation includes uniqueness in areas such as product quality, design, and level of after-sales service. Examples of products that customers commonly purchase because they perceive them as being different are Apple's iPhones (because of their design and technology) and Porsche automobiles (because of their styling and performance characteristics).

Cost Leadership

Cost leadership is a strategy that focuses on making an organization more competitive by producing products more cheaply than competitors can. According to the logic behind this strategy, producing products more cheaply than its competitors means that an organization will then be able to offer products to customers at lower prices than competitors can and will thereby increase its market share. Examples of tactics managers might use to gain cost leadership are obtaining lower prices on product parts purchased from suppliers and using technology such as robots to increase organizational productivity. Wal-Mart is an example of a company that employs a cost leadership strategy.[30]

Focus

Focus is a strategy that emphasizes making an organization more competitive by targeting a particular segment of customers. Magazine publishers commonly use a focus strategy in offering their products to specific customers. *Working Woman* and *Ebony* are examples of magazines that are aimed, respectively, at the target markets of employed women and African Americans.

Sample Organizational Strategies

Analyzing the organizational environment and applying one or more of the strategy tools—critical question analysis, SWOT analysis, business portfolio analysis, and Porter's Model—give managers a foundation on which to formulate an organizational strategy. The four common organizational strategies that evolve this way are growth, stability, retrenchment, and divestiture.

The following discussion of these organizational strategies features business portfolio analysis as the tool used to arrive at the strategy, although the same strategies could result from critical question analysis, SWOT analysis, and Porter's Model.

Growth

Growth is a strategy adopted by management to increase the amount of business that an SBU is currently generating. The growth strategy is generally applied to star SBUs or to question mark SBUs that have the potential to become stars. Management generally invests substantial amounts of money to implement this strategy and may even sacrifice short-term profit to build long-term gain.[31]

Managers can also pursue a growth strategy by purchasing an SBU from another organization. Black & Decker held the leadership position in power tools for many years, but the company wanted to extend its reach beyond that product line. Rather than attempt to develop its own line of power tools, Black & Decker purchased General Electric's small-appliance business. Through this purchase, Black & Decker hoped that the amount of business it did would grow significantly over the long term. Similarly, President Enterprises, the largest food company in Taiwan, bought the American Famous Amos brand of chocolate chip cookies. Despite a downturn in the U.S. cookie market, management at President Enterprises saw the purchase as important for company growth because it would give the company a nationally recognized product line in the United States.[32]

Stability

Stability is a strategy adopted by management to maintain or slightly improve the amount of business that an SBU is generating. This strategy is generally applied to cash cows because these SBUs are already in an advantageous position. Management must be careful, however, that in its pursuit of stability, it does not turn cash cows into dogs.

Retrenchment

In this strategy, *retrench* is used in the military sense: to defend or fortify. Through **retrenchment** strategy, management attempts to strengthen or protect the amount of business an SBU is currently generating. This strategy is generally applied to cash cows or stars that are beginning to lose market share.

Divestiture

Divestiture is a strategy adopted to eliminate an SBU that is not generating a satisfactory amount of business and that has little hope of doing so in the near future. In essence, the organization sells or closes down the SBU in question. This strategy is usually applied to SBUs that are dogs or question marks that have failed to increase market share but still require significant amounts of cash.[33]

Strategy Implementation

Strategy implementation, the fourth step of the strategic management process, involves putting formulated strategies into action.[34] Without successful implementation, valuable strategies developed by managers are virtually worthless.[35]

9-6   Insights regarding strategy implementation

The successful implementation of strategy requires four basic skills:[36]

a. **Interacting skill** is the ability to manage people during implementation. Managers who are able to understand the fears and frustrations others feel during the implementation of a new strategy tend to be the best implementers. These managers empathize with organization members and bargain for the best way to put a strategy into action.

TIPS FOR MANAGING AROUND THE GLOBE

Ryanair Utilizes Cost Leadership Strategy

Ryanair, based in Swords, Ireland, has recently become the largest airline in Europe through its cost leadership strategy. Founded in 1984, the airline has slowly gained ground on all the other major airlines in Europe through its very low airfares. It now flies into just about every major European city. The company flew well over 100 million passengers in 2016 and continues to grow each quarter.

The CEO, Michael O'Leary, credits the low-cost strategy with the airline's success. "If we don't keep challenging ourselves, and we don't keep challenging rival airlines, and we don't commit to keeping driving down prices, then we will become fat, numb and stupid like the rest of the industry." The low-cost strategy is working. At an average fare of less than fifty euros, many customers simply cannot beat their prices. And with revenues at $1.4 billion, the low-cost airline plans to double in size over the next eight years and hopes to move over 220 million passengers by 2024.[37]

b. **Allocating skill** is the ability to provide the organizational resources necessary to implement a strategy. Successful implementers are talented at scheduling jobs, budgeting time and money, and allocating other resources that are critical for implementation.

c. **Monitoring skill** is the ability to use information to determine whether a problem has arisen that is blocking strategy implementation. Good strategy implementers set up feedback systems that continually tell them about the status of strategy implementation.

d. **Organizing skill** is the ability to create throughout the organization a network of people who can help solve implementation problems as they occur. Good implementers customize this network to include individuals who can handle the special types of problems anticipated in the implementation of a particular strategy.

Overall, then, the successful implementation of a strategy requires handling people appropriately, allocating the resources necessary for implementation, monitoring implementation progress, and solving implementation problems as they occur. Perhaps the most important requirements are knowing which people can solve specific implementation problems and being able to involve those people when implementation problems arise.

Strategic Control

9-7   An appreciation for the importance of strategic control

Strategic control, the last step of the strategic management process, consists of monitoring and evaluating the strategic management process as a whole to ensure that it is operating properly. Strategic control focuses on the activities involved in environmental analysis, organizational direction, strategy formulation, strategy implementation, and strategic control itself—checking that all steps of the strategic management process are appropriate, compatible, and functioning properly.[38] Strategic control is a special type of organizational control, a topic that is featured in Chapters 19 and 20.

Tactical Planning

9-8   Insights into what tactical planning is and how strategic and tactical planning should be coordinated

Tactical planning is short-range planning that emphasizes the current operations of various parts of an organization. *Short range* is defined as a period of time extending about one year or less into the future. Managers use tactical planning to indicate what the various parts of the organization must do for the organization to be successful at some point one year or less into the future.[39] Tactical plans are usually developed in the areas of production, marketing, personnel, finance, and plant facilities.

TABLE 9.3   Major Differences between Strategic and Tactical Planning

Area of Difference	Strategic Planning	Tactical Planning
Individuals involved	Developed mainly by upper-level management	Developed mainly by lower-level management
Facts on which to base planning	Facts are relatively difficult to gather	Facts are relatively easy to gather
Amount of detail in plans	Plans contain relatively little detail	Plans contain substantial amounts of detail
Length of time plans cover	Plans cover long periods of time	Plans cover short periods of time

Comparing and Coordinating Strategic and Tactical Planning

In striving to implement successful planning systems within organizations, managers must keep in mind several basic differences between strategic planning and tactical planning:

- Because upper-level managers generally have a better understanding of the organization as a whole than lower-level managers do, and because lower-level managers generally have a better understanding of the day-to-day organizational operations than upper-level managers do, strategic plans are usually developed by upper-level management and tactical plans by lower-level management.
- Because strategic planning emphasizes analyzing the future and because tactical planning emphasizes analyzing the everyday functioning of the organization, facts on which to base strategic plans are usually more difficult to gather than are facts on which to base tactical plans.
- Strategic plans are based primarily on a prediction of the future, and tactical plans are based primarily on known circumstances that exist within the organization; thus, strategic plans are generally less detailed than tactical plans.
- Because strategic planning focuses on the long term and tactical planning focuses on the short term, strategic plans cover a relatively long period of time, whereas tactical plans cover a relatively short period of time.

These major differences between strategic and tactical planning are summarized in **Table 9.3**.

Despite their differences, tactical planning and strategic planning are interrelated. As Russell L. Ackoff states, "We can look at them separately, even discuss them separately, but we cannot separate them in fact."[40] In other words, managers need both tactical and strategic planning programs, and these programs must be closely related to be successful. Tactical planning should focus on what to do in the short term to help the organization achieve the long-term objectives determined by strategic planning.

Competitive Dynamics

In the previous sections, we examined the first two components of strategic planning: strategic and tactical actions. In this section, we discuss the final component of strategic planning, which is gaining more attention from both researchers and practitioners: competitive dynamics. **Competitive dynamics** refers to the process by which firms undertake strategic and tactical actions and how competitors respond to these actions.[41] Although the previous sections do distinguish between and classify different types of strategic and tactical actions, the study of competitive dynamics is important in order to understand *why* managers undertake such actions. Inevitably, these actions and reactions influence a firm's ultimate financial performance.

Many studies of strategic planning and competition involve the analysis of industries. In contrast, research in competitive dynamics focuses on competitive dyads, which are groups of two companies competing vigorously within a particular industry.[42] By focusing on only two firms, researchers are able to isolate the factors that affect the competitive actions of both the

9-9   An awareness of how competitive dynamics can influence an organization's financial performance

PRACTICAL CHALLENGE: COMPETITIVE DYNAMICS FOR OIL

Shale Boom Shakes the Sheiks

The U.S. shale revolution triggered a wake-up call for the Organization of Petroleum-Exporting Countries (OPEC), a group of 12 global oil producers. The changing competitive dynamics caused by the entry of the United States into the global oil market required OPEC to reanalyze its management processes. The demand for oil in the Middle East is predicted to grow by 77 percent by 2035, leaving only 65 percent of its oil production available for export. The U.S. energy market has received a massive boost from its domestic shale oil and gas industry. It brought a supply of cheaper gas and oil into the market, leading to greater competition for traditional producers like Saudi Arabia. Countries like Iran and Venezuela have demanded that fellow OPEC members reduce oil output to curtail falling prices; however, OPEC's biggest producer and exporter, Saudi Arabia, has shown little sign of agreeing. By 2018, the U.S. crude oil being shipped overseas has reached over 1.3 million barrels per day, much of it going to Asia. By the mid-2020s, this is expected to rise to 4 million per day.[43]

attacker—the first firm to make a strategic or tactical action—and the defender—the second firm, which must choose whether or not to respond to the attacker.[44]

The following example may help clarify the influence of competitive dynamics on strategic planning: On a recent Monday morning, Barnes & Noble reduced the price of its e-book reader—the Nook—by 23 percent. This decision resulted after careful deliberation by the top managers at Barnes & Noble. Hours later, Amazon.com announced through a press release that it would reduce the price of its e-book reader—the Kindle—by an even larger amount, 27 percent.[45] The price war between Barnes & Noble and Amazon.com illustrates the intense rivalry between the two companies as they compete in the market for e-book readers as well as in the market for e-book sales. In this example, Barnes & Noble represents the attacker, and Amazon .com represents the defender.

Research suggests that three primary factors influence a firm's action or reaction: awareness, motivation, and capability.[46] These factors are illustrated in **Figure 9.6**. **Competitor awareness**

Figure 9.6
Competitive dynamics

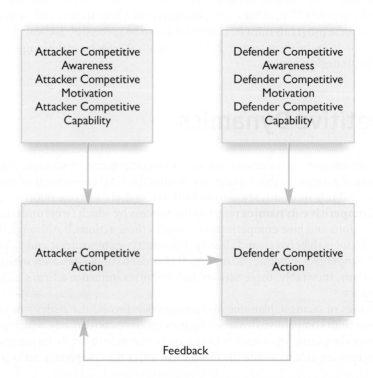

refers to how mindful a company is of its competitor's actions. In the example above, Amazon.com was clearly aware of Barnes & Noble's price cuts, which garnered a great deal of media attention. This media coverage was not a surprise because larger firms typically receive higher levels of media attention than do smaller firms.[47] In addition to media coverage, companies may learn about competitors' actions by taking note of a competitor's press releases. Alternatively, companies may learn about their competitors' actions by seeking information from shared customers or suppliers or from employees who previously worked for the competitor.

Competitor motivation refers to the incentives that drive an organization to take action. Extending the e-book example, Amazon.com was highly motivated to respond to Barnes & Noble's price cuts. If Amazon.com had not responded to these price cuts, many customers may have opted to purchase a Nook instead of a Kindle. This buyer decision becomes important because sales of e-book readers lead to subsequent e-book sales. A customer purchasing a Nook, for instance, is likely to make multiple e-book purchases from Barnes & Noble. Considering such future sales highlights just how motivated both companies are in the market for e-book readers. In addition, managers' incentives (e.g., pay packages) may also increase their motivation to engage in particular competitive actions.

Finally, **competitor capability** refers to a firm's ability to undertake an action. Often, capability refers to the resources that a firm has to take an action. For instance, a firm's competitor capability includes items such as available cash or the experience of the firm's management team. By extending the previous example, we can see that Amazon.com does not necessarily need cash to implement a price reduction for its Kindle. Nonetheless, Amazon.com does have to consider the long-term financial effects stemming from selling Kindles at a reduced price. Even though tactical actions may not require substantial resources, strategic actions may require large investments and thus high levels of resources.

Effective strategic planning requires an understanding of competitors' competitive actions. The competitor awareness, motivation, and capability framework provides a useful tool that managers may use to forecast competitor actions and reactions. To the extent that managers can measure their organization's activities (and those of its competitors) in an extremely precise manner, they will be able to gain insights about organizational performance and enhance their growth strategies.[48]

CHALLENGE CASE SUMMARY

In developing a plan to compete in its industry, management at Facebook should begin by thinking strategically. That is, management should try to determine what it can do to ensure that Facebook will continue to be successful at some point three to five years in the future. For example, building capabilities to create software for mobile devices should be part of this thinking. Facebook managers must be careful, however, to spend funds on strategic planning only if they can anticipate a return on these expenses in the foreseeable future.

The end result of Facebook's overall strategic planning will be a strategy—a broad plan that indicates what must be done to reach long-range objectives and carry out the organizational purpose of the company. This strategy will focus on many organizational areas, one of which will be competing with other companies that develop strategies in the same industry as Facebook. Once the strategy has been formulated using the results of an environmental analysis, Facebook management must conscientiously carry out the remaining steps of the strategic management process: strategy implementation and strategic control.

As part of the strategy development process, Facebook management should spend time analyzing the environment in which the organization exists. Naturally, these managers should focus on Facebook's general, operating, and internal environments. Environmental factors that probably would be important for Facebook's managers to consider as they pursue strategic planning include the companies with which Facebook competes and the kinds of software those companies are developing or the ads they are selling, strengths and weaknesses of Facebook's services when compared with those of competitors, the technologies that consumers are using for social networking, and the social and legal trends affecting the expectations for social media. Obtaining information about environmental issues such as these will increase the probability that any strategy developed for Facebook will be appropriate for the environment in which the company operates and that the company will be successful in the long term.

Based on the previous information, after Facebook has performed its environmental analysis, it must determine the direction in which the organization should move regarding its competitors' positions. Facebook has begun this process by developing a mission statement that describes the purpose for which the company exists. Facebook's managers have several tools available to assist them in formulating strategy. If they are to be effective in this area, however, they must use the tools in conjunction with environmental analysis. One of the tools, critical question analysis, would require management to analyze the purpose of Facebook, the direction in which the company is going, the environment in which it exists, and how the goals might be better achieved.

SWOT analysis, another strategy development tool, would require management to compile information regarding the internal strengths and weaknesses of Facebook, as well as the opportunities and threats that exist within the company's environment. In recent years, for example, Facebook would likely have seen a strength in the widespread growth of active users and a weakness in its lack of capabilities to develop popular mobile apps. Management probably would classify up-and-coming mobile apps that lure away young users as threats and competition with television in mobile advertising as an opportunity.

One approach to business portfolio analysis would suggest that Facebook management classify each major product line (SBU) within the company as a star, cash cow, question mark, or dog, depending on the growth rate of the market and the market share the Facebook product line possesses. Management could decide, for example, to consider the main Facebook website, the Facebook mobile apps, and Instagram as separate units for SBU analysis and categorize them according to the four classifications. As a result of this categorization process, managers could develop growth, stability, retrenchment, or divestiture strategies for each unit. Facebook management should use whichever strategy development tools it thinks would be most useful. Their objective, of course, is to develop an appropriate strategy for the evolution of Facebook's product lines.

To be successful at using the strategy they develop, managers at Facebook must apply the set of skills needed for implementation: interacting skill, allocating skill, monitoring skill, and organizing skill. In addition, management must be able to improve the strategic management process when necessary.

In addition to developing strategic plans for the organization, Facebook managers should consider tactical, or short-range, plans that would complement its strategic plans. Tactical plans for Facebook should focus on what can be done within approximately the next year to reach the organization's three- to five-year objectives and to take business away from its competitors. For example, tactical plans could include how the company will sell video advertising and what price it will charge advertisers. Other tactical plans could include adding features to Facebook's website and mobile apps to entice users to spend more time in each online location.

In addition, Facebook management must closely coordinate strategic and tactical planning within the company. Managers must keep in mind that strategic planning and tactical planning are different types of activities, may involve different people within the organization, and may result in plans with different degrees of detail. Yet they must also remember that these two types of planning are interrelated. Whereas lower-level managers would be mostly responsible for developing tactical plans, upper-level managers would mainly spend time on long-range planning and developing strategic plans that reflect company goals.

MyLab Management Assessing Your Management Skill

If your instructor has assigned this activity, go to www.pearson.com/mylab/management to complete the exercise related to the Challenge Case.

DEVELOPING STRATEGIC PLANNING SKILL

This section is specially designed to help you develop strategic planning skills. An individual's strategic planning skill is based on an understanding of the concepts and the ability to apply those concepts. The following activities will help to enhance your strategic planning skills in various organizational situations.

Class Preparation and Personal Study

To help you prepare for class, perform the activities outlined in this section. Performing these activities will help you enhance your classroom performance significantly.

Reflecting on Target Skill

On page 220, this chapter opens by presenting a target management skill along with a list of related objectives outlining knowledge and understanding that you should aim to acquire related to that skill. Review this target skill and the list of objectives to make sure that you've acquired all pertinent information within the chapter. If you do not feel that you've reached a particular objective(s), study related chapter coverage until you do.

Know Key Terms

Understanding the following key terms is critical to your preparing for class. Define each of these terms. Refer to the page(s) referenced after a term to check your definition or to gain further insight regarding the term.

Know How Management Concepts Relate

This section comprises activities that will further sharpen your understanding of management concepts. Answer these essay questions as completely as possible.

9-1 Name one of the best-known industry analysis tools. List and describe its main components. What is its analysis value?

9-2 The Boston Consulting Group uses SBUs. What are SBUs and their identifying characteristics? Using the BCG Growth-Share Matrix, classify the SBUs of a company of your choice.

Management Skills Exercises

Learning activities in this section are aimed at helping you develop strategic planning skills.

MyLab Management
Discussion Questions

Go to www.pearson.com/mylab/management to complete the problems marked with this icon ⭐.

⭐ Cases

Facebook Positions Itself to Stay Relevant

The Challenge Case "Facebook Positions Itself to Stay Relevant" (p. 221) and its related Challenge Case Summary were written to help you better understand the management concepts contained in this chapter. Answer the following discussion questions about the Challenge Case to better understand how strategic planning concepts can be applied in a company such as Facebook.

9-3 For Facebook's managers, is acquiring a business such as Instagram a strategic management issue? Explain.

9-4 Give three factors in Facebook's internal environment that managers should be assessing in determining the company's organizational direction. Why are these factors important?

9-5 Using the business portfolio matrix, categorize Facebook's recently acquired Instagram unit as a dog, question mark, star, or cash cow. From a strategic planning viewpoint, what do you recommend Facebook managers do with Instagram, given this categorization? Why?

Dyson: All about the Technology

Read the case and answer the questions that follow. Studying this case will help you better understand how concepts relating to strategic planning can be applied in an organization like Dyson.

There are hundreds, if not thousands, of vacuum cleaners in the global market. British inventor James Dyson entered this highly competitive market in 1991 and began selling his first mass-market vacuum cleaner two years later. Since then, Dyson has achieved global recognition for his imaginative re-designing of hand dryers, hair dryers, heaters, and bladeless fans. More recently, he has focused on the vexed issue of reliable batteries for automobiles.

Since 2015, Dyson has had 400 engineers working on his new electric car, which he plans to launch in 2020. The company claims that their new batteries will be twice as efficient as existing batteries and that the design of both the battery and the vehicle are radically different. So far, Dyson has invested $3.32 billion in the project. Just under half of the investment has been devoted to the actual design of the car; the rest, to battery research and associated projects. The most immediate competitor is likely to be the more upmarket Tesla cars. However, Tesla vehicles are currently out of most customers' price range—the cheapest is the Model 3, at $46,000, and the Model S starts at $80,000.

Dyson claims that his desire to produce a clean automobile dates back to the late 1990s, when he was involved in designing filters for conventional engines. From the outset, Dyson's business has held several interconnecting mission statements close to all their activities that succinctly encapsulate the ideal of sustainability.

The company has recruited heavily from the automobile manufacturing industry while simultaneously increasing its investment in battery technology. As an organization, although UK-based, Dyson takes a very pragmatic view regarding manufacturing location. It has recognized the fact that many Asian countries are ahead of the adoption curve in terms of electric car demand and actual purchases—there is a demand for low-particulate automobiles and systems to protect drivers, so Dyson has incorporated an air-purifying system into the car design. Dyson has also made clear that batteries for the automobiles will be manufactured at the same location that the vehicle is. Dyson's new solid-state batteries are unlike those that are used in smartphones and existing electric vehicles, which rely on lithium-ion. Dyson is not alone in pursuing this approach, as Toyota aims to release its own solid-state batteries in 2020.

These imminent decisions by Dyson come at a time when Indian-owned Jaguar Land Rover has already made the commitment to produce their electric cars in the United Kingdom from 2020 onward. Similarly, German-owned BMW has committed to manufacturing their new electric Mini in Oxford, and Japan's Nissan has decided that Sunderland is the prime location for their electric Leaf automobile. Volkswagen plans to invest over $24 billion in electric vehicle research and manufacturing by 2030 and other automobile manufacturers are scrambling to bring their own electric vehicles and better batteries to market first.

Ultimately, the success or failure of Dyson's foray into electric vehicles will be determined by timing, its ability to offer a solid and reliable product, a better battery range and quicker charging time, and immediate access to the biggest markets. The last factor is hugely significant as Dyson already has manufacturing facilities in Malaysia. Many industry analysts are confident that China will be the preferred manufacturing location as it already has a significant and growing market for plug-in hybrid-electric vehicles (PHEVs). The Chinese market for PHEVs in 2016 was some 507,000, an increase of 53 percent compared to 2015. Most of the car sales were secured by Chinese manufacturers. Across Europe, sales were also up by 14 percent, but at 222,200, far less than in China. Meanwhile, the U.S. market, up by 36 percent, nonetheless lagged behind with just 157,000 sales.[49]

Questions

9-6 Why is it important for Dyson to have a mission statement? How do the strategic decisions described in this case support Dyson's mission?

9-7 Using examples from the case, describe how Dyson's managers can use critical question analysis to formulate a strategy.

9-8 Which of the three generic strategies identified by Porter best describes Dyson's strategy? Explain your reasons for choosing this strategy.

Experiential Exercises

Examining Lush's Operating Environment

Directions. Read the following scenario and then perform the listed activities. Your instructor may wish you to perform the activities as an individual or in groups. Follow all of your instructor's directions carefully.

Established in 1995, the fresh-cosmetics company Lush now has over 900 stores worldwide. It is a highly competitive market. Beyond the day-to-day internal working environment of a business and within the broader external environment is the operating environment in which businesses like Lush exist. The international suppliers, labor, competition, and customer environments are strong determinants of Lush's decision-making and actions. Examine these five areas of concern and suggest how they impact on the company using the PESTLE framework as a guide.

You and Your Career

SWOT analysis represents an important tool in your strategic planning skill. Using SWOT analysis, top executives can better understand the strengths and weaknesses of their organization as well as the opportunities and threats in the external environment. Suppose you are interviewing for a position in an organization. How might SWOT analysis help you prepare for an interview? Now suppose you have just started working at an organization. How might SWOT analysis help you better understand your position and role in the organization?

Building Your Management Skills Portfolio

Your management skills portfolio is a collection of activities specially designed to demonstrate your management knowledge and skill. Be sure to save your work. Taking your printed portfolio to an employment interview could prove helpful.

The portfolio activity for this chapter is strategic planning at House of Fraser. Study this information and complete the exercises that follow.

In June 2018, House of Fraser, the UK-based department store chain, was on the verge of collapse. Some 17,500 jobs were at risk. To save the business, the decision was made to close 31 stores, including the flagship Oxford Street branch, at a cost of 6,000 jobs.

While announcing the decision, Frank Slevin, the chairman of House of Fraser, spoke generally about the traditional bricks-and-mortar retail industry and recognized a need to make serious changes and adapt at the earliest opportunity. Turning to House of Fraser itself, he said that the large department-store format meant that the business was hemorrhaging money and that it was a question of restricting or closing for good. Slevin has contacted you and asked you to help the company devise a new strategic plan.

The following questions will help you apply the strategic planning process to a real scenario.

9-9 Perform an environmental analysis for House of Fraser. Which segment of the environment is causing the company's problem(s)?

_____

_____

_____

9-10 Based on this analysis, develop a mission statement for the company and develop three objectives that will help the company fulfill its mission.

_____

_____

_____

9-11 Review Porter's generic strategies. Which one of these strategies would you recommend for the House of Fraser? Explain.

_____

_____

_____

9-12 Which of the four strategy implementation skills do you think will be most important for the company as it moves forward? Why?

_____

_____

_____

MyLab Management
Writing Assignments

If your instructor has assigned this activity, go to www.pearson.com/mylab/management for the following assisted-graded writing assignments:

Assisted-Graded Questions

9-13 Describe how an organization might use the BCG Growth-Share Matrix to evaluate its different strategic business units. Now, explain how an organization might use the GE Multifactor Portfolio Matrix to evaluate its strategic business units.

9-14 Describe Porter's generic business strategies and provide an example of each strategy.

9-15 Describe Porter's Five Forces Model. Why do organizations use Porter's Model?

9-16 In your local newspaper or a national publication like *Bloomberg Businessweek* or the *Wall Street Journal*, choose a company featured in the news. Analyze the company's actions. In your opinion, how did competitive dynamics play a role in the company's recent behavior?

Endnotes

1. Facebook, "About," https://www.facebook.com/facebook?v=info, accessed December 20, 2013; Facebook, "Key Facts," Facebook Newsroom, http://newsroom.fb.com/Key-Facts, accessed December 20, 2013; Evelyn M. Rusli, "Even Facebook Must Change," *Wall Street Journal*, January 29, 2013, http://online.wsj.com; Ben Fox Rubin, "Facebook Earnings: Profit Rises Amid Growth in Mobile," *Wall Street Journal*, May 1, 2013, http://online.wsj.com; Reed Albergotti, "Instagram Strikes Back at Snapchat," *Wall Street Journal*, December 13, 2013, http://online.wsj.com; Joshua Brustein, "Facebook Crosses the Advertising Frontier into TV's Turf," *Bloomberg Businessweek*, December 18, 2013, http://www.businessweek.com; Cooper Smith, "Seven Statistics about Facebook Users That Reveal Why It's Such a Powerful Marketing Platform," *Slate*, October 29, 2013, http://www.slate.com; Jessica Guynn, "Facebook, Twitter Try to Grab Teens' Attention with New Features," *Los Angeles Times*, December 12, 2013, http://articles.latimes.com.

2. For a model of learning to think strategically, see Andrea J. Casey and Ellen F. Goldman, "Enhancing the Ability to Think Strategically: A Learning Model," *Management Learning* 41, no. 2 (April 2010): 167–185.

3. To better understand the different dimensions of strategic planning, see Peter Brews and Devavrat Purohit, "Strategic Planning in Unstable Environments," *Long Range Planning* 40 (2007): 64–83.

4. For an article on the importance of strategic planning, see Sarah Kaplan and Eric Beinhocker, "The Real Value of Strategic Planning," *MIT Sloan Management Review* 44 (2003): 71. To better understand the influence of strategic planning in developing countries, see Jose Santos, "Strategy Lessons from Left Field," *Harvard Business Review* (2007): 20–21.

5. Ed Barrows, "Four Fatal Flaws of Strategic Planning," *Harvard Business Review*, March 13, 2009, http://blogs.hbr.org. For a review of research on strategic planning, see C. Wolf and S. W. Floyd, "Strategic Planning Research: Toward a Theory-Driven Agenda," *Journal of Management*, 2014, http://jom.sagepub.com/content/early/2013/03/26/0149206313478185.

6. For more information about how backup plans might influence the commitment principle, see J. Shin and K. L. Milkman, "How Backup Plans Can Harm Goal Pursuit: The Unexpected Downside of Being Prepared for Failure," *Organizational Behavior and Human Decision Processes* 135 (2016): 1–9.

7. Dyan Machan, "The Strategy Thing," *Forbes* (May 23, 1994): 113–114. For an example of a successful business strategy, see Laura Haller, "Target Reiterates Stable Strategy," *DSN Retailing Today* (June 4, 2001): 6.

8. For a detailed discussion of strategy formulation in small family-owned businesses, see Nancy Drozdow and Vincent P. Carroll, "Tools for Strategy Development in Family Firms," *Sloan Management Review* 39, no. 1 (Fall 1997): 75–88; see also Michael Beer and Russell Eisenstat, "How to Have an Honest Conversation about Your Business Strategy," *Harvard Business Review* 82 (2004): 82.

9. To better understand how the field of strategic management has evolved, see R. Durand, R. M. Grant, and T. M. Madsen, "The Expanding Domain of Strategic Management Research and the Quest for Integration," *Strategic Management Journal* 38 (2017): 4–16.

10. This section is based on Samuel C. Certo and J. Paul Peter, *Strategic Management: Concepts and Applications* (Chicago: Austen Press/Irwin, 1995), 3–27.

11. Samuel C. Certo and J. Paul Peter, *The Strategic Management Process*, 4th ed. (Chicago: Austen Press/Irwin, 1995), 32; William Drohan, "Principles of Strategic Planning," *Association Management* 49, no. 1 (January 1997): 85–87.

12. This section is based on William F. Glueck and Lawrence R. Jauch, *Business Policy and Strategic Management* (New York: McGraw-Hill, 1984), 99–110.

13. John F. Watkins, "Retirees as a New Growth Industry? Assessing the Demographic and Social Impact," *Review of Business* (Spring 1994): 9–14.

14. Patrick J. Kiger, "Serious Progress in Strategic Workforce Planning," *Workforce Management*, July 2010, http://www.workforce.com.

15. Editorial Board, "China's Dirty Air," *New York Times*, November 7, 2013, http://www.nytimes.com/2013/11/08/opinion/ chinas-dirty-air.html, accessed January 4, 2014. For more information on the influence of political activity on strategy in China, see N. Jia, "Are Collective Political Actions and Private Political Actions Substitutes or Complements? Empirical Evidence from China's Private Sector," *Strategic Management Journal* 35 (2014): 292–315.

16. Inga S. Baird, Marjorie A. Lyles, and J. B. Orris, "The Choice of International Strategies by Small Businesses," *Journal of Small Business Management* 32, no. 1 (January 1994): 48–60.

17. "Hershey Goes to China for Its Biggest-Ever Deal," *New York Times*, December 19, 2013, http://dealbook.nytimes.com/2013/12/19/hershey-goes-to-china-for-biggest-ever-deal/, accessed January 4, 2014; Laurie Burkitt, "Hershey to Buy China Candy Maker," *Wall Street Journal*, December 19, 2013, http://online.wsj.com/news/articles/SB10001424052702304773104579267634226586204, accessed January 4, 2014.

18. This discussion of Porter's Model is based on Chapters 1 and 2 of Porter's *Competitive Strategy* (New York: The Free Press, 1980); and Chapter 1 of Porter's *Competitive Advantage: Creating and Sustaining Superior Performance* (New York: The Free Press, 1985). For a review of how managers use Porter's Model, see R. P. Wright, S. E. Paroutis, and D. P. Blettner, "How Useful Are the Strategic Tools We Teach in Business Schools?," *Journal of Management Studies* 50 (2013): 92–125.

19. M. Klemm, S. Sanderson, and G. Luffman, "Mission Statements: Selling Corporate Values to Employees," *Long-Range Planning* (June 1991): 73–78.

20. Forest David and Fred Davis, "It's Time to Redraft Your Mission Statement," *Journal of Business Strategy* 24 (2003): 11. See also B. Blair-Loy, A. Wharton, and J. Goodstein, "Exploring the Relationship Between Mission Statements and Work-Life Practices in Organizations," *Organization Studies* 32 (2011): 427–450.

21. Colin Coulson-Thomas, "Strategic Vision or Strategic Cons: Rhetoric or Reality," *Long-Range Planning* (February 1992): 81–89; Rhymer Rigby, "Mission Statements," *Management Today* (March 1998): 56–58; Jeffrey Abrahams, *101 Mission Statements from Top Companies* (Berkeley, CA: Ten Speed Press, 2007).

22. For an interesting discussion of holding leaders accountable for attaining the objective of developing organizational integrity as a strategic asset, see Joseph A. Petrick and John F. Quinn, "The Challenge of Leadership Accountability for Integrity Capacity as a Strategic Asset," *Journal of Business Ethics* 34 (2001): 331–343.

23. Les McKeown, "Ten Questions to Jumpstart Your Strategic Planning Process," *Inc.*, August 13, 2013, http://www.inc.com; Mark Suster, "Every Start-Up Needs a Well-Articulated Strategy," *Inc.*, June 4, 2013, http://www.inc.com; Aileron, "Turning Your Dream into a Strategic Plan," *Forbes*, October 2, 2013, http://www.forbes.com; Small Business Administration, "Starting a Business: Creating Your Business Plan," *Starting and Managing a Business*, http://www.sba.gov, accessed December 18, 2013.

24. This section is based primarily on Thomas H. Naylor and Kristin Neva, "Design of a Strategic Planning Process," *Managerial Planning* (January/February 1980): 2–7; Donald W. Mitchell, "Pursuing Strategic Potential," *Managerial Planning* (May/June 1980): 6–10; Benton E. Gup, "Begin Strategic Planning by Asking Three Questions," *Managerial Planning* (November/December 1979): 28–31, 35; Rainer Feurer and Kazem Chaharbaghi, "Dynamic Strategy Formulation and Alignment," *Journal of General Management* 20, no. 3 (Spring 1995): 76–91.

25. Paula Jarzabkowski and Julia Balogun, "The Practice and Process of Delivering Integration through Strategic Planning," *Journal of Management Studies* 46, no. 8 (July 6, 2009): 1255–1288.

26. Doug Leigh, "SWOT Analysis," *Handbook of Improving Performance in the Workplace*, Wiley Online Library, February 2, 2010.

27. Philip Kotler, *Marketing Management Analysis, Planning and Control*, 7th ed. (Upper Saddle River, NJ: Prentice Hall, 1991), 39–41.

28. For an interesting discussion of international SBUs, see R. Belderbos, T. W. Tong, and S. Wu, "Multinationality and Downside Risk: The Roles of Option Portfolio and Organization," *Strategic Management Journal* 35 (2014): 88–106.

29. For an in-depth example of a differentiation strategy, see G. Cattani, R. L. M. Dunbar, and Z. Shapria, "How Commitment to Craftsmanship Leads to Unique Value: Steinway & Sons' Differentiation Strategy," *Strategy Science* 2 no. 1 (2017): 13–38.

30. One of the biggest challenges of business-level strategy is being "stuck in the middle." For more information on this topic, see

R. Adner, F. Ruiz-Aliseda, and P. Zemsky, "Specialist versus Generalist Positioning: Demand Heterogeneity, Technology Scalability and Endogenous Market Segmentation," *Strategy Science* 1 no. 3 (2016): 184–206.

31. Ian C. MacMillan, Donald C. Hambrick, and Diana L. Day, "The Product Portfolio and Profitability—A PIMS-Based Analysis of Industrial-Product Businesses," *Academy of Management Journal* (December 1982): 733–755. For more information on establishing growth businesses, see Y. Eshima and B. S. Anderson, "Firm Growth, Adaptive Capability, and Entrepreneurial Orientation," *Strategic Management Journal* 38 (2017): 770–779.

32. Walecia Konrad and Bruce Einhorn, "Famous Amos Gets a Chinese Accent," *BusinessWeek* (September 28, 1992): 76.

33. For more on how companies redeploy resources after divestitures, see M. B. Lieberman, G. K. Lee, and T. B. Folta, "Entry, Exit, and the Potential for Resource Redeployment," *Strategic Management Journal* 38 (2017): 526–544.

34. For a practical discussion of strategy implementation, see Brooke Dobni, "Creating a Strategy Implementation Environment," *Business Horizons* 46 (2003): 43.

35. William Sandy, "Avoid the Breakdowns Between Planning and Implementation," *Journal of Business Strategy* (September/October 1991): 30–33.

36. Thomas V. Bonoma, "Making Your Marketing Strategy Work," *Harvard Business Review* (March/April 1984): 69–76. Siddharth Philip, "Tata Signals Pricier Nano after 'Cheapest Car' Tag Flops," *Bloomberg Businessweek*, April 11, 2013, http://www.businessweek.com; Sean McLain, "Why the World's Cheapest Car Flopped," *Wall Street Journal*, October 14, 2013, http://online.wsj.com; Dana O'Donovan and Noah Rimland Flower, "The Strategic Plan Is Dead; Long Live Strategy," *Stanford Social Innovation Review*, January 10, 2013, http://www.ssireview.org.

37. Oliver Clark, "O'Leary: We Won't Mimic 'Fat, Numb, Stupid' Rivals," *Airline Business*, February 24, 2017, p.1.

38. For more on the distinction between formal and informal controls, see M. Kreutzer, L. B. Cardinal, J. Walter, and C. Lechner, "Formal and Informal Control as Complement or Substitute? The Role of the Task Environment," *Strategy Science* 1 no. 4 (2016): 235–255.

39. For a detailed discussion of the characteristics of strategic and tactical planning, see George A. Steiner, *Top Management Planning* (Toronto, Canada: Collier-Macmillan, 1969), 37–39.

40. Russell L. Ackoff, *A Concept of Corporate Planning* (New York: Wiley, 1970), 4.

41. Ming-Jer Chen and Danny Miller, "Competitive Dynamics: Themes, Trends, and a Prospective Research Platform," *The Academy of Management Annals* (2012), doi:10.1080/19416520.2012.660762. See also A. R. Menon and D. A. Yao, "Elevating Repositioning Costs: Strategy Dynamics and Competitive Interactions," *Strategic Management Journal*, in press, doi:10.1002/smj.2635.

42. M. J. Chen, "Competitive Dynamics Research: An Insider's Odyssey," *Asia Pacific Journal of Management* 26 (2009): 5–25.

43. Grant Smith, "U.S. to Be Top Oil Producer by 2015 on Shale, IEA Says," *Bloomberg*, November 12, 2013; Alex Lawler and Stephen Eisenhammer, "Middle East Faces Oil Challenges from Shale and Within – BP," Reuters, January 15, 2014; "OPEC Cuts 2015 Demand Forecast for Its Oil as Shale Boom Persists," Reuters with CNBC.com, December 10, 2014; Paul Horsnell, "Oil Prices: Boom, Bust and Boom Again," *The Financial Times*, December 9, 2014; Holly Ellyatt, "OPEC Needs to 'Wake Up' to Shale Revolution," CNBC, November 25, 2014.

44. M. J. Chen, K. H. Su, and W. Tsai, "Competitive Tension: The Awareness-Motivation-Capability Perspective," *Academy of Management Journal* 50 (2007): 101–118.

45. Geoffrey A. Fowler, "Price Cuts Electrify E-Reader Market," *Wall Street Journal*, June 21, 2010, http://online.wsj.com.

46. See K. G. Smith, W. J. Ferrier, and H. Ndofor, "Competitive Dynamics Research: Critique and Future Directions," in M. Hitt, R. E. Freeman, and J. Harrison, eds., *Handbook of Strategic Management* (London: Blackwell, 2001).

47. For further information on the relationship between firm size and media coverage, see L. Fang and J. Peress, "Media Coverage and the Cross-Section of Stock Returns," *Journal of Finance* 64, no. 5 (2009): 2023–2052.

48. Mehrdad Baghai, Sven Smit, and Patrick Viguerie, "Is Your Growth Strategy Flying Blind?," *Harvard Business Review*, May 2009, http://hbr.org.

49. Gwyn Topham, "James Dyson to Invest £2.5bn on 'Radically Different' Electric Car," *The Guardian*, September 26, 2017, https://www.theguardian.com/technology/2017/sep/26/james-dyson-electric-car-2020; Karl West, "Dyson: Industry Experts Cast Doubt on Electric Car Project," *The Guardian*, September 29, 2017, https://www.theguardian.com/technology/2017/sep/29/dyson-electric-car-project-industry-experts-2020-engineering-manufacturing-regulatory-hurdles; Dyson Institute, Home, www.dysoninstitute.com.

10 Fundamentals of Organizing

TARGET SKILL

Organizing Skill: the ability to establish orderly uses for resources within the management system

ORGANIZING SKILL AND YOUR CAREER

Organizing skill will be of great value to you in enhancing your career. This skill can help you establish orderly uses for resources within your organization. This ability contributes to organizational success, builds your image as a competent manager, makes you valuable to your organization, and supports promotions as you build your career.

OBJECTIVES

To help build my *organizing skill*, when studying this chapter, I will attempt to acquire:

10-1 An understanding of the organizing function

10-2 Knowledge regarding the benefits and costs of bureaucracy

10-3 Insights into the advantages and disadvantages of division of labor

10-4 An appreciation for the complexities of determining appropriate organizational structure

10-5 An appreciation for the advantages and disadvantages associated with the different types of departmentalization

---

MyLab Management Chapter Warm Up

If your instructor has assigned this activity, go to www.pearson.com/mylab/management to complete the chapter warm up.

Microsoft Tries to Program Unity with Its New Structure

Microsoft can boast of operating systems that are installed on the vast majority of desktop computers; on the popular Xbox gaming system; and on the Office suite of software, which dominates the market for word-processing and other business applications. The 100,000-employee company has enjoyed steady growth in revenues, recently exceeding $73 billion. However, profits have lagged revenue growth as Microsoft has struggled to keep up with the pace of technological change.

The top managers at Microsoft, under new CEO Satya Nadella, determined that what was holding the company back was a structure that did not foster a shared vision. Microsoft had eight divisions focused on specific products, and each division pursued its own strategy. The solution would be to reorganize work into fewer divisions aimed at a unified strategy.

The organization's new shared strategy is to create "a family of devices and services."[1] In other words, instead of one division handling, say, the Bing search engine while another handles the Windows operating system, Microsoft's hardware, software, and online services divisions should work together to let users perform computer-related activities on all their devices. This would require a new level of cooperation among employees across divisions.

The major change to Microsoft's structure involved shrinking the number of divisions and combining activities. Instead of eight divisions based on product lines, the new structure has four divisions based on ways groups of products are used:

- Applications—This group, headed by Qi Lu, has been assigned to manage work related to Office and Skype. Lu was formerly in charge of Bing.
- Cloud and enterprise—"Cloud" refers to online software and computing systems, including Microsoft's network of data centers running cloud systems. "Enterprise" includes databases and other technologies used primarily by businesses.
- Devices and studios—Under Julie Larson-Green, this group includes Xbox, Surface tablets, hardware accessories, and games. Larson-Green formerly headed the group in charge of the Windows operating system.
- Operating systems—Terry Myerson was chosen to head this group, which aims to unify operating systems across computers, Xbox, and mobile devices. Myerson previously led engineering for Windows Phone.

Jstone/Shutterstock

New Microsoft CEO Satya Nadella reorganized the company's structure into fewer divisions with a unified strategy to create "a family of devices and services."

Besides these product-use divisions, the reorganized Microsoft has divisions providing support functions for all employees and groups. These divisions include finance, marketing, and human resources. The goal of setting up company-wide functional divisions is for managers to collaborate and create marketing plans and finance projects in support of Microsoft's corporate strategy rather than pursuing divisional strategies that might conflict.

With this plan sketched out, the challenge now is implementing the new structure. Besides spelling out the details of each new job, Microsoft's managers, including Lu, Larson-Green, Myerson, and the heads of the functional departments, must convince their employees that collaboration is the new way of life at Microsoft.[2]

THE ORGANIZING CHALLENGE

The Challenge Case illustrates many different organizing challenges that Satya Nadella, the CEO, will have to meet if Microsoft is to be successful.

> The remaining material in this chapter explains organizing concepts and helps develop the corresponding organizing skill that you will need to meet organizing challenges throughout your career. After studying chapter concepts, read the Challenge Case Summary at the end of the chapter to help you relate chapter content to meeting organizing challenges at Microsoft.

Definitions of Organizing and Organizing Skill

10-1 An understanding of the organizing function

Organizing is the process of establishing orderly uses for resources within the management system. Correspondingly, **organizing skill** is the ability to create throughout the organization a network of people who can help solve implementation problems as they occur. This chapter focuses on organizing and helping you develop the target skill for this chapter, organizing skill.

Orderly uses of resources emphasize the attainment of management system objectives and assist managers not only in making objectives apparent but also in clarifying which resources will be used to attain those objectives.[3] A primary focus of organizing is determining what individual employees will do in an organization and how their individual efforts should best be combined to advance the attainment of organizational objectives.[4] *Organization* refers to the result of the organizing process. Henri Fayol presents a number of guidelines for effective organizations; these guidelines are displayed in **Figure 10.1**.

The Importance of Organizing

The organizing function is extremely important to the management system because it is the primary mechanism that managers use to activate plans.[5] Organizing creates and maintains relationships among all organizational resources by indicating which resources are to be used for specified activities and when, where, and how they are to be used. A thorough organizing effort helps managers minimize costly weaknesses, such as duplication of effort and idle organizational resources.

Some management theorists consider the organizing function so important that they advocate the creation of an organizing department within the management system. Typical duties of

Figure 10.1

Organization: Fayol's guidelines

In essence, each organizational resource represents an investment from which the management system must get a return. Appropriate organization of these resources increases the efficiency and effectiveness of their use. Henri Fayol developed 16 general guidelines for organizing resources:

1. Judiciously prepare and execute the operating plan.
2. Organize the human and material facets so that they are consistent with objectives, resources, and requirements of the concern.
3. Establish a single competent, energetic guiding authority (formal management structure).
4. Coordinate all activities and efforts.
5. Formulate clear, distinct, and precise decisions.
6. Arrange for efficient selection so that each department is headed by a competent, energetic manager, and all employees are placed where they can render the greatest service.
7. Define duties.
8. Encourage initiative and responsibility.
9. Offer fair and suitable rewards for services rendered.
10. Make use of sanctions against faults and errors.
11. Maintain discipline.
12. Ensure that individual interests are consistent with the general interests of the organization.
13. Recognize the unity of command.
14. Promote both material and human coordination.
15. Institute and effect controls.
16. Avoid regulations, red tape, and paperwork.

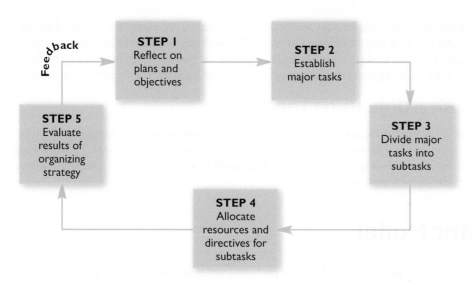

Figure 10.2
The five main steps of the
organizing process

this department would include three primary responsibilities.[6] First, the department should periodically formulate reorganization plans that make the management system more effective and efficient. For example, companies typically restructure to devote more resources to profitable divisions and fewer resources to divisions losing money. Second, the department should foster and support an advantageous organizational climate within the management system. Third, the department should develop plans to improve managerial skills so that they fit current management system needs.

General Electric (GE) is known the world over for its ability to develop managerial talent. Although GE is famous for its products and services, ranging from light bulbs to NBC television, many suggest that the key to GE's success is primarily the company's ability to identify and develop managers.[7]

The Organizing Process

The five main steps of the organizing process are presented in **Figure 10.2**: reflect on plans and objectives, establish major tasks, divide major tasks into subtasks, allocate resources and directives for subtasks, and evaluate the results of implemented organizing strategy.[8] As the figure implies, managers should continually repeat these steps. Through repetition, managers obtain feedback that will help them improve the existing organization.[9]

The management of a restaurant can serve as an illustration of how the organizing process works. The first step that the restaurant manager would take to initiate the organizing process would be to reflect on the restaurant's plans and objectives. Because planning involves determining how the restaurant will attain its objectives, and organizing involves determining how the restaurant's resources will be used to activate plans, the restaurant manager must start to organize by understanding planning.

The second and third steps of the organizing process focus on tasks to be performed within the management system. The manager must designate major tasks or jobs to be done within the restaurant. Two such tasks are serving customers and cooking food. Then the tasks must be divided into subtasks. For example, the manager might decide that serving customers includes the subtasks of taking orders and clearing tables.

The fourth organizing step is determining who will take orders and who will clear the tables, and the details of the relationship between these individuals. The size of tables and how they are to be set are other factors to consider at this point.

Managers have to improve organizational structure based on results. Avon cut layers of management and pushed decision making to lower levels as it needed to cut costs while stimulating growth on an international scale.

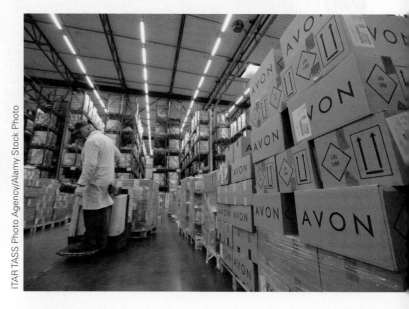

ITAR TASS Photo Agency/Alamy Stock Photo

In the fifth step, evaluating the results of the implemented organizing strategy, the manager gathers feedback on how well the strategy is working. This feedback should furnish information that can be used to improve the existing organization. For example, the manager may find that a particular type of table is not large enough and that larger ones must be purchased if the restaurant is to attain its goals.

Classical Organizing Theory

Classical organizing theory comprises the cumulative insights of early management writers on how organizational resources can best be used to enhance goal attainment. The following sections discuss three major components of classical organizing theory: Weber's bureaucratic model, division of labor, and structure.

Weber's Bureaucratic Model

10-2 Knowledge regarding the benefits and costs of bureaucracy

The writer who probably had the most profound influence on classical organizing theory was Max Weber. Most agree that Weber's most notable contribution to classical organizing theory was his concept of bureaucracy.[10] Specifically, Weber used the term **bureaucracy** to describe the management system that includes three primary components: detailed procedures and rules, a clearly outlined organizational hierarchy, and impersonal relationships among organization members.

Although he firmly believed in the bureaucratic approach to organizing, he was concerned that managers are inclined to overemphasize the merits of a bureaucracy. He cautioned that a bureaucracy is not an end in itself but rather a means to the end of management system goal attainment. The main criticism of Weber's bureaucracy model, as well as the concepts of other classical organizing theorists, is that they give short shrift to the human variable within organizations. In fact, it is recognized today that the bureaucratic approach without an appropriate emphasis on the human variable is almost certainly a formula for organizational failure.[11]

MyLab Management Watch It

If your instructor has assigned this activity, go to www.pearson.com/mylab/management to complete the video exercise.

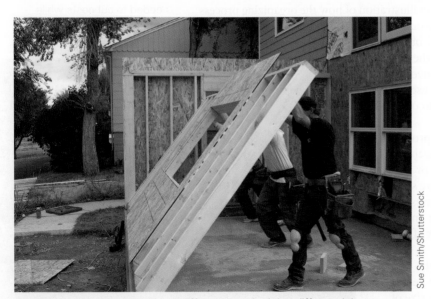

Sue Smith/Shutterstock

A company typically would have different people doing different jobs, so everyone can specialize and be efficient. Finding a balance between specialization and human motivation is important for managers.

Another criticism of bureaucracy is that it may have a negative influence on organizational effectiveness.[12] For an example of bureaucracy negatively influencing organizational effectiveness, consider General Motors (GM). For years, GM was not only one of the world's largest companies but also a huge bureaucracy. Although over the years various GM chief executives tried to cut layers of management, the company continued to post losses and, by 2009, faced bankruptcy. Before the U.S. government would provide further aid, GM was ordered to make significant and deep organizational cuts. With a slimmed-down GM emerging from bankruptcy, company vice chair Bob Lutz pledged that GM would maintain its focus on eliminating bureaucracy, saying, "If you tell yourself you're done [cutting costs], that probably means you're complacent."[13] Even though appropriate organization can improve efficiency and effectiveness, this example illustrates the potential problems associated with inappropriate organization.

Division of Labor

A primary consideration of any organizing effort is how to divide labor. **Division of labor** is the assignment of various portions of a particular task among a number of organization members.[14] Rather than one individual doing the entire job, several individuals perform different parts of the job. Production is divided into a number of steps, with the responsibility for completing various steps assigned to specific individuals. The essence of division of labor is that individuals specialize in doing part of a task rather than the entire task.[15]

A commonly used illustration of division of labor is the automobile production line. Rather than one person assembling an entire car, specific portions of the car are assembled by various workers. Although most associate division of labor with automobiles, division of labor plays an important role in a variety of businesses. For example, division of labor plays an important role in the manufacturing of art in China. At some manufacturing facilities, several artists help to paint copies of the same picture. When individuals finish painting their particular sections, they pass the painting on to other members to finish their own sections.[16] This approach allows Chinese galleries, such as the Ji Yi Yuang Gallery, to sell paintings for lower prices. It is clear, then, that the division of labor influences a variety of organizations. The following sections discuss the advantages and disadvantages of division of labor, the relationship between division of labor and coordination, and Mary Parker Follett's coordination guidelines.

10-3 Insights into the advantages and disadvantages of division of labor

Advantages and Disadvantages of Division of Labor

Even the peerless physicist Albert Einstein, famous for his independent theorizing, believed that division of labor could be advantageous in many undertakings.[17] Several explanations have been offered for the usefulness of division of labor. First, when workers specialize in a particular task, their skill at performing that task tends to increase. Second, workers who have one job and one place in which to do that job do not lose valuable time changing tools or locations. Third, when workers concentrate on performing only one job, they naturally try to make the job easier and more efficient. Division of labor also creates a situation in which workers need to know how to perform only their part of the work task rather than the entire process for producing the end product. Thus, the task of understanding their work does not become too burdensome.

Arguments against the use of an extreme division of labor have also been presented.[18] Essentially, these arguments contend that division of labor focuses solely on efficiency and economic benefit, and overlooks the human variable in organizations. Work that is extremely specialized tends to be boring and therefore will eventually cause production rates to go down as workers become resentful of being treated like machines. Clearly, managers need to find a reasonable balance between specialization and human motivation. Finding this balance is an ongoing challenge for organizations and an area of continued study.[19]

Division of Labor and Coordination

In a division-of-labor situation, the importance of effective coordination of the different individuals doing portions of the task is obvious. Mooney has defined **coordination** as "the orderly arrangement of group effort to provide unity of action in the pursuit of a common purpose." In essence, coordination is a means for achieving any and all organizational objectives.[20] It involves encouraging the completion of individual portions of a task in a synchronized order that is appropriate for the overall task. Groups cannot maintain their productivity without coordination.[21] Part of the synchronized order of assembling an automobile, for example, is that seats are installed only after the floor has been installed; adhering to this order of installation is an example of coordination.

Establishing and maintaining coordination may require close supervision of employees, although managers should try to break away from the idea that coordination can be achieved only in this way.[22] They can instead establish and maintain coordination through bargaining, formulating a common purpose for the group, or improving on specific solutions so that the group will know what to do when it encounters those problems. Each of these efforts is considered a specific management tool.

PRACTICAL CHALLENGE: COORDINATION

How the MBTA Moved Forward with Security

The Massachusetts Bay Transportation Authority (MBTA) offers an illustration of how a common purpose can support better coordination. The MBTA provides bus and rail transit services to almost 5 million people in Boston and eastern Massachusetts. With a thousand buses and hundreds of other vehicles carrying a million passengers every day, keeping everyone safe is a major concern, which was tragically heightened in April 2013, when bombs disrupted the finish of the Boston Marathon.

Several years before that event, the MBTA had improved coordination of security activities by setting up centralized management for all security operations. The security and emergency management department started by bringing together the MBTA transit police with people from operations and information technology to establish priorities for protecting workers, passengers, and property. Because management and the police appreciate the importance of security, they readily supported the efforts.[23]

Follett's Guidelines on Coordination

Mary Parker Follett provided valuable advice on how managers can establish and maintain coordination within the organization. First, Follett said that coordination can be attained with the least difficulty through direct horizontal relationships and personal communications. In other words, when a coordination problem arises, peer discussion may be the best way to resolve it. Second, Follett suggested that coordination be a discussion topic throughout the planning process. In essence, managers should plan for coordination. Third, maintaining coordination is a continuing process and should be treated as such. Managers cannot assume that just because their management system shows coordination today, it will also show coordination tomorrow.

Follett also noted that coordination can be achieved only through purposeful management action—it cannot be left to chance. Finally, she stressed the importance of the human element and advised that the communication process is an essential consideration in any attempt to encourage coordination. Primary considerations include employee skill levels, employee motivation levels, and the effectiveness of the human communication process used during coordination activities.[24]

Structure

10-4 An appreciation for the complexities of determining appropriate organizational structure

In any organizing effort, managers must choose an appropriate structure. **Structure** refers to the designated relationships among resources of the management system. Its purpose is to facilitate the use of each resource, individually and collectively, as the management system attempts to attain its objectives.[25] The two basic types of structure within management systems are formal and informal structures. **Formal structure** is defined as the relationships among organizational resources as outlined by management; formal structure is represented primarily by the organization chart. In contrast, **informal structure** is defined as the patterns of relationships that develop because of the informal activities of organization members. It evolves naturally and tends to be shaped by individual norms and values and social relationships. Essentially, an organization's informal structure is the system or network of interpersonal relationships that exists within, but is not usually identical to, the organization's formal structure.[26]

Informal Organizational Structures

A **mechanistic structure** is a formal organizational structure such as those discussed in this chapter. In contrast, an **organic structure** is less formal and represents loosely coupled networks of workers. Some researchers suggest that mechanistic structures are better suited for some organizations and organic structures are better suited for other organizations. In particular, research indicates that a mechanistic structure is better for large companies and those operating in stable industries. In contrast, organic structures are better for smaller companies and those operating in more volatile industries.[27]

Organizational structure is represented primarily by means of a graphic illustration called an **organization chart**. Traditionally, an organization chart is constructed in pyramid form, with individuals toward the top of the pyramid having more authority and responsibility than do those toward the bottom.[28] The relative positioning of individuals within boxes on the chart indicates broad working relationships, and lines between boxes designate formal lines of communication between individuals. In addition to specifying formal relationships within the firm, an organization chart can also communicate to outsiders the complexity of the organization. Structure involves two primary dimensions: the vertical dimension and the horizontal dimension. The following sections discuss each dimension in detail.[29]

Vertical Dimensioning

Vertical dimensioning refers to the extent to which an organization uses vertical levels to separate job responsibilities. Vertical dimensioning is directly related to the concept of the **scalar relationship**—that is, the chain of command. Every organization is built on the premise that the individual at the top possesses the most authority and that other individuals' authority is scaled downward according to their relative position on the organization chart. The lower a person's position on the organization chart, the less authority that person possesses.[30]

The scalar relationship, or chain of command, is related to the unity of command. **Unity of command** is the management principle that recommends that an individual have only one boss. If too many bosses give orders, the result will probably be confusion, contradiction, and frustration—a sure recipe for ineffectiveness and inefficiency in an organization. Although the unity-of-command principle made its first appearance in management literature well over 75 years ago, it is still discussed today as a critical ingredient of successful organizations.[31]

Span of Management

When examining the vertical dimensioning of an organization chart, it is important for managers to consider the influence of **span of management**—the number of individuals a manager supervises. The more individuals a manager supervises, the greater the span of management. Conversely, the fewer individuals a manager supervises, the smaller the span of management. The span of management has a significant effect on how well managers carry out their responsibilities. Span of management is also called *span of control, span of authority, span of supervision,* and *span of responsibility*.[32]

The central concern of span of management is to determine how many individuals a manager can supervise effectively.[33] To use the organization's human resources effectively, managers should supervise as many individuals as they can best guide toward production quotas. If they are supervising too few people, however, they are wasting a portion of their productive capacity. If they are supervising too many, they are losing part of their effectiveness.

Designing Span of Management: A Contingency Viewpoint

As reported by Harold Koontz, several important situational factors influence the appropriateness of the size of an individual's span of management:[34]

- **Similarity of functions**—the degree to which activities performed by supervised individuals are similar or dissimilar. As the similarity of subordinates' activities

Employees at call centers like this one perform similar activities, are physically close, and need little coordination, so supervisors tend to have a greater span of management.

David Pearson/Alamy Stock Photo

TABLE 10.1   **Major Factors That Influence the Span of Management**

Factor	Factor Has Tendency to Increase Span of Management When—	Factor Has Tendency to Decrease Span of Management When—
1. Similarity of functions	1. Subordinates have similar functions	1. Subordinates have different functions
2. Geographic contiguity	2. Subordinates are physically close	2. Subordinates are physically distant
3. Complexity of functions	3. Subordinates have simple tasks	3. Subordinates have complex tasks
4. Coordination	4. Work of subordinates needs little coordination	4. Work of subordinates needs much coordination
5. Planning	5. Manager spends little time planning	5. Manager spends much time planning

increases, the span of management appropriate for the situation widens. The converse is also generally true.

- **Geographic contiguity**—the degree to which subordinates are physically separated. In general, the closer subordinates are to each other physically, the more of them managers can supervise effectively.
- **Complexity of functions**—the degree to which workers' activities are difficult and involved. The more difficult and involved the activities are, the more difficult it is to manage a large number of individuals effectively. This is particularly true for research and development departments, which typically include a number of engineers and scientists.[35]
- **Coordination**—the amount of time managers must spend synchronizing the activities of their subordinates with the activities of other workers. The greater the amount of time that must be spent on such coordination, the smaller the span of management.
- **Planning**—the amount of time managers must spend developing management system objectives and plans, and integrating them with the activities of their subordinates. The more time managers must spend on planning activities—whether those activities are repetitive and routine or infrequent but complex—the fewer individuals they can manage effectively.[36]

Table 10.1 summarizes the factors that tend to increase and decrease the span of management.

Graicunas and Span of Management

Perhaps the best-known contribution to the span-of-management literature was made by the management consultant V. A. Graicunas.[37] He developed a formula for determining the number of *possible* relationships between a manager and subordinates when the number of subordinates is known. **Graicunas's formula** is as follows:

$$C = n\left(\frac{2^n}{2} + n - 1\right)$$

C is the total number of possible relationships between manager and subordinates, and *n* is the known number of subordinates. As the number of subordinates increases arithmetically, the number of possible relationships between the manager and those subordinates increases geometrically.

A number of criticisms have been leveled at Graicunas's work. Some have argued that he failed to take into account a manager's relationships outside the organization and that he considered only *potential* relationships rather than *actual* relationships. These criticisms have some validity, but the real significance of Graicunas's work lies outside them. His main contribution involved pointing out that span of management is an important consideration that can have a far-reaching impact on the organization.[38]

Height of Organization Chart

Span of management directly influences the height of an organization chart. Normally, the greater the height of the organization chart, the smaller the span of management, and the lower the height of the chart, the greater the span of management.[39] Organization charts with little height are usually referred to as *flat*, whereas those with much height are usually referred to as *tall*.[40]

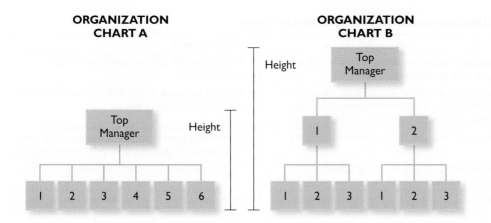

Figure 10.3 is a simple example of the relationship between organization chart height and span of management. Organization chart A has a span of management of six, and organization chart B has a span of management of two. As a result, chart A is flatter than chart B. Note that both charts have the same number of individuals at the lowest level. The larger span of management in A is reduced in B merely by adding a level to organization chart B.

An organization's structure should be built from top to bottom to ensure that appropriate spans of management are achieved at all levels. Increasing spans of management merely to eliminate certain management positions and thereby reduce salary expenses may prove to be a short-sighted move. Increasing spans of management to achieve objectives such as speeding up organizational decision making and building a more flexible organization is more likely to help the organization achieve success in the long run.[41] A survey of organization charts of the 1990s reveals that top managers were creating flatter organizational structures than top managers used in the 1980s. Overall, managers seem to be using flatter organizational structures now than in the past.

One company that created a flatter organizational structure is the news and information provider Thomson Reuters. In an effort to simplify operations and decrease inefficiencies, the company recently removed several layers from its organizational structure. According to the company's chief executive, this change will simplify operations and remove bureaucracy.[42]

Horizontal Dimensioning

The **horizontal dimensioning** of an organization refers to the extent to which firms use lateral subdivisions or specialties within the organization. Overall, to build organizations horizontally, organizations establish departments. A **department** is a unique group of resources established by management to perform some organizational task. **Departmentalizing** is the process of establishing departments within the management system. Typically, these departments are based, or contingent, on situational factors such as the work functions being performed, the product or service being offered, the territory being covered, or the customer being targeted.

Types of Departmentalization

The following sections highlight several different ways in which managers may departmentalize their organizations. In particular, the following illustrate how Sony might employ the various departmental structures discussed. **Table 10.2** summarizes the major advantages and disadvantages associated with each type of departmentalization.

10-5 An appreciation for the advantages and disadvantages associated with the different types of departmentalization

Departments Based on Function

Perhaps the most widely used basis for establishing departments within the formal structure is the type of *work functions* (activities) being performed within the management system.[43] Functions are typically divided into the major categories of marketing, production, and

TABLE 10.2 **Advantages and Disadvantages of Departmentalization Modes**

Departmentalization	Advantages	Disadvantages
Functional	• Power of functional heads promotes consistency (i.e., consistent marketing messages) • Relatively easy to assign blame or credit for the performance of a function (i.e., the performance of the company's marketing program)	• May prove difficult to coordinate between various functions • Difficult to assign credit or blame when a product performs well or poorly
Product	• Allows managers to focus on the products sold by the company • Relatively easy to assign credit or blame based on the performance of a product	• Focus on product may force managers to miss differences in customers or geographic regions • May be difficult to coordinate across products
Geographic	• Managers can focus on the various regions (and their differences) served by the company • Allows firms to develop human resources by rotating managers across different regions	• May prove difficult to coordinate between various regions • May prove difficult to assign credit or blame based on the performance of a particular product
Customer	• Allows managers to focus on and cater to the most important customers • Relatively easy to assign blame or credit regarding customer relationships	• May prove difficult to coordinate across various customers • May introduce complexities as customers span different products and geographic areas
Matrix	• Allows firm to pool human resources for both short-term and long-term projects • Allows firm to maintain flexibility over time	• Difficult for employees to understand power structure within the firm • Difficult for employees to prioritize responsibilities based on multiple authority figures

finance. **Figure 10.4** is an organization chart showing structure based primarily on function for Sony.

Functional departmentalizing brings with it both advantages and disadvantages. Perhaps the primary advantage of functional departmentalizing is the control conferred to the various functional heads. The vice president of marketing for Sony, for example, is able to control and coordinate the marketing plan for all of the organization's products, geographic regions, and customers. This structure allows for consistent marketing messages throughout the company. At the same time, however, the marketing plan emanating from such a structure may not be differentiated enough to suit the needs of Sony's diverse products, geographic regions, and customers. In other words, this structure may implicitly impose functional standardization that may not meet the needs of the organization's various products and services.

TIPS FOR MANAGING AROUND THE GLOBE

France Bans E-Mails after Work

There was once a time (before the Internet) when employees left work for home, they were no longer connected to work until the next day. With the proliferation of the Web and the ability, through cell phones, to remain constantly connected to work, employees are essentially "at work" 24 hours a day, seven days a week.

Recently, the French government recognized this and passed a new law that permits employees of companies who have 50 or more associates to "disconnect" from work. The law forbids associates from checking or responding to e-mails or utilizing a work phone outside the normal 35-hour workweek: specifically, the hours after 6:00 p.m. and before 9:00 a.m. during the week. Only in what the law calls "exceptional circumstances" can employees make or respond to work-related e-mails or phone calls. Other countries throughout Europe are also considering a similar law.[44]

Figure 10.4
Departments by function at Sony

Departments Based on Product or Service

Organizational structure based primarily on *product or service* departmentalizes resources according to the products or services being offered. As more and more products are offered by a company, it becomes increasingly difficult for management to coordinate activities across the organization. However, organizing according to product or service permits the logical grouping of resources necessary to produce and market each product or service. **Figure 10.5** is an organization chart for Sony showing structure based primarily on product.[45]

Product or service departmentalizing also has both advantages and disadvantages. One of the primary advantages is the ability to focus the organization's efforts on each of the firm's products or services. With this structure, for example, the vice president of electronics for Sony has the power and authority to control all aspects of the electronics business. In addition, this type of structure directly associates responsibility for each of the firm's products. If the electronics division does not perform well, for example, it is relatively easy for Sony's CEO to determine responsibility for the poor performance.

One of the primary disadvantages of this structure, though, is that the different units may result in duplication of efforts, which may lead to higher costs. Continuing the example of Sony, the managers of the electronics division and the music division may both request more capital for marketing expenditures. They also may both create marketing positions within their units to aid in the marketing efforts. Taken together, these types of requests may strain the organization's resources.

Figure 10.5
Departments by product at Sony

Figure 10.6

Departments by geography
at Sony

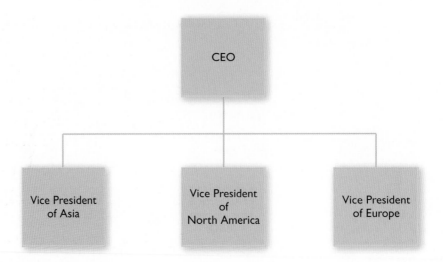

Departments Based on Geography

Structure based primarily on *territory* departmentalizes according to the places where the work is being done or the geographic markets on which the management system is focusing. The physical distances can range from quite short (between two points in the same city) to quite long (between two points in the same state, in different states, or even in different countries).[46] As market areas and work locations expand, the physical distances between places can make the management task extremely cumbersome. To minimize this problem, resources can be departmentalized according to territory. **Figure 10.6** is an organization chart for Sony based primarily on territory.

Several advantages and disadvantages are associated with geographic departmentalizing. One of the primary advantages of this structure is that it helps the organization focus equally on the organization's various geographic locations. For a company such as Sony, for example, the vice president of North America is in charge of operations in North America, and the vice president of Asia is in charge of operations in Asia. The organization defines clearly the individuals responsible for these various regions.

At the same time, however, this type of departmentalizing brings with it disadvantages. One of the main disadvantages, for example, is the lack of focus on products and services. In this example, the vice president of North America is responsible for selling movies, electronics, and music in North America. At the same time, the vice president of Asia is responsible for selling these same products in Asia; thus, no single manager is responsible for the performance of movies, electronics, and music. Instead, the responsibility is shared among various divisional vice presidents; this dispersion of responsibility may produce coordination problems.

Departments Based on Customer

Structure based primarily on the *customer* establishes departments in response to the organization's major customers. This structure, of course, assumes that major customers can be identified and divided into logical categories. **Figure 10.7** is an organization chart for Sony based primarily on customers. Sony can clearly identify its customers and divide them into logical categories.

Consider the new organizational structure created at Salt Lake City–based Energy*Solutions*, a firm in the nuclear energy industry. Formerly, the company consisted of four operating groups, organized by function, and reporting to a chief operating officer (COO). Reorganizing as three customer-focused groups has permitted the company to integrate its service offerings for customers—and eliminate the role of COO.[47]

Like the previously discussed organizational structures, customer departmentalization has both advantages and disadvantages. One of the primary advantages of customer departmentalization is that the firm focuses explicitly on its customers. Sony, for example, could follow this structure and include a vice president for each of its largest customers. This structure would increase the likelihood that Sony would maintain its focus on its most important sources of sales. At the same time, however, this structure could create some redundancies and increased

Figure 10.7
Departments by customer at Sony

costs. For example, the vice presidents might require their own marketing departments, which would increase the likelihood of duplicated efforts.

Departments by Matrix

The previous sections discussed several different types of departmentalizing; the potential advantages and disadvantages associated with each type were pointed out. These potential disadvantages have in part driven research examining "postbureaucratic" forms of organization.[48] These various organizational forms have arisen as a way to circumvent the possible disadvantages of the previously mentioned types of departmentalizing.

One of the most popular examples of postbureaucratic organizational forms is a matrix structure. The matrix structure is best understood by first visualizing a more traditional form of organizational structure. Figure 10.4, for example, shows a more traditional organizational form for Sony departmentalized by function. **Figure 10.8** adds a series of projects (PlayStation 3, Spider-Man 3, and Portable Digital Music Player) and a manager for each project to the original organization structure to form a matrix organization for Sony. Essentially, a matrix organization is one in which a project manager borrows workers from various parts of the organization to complete a specific project.[49] For this reason, matrix organizations are also called *project organizations*. The project itself may be either long term or short term, and once the project is finished, the employees borrowed to complete it return to their original jobs. Within a matrix structure, the workers are responsible for their original activities along with project activities.

STEPS FOR SUCCESS

Managing in a Matrix Structure

The complexities of a matrix organization are intimidating, and old-fashioned command-and-control managers may struggle to get results. The following ideas can help managers succeed in a matrix:[50]

- Build strong, positive relationships with colleagues. A matrix requires collaboration, and it is easier to collaborate when you are in the habit of staying in touch.
- Identify and reinforce shared goals, such as serving customers and fulfilling the organization's mission.

- Increase trust by making and keeping promises. This is especially important for managers who do not work face-to-face with the people they are linked to in the matrix.
- Get coaching on interpersonal skills such as empathy, influence, and conflict management. Use those skills instead of relying on your position in the organization to get results.

Figure 10.8
Matrix departments at Sony

Because of the importance of matrix structure projects, project managers generally report directly to the company CEO.

As with other types of departmentalizing, departmentalizing by matrix has both advantages and disadvantages. Perhaps the chief advantage of the matrix structure is that it allows the organization to focus on various projects simultaneously. For example, the matrix structure in Figure 10.8 allows Sony to focus on PlayStation 3, Spider-Man 3, and the Portable Digital Music Player at the same time.

As just mentioned, the matrix structure also has disadvantages. For example, the matrix structure can be confusing, and employees may not be able to cope effectively with two bosses. In the Sony example, assume that the PlayStation 3 project manager and the vice president of marketing both ask the same employee to complete different tasks. Which task should the employee complete first? Issues such as these can make the matrix structure confusing.

Forces Influencing Formal Structure
According to Y. K. Shetty and Howard M. Carlisle, the formal structure of a management system is continually evolving. Four primary forces influence this evolution: forces in the manager, forces in the task, forces in the environment, and forces in the subordinates.[51] The evolution of a particular organization is actually the result of a complex and dynamic interaction among these forces.

Forces in the manager are the unique ways in which a manager perceives organizational problems.[52] Naturally, background, knowledge, experience, and values influence the manager's perception of what the organization's formal structure should be or how it should be changed. In the same way, similar forces influence the employee and play a key role in how he or she views work.[53]

Forces in the task include the degree of technology involved in performing the task and the task's complexity. As task activities change, a force is created to change the existing organization. Forces in the environment include the customers and suppliers of the management system along with existing political and social structures. Forces in the subordinates include their needs and skill levels. Obviously, as the environment and subordinates change, forces are created simultaneously to change the organization.

Fayol's Advice on Using Formal Structure   The preceding discussion emphasized how to establish organizational structure and the related chain of command. Should a manager always adhere to established organizational structure and related chain of command? Fayol indicated that strict adherence to a particular chain of command is not always advisable.[54] **Figure 10.9** illustrates his rationale. If individual F needs information from individual G and follows the concept of chain of command, F has to go through individuals D, B, A, C, and E before reaching G. The information would get back to F only by going from G through E, C, A, B, and D. Obviously, this long, involved process can be time-consuming and therefore expensive for the organization.

To avoid this lengthy process, Fayol recommended that a bridge, or gangplank, be used to allow F to go directly to G for information. This bridge is represented in Figure 10.9 by the dotted line connecting F and G. Managers should be careful in allowing the use of these organizational bridges, however: although F might get the information from G more quickly and cheaply that way, individuals D, B, A, C, and E would be excluded from the communication channel, and their ignorance might prove more costly to the organization in the long run than would following the established chain of command. Thus, when managers allow the use of an organizational bridge, they must be extremely vigilant about informing all other appropriate individuals within the organization of any information transmitted that way.

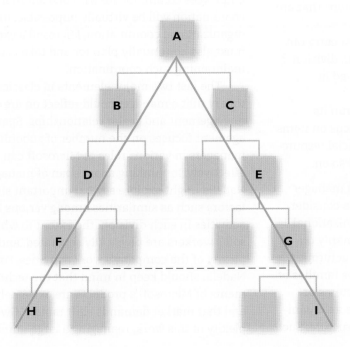

Figure 10.9

Sample organization chart showing that adhering to the chain of command is not advisable

CHALLENGE CASE SUMMARY

The Challenge Case at the beginning of this chapter generally describes how Microsoft has reorganized to be more competitive. Concepts in this chapter would be useful to a manager such as Microsoft's CEO in charge of the reorganization, Satya Nadella, and to his successor in meeting organizing challenges similar to those discussed in the case.

In contemplating how Microsoft should be organized, a manager such as Nadella should focus on answering several important questions. These questions should be aimed at establishing an orderly use of Microsoft's organizational resources. Because these resources represent an investment on which the company must get a return, Nadella should ask questions geared toward gaining information that will be used to maximize this return. Overall, such questions should focus on determining which use of Microsoft's resources will best accomplish its goals.

Some preliminary questions could be the following:

1. What organizational objectives exist at Microsoft? For example, does Microsoft want to focus more on currently successful products such as operating systems or on new technologies such as mobile devices and cloud computing? Does Microsoft want to grow or maintain its present size?
2. What plans does Microsoft have to accomplish these objectives? Is the company going to invest more in product development? Will it shed divisions that are no longer growing?
3. What are the major tasks Microsoft must carry out to establish profitable linkages among its divisions? For example, how many steps are involved in launching a new product line?
4. What resources does Microsoft have to run its operations? Answers to this question focus on items such as the number of employees, financial resources available, equipment being used, and so on.

To develop a sound organizing effort, a manager should take classical organizing theory into consideration. Nadella's effort started with an organizational structure for Microsoft that was based primarily on product categories. In its most recent restructuring, the company brought together work that unites families of devices and services, such as operating systems or cloud computing. A manager typically uses an organization chart to represent organizational structure. Such a chart would allow Nadella not only to see the lines of authority and responsibility at Microsoft but also to understand the broad working relationships among the company's employees.

In developing the most appropriate way to organize Microsoft employees, a manager can reflect on another major element in classical organizing theory: division of labor. Nadella could decide, for example, that instead of having one person do all the work involved in managing operating systems across devices, the labor could be divided so that different managers oversee operating systems for particular devices, and they would report to the divisional manager who has the larger picture in mind. In this way, the managers of particular products could focus on the issues that arise with those products, while the divisional manager could focus on larger strategic issues.

In considering the appropriateness of division of labor at Microsoft, a manager could also consider creating a mechanism for enhancing coordination. To develop such a mechanism, Nadella and his vice presidents must have a thorough understanding of how various Microsoft business processes occur so that they can divide various tasks and maintain coordination among the various divisions. In addition, managers like Microsoft executives must stress communication as a prerequisite for coordination. Unless Microsoft employees communicate with one another continually, coordination will be virtually impossible. In enhancing organizational coordination, Microsoft's executives must also continually plan for and take action toward maintaining such coordination.

The last two major elements in classical organizing theory that a manager could reflect on are span of management and scalar relationships. Span of management focuses on the number of subordinates that managers in various roles at Microsoft can supervise effectively. In thinking about span of management, Nadella might explore several important situational factors such as similarities among various Microsoft activities in each division, the extent to which Microsoft's workers are physically separated, and the complexity of the company's work activities. For example, Nadella should keep in mind that the technical requirements of Microsoft's products are extremely complex and that market demands shift rapidly. Given the complexity of this work, managing a large number of workers is difficult, so the span of management for technical employees should generally be relatively small. Other important factors that Nadella and his vice presidents should consider when determining spans of management are the amount of time

managers must spend coordinating workers' activities and the amount of time managers spend planning. With all this information, Microsoft's executives should be capable of determining the appropriate spans of management for their managers.

MyLab Management Assessing Your Management Skill

If your instructor has assigned this activity, go to www.pearson.com/mylab/management to complete the exercise related to the Challenge Case.

DEVELOPING ORGANIZING SKILL

This section is specially designed to help you develop organizing skills. An individual's organizing skill is based on an understanding of the concepts and the ability to apply those concepts. The following activities will help to enhance your organizing skills in various organizational situations.

Class Preparation and Personal Study

To help you prepare for class, perform the activities outlined in this section. Performing these activities will help you enhance your classroom performance significantly.

Reflecting on Target Skill

On page 244, this chapter opens by presenting a target management skill along with a list of related objectives outlining knowledge and understanding that you should aim to acquire related to that skill. Review this target skill and the list of objectives to make sure you've acquired all pertinent information within the chapter. If you do not feel that you've reached a particular objective(s), study related chapter coverage until you do.

Know Key Terms

Understanding the following key terms is critical to your preparing for class. Define each of these terms. Refer to the page(s) referenced after a term to check your definition or to gain further insight regarding the term.

organizing **246**
organizing skill **246**

Know How Management Concepts Relate

This section comprises activities that will further sharpen your understanding of management concepts. Answer these essay questions as completely as possible.

10-1 Each resource is an investment and must produce a return. Choose a business organization with which you are familiar and use Fayol's 16 guidelines to explain how they organize resources.

10-2 Managers may opt to departmentalize their organizations for various reasons on the basis of elements such as products, functions, and geography. However, there are other options, and some organizations may change from one to the other. Find examples of organizations that match the characteristics of the five departmentalization options.

> ### MyLab Management
> #### Personal Inventory Assessment
>
> Go to www.pearson.com/mylab/management to complete the Personal Inventory Assessment related to this chapter.
>
> PERSONAL INVENTORY ASSESSMENT

Management Skills Exercises

Learning activities in this section are aimed at helping you develop your organizing skills.

> ### MyLab Management
> #### Discussion Questions
>
> Go to www.pearson.com/mylab/management to complete the problems marked with this icon ✪.

✪ Cases

Microsoft Tries to Program Unity with Its New Structure

The Challenge Case "Microsoft Tries to Program Unity with Its New Structure" (p. 245) and its related Challenge Case Summary were written to help you understand the organizing concepts contained in this chapter. Answer the following discussion questions about the Challenge Case to explore how basic organizational principles can be applied in a company such as Microsoft.

10-3 Does it seem reasonable that Satya Nadella and his leadership team were attempting to reorganize Microsoft to make it more competitive? Explain.

10-4 List five questions that Nadella should have asked himself in exploring the best way to reorganize Microsoft.

10-5 Explain why it would be important for Nadella to ask each of the questions you listed.

Shutterstock's Image of a Great Organization

Read the case and answer the questions that follow. Studying this case will help you better understand how concepts relating to organizational structure can be applied in a company such as Shutterstock.

The idea for Shutterstock came from founder Jon Oringer's experience as a "serial entrepreneur."[55] Oringer saw that prospects are much likelier to look at information about a company if stories about it include pictures, but buying professional photographs is expensive for a start-up. One stock image could cost hundreds of dollars. Oringer thought that if he could make photographs easy and affordable to buy online, the volume of sales could make an attractive market for buyers and sellers alike.

Oringer got started on his own. He bought a camera, took 100,000 photos, and chose 30,000 to upload into an online database. He sold customers $49 subscriptions for the right to use any of the photos. Even with his limited photography skill, Oringer soon had a growing business. He began signing up professional photographers, eventually building his database to contain more than 32 million images, including illustrations and videos. Now the standard subscription rate is $249 for the right to use up to 25 images a month, with extensive users paying more. Even with the higher prices, Shutterstock boasts about half a million users. The cost is still a bargain compared with other art/photograph sources, and the volume of sales has generated a comfortable living for many of the artists and photographers who work with Shutterstock. Being online has helped Shutterstock build an international customer base, and it now operates in 14 languages and obtains work from 100 countries.

To serve the growing demand, Shutterstock hired software engineers to build the system's capabilities and then hired specialists in support functions. (The photographers are not employees but have contracts with Shutterstock and may sell their work to other agencies as well.) Although Shutterstock's growth strategy focuses on automation, the company has grown to include more than 200 employees.

To handle the growth, Oringer has had to figure out how to organize the company. The company's basic structure involves functional divisions such as products, marketing, technology, and finance. About two-fifths of staff members work on either the technology or the product line. For example, engineering employees figure out new ways for users to search the database—say, generating results by color. Product-focused employees include reviewers of submitted photos; only approved images go on the site. Each division has its own objectives to meet and functions independently.

With a functional structure, coordination is especially important because employees in different functions may not share the same outlook. Once a year, Shutterstock brings employees together in 24-hour hackathons to develop new product ideas. The idea of a hackathon is to be resourceful and pull an idea together quickly; teams of employees all present their ideas (in just two minutes per team), and managers select the best ones for possible development. Although this kind of activity is traditionally associated with programmers and software engineers, the teams include employees from different divisions, and nontechnical employees find that they have valuable ideas to share. For example, in a recent hackathon, the senior manager of business development saw that she could contribute an understanding of business needs while her team members focused on the software.

So far, the structure is working for Shutterstock. The company is growing quickly, began selling stock to the public in 2012, and has posted profits above $30 million. A key question will be whether the structure needs tweaking as Shutterstock's horizons continue to widen.[56]

Questions

10-6 Do you feel that a functional departmentalization structure is best for Shutterstock? Why or why not?

10-7 How might continuing growth affect the choice of the best organizational structure for Shutterstock?

10-8 Besides running hackathons, what else should Shutterstock's managers consider for maintaining coordination among departments and employees?

Experiential Exercises

Frogs of the World

Directions. Read the following scenario and then perform the listed activities. Your instructor may ask you to perform the activities as an individual or within groups. Follow all of your instructor's directions carefully.

Your company, Frogs of the World, has been manufacturing and selling plastic toy frogs for more than 15 years. Overall, the company has been successful and has become a market leader in the toy industry. Exploring the introduction of a new product, top management has just decided to begin manufacturing and selling a paper frog that hops. Mr. Hopper is the name of the new product. Your instructor will distribute design specifications for producing Mr. Hopper.

Top management has informed your group that it will begin manufacturing Mr. Hopper immediately. The department will include only the people in your group. At some point your instructor will appoint a leader for your group, give each member the raw materials needed to produce Mr. Hopper, and instruct you to begin the production process.

Your team will be judged by the number and quality of the Mr. Hoppers that you produce.

You and Your Career

One of the topics discussed in this chapter is the concept of a "flat" and a "tall" organization chart. Flat organizations have few layers of management, while tall organizations have multiple layers of management. Think about what this concept entails as you begin your career and start moving into higher positions within an organization. Would you prefer to work in a company with a flat organization chart or one with a tall organization chart? Explain.

Building Your Management Skills Portfolio

Your Management Skills Portfolio is a collection of activities specially designed to demonstrate your management knowledge and skill. Be sure to save your work. Taking your printed portfolio to an employment interview could be helpful in obtaining a job.

The portfolio activity for this chapter is Organizing Skill: Examining Organization Charts. Search the Internet for an organization chart of your choosing. Then complete the exercises that follow.

10-9 Is the organization chart based mainly on function, product, geography, or customer? Argue why this basis might be appropriate for the operations of the organization you chose.

_____

_____

10-10 Does the organization chart reflect an emphasis on division of labor? Explain.

_____

_____

10-11 Give an example of how coordination is important to the success of the organization.

_____

_____

10-12 Present an argument discussing why the span of management for this organization is appropriate or inappropriate.

_____

_____

MyLab Management
Writing Assignments

If your instructor has assigned this activity, go to www.pearson.com/mylab/management for the following assisted-graded writing assignments:

Assisted-Graded Questions

10-13 Describe the fundamental components of the organizing process. In your opinion, which of these components is most important? Which is least important? Explain.

10-14 Compare and contrast the various types of departmentalization. In your opinion, which type of departmentalization is best?

10-15 Discuss the advantages and disadvantages associated with the concept of division of labor. How is the concept of span of management related to division of labor?

Endnotes

1. Steve Ballmer, "One Microsoft: Company Realigns to Enable Innovation at Greater Speed, Efficiency," e-mail, July 11, 2013, accessed at Microsoft Company News, http://www.microsoft.com/en-us/news/press/2013/jul13/07-11onemicrosoft.aspx.

2. Ibid.; Michael Endler, "Microsoft Reorganization Signals Big Challenges Ahead," *InformationWeek*, July 11, 2013, http://www.informationweek.com; Nick Wingfield, "Microsoft Overhauls, the Apple Way," *New York Times*, July 11, 2013, http://www.nytimes.com; "Will Microsoft's Reorganization Pay Off?," *Knowledge@Wharton*, July 17, 2013, http://www.knowledge.wharton.upenn.edu; J. P. Mangalindan, "Microsoft's Reorganization Is Only Step One," *Fortune*, July 11, 2013, http://tech.fortune.cnn.com; David Goldman, "Microsoft Shakes Up Management—Again," *CNNMoney*, July 15, 2013, http://money.cnn.com; Tom Warren, "Microsoft Announces Massive Company-Wide Reorganization," *The Verge*, July 11, 2013, http://www.theverge.com.

3. A. Tacket, "Organizing and Organizations: An Introduction," *Journal of the Operational Research Society* 53 (2002): 1401.

4. Douglas S. Sherwin, "Management of Objectives," *Harvard Business Review* (May/June 1976): 149–160. See also Lloyd Sandelands and Robert Drazin, "On the Language of Organization Theory," *Organizational Studies* 10 (1989): 457–477.

5. Tim Peakman, "Organizing the Organization," *Drug Discovery Today* 8 (2003): 673.

6. For a discussion emphasizing the importance of continually adapting organizational structure, see Michael A. Vercspej, "When Change Becomes the Norm," *Industry Week* (March 16, 1992): 35–36.

7. Betsy Morris, "The GE Mystique," *Fortune* (March 6, 2006): 98–102. For an interesting analysis of General Electric's management development process, see Derek Lehmberg, W. Glenn Rowe, Roderick E. White, and John R. Phillips, "The GE Paradox: Competitive Advantage through Fungible Non-Firm-Specific Investment," *Journal of Management* 35, no. 5 (October 1, 2009): 1129–1153.

8. Saul W. Gellerman, "In Organizations, as in Architecture, Form Follows Function," *Organizational Dynamics* 18 (Winter 1990): 57–68.

9. For an example of how organizing principles can be applied to the educational arena, see A. Georges Romme, "Organizing Education by Drawing on Organization Studies," *Organization Studies* 24 (2003): 697.

10. Max Weber, *Theory of Social and Economic Organization*, trans. and ed. A. M. Henderson and Talcott Parsons (London: Oxford University Press, 1947); P. A. Saparito and J. E. Coombs, "Bureaucratic

11. Sandra T. Gray, "Fostering Leadership for the New Millennium," *Association Management* (January 1995): L78–L82.

12. David Courpasson and Stewart Clegg, "Dissolving the Iron Cages? Tocqueville, Michels, Bureaucracy and the Perpetuation of Elite Power," *Organization* 13 (2006): 319–343.

13. "GM Timeline," MSNBC.com, http://www.msnbc.com, accessed June 3, 2010; Ryan Chilcote and Steve Rothwell, "GM to Focus on Cutting Spending, Reducing Bureaucracy," Bloomberg.com, March 2, 2010, http://www.bloomberg.com.

14. For a review focusing on division of labor, see "Division of Labor Welcomed," *Business Insurance* 34, no. 10 (March 6, 2000): 8. See also S. K. Parker, F. P. Morgeson, and G. Johns, "One Hundred Years of Work Design Research: Looking Back and Looking Forward," *Journal of Applied Psychology* 102 (2017): 403–420.

15. T. W. Malone, R. J. Laubacher, and T. Johns, "The Age of Hyperspecialization," *Harvard Business Review* 89 (2011): 57–65. For more information on the role of emotions in understanding division of labor, see H. A. Elfenbein, "Emotional Division of Labor: A Theoretical Account," *Research in Organizational Behavior* 36 (2017): 1–26.

16. Example based on "Painting by Numbers: China's Art Business," *The Economist* (June 10, 2006): 77.

17. Carol Ann Dorn, "Einstein: Still No Equal," *Journal of Business Strategy* (November/December 1994): 20–23.

18. C. R. Walker and R. H. Guest, *The Man on the Assembly Line* (Cambridge, MA: Harvard University Press, 1952).

19. For an interesting analysis of how structural organizational factors such as specialization influence organizational memory, see Marina Fiedler and Isabell Welpe, "How Do Organizations Remember? The Influence of Organizational Structure on Organizational Memory," *Organization Studies* 31, no. 4 (2010): 381–407.

20. J. Mooney, "The Principles of Organization," in D. Waldo, ed., *Ideas and Issues in Public Administration* (New York: McGraw-Hill, 1953), 86. See also L. Pierce, "Organizational Structure and the Limits of Knowledge Sharing: Incentive Conflict and Agency in Car Leasing," *Management Science* (2012).

21. Bruce D. Sanders, "Making Work Groups Work," *Computerworld* 24 (March 5, 1990): 85–89; L. Garicano and Y. Wu, "Knowledge, Communication, and Organizational Capabilities," *Organization Science* 23, no. 5 (2012): 1382–1397.

22. George D. Greenberg, "The Coordinating Roles of Management," *Midwest Review of Public Administration* 10 (1976): 66–76; Stephen Ackroyd, "How Organizations Act Together: Interorganizational Coordination in Theory and Practice," *Administrative Science Quarterly* 43, no. 1 (March 1998): 217–221.

23. Steve Lasky, "Collaboration Gets the MBTA Moving into the Security Fast Lane," *Security Technology Executive*, September 2013, Business Insights: Global, http://bi.galegroup.com; Susan Bregman, "MBTA Takes Steps to Upgrade Safety and Security," *Transit Wire*, May 3, 2013, http://www.thetransitwire.com; Peter Schworm, "US Slices Federal Funds for MBTA Security," *Boston Globe*, September 3, 2013, http://www.bostonglobe.com.

24. Henry C. Metcalf and Lyndall F. Urwich, eds., *Dynamic Administration: The Collected Papers of Mary Parker Follett* (New York: Harper & Bros., 1942), 297–299; James F. Wolf, "The Legacy of Mary Parker Follett," *Bureaucrat Winter* (1988–1989): 53–57. For a more recent discussion of the work of Mary Parker Follett, see David M. Boje and Grace Ann Rosile, "Where's the Power in Empowerment? Answers from Follett and Clegg," *Journal of Applied Behavioral Science* 37, no. 1 (March 2001): 90–117.

25. Lyndall Urwich, *Notes on the Theory of Organization* (New York: American Management Association, 1952).

26. David Stamps, "Off the Charts," *Training* 34, no. 10 (October 1997): 77–83. To understand the role of huddles in informal structures, see R. W. Quinn and J. S. Bunderson, "Could We Huddle on This Project? Participant Learning in Newsroom Conversations," *Journal of Management* 42 (2016): 386–418.

27. Xiaowen Huang, Mehment Kristal, and Roger Schroeder, "The Impact of Organzational Structure on Mass Customization Capability: A Contingency View," *Production and Operations Management* 19, no. 5 (2010): 515–530.

28. "Organizational Chart," *Encyclopedia of Management* (2010).

Systems' Facilitating and Hindering Influence on Social Capital," *Entrepreneurship Theory and Practice* 37: 625–639.

29. Eric J. Walton, "The Persistence of Bureaucracy: A Meta-Analysis of Weber's Model of Bureaucratic Control," *Organization Studies* 26, no. 4: 569–600.

30. S. R. Maheshwari, "Hierarchy: Key Principle of Organization," *Employment News* 21, no. 49 (March 8–14, 1997): 1–2. To see how hierarchies and formal structures change when companies form strategic alliances, see S. Albers, F. Wohlgezogen, and E. J. Zajac, "Strategic Alliance Structures: An Organization Design Perspective," *Journal of Management* 42 (2016): 582–614.

31. Cass Bettinger, "The Nine Principles of War," *Bank Marketing* 21 (December 1989): 32–34; Donald C. Hambrick, "Corporate Coherence and the Top Management Team," *Strategy & Leadership* 25, no. 5 (September/October 1997): 24–29.

32. Leon McKenzie, "Supervision: Learning from Experience," *Health Care Supervisor* 8 (January 1990): 1–11. For an example of how span of control influences interactions in hospitals, see C. Holm-Petersen, S. Ostergaard, and P. B. N. Andersen, "Size Does Matter—Span of Control in Hospitals," *Journal of Health Organization and Management* 31, no. 2: 192–206.

33. For a look at the concept of span of management in public organizations, see Kenneth Meier and John Bohte, "Span of Control and Public Organizations: Implementing Gulick's Research Design," *Public Administration Review* 63 (2003): 61.

34. Harold Koontz, "Making Theory Operational: The Span of Management," *Journal of Management Studies* (October 1966): 229–243. See also John S. McClenahen, "Managing More People in the '90s," *Industry Week* 238 (March 1989): 30–38.

35. For more information on the effects of job complexity, see J. Li, T. C. Burch, and T. W. Lee, "Intra-Individual Variability in Job Complexity over Time: Examining the Effect of Job Complexity Trajectory on Employee Job Strain," *Journal of Organizational Behavior* 38 (2017): 671–691.

36. The U.S. space program offers an interesting study of the forms of work organization—both simple and complex—required to ultimately succeed in putting an astronaut on the moon. See Martin Parker, "Space Age Management," *Management & Organizational History* 4, no. 3 (2009): 317–332.

37. V. A. Graicunas, "Relationships in Organization," *Bulletin of International Management Institute* (March 1933): 183–187; L. F. Urwick, "V. A. Graicunas and the Span of Control," *Academy of Management Journal* 17 (June 1974): 349–354; see also N. J. Foss, J. Lyngsie, and S. A. Zahara, "The Role of External Knowledge Sources and Organizational Design in the Process of Opportunity Exploitation," *Strategic Management Journal* 34: 1453–1471.

38. For a discussion about why managers should increase spans of management, see Stephen R. Covey, "The Marketing Revolution," *Executive Excellence* 14, no. 3 (March 1997): 3–4.

39. John R. Brandt, "Middle Management: 'Where the Action Will Be,'" *Industry Week* (May 2, 1994): 30–36.

40. For a discussion of the benefits of tall structures, see Harold J. Leavitt, "Why Hierarchies Thrive," *Harvard Business Review* 81, no. 3 (2006): 96–102.

41. Philip R. Nienstedt, "Effectively Downsizing Management Structures," *Human Resources Planning* 12 (1989): 155–165.

42. J. Toonkel, "Thomson Reuters to Cut 2,000 Jobs; Profit Tops Estimates," November 1, 2016, http://www.reuters.com/article/us-thomsonreuters-results-idUSKBN12W3PE. For more information on how social responsibility influences organizational structure, see A. Rasche, F. G. A. de Bakker, and J. Moon, "Complete and Partial Organizing for Corporate Social Responsibility," *Journal of Business Ethics* 115 (2013): 651–663.

43. Geary A. Rummler and Alan P. Brache, "Managing the White Space on the Organization Chart," *Supervision* (May 1991): 6–12.

44. Robert Crawford, "French Firms Ban Work Emails after 6pm," *Employee Benefits*, April 11, 2014, 6.

45. Y. M. Zhou, "Synergy, Coordination Costs, and Diversification Choices," *Strategic Management Journal* 32, no. 6 (2011): 624–639.

46. Roderick E. White and Thomas A. Poynter, "Organizing for Worldwide Advantage," *Business Quarterly* 54 (Summer 1989): 84–89.

47. "EnergySolutions Announces New Organizational Structure," *Marketwire*, March 30, 2010, http://www.marketwire.com.

48. M. Lindgren and J. Packendorff, "What's New in New Forms of Organizing? On the Construction of Gender in Project-Based Work," *Journal of Management Studies* 43, no. 4 (2006): 841–866.

49. C. J. Middleton, "How to Set Up a Project Organization," *Harvard Business Review* (March/April 1967): 73. See also George J. Chambers, "The Individual in a Matrix Organization," *Project Management Journal* 20 (December 1989): 37–42, 50.

50. Jon R. Katzenbach and Adam Michaels, "Life in the Matrix," *Strategy + Business*, Autumn 2013, http://www.strategy-business.com; Kevan Hall, "Revisiting Matrix Management," *People & Strategy* 36, no. 1 (2013): 4–5; Ruth Malloy, "Managing Effectively in a Matrix," *Harvard Business Review*, August 10, 2012, http://blogs.hbr.org.

51. Y. K. Shetty and Howard M. Carlisle, "A Contingency Model of Organization Design," *California Management Review* 15 (1972): 38–45.

52. For insights on how Ralph Larsen, CEO of Johnson & Johnson, views problems and how his view might influence the formal structure of his organization, see Brian Dumaine, "Is Big Still Good?," *Fortune* (April 30, 1992): 50–60.

53. An employee's *locus of control*—that is, those aspects that an individual perceives to be within his or her own ability to modify—figures strongly into work outcomes. For a study of the influences on work outcomes, see Steven M. Elias, "Restrictive versus Promotive Control and Employee Work Outcomes: The Moderating Role of Locus of Control," *Journal of Management* 35, no. 2 (March 1, 2009): 369–392. Elias also provides another interesting study of employee perceptions during the restructuring of their organization's design. See "Employee Commitment in Times of Change: Assessing the Importance of Attitudes toward Organizational Change," *Journal of Management* 35, no. 1 (February 1, 2009): 37–55.

54. Henri Fayol, *General and Industrial Administration* (Belmont, CA: Pitman, 1949). For more information about combining both formal and informal structures, see C. A. O'Reilly III and M. L. Tushman, "Organizational Ambidexterity: Past, Present, and Future," *Academy of Management Perspectives* 27: 327–338.

55. Jennifer Wang, "Picture Perfect," *Entrepreneur* (April 2013): 30–36.

56. Ibid.; Will Yakowicz, "Under Pressure: Inside Shutterstock's High Stakes Hackathon," *Inc.*, July 30, 2013, http://www.inc.com; Christine Lagorio-Chafkin, "How Shutterstock Went from Zero to IPO," *Inc.*, October 29, 2012, http://www.inc.com; Shutterstock, "About Us," http://www.shutterstock.com, accessed January 10, 2014.

11 Responsibility, Authority, and Delegation

TARGET SKILL

Responsibility and Delegation Skill: the ability to understand one's obligation to perform assigned activities and to enlist the help of others to complete those activities

RESPONSIBILITY AND DELEGATION SKILL AND YOUR CAREER

Responsibility and delegation skill will be of great value to you in enhancing your career. This skill helps you understand your obligation to perform activities in the workplace and how to gain the support of others to help you complete these activities. This ability contributes to organizational success, builds your image as a competent manager, makes you valuable to your organization, and supports promotions as you build your career.

OBJECTIVES

To help build my *responsibility and delegation skill*, when studying this chapter, I will attempt to acquire:

11-1 An understanding of responsibility and its relationship to job description

11-2 Information on how to divide job activities of individuals working within an organization

11-3 An understanding of the benefits of clarifying the job activities of managers

11-4 Insights regarding the importance of authority within an organization

11-5 An understanding of how to delegate

11-6 A recognition of the advantages and disadvantages of centralization and decentralization

MyLab Management Chapter Warm Up

If your instructor has assigned this activity, go to www.pearson.com/mylab/management to complete the chapter warm up.

CHALLENGE CASE

Autonomy at Hy-Vee Supermarkets

Hy-Vee Supermarkets have been around since 1930, serving eight midwestern states. Constantly being challenged by giants such as Wal-Mart as well as small, regional chains, the company has consistently grown and has nearly $10 billion in annual sales. But what keeps a nearly 90-year-old company thriving?

"People are allowed to share in the success of the company," says Ron Taylor, the chain's senior vice president of corporate procurement and logistics. "Not only economically," he says, "but in having knowledge about how the company runs." Taylor is referring to the degree of autonomy experienced by store managers and the authority they have to ensure that their store is successful.

According to Taylor, the store managers are essentially the CEOs of their respective stores. Not only do they handle all the hiring of staff, but they can even change the pricing and marketing from what is produced at the corporate office. Typically, retailers are required to follow a planogram (a pictorial description of how products should appear on the store shelves) created by the company's headquarters. But at Hy-Vee, store managers can elect to change the planogram to better suit the local customers. This may also result in changes to the prices as well as in-store promotions.

Store managers can also choose to stock products that are localized. "We do a lot with local vendors," Taylor states. "Stores are given freedom to bring in their local items. If you go to Kansas City, for example, you'll see an entirely different mix of product than you'll see in [another] store." This means that store managers are working closely with vendors in the store's hometown—featuring hometown products in addition to national brands.

Employees, including store managers, having the ability to make their own decisions is known as autonomy. Hy-Vee's store managers have the autonomy to determine what products are on their store shelves, how to price those products effectively, and what marketing approaches work best with their particular customers. That autonomy has been delegated to them from the corporate office.

Hy-Vee is a chain of over 240 midwestern supermarkets. Each store manager is the equivalent of a CEO of his or her store, having the authority to make decisions that are best for the store.

Unlike larger chains, such as Wal-Mart, Hy-Vee's managers make decisions that make the most business sense for their store. With more than 240 stores, Hy-Vee essentially has over 240 presidents of small companies making the best decisions they can to affect the company's success.

"There's real pride here," says Taylor, "and it helps everyone do a better job."[1]

THE RESPONSIBILITY AND DELEGATION CHALLENGE

The Challenge Case describes Hy-Vee's efforts to delegate autonomy to store managers throughout the company. Being able to make decisions at the store level that ensure an individual store's success is very important. Hy-Vee executives must answer questions such as the following: How should responsibility be established at each store and across the organization? How should authority be distributed within the organization? The information in this chapter should be of great value to a manager in answering such questions.

Responsibility and Job Descriptions

11-1 An understanding of responsibility and its relationship to job description

Perhaps the most fundamental method of channeling the activities of individuals within an organization, **responsibility** is the obligation to perform assigned activities. It is the self-assumed commitment to handle a job to the best of one's ability. The source of responsibility lies within the individual. A person who accepts a job agrees to carry out a series of duties or activities or to see that someone else carries them out.[2] The act of accepting the job means that the person is obligated to a superior to see that job activities are completed successfully. Even though a manager may delegate a task to another employee, the manager still remains responsible for the completion of the task. In a sense, responsibility is shared by both the manager and the employee.

Nonetheless, responsibility is often difficult to identify.

Some believe that the actions of investment firm Goldman Sachs helped fuel the nation's recent financial meltdown. Goldman Sachs executives defended their practice of selling an investment to a client, while simultaneously "betting" that the investment would falter, and making a profit when the investment declined in value by saying that the practice is common in the investment industry. Only after a six-hour grilling by a Senate investigation panel did an executive acknowledge that his company may have had some responsibility for the economic crisis. In this example, although the firm's executive officers did bear some responsibility for the company's actions, the Goldman Sachs employees who processed these transactions for investors also bore some responsibility.[3]

An individual's job activities within an organization are usually summarized in a formal statement called a **job description**—a list of specific activities that must be performed by whoever holds the position. Unclear job descriptions can confuse employees and may cause them to lose interest in their jobs. On the other hand, a clear job description can help employees to become successful by focusing their efforts on the issues that are important for their position. When properly designed, job descriptions communicate job content to employees, establish performance levels that employees must maintain, and act as guides that employees should follow to help the organization reach its objectives.[4]

Job activities are delegated by management to enhance the accomplishment of management system objectives. Management analyzes its objectives and assigns specific duties that will lead to reaching those objectives. A sound organizing strategy delineates specific job activities for every individual in the organization. Note, however, that as objectives and other conditions within the management system change, so will individual job activities.

The three areas related to responsibility include dividing job activities, clarifying the job activities of managers, and being responsible. Each of these topics is discussed in the sections that follow.

STEPS FOR SUCCESS

Tips for Delegating Tasks

Delegating particular tasks to employees helps them grow and learn new skills. The following suggestions can help managers delegate more effectively:[5]

- Realize that you cannot do it all. Experienced managers know that they have to delegate tasks in order to be able to carry out key managerial responsibilities.
- Learn the strengths of your employees. Know what each employee is capable of.
- Make sure you spread the wealth. Assign tasks to all your employees so that you can determine which

skills among your team members need further development.
- Don't delegate a task because you don't want to do it. Be a good example for your employees by being willing to do the tasks as well.
- Don't delegate a task because you don't know how to do it. Learn how to do certain tasks before delegating them.
- Don't use delegation as punishment. If there is a troublesome employee, discipline that individual appropriately rather than piling on additional tasks.

Dividing Job Activities

Obviously, one person cannot be responsible for performing all the activities that need to take place within an organization. Because so many people work in a given management system, organizing necessarily involves dividing job activities among individuals. Some method of distributing these job activities is essential.

11-2 Information on how to divide job activities of individuals working within an organization

The Functional Similarity Method

The **functional similarity method** is, according to many management theorists, the most basic method of dividing job activities. Simply stated, the method suggests that management should take four basic, interrelated steps to divide job activities in the following sequence:

1. Examine management system objectives.
2. Designate the appropriate activities that must be performed to reach those objectives.
3. Design specific jobs by grouping similar activities.
4. Make specific individuals responsible for performing those jobs.

Figure 11.1 illustrates this sequence of activities.

Functional Similarity and Responsibility

At least three additional guides can be used to supplement the functional similarity method.[6] The first of these supplemental guides suggests that overlapping responsibility should be avoided when making job activity divisions. **Overlapping responsibility** refers to a situation in which more than one individual is responsible for the same activity. Generally speaking, only one person should be responsible for completing any one activity. When two or more employees are unsure about who should do a job because of overlapping responsibility, the result is usually conflict and poor working relationships.[7] Often, the job does not get done because each employee assumes that the other will do the job.

The second supplemental guide suggests that responsibility gaps should be avoided. A **responsibility gap** exists when certain tasks are not included in the responsibility area of any individual organization member. In this situation, nobody within the organization is obligated to perform certain necessary activities.[8]

The third supplemental guide suggests that management should avoid creating job activities to accomplish tasks that do not enhance goal attainment. Organization members should be obligated to perform *only* those activities that lead to goal attainment.

The absence of clear, goal-related, nonoverlapping responsibilities undermines organizational efficiency and effectiveness.[9] When job responsibilities are distributed inappropriately, the organization will have both responsibility gaps and overlapping responsibilities. The effects of responsibility gaps on product quality are obvious, but overlapping responsibilities also impair product quality. When two (or more) employees are uncertain about who is responsible for a task, four outcomes are possible:

1. One of the two may perform the job. The other may either forget to or choose not to do the job—and neither of these is a desirable outcome for product quality control.
2. Both employees may perform the job. At the least, this situation results in duplicated effort, which dampens employee morale. At worst, one employee may diminish the value of the other employee's work, resulting in a decrement in product quality.
3. Neither employee may perform the job because each assumed the other would do it.

Figure 11.1

Sequence of activities for the functional similarity method of dividing job activities

4. The employees may spend valuable time negotiating each aspect and phase of the job to carefully mesh their job responsibilities, thus minimizing both duplication of effort and responsibility gaps. Though time-consuming, this is actually the most desirable option in terms of product quality.

Note that each of these outcomes negatively affects both product quality and overall productivity.

Clarifying Job Activities of Managers

11-3 An understanding of the benefits of clarifying the job activities of managers

Clarifying the job activities of managers is even more important than dividing the job activities of nonmanagers because managers have an impact on large portions of resources within the management system. Responsibility gaps, for instance, usually have a more significant impact on the management system when they relate to managers than when they relate to nonmanagers.

One process used to clarify management job activities "enables each manager to actively participate with his or her superiors, peers, and subordinates in systematically describing the managerial job to be done and then clarifying the role each manager plays in relationship to his or her work group and to the organization."[10] The purpose of this interaction is to eliminate overlaps or gaps in perceived management responsibilities and to ensure that managers are performing only those activities that lead to the attainment of management system objectives. Although this process is typically used to clarify the responsibilities of managers, it can also be effective in clarifying nonmanagers' responsibilities.

Management Responsibility Guide

A specific tool developed to implement this interaction process is the **management responsibility guide**, a version of which is used in most organizations. This guide helps management to describe the various responsibility relationships that exist in the organization and to summarize how the responsibilities of various managers relate to one another.

The seven main organizational responsibility relationships covered by the management responsibility guide are listed in **Table 11.1**. Once it is decided which of these relationships exist within the organization, the relationships among these responsibilities can be defined.

MyLab Management Watch It

If your instructor has assigned this activity, go to www.pearson.com/mylab/management to complete the video exercise.

TABLE 11.1   **Seven Responsibility Relationships among Managers, as Used in the Management Responsibility Guide**

1. General Responsibility—The individual who guides and directs the execution of the function through the person accepting operating responsibility

2. Operating Responsibility—The individual who is directly responsible for the execution of the function

3. Specific Responsibility—The individual who is responsible for executing a specific or limited portion of the function

4. Must Be Consulted—The individual whose area is affected by a decision and who must be called on to render advice or relate information before any decision is made or approval is granted (This individual does not, however, make the decision or grant approval.)

5. May Be Consulted—The individual who may be called on to relate information, render advice, or make recommendations before the action is taken

6. Must Be Notified—The individual who must be notified of any action that has been taken

7. Must Approve—The individual (other than persons holding general and operating responsibility) who must approve or disapprove the decision

Responsible Managers   Managers can be described as responsible if they perform the activities they are obligated to perform.[11] Because managers have more impact on an organization than nonmanagers do, responsible managers are a prerequisite for management system success. Several studies have shown that responsible management behavior is highly valued by top executives because the responsible manager guides many other individuals within the organization in performing their duties appropriately.

The degree of responsibility that a manager possesses can be determined by appraising the manager on the following four dimensions:

1.   Attitude toward and conduct with subordinates
2.   Behavior with upper management
3.   Behavior with other groups
4.   Personal attitudes and values

Table 11.2 summarizes what each of these dimensions entails.

Authority

Individuals are assigned job activities to channel their behavior within the organization appropriately. Once they have been given specific assignments, they must be given a commensurate amount of authority to perform those assignments satisfactorily.

Authority is the right to perform or command. It allows its holder to act in certain designated ways and to influence the actions of others directly through orders. It also allows its holder to allocate the organization's resources to achieve organizational objectives.[12]

11-4 Insights regarding the importance of authority within an organization

Authority on the Job

The following example illustrates the relationship between job activities and authority: Two primary tasks for which a particular service station manager is responsible are pumping gasoline and repairing automobiles. The manager has the authority necessary to perform both tasks, or he or she may choose to delegate automobile repair to the assistant manager. Along with the activity of repairing, the assistant should also be delegated the authority to order parts, to command certain attendants to help, and to do anything else necessary to perform repair jobs. Without this authority, the assistant manager may find it impossible to complete the delegated job activities.

Practically speaking, authority merely increases the probability that a specific command is obeyed.[13] The following excerpt emphasizes that authority does not always lead to obedience:[14]

TABLE 11.2   **Four Key Dimensions of Responsible Management Behavior**

Attitude toward and Conduct with Subordinates	Behavior with Upper Management	Behavior with Other Groups	Personal Attitudes and Values
Responsible managers—	Responsible managers—	Responsible managers—	Responsible managers—
1. Take complete charge of their work groups	1. Accept criticism for mistakes and buffer their groups from excessive criticism	1. Make sure that any gaps between their areas and those of other managers are securely filled	1. Identify with the group
2. Pass praise and credit along to subordinates	2. Ensure that their groups meet management expectations and objectives		2. Put organizational goals ahead of personal desires or activities
3. Stay close to problems and activities			3. Perform tasks that offer no immediate reward but help subordinates, the company, or both
4. Take actions to maintain productivity and are willing to terminate poor performers if necessary			4. Conserve corporate resources as if the resources were their own

People who have never exercised power have all kinds of curious ideas about it. The popular notion of top leadership is a fantasy of capricious power: the top man [or woman] presses a button and something remarkable happens; he [or she] gives an order as the whim strikes him [or her], and it is obeyed. Actually, the capricious use of power is relatively rare except in some large dictatorships and some small family firms. Most leaders are hedged around by constraints—tradition, constitutional limitations, the realities of the external situation, rights and privileges of followers, the requirements of teamwork, and most of all, the inexorable demands of large-scale organization, which does not operate on capriciousness. In short, most power is wielded circumspectly.

Acceptance of Authority

As Chapter 10 showed, the positioning of individuals on an organization chart indicates their relative amounts of authority. Those positioned toward the top of the chart possess more authority than those positioned toward the bottom. Chester Barnard wrote, however, that the exercise of authority is determined less by formal organizational decree than by acceptance among those under the authority. According to Barnard, authority exacts obedience only when it is accepted.

In line with this rationale, Barnard defined *authority* as the character of communication by which an order is accepted by an individual as governing the actions that individual takes within the system. Barnard maintained that authority will be accepted only under the following conditions:

1. The individual can understand the order being communicated.
2. The individual believes the order is consistent with the purpose of the organization.
3. The individual sees the order as compatible with his or her personal interests.
4. The individual is mentally and physically able to comply with the order.

The fewer of these four conditions that are present, the lower the probability that authority will be accepted and obedience will be exacted.

Barnard offered some guidance on what managers can do to raise the odds that their commands will be accepted and obeyed. He maintained that more and more of a manager's commands will be accepted over the long term if:[15]

1. The manager uses formal channels of communication that are familiar to all organization members.
2. Each organization member has an assigned formal communication channel through which orders are received.
3. The line of communication between manager and subordinate is as direct as possible.
4. The complete chain of command is used to issue orders.
5. The manager possesses adequate communication skills.
6. The manager uses formal communication lines only for organizational business.
7. A command is authenticated as coming from a manager.

Types of Authority

Three main types of authority can exist within an organization: line authority, staff authority, and functional authority. Each type exists only to enable individuals to carry out the different types of responsibilities with which they have been charged.[16]

Line and Staff Authority
Line authority, the most fundamental authority within an organization, reflects existing superior–subordinate relationships. It consists of the right to make decisions and to give orders concerning the production-, sales-, or finance-related behavior of subordinates. In general, line authority pertains to matters directly involving management system production, sales, and finance and, as a result, the attainment of objectives. People directly responsible for these areas within the organization are delegated line authority to assist them in performing their obligatory activities.[17]

Whereas line authority involves giving orders concerning production activities, **staff authority** consists of the right to advise or assist those who possess line authority as well as other staff personnel. Staff authority enables those responsible for improving the effectiveness of line personnel to perform their required tasks. Examples of organization members with staff authority are people working in the accounting and human resource departments. Obviously, line and staff personnel must work together closely to maintain the efficiency and effectiveness of the organization. To ensure that line and staff personnel work together productively, management must make sure that both groups understand the organizational mission, have specific objectives, and realize that they are partners in helping the organization reach its objectives.[18]

Size is perhaps the most significant factor in determining whether an organization will have staff personnel. Generally speaking, the larger the organization, the greater the need and the ability to employ staff personnel. As an organization expands, it usually needs employees with expertise in diverse areas. Although small organizations may also require this kind of diverse expertise, they often find it more practical to hire part-time consultants to provide this expertise as needed rather than to hire full-time staff personnel, who may not always be kept busy.

Carlos Osorio/AP Images

In an automobile plant, a production manager has line authority over each supervisor. A quality control manager has staff authority to suggest process modifications.

Line-Staff Relationships   **Figure 11.2** shows how line–staff relationships can be presented on an organization chart. The plant manager on this chart has line authority over each immediate subordinate—the human resource manager, the production manager, and the sales manager. However, the human resource manager has staff authority in relation to the plant manager, meaning the human resource manager possesses the right to advise the plant manager on human resource matters. Still, final decisions concerning human resource matters are in the hands of the plant manager, the person holding line authority. Similar relationships exist between the sales manager and the sales research specialist, as well as between the production manager and the quality control manager.

Roles of Staff Personnel   Harold Stieglitz has pinpointed three roles that staff personnel typically perform to assist line personnel:[19]

1. **The advisory or counseling role**—In this role, staff personnel use their professional expertise to solve organizational problems. The staff personnel are, in effect, internal consultants whose relationship with line personnel is similar to that of a professional and a

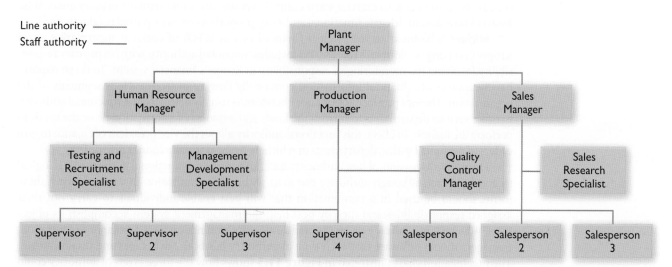

Line authority ——————
Staff authority ——————

Figure 11.2 Possible line–staff relationships in selected organizational areas client. For example, the staff quality control manager might advise the line production manager on possible technical modifications to the production process that would enhance the quality of the organization's products.

2. **The service role**—Staff personnel in this role provide services that can be provided by a single centralized staff group more efficiently and effectively than those services can be provided by many individuals scattered throughout the organization. This role can probably best be understood if staff personnel are viewed as suppliers, and line personnel are viewed as customers. For example, members of a human resource department recruit, employ, and train workers for all organizational departments. In essence, they are the suppliers of workers, and the various organizational departments needing workers are their customers.

3. **The control role**—In this role, staff personnel help establish a mechanism for evaluating the effectiveness of organizational plans. Staff personnel exercising this role are representatives, or agents, of top management.

These three are not the only roles performed by staff personnel, but they are the major ones. In the final analysis, the roles of staff personnel in any organization should be specially designed to best meet the needs of that organization. In some organizations, the same staff people must perform all three major roles.

Conflict in Line-Staff Relationships
Most management practitioners readily admit that a noticeable amount of organizational conflict centers around line–staff relationships.[20] From the viewpoint of line personnel, conflict is created because staff personnel tend to assume line authority, do not give sound advice, steal credit for success, fail to keep line personnel informed of their activities, and do not see the whole picture. From the viewpoint of staff personnel, conflict is created because line personnel do not make proper use of staff personnel, resist new ideas, and refuse to give staff personnel enough authority to do their jobs. In some organizations, the distribution and use of authority is a matter requiring careful negotiation.[21]

Staff personnel can often avert line–staff conflicts if they strive to emphasize the objectives of the organization as a whole, encourage and educate line personnel in the appropriate use of staff personnel, obtain any necessary skills they do not already possess, and deal intelligently with resistance to change rather than view it as an immovable barrier. Line personnel can do their part to minimize line–staff conflict by using staff personnel wherever possible, making proper use of the staff abilities, and keeping staff personnel appropriately informed.[22]

Functional Authority
Functional authority consists of the right to give orders within a segment of the organization in which this right is normally nonexistent. This authority is usually assigned to individuals to complement the line or staff authority they already possess. Functional authority generally covers only specific task areas and is operational only for designated amounts of time. Typically, it is given to individuals who, in order to meet responsibilities in their own areas, must be able to exercise some control over organization members in other areas. Wise leaders know how to delegate functional authority properly to ensure optimal productivity.[23]

Michael Schlotman serves as chief financial officer (CFO) of national supermarket chain Kroger Company. Schlotman's role as CFO includes functional authority, with his primary responsibility involving the monitoring of responsibility in Kroger's financial system. To do so requires having appropriate financial information continually flowing in from various segments of the organization. The vice president of finance, therefore, is usually delegated the functional authority to order various departments to furnish the kinds and amounts of information he or she needs to perform an analysis. In effect, this functional authority allows the vice president of finance to give orders to personnel within departments in which he or she normally cannot give orders.

From this discussion of line authority, staff authority, and functional authority, it is logical to conclude that, although authority can exist within an organization in various forms, these forms should be used in a combination that will best enable individuals to carry out their assigned responsibilities and thereby best help the management system accomplish its objectives. When trying to decide on an optimal authority combination for a particular organization, managers should be aware that each type of authority has both advantages and disadvantages. The organization chart illustrated in **Figure 11.3** shows how the three types of authority could be combined for the overall benefit of a hospital management system.[24]

PROPOSED LARGE HOSPITAL ORGANIZATION AUTHORITY AND RELATIONSHIPS

Figure 11.3 Proposed design for incorporating three types of authority in a hospital

Accountability

Accountability refers to the management philosophy whereby individuals are held liable, or accountable, for how well they use their authority and live up to their responsibility of performing predetermined activities.[25] The concept of accountability implies that, if an individual does not perform predetermined activities, some type of penalty, or punishment, is justifiable.[26] The punishment theme of accountability has been summed up by one company executive: "Individuals who do not perform well simply will not be around too long."[27] The accountability concept also implies that some kind of reward will follow if predetermined activities are performed well. Accountability is especially important for successful knowledge management in an organization.[28]

Delegation

So far in this chapter, we have discussed responsibility and authority as complementary factors that channel activity within an organization. **Delegation** is the actual process of assigning job activities and corresponding authority to specific individuals within the organization.[29] This

11-5 An understanding of how to delegate

PRACTICAL CHALLENGE: ACCOUNTABILITY

Airport Authority Hong Kong and Accountability

The Airport Authority Hong Kong (AAHK) has consistently advertised their commitment to maintaining high standards of corporate governance. The AAHK recognizes the fact that this is not only the reasonable expectation of their stakeholders but also the means by which it will ensure long-term growth. This indicates the presence of a clear framework that aims to encourage ethical and responsible behavior at all levels within the organization. An essential part of this is transparency and accountability.

As the AAHK considers accountability to be one of the fundamentals of corporate governance, much of its corporate structure and the management culture are based on this concept. Ultimately, it is the AAHK board that is held accountable for performance and behavior. The board, in turn, has set operating parameters for each department, making them clearly accountable for their actions.[30]

section focuses on the steps in the delegation process, obstacles to the delegation process, and elimination of obstacles to the delegation process. The next section focuses on centralization and decentralization.

Steps in the Delegation Process

According to Newman and Warren, the delegation process consists of three steps, all of which may be either observable or implied.[31] The first step is assigning specific duties to the individual. In all cases, the manager must be sure that the subordinate assigned to the specific duties has a clear understanding of what these duties entail. Whenever possible, the activities should be stated in operational terms so that the subordinate knows exactly what actions must be taken to perform the assigned duties. The second step of the delegation process involves granting the appropriate authority to the subordinate—that is, the subordinate must be given the right and power within the organization to accomplish the duties assigned. The last step involves creating the obligation for the subordinate to perform the duties assigned. The subordinate must be aware of his or her responsibility to complete the duties assigned and must accept that responsibility. **Table 11.3** offers several guidelines that managers can follow to ensure the success of the delegation process.

Obstacles to the Delegation Process

Obstacles that can make delegation within an organization difficult or even impossible can be classified into three general categories: (1) obstacles related to the supervisor, (2) obstacles related to subordinates, and (3) obstacles related to organizations.

An example of the first category is the supervisor who resists delegating his authority to subordinates because he cannot bear to part with any authority. Two other supervisor-related obstacles are the fear that subordinates will not do a job well and the suspicion that surrendering some authority may be seen as a sign of weakness. If supervisors are insecure in their jobs or believe certain activities are extremely important to their personal success, they may find it hard to put the performance of these activities into the hands of others.

Supervisors who do want to delegate to subordinates may encounter several subordinate-related roadblocks. First, subordinates may be reluctant to accept delegated authority because they are afraid of failing, lack self-confidence, or feel the supervisor doesn't have confidence in them.[32] These obstacles will be especially apparent in subordinates who have never before used

TABLE 11.3   **Guidelines for Making Delegation Effective**

- Give employees the freedom to pursue tasks in their own way.
- Establish mutually agreed-upon results and performance standards for delegated tasks.
- Encourage employees to take an active role in defining, implementing, and communicating progress on tasks.
- Entrust employees with completion of whole projects or tasks whenever possible.
- Explain the relevance of delegated tasks to larger projects or to department or organization goals.
- Give employees the authority necessary to accomplish tasks.
- Allow employees access to all information, people, and departments necessary to perform delegated tasks.
- Provide the training and guidance necessary for employees to complete delegated tasks satisfactorily.
- When possible, delegate tasks on the basis of employee interests.

delegated authority. Other subordinate-related obstacles are the fear that the supervisor will be unavailable for guidance when needed and the reluctance to exercise authority that may complicate congenial working relationships.[33]

Characteristics of the organization itself may also make delegation difficult. For example, a very small organization may present the supervisor with only a minimal number of activities to be delegated. In organizations where few job activities and little authority have been delegated in the past, an attempt to initiate the delegation process may make employees uncooperative and apprehensive because the supervisor is introducing a significant change in procedure—and change is often strongly resisted.[34]

Eliminating Obstacles to the Delegation Process

Because delegation has significant advantages for an organization, eliminating obstacles to the delegation process is something managers must do. Among the advantages of delegation are enhanced employee confidence; improved subordinate involvement and interest; more free time for the supervisor to accomplish tasks; and, as the organization gets larger, assistance from subordinates in completing tasks the manager simply doesn't have time for. True, there are potential disadvantages to delegation—such as the possibility that the manager will lose track of the progress of a delegated task—but the potential advantages of some degree of delegation generally outweigh the potential disadvantages.[35]

What can managers do to eliminate obstacles to the delegation process? First, they must continually strive to uncover any obstacles to delegation. Then they should approach taking action to eliminate these obstacles with the understanding that they may be deeply ingrained and therefore might require much time and effort to overcome. Among the most effective managerial actions that can be taken to eliminate obstacles to delegation are building subordinate confidence in the use of delegated authority, minimizing the impact of delegated authority on established working relationships, and helping delegatees cope with problems whenever necessary.[36] In this sense, some suggest that effective delegation requires coaching.[37]

Koontz, O'Donnell, and Weihrich believe that overcoming the obstacles to delegation requires managers to have certain critical characteristics. These characteristics include the willingness to consider seriously the ideas of others, the insight to allow subordinates the free rein necessary to carry out their responsibilities, the capacity to trust subordinates' abilities, and the wisdom to allow people to learn from their mistakes rather than instituting unreasonable penalties because they made mistakes. Frequently, the lack of such personal attributes in a manager spells the difference between a productive, cohesive team and one that is perennially dysfunctional.[38]

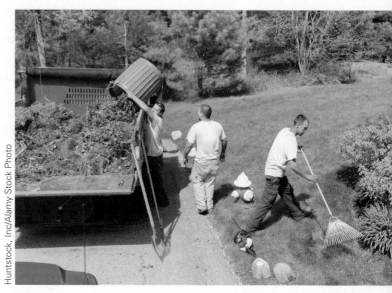

Huntstock, Inc/Alamy Stock Photo

In a small company, it can be hard for managers to learn to delegate when they've been used to doing the work themselves.

Centralization and Decentralization

Noticeable differences can be found from organization to organization in the relative number of job activities and the relative amount of authority delegated to subordinates. These differences are seldom a case of delegation existing in one organization and not existing in another. Rather, the differences come from degree of delegation.[39]

The terms **centralization** and **decentralization** describe the general degree to which delegation exists within an organization. They can be visualized as opposite ends of the delegation continuum depicted in **Figure 11.4**. It is apparent from this figure that centralization implies that a minimal number of job activities and a minimal amount of authority have been delegated to subordinates by management, whereas decentralization implies the opposite.

11-6 A recognition of the advantages and disadvantages of centralization and decentralization

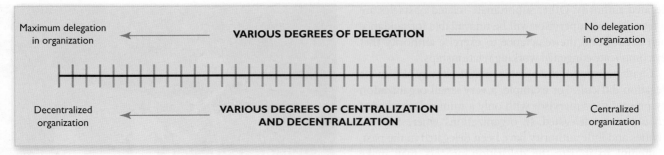

Figure 11.4 Centralized and decentralized organizations on delegation continuum

The issues practicing managers usually face are determining whether to decentralize an organization further and, if that course of action is advisable, deciding how to decentralize it.[40] The section that follows presents practical suggestions on both issues.

Decentralizing an Organization: A Contingency Viewpoint

The appropriate degree of decentralization in an organization depends on the unique situation of that organization. Some specific questions managers can ask to determine the amount of decentralization appropriate for a situation are as follows:

1. **What is the present size of the organization?** As noted earlier, the larger the organization, the greater the likelihood that decentralization will be advantageous. As an organization increases in size, managers have to assume increasing responsibility and different types of tasks. Delegation is typically an effective means of helping them manage this increased workload.

   In some cases, however, top management will conclude that the organization is actually too large and decentralized. One indication that an organization is too large is that labor costs are high relative to other organizational expenses. In this instance, increased centralization of certain organizational activities could reduce the need for some workers and thereby lower labor costs to a more acceptable level.[41]

2. **Where are the organization's customers located?** As a general rule, the more physically separated the organization's customers are, the more viable a significant amount of decentralization is. Decentralization places appropriate management resources close to customers and thereby makes quick customer service possible. For example, by decentralizing its decision making in different continents, Samsonite gives its managers the authority to concentrate on the demands of local customers in each of the different countries in which it sells its luggage products.[42]

3. **How homogeneous is the organization's product line?** Generally, as the product line becomes more heterogeneous, or diversified, the appropriateness of decentralization increases. Different kinds of decisions, talents, and resources are needed to manufacture different products.

   Johnson & Johnson, the world's largest health-care company, consists of more than 250 companies in 57 countries. With such a comprehensive array of products and services, the decision to decentralize authority enables Johnson & Johnson to recruit high-performing individuals whose leadership and expertise drive the company's business.[43] By separating organizational resources by product and keeping pertinent decision making close to the manufacturing process, decentralization usually minimizes the confusion that can result from diversification.[44]

4. **Where are organizational suppliers?** The location of the raw materials needed to manufacture the organization's products is another important consideration. Time lost and high transportation costs associated with shipping raw materials over great distances from supplier to manufacturer could signal the need to decentralize certain functions.

   For example, the wood necessary to manufacture a certain type of bedroom set may be available only from tree growers in certain northern states. If the bedroom set in question is an important product line for a furniture company and if the costs of transporting the

TIPS FOR MANAGING AROUND THE GLOBE

Decentralizing for Diverse Markets: The Four Seasons Example

Should an international business be more centralized or decentralized? A survey by global consultancy Ernst & Young found that the most successful global companies choose decentralization. Decentralized authority puts decision making in the hands of the employees who are closest to the local cultures of the people affected.

Decentralization and a high degree of delegation are central to the management approach of Four Seasons Hotels and Resorts. The Toronto-based chain of luxury hotels in 36 countries empowers employees to act independently to satisfy customers. The company's founder and chair, Isadore Sharp, built the company's reputation on innovation and extraordinary attention to guests' comfort. Four Seasons maintains that approach by hiring employees who share that commitment and then letting them make their own decisions.[45]

lumber are substantial, a decision to decentralize may be a sound one. The effect of this decision would probably be the need to build a plant that produces only bedroom sets in a northern state, close to where the necessary wood is readily available. The advantages of such a costly decision, of course, would accrue to the organization only over the long term.

5. **Are quick decisions needed in the organization?** If speedy decision making is essential, a considerable amount of decentralization is probably in order. Decentralization cuts red tape and allows the subordinate to whom authority has been delegated to make on-the-spot decisions when necessary. It goes without saying that this delegation is advisable only if the potential delegatees have the ability to make sound decisions. If they don't, faster decision making will result in no advantage for the organization but quite the contrary: The organization may find itself saddled with the effects of unsound decisions.

6. **Is creativity a desirable feature of the organization?** If creativity is desirable, then some decentralization is advisable because decentralization allows delegatees the freedom to find better ways of doing things. The mere existence of this freedom encourages the incorporation of new and more creative techniques within the task process.[46]

Decentralization at Massey-Ferguson: A Classic Example from the World of Management

Beneficial decentralization is decentralization that is advantageous for the organization in which it is being implemented; detrimental decentralization is disadvantageous for the organization. To see how an organization should be decentralized, it is worthwhile to study a classic example of an organization that achieved beneficial decentralization: Massey-Ferguson.[47]

Guidelines for Decentralization
Massey-Ferguson is a worldwide farm equipment manufacturer that has enjoyed noticeable success with decentralization over the past several decades. The company has three guidelines for determining the degree of decentralization of decision making that is appropriate for a situation:

1. The competence to make decisions must be possessed by the person to whom authority is delegated. A derivative of this principle is that the superior must have confidence in the subordinate to whom authority is delegated.
2. Adequate and reliable information pertinent to the decision is required by the person making the decision. Decision-making authority therefore cannot be pushed below the point at which all information bearing on the decision is available.
3. If a decision affects more than one unit of the enterprise, the authority to make the decision must rest with the manager accountable for the most units affected by the decision.

Delegation as a Frame of Mind
Massey-Ferguson also encourages in its managers a positive attitude toward decentralization. The company's organization manual states that delegation is not delegation in name only but is a frame of mind that includes both what a supervisor says to subordinates and how the supervisor acts toward them. Managers at Massey-Ferguson are encouraged to allow subordinates to make a reasonable number of mistakes and to help them learn from these mistakes.

Complementing Centralization
Another feature of the beneficial decentralization at Massey-Ferguson is that decentralization is complemented by centralization:

> The organization plan that best serves our total requirements is a blend of centralized and decentralized elements. Marketing and manufacturing responsibilities, together with supporting service functions, are located as close as possible to local markets. Activities that determine the long-range character of the company, such as the planning and control of the product line, the planning and control of facilities and money, and the planning of the strategy to react to changes in the patterns of international trade, are highly centralized.

Thus, Massey-Ferguson management recognizes that decentralization is not necessarily an either/or decision and uses the strengths of both centralization and decentralization to its advantage.

Management Responsibilities
Not all activities at Massey-Ferguson are eligible for decentralization. Only management is allowed to follow through on the following responsibilities:

1. Responsibility for determining the overall objectives of the enterprise
2. Responsibility for formulating the policies that guide the enterprise
3. Final responsibility for control of the business within the total range of the objectives and policies, including control over any changes in the nature of the business
4. Responsibility for product design when a product decision affects more than one area of accountability
5. Responsibility for planning for achievement of overall objectives and for measuring actual performance against those plans
6. Final approval of corporate plans or budgets
7. Decisions pertaining to availability and application of general company funds
8. Responsibility for capital investment plans

CHALLENGE CASE SUMMARY

Hy-Vee executives have been faced with the challenge of organizing the activities of their expanding firm. With over 240 locations, the company has delegated authority and autonomy to each store manager, permitting each one to make key decisions that affect their respective store. Store managers must determine which products should be stocked at their store, how much to price those items, and how they should be displayed to attract customers.

In organizing the activities of employees in a growing organization like Hy-Vee, leadership must recognize, for example, that a manager's activities, as well as those of subordinates, are a major factor in the company's success. Because the activity of a store manager can affect all personnel within that store, the activities of the store manager must be well defined.

Overall, for store managers to be responsible, they must perform the activities they are obligated to perform. Store managers, even though they have been delegated some autonomy, must still follow all company policies and procedures. They must also ensure that employees working at their particular store receive necessary training and are compensated appropriately.

Hy-Vee's corporate office must be sure that any individuals within the company who are delegated job activities are given a commensurate amount of authority to give orders and carry out those activities. Managers throughout the company must recognize, however, that authority must be accepted if obedience is to be exacted. To increase the probability of acceptance, care should be taken to ensure that individuals understand internal orders and regard those orders as being consistent with the objectives of the store they work in and the objectives of the company. Employees should also perceive the orders they receive as being compatible with their individual interests and should consider themselves mentally and physically able to follow those orders. Management must be careful to delegate jobs only to those organization members who are mentally and physically able to carry them out.

Assuming that one of Hy-Vee's main objectives is to sell safe and fairly priced groceries, company personnel who are directly responsible for achieving this objective should possess line authority so that they can perform their responsibilities. For example, individuals responsible for procuring national brands must be given the right to do everything necessary to secure the best-selling brands possible.

Functional authority and accountability are two additional factors that Hy-Vee must consider when organizing employee activities. Some employees may have to be delegated functional authority to supplement the line or staff authority they already have. A Hy-Vee human resource manager (staff person), for example, may need to gather information from the company's sales department in order to understand whether the company needs to hire additional people. Functional authority would enable human resource staff to command that this information be channeled to them.

In organizing employee activity, Hy-Vee should also stress the concept of accountability—the idea that fulfilling assigned responsibilities brings rewards and not fulfilling them brings negative consequences.

To delegate activities effectively, Hy-Vee must assign specific duties to individuals, grant the corresponding authority to these individuals, and make sure these individuals are aware that they are obligated to perform these activities.

In encouraging the use of delegation, Hy-Vee must be aware that obstacles to delegation may exist on the part of store managers, their subordinates, or the departments in which they work. Leadership must be sure that managers can meet the delegation challenges of discovering which obstacles exist in their work environments and taking steps to eliminate them. If Hy-Vee store managers are to be successful delegators, they also must be willing to consider the ideas of subordinates, allow them the free rein necessary to perform their assigned tasks, trust them, and help them learn from their mistakes rather than instituting unreasonable penalties.

Centralization implies that few job activities and little authority have been delegated to subordinates; decentralization implies that many job activities and much authority have been delegated. Hy-Vee corporate leadership will have to determine the best degree of delegation for store managers regarding all job activities. For guidelines, Hy-Vee leaders can rely on certain rules of thumb that say greater degrees of delegation will be appropriate for the company (1) as stores become larger, (2) as store locations become more geographically dispersed and diversified, and (3) as the needs for quick decision making and creativity increase.

At the store level, managers should also determine how decentralized the store should be. First, store managers should use specific guidelines to decide whether their situation warrants additional decentralization. In general, additional delegation will probably be warranted within the store as the competence of subordinates increases, as managers' confidence in their subordinates increases, and as more adequate and reliable decision-making information within the company becomes available to subordinates. For delegation to be advantageous for Hy-Vee, store managers must help subordinates learn from their mistakes. Depending on their situations, individual managers may want to consider supplementing decentralization with centralization.

MyLab Management Assessing Your Management Skill

If your instructor has assigned this activity, go to www.pearson.com/mylab/management to complete the exercise related to the Challenge Case.

DEVELOPING RESPONSIBILITY AND DELEGATION SKILL

This section is specially designed to help you develop responsibility and delegation skills. An individual's responsibility and delegation skill is based on an understanding of the concepts and the ability to apply those concepts. The following activities will help to enhance your responsibility and delegation skills in various organizational situations.

Class Preparation and Personal Study

To help you prepare for class, perform the activities outlined in this section. Performing these activities will help you enhance your classroom performance significantly.

Reflecting on Target Skill

On page 266, this chapter opens by presenting a target management skill along with a list of related objectives outlining knowledge and understanding that you should aim to acquire related to that skill. Review this target skill and the list of objectives to make sure that you've acquired all pertinent information within the chapter. If you do not feel that you've reached a particular objective(s), study related chapter coverage until you do.

Know Key Terms

Understanding the following key terms is critical to your preparing for class. Define each of these terms. Refer to the page(s) referenced after a term to check your definition or to gain further insight regarding the term.

responsibility **268**
job description **268**
functional similarity method **269**
overlapping responsibility **269**
responsibility gap **269**
management responsibility guide **270**
authority **271**
line authority **272**
staff authority **272**
functional authority **274**
accountability **275**
delegation **275**
centralization **277**
decentralization **277**

Know How Management Concepts Relate

This section comprises activities that will further sharpen your understanding of management concepts. Answer essay questions as completely as possible.

11-1   On the basis of which four dimensions can a manager's degree of responsibility be assessed? Describe the qualities a responsible manager should have in terms of attitudes and values.

11-2   Why is it desirable for authority to exist in a variety of different forms?

11-3   Explain the three major steps in the delegation process.

MyLab Management
Personal Inventory Assessment

Go to www.pearson.com/mylab/management to complete the Personal Inventory Assessment related to this chapter.

 PERSONAL INVENTORY ASSESSMENT

Management Skills Exercises

Learning activities in this section are aimed at helping you develop responsibility and delegation skills.

MyLab Management
Discussion Questions

Go to www.pearson.com/mylab/management to complete the problems marked with this icon ✪.

✪ Cases

Autonomy at Hy-Vee Supermarkets

The Challenge Case "Autonomy at Hy-Vee Supermarkets" (p. 267) and its related Challenge Case Summary were written to help you understand the management concepts contained in this chapter. Answer the following discussion questions about the Challenge Case to better understand how responsibility, authority, and delegation concepts can be applied in a company such as Hy-Vee Supermarkets.

11-4 Discuss the roles of responsibility, authority, and accountability among store managers at Hy-Vee Supermarkets.

11-5 What are the drawbacks to delegating so much authority to Hy-Vee store managers?

11-6 What are the advantages to delegating authority to Hy-Vee store managers?

Warby Parker Lets Employees Choose Projects

Read the case and answer the questions that follow. Studying this case will help you better understand how concepts relating to responsibility and delegation can be applied in an organization such as Warby Parker.

Warby Parker is a very trendy eyewear company started in 2010. The young founders of the firm all attended the University of Pennsylvania's Wharton School of Business and started the venture with just $2,500 in seed money. Today, the company is valued at over $1 billion.

The business model is primarily prescription glasses sold online and in a few on-site boutiques in the United States and Canada. They even have a "try it at home" approach where customers can receive five frames free of charge for five days to see which frame they like best.

Like any growing company, there are always big and small issues for employees to tackle. But how can employees know which projects are most important for the company's success or will be highly valued by management? Warby Parker recently instituted *Warbles* that does just that. Warbles permits all 800 employees to help determine which projects should be addressed first. As projects are developed, managers assign points to the projects they think are the most important for the company. Next, associates can choose among those projects: whichever one they like or have the necessary skills to address. If they select and complete the projects that have the most points, they are rewarded. Individuals and teams collect points as they choose one project after another. Finally, each quarter, the team with the most points wins a prize, such as a free dinner for the team.

Before Warbles was introduced, some projects sat untouched for weeks or even months. Other projects were completed quickly, but they added little value to the company. Also, in many cases, employees had little say in which projects they were assigned. According to co-CEO, Dave Gilboa, Warbles "ensures that we're getting a lot of value" and that employees are "much happier; they love the idea that they have autonomy and they can select ideas that they find most interesting."

As an example of how Warbles works, a project was inspired by one associate's idea to allow customers to select a favorite pair of glasses on the company's website by clicking on a "heart icon." Even if the customer didn't buy that item, it would still appear as a favorite item when the customer returned to the site. It was a great idea, but it would require a team of individuals to do the appropriate

programming to the website to enable this new feature. And, of course, there were numerous other projects that also needed to be completed. Warby Parker's 31 managers are the ones who assign point values, typically up to five points. However, the co-CEOs each get 10 to 30 points. Everyone who uses the Warbles system can see what anyone else is voting on and the current point value. Managers use their points to "upvote" or "downvote" certain projects. After nearly two weeks, the "heart icon" feature for the website was up to 80 Warbles points, which is a fairly high value, and one recently hired web developer snagged the project. Within a few months, the "heart icon" was beta-tested, and after proving popular with users, was added as a permanent feature on the Warby Parker website.[48]

Questions

11-7 What challenges do you see with Warby Parker's use of Warbles? How can the company overcome these challenges?

11-8 Compare and contrast the Warbles system at Warby Parker with what you have learned in this chapter about delegation.

11-9 Within what kinds of companies would Warby Parker's Warbles system work best? Within what kinds of companies would it not work? Explain your answers.

Experiential Exercises

Centralization versus Decentralization at Dairy Queen

Directions. Read the following scenario and then perform the listed activities. Your instructor may want you to perform the activities as an individual or within groups. Follow all of your instructor's directions carefully.

As discussed in this chapter, scholars have long debated the advantages and disadvantages of centralization and decentralization. Executives at the restaurant chain Dairy Queen have contacted your group to help them better understand whether the company should be either more centralized or more decentralized. Visit Dairy Queen's website and learn more about the company, its number of locations, and what it offers on the menu. After studying the company, revisit the discussion of centralization and decentralization in the chapter. How centralized or decentralized should Dairy Queen be with regard to individual locations and franchises? Use the guidelines presented in the text to frame and support your arguments.

You and Your Career

A job description is a list of specific activities performed by whoever holds a particular position within an organization. Request a copy of your job description from your employer; if you are unable to obtain a copy or you are currently not working, search online for a similar job description to your most recent job. Examine your own job description. Then answer the following questions: How accurate is the job description? Does it capture every major activity you perform? What is missing? Is the job description outdated? What would it require to bring it up to date? Why is a job description important?

Building Your Management Skills Portfolio

Your Management Skills Portfolio is a collection of activities specially designed to demonstrate your management knowledge and skill. Be sure to save your work. Taking your printed portfolio to an employment interview could be helpful in obtaining a job.

The portfolio activity for this chapter is Delegating Duties at Etsy. Study the following information and complete the exercises that follow.[49]

Etsy is a peer-to-peer e-commerce website focusing primarily on handmade and craft items. With nearly 60 million registered users and almost 700 employees, the company has recently changed its leadership. In 2017, the new CEO is Josh Silverman. Part of the reason for the change has been a decline in revenue under the former CEO. Before Etsy, Silverman was the CEO of Skype and Evite. Silverman is taking over at a time when the company is attempting to regain its former growth patterns while laying off 80 employees. According to Silverman, "In the coming weeks, I look forward to listening and learning from our employees, buyers and shareholders to help ensure we are focusing on the most value-enhancing near- and long-term opportunities."

As the new CEO of Etsy, Silverman has asked you to help him perform his job both efficiently and effectively. Specifically, Silverman believes that he needs to delegate tasks, but he needs guidance in how to do so. In the following exercise, answer the questions related to the delegation process.

11-10 What are some of the responsibilities of a CEO? List at least seven.

_____

_____

_____

11-11 The first step in the delegation process is to assign specific duties to individuals. What are Silverman's primary duties, and to whom can he assign these duties? Which of Silverman's duties cannot be assigned to others?

_____

_____

_____

11-12 The second step in the delegation process involves granting authority to subordinates. How would Silverman grant authority to others? How would he make sure that others accept this new authority?

_____

_____

_____

11-13 The third step of the delegation process entails making sure the subordinate accepts responsibility

for the delegated tasks. How would Silverman ensure that subordinates accept responsibility?

_____

_____

11-14 Many obstacles could damage the effectiveness of Silverman's delegation efforts. List the primary obstacles that Silverman must overcome.

_____

_____

MyLab Management
Writing Assignments

If your instructor has assigned this activity, go to www.pearson.com/mylab/management for the following assisted-graded writing assignments:

Assisted-Grading Questions

11-15 Compare and contrast centralization versus decentralization. In your opinion, which is better for organizations?

11-16 What is acceptance of authority, and under which conditions will employees accept authority?

Endnotes

1. Warren Thayer, "How Hy-Vee Stays Young," *Refrigerated & Frozen Foods Retailer* (August 2007): 16–23.
2. Andre Nelson, "Have I the Right Stuff to Be a Supervisor?" *Supervision* 51 (January 1990): 10–12. For a more recent responsibility-related trend, see "Office Professionals' Responsibilities Set to Soar," *British Journal of Administrative Management* (May/June 2001): 6.
3. "Goldman Sachs: Key Executive Accepts Some Responsibility for Meltdown," *Los Angeles Times*, April 27, 2010, http://www.latimes.com. For a general discussion of the accountability of top executives in the context of company performance, see C. Crossland and G. Chen, "Executive Accountability around the World: Sources of Cross-National Variation in Firm Performance—CEO Dismissal Sensitivity," *Strategic Organization* 11 (2013): 78–109.
4. J. E. Osborne, "Job Descriptions Do More Than Describe Duties," *Supervisory Management* (February 1992): 8. For more information on crafting jobs, see D. T. A. M. Kooij, M. van Woerkom, J. Wilkenloh, L. Dorenbosch, and J. J. A. Denissen, "Job Crafting towards Strengths and Interests: The Effects of a Job Crafting Intervention on Person-Job Fit and the Role of Age," *Journal of Applied Psychology* 102 (2017): 971–981.
5. "Delegation: A Win-Win Situation for Managers and Employees," *Health Care Collector: The Monthly Newsletter for Health Care Collectors* 3, no. 5: 8–10.
6. Robert J. Theirauf, Robert C. Klekamp, and Daniel W. Geeding, *Management Principles and Practices: A Contingency and Questionnaire Approach* (New York: Wiley, 1977), 334.
7. Deborah S. Kezsbom, "Managing the Chaos: Conflict among Project Teams," *AACE Transactions* (1989): A4.1–A4.8. To better understand the relationship between delegation and shared responsibility, see M. P. Haselhuhn, E. M. Wong, and M. E. Ormiston, "With Great Power Comes Shared Responsibility: Psychological

Power and Delegation of Authority," *Personality and Individual Differences*, 108 (2017): 1–4.

8. Richard Korman, "A Responsibility Gap Crashes at Location C3," *ENR* 250 (2003): 12.

9. Chuck Douros, "Clear Division of Responsibility Defeats Inefficiency," *Nation's Restaurant News* (February 21, 1994): 20.

10. Robert D. Melcher, "Roles and Relationships: Clarifying the Manager's Job," *Personnel* 44 (May/June 1967): 34–41.

11. This section is based primarily on John H. Zenger, "Responsible Behavior: Stamp of the Effective Manager," *Supervisory Management* (July 1976): 18–24.

12. Stephen Bushardt, David Duhon, and Aubrey Fowler, "Management Delegation Myths and the Paradox of Task Assignment," *Business Horizons* (March/April 1991): 37–43.

13. Max Weber, "The Three Types of Legitimate Rule," trans. Hans Gerth, *Berkeley Journal of Sociology* 4 (1953): 1–11. For a current illustration of this concept, see Gail DeGeorge, "Yo, Ho, Ho, and a Battle for Bacardi," *BusinessWeek* (April 16, 1990): 47–48.

14. John Gardner, "The Anti-Leadership Vaccine," *Carnegie Foundation Annual Report* (1965).

15. Chester I. Barnard, *The Functions of the Executive* (Cambridge, MA: Harvard University Press, 1938).

16. To better understand the interplay between incentives and authority, see Jan Bouwens and Laurence Van Lent, "Assessing the Performance of Business Unit Managers," *Journal of Accounting Research* 45, no. 4 (2007): 667–697.

17. For an illustration of how line authority issues can have an impact on the operation of the IRS, see "TEI Recommends Changes in IRS Appeals Large Case Program," *Tax Executive* 48, no. 4 (July/August 1996): 265.

18. Patti Wolf, Gerald Grimes, and John Dayani, "Getting the Most Out of Staff Functions," *Small Business Reports* 14 (October 1989): 68–70.

19. Harold Stieglitz, "On Concepts of Corporate Structure," *Conference Board Record* 11 (February 1974): 7–13.

20. Wendell L. French, *The Personnel Management Process: Human Resource Administration and Development* (Boston: Houghton Mifflin, 1987), 66–68.

21. For a discussion of how supervisors empower the employees they manage, see D. R. Avery, M. Wang, S. D. Volpone, and L. Zhou, "Different Strokes for Different Folks: The Impact of Sex Dissimilarity in the Empowerment-Performance Relationship," *Personnel Psychology* 66 (2013): 757–784.

22. Derek Sheane, "When and How to Intervene in Conflict," *Personnel Management* (November 1979): 32–36. For an interesting discussion highlighting the potential benefits of conflict, see B. H. Bradley, A. C. Klotz, B. E. Postlethwaite, and K. G. Brown, "Ready to Rumble: How Team Personality Composition and Task Conflict Interact to Improve Performance," *Journal of Applied Psychology* 98: 385–392.

23. For a discussion of how giving up authority can be good for an organization, see A. D. Amar, Carsten Hentrich, and Vlatka Hlupic, "To Be a Better Leader, Give Up Authority," *Harvard Business Review*, December 2009, http://hbr.org.

24. Researchers have devised an interesting way to map the distribution of authority within an organization. For a description of this technique, see Michael Segalla, "Find the Real Power in Your Organization," *Harvard Business Review* (May 2010): 34–35.

25. Robert Albanese, *Management* (Cincinnati, OH: South-Western Publishing, 1988), 313. To learn more about how CEOs are accountable for ethical actions, see J. Chen, D. Cumming, W. Hou, and E. Lee, "CEO Accountability for Corporate Fraud: Evidence from the Split Share Structure Reform in China," *Journal of Business Ethics* 138 (2016): 787–806.

26. Anthony Buono, "Accountability: Freedom and Responsibility Without Control," *Personnel Psychology* 56 (2003): 546. To learn more about how individuals remain accountable for actions they delegate, see A. Masli, V. J. Richardson, M. W. Watson, and R. W. Zmud, "Senior Executives' IT Management Responsibilities: Serious IT-Related Deficiencies and CEO/CFO Turnover," *MIS Quarterly* 40 (2016): 687–708.

27. "How Ylvisaker Makes 'Produce or Else' Work," *BusinessWeek* (October 27, 1973): 112; N. P. Mero, R. M. Guidice, and S. Werner, "A Field Study of the Antecedents and Performance Consequences of Perceived Accountability," *Journal of Management* 40 (2014): 1627–1652.

28. See Chris Rivinus, "Ignorance Management," *Business Information Review* 27, no. 1 (2010): 33–38.

29. For a practical discussion related to the delegation process, see Kenneth Corts and Darwin Neher, "Credible Delegation," *European Economic Review* 47 (2003): 395. See also M. Steffel, E. F. Williams, and J. Perrmann-Graham, "Passing the Buck: Delegating Choices to Others to Avoid Responsibility and Blame," *Organizational Behavior and Human Decision Processes* 135 (2016): 32–44.

30. Hong Kong Airport Web site, https://www.hongkongairport.com/eng/pdf/media/publication/report/11_12/E_09_Corporate_Governance.pdf.

31. William H. Newman and E. Kirby Warren, *The Process of Management: Concepts, Behavior, and Practice*, 4th ed. (Upper Saddle River, NJ: Prentice Hall, 1977), 39–40; Dave Wiggins, "Stop Doing It All Yourself! Some Keys to Effective Delegation," *Journal of Environmental Health* 60, no. 9 (May 1998): 29–30. See also Kristin Gilpatrick, "Step Up to Delegation," *Credit Union Management* 24, no. 4 (April 2001): 18.

32. R. S. Drever, "The Ultimate Frustration," *Supervision* (May 1991): 22–23.

33. To better understand the intricacies of delegation in international contexts, see Zhen Xiong Chen and Samuel Aryee, "Delegation and Employee Work Outcomes: An Examination of the Cultural Context of Mediating Processes in China," *Academy of Management Journal* 50, no. 1 (2007): 226–238.

34. For more recommendations regarding delegation, see Joni Youngworth, "Delegation Dilemmas," *Journal of Financial Planning* 20 (September 2007): 10–12.

35. Ted Pollock, "Secrets of Successful Delegation," *Production* (December 1994): 10–11; Robert B. Nelson, "Mastering Delegation," *Executive Excellence* 7 (January 1990): 13–14.

36. Roz Ayres-Williams, "Mastering the Fine Art of Delegation," *Black Enterprise* (April 1992): 91–93.

37. S. Nawaz, "For Delegation to Work, It Has to Come with Coaching," *Harvard Business Review*, May 5, 2016, published on HBR.ORG (reprint: H02V8H).

38. Harold Koontz, Cyril O'Donnell, and Heinz Weihrich, *Essentials of Management*, 8th ed. (New York: McGraw-Hill, 1986), 231–233. See also Robert I. Sutton, "Some Bosses Live in a Fool's Paradise," *Harvard Business Review*, June 3, 2010, http://blogs.hbr.org; Andrew O'Connell, "Why Controlling Bosses Have Unproductive Employees," *Harvard Business Review*, May 25, 2010, http://blogs.hbr.org.

39. For a practical look at the process of centralization, see "Pros and Cons of Centralization," *Nature* 423 (2003): 787. See also Marco Adria and Shamsud Chowdhury, "Centralization as a Design Consideration for the Management of Call Centers," *Information and Management* 41 (2004): 497.

40. For an interesting discussion of the role of centralization in franchising, see M. Herz, C. Hutzinger, H. Seferagic, and J. Windpserger, "Trust, Decision Rights Delegation, and Performance—The Case of Franchising, *Journal of Small Business Management* 54 (2016): 973–991.

41. Steve Weinstein, "A Look at Fleming's New Look," *Progressive Grocer* 74 (1995): 47–49. To understand the interplay between decentralization and innovation, see B. Ecker, S. van Triest, and C. Williams, "Management Control and the Decentralization of R&D," *Journal of Management* 39 (2013): 906–927.

42. T. Derpinghaus and A. Bhattacharya, "Samsonite Sees Rapid Growth in Asia," *Wall Street Journal*, December 29, 2013, http://online.wsj.com/news/articles/SB1000142405270230334510457928 3621990013420?KEYWORDS=decentralize, accessed February 10, 2014.

43. Jack Neff, "What's Ailing J&J—and Why Isn't Its Rep Hurting?," *Advertising Age*, May 10, 2010, http://www.adage.com.

44. To better understand how decentralization influences the empowerment of employees, see P. S. Hempel, Z. Zhang, and Y. Han, "Team Empowerment and the Organizational Context: Decentralization and the Contrasting Effects of Formalization," *Journal of Management* 38 (2012): 475–501.

45. Scott S. Smith, "Hotelier Isadore Sharp, a Man for Four Seasons," *Investor's Business Daily*, May 20, 2013, Business Insights: Global, http://bi.galegroup.com; Robert J. Thomas, Joshua Bellin, Claudy Jules, and Nandani Lynton, "Four Blueprints for Ensemble Decision-Making," *Ivey Business Journal*, May 2013, Business Insights: Global, http://bi.galegroup.com; EY (Ernst & Young Global Ltd.),

"Talent Management Sea Change Needed for Global Growth, Says Survey," news release, November 12, 2012, http://www .ey.com.

46. Donald O. Harper, "Project Management as a Control and Planning Tool in the Decentralized Company," *Management Accounting* (November 1968): 29–33. For a detailed description of the effects of decentralization on research and development (R&D), see B. Ecker, S. van Triest, and C. Williams, "Management Control and the Decentralization of R&D," *Journal of Management* 39, no. 4 (2013): 906–927.

47. Information for this section is mainly from John G. Staiger, "What Cannot Be Decentralized," *Management Record* 25 (January 1963):

19–21. At the time the article was written, Staiger was vice president of administration, North American Operations, Massey-Ferguson, Limited.

48. "Warby Parker Is Getting Better Results by Reducing Managers' Control over Workers," https://qz.com/1016992/ george-soros-ray-dalio-and-charlie-munger-three-of-the-worlds-most-powerful-billionaires-agree-theres-one-trait-you-need-to-succeed/.

49. This exercise was based on Anthony Ha, "Etsy Names Josh Silverman as Its New CEO," May 2, 2017, https://techcrunch .com/2017/05/02/etsy-new-ceo/.

Human Resource Management

TARGET SKILL

 Human Resource Management Skill: the ability to take actions that increase the contributions of individuals within the organization

HUMAN RESOURCE MANAGEMENT SKILL AND YOUR CAREER

Human resource management skill will be of great value to you in enhancing your career. This skill will help you take actions that increase the contributions of other individuals within the organization. In addition, it will help you understand your role in the organization. This ability contributes to organizational success, builds your image as a competent manager, makes you valuable to your organization, and supports promotions as you build your career.

OBJECTIVES

To help build my *human resource management skill,* when studying this chapter, I will attempt to acquire:

12-1 An overall understanding of how appropriate human resources can be provided for the organization

12-2 An appreciation for the relationship among recruitment efforts, an open position, sources of human resources, and the law

12-3 Insights into the use of tests and assessment centers in employee selection

12-4 An understanding of how the training process operates

12-5 A concept of what performance appraisals are and how they can best be conducted

---

MyLab Management Chapter Warm Up

If your instructor has assigned this activity, go to www.pearson.com/mylab/management to complete the chapter warm up.

Netflix Revamps Its Human Resources

Netflix, the online streaming and DVD subscription service, was started in 1997 by Reed Hastings and Marc Randolph. Since then, the company has grown to nearly $9 billion in revenue and close to 100 million subscribers worldwide. In addition to renting or streaming movies, documentaries, stand-up comic performances, and TV shows, the firm also develops its own original programming, such as *House of Cards* and *Orange Is the New Black*.

Like any major company, Netflix has struggled with managing the human resources that are so important to the firm's success. Patty McCord, former chief talent officer for the organization, shared her insights into how Netflix took a unique approach to hiring, retaining, and developing its human resources. According to McCord, the secret to an outstanding human resource department is in making certain that the best associates are hired in the first place. "The best thing you can do for employees—a perk better than foosball or free sushi—is hire only 'A' players to work alongside them. Excellent colleagues trump everything else." This meant recruiting and selecting talent that is a right fit from the start. Rather than hoping an employee might be productive, the selection process at Netflix attempts to find the perfect employee right away. "We continually told managers," she said, "that building a great team was their most important task. We didn't measure them on whether they were excellent coaches or mentors or got their paperwork done on time. Great teams accomplish great work, and recruiting the right team was the top priority."

With a solid group of employees on the team, McCord next turned to how these talented individuals were managed within the company. She asked managers to think about what is required of teams and specific employees—in other words, what skills do they need to possess in order to be successful in what they do? "If you're in a fast-changing business environment," said McCord, "you're probably looking at a lot of mismatches. In that case, you need to have honest conversations about letting some team members find a place where their skills are a better fit."

As employees were being developed and trained at Netflix, the company also examined its other human resource practices and improved upon them. For example, rigid complex policies regarding vacation time were reduced simply to having employees and managers

Bernd von Jutrczenka/dpa/picture-alliance/Newscom

Netflix is a company that provides online streaming and DVD rental of movies and television programming. It has about 100 million subscribers worldwide and nearly $9 billion in revenue.

mutually agree upon what is an appropriate number of days to be away from work. Also, when it came to compensation, Netflix tries to pay at least what the market is paying and actually encourages associates to see what other companies are paying. This may seem counterintuitive, but McCord believes it's important for employees and human resource professionals to know the prevailing salaries in the labor market.

For McCord, these unique approaches to human resources embody the importance of the human resource function in modern organizations. Simply utilizing the same practices from decades ago might not suffice in a highly competitive industry such as the technology sector. Instead, reinventing how human resources are hired and developed has helped Netflix become an Internet powerhouse. With advances in cloud data storage and improvements in the streaming services the company provides, innovations in technology are vital. But according to McCord, "there's no reason the HR team can't be innovative, too."[1]

THE HUMAN RESOURCE MANAGEMENT CHALLENGE

The Challenge Case discusses tactics that managers at Netflix have used to hire and retain its brightest employees. The task of hiring and retaining the right people—particularly top performers—is part of managing human resources in any organization. This chapter explores the process of managing human resources within an organization, emphasizes how hiring and retaining the right people is part of this process for managers at a company such as Netflix, discusses this process by first defining appropriate human resources, and then examines the steps to be followed in providing these resources.

Defining Appropriate Human Resources

The phrase **appropriate human resources** refers to the individuals within the organization who make valuable contributions to management system goal attainment. These contributions result from their productivity in the positions they hold. The phrase *inappropriate human resources* refers to organization members who do not make valuable contributions to the attainment of management system objectives. For one reason or another, these individuals are ineffective in their jobs.

Productivity in all organizations is determined by how well human resources interact and work together to use all other management system resources. Factors such as background, age, job-related experience, and level of formal education all play a role in determining how appropriate an individual is for the organization. Although the process of providing appropriate human resources for the organization is involved and is somewhat subjective, the following sections offer insights on how to increase the success of this process.

To provide appropriate human resources to fill both managerial and nonmanagerial openings, managers follow four sequential steps:[2]

1. Recruitment
2. Selection
3. Training
4. Performance appraisal

Figure 12.1 illustrates these steps.

12-1 An overall understanding of how appropriate human resources can be provided for the organization

Recruitment

Recruitment is the initial attraction and screening of the supply of prospective human resources available to fill a position. Its purpose is to narrow a large field of prospective employees to a relatively small group of individuals from which someone eventually will be hired. To be effective, recruiters must know the job they are trying to fill, where potential human resources can be located, and how the law influences recruiting efforts. What's more, with advances in technology, recruiting continues to evolve and change. To maintain appropriate human resources, today's managers must keep abreast of the trends.[3]

12-2 An appreciation for the relationship among recruitment efforts, an open position, sources of human resources, and the law

Knowing the Job

Recruitment activities must begin with a thorough understanding of the position to be filled so that the broad range of potential employees can be narrowed appropriately. The technique commonly used to gain that understanding is known as **job analysis**. Basically, job analysis is aimed at determining a job description (the activities that a job entails)—which was discussed in the previous chapter—and a **job specification** (the characteristics of the individual who should be hired for the job).[4] **Figure 12.2** shows the relationship of job analysis to job description and job specification.[5]

STEP 1	STEP 2	STEP 3	STEP 4
Recruitment	Selection	Training	Performance Appraisal

Figure 12.1

Four steps to providing appropriate human resources for an organization

Figure 12.2
Relationship among job
analysis, job description,
and job specification

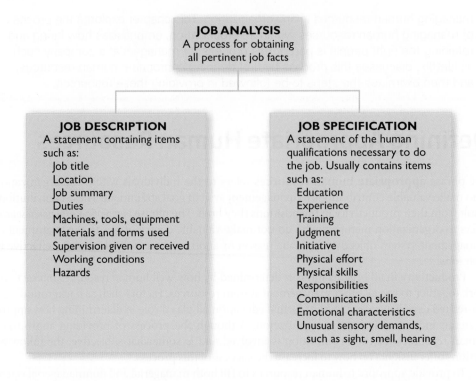

The U.S. Civil Service Commission has developed a procedure for performing a job analysis. As with all job analysis procedures, the Civil Service procedure uses information gathering as the primary means of determining what workers do and how and why they do it. Naturally, the quality of the job analysis depends on the accuracy of the information gathered. This information is used to develop both a job description and a job specification.[6]

Knowing Sources of Human Resources

Besides a thorough knowledge of the position the organization is trying to fill, recruiters must be able to pinpoint sources of human resources. The supply of individuals from which to recruit is continually changing, which means that finding appropriate human resources will sometimes be much harder than at other times. Human resource specialists in organizations must continually monitor the labor market so that they know where to recruit appropriate people and what kinds of strategies and tactics to use to attract job applicants in a competitive marketplace.[7]

Sources of human resources available to fill a position can generally be categorized in two ways: sources inside the organization and sources outside the organization.

Sources Inside the Organization
The pool of employees within the organization is one source of human resources. Some individuals who already work for the organization may be well qualified for an open position. Although existing personnel are sometimes moved laterally within an organization, most internal movements are promotions. Promotion from within has the advantages of building employee morale, encouraging employees to work harder in hopes of being promoted, and enticing employees to stay with the organization because of the possibility of future promotions. Companies such as Exxon and General Electric find it especially rewarding to train their managers for advancement within the organization.[8]

Human Resource Inventory.   A **human resource inventory** consists of information about the characteristics of organization members. The focus is on past performance and future potential, and the objective is to keep management up to date about the possibilities for filling a position from within. This inventory should indicate which individuals in the organization would be appropriate for filling a position if it becomes available. In a classic article, Walter S. Wikstrom proposed that organizations keep three types of records that can be combined to

Figure 12.3
Management inventory card

maintain a useful human resource inventory.[9] Although Wikstrom focused on filling managerial positions, slight modifications to his inventory forms would make his records equally useful for filling nonmanagerial positions. To make their human resource inventory system more efficient and effective, many organizations computerize records like the ones Wikstrom suggested.

- The first of Wikstrom's three types of records for a human resource inventory is the **management inventory card**. The management inventory card in **Figure 12.3** has been completed for a fictional manager named Mel Murray. It indicates Murray's age, year of employment, present position and the length of time he has held it, performance ratings, strengths and weaknesses, the positions to which he might move, when he would be ready to assume these positions, and additional training he would need to fill the positions. In short, this card contains an organizational history of Murray and an indication of what positions he might hold in the future. (Note that Figures 12.3 through 12.5 depict a computerized version of Wikstrom's human resource inventory system.)
- **Figure 12.4** shows Wikstrom's second type of human resource inventory record—the **position replacement form**. This record focuses on position-centered information rather than the people-centered information maintained on the management inventory card. Note that the form in Figure 12.4 indicates little about Murray but much about the two individuals who could replace him. The position replacement form is helpful in determining what would happen to Murray's present position if he were selected to be moved within the organization or if he decided to leave the organization.
- Wikstrom's third human resource inventory record is the **management manpower replacement chart** (see **Figure 12.5**). This chart presents a composite view of the individuals management considers significant for human resource planning. Note in Figure 12.5 how Murray's performance rating and promotion potential can easily be compared with those of other employees when the company is trying to determine which individual would most appropriately fill a particular position.

Figure 12.4
Position replacement form

Present Performance

▨ Outstanding   ☑ Satisfactory   ☐ Needs improvement   ◖ Ready now   ◑ Needs further   ● Questionable
training

Promotion Potential

Figure 12.5 Management manpower replacement chart

The management inventory card, the position replacement form, and the management manpower replacement chart are three separate record-keeping devices for a human resource inventory. Each form furnishes different data on which to base a hiring-from-within decision. These forms help management answer the following questions:

1. What is the organizational history of an individual, and what potential does that person possess (management inventory card)?
2. If a position becomes vacant, who might be eligible to fill it (position replacement form)?
3. What are the merits of one individual being considered for a position compared to those of another individual under consideration (management manpower replacement chart)?

Overall, Wikstrom's human resource inventory system can serve as the foundation for succession planning in organizations. **Succession planning** is the process of determining who will follow whom in various organizational positions. Studies show that such planning will be among the top five challenges executives face in the future.[10] Gene Diedrich, CEO of Moneta Group, has made succession planning a priority at his company.[11] Several years ago, he realized that many of the company's top employees would be retiring within a few years. To address this challenge, his company formalized a plan to select and mentor younger employees to eventually assume those roles, and today, many of those younger employees *are* assuming those roles. At companies like Moneta Group, computer software is available to aid managers in keeping track of the organization's complex human resource inventories and in making better decisions about how employees can best be deployed and developed.[12]

GM's new CEO, Mary Barra, appears here. GM needed succession planning to fill the shoes of her predecessor, Dan Akerson, when he retired, as well as a succession plan for who would fill Barra's previous role as senior VP for global product development.

Sources Outside the Organization

If a position cannot be filled by someone currently employed by the organization, management has available numerous sources of human resources outside the organization. These sources include the following:

1. **Competitors**—One often-tapped external source of human resources is competing organizations. Because of several advantages in luring human resources away from competitors, this type of piracy has become a common practice. Among the advantages are the following:
   - The individual knows the business.
   - The competitor will have paid for the individual's training up to the time of hire.
   - The competing organization will probably be weakened somewhat by the loss of the individual.
   - Once hired, the individual will be a valuable source of information about how best to compete with the other organization.
2. **Employment agencies**—Employment agencies help people find jobs and help organizations find job applicants. Such agencies can be either public or private. Public employment agencies do not charge fees, whereas private ones collect a fee from either the person hired or the organization doing the hiring, once the hire has been finalized.
3. **Readers of certain publications**—Perhaps the most widely used external source of human resources is the readership of certain publications. To tap this source, recruiters simply place an advertisement in a suitable publication. The advertisement describes the open position in detail and announces that the particular organization is accepting applications from qualified individuals. The type of position to be filled determines the type of

TIPS FOR MANAGING AROUND THE GLOBE

European Companies Need Women on Their Boards

International companies need to be aware of the human resource laws and regulations governing all the locations where they operate. In Europe, for example, the parliament of the European Union (EU) has been moving toward requiring that boards of directors be 40 percent female by 2020. Even without the EU requirement, some individual nations impose their own quotas. In France, for example, corporate boards must have at least 20 percent women, and in Italy, boards needed to be one-third female by 2015.

On average, at the EU's largest companies, only 17.6 percent of board members are women, but companies are actively recruiting qualified women for their boards. Some, such as the French food services company Sodexo and the British technology company Smiths Group, have selected American executives as a way to gain a greater understanding of the U.S. market.[13]

publication in which the advertisement is placed. The objective is to advertise in a publication whose readers are likely to be interested in filling the position. An opening for a top-level executive might be advertised in the *Wall Street Journal*, a training director opening might be advertised in the *Journal of Training and Development*, and an educational opening might be advertised in the *Chronicle of Higher Education*.

4. **Educational institutions**—Many recruiters go directly to schools to interview students who will soon graduate. Liberal arts schools, business schools, engineering schools, junior colleges, and community colleges all have somewhat different human resources to offer. Recruiting efforts should thus focus on the schools with the highest probability of providing human resources appropriate for the open position.

To increase their hiring from educational institutions, Intel Corp. and 24 venture capital firms have created a $3.5 billion strategic alliance called "Invest in America." The alliance has enlisted 18 technology firms, including Cisco Systems, eBay, Google, and Yahoo!, who have committed to increase their hiring of college graduates. Offering more opportunities to recent graduates is one way U.S. businesses can help support the economy.[14]

Knowing the Law

Legislation has had a major impact on modern organizational recruitment practices. Managers need to be aware of the laws that govern recruitment efforts. The Civil Rights Act, passed in 1964 and amended in 1972, created the **Equal Employment Opportunity Commission (EEOC)** to enforce federal laws prohibiting discrimination on the basis of race, color, religion, gender, disability, sexual orientation, national origin, and genetic information in recruitment, hiring, firing, layoffs, and all other employment practices. Such laws include the Pregnancy Discrimination Act,[15] requiring the treatment of pregnancy as a medical disability; the Age Discrimination in Employment Act, prohibiting the arbitrary setting of age limits for job holders; and the Americans with Disabilities Act, prohibiting discrimination against individuals with mental or physical disabilities in the area of employment.

Equal opportunity legislation protects the right of a citizen to work and obtain a fair wage based primarily on merit and performance. The EEOC seeks to uphold this right by overseeing the employment practices of labor unions, private employers, educational institutions, and government bodies.

Affirmative Action   In response to equal opportunity legislation, many organizations have established an **affirmative action program**.[16] Literally, *affirmative action* means positive movement: "In the area of equal employment opportunity, the basic purpose of positive movement or affirmative action is to eliminate barriers and increase opportunities for the purpose of increasing the utilization of underutilized and/or disadvantaged individuals."[17] An organization can judge how much progress it is making toward eliminating such barriers by taking the following steps:

1. Determining how many minority and disadvantaged individuals it presently employs
2. Determining how many minority and disadvantaged individuals it should be employing according to EEOC guidelines

3. Comparing the numbers obtained in steps 1 and 2

If the two numbers obtained in step 3 are nearly the same, the organization's employment practices probably should be maintained; if they are not nearly the same, the organization should modify its employment practices accordingly.

Modern management writers recommend that managers follow the guidelines of affirmative action not merely because they are mandated by law but also because of the characteristics of today's labor supply.[18] According to these writers, more than half of the U.S. workforce now consists of minorities, immigrants, and women. Because the overall workforce is so diverse, it follows that employees in today's organizations will also be more diverse than in the past. Thus, today's managers face the challenge of forging a productive workforce out of an increasingly diverse labor pool, and this task is more formidable than simply complying with affirmative action laws.

Diversity also includes diversity in age, and with the aging of America's baby boom generation, recruiting managers are increasingly paying attention to real and perceived differences in the work values among younger and older generations of workers.[19]

Selection

The second major step involved in providing human resources for the organization is **selection**—choosing an individual to hire from all those who have been recruited. Selection, obviously, depends on the first step, recruitment.

Selection is represented as a series of stages through which job applicants must pass to be hired.[20] Each stage reduces the total group of prospective employees until, finally, one individual is hired. **Figure 12.6** lists the specific stages of the selection process, indicates reasons for eliminating applicants at each stage, and illustrates how the group of potential employees is narrowed to the individual who ultimately is hired. Two tools often used in the selection process are testing and assessment centers.

12-3 Insights into the use of tests and assessment centers in employee selection

Testing

Testing is examining human resources for qualities relevant to performing available jobs. Although many different kinds of tests are available for organizational use, they generally can be divided into the following four categories:[21]

1. **Aptitude tests**—Tests of aptitude measure the potential of an individual to perform a task. Some aptitude tests measure general intelligence, whereas others measure special abilities, such as mechanical, clerical, or visual skills.[22]

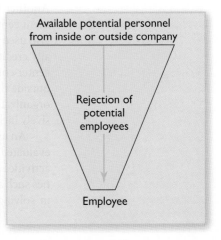

STAGES OF THE SELECTION PROCESS	REASONS FOR ELIMINATION
Preliminary screening from records, data sheets, and so on	Lack of adequate educational and performance record
Preliminary interview	Obvious misfit from outward appearance and conduct
Intelligence tests	Failure to meet minimum standards
Aptitude tests	Failure to have minimum necessary aptitude
Personality tests	Negative aspects of personality
Performance references	Unfavorable or negative reports on past performance
Diagnostic interview	Lack of necessary innate ability, ambition, or other qualities
Physical examination	Physically unfit for job
Personal judgment	Remaining candidate placed in available position

Figure 12.6 Summary of major factors in the selection process

Monkey Business/Fotolia

Tests of vocational interests try to measure a person's interest in performing a variety of jobs. These applicants are testing their computer or keyboarding skills.

2. **Achievement tests**—Tests that measure the level of skill or knowledge an individual possesses in a certain area are called *achievement tests*. This skill or knowledge may have been acquired through various training activities or through experience in the area. Examples of skill tests are typing and keyboarding tests. As the "big data movement" progresses, companies are also relying on software that allows computers to process and evaluate job candidates' complex writing tasks and writing assignments.[23]

3. **Vocational interest tests**—Tests of vocational interest attempt to measure an individual's interest in performing various kinds of jobs. They are administered on the assumption that certain people perform jobs well because they find the job activities stimulating. The basic purpose of this type of test is to select for an open position the individual who finds most aspects of that position interesting.

4. **Personality tests**—Personality tests attempt to describe an individual's personality dimensions in areas such as emotional maturity, subjectivity, honesty, and objectivity. These tests can be used advantageously if the personality characteristics needed to do a particular job properly are well defined and if individuals possessing those characteristics can be identified and selected. Managers must be careful, however, not to expose themselves to legal prosecution by basing employment decisions on personality tests that are invalid and unreliable.[24]

Testing Guidelines   Several guidelines should be followed when tests are part of the selection process. First, care must be taken to ensure that the test being used is both valid and reliable. A test is *valid* if it measures what it is designed to measure; the test is *reliable* if it measures accurately time after time.[25] Second, test results should not be used as the sole basis of a hiring decision. People change over time, and someone who doesn't score well on a particular test might still develop into a productive employee. Factors such as potential and desire to obtain a position should be assessed subjectively and considered along with test scores in the final selection decision. Third, care should be taken to ensure that tests are nondiscriminatory; many tests contain language or cultural biases that may discriminate against minorities, and the EEOC has the authority to prosecute organizations that use discriminatory testing practices. Finally, employers should acknowledge that such tests may increase applicants' anxiety and cause them to worry about the potential effects of such testing.[26]

Assessment Centers

Another tool often used in employee selection is the assessment center. Although the assessment center concept is discussed in this chapter primarily as an aid to selection, this concept is also used in areas such as human resource training and organization development. AT&T is usually credited with first using an assessment center. Since AT&T's initial efforts, the assessment center concept has expanded greatly, and today it is used not only to identify individuals from outside the organization who should be hired but also to identify individuals from inside the organization who should be promoted. Corporations that have used assessment centers extensively include JCPenney, Standard Oil of Ohio, and IBM.[27]

An **assessment center** is a program (not a place) in which participants engage in, and are evaluated on, a number of individual and group exercises constructed to simulate important activities at the organizational levels to which they aspire.[28] These exercises can include activities such as participating in leaderless discussions, giving oral presentations, and leading a group in solving an assigned problem.[29] The individuals performing the activities are observed by managers or trained observers, who evaluate the individuals' abilities and potential. In general, participants are assessed according to job-related criteria such as oral communication, conflict resolution, leadership, persuasion, and problem solving.[30]

MyLab Management Watch It

If your instructor has assigned this activity, go to www.pearson.com/mylab/management to complete the video exercise.

Training

After recruitment and selection, the next step in providing appropriate human resources for the organization is training. **Training** is the process of developing qualities in human resources that will enable them to be more productive and thus contribute more to organizational goal attainment. The purpose of training is to increase the productivity of employees by influencing their behavior. **Table 12.1** provides an overview of the types of training being offered by organizations today.

12-4 An understanding of how the training process operates

The training of individuals is essentially a four-step process:

1. Determining training needs
2. Designing the training program
3. Administering the training program
4. Evaluating the training program

These steps are presented in **Figure 12.7** and are described in the sections that follow.

Determining Training Needs

The first step of the training process is determining the organization's training needs.[31] **Training needs** are the information or skill areas of an individual or group that require further development to increase the productivity of that individual or group. Only if training focuses on those needs can it be productive for the organization.

The training of organization members is typically a continuing activity. Even employees who have been with the organization for some time and who have undergone initial orientation and skills training need continued training to improve their skills.

Determining Needed Skills   Several methods are available for determining on which skills to focus with established human resources. One method calls for evaluating the production process within the organization. Factors such as excessive numbers of rejected products, unmet deadlines, and high labor costs are clues to deficiencies in production-related

TABLE 12.1   **Management Training Topics for Police within the Alabama Department of Public Safety**

Organization theory	Effective communication
Leadership	Hiring practices
Organizational goals	Training process
Media relations	Measuring productivity
Problem solving	Employee evaluations
Decision making	Discipline
Time management	Legal aspects of discipline and termination
Stress management	Motivation
Ethics and integrity	Contingency planning

Figure 12.7
Steps of the training process

expertise. Another method for determining training needs calls for getting direct feedback from employees on what they believe are the organization's training needs. Organization members are often able to verbalize clearly and accurately exactly what types of training they require to do a better job. A third way of determining training needs involves looking into the future. If the manufacture of new products or the use of newly purchased equipment is foreseen, some type of corresponding training almost certainly will be needed.

For example, South Coast Health System in New Bedford, Massachusetts, recently adopted a paperless system shortly after a round of layoffs. For the remaining IT employees to be able to use the new system, management at South Coast recognized that they would need additional training. As a result, the company made a significant investment in outside training programs.[32]

Designing the Training Program

Once training needs have been determined, a training program aimed at meeting those needs must be designed. Basically, designing a training program entails assembling various types of facts and activities that will meet the established training needs. Obviously, as training needs vary, so will the facts and activities designed to meet those needs.

Administering the Training Program

The next step in the training process is administering the training program—that is, actually training the individuals selected to participate in the program. Various techniques exist for both transmitting necessary information and developing needed skills in training programs, and several of these techniques are discussed in the pages that follow.

Techniques for Transmitting Information   Two techniques for transmitting information in training programs are lectures and programmed learning. Although it could be argued that these techniques develop skills in individuals as well as transmit information to them, they are primarily devices for the dissemination of information.

1. **Lectures**—Perhaps the most widely used technique for transmitting information in training programs is the lecture. The **lecture** is primarily a one-way communication situation in which an instructor orally presents information to a group of listeners. The instructor typically does most of the talking, and trainees participate primarily through listening and note taking.

   An advantage of the lecture is that it allows the instructor to expose trainees to a maximum amount of information within a given time period. The lecture, however, has some serious disadvantages:[33]

   The lecture generally consists of a one-way communication: The instructor presents information to a group of passive listeners. Thus, little or no opportunity exists to clarify meanings, to check on whether trainees really understand the lecture material, or to take into account the wide diversity of abilities, attitudes, and interests that may prevail among the trainees. Also, this format permits little or no opportunity for practice, reinforcement, knowledge of results, or overlearning. Ideally, the competent lecturer makes the material meaningful and intrinsically motivating to his or her listeners. However, whether most lecturers achieve this goal is a moot question. These limitations, in turn, impose further limitations on the lecture's actual content. A skillful lecturer may be fairly successful in transmitting conceptual knowledge to a group of trainees who are ready to receive it; however, all the evidence available indicates that the nature of the lecture situation makes the lecture of minimal value in promoting attitudinal or behavioral change.

2. **Programmed learning**—Another commonly used technique for transmitting information in training programs is called programmed learning. **Programmed learning** is a technique for instructing without the presence or intervention of a human instructor.[34] Small amounts of information that require responses are presented to individual trainees. The trainees determine, from comparing their responses to provided answers, whether their understanding of the information is accurate. The types of questions posed to trainees vary from situation to situation, but they are usually multiple choice, true/false, or fill in the blank.

With advances in technology, some training professionals are developing new forms of programmed learning. Selected employers, for example, are incorporating the use of virtual-world programs like Second Life into their training programs.[35]

Like the lecture method, programmed learning has both advantages and disadvantages. Among the advantages are that it can be computerized, and thus students can learn at their own pace, know immediately whether they are right or wrong, and participate actively in the learning process. The primary disadvantage of this method is that no one is present to answer a confused learner's questions.

Techniques for Developing Skills   Techniques for developing skills in training programs can be divided into two broad categories: on the job and classroom. Techniques for developing skills on the job, referred to as **on-the-job training**, reflect a blend of job-related knowledge and experience. These techniques include coaching, position rotation, and special project committees. *Coaching* is direct critiquing of how well an individual is performing a job.[36] *Position rotation* involves moving an individual from job to job to enable the person to gain an understanding of the organization as a whole. *Special project committees* are vehicles in which a particular task is assigned to an individual to furnish him or her with experience in a particular area.[37]

Classroom techniques for developing skills also reflect a blend of job-related knowledge and experience. The skills addressed through these techniques can range from technical, such as

---

STEPS FOR SUCCESS

Tips for Being an Effective Interviewer

To find the right people, organizations use interviews as a selection technique. Some suggestions for being an effective interviewer include:[38]

- Read over the candidate's résumé . It is important to be prepared for the interview, so reading the résumé ahead of time helps ensure a more productive interview.
- Be up front with the candidate. Let him or her know what is expected for the job, the hours, tight deadlines, or company benefits.
- Have a standard set of interview questions. To avoid treating some candidates unfairly, have a certain group of questions that are asked of every candidate.

- Pay attention to nonverbal behaviors and tone. A candidate who is late to the interview, is overly nervous, or doesn't make eye contact may not have the passion needed for the job.
- Involve other managers. Getting others' perspectives on a candidate facilitates choosing the right candidate the first time. A single interviewer might miss something important.
- Don't be too hasty. Interviewers should take their time in interviewing a number of candidates before making a job offer to one.

computer programming skills, to interpersonal, such as leadership skills. Specific classroom techniques aimed at developing skills include various types of management games and role-playing activities. The most common format of *management games* requires small groups of trainees to make and then evaluate various management decisions. The *role-playing format* typically involves acting out and then reflecting on some people-oriented problem that must be solved in the organization.

In contrast to the typical one-way communication of the lecturer, the skills instructor in the classroom encourages large amounts of discussion and interaction among trainees, develops an atmosphere in which trainees learn new behavior by carrying out various activities, clarifies related information, and facilitates learning by eliciting trainees' job-related knowledge and experiences in applying that knowledge. The difference between the instructional role in information dissemination and the instructional role in skill development is striking.[39]

Evaluating the Training Program

After the training program has been completed, management should evaluate its effectiveness.[40] Because training programs represent a considerable investment—costs include materials, trainer time, and production lost while employees are being trained rather than doing their jobs—a reasonable return is essential.

Basically, management should evaluate the training program to determine whether it met the needs for which it was designed. Answers to questions such as the following help determine the effectiveness of a training program:

1. Has the excessive rejection rate of products declined?
2. Are deadlines being met more regularly?
3. Are labor costs per unit produced decreasing?

If the answer to such questions is "yes," the training program can be judged as at least somewhat successful, although perhaps its effectiveness could be enhanced through certain selective changes. If the answer is "no," significant modification to the training program is warranted.

In a noteworthy survey of businesspeople, 50 percent of respondents thought their sales per year would be unaffected if training programs for experienced salespeople were halted.[41] Management needs to seek and scrutinize this kind of feedback to see whether present training programs should be discontinued, slightly modified, or drastically altered to make them more valuable to the organization. The results of the survey just mentioned indicate a need to make significant changes in sales training programs at the companies covered by the survey.

Performance Appraisal

12-5 A concept of what performance appraisals are and how they can best be conducted

Even after individuals have been recruited, hired, and trained, the task of making them maximally productive within the organization is not finished. The fourth step in the process of providing appropriate human resources for the organization is **performance appraisal**—the process of reviewing individuals' past productive activities to evaluate the contributions they have made toward attaining management system objectives. Like training, performance appraisal—which is also called *performance review* and *performance evaluation*—is a continuing activity that focuses on both established human resources within the organization and newcomers. Its main purpose is to furnish feedback to organization members about how they can become more productive and useful to the organization in its quest for quality.[42] **Table 12.2** describes several methods of performance appraisal.

TABLE 12.2 **Descriptions of Several Methods of Performance Appraisal**

Appraisal Method	Description
Rating scale	Individuals appraising performance use a form containing several employee qualities and characteristics to be evaluated (e.g., dependability, initiative, leadership). Each evaluated factor is rated on a continuum or scale ranging, for example, from 1 to 7.
Employee comparisons	Appraisers rank employees according to such factors as job performance and value to the organization. Only one employee can occupy a particular ranking. This method is also known as a "forced distribution" or "forced ranking" system.[43]
Free-form essay	Appraisers simply write down their impressions of employees in paragraph form.
Critical-form essay	Appraisers write down particularly good or bad events involving employees as these events occur. Records of all documented events for any one employee are used to evaluate that person's performance.

Why Use Performance Appraisals?

Most U.S. firms engage in some type of performance appraisal. Douglas McGregor has suggested the following three reasons for using performance appraisals:[44]

1. They provide systematic judgments to support salary increases, promotions, transfers, and sometimes demotions or terminations.
2. They are a means of telling subordinates how they are doing and of suggesting needed changes in behavior, attitudes, skills, or job knowledge; they let subordinates know where they stand with the boss.
3. They furnish a useful basis for the coaching and counseling of individuals by superiors.

Multisource Feedback

In some cases, performance appraisals include feedback from only employees' supervisors. In contrast, multisource feedback occurs when recipients receive feedback from subordinates, peers, supervisors, and/or external stakeholders such as customers and suppliers.[45] Receiving information from multiple sources prevents any bias (positive or negative) that may occur when only a supervisor provides feedback. Evidence indicates that approximately 90 percent of *Fortune* 500 companies use multisource feedback in performance appraisals.[46]

PRACTICAL CHALLENGE: POLITICIZED APPRAISALS

Is Organizational Politics a Fact of Life?

A study in South Africa investigated the political dimension of performance appraisals within a regional health-care system. Unsurprisingly, it was discovered that appraisals were, in some cases, politicized. After all, how many can honestly say that internal politics do not exist within their organization?

One of the first things discovered was the lack of personalized criteria in the process. There were numerous instances of appraisals being the result of manipulation. Another issue was that the appraisals had too clear a link with promotion prospects, increased salaries, and other rewards. There were no review mechanisms in place. This meant that issues related to bias, discrimination, favoritism, and other behaviors were not picked up unless the person being appraised made them public.

The creation of an independent appeals process was recommended in order to protect employees from unfair appraisals, protect the organization against claims of unfairness, and ensure that managers would conduct fair reviews in the first place.[47]

Handling Performance Appraisals

If performance appraisals are not handled properly, their benefits to the organization are minimal.[48] Several guidelines can assist management in increasing the appropriateness with which appraisals are conducted. The first guideline is that performance appraisals should focus on performance in the position that the individual holds and on the success with which the individual is attaining organizational objectives. Although conceptually separate, performance and objectives should be inseparable topics of discussion during performance appraisals. The second guideline is that appraisals should focus on how well the individual is doing the job, not on the evaluator's impression of the individual's work habits. In other words, the appraisal should be an objective analysis of the employee's performance rather than a subjective evaluation of the employee's work habits.

The third guideline is that the appraisal should be acceptable to both the evaluator and the subject—that is, both should agree that it has benefit for the organization and the worker. The fourth and last guideline is that performance appraisals should provide a foundation on which to improve individuals' productivity within the organization by making them better equipped to be productive.[49]

Potential Weaknesses of Performance Appraisals

To maximize the benefit of performance appraisals to the organization, managers must eliminate several potential weaknesses of the appraisal process, including the following pitfalls:[50]

1. Performance appraisals encourage employees to focus on short-term rewards rather than on issues that are important to the long-run success of the organization.
2. Individuals involved in performance appraisals view them as a reward–punishment process.
3. The emphasis of the performance appraisal is on completing paperwork rather than on critiquing the individual's performance.
4. Individuals being evaluated view the process as unfair or biased.
5. Subordinates react negatively when evaluators offer unfavorable comments.

To eliminate these potential weaknesses, supervisors and employees should regard the performance appraisal process as an opportunity to increase the value of the employee's contributions through constructive feedback rather than as a means of rewarding or punishing the employee through positive or negative comments. In addition, paperwork should be viewed only as an aid in providing this feedback, not as an end in itself. Also, care should be taken to make appraisal feedback as tactful and objective as possible to minimize negative reactions.

CHALLENGE CASE SUMMARY

In hiring new employees for an organization like Netflix, management must be careful to emphasize not just hiring workers but hiring the right workers. For Netflix, appropriate human resources are those people who will make valuable contributions to the attainment of the company's organizational objectives. In hiring associates, management should hire only those people who will best help the organization become successful. In finding the appropriate human resources, management at Netflix has to follow four basic steps: (1) recruitment, (2) selection, (3) training, and (4) performance appraisal.

Basically, recruitment entails the initial screening of individuals available to fill open positions at Netflix. For recruitment efforts to be successful, recruiters have to know the jobs they are trying to fill, where potential human resources can be located, and how the law influences recruiting efforts.

Recruiters could acquire an understanding of open positions at a company such as Netflix by performing a job analysis. This job analysis would force them to determine the job description of each open position—the activities of an engineer, programmer, or salesperson, for example—and the job specification of the position, including the type of individual who should be hired to fill that position. A successful recruitment effort at Netflix would also require recruiters to know where to find the available human resources to fill open positions at Netflix. These sources may be found both within Netflix and outside it.

To ensure that Netflix maintains its position as one of the best technology companies in the world, management must plan for obtaining the needed appropriate human resources along with the other needed resources such as equipment and computer hardware and software. To do this, management must keep current on the possibilities of filling positions from within by maintaining some type of human resource inventory. This inventory can help management coordinate information about the organizational histories and potentials of various Netflix employees as well as the relative abilities of various Netflix employees to fill the necessary openings. Some of the sources of potential human resources outside Netflix that management should be aware of are competitors' current employees, public and private employment agencies, the readership of industry-related publications, and various types of educational institutions.

Netflix management must also be aware of how the law influences its recruitment efforts. Basically, the law says that Netflix's recruitment practices cannot discriminate on the basis of race, color, religion, sex, or national origin. If recruitment practices at Netflix were found to be discriminatory, the company would be subject to prosecution by the Equal Employment Opportunity Commission.

After the initial screenings of potential human resources, Netflix will be faced with the task of selecting the individuals from those who have been screened to be hired. Two tools that Netflix could use to help in this selection process are testing and assessment centers.

For example, after screening potential employees for positions at Netflix, management could use aptitude tests, achievement tests, vocational interest tests, or personality tests to see whether any of the screened individuals have the qualities necessary to fill a specific job opening. In using these tests, however, management must make sure that the tests are both valid and reliable, that they are not the sole basis on which a selection decision is made, and that they are nondiscriminatory.

Netflix can also use assessment centers to simulate the tasks necessary to succeed at the jobs that need to be done. Individuals who perform well on these tasks will probably be more appropriate for the positions than those who perform poorly. The use of assessment centers might be particularly appropriate for evaluating applicants for sales positions. Simulating this job would probably give management an excellent idea of how prospective salespeople would actually interact with customers during sales presentations.

After hiring, Netflix must train the new employees—including those who simply transferred to new positions within the company—to be productive organization members. To conduct effective training, Netflix must determine training needs, design a corresponding training program, and administer and evaluate the training program.

Designing a training program requires Netflix to assemble facts and activities that address specific company training needs. These needs include information or skill areas that must be developed in Netflix employees to make them productive. After training needs at Netflix have been determined and programs have been designed to meet those needs, the programs must be administered. Administering training programs at Netflix might involve the lecture technique as well as the programmed learning technique to transmit the necessary information to trainees. To develop skills in trainees, Netflix could use on-the-job training methods such as coaching, position rotation, or special project committees. To develop skills in a classroom setting, Netflix could use instructional techniques such as role-playing activities. For example, salespeople could be asked to deal with customers who have various needs and budgets. These situations then could be analyzed from the viewpoint of how to improve salespeople–customer relationships.

Once a Netflix training program has been completed, it must be evaluated to determine whether it met the training need for which it was designed. Training programs aimed at teaching specific skills such as computer programming would be much easier to evaluate than training programs aimed at teaching interpersonal skills such as developing customer relations. Of course, the evaluation of any training program at Netflix should emphasize how to improve the program the next time it is implemented.

The last step of acquiring appropriate human resources at Netflix is performance appraisal, in which the contributions that Netflix employees make toward the attainment of management system objectives are evaluated. Because of Netflix's rapid growth, employees will have various levels of experience at Netflix. As such, the performance appraisal process at Netflix should focus on new as well as established employees.

It would be difficult to imagine a Netflix employee who would not benefit from a properly conducted performance appraisal. Such an appraisal would focus on activities on the job and the employee's effectiveness in accomplishing job objectives. Objective appraisals would provide Netflix employees with tactful, constructive criticism that should help them increase their productivity. Handled properly, Netflix's appraisals would not be rewards or punishments in themselves but rather opportunities to increase employees' value to the company. Objective analysis of performance in a company such as Netflix should help employees become more productive over time rather than function without guidance and perhaps proceed to the inevitable outcome of being fired. Overall, if these performance appraisal issues, as well as issues related to recruitment, selection, and training, are addressed at Netflix, management should be successful in providing appropriate human resources for the company.

MyLab Management Assessing Your Management Skill

If your instructor has assigned this activity, go to www.pearson.com/mylab/management to complete the exercise related to the Challenge Case.

DEVELOPING HUMAN RESOURCE MANAGEMENT SKILL

This section is specially designed to help you develop human resource management skills. An individual's human resource management skill is based on an understanding of the concepts and the ability to apply those concepts. The following activities will help to enhance your human resource management skills in various organizational situations.

Class Preparation and Personal Study

To help you prepare for class, perform the activities outlined in this section. Performing these activities will help you enhance your classroom performance significantly.

Reflecting on Target Skill

On page 287, this chapter opens by presenting a target management skill along with a list of related objectives outlining knowledge and understanding that you should aim to acquire related to that skill. Review this target skill and the list of objectives to make sure that you've acquired all pertinent information within the chapter. If you do not feel that you've reached a particular objective(s), study related chapter coverage until you do.

Know Key Terms

Understanding the following key terms is critical to your preparing for class. Define each of these terms. Refer to the page(s) referenced after a term to check your definition or to gain further insight regarding the term.

Know How Management Concepts Relate

This section comprises activities that will further sharpen your understanding of management concepts. Answer essay questions as completely as possible.

12-1 Describe the four steps in the human resource management process. In your opinion, which step is most important? Explain.

12-2 What are the relationships between job analysis, job description, and job specification?

12-3 Where might an organization look for employees or managers if its usual sources for high-caliber candidates provide no results?

MyLab Management
Personal Inventory Assessment

Go to www.pearson.com/mylab/management to complete the Personal Inventory Assessment related to this chapter.

PERSONAL INVENTORY ASSESSMENT

Management Skills Exercises

Learning activities in this section are aimed at helping you develop your human resource management skills.

MyLab Management
Discussion Questions

Go to www.pearson.com/mylab/management to complete the problems marked with this icon ✪.

✪ Cases

Netflix Revamps Its Human Resources

The Challenge Case "Netflix Revamps Its Human Resources" (p. 288) and its related Challenge Case Summary were written to help you understand the management concepts contained in this chapter. Answer the following discussion questions about the Challenge Case to better understand how managing human resources can be applied in a company such as Netflix.

12-4 How important to an organization such as Netflix is the hiring of talented employees? Explain.

12-5 Do you agree with Patty McCord's statement that the most important role for the managers at Netflix is to build a great team? Why or why not?

12-6 Based on the information in the Challenge Case, what do you think is the biggest challenge for Netflix management in successfully providing appropriate human resources for the organization? Explain.

Disney Uses Social Media to Recruit Employees

Read the case and answer the questions that follow. Studying this case will help you better understand how concepts related to recruiting can be applied in a company such as Disney.

The Walt Disney Company is approaching its 100-year anniversary in 2023, but the firm is operating its human resource function in a manner that is nothing like it did a century ago. The company employs nearly 200,000 individuals and has well over $50 billion in revenue. The firm's holdings include not only amusement parks but also movie and television show production companies; the ABC network; ESPN; and LucasFilms, creator of the *Star Wars* franchise.

Disney has stepped up its use of social media as a recruiting tool for the company. Using applications such as LinkedIn, YouTube, Twitter, Facebook, and Instagram, the organization is tapping into a labor market that just a decade ago did not exist the way it does today. According to Bruce Jones, senior programming director for the Disney Institute, for customers, "we create happiness," but when it comes to recruiting talent, the company is more specific. "At Disney," Jones said, "we are intentional about our recruiting; we hire candidates based on required skills and desired behaviors." And they are increasingly doing this through the use of social media.

It is more than simply posting "Help Wanted" on Facebook. The firm is thoughtful in its approach. "We have noticed a shift in the way companies are using social media for recruiting. It's a more strategic approach that leverages the visual nature of these platforms, creating an opportunity for candidates to obtain a clearer understanding of an organization's expectations and the qualifications for open positions up front . . . even before candidates have submitted their applications and set foot in the door."

As an example, Disney was looking for bus drivers to move guests to and from various Disney properties. On a variety of social media sites, the company used vivid graphics and short phrases to convey the need for quality drivers. One post included the silhouette of a bus with Epcot Center in the background. Above the illustration were the words, "It's not just about the destination," and then on the silhouette of the bus, "it's about the journey." It is important for Disney to craft carefully worded and graphically illustrated recruitment posts that will attract the best candidates. "The text, graphics, images, and videos," said Jones, "of the organization's social media posts should deliberately speak to the type of person who will be a 'best-fit' for an open position—and for the culture."

Followers of Disney on social media already have a connection to the company. They may admire Disney's movies or are guests at its parks. Regardless, the connection is there and these individuals want to engage with Disney on their phones, tablets, or computers. Some of them, at some point in their careers, may even want to work for Disney. Sending employment messages to these social media followers opens up recruiting doors for potential candidates. "Why is this important?" asked Jones. "Because, organizations not only want to find the best employees with the skills to do the job, they also want to create long-term value for the organization by finding those who most perfectly align with their organizational culture, values, and desired behaviors."

Being consistent across all social media platforms with a recruiting message is vital. The consistency of message ensures that users of social media understand the company's values and may even have a grasp of the culture, too. According to Jones, "This strategy will help the organization determine whether or not a candidate will be a great fit, and it will help the candidate determine if the organization is right for them."[51]

Questions

12-7 How important is social media in attracting qualified candidates for jobs? Explain.

12-8 If a company were to rely on social media exclusively as a recruiting tool, what challenges would it encounter? What would you recommend to overcome these challenges?

12-9 Based on what you just read, is Disney the kind of organization for which you would enjoy working? Why or why not?

Experiential Exercises

Determining Training Needs at Wal-Mart

Directions. Read the following scenario and then perform the listed activities. Your instructor may want you to perform the activities as an individual or within groups. Follow all of your instructor's directions carefully.

Wal-Mart and Dell recently reached an agreement to sell Dell computers in Wal-Mart stores. However, top executives at Wal-Mart and Dell are somewhat concerned because most of Wal-Mart's sales associates do not have any experience selling computers.

As such, Wal-Mart has contacted your group to help design the training program that will be used in all Wal-Mart locations. Specifically, the executives want you to determine the training needs, which is the first step in the training process. Your group should describe the process you would use to determine these training needs. Assume that Wal-Mart and Dell will give you the resources necessary to implement your process (i.e., access to employees, managers, etc.). Also, rely on your own experiences with purchasing and using personal computers to describe some of the training needs from a customer's perspective.

You and Your Career

The beginning of this chapter distinguished between appropriate and inappropriate human resources and implied that employees should focus on demonstrating how they contribute to the organization's goals. The previous section suggested that training can help employees improve their job skills. How might training influence whether your employer (or future employer) considers you an "appropriate" human resource? How might your view of the training process affect your performance as an employee?

Building Your Management Skills Portfolio

Your management skills portfolio is a collection of activities specially designed to demonstrate your management knowledge and skill. Be sure to save your work. Taking your printed portfolio to an employment interview could prove helpful.

The portfolio activity for this chapter is human resources at Java House. Study this information and complete the exercises that follow.

In 2017, the Abraaj Group, a Dubai-based private equity business, bought the Kenya-based Java House Group. Java House is the largest casual dining and food service chain across East Africa, with around 60 stores in Kenya, Uganda, and Rwanda. With 2,000 employees, Java House has three brands: the original Java House (coffee-based all-day dining), Planet Yogurt (a self-service yogurt chain), and 360 Degrees Artisan Pizza (an upmarket pizzeria).

Abraaj aims to expand the chains across the whole of sub-Saharan Africa to take advantage of the growing middle class in this region. Abraaj's managing director, Mustafa Abdel-Wadood, has asked you for help in growing the brand.

Use the knowledge you have developed in this chapter to answer the following questions.

12-10 If the company were to add new outlets to the group, what recruitment strategies should the chain use to find applicants (managers, cooks, and servers)?

12-11 Once appropriate applicants are found for the new locations, what selection procedures should the company use? Be specific.

12-12 How will the hired candidates be trained? What is the best way to train these new associates?

12-13 Describe how each employee should have their performance appraised. What performance appraisal system is best?

MyLab Management
Writing Assignments

If your instructor has assigned this activity, go to www.pearson.com/mylab/management for the following assisted-graded writing assignments:

Assisted-Grading Questions

12-14 Review and describe the different types of tests that organizations might use in the selection process.

12-15 What are performance appraisals, and why are they important? Use an example from your life to illustrate either an effective or an ineffective performance appraisal.

Endnotes

1. This case was based on Patty McCord, "How Netflix Reinvented HR," *Harvard Business Review* 92 (January/February 2014): 70–76.
2. To see how the performance of these steps can be shared in an organization, see Brenda Paik Sunoo, "Growing without an HR Department," *Workforce* 77, no. 1 (January 1998): 16–17. For a look at job descriptions, see Jeff Archer, "New Job Description?," *Education Week* 22 (2003): 18. For another view, see Man-Ki Yoon, Chang-Gun Lee, and Junghee Han, "Migrating from Per-Job Analysis to Per-Resource Analysis for Tighter Bounds of End-to-End Response Times," *IEEE Transactions on Computers* 59, no. 7 (July 2010): 933–942.

3. As an example, research suggests that, compared to men, women prefer to work in smaller organizations. For a detailed study of this effect, see K. J. Hanek, S. M. Garcia, and A. Tor, "Gender and Competitive Preferences: The Role of Competition Size," *Journal of Applied Psychology* 101: 1122–1133.

4. For a look at job descriptions, see Jeff Archer, "New Job Description?," *Education Week* 22 (2003): 18. For another view, see Man-Ki Yoon, Chang-Gun Lee, and Junghee Han, "Migrating from Per-Job analysis to Per-Resource Analysis for Tighter Bounds of End-to-End Response Times."

5. Bruce Shawkey, "Job Descriptions," *Credit Union Executive* 29 (Winter 1989–1990): 20–23; Howard D. Feldman, "Why Are Similar Managerial Jobs So Different?," *Review of Business* 11 (Winter 1989): 15–22.

6. "Job Analysis," *Bureau of Intergovernmental Personnel Programs* (December 1973): 135–152. For a better understanding of how internships help applicants learn about a job, see H. Zhao and R. C. Liden, "Internship: A Recruitment and Selection Perspective," *Journal of Applied Psychology* 96, no. 1 (2011): 221–229. For an excellent review of research on employee recruitment, see J. A. Breaugh, "Employee Recruitment," *Annual Review of Psychology* 64 (2013): 389–416.

7. Bob Gatewood, Hubert Feild, and Murray Barrick, *Human Resource Selection* (Mason, OH: South-Western Cengage Learning, 2010), 307–332. To better understand how potential employees view the recruitment process, see H. J. Walker, T. N. Bauer, M. S. Cole, J. B. Bernerth, H. S. Feild, and J. C. Short, "Is This How I Will Be Treated? Reducing Uncertainty through Recruitment Interactions," *Academy of Management Journal* 56 (2013): 1325–1347.

8. Fred K. Foulkes, "How Top Nonunion Companies Manage Employees," *Harvard Business Review* (September/October 1981): 90.

9. Walter S. Wikstrom, "Developing Managerial Competence: Concepts, Emerging Practices," *Studies in Personnel Policy* (National Industrial Conference Board), no. 189 (1964): 95–105.

10. Robert Kleinsorge, "Expanding the Role of Succession Planning," *T + D* 64, no. 4 (April 2010): 66–69.

11. K. Kearsley, "Firm Shares Tips for Succession Planning," *Wall Street Journal*, January 24, 2014, http://online.wsj.com/news/articles/SB10001424052702303947904579340522630841530, accessed February 15, 2014.

12. Patricia Panchak, "Resourceful Software Boosts HR Efficiency," *Modern Office Technology* 35 (April 1990): 76–80.

13. Joann S. Lublin, "'Pink Quotas' Alter Europe's Boards," *Wall Street Journal*, September 11, 2012, http://online.wsj.com; European Parliament, "Women on Company Boards: Go for 40% of Non-Executive Posts by 2020, Urge MEPs," news release, October 14, 2013, http://www.europarl.europa.eu; Stephanie Bodoni, "EU Plan for 40 Percent Quota of Women on Boards Gets Win," *Bloomberg News*, November 20, 2013, http://www.bloomberg.com.

14. James Temple, "Alliance to Boost Startups, Hire More Grads," SFGate.com, February 24, 2010, http://articles.sfgate.com.

15. For an overview of the EEOC guidelines, see "Facts about Discrimination in Federal Government Employment Based on Marital Status, Political Affiliation, Status as a Parent, Sexual Orientation, or Transgender (Gender Identity) Status," http://www.eeoc.gov/federal/otherprotections.cfm, accessed February 20, 2014.

16. For issues regarding affirmative action, see Glenn Cook, "A Victory for Affirmative Action," *American School Board Journal* 190 (2003): 7. For more information regarding the potential legal issues associated with discrimination, see Richard A. Posthuma, Mark V. Roehling, and Michael A. Campion, "Applying U.S. Employment Discrimination Laws to International Employers: Advice for Scientists and Practitioners," *Personnel Psychology* 59, no. 3 (2006): 705–739. For a history of employment discrimination, including affirmative action, see Walter Vertreace, "Equal Employment Opportunity: Mission Accomplished, or Dream Deferred?," *Black Collegian* 40, no. 2 (January 2010): 57–60.

17. Ray H. Hodges, "Developing an Effective Affirmative Action Program," *Journal of Intergroup Relations* 5 (November 1976): 13. For a discussion of EEOC operations, see Ellen Rettig, "EEOC Gets Tough with Employers," *Indianapolis Business Journal* 20, no. 46 (January 24, 2000): 1.

18. R. Roosevelt Thomas, Jr., "From Affirmative Action to Affirming Diversity," *Harvard Business Review* 68 (March/April 1990): 107–117.

19. For a different view of generational differences among those entering the workforce, see Jean M. Twenge, Stacy M. Campbell, Brian J. Hoffman, and Charles E. Lance, "Generational Differences in Work Values: Leisure and Extrinsic Values Increasing, Social and Intrinsic Values Decreasing," *Journal of Management*, March 1, 2010, http://jom.sagepub.com.

20. For an extensive overview of research on selection, see A. M. Ryan and R. E. Ployhart, "A Century of Selection," *Annual Review of Psychology* 65 (2014): 693–717. To better understand the importance of structured interviews, see E. E. Kausel, S. S. Culbertson, and H. P. Madrid, "Overconfidence in Personnel Selection: When and Why Unstructured Interview Information Can Hurt Hiring Decisions," *Organizational Behavior and Human Decision Processes*, 137 (2016): 27–44.

21. This section is based on Andrew F. Sikula, *Personnel Administration and Human Resource Management* (New York: Wiley, 1976), 188–190. For an interesting article on how interviewers try to manage impressions in the interview process, see B. W. Swider, M. R. Barrick, and T. B. Harris, "Initial Impressions: What They Are, What They Are Not, and How They Influence Structured Interview Outcomes," *Journal of Applied Psychology* 101 (2016): 625–638.

22. For an example of an aptitude test for accident proneness, see Hiroshi Matsuoka, "Development of a Short Test for Accident Proneness," *Perceptual and Motor Skills* 85, no. 3 (December 1997): 903–906.

23. M. C. Campion, M. A. Campion, E. D. Campion, and M. H. Reider, "Initial Investigation into Computer Scoring of Candidate Essays for Personnel Selection," *Journal of Applied Psychology* 101 (2016): 958–975.

24. Daniel P. O'Meara, "Personality Tests Raise Questions of Legality and Effectiveness," *HR Magazine* (January 1994): 97–100. See also Joyce Hogan, Paul Barrett, and Robert Hogan, "Personality Measurement, Faking, and Employment Selection," *Journal of Applied Psychology* 92, no. 5 (2007): 1270–1285.

25. Clive Fletcher, "Testing the Accuracy of Psychometric Measures," *People Management* 3, no. 21 (October 23, 1997): 64–66.

26. Julie McCarthy, Coreen Hrabluik, and R. Blake Jelley, "Progression Through the Ranks: Assessing Employee Reactions to High-Stakes Employment Testing," *Personnel Psychology* 62 (2009): 793–832.

27. David Littlefield, "Menu for Change at Novotel," *People Management* (January 26, 1995): 34–36; Susan O. Hendricks and Susan E. Ogborn, "Supervisory and Managerial Assessment Centers in Health Care," *Health Care Supervisor* 8 (April 1990): 65–75.

28. Barry M. Cohen, "Assessment Centers," *Supervisory Management* (June 1975): 30. See also D. J. R. Jackson, G. Michaelides, and C. Dewberry, "Everything That You Have Ever Been Told about Assessment Center Ratings Is Confounded," *Journal of Applied Psychology* 101 (2016): 976–994.

29. To examine the possible impact on inmates of assessment centers, see Ralph Fretz, "New Jersey's Assessment Centers Helping Inmates Take the Final Step toward Release," *Corrections Today* 64 (2002): 78.

30. A. M. Gibbons and D. E. Rupp, "Dimension Consistency as an Individual Difference: A New (Old) Perspective on the Assessment Center Construct Validity Debate," *Journal of Management* 35 (2009): 1154–1180.

31. William Umiker and Thomas Conlin, "Assessing the Need for Supervisory Training: Use of Performance Appraisals," *Health Care Supervisor* 8 (January 1990): 40–45.

32. Jim Schakenbach, "Employee Training Programs Show Signs of Improvement," *Mass High Tech*, January 6, 2010, http://www.masshightech.com.

33. Bass and Vaughn, *Training in Industry*. For discussion on using technology to improve lecture effectiveness, see "Switches Offer Classroom Control," *Computer Dealer News* 14, no. 17 (May 4, 1998).

34. David Sutton, "Further Thoughts on Action Learning," *Journal of European Industrial Training* 13 (1989): 32–35. For additional information regarding the relationship between training and learning, see Andrew Neal, Stuart T. Godley, Terry Kirkpatrick, and Graham Dewsnap, "An Examination of Learning Processes during Critical Incident Training: Implications for the Development of Adaptable Trainees," *Journal of Applied Psychology* 91, no. 6 (2007): 1276–1291.

35. Garry Kranz, "It's 'Game On' for Training in Virtual Worlds," *Workforce Management* (May 2010): 4.

36. Anne Fisher, "Don't Blow Your New Job," *Fortune* (June 22, 1998): 159–162.

37. For an example of how training improves the effectiveness of consultants, see F. Lievens and J. I. Sanchez, "Can Training Improve the Quality of Inferences Made by Raters in Competency Modeling? A Quasi-Experiment," *Journal of Applied Psychology* 92, no. 3 (2007): 812–819.

38. Theresa Hegel, "How Can I Conduct a Foolproof Job Interview?," *Wearables* 103, no. 5 (September/October 2015): 9.

39. Samuel C. Certo, "The Experiential Exercise Situation: A Comment on Instructional Role and Pedagogy Evaluation," *Academy of Management Review* (July 1976): 113–116.

40. "Training Program's Results Measured in Unique Way," *Supervision* (February 1992): 18–19.

41. William Keenan, Jr., "Are You Overspending on Training?," *Sales and Marketing Management* 142 (January 1990): 56–60.

42. For a review of the literature linking performance appraisal and training needs, see Glenn Herbert and Dennis Doverspike, "Performance Appraisal in the Training Needs Analysis Process: A Review and Critique," *Public Personnel Management* (Fall 1990): 253–270. For a comprehensive review of research on performance appraisals, see A. DeNisi and C. E. Smith, "Performance Appraisal, Performance Management, and Firm-Level Performance: A Review, a Proposed Model, and New Directions for Future Research," *The Academy of Management Annals* 8, no. 1 (2014): 127–179.

43. A "forced distribution" or "forced ranking" rating system was put in place at General Electric years ago, and its value has been the subject of some debate ever since. For the findings of a study of employees' reactions to this methodology, see Deidra J. Schleicher, "Rater Reactions to Forced Distribution Rating Systems," *Journal of Management* 35, no. 4 (August 1, 2009): 899–927.

44. D. McGregor, "An Uneasy Look at Performance Appraisal," *Harvard Business Review* (September/October 1972): 133–134. For an interesting look at gender differences in the context of performance appraisals, see D. Motro and A. P. J. Ellis, "Boys, Don't Cry: Gender and Reactions to Negative Performance Feedback," *Journal of Applied Psychology* 102 (2017): 227–235.

45. K. Y. Kim, L. Atwater, P. C. Patel, and J. W. Smither, "Multisource Feedback, Human Capital, and the Financial Performance of O\organizations," *Journal of Applied Psychology* 101 (2016): 1569–1584.

46. T. Maylett, "360-Degree Feedback Revisited: The Transition from Development to Appraisal," *Compensation and Benefits Review* 41 (2009): 52–59.

47. Sonia Swanepoel, Petrus A. Botha, and Nancy B. Mangonyane, "Politicisation of Performance Appraisals," *SA Journal of Human Resource Management* 12, no. 1 (2014), http://www.sajhrm.co.za/index.php/sajhrm/article/view/525/.

48. For information regarding the role of documentation in handling performance appraisals, see Brian Crawford, "Performance Appraisals: The Importance of Documentation," *Fire Engineering* 156 (2003): 100.

49. Linda J. Segall, "KISS Appraisal Woes Goodbye," *Supervisory Management* 34 (December 1989): 23–28. For an example of how appraisal systems work for nonprofits (in this case, a police department), see Victor M. Catano, Wendy Darr, and Catherine A. Campbell, "Performance Appraisal of Behavior-Based Competencies: A Reliable and Valid Procedure," *Personnel Psychology* 60, no. 1 (2006): 201–230.

50. Robert M. Gerst, "Assessing Organizational Performance," *Quality Progress* (February 1995): 85–88. For a better understanding of how employee turnover influences organizational performance, see J. I. Hancock, D. G. Allen, F. A. Bosco, K. R. McDaniel, and C. A. Pierce, "Meta-Analytic Review of Employee Turnover as a Predictor of Firm Performance," *Journal of Management* 39 (2013): 573–603.

51. Bruce Jones, "How Strategic Is Your Social Media Recruiting? Why You Should D'Think It" (July 8, 2014); https://disneyinstitute.com/blog/2014/07/how-strategic-is-your-social-media-recruiting-why-you-should-dthink-it/279/.

Changing Organizations: Stress, Conflict, and Virtuality

13

TARGET SKILL

 Organizational Change Skill: the ability to modify an organization in order to enhance its contribution to reaching company goals

ORGANIZATIONAL CHANGE SKILL AND YOUR CAREER

Organizational change skill can be of great value to you in enhancing your management career. For example, this skill can help you improve an organization to be more effective and efficient in reaching organizational goals. Improving organizations in this way contributes to organizational success, builds your image as a competent manager, makes you valuable to your organization, and supports promotions as you build your career.

OBJECTIVES

To help build my *organizational change skill*, when studying this chapter, I will attempt to acquire:

13-1 Fundamental principles of *changing an organization*

13-2 Insights about factors to consider when changing an organization

13-3 An appreciation for the relationship between change and stress

13-4 Insights concerning how to handle conflict as a factor related to organizational change

13-5 Knowledge about virtuality as a vehicle for organizational change

---

MyLab Management Chapter Warm Up

If your instructor has assigned this activity, go to www.pearson.com/mylab/management to complete the chapter warm up.

How Huntington Hospital Introduced Electronic Health Records

Huntington Memorial Hospital, a 635-bed hospital located in Pasadena, California, has a mission expressed by the phrase "right care, right place, right time." Fulfilling that mission requires highly qualified professionals with access to the most up-to-date and accurate information on patients and treatment options. Huntington's management realized that the traditional paper-based approach to record keeping did not adequately support that mission.

Management thus determined that it was time to begin the switch to electronic health records. Such records could make health information easily available to the hospital's professionals at the point of care, whether that was a doctor's office or a patient's bedside. It could help physicians manage the increasing complexity of their work. Patient outcomes could improve, assuming the electronic records would give doctors faster access to lab results, imaging studies, and other documents.

Despite these advantages, the changeover from paper to electronic records can be a trying experience. Perhaps the highest hurdle is getting the professional staff members to adopt new ways of carrying out their work. Busy doctors, nurses, and therapists may not appreciate the added time required to learn a computer system. Working on a computer may feel especially awkward for those who have many years of experience using paper records.

Huntington's administrators tackled the challenge by engaging the doctors in the change process. They started by conducting a survey of the physicians to learn how they handled record keeping, what value they placed on existing technologies, and what challenges they faced with keeping records. Based on that feedback, the hospital determined that electronic medical records could offer physicians the most and the fastest advantages in the area of electronic prescription data. To choose a software vendor, Huntington invited doctors to participate in a "click-off" event in which they counted how many mouse clicks they needed to complete various tasks. This event helped Huntington select a program that the doctors would be most comfortable using while also engaging them in the change process.

Huntington contracted with a software company called Allscripts to develop its electronic health records system, which it named Huntington Health eConnect. The

Staff at Huntington Memorial Hospital keep and access electronic health records to fulfill the hospital's mission, "right care, right place, right time."

software is offered first to interested physicians in their practices as a pilot program. By starting first with the e-prescribing application, an application doctors can use to prescribe medicine to patients, the hospital eases the doctors into the use of computer technology. As each program gets up and running, it is expanded to other physicians.

One group of physicians that has embraced the program is the Huntington Medical Foundation (HMF), which brings together 60 physicians affiliated with Huntington Hospital. HMF was an early adopter of electronic medical records and uses the system to track physicians' prescriptions, keep up with tests and procedures ordered, and transmit information to the hospital emergency room or to the specialists the patient is consulting. HMF's chief executive officer credits the system for helping doctors reduce medication errors and improve patient care.[1]

THE ORGANIZATIONAL CHANGE CHALLENGE

The Challenge Case illustrates the organizational change challenges that Huntington administrators must meet. Huntington administrators must constantly assess the condition of their organization and make appropriate organizational changes that enhance goal attainment. Recent changes at Huntington have focused on transitioning away from

Mckyartstudio/Shutterstock

paper-based record keeping. Huntington administrators know, however, that the company will need to institute other types of changes in the future in order to maintain the company's competitiveness. Managers who are faced with meeting organizational change challenges, such as those at Huntington, would find the major topics in this chapter useful and practical. These topics are (1) fundamentals of changing an organization, (2) factors to consider when changing an organization, (3) change and stress, (4) change and conflict, and (5) virtuality.

Fundamentals of Changing an Organization

Thus far, the discussion in this "Organizing" section of the text has centered on the fundamentals of organizing; on authority, delegation, and responsibility; and on furnishing appropriate human resources for the organization. This chapter focuses on changing the organization.

13-1 Fundamental principles of *changing an organization*

Defining Changing an Organization

Changing an organization is the process of modifying an existing organization to increase organizational effectiveness—that is, the extent to which an organization accomplishes its objectives. These modifications can involve virtually any organizational segment, but they typically affect the lines of organizational authority, the levels of responsibility held by various organization members, and the established lines of organizational communication. Driven by proactivity to build more effective and efficient organizations, almost all modern organizations are changing in some way.[2]

The Importance of Change   Most managers agree that if an organization is to thrive, it must change continually in response to significant developments in the environment, such as changing customer needs, technological breakthroughs, and new government regulations. The study of organizational change is extremely important because managers at all organizational levels are faced throughout their careers with the task of changing their organizations. Managers who can determine appropriate changes and then implement such changes successfully enable their organizations to be more flexible and innovative.[3] Because change is such a fundamental part of organizational existence, those managers are valuable to organizations of all kinds.[4]

Many managers consider change to be so critical to organizational success that they encourage employees to search continually for areas in which beneficial changes can be made. To take a classic example, General Motors has traditionally provided employees with a "think list" to encourage them to develop ideas for organizational change and to remind them that change is vital to the continued success of GM. The think list contains the following questions:[5]

1. Can a machine be used to do a better or faster job?
2. Can the fixture now in use be improved?
3. Can handling of materials for the machine be improved?
4. Can a special tool be used to combine the operations?
5. Can the quality of the part being produced be improved by changing the sequence of the operation?
6. Can the material used be cut or trimmed differently for greater economy or efficiency?
7. Can the operation be made safer?
8. Can paperwork regarding this job be eliminated?
9. Can established procedures be simplified?

The recent changes at GM—brought about by its financial collapse, bankruptcy filing, and subsequent bailout by the U.S. government—demonstrate that organizations sometimes need to take radical steps to restructure, or "reengineer," their operations in order to stay in business.[6]

Figure 13.1
Adaptation, stability, and
organizational survival

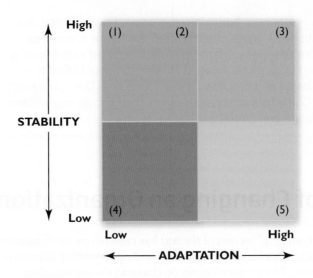

(1) High death probability
(slow)
(2) High survival probability
(3) High survival and growth
probability
(4) Certainty of death (quick)
(5) Certainty of death (quick)

Change versus Stability

In addition to organizational change, some degree of stability is a prerequisite for long-term organizational success. **Figure 13.1** presents a model developed by Hellriegel and Slocum that shows the relative importance of change and stability to organizational survival. Although these authors use the word *adaptation* in their model rather than *change*, the two terms are essentially synonymous.

The model stresses that organizational survival and growth are most probable when both stability and adaptation are high within the organization (number 3 on the model depicted in Figure 13.1). The organization without enough stability to complement change is at a definite disadvantage. When stability is low, the probability of organizational survival and growth declines. Change after change without regard for the essential role of stability typically results in confusion and employee stress.[7]

Factors to Consider When Changing an Organization

13-2 Insights about factors to consider when changing an organization

How managers deal with the major factors that need to be considered when an organizational change is being made will largely determine the success of that change. The following factors should be considered whenever change is being contemplated: (1) the change agent, (2) determining what should be changed, (3) the kind of change to make, (4) individuals affected by the change, and (5) evaluation of the change. Although the following sections discuss each of these factors individually, **Figure 13.2** makes the point that the collective influence of these factors' ultimately determines the success of a change.[8]

The Change Agent

Perhaps the most important factor that managers need to consider when changing an organization is who will be the **change agent**—the individual inside or outside the organization who tries to modify the existing organizational situation.[9] The change agent might be a self-designated manager within the organization or an outside consultant hired because of special expertise in a particular area. This individual might be responsible for making broad changes, such as altering the culture of the whole organization, or more narrow changes, such as designing and implementing a new safety program or a new quality program.[10] Although in some circumstances the change agent will not be a manager, the terms *manager* and *change agent* are used synonymously throughout this chapter.

Special skills are necessary to be successful as a change agent. Among them are the ability to determine how a change should be made, the skill to solve change-related problems, and the experience of using behavioral science tools to influence people appropriately during the change

Figure 13.2

The collective influence of five major factors on the success of changing an organization

process.[11] Perhaps the most overlooked skill of successful change agents, however, is the ability to determine how much change employees can withstand.[12]

Managers should choose as change agents those employees who have the most expertise in all of these areas. A potentially beneficial change might not result in any advantages for the organization if a person without expertise in these areas is designated as the change agent.

Determining What Should Be Changed

Another major factor managers need to consider is exactly what should be changed within the organization. In general, managers should make only those changes that will increase organizational effectiveness.

It has been generally accepted for many years that organizational effectiveness depends primarily on activities centering around three classes of factors:

1. People
2. Structure
3. Technology

People factors are attitudes, leadership skills, communication skills, and all other characteristics of the human resources within the organization; **structural factors** are organizational controls, such as policies and procedures; and **technological factors** are types of equipment or processes that assist organization members in the performance of their jobs.

For an organization to maximize its effectiveness, the appropriate people must be matched with the appropriate technology and the appropriate structure. Thus, people factors, technological factors, and structural factors are not independent determinants of organizational effectiveness. Instead, as **Figure 13.3** shows, organizational effectiveness is determined by the relationship among these three factors.

As an example of technological change, consider the situation faced by University Health System in San Antonio, Texas. The organization needed a data technology system that would allow clinical staff members to operate more efficiently. Previously, staff members at its University Hospital and 20 off-site clinics had to input critical temperature data for refrigerated medications manually. With 172 cold-storage facilities in the hospital alone, this hourly recording was not only subject to human error but also took valuable time away from patient care. By upgrading the organization's technology with special health-care software, University Health System was able to automate this process and many others, streamlining staff operations.[13]

The Kind of Change to Make

The kind of change to make is the third major factor that managers need to consider when they set out to change an organization. Most changes can be categorized as technological, structural, or people. Note that these three kinds of change correspond to the three main determinants of organizational effectiveness—each change is named for the determinant it emphasizes.

Figure 13.3
Determination of organizational effectiveness by the relationship among people, technological, and structural factors

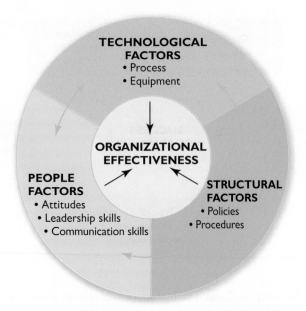

For example, **technological change** emphasizes modifying the level of technology in the management system. Because this kind of change so often involves outside experts and highly technical language, it is more profitable to discuss structural change and people change in detail in this text.

Structural Change

Structural change emphasizes increasing organizational effectiveness by changing the controls that influence organization members during the performance of their jobs. The following section further describes this approach and provides managers with insights regarding how to deal with structural change issues.

Describing Structural Change

Structural change is change aimed at increasing organizational effectiveness through modifications to the existing organizational structure. These modifications can take several forms:

1. Clarifying and defining jobs
2. Modifying organizational structure to fit the communication needs of the organization
3. Decentralizing the organization to reduce the cost of coordination, increase the controllability of subunits, increase motivation, and gain greater flexibility

Although structural change must take into account people and technology in order to be successful, its primary focus is obviously on changing organizational structure. In general, managers should choose to make structural changes within an organization if the information they have gathered indicates that the present structure is the main cause of organizational ineffectiveness. The precise structural changes they choose to make will vary from situation to situation, of course. After changes to organizational structure have been made, management should conduct periodic reviews to make sure the changes are accomplishing their intended purposes.[14]

People Change

Although successfully changing people factors necessarily involves some consideration of structure and technology, the primary emphasis is on people. The following sections discuss people change and examine grid organization development, one commonly used means of changing organization members.

Describing People Change: Organization Development (OD)

People change emphasizes increasing organizational effectiveness by changing certain characteristics of organization members such as their attitudes and leadership skills. In general, managers should attempt to make this kind of change when human resources are shown to be the main cause of organizational ineffectiveness.

The process of people change can be referred to as **organization development (OD)**. Although OD focuses mainly on changing certain aspects of people, these changes are based on an overview of structure, technology, and all other organizational components.

Grid OD   One traditionally used OD technique for changing people in organizations is called **grid organization development (grid OD)**.[15] The **managerial grid**, a theoretical model describing various managerial styles, is used as the foundation for grid OD. The managerial grid is based on the premise that various managerial styles can be described by means of two primary attitudes of the manager: concern for people and concern for production. Within this model, each attitude is placed on an axis, which is scaled 1 through 9 and is used to generate five managerial styles. **Figure 13.4** shows the managerial grid, its five managerial styles, and the factors that characterize each of these styles.

THE IDEAL STYLE

The central theme of this managerial grid is that 9,9 management (as shown on the grid in Figure 13.4) is the ideal managerial style. Managers using this style have a high concern for both people and production. Managers using any other style have lesser degrees of concern for people or production and are thought to reduce organizational success accordingly. The purpose of grid OD is to change the thinking of organization managers so that they will adopt the 9,9 management style.

MAIN TRAINING PHASES

How is a grid OD program conducted? The program has six main training phases that are used with all managers within the organization. The first two phases focus on acquainting managers with the managerial grid concept and assisting them in determining which managerial style they most commonly use. The last four phases of the grid OD program concentrate on encouraging managers to adopt the 9,9 management style and showing them how to use this style

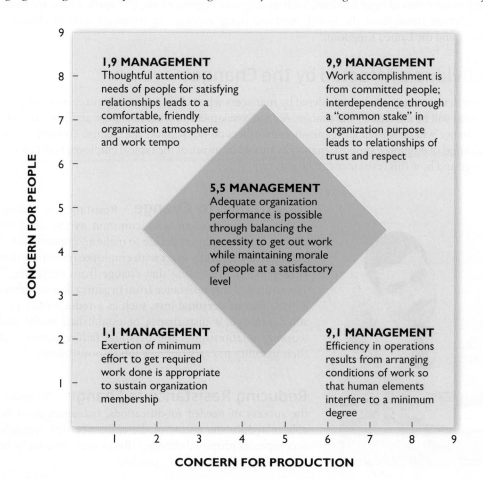

Figure 13.4
The managerial grid

within their specific job situations. Emphasis throughout the program is on developing team-work within the organization.

Some evidence suggests that grid OD is effective in enhancing profit, positively changing managerial behavior, and positively influencing managerial attitudes and values.[16] However, grid OD will have to undergo more rigorous testing for an extended period of time before conclusive statements can be made about it.

The Status of Organization Development   If the entire OD area is taken into consideration, changes that emphasize both people and the organization as a whole seem to have inherent strength. However, several commonly voiced weaknesses of OD efforts include the following:[17]

1. The effectiveness of an OD program is difficult to evaluate.
2. OD programs are generally too time-consuming.
3. OD objectives are commonly too vague.
4. The total costs of an OD program are difficult to gauge at the time the program starts.
5. OD programs are generally too expensive.

These weaknesses should not eliminate OD from consideration but should instead indicate areas to perfect within it. Managers can improve the quality of their OD efforts by doing the following:[18]

1. Systematically tailoring OD programs to meet the specific needs of the organization
2. Continually demonstrating exactly how people should change their behavior
3. Conscientiously changing organizational reward systems so that organization members who change their behavior in ways suggested by the OD program are rewarded

Managers have been employing OD techniques for several decades, and broad and useful applications of these techniques continue to be documented in more recent management literature.[19] OD techniques are currently being applied not only to business organizations but also to many other types of organizations, such as religious organizations. OD applications are being documented throughout the world, with use being reported in countries such as Hungary, Poland, and the United Kingdom.[20]

Individuals Affected by the Change

A fourth major factor to be considered by managers when changing an organization is the people who will be affected by the change. A good assessment of what to change and how to make the change will be wasted if organization members do not support the change. To increase the likelihood of employee support, managers should be aware of the typical employee resistance to change and how this resistance can be reduced.

Fear often causes employees to resist change.

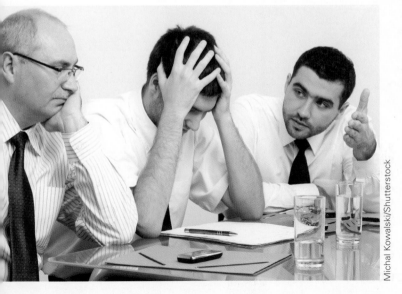

Michal Kowalski/Shutterstock

Resistance to Change   Resistance to change within an organization is as common as the need for change. After managers decide to make an organizational change, they typically meet with employee resistance that is targeted at preventing that change from occurring.[21] The source of this resistance from organization members is their fear of personal loss, such as a reduction in personal prestige, a disturbance of established social and working relationships, and personal failure because of their inability to carry out new job responsibilities.[22]

Reducing Resistance to Change   To ensure the success of needed modifications, managers must be able to reduce the effects of the resistance that typically accompanies proposed change.[23] Resistance can usually be reduced by following these guidelines:[24]

1. **Avoid surprises**—People need time to evaluate a proposed change before management implements that change. Unless they are given time to evaluate and understand how the change will affect them, employees are likely to be automatically opposed to it. Whenever possible, therefore, individuals who will be affected by a change should be informed of the kind of change being considered and the probability that it will be adopted.

2. **Promote genuine understanding**—When fear of personal loss related to a proposed change is reduced, opposition to the change is also reduced. Most managers find ensuring that organization members thoroughly understand a proposed change is a major step in reducing this fear. Understanding may even generate enthusiastic support for the change if such understanding leads employees to focus on the individual gains that could materialize as a result of the change. People should be given information that will help them answer the following change-related questions they invariably will have:

   - Will I lose my job?
   - Will my old skills become obsolete?
   - Am I capable of producing effectively under the new system?
   - Will my power and prestige decline?
   - Will I be given more responsibility than I care to assume?
   - Will I have to work longer hours?
   - Will it force me to betray or desert my good friends?

3. **Set the stage for change**—Perhaps the most powerful tool for reducing resistance to change is management's positive attitude toward the change. This attitude should be displayed openly by top and middle management as well as by lower management. In essence, management should convey that change is one of the basic prerequisites for a successful organization. Management should also strive to encourage change for increasing organizational effectiveness rather than for the sake of trying something new.

   Storytelling—the sharing of anecdotes or personal narratives to create emotional connections among work groups—is a useful communication technique that can help set the stage for organizational change. By breaking down barriers and resistance to change, storytelling also enables management to honor organizational traditions of the past and helps employees accept new ways of doing things.[25]

   To encourage employees to have a positive attitude toward change, some portion of organizational rewards should be earmarked for those organization members who are most instrumental in implementing constructive change.

4. **Make the change tentative**—Resistance to change can also be reduced if the changes are made on a tentative basis. This approach establishes a trial period during which organization members spend some time incorporating a proposed change into their work before voicing support or nonsupport of it. Tentative change is based on the assumption that a trial period during which organization members incorporate a change is the best way of reducing employees' fears of personal loss. Judson has summarized the benefits of using the tentative approach:

   - Employees affected by the change are able to consider their reactions to the new situation before committing themselves irrevocably to it.
   - Those who will work with the change are able to acquire more facts on which to base their attitudes toward the change.
   - Those who had strong preconceptions about the change are in a better position to assess it with objectivity. Consequently, they may review and modify some of their preconceptions.
   - Those involved are less likely to regard the change as a threat.
   - Management is better able to evaluate the method of change and make any necessary modifications before carrying it out more fully.[26]

Evaluation of the Change

As with all other managerial actions, managers should spend time evaluating the changes they want to make. The purpose of this evaluation is not only to gain insight into how the change itself might be modified to further increase its organizational effectiveness but also to determine

TIPS FOR MANAGING AROUND THE GLOBE

Sincere Changes: Managing Change in a 118-Year-Old Department Store

In recent years, Hong Kong has proved to be a challenging environment for the retail industry. Rents have increased to unprecedented levels, and competition from Internet sales and global brands have eaten into the profits.

King Huen Ma is the chairman of the Sincere Company, which was founded in 1900 as Hong Kong's first Chinese-owned department store. Sincere has always had a dedication to quality service and customer satisfaction. It can, and does, charge premium prices for premium brands, but at many levels of competition, it has to offer products at affordable prices.

Under Ma's leadership, the company has diversified into property investment and development and securities trading, but retailing continues to be the core activity of the business. Ma is never afraid to make changes to match market demands and customer expectations. For example, recognizing that children needed school, sport, and recreational footwear, Ma increased the store's focus on children's shoes, resulting in increased sales. Introducing European fashions and high-quality craftsmanship from around the world also paid off, as did the introduction of women's fashion from Korea in 2013. Korean apparel now accounts for 20 percent of its revenue.[27]

whether the steps taken to make the change should be modified to increase organizational effectiveness the next time those steps are used.

According to Margulies and Wallace, making this evaluation may be difficult because the data from individual change programs may be unreliable.[28] Nevertheless, managers must do their best to evaluate the desired change in order to increase the benefits the organization will gain from the change.[29]

Evaluation of change often involves watching for signs that indicate further change is necessary. For example, if organization members continue to be oriented more to the past than to the future, if they adhere to the obligations of rituals more readily than they do to the challenges of current problems, or if they pay greater allegiance to departmental goals than to overall company objectives, the probability is high that further change is necessary.

A word of caution is needed at this point. Although signs such as those listed in the preceding paragraph generally indicate that further change is warranted, the decision to make additional changes should not be made solely on that basis. More objective information should be considered. In general, additional change is justified if that change will accomplish goals like increasing profitability, raising job satisfaction, or contributing to the general welfare of society. Increasing customer satisfaction with products is also a commonly cited goal for initiating added organizational change.[30]

Change and Stress

13-3 An appreciation for the relationship between change and stress

Whenever managers implement changes, they should be concerned about the stress the changes may be creating. If the stress is significant enough, it may well cancel out the improvement that was anticipated from the change. In fact, stress could result in the organization being *less* effective than it was before the change was implemented. This section defines stress and discusses the importance of studying and managing it.

Defining Stress

The bodily strain that an individual experiences as a result of coping with some environmental factor is **stress**.[31] Hans Selye, an early authority on this subject, said that stress constitutes the factors resulting in wear and tear on the body. In organizations, this wear and tear is caused primarily by the body's subconscious mobilization of energy whenever an individual is confronted with new organizational or work demands.[32]

The Importance of Studying Stress

The study of stress is important for several reasons:[33]

- Stress can have damaging psychological and physiological effects on employees' health and on their contributions to organizational effectiveness. It can cause heart disease and also prevent employees from concentrating or making decisions. Increased levels of stress have also been associated with adverse effects on family relationships,[34] decreased productivity in the workplace, and increased psychiatric symptoms.[35]
- Stress is a major cause of employee absenteeism and turnover. Certainly, such factors severely limit the potential success of an organization.
- A stressed employee can affect the safety of other workers or even the public.
- Stress represents a significant cost to organizations. Some estimates put the cost of stress-related problems in the United States at $150 billion a year. For example, many organizations spend a great deal of money treating stress-related employee problems through medical programs, and they must also absorb expensive legal fees when handling stress-related lawsuits.

The strain of coping with heavy work demands causes stress-related wear and tear on the body.

Managing Stress in Organizations

Because stress is felt by almost all employees in all organizations, insights about managing stress are valuable to all managers. This section centers on the assumption that to manage employees' stress appropriately in organizations, managers must understand how stress influences worker performance, identify where unhealthy stress exists in organizations, and help employees handle stress.

Understanding How Stress Influences Worker Performance   To deal with stress among employees, managers must understand the relationship between the amount of stress felt by a worker and the worker's performance. This relationship is shown in **Figure 13.5**. Note that extremely high and extremely low levels of stress tend to have negative effects on production. Also note that, although increasing stress tends to bolster worker performance up to a point (Point A in the figure), when the level of stress increases beyond that point, worker performance begins to deteriorate.

In sum, a certain amount of stress among employees is generally considered to be advantageous for an organization because it tends to increase production. However, too much or too little stress for employees is generally disadvantageous for the organization because it tends to decrease production.

WORKER STRESS

Figure 13.5

The relationship between worker stress and the level of worker performance

STEPS FOR SUCCESS

Managing Stress

Experts on stress management realize that stress is a normal part of life and can even help us learn and motivate us to make changes for the better. Here are some of their ideas for making stress a positive force in the lives of managers and their employees:[36]

- Look for meaning in your work. Define what you do in terms of the benefits you provide to others. Use this perspective when talking to employees about the importance of what they do.

- Build ties to people who offer support and encouragement. Get coaching or training in handling stressful situations.
- Keep a positive attitude. For example, when noticing a faster heartbeat and sweaty palms in a new situation, think of them as signs of the excitement and energy of an important challenge, not as signs of fear in the face of a threat.

Identifying Unhealthy Stress in Organizations

Once managers understand the impact of stress on performance, they must identify where stress exists within the organization.[37] After areas of stress have been pinpointed, managers must then determine whether the stress is at an appropriate level or is too high or too low. Because most stress-related organizational problems result from too much stress rather than too little, the remainder of this section focuses on how to relieve undesirably high levels of stress.

Managers often find it difficult to identify the people in the organization who are experiencing detrimentally high levels of stress. This difficulty comes about partly because people respond to high stress levels in different ways and partly because physiological reactions to stress—such as high blood pressure, a pounding heart, and gastrointestinal disorders—are hard, if not impossible, for managers to observe and monitor.

Nevertheless, managers can learn to recognize several observable signs of undesirably high stress levels:[38]

- Constant fatigue
- Low energy
- Moodiness
- Increased aggression
- Excessive use of alcohol
- Temper outbursts
- Compulsive eating
- High levels of anxiety
- Chronic worrying

A manager who observes one or more of these signs in employees should investigate to determine whether those exhibiting the signs are indeed under too much stress. If they are, the manager should try to help those employees handle their stress or should attempt to reduce stressors in the organization.[39]

Helping Employees Handle Stress

A **stressor** is an environmental demand that causes people to feel stress. Stressors are common in situations where individuals are confronted by circumstances in which their usual behaviors are inappropriate or insufficient and where negative consequences are associated with the failure to deal properly with the situation. Organizational change characterized by continual layoffs or firings is an obvious stressor, but many other factors related to organizational policies, structure, physical conditions, and processes can also act as stressors.[40]

A recent study identified workplace bullying as a stressor in the work lives of doctors in India and Malaysia. **Workplace bullying** refers to individuals being isolated or excluded socially and having their work efforts devalued. According to study results, workplace bullying is frequently experienced by junior doctors and leads to reduced job satisfaction, depression and anxiety, sickness, and absence. Although this stressor may lead to positive outcomes, such as doctors feeling challenged and thereby increasing their productivity, this stressor might also lead to undesirable consequences, such as doctors exhibiting low morale and poor work performance, which can negatively affect patient care. Because workplace bullying is generally seen as having a negative effect on doctors, countries such as England, Sweden, Norway, and Finland have implemented programs to eliminate workplace bullying.

MyLab Management Watch It

If your instructor has assigned this activity, go to www.pearson.com/mylab/management to complete the video exercise.

Stress is seldom reduced significantly until the stressors causing it have been coped with satisfactorily or withdrawn from the environment. For example, if too much organizational change is causing undesirably high levels of stress, management may be able to reduce that stress by improving organizational training aimed at preparing workers to deal with job demands resulting from the change. Management might also choose to reduce such stress by temporarily refraining from making further organizational changes.[41]

Management can also adopt several strategies to help prevent the initial development of unwanted stressors in their organizations. Four such strategies follow:[42]

1. **Create an organizational climate that is supportive of individuals**—Organizations commonly evolve into large bureaucracies with formal, inflexible, impersonal climates. This environment leads to considerable job stress. Making the organizational environment less formal and more supportive of employee needs helps prevent the development of unwanted organizational stressors.

2. **Implement stress management courses**—Recent research has demonstrated that employees who participated in a stress management course were less depressed than employees who did not participate in such a course.[43] The stress management course involved a group session in which educational materials about coping strategies and stress prevention were presented. An additional part of the course involved teaching employees about the benefits of relaxation. Those employees who participated in the course demonstrated a significant reduction in their depressive symptoms. Clearly, implementing a stress management course would be beneficial for the workplace.

3. **Make jobs interesting**—Routine jobs that do not allow employees some degree of freedom often result in undesirable employee stress. A management focus on making jobs as interesting as possible should help prevent the development of stressors related to routine, boring jobs.

4. **Design and operate career counseling programs**—Employees often experience considerable stress when they do not know what their next career step might be or when they might realistically be able to take it. If managers can show employees that next step and when it can realistically be achieved, they can discourage unwanted organizational stressors in this area.

IBM is an example of a company that for many years has focused on career planning for its employees as a vehicle for reducing employee stress.[44] IBM has a corporation-wide program to encourage supervisors to conduct annual voluntary career planning sessions with employees that result in one-page career action plans. Thus, IBM employees have a clear idea of where their careers are headed.

Change and Conflict[45]

Defining Conflict

Managers often encounter conflict as a result of planning and making organizational changes. **Conflict** is defined in this context as a struggle that results from opposing needs or feelings of two or more people. In the case of organizational change, conflict generally results from managers making changes that threaten employees or create competing views between employees and

13-4 Insights concerning how to handle conflict as a factor related to organizational change

Figure 13.6
Techniques for handling conflict

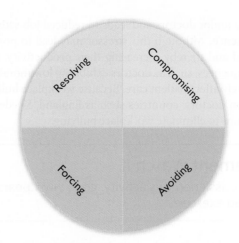

managers concerning when, how, or if a particular organizational change should be made. Note, however, that conflict sometimes results in a positive outcome for the organization. For example, a manager in conflict with a subordinate regarding how the subordinate's job will change might garner good suggestions from the subordinate regarding how to improve the planned change. On the other hand, conflict sometimes results in a negative outcome for the organization. For example, the situation regarding conflict between manager and subordinate could destroy their work relationship and frustrate the employee to the point where he or she, in order to get back at the manager, finds ways to sabotage the success of the planned change.

Strategies for Settling Conflict

Fortunately for managers, several useful techniques are available for handling conflict. These techniques, depicted in **Figure 13.6**, include *compromising*, *avoiding*, *forcing*, and *resolving*. Each of these techniques is discussed in the following sections.

Compromising
One conflict management strategy a manager can use is to **compromise**, which means the parties to the conflict settle on a solution that gives both of them *part* of what they wanted. Neither the manager nor the employees get exactly what they initially wanted. Instead, all parties agree to an organizational change that they presumably can accept.

Managers who choose to compromise generally feel that a solution completely acceptable to everyone would be difficult to reach and that they would rather not force someone to accept a completely unwanted choice. Compromise is generally appropriate to adopt as a conflict management technique if a planned change is relatively minor and the time in which to make the organizational change is somewhat limited.

PRACTICAL CHALLENGE: MANAGING CONFLICT

Southwest Airlines Embraces Positive Conflict

Experts, including executive coach Judith Glaser and recruiting executive Theodore Dysart, say that successful managers do not run from conflict. Rather, they recognize when conflict may be a positive force and know how to handle it constructively. Some companies openly acknowledge the importance of these skills.

An example is Southwest Airlines. In training its managers, Southwest instructs them in how to encourage employees to debate ideas forcefully but respectfully. This value arose in part from founder Herb

Kelleher's view of his company as being at war with its larger competitors. He expressed the company's mission in terms that united his people in a cause where conflict (with competitors) was highly motivating. Southwest's attitude toward conflict is also connected to its business strategy. Southwest's low-cost, high-efficiency strategy requires problem solving through innovation and close cooperation. When the company hires, it looks for individuals who demonstrate skill in respectfully sorting out conflicts with others.[46]

Avoiding

Some managers use the avoiding technique as a means to manage conflict. **Avoiding** is a conflict management technique whereby managers simply ignore the conflict. For example, if a sales manager finds that individuals in the human resource department are a continual source of conflict because they are inflexible and resist proposed changes, the manager might choose to avoid dealing with the department. The manager can opt to propose and implement desirable changes by dealing with others in the organization besides the human resource personnel.

This strategy makes sense if you assume that all conflict is bad. If you successfully avoid all conflicts, the work environment might seem positive on the surface. However, managers often disagree with others in the organization, and sometimes people with opposing, conflicting viewpoints have important ideas to share. Managers should thus be selective in avoiding conflict. The avoiding technique is perhaps most appropriate when the potential conflict will not limit organizational goal attainment.

When organizational change results in conflict and managers settle it wisely, it can have a positive impact on the organization.

The avoiding technique should also be assessed in relation to the high level of workforce diversity that exists in most modern organizations. An employee's point of view can often seem puzzling, irritating, or completely incorrect to a manager if the employee is of another race, age, or sex. Managers must work hard to understand people who are different and must give equal attention to the views of all employees, not just those the manager easily understands. Pretending that everyone views a situation the same way is inappropriate and may give some employees the belief that their manager is discriminating against them.

Managers must keep in mind that people from many non-Western cultures believe it is best to avoid conflicts, and they thus place a higher value on harmony than on confrontation. Employees with such values are less likely than employees from Western cultures to become involved in conflict with a manager regarding an organizational change that is being implemented. To make sure that organizational change is designed and implemented most effectively and efficiently, a manager must ensure that employees know that he or she wants to be informed of all employees' thoughts about how to improve organizational change.

Forcing

Rather than avoid conflict, a manager may try a more direct approach to manage conflict. **Forcing** is a technique for managing conflict in which managers use their authority to declare that conflict is ended. In essence, managers can declare this because they have the authority to do so. For example, assume that a worker complains to a manager that a recently changed and implemented procedure is unfair because the procedure does not allow the worker a fair share of overtime hours. Managers can force the acceptance of a change simply by declaring, "I make the assignments, and your job is to do what you're told."

The management of work teams also illustrates how managers can force an end to conflict. For example, assume that a manager is leading his employees in a project to reduce the time needed to deliver a product; also assume that because of conflict within the team regarding what change should be made and how it should be made, the team is deadlocked about what to do. In such situations, managers may simply force or dictate what organizational change needs to be made and how it should be made.

Forcing a solution is a relatively fast way to manage a conflict, and it may be the best approach in an emergency. However, forcing a solution can frustrate employees, and this frustration might lead to future management–employee conflict.

Resolving

Perhaps the most direct—and sometimes the most difficult—way to manage conflict is to work out the difference(s) between managers and employees. This conflict management strategy is called **resolving**. The manager initiates this technique by pinpointing differences related to organizational change that exist between managers and employees. Pinpointing these differences requires managers and employees to listen to others' viewpoints in a sincere effort to understand rather than to argue. Next, managers and employees should identify the issues on which they agree and the ways they can both benefit from implementing the change. Both management and employees should examine their own thoughts honestly and carefully to reach a mutually agreed-upon, change-related strategy.

Resolving is based on an assumption about the conflict that is somewhat different from the assumptions of other strategies for conflict management. The other techniques tend to assume managers and employees are in a *win–lose conflict*. In other words, the outcome of the conflict will be that one side wins (achieves a desired outcome) and the other side loses (does not achieve a desired outcome). In contrast, *resolving* assumes that many conflicts are *win–win conflicts*, in which the resolution can leave both management and employees achieving desirable outcomes and thus can help the organization maximize organizational success.

Virtuality

13-5 Knowledge about virtuality as a vehicle for organizational change

One specific, commonplace type of organizational change being made in modern organizations throughout the world is the trend toward "virtuality." Because this trend is significant and is expected to grow in use even more in the future, this section focuses on it by defining a virtual organization, discussing degrees of virtuality in organizations, and describing the virtual office.[47]

Defining a Virtual Organization

Overall, a **virtual organization** has the essence of a traditional organization but lacks some aspect of traditional boundaries and structure.[48] Virtual organizations are also referred to as *network organizations* or *modular corporations*.[49] In essence, managers extend beyond traditional boundaries and structure for the good of the organization by using developments in information technology. Perhaps the most prominent of these developments are the Internet and hardware and software tools that enable managers to go beyond traditional boundaries and structure more easily.[50] Both large and small organizations can have virtual aspects.[51]

Degrees of Virtuality

Organizations can vary drastically in terms of their degrees of virtuality. Perhaps the company exhibiting the most extensive degree is known as the **virtual corporation**, an organization that extends significantly beyond the boundaries and structure of a traditional organization by comprehensively "tying together" its stakeholders—employees, suppliers, and customers—via an elaborate system of e-mail and other Internet-related methods such as videoconferencing. This tying together allows all stakeholders to communicate and participate in helping the organization become more successful.

On the other hand, some organizations have much lesser degrees of virtuality. For example, some organizations limit their virtuality to **virtual teams**, groups of employees formed by managers that extend beyond the boundaries and structure of traditional teams in that members in geographically dispersed locations "meet" via real-time messaging on an intranet or on the Internet to discuss special or unanticipated organizational problems.[52] As another example, organizations may limit their virtuality to **virtual training**, a training process that extends beyond the boundaries and structure of traditional training by, for example, instructing employees via Internet-assisted learning materials.[53] The following sections discuss virtual offices, a popular type of virtuality being introduced into many organizations.

The Virtual Office

An exciting component of organization virtuality is the virtual office.[54] The following sections discuss the definition of the term, various reasons for establishing a virtual office, and the challenges of managing a virtual office.

Figure 13.7 Continuum of alternative work arrangements

Defining a Virtual Office

A **virtual office** is a work arrangement that extends beyond the structure and boundaries of the traditional office arrangement. Specifics of the arrangements vary from organization to organization but can be conceptualized using the alternative work arrangements continuum shown in **Figure 13.7**. This continuum is based on the degree of worker mobility present within a particular virtual office, ranging from "occasional telecommuting" to "fully mobile." The definitions of the alternative work arrangements shown on the continuum follow.

OCCASIONAL TELECOMMUTING

Workers have fixed, traditional offices and work schedules but occasionally work at home. In this situation, most are traditional workers in traditional office situations.

HOTELING

Workers come into the traditional office frequently, but because they are not always physically present, they are not allocated permanent office space. Instead, in advance of their arrival, these workers reserve a room or cubicle, sometimes called a "hotel room," where they can receive and return telephone calls and link to a computer network.

TETHERED IN OFFICE

"Tethered" workers have some mobility but are expected to report to the office on a regular basis. For example, some tethered workers are expected to be at the office in the morning to each receive a cellular phone and a portable computer. Each worker returns the equipment to the office in the afternoon, sometimes accompanied by a meeting or progress report for the workday.

HOME-BASED, SOME MOBILITY

A home-based worker has no traditional office. The work space of this type of worker could be a kitchen table or a bedroom desk. A home-based worker may visit customers or go outside the home occasionally, but his or her work is mainly done via the telephone or computer inside the home. Some companies support home-based workers by leasing office furniture, providing computers, and procuring high-speed phone lines.

FULLY MOBILE

A worker who is fully mobile works out of a car. In essence, the car is an office containing equipment such as a cellular phone, portable computer, and fax machine. This type of worker, typically a field sales representative or customer service specialist, is expected to be on the road or at work areas such as customer locations during the entire workday.

Reasons for Establishing a Virtual Office

Managers design and implement virtual offices for many different reasons. Cost reduction, usually in the areas of real estate or rental costs, is the most commonly cited reason. Traditional office space needed for an organization can be reduced by more than 50 percent by using virtual offices. Managers also use virtual offices to increase productivity. The history of some organizations shows that people work faster and are interrupted less when working at home. Third, firms establish virtual offices as part of redesigning jobs to make employees more effective and efficient. For example, some organizations need to reduce the amount of time taken to address customer problems. Some managers meet this need by establishing fully mobile customer service employees. According to this rationale, fully mobile customer service employees have a better chance of arriving quickly at customer locations than do customer service employees in traditional offices and thereby have a better chance of solving problems quickly.

Challenges of Managing a Virtual Office

Managers face many new and different challenges when using the virtual office concept. For example, virtual offices make it more difficult to create a desired corporate culture. Due simply to their lack of proximity, employees working in virtual offices are more difficult for managers to integrate into the fabric of the organizational culture. Virtual offices also make communication more difficult. Planned or unplanned face-to-face communication that takes place in a traditional office is essentially non-existent in a virtual office. As a result, management may experience more difficulty gathering information that is relevant to employee attitudes and work concerns.

There is some evidence that managers are having difficulty meeting such challenges and have opted to avoid them by moving back to traditional office arrangements. Organizations like IBM and Yahoo! are abandoning their virtual office organizational structures and requiring employees to move back into traditional office settings. The rationale for the move is that putting employees in the same physical space hastens the speed of work and sparks innovation.[55]

CHALLENGE CASE SUMMARY

The information in this chapter furnishes several insights into how Huntington Memorial Hospital's administrators should reach decisions about enacting a change at the hospital. These administrators should evaluate the change in relation to the degree that it better enables the hospital to fulfill its mission. Administrators should focus only on making changes that help the hospital to accomplish its mission better. If the hospital wants continued success over the long run, major changes will have to be made many times. In fact, appropriate change is so important to an organization that the administrators might want to consider initiating a program to encourage employees to submit their ideas on a continuing basis regarding how the hospital could continue to improve its performance. When considering possible changes, however, the administrators need to remember that some level of stability is also necessary if the hospital is to survive and serve the community over the long term.

In the Challenge Case, it was clear that there needed to be change agents in Huntington's administration. Given the impact of electronic health records on all levels of the organization, including its physicians, it was important that change agents existed at the highest as well as at the lowest levels of the administration. These individuals needed to evaluate the overall advantages and disadvantages of converting each part of the paper-based record-keeping system to an electronic record-keeping system and then to make the changes if advisable. Like the administrators in the case, change agents must recognize that people affected by organizational change, like the physicians, should be involved in helping to make needed changes. Such involvement

helps to lower the resistance to proposed changes and increases the commitment to making the changes work.

In general, change agents must be able to use behavioral science tools to influence organization members during the implementation of a planned change. For example, they must determine how much change an organization's employees can withstand and perhaps implement each change gradually so that employees will not be overwhelmed. Huntington seemed to address these issues by identifying an appropriate type of electronic record to start with and by phasing in the system gradually. Overall, the ability to use behavioral science tools will help the change agent succeed in implementing needed change at an organization.

Huntington's administrators can make many different types of changes. They can change technological factors, people factors, and structural factors to increase the organization's effectiveness. Huntington's record-keeping decisions discussed in the Challenge Case emphasized technological factors, but these decisions often have an impact on people and structure as well. For example, the hospital needs people to work with the software vendor and probably will need an information technology staff with the skill to keep the system working on a day-to-day basis. It will have to continue making training available as new people come on board and need to learn how to use the system. If the paper system was less efficient than the electronic one is, perhaps there were people whose jobs involved managing the paper and moving it from place to place. If so, the hospital may need to eliminate such jobs in the future, and those who do manage the new flow of information may require a different, perhaps more advanced, set of skills.

The complete changeover from paper to electronic medical records could radically change how the hospital carries out its mission. As a result, Huntington may find it useful to implement organization development (OD) to spur the people change that will be required. Alternatively, Huntington may use grid OD to modify management styles. Of course, the hospital could use both techniques to train the managers needed to ensure that the organizational change succeeds.

Huntington's administrators realize that, even though they may formulate structural change that would benefit the organization, any attempt to implement this change could prove unsuccessful if the implementation does not consider the people affected by the change. For example, creating a new department to coordinate electronic patient record keeping might cause doctors and their staff to worry that using electronic records may interfere with their ability to deliver patient care in the ways they did in the past. As a result, they may subtly resist the change.

To overcome such resistance, Huntington could use strategies such as giving employees enough time to evaluate and understand the change fully. In fact, the hospital has offered extensive training and has involved doctors in the evaluation process. Huntington's administrators could also present a positive attitude about the change. If resistance is strong, administrators could say that the proposed change will be tentative until it is fully evaluated.

All changes at Huntington Hospital need to be evaluated after implementation to learn whether further organizational change is necessary and whether the change process used might be improved for the future. For example, the hospital could collect data on doctors' satisfaction, treatment costs, and patient outcomes to measure whether the system is improving financial performance and patients' health. If it is not, further changes to the system might be necessary.

Huntington should be careful not to create too much stress for other organization members as a result of planned change. Such stress could be significant enough to eliminate any planned improvement at the hospital and could eventually result in employees having physical symptoms and the inability to make sound decisions. These stress impacts are especially detrimental in caregiving situations such as a hospital. Although some additional stress on employees as a result of changes might improve the organization's effectiveness, too much stress could have a negative impact on the care given to patients. Signs to look for include constant fatigue, increased aggression, temper outbursts, and chronic worrying.

If Huntington's administrators determine that undesirably high levels of stress have resulted from implementing the electronic medical records, they should try to reduce the stress. They may be able to do so through training programs aimed at better equipping employees to execute the new job demands, or they may simply decide to slow the implementation rate of the change.

It would probably be wise for Huntington to take action to prevent unwanted, damaging stressors from developing as a result of planned change. To do so, the hospital could ensure that its organizational climate is supportive of individual needs and that jobs resulting from the planned change are as effective and as interesting as possible.

The administrators should also keep in mind that conflict is a usual by-product of planning and implementing organizational change. In handling this conflict, the administrators can *compromise* (settle on a modified solution that reflects a change in the ideas of all conflicting parties but that all parties find acceptable), *avoid* (pretend that no conflict exists), *force* (demand that a change be made), or *resolve* (confront the problems causing the conflict and resolve them).

The introduction of electronic medical records is intended to improve both patient care outcomes and efficiency in the delivery of care. Sharing electronic information online also creates the possibility of using virtual work arrangements. It is unlikely that the hospital would become a virtual corporation, but it could establish virtual teams.

Huntington could choose among various options to have a virtual dimension. For example, it could set up a virtual office in which the billing department employees telecommute. Other options for a virtual office include workers "hoteling," being tethered in the office, being home-based with some mobility, or being fully mobile. The rationale for establishing this type of virtual office probably would include cost savings in rent and enhanced worker productivity.

As with any type of change, establishing a virtual dimension at Huntington Hospital would include a number of important challenges that need to be overcome. Perhaps the most significant challenge would be integrating virtual employees appropriately into the hospital's organizational culture. Building good communication among Huntington's managers and virtual workers would be an important step in integrating these workers into the culture and maintaining their continued presence. To create this communication, Huntington's administrators could take steps that include establishing regular communication times with virtual workers, publishing an online newsletter aimed at helping virtual workers deal with their precise problems, and having regular social events where virtual workers could meet and interact with one another and with the hospital's on-location employees.

> **MyLab Management** Assessing Your Management Skill
>
> If your instructor has assigned this activity, go to www.pearson.com/mylab/management to complete the exercise related to the Challenge Case.

DEVELOPING ORGANIZATIONAL CHANGE MANAGEMENT SKILL

This section is specially designed to help you develop organizational change skills. An individual's organizational change skill is based on an understanding of organizational change concepts and on the ability to apply those concepts in management situations. The following activities are designed both to heighten your understanding of organizational change fundamentals and to develop your ability to apply those concepts in various management situations.

Class Preparation and Personal Study

To help you prepare for class, perform the activities outlined in this section. Performing these activities will help you enhance your classroom performance significantly.

Reflecting on Target Skill

On page 309, this chapter opens by presenting a target management skill along with a list of related objectives outlining knowledge and understanding that you should aim to acquire related to that skill. Review this target skill and the list of objectives to make sure that you've acquired all pertinent information within the chapter. If you do not feel that you've reached a particular objective(s), study related chapter coverage until you do.

Know Key Terms

Understanding the following key terms is critical to your preparing for class. Define each of these terms. Refer to the page(s) referenced after a term to check your definition or to gain further insight regarding the term.

changing an organization **311**
change agent **312**
people factors **313**
structural factors **313**
technological factors **313**
technological change **314**
structural change **314**
people change **314**
organization development (OD) **315**
grid organization development (grid OD) **315**
managerial grid **315**
stress **318**
stressor **320**
workplace bullying **320**
conflict **321**
compromise **322**
avoiding **323**

forcing **323**
resolving **323**
virtual organization **324**
virtual corporation **324**
virtual teams **324**
virtual training **324**
virtual office **325**

Know How Management Concepts Relate

This section comprises activities that will further sharpen your understanding of management concepts. Answer essay questions as completely as possible.

13-1 Is it important for organizational change to occur on a regular basis? Why or why not?

13-2 List and discuss four ways that you might settle conflict that results from an organizational change that you make.

13-3 Discuss grid OD as a technique for changing people in organizations.

> ### MyLab Management
> #### Personal Inventory Assessment
>
> Go to www.pearson.com/mylab/management to complete the Personal Inventory Assessment related to this chapter.
>
> PERSONAL INVENTORY ASSESSMENT

Management Skills Exercises

Learning activities in this section are aimed at helping you develop organizational change skills.

MyLab Management
Discussion Questions

Go to www.pearson.com/mylab/management to complete the problems marked with this icon ✪.

✪ Cases

How Huntington Hospital Introduced Electronic Health Records

The Challenge Case "How Huntington Hospital Introduced Electronic Health Records" (p. 310) and its related Challenge Case Summary were written to help you better understand the management concepts contained in this chapter. Answer the following discussion questions about the Challenge Case to better understand how concepts relating to organizational change and stress can be applied in a company such as Huntington.

13-4   How difficult would it be for a lower-level administrator to spearhead an effort to find new electronic applications for record keeping throughout Huntington and actually implement the changes? Explain.

13-5   Do you think that employees at Huntington would tend to resist the efforts of this lower-level administrator more than they would resist those of a higher-level administrator? Why or why not?

13-6   What elements of the change process at Huntington described in the case might cause organization members to experience stress? What could a change agent do to help alleviate this stress? Be specific.

Business Management Resource Group's Virtual Offices

Read the case and answer the questions that follow. Studying this case will help you better understand how concepts relating to organizational change and virtuality can be applied in a company such as Business Management Resource Group (BMRG).

Business Management Resource Group (BMRG) is not your ordinary accounting firm. Typically, this kind of business rents office space, which projects an image of stability and prosperity. In this office space, accountants and support staff work together to meet with clients and prepare reports. BMRG, however, does not operate out of a brick-and-mortar office. Instead, the Connecticut-based company's two dozen employees operate in their own locations and keep in touch mainly online.

Although BMRG is prospering today, starting any business is full of challenges and stresses. The company's founder, Jennifer Katrulya, initially worked out of her home and struggled to teach herself about computer hardware as technology advanced and her business grew. She had a background in accounting, not technology, but she knew she needed a smoothly running computer system to meet her clients' needs. Katrulya persevered, began hiring employees, and opened an office. She built BMRG into a successful firm that specializes in handling the controlling activities (overseeing all of a company's accounting functions) at growing start-ups and midsized businesses across the United States and in several other countries. BMRG stores the data online so that clients can look up their financial data from wherever they are located.

Katrulya's decision to go virtual followed developments in the firm's growth. As investors referred businesses to BMRG, she needed employees in locations convenient to those clients. However, setting up an office for each new employee would have been expensive. Meanwhile, at the main office, some employees increasingly wanted to work from home. Katrulya also observed that more and more of the space she was renting was unoccupied. In addition, BMRG had been moving data and software online and eventually found the technology that made remote accounting painless. Virtual offices looked like a logical and practical next step.

Katrulya planned the transition to virtual offices to take place over a year. During that time, she shrank the company's office space by half before eventually moving out. That way, until employees became comfortable with working from remote locations, they had the option to go into the office occasionally. Even so, Katrulya encountered resistance and conflict. She admits that she did not fully anticipate the human relations challenges of implementing this organizational change. Instead, she presented employees with her entire vision and expected them to be on board. Several employees left, however, and by the end of the change process, only two of the staff members remained. BMRG has since rebuilt with employees who appreciate the work arrangement.

Running virtual offices poses some management challenges. Building team spirit is harder from remote locations. Katrulya addresses the problem by holding staff meetings at least twice a year and sending employees to conferences, where they can get better acquainted. Another challenge is that some kinds of communication, such as performance feedback, are difficult to convey over a distance. Katrulya also must help her employees learn that it is acceptable—even beneficial—to switch off work-related devices and take a break.

According to Katrulya, the shift to working from virtual offices and sharing work online is saving BMRG more than $95,000 a year. Besides the savings, she says, the other major advantage of the arrangement is that BMRG can attract talented employees across the United States. In addition to the recruitment advantage, Katrulya views the financial savings as freeing up money to spend on employees' compensation and development.[56]

Questions

13-7 The chapter discusses three classes of factors (people, structure, and technology) to consider when determining what should be changed. How has BMRG's growth brought changes affecting each of these factors?

13-8 How can Jennifer Katrulya help her employees manage the stress of working in a growing organization with virtual offices?

13-9 If you had been advising Katrulya about her plans to set up virtual offices, what advice would you have given her for overcoming resistance to change and for meeting the challenges of managing virtual offices?

Experiential Exercises

Being a Change Agent

Directions. Read the following scenario and then perform the listed activities. Your instructor may want you to perform the activities as an individual or in a group. Follow all of your instructor's directions carefully.

In this chapter, you learned about change agents: individuals inside or outside the organization who try to modify the existing organizational situation. This is an important role for any person in an organization.

For this exercise, choose a student organization at your school. Select one that you are already familiar with and assume the role of change agent for that organization. Determine what elements of that student organization you would alter if you were the change agent. Be specific in your approach. Assess what you would change and how that change would occur.

Questions

13-10 Discuss the changes you would make in the student organization if you were to assume the role of change agent. How would you effect these changes?

13-11 What challenges do you envision for each of your changes? Do you anticipate that the student organization would welcome these changes? Why or why not?

13-12 For your particular student organization, would change occur more readily if the change agent were also the president of the organization? Discuss.

13-13 In your opinion, why do some people avoid the role of change agent? Why do others choose the role? Explain.

You and Your Career

Assume that, immediately after graduating, you become the store manager of a major retail or restaurant chain. After six months on the job, as you might anticipate, your stress levels begin to rise. Issues with achieving revenue targets, keeping costs in line, dealing with personnel issues, implementing corporate policies, and at the same time trying to maintain a vibrant personal life are all taking their toll on your physical and mental well-being. Clearly, the problems just mentioned will not go away: they are inherent in both the retail and restaurant industries. However, it is critical that you find ways to reduce your stress. Discuss the techniques you would utilize to reduce your stress levels. Be specific. Which of these stress-reducing techniques are you currently using in your roles as a student and employee? What makes these techniques useful?

Building Your Management Skills Portfolio

Your Management Skills Portfolio is a collection of activities specially designed to demonstrate your management knowledge and skill. Be sure to save your work. Taking your printed portfolio to an employment interview could prove helpful.

The portfolio activity for this chapter is about the restructuring of Jaguar Land Rover. Study the information provided and complete the exercises that follow.

In 2015, the India-based Tata Group, owners of the global brand Jaguar Land Rover, announced their intentions to build a new $1.2 billion manufacturing facility in Slovakia. The factory came online in 2018 with the goal of producing 150,000 vehicles a year and employing around 2,800 people. At the time of the announcement, Tata was insistent that the new factory would complement the major manufacturing plants in the United Kingdom and not replace them. Understandably, workers and trade unions were skeptical.

The Jaguar Land Rover group employs around 36,000 people, the majority of them in the United Kingdom, with factories in Liverpool and the West Midlands. The company also operates factories in China, Brazil, and India. While the factory was being constructed in Slovakia, Tata launched a major cost review as a result of falling sales in China. It concluded that some $6 billion could be cut.

In 2018, Tata announced that all production of the Land Rover Discovery would shift to Slovakia, meaning hundreds of job losses in the United Kingdom. Tata cited the decline in sales of diesel vehicles, previously accounting for 90 percent of their UK and European sales, as the reason for their decisions.

Tata were keen to point out that it was temporary agency staff that had been affected by the job losses, but that was little comfort for the hundreds of skilled workers who suddenly found themselves out of work.

Use the knowledge you have developed in this chapter to answer the following questions:

13-14 How would you have informed the employees about the decision to shift production to Slovakia? Be specific. What actual words would you have said to them?

_____

_____

_____

_____

13-15 Are there any steps that you could take to help the employees cope with this change? Explain.

_____

_____

_____

_____

13-16 Jaguar Land Rover signalled their intent to use the Slovakian factory to complement the manufacturing in the United Kingdom. What are the four key areas that this approach may have impacted on in terms of reducing resistance to change?

_____

_____

_____

13-17 How would you advise Jaguar Land Rover about developing a strategy to deal with any resistance to change? How would you describe the likely reactions of those resisting change?

_____

_____

_____

_____

MyLab Management
Writing Assignments

If your instructor has assigned this activity, go to www.pearson.com/mylab/management for the following assisted-graded writing assignments:

Assisted-Grading Questions

13-18 List and explain five reasons why organizations should undergo change.

13-19 Why is handling conflict an important part of making an organizational change?

Endnotes

1. Rebecca Armato, "Grassroots Approach Builds Connected Health Community," *Health Management Technology* (September 2011): 16–17; Rebecca Armato, "For Doctors, EHR Adoption Isn't a Spectator Sport," *InformationWeek*, February 1, 2011, Business & Company Resource Center, http://galenet.galegroup.com; Huntington Medical Foundation, "The Huntington Medical Foundation (HMF): A Collaborative Healthcare Group," news release, December 12, 2011, http://www.huntingtonhospital.com; Farrah Jolly and Neil Versel, "So Many Choices," *InformationWeek*, February 1, 2011, Business & Company Resource Center, http://galenet.galegroup.com.

2. Sharon K. Parker and Uta K. Bindl (eds.), *Proactivity at Work: Making Things Happen in Organizations* (Routledge: New York, 2017).

3. For an in-depth analysis of effective change in the workplace, see Angela Mansell, Paula Brough, and Kevin Cole, "Stable Predictors of Job Satisfaction, Psychological Strain, and Employee Retention: An Evaluation of Organizational Change within the New Zealand Customs Service," *International Journal of Stress Management* 13 (2006): 84–107.

4. Rosabeth Moss Kanter, "The New Managerial Work," *Harvard Business Review* (November/December 1989): 85–92. For further discussion of organizational change, see William Kahn, "Facilitating and Undermining Organizational Change: A Case Study," *Journal of Applied Behavioral Science* 40 (2004): 7.

5. John S. Morgan, *Managing Change: The Strategies of Making Change Work for You* (New York: McGraw-Hill, 1972), 99; to see an interesting discussion about building processes to facilitate change, see C. G. Worley, T. Williams, and E. E. Lawler, "Creating Management Processes Built for Change," *MIT Sloan Management Review* 58, no. 1 (2016): 77–82.

6. Jeremy Smerd, "General Motors Shakes Up HR Leadership," *Workforce Management*, July 30, 2009, http://www.workforce.com. For additional information on radical change, see Mark Hughes, "Reengineering Works: Don't Report, Exhort," *Management & Organizational History* 4, no. 1 (2009): 105–122.

7. Bart Nooteboom, "Paradox, Identity, and Change in Management," *Human Systems Management* 8 (1989): 291–300.

8. For a discussion of the importance of change, see Freek Vermeulen, Phanish Puranam, and Ranjay Gulati, "Change for Change's Sake," *Harvard Business Review*, June 2010, http://www.hbr.org.

9. For a different perspective on the behaviors required for change agents, see Sharon K. Parker and Catherine G. Collins, "Taking Stock: Integrating and Differentiating Multiple Proactive Behaviors," *Journal of Management* 36, no. 3 (May 2010): 633–662.

10. For discussion of change agents in academia, see J. A. Gaubatz and D. C. Ensminger, "Department Chairs as Change Agents," *Educational Management Administration & Leadership* 45, no. 1 (2017): 141–163.

11. For an article on being an effective change agent, see Shelley Cohen, "Change Agents Bolster New Practices in the Workplace," *Nursing Management* 37 (2006): 16–17.

12. Myron Tribus, "Changing the Corporate Culture—A Roadmap for the Change Agent," *Human Systems Management* 8 (1989): 11–22. For research focusing on an internal change agent, see Choi Sang Long, Wan Khairuzzaman Wan Ismail, and Salmiah Mohd Amin, "The Role of Change Agent as Mediator in the Relationship Between HR Competencies and Organizational Performance," *The International Journal of Human Resource Management* 24, no. 10 (2013): 2019.

13. "University Health System Modernizes Operations with Technology Upgrades," *San Antonio Business Journal*, April 20, 2010, http://www.bizjournals.com.

14. For an interesting case illustrating the changing nature of organizational structure at Procter & Gamble, see Aelita G. B. Martinsons and Maris G. Martinsons, "In Search of Structural Excellence," *Leadership & Organization Development Journal* 15 (1994): 24–28. See also Saul W. Gellerman, "In Organizations, as in Architecture, Form Follows Function," *Organizational Dynamics* 18 (Winter 1990): 57–68.

15. This section is based primarily on R. Blake, J. Mouton, and L. Greiner, "Breakthrough in Organization Development," *Harvard Business Review* (November/December 1964): 133–155.

16. Ibid.

17. W. J. Heisler, "Patterns of OD in Practice," *Business Horizons* (February 1975): 77–84; P. F. Sorensen, T. Yaeger, and R. Narel, "The New Golden Age of Organization Development Research and Knowledge," *Organization Development Journal* 35 no. 1 (2017): 47–55.

18. Martin G. Evans, "Failures in OD Programs—What Went Wrong," *Business Horizons* (April 1974): 18–22; for a useful history of OD, see R. J. Torraco, "Early History of the Fields of Practice of Training and Development and Organization Development," *Advances in Developing Human Resources* 18, no. 4 (2016): 439–453.

19. For one such article on organization development, see Jeana Wirtenberg, David Lipsky, Lilian Abrams, Malcolm Conway, and Joan Slepian, "The Future of Organizational Development: Enabling Sustainable Business Performance through People," *Organization Development* 25 (Summer 2007): 11–22.

20. For discussion of training and development issues in Jordanian banking, see C. A. Rowland, R. D. Hall, and I. Altarawneh, "Training and Development," *EuroMed Journal of Business* 12 (2017): 36–51.

21. For an interesting discussion of resistance to change, see B. Mathews and C. M. Linski, "Shifting the Paradigm: Reevaluating Resistance to Organizational Change," *Journal of Organizational Change Management* 29, no. 6 (2016): 963–972.

22. For an interesting article on resistance to change in the workplace, see David Stanley, John Meyer, and Laryssa Topolnytsky, "Employee Cynicism and Resistance to Organizational Change," *Journal of Business and Psychology* 19 (2005): 429–459.

23. For more information about internal resistance to change, see Robert Sevier, "Overcoming Internal Resistance to Change," *University Business* 6 (2003): 23.

24. This strategy for minimizing resistance to change is based on "How Companies Overcome Resistance to Change," *Management Review* (November 1972): 17–25. See also Dennis G. Erwin and Andrew N. Garman, "Resistance to Organizational Change: Linking Research and Practice," *Leadership & Organization Development Journal* 31, no. 1 (2010): 39–56.

25. For discussions on how storytelling can facilitate change and help an organization's workforce through transitions, see Andrew D. Brown, Yiannis Gabriel, and Silvia Gherardi, "Storytelling and Change: An Unfolding Story," *Organization* 16, no. 3 (2009): 323–333; Michaela Driver, "From Loss to Lack: Stories of Organizational Change as Encounters with Failed Fantasies of Self, Work and Organization," *Organization* 16, no. 3 (2009): 353–369.

26. Arnold S. Judson "A Manager's Guide to Making Changes" (New York: John Wiley and Sons, 1966), 118. To complement Judson's classic discussion and learn about the role of vision in making organizational change, see M. D. Haque, A. TitiAmayah, and L. Liu, "The Role of Vision in Organizational Readiness for Change and Growth," *Leadership & Organization Development Journal* 37, no. 7 (2016): 983–999.

27. "The Sincere Company Ltd," http://www.sincere.com.hk/department/lang_en.

28. Newton Margulies and John Wallace, *Organizational Change: Techniques and Applications* (Chicago: Scott, Foresman, 1973), 14.

29. For an article on evaluating change within a pharmaceutical organization, see Bill Cowley, "Why Change Succeeds: An Organizational Self-Assessment," *Organization Development Journal* 25 (2007): 25–30.

30. T. L. Stanley, "Only When Necessary," *SuperVision* 66, no. 11 (November 2005): 7–9.

31. For an article on developments concerning stress in the workplace, see "CEO's Stress Worried Pfizer; Board Was Seeking Lieutenant to Share Load, but Kindler Decided to Retire," *Wall Street Journal Online*, December 7, 2010; see also Patricia Sikora, David Beaty, and John Forward, "Updating Theory on Organizational Stress: The Asynchronous Multiple Overlapping Change (AMOC) Model of Workplace Stress," *Human Resource Development Review* 3 (2004): 3.

32. Hans Selye, *The Stress of Life* (New York: McGraw-Hill, 1956). See also James C. Quick and Jonathan D. Quick, *Organizational Stress and Preventive Management* (New York: McGraw-Hill, 1984).

33. James D. Bodzinski, Robert F. Scherer, and Karen A. Gover, "Workplace Stress," *Personnel Administrator* 34 (July 1989): 76–80.

34. For an article regarding the role of stress in the overall quality of life of employees, see Cary Cooper, "The Challenges of Managing the Changing Nature of Workplace Stress," *Journal of Public Mental Health* 5 (2005): 6–9.

35. For an article that describes the relationship between workplace stress and psychiatric disorders, see Carolyn Dewa, Elizabeth Lin, Mieke Kooehoorn, and Elliot Goldner, "Association of Chronic Work Stress, Psychiatric Disorders, and Chronic Physical Conditions with Disability among Workers," *Psychiatric Services* 58 (2007): 652–658.

36. Sue Shellenbarger, "Turn Bad Stress into Good," *Wall Street Journal*, May 7, 2013, http://online.wsj.com; Annie Murphy Paul, "Good or Bad? It Depends on How You Think about It," *European Union News*, February 28, 2014, Business Insights: Global, http://bi.galegroup.com; Mayo Clinic, "Healthy Lifestyle: Stress Management," March 4, 2014, http://www.mayoclinic.org; Robert Sanders, "Researchers Find Out Why Some Stress Is Good for You," University of California–Berkeley News Center, April 16, 2013, http://newscenter.berkeley.edu.

37. Identifying and dealing with stressors is critical because stress can have a negative impact on work skills; see M. Carmen Martinez, S. A. Dias de Oliveira Latorre, Maria do Rosario, and F. M. Fischer, "Longitudinal Associations between Stressors and Work Ability in Hospital Workers," *Chronobiology International* 33, no. 6 (2016), 754–758.

38. J. Clifton Williams, *Human Behavior in Organizations* (Cincinnati: South-Western, 1982), 212–213; Thomas L. Brown, "Are You Living in 'Quiet Desperation'?," *Industry Week* (March 16, 1992): 17.

39. For more information about the relationship among stress, burnout, and depression, see A. Iacovides, K. Fountoulakis, S. Kaprinis, and G. Kaprinis, "The Relationship between Job Stress, Burnout and Clinical Depression," *Journal of Affective Disorders* 75 (2003): 209; see also Arla L. Day, Aaron Sibley, Natasha Scott, John M. Tallon, and Stacy Ackroyd-Stolarz, "Workplace Risks and Stressors as Predictors of Burnout: The Moderating Impact of Job Control and Team Efficacy," *Canadian Journal of Administrative Sciences* 26, no. 1 (March 2009): 7–22.

40. Stewart L. Stokes, Jr., "Life after Rightsizing," *Information Systems Management* (Fall 1994): 69–71. For an interesting discussion of stressors, see Chau-kiu Cheung, Lih-rong Wang, and Raymond Kwok-hong Chan, "Differential Impacts of Stressors on Sense of Belonging," *Social Indicators Research* 113, no. 1 (August 2013): 277–297.

41. For interesting discussion of workplace bullying as a stressor and how to deal with it, see D. B. Van, E. Baillien, H. De Witte, T. V. Elst, and L. Godderis, "The Role of Work Stressors, Coping Strategies and Coping Resources in the Process of Workplace Bullying: A Systematic Review and Development of a Comprehensive Model," *Aggression and Violent Behavior* 29 (2016): 61–71.

42. Fred Luthans, *Organizational Behavior* (New York: McGraw-Hill, 1985), 146–148. For one successful method of reducing workplace stress, see J. Michael Krivyanski, "Employer-Sponsored Programs Try to Keep Workplace Stress in Check," *Business Times Journal* 20, no. 38 (April 6, 2001): 34.

43. For an article outlining the advantages of workplace stress management classes, see Yoshio Mino, Akira Babazono, Toshihide Tsuda, and Nobufumi Yasuda, "Can Stress Management at the Workplace Prevent Depression? A Randomized Controlled Trial," *Psychotherapy and Psychosomatics* 75 (2006): 177–182.

44. Donald B. Miller, "Career Planning and Management in Organizations," *S.A.M. Advanced Management Journal* 43 (Spring 1978): 33–43.

45. This section is based on Samuel C. Certo, *Supervision: Concepts and Skill-Building* (Burr Ridge, IL: McGraw-Hill Irwin, 2010), 379–381.

46. Joann S. Lublin, "The High Cost of Avoiding Conflict at Work," *Wall Street Journal*, February 14, 2014, http://online.wsj.com; Greg J. Bamber and Jody Hoffer Gittell, "A Tale of Two Airlines: Can Low-Cost Carriers Be Sustainable and Good Places to Work?," *The Conversation*, March 6, 2012, http://theconversation.com; Marina Krakovsky, "Nir Halevy: How Do You Resolve a Conflict?," *Stanford Graduate School of Business News*, December 16, 2013, http://www.gsb.stanford.edu.

47. William H. Davidow and Michael S. Malone, *The Virtual Corporation* (New York: HarperCollins, 1992).

48. P. Maria Joseph Christie and Reuven R. Levary, "Virtual Corporations: Recipe for Success," *Industrial Management* (July/August 1998): 7–11.

49. Charles C. Snow, Raymond E. Miles, and Henry J. Coleman, Jr., "Managing 21st Century Network Organizations," *Organizational Dynamics* (Winter 1992): 5–20.

50. Judith R. Gordon, *Organizational Behavior: A Diagnostic Approach* (Upper Saddle River, NJ: Prentice Hall, 1999), 385.

51. Christopher Barnatt, "Virtual Organizations in the Small Business Sector: The Case of Cavendish Management Resources," *International Small Business Journal* 15, no. 4 (July/September 1997): 36–47.

52. Anthony M. Townsend, Samuel M. DeMarie, and Anthony R. Hendrickson, "Virtual Teams: Technology and the Workplace of the Future," *Academy of Management Executive* 12, no. 3 (August 1998): 17–29. For an article that examines the role of culture in the virtual workplace, see John Symons and Claudia Stenzel, "Virtually Borderless: An Examination of Culture in Virtual Teaming," *Journal of General Management* 32 (2007): 1–17.

53. For other examples of types of virtuality in organizations, see Daniel E. O'Leary, Daniel Kuokka, and Robert Plant, "Artificial Intelligence and Virtual Organizations," *Communication of the Ach* 40, no. 1 (January 1997): 52–59.

54. This section draws from Thomas H. Davenport and Keri Pearlson, "Two Cheers for the Virtual Office," *Sloan Management Review* (Summer 1998): 51–65. For a further look at the advantages of a virtual

office, see Stephen Roth, "Consultants Use a Virtual Office to Make New Services a Reality," *Business Journal* 19, no. 20 (January 26, 2001): 8; Jeanne Wilson, C. Brad Crisp, and Mark Mortensen, "Extending Construal-Level Theory to Distributed Groups: Understanding the Effects of Virtuality," *Organization Science* 24, no. 2 (March/April 2013): 629–644.

55. "IBM Says No to Home Work," Dow Jones Newswire, May 19, 2017.
56. Jeff Drew, "How to Open New Doors by Closing Your Office," *Journal of Accountancy*, July 2013, EBSCOhost, http://web.a.ebscohost

.com; Kristy Short, "Cornering the Market on Premium Outsourced Accounting Services," *CPA Practice Advisor*, March 2013, Business Insights: Global, http://bi.galegroup.com; Jennifer Katrulya, "The Last Word: Jennifer Katrulya, CPA/CITP, CGMA," *Journal of Accountancy*, September 2012, http://www.journalofaccountancy.com; Business Management Resource Group (BMRG), "About Us," http://bmrg.homestead.com/About-Our-Firm.html, accessed March 19, 2014; BMRG, "Career Opportunities with BMRG," http://bmrg.homestead.com/Careers.html, accessed March 19, 2014.

14

Influencing and Communication

TARGET SKILL

 Communication Skill: the ability to share information with other individuals

COMMUNICATION SKILL AND YOUR CAREER

Communication skill will be of great value to you in enhancing your career. For example, this skill can help you to share clearly expectations that you have for worker performance and to coach workers in how to better meet those expectations. Successfully communicating with others in organizations contributes to organizational success, builds your image as a competent manager, makes you valuable to your organization, and supports promotions as you build your career.

OBJECTIVES

To help build my *communication skill*, when studying this chapter, I will attempt to acquire:

14-1 A fundamental understanding of influencing

14-2 Insights about emotional intelligence

14-3 An understanding of how communication works

14-4 Hints for communicating in organizations

14-5 Useful ideas for encouraging organizational communication

---

MyLab Management Chapter Warm Up

If your instructor has assigned this activity, go to www.pearson.com/mylab/management to complete the chapter warm up.

CHALLENGE CASE

How Evernote's Phil Libin Keeps Communication Flowing

Phil Libin modestly submits himself as an example of a manager who has learned a lot about communicating with and influencing employees. After Libin and two other computer programmers started a business, the three founders realized that someone needed to focus full-time on leading employees. Libin was, in his words, "the weakest programmer," so he took over the management duties.[1]

Today, as CEO of Evernote, Libin shows that he learned quickly. Evernote—which sells software that collects images of all kinds of notes and converts images of the notes into electronic data that users can search—is the third company Libin has started. He defines his role as focusing on company culture and eliminating the obstacles that hold employees back. He also aims to maintain the culture of a start-up by ensuring that employees understand how their work contributes to the company's larger vision. He reinforces those values by making communication skills the top consideration in choosing employees.

At the heart of Libin's effort to foster a start-up culture is ensuring that communication flows without barriers. Employees are assigned to teams of up to eight workers, which is a small enough number for easy conversation. They gather for weekly meetings to learn what is new at the company. Managers do not get status symbols like private offices because private offices create physical barriers that discourage communication. Instead, everyone works in an open space. The company provides no phones on desks because ringing phones and phone conversations are noisy distractions. Instead, employees who want to call someone at another location can do so from a conference room, and employees who want to talk to others in the office can walk a few feet to talk face-to-face.

Another way Libin breaks down barriers and promotes communication is with a program called Evernote Officer Training. Employees who choose to participate receive random assignments to attend meetings outside those of their work teams. They are encouraged to participate actively in the meetings so that they have a deeper understanding of what the company is doing.

Libin also establishes the conditions for spontaneous conversations. The company expanded from its headquarters in Mountain View, California, by adding an office in Austin, Texas. After that, Libin had giant video screens installed on a wall of each location. A camera on each screen displays the room to employees at the other

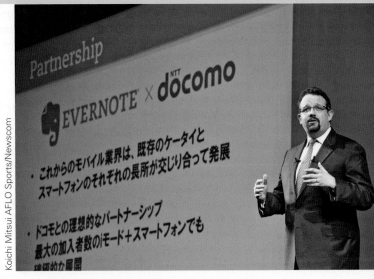

Koichi Mitsui AFLO Sports/Newscom

Evernote is committed to open and timely communication to help create an organization employees can be proud of.

location. When employees see one another on screen, they can use microphones and speakers to chat. Libin can even start chats via a six-foot-tall robot he operates remotely when he is away from the office. He can move the robot around to visit employees' desks and see what is happening. In addition, Libin sets standards for informal messages: Annoying notes like "Wash your dishes" in the break room are forbidden in favor of positive messages.

Effective communication and a commitment to excellence are helping Evernote grow. It now has more than 65 million users and hundreds of employees working in eight countries. The company has expanded from selling software to selling tangible products that help workers stay organized and productive. As Evernote continues to grow, Libin knows that his commitment to open communication will become more important.[2]

THE COMMUNICATION CHALLENGE

As described in the Challenge Case, Evernote CEO Phil Libin understands the importance of information flow within an organization. According to the case, Libin sees open communication as a means of fostering employee commitment and innovation. This chapter focuses on the challenge of improving communication within organizations such as Evernote and offers some insights into how this challenge can be conquered. The chapter is divided into two main parts: fundamentals of influencing and fundamentals of communication.

Fundamentals of Influencing

14-1 A fundamental understanding of influencing

The four basic managerial functions—planning, organizing, influencing, and controlling—were introduced in Chapter 1. *Planning* and *organizing* have already been discussed; *influencing* is the third of these basic functions covered in this text. A definition of *influencing* and a discussion of the influencing subsystem follow.

Defining Influencing

Influencing is the process of guiding the activities of organization members in appropriate directions. *Appropriate directions*, of course, are those that lead to the attainment of management system objectives. Influencing thus involves focusing on organization members as people and dealing with issues such as morale, arbitration of conflicts, and the development of good working relationships.[3] Influencing is a critical part of a manager's job; in fact, the ability to influence others is a primary determinant of a successful manager.[4]

The Influencing Subsystem

Like the planning and organizing functions, the influencing function can be viewed as a subsystem within the overall management system (see **Figure 14.1**). The primary purpose of the influencing subsystem, as already stated, is to enhance the attainment of management system objectives by guiding the activities of organization members in appropriate directions.[5]

Figure 14.2 shows the constituent parts of the influencing subsystem. The input of this subsystem is composed of a portion of the total resources of the overall management system, and its output is appropriate organization member behavior. The process of the influencing subsystem involves the performance of six primary management activities:

1. Leading
2. Motivating
3. Considering groups
4. Communicating
5. Encouraging creativity and innovation
6. Building corporate culture

Figure 14.1

Relationship between overall management system and influencing subsystem

Figure 14.2
The influencing subsystem

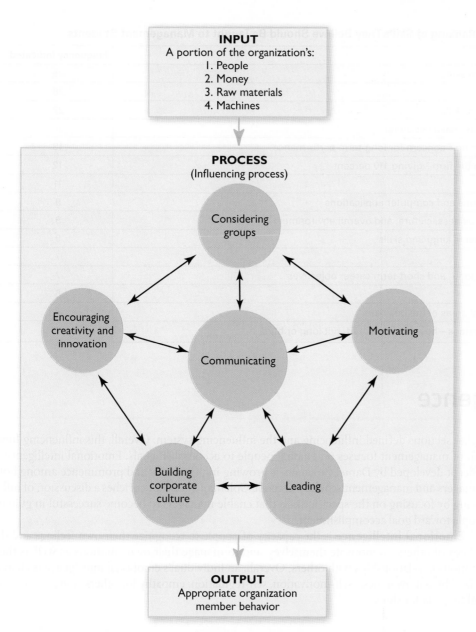

INPUT
A portion of the organization's:
1. People
2. Money
3. Raw materials
4. Machines

PROCESS
(Influencing process)

Considering groups

Encouraging creativity and innovation

Communicating

Motivating

Building corporate culture

Leading

OUTPUT
Appropriate organization member behavior

Managers transform a portion of organizational resources into appropriate organization member behavior mainly by performing these activities.

As Figure 14.2 shows, leading, motivating, considering groups, building corporate culture, communicating, and encouraging creativity and innovation are interrelated. To some extent, managers accomplish each of these influencing activities by communicating with organization members. For example, managers can decide what kinds of leaders they need to be only after they first analyze the characteristics of the various groups with which they will interact and second determine how those groups can best be motivated. Then, regardless of the leadership strategy they adopt, their leading, motivating, and working with groups, for example, will be accomplished—at least partly—through communication with other organization members.

In fact, *all* management activities are accomplished at least partly through communication or communication-related endeavors. Because communication is used repeatedly by managers, the ability to communicate is often referred to as the *fundamental management skill*.

A recent survey of chief executives supports this notion that communication is the fundamental management skill. The results, which appear in **Table 14.1**, show that CEOs ranked oral and written communication skills first (along with interpersonal skills) among those that should be taught to management students.

TABLE 14.1   **Chief Executives' Ranking of Skills They Believe Should Be Taught to Management Students**

Rank*	Key Learning Area	Frequency Indicated
1	Oral and written communication skills	25
1	Interpersonal skills	25
3	Financial/managerial accounting skills	22
4	Ability to think, be analytical, and make decisions	20
5	Strategic planning and goal setting—concern for long-term performance	13
6	Motivation and commitment to the firm—giving 110 percent	12
7	Understanding of economics	11
8	Management information systems and computer applications	9
8	Thorough knowledge of your business, culture, and overall environment	9
8	Marketing concept (the customer is king) and skills	9
11	Integrity	7
11	Knowledge of yourself: setting long- and short-term career objectives	7
13	Leadership skills	6
13	Understanding of the functional areas of the business	6
15	Time management: setting priorities—how to work smart, not long or hard	1

*1 is most important.

Emotional Intelligence

14-2   Insights about emotional intelligence

Earlier sections defined influencing and the influencing system. Overall, this influencing function of management focuses on guiding people to accomplish goals. Emotional intelligence, a concept developed by Daniel Goleman, is growing in popularity and prominence among both managers and management scholars. Overall, Goleman's concept enriches a discussion of influencing by focusing on the specific skills that enable managers to become successful in guiding people toward goal accomplishment.[6]

Emotional intelligence is the capacity of people to recognize their own feelings and the feelings of others, to motivate themselves, and to manage their own emotions as well as their emotions in relationships with others. Overall, an individual's emotional intelligence is characterized by self-awareness, self-motivation, self-regulation, empathy for others, and adeptness in building relationships.

PRACTICAL CHALLENGE: EMOTIONAL INTELLIGENCE

PepsiCo Pilot Project

Regardless of region or industry, all businesses face unprecedented challenges, and managers constantly seek ways to adapt to rapid global economic changes. In such situations, emotional intelligence matters more than ever. A study by Gallup shows that almost 63 percent of employees worldwide are "not engaged," lack motivation, and invest less effort in organizational goals. For cross-cultural teams, motivational methods have to be tailored to the cultural ethos of the region. For higher levels of productivity; smooth and effective teamwork; and widening bases in different social, cultural, and economic regions, managers must learn to regularly empathize with different cultures.

A pilot project at PepsiCo revealed that certain executives selected for EQ competencies had far outperformed their colleagues, delivering a 10-percent increase in productivity, $3.75 million in added economic value, and over 100 percent return on investment. In addition, the SharePower program at PepsiCo—where employees may earn stock options totaling 10 percent of their previous year's pay in the current year—encouraged employees worldwide to work as though they own the business. This created a culture where everyone felt a greater sense of responsibility and as a result contributed to the success of the larger organization.[7]

Figure 14.3

Ten skills possessed by emotionally intelligent managers

Emotionally intelligent managers:

1. Motivate others
2. Focus on personal and organizational achievement
3. Understand others
4. Communicate efficiently and effectively
5. Lead others
6. Build successful teams
7. Handle conflict appropriately
8. Change organizations appropriately
9. Manage diversity
10. Manage creativity and innovation

Studies highlight many interesting points regarding emotional intelligence. Some research indicates that managers with high levels of emotional intelligence are likely to be successful because they are likely to create an organization culture that is characterized by trust, learning, information sharing, and desirable risk taking. Other studies reveal that managers with high levels of emotional intelligence are more interpersonally effective than are managers with low levels of emotional intelligence.[8] Studies have also shown that managers with high levels of emotional intelligence are likely to be more satisfied in their jobs than are other managers, and that employees who work for managers with high levels of emotional intelligence are more satisfied with their jobs than are employees who work for managers with low levels of emotional intelligence. Ongoing studies reveal that a steady, five-year increase in emotional intelligence seems to be leveling off, perhaps implying that more training in this area needs to take place.[9]

In some ways, research in the area of emotional intelligence has produced somewhat puzzling results. On the one hand, emotional intelligence research traditionally seems to indicate that managers with low levels of emotional intelligence are likely to be relatively unsuccessful because they are less likely to produce a positive work culture.[10] On the other hand, another study suggests that the further an individual goes up the corporate ladder, the lower his or her emotional intelligence because some organizations promote employees based on their financial performance rather than their people skills.[11]

At first glance, the relationship between the traditional influencing function of management and Goleman's emotional intelligence may be hard to identify. Upon inspecting the skills that Goleman outlines as necessary to be an emotionally intelligent manager, however, the relationship becomes clearer. **Figure 14.3** lists several of the skills of the emotionally intelligent manager. As you can see by inspecting the figure, the influencing section of this text and the concept of emotional intelligence both emphasize critical management concepts and skills in areas of motivation, communication, leadership, teamwork, creativity, and innovation—all important attributes in building positive psychological capital in an organization.[12]

Communication is discussed further in the rest of this chapter. Leading, motivating, and considering groups and teams; corporate culture; and creativity and innovation are discussed in Chapters 15, 16, 17, and 18 and in Appendix 1.

Communication

Communication is the process of sharing information with other individuals. Information, as understood here, is any thought or idea that managers want to share with others. In general, communication involves the process of one person projecting a message to one or more other people, which results in everyone arriving at a common understanding of the message. Because communication is a commonly used management skill and ability, and because it is often cited as the skill most responsible for a manager's success, prospective managers must learn how to

14-3   An understanding of how communication works

communicate.[13] To help managers become better interpersonal communicators, new training techniques are constantly being developed and evaluated.[14]

The communication activities of managers generally involve interpersonal communication—sharing information with other organization members.[15] The following sections feature both the general topic of interpersonal communication and the more specific topic of interpersonal communication in organizations.

Interpersonal Communication

To be a successful interpersonal communicator, a manager must understand the following:

1. How interpersonal communication works
2. The relationship between feedback and interpersonal communication
3. The importance of verbal versus nonverbal interpersonal communication

How Interpersonal Communication Works

Interpersonal communication is the process of transmitting information to others.[16] To be complete, the process must have the following three basic elements:[17]

1. **The source/encoder**—The **source/encoder** is the person in the interpersonal communication situation who originates and encodes information to be shared with others. Encoding is putting information into a form that can be received and understood by another individual. Putting one's thoughts into a letter is an example of encoding. Until information is encoded, it cannot be shared with others. (From this point on, the *source/encoder* will be referred to simply as the *source*.)
2. **The signal**—Encoded information that the source intends to share constitutes a **message**. A message that has been transmitted from one person to another is called a **signal**.
3. **The decoder/destination**—The **decoder/destination** is the person or persons with whom the source is attempting to share information. This person receives the signal and decodes, or interprets, the message to determine its meaning. Decoding is the process of converting messages back into information. In all interpersonal communication situations, message meaning is the result of decoding. (From this point on, the *decoder/destination* will be referred to simply as the *destination*.)

The classic work of Wilbur Schramm clarifies the role played by each of the three elements of the interpersonal communication process. As implied in **Figure 14.4**, the source determines what information to share, encodes that information in the form of a message, and then transmits the message as a signal to the destination. The destination decodes the transmitted message to determine its meaning and then responds accordingly.

A manager who desires to assign the performance of a certain task to a subordinate would use the communication process in the following way: First, the manager would determine exactly what task he or she wants the subordinate to perform. Then the manager would encode and transmit to the subordinate a message that would accurately reflect this assignment. The message transmission itself could be as simple as the manager telling the subordinate what the new responsibilities include. Next, the subordinate would decode the message transmitted by the manager to ascertain its meaning and then respond to it appropriately.

Successful and Unsuccessful Interpersonal Communication

Successful communication refers to an interpersonal communication situation in which the information that the source intends to share with the destination and the meaning that the

Figure 14.4

Roles of the source, signal, and destination in the communication process

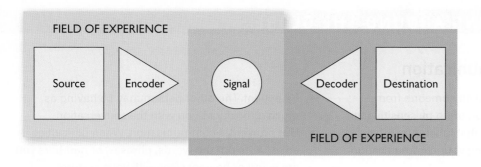

destination derives from the transmitted message are the same. Conversely, **unsuccessful communication** is an interpersonal communication situation in which the information that the source intends to share with the destination and the meaning that the destination derives from the transmitted message are different.

To increase the probability that communication will be successful, the message must be encoded so that the source's experience of the way a signal should be decoded is equivalent to the destination's experience of the way it should be decoded. If these experiences match up, the probability is high that the destination will interpret the signal as intended by the source. **Figure 14.5** illustrates these overlapping fields of experience that ensure successful communication.

Barriers to Successful Interpersonal Communication
Factors that decrease the probability that communication will be successful are called *communication barriers.* A clear understanding of these barriers will help managers maximize their communication success. The following sections discuss both communication macrobarriers and communication microbarriers.

MACROBARRIERS

Communication macrobarriers are factors that hinder successful communication in a general communication situation.[18] These factors relate primarily to the communication environment and to the larger world in which communication takes place. Some common macrobarriers include the following:[19]

1. **The increasing need for information**—Because society is changing constantly and rapidly, individuals have an increasingly greater need for information. This growing need tends to overload communication networks, thereby distorting communication. To minimize the effects of this barrier, managers should take steps to ensure that organization members are not overloaded with information. Only information critical to the performance of their jobs should be transmitted to them.

   The White House is an example of an organization that regularly faces an increasing need for information from a variety of audiences, including the American public. After an evaluation of President Barack Obama's first year in office, the White House staff decided to retool elements of its communication strategy to better meet increasing needs for information that others might have. As a result of this evaluation, the White House staff decided to take specific steps to better meet such increasing needs—for example, staffers should be more aggressive in taking initiative in sending out information before it's requested. In addition, they should provide speedier, more exact responses to information requests and help the president be more efficient when communicating with others.[20]

2. **The need for increasingly complex information**—Because of today's rapid technological advances, most people are confronted with complex communication situations in their everyday lives. However, if managers take steps to emphasize simplicity in communication, the effects of this barrier can be lessened. Furnishing organization members with adequate training to deal with more technical areas is another strategy for overcoming this barrier.

3. **The reality that people in the United States are increasingly coming into contact with people who use languages other than English**—As U.S. business becomes more international in scope and as organization members travel more frequently, the need to

TIPS FOR MANAGING AROUND THE GLOBE

Cross-Cultural Communication

When talking one-on-one with someone from another culture, it's important to be sensitive to the barriers of communication that inherently exist. Some suggestions for improving your communication experience are:[21]

- Talk clearly. Though the other individual may speak English, it may be his or her second or third language, so speak slowly and clearly so you can be understood.
- Avoid colloquialisms. The use of slang and industry-specific jargon can be confusing to another person.
- Be professional. Different cultures may be more formal or more relaxed than you, so err on the side of being more formal.

- Be patient. The other person may be having as much difficulty as you with the conversation.
- Use nonverbal communication. When difficulties arise, write out the words, phrases, or numbers you are using or be very clear with your gestures.
- Repeat what you have heard. Ensure there is no confusion by repeating what you have understood from the other individual.
- Show respect. If possible, do some research ahead of time in order to acknowledge and respect the other person's culture.
- Be aware of personal space. Some cultures may stand closer or further away during personal conversations.

know languages other than English increases. The potential communication barrier of this multilanguage situation is obvious. People who deal with foreigners need to be familiar with not only their languages but also their cultures. Formal knowledge of a foreign language is of little value unless the individual also knows which words, phrases, and actions are culturally acceptable.[22]

4. **The constant need to learn new concepts, which cuts down on the time available for communication**—Many managers feel pressured to learn new and important concepts that they did not need to know in the past. Learning about the intricacies of international business or computer usage, for example, takes up significant amounts of managerial time. Many managers also find that the increased demands that training employees makes on their time leaves them with little time to communicate with other organization members.

MICROBARRIERS

A **communication microbarrier** is a factor that hinders successful communication in a specific communication situation.[23] This factor relates directly to variables such as the communication message, the source, and the destination. Among the microbarriers are the following:[24]

1. **Source's view of the destination**—The source in any communication situation has a tendency to view the destination in a specific way, and this view influences the messages sent. For example, individuals usually speak one way to people they think are informed about a subject and another way to those they believe are uninformed. The destination can sense the source's attitudes, which often blocks successful communication. Managers should thus keep an open mind about the people with whom they communicate and be careful not to imply negative attitudes through their communication behaviors. **Figure 14.6** lists several examples of negative attitudes or stereotypes that managers in our society might possess regarding various types of employees. If managers possess such negative feelings about employees, those feelings will inevitably have a negative impact on the managers' communications with those employees and ultimately limit organizational success. Such negative attitudes or stereotypes have no place in the world of modern management.

2. **Message interference**—A stimulus that competes with the communication message for the attention of the destination is called **message interference**, or noise. An example of message interference is a manager talking to a worker while the worker is trying to input

Employee Type	Possible Negative Attitude Held
Women	Women have weak math ability
Senior citizens	Older people have bad memory
Gay men	Gay men are dangerous to young children
Whites	Whites are racists
Men	Men are less capable than women in dealing with emotional issues
Black men	Black men are more coordinated than white men

Figure 14.6

Examples of managers' potentially negative attitudes toward employees[25]

data into a computer. The inputting of data is the message interference because it is competing with the manager's communication message. Managers should attempt to communicate only when they have the total attention of the individuals with whom they wish to share information.

3. **Destination's view of the source**—Certain attitudes of the destination toward the source can also hinder successful communication. If, for example, a destination believes that the source has little credibility in the area about which the source is communicating, the destination may filter out much of the source's message and pay only slight attention to that part of the message actually received. Managers should attempt to consider the worth of messages transmitted to them independently of their personal attitudes toward the source. Many valuable ideas will escape them if they allow their personal feelings toward others to influence which messages they attend to.

4. **Perception**—**Perception** is an individual's interpretation of a message. Different individuals may perceive the same message in different ways. The two primary factors that influence how a message is perceived are the destination's education level and the destination's amount of experience. To minimize the negative effects of this perceptual factor on interpersonal communication, managers should try to send messages with precise meanings. Ambiguous words generally tend to magnify negative perceptions. What's more, trite or insincere messages are easy for employees to detect.[26]

5. **Multimeaning words**—Because many words in the English language have several meanings, a destination may have difficulty deciding which meaning should be attached to the words of a message. A manager should not assume that a word means the same thing to all the people who use it.

A classic study by Lydia Strong substantiates this point. Strong concluded that for the 500 most common words in the English language, there are 4,070 different dictionary definitions. On average, each of these words has more than eight usages. The word *run* is an example:[27]

Babe Ruth scored a run.

Did you ever see Jesse Owens run?

I have a run *in my stocking.*

There is a fine run *of salmon this year.*

Are you going to run *this company or am I?*

You have the run *of the place.*

What headline do you want to run?

There was a run *on the bank today.*

Did he run *the ship aground?*

I have to run *[drive the car] downtown.*

Who will run *for president this year?*

Joe flies the New York–Chicago run *twice a week.*

You know the kind of people they run *around with.*

The apples run *large this year.*

Please run *my bathwater.*

Employees being more proactive and exact in dispensing of information helps managers communicate more efficiently.

When encoding information, managers should be careful to define whenever possible the terms they are using, avoid using obscure meanings for words when designing messages, and strive to use words in the same way that their destination uses them.

Feedback and Interpersonal Communication
Feedback is the destination's reaction to a message. Feedback can be used by the source to ensure successful communication. For example, if the destination's message reaction is inappropriate, the source can conclude that communication was unsuccessful and that another message should be transmitted. If the destination's message reaction is appropriate, the source can conclude that communication was successful (assuming, of course, that the appropriate reaction did not happen merely by chance). Because of its potentially high value, managers should encourage feedback whenever possible and evaluate it carefully.[28]

Gathering and Using Feedback
Feedback can be either verbal or nonverbal.[29] To gather verbal feedback, the source can simply ask the destination pertinent message-related questions; the destination's answers should indicate whether the message was perceived as intended. To gather nonverbal feedback, the source can observe the destination's nonverbal response to a message.[30] Let's say that a manager has transmitted a message to a subordinate, specifying new steps that must be taken in the normal performance of the subordinate's job. The subordinate's failure to follow the steps accurately constitutes nonverbal feedback telling the manager that the initial message needs to be clarified.

If managers discover that their communication effectiveness is relatively low over an extended period of time, they should assess the situation to determine how to improve their communication skills. It may be that their vocabulary is confusing to their destinations. For example, a study conducted by Group Attitudes Corporation found that when managers used certain words repeatedly in communicating with steelworkers, the steelworkers usually became confused.[31] Among the words causing confusion were *accrue*, *contemplate*, *designate*, *detriment*, *magnitude*, and *subsequently*.

Achieving Communication Effectiveness
In general, managers can sharpen their communication skills by adhering to the following "10 commandments of good communication" as closely as possible:[32]

1. **Seek to clarify your ideas before communicating**—The more systematically you analyze the problem or idea to be communicated, the clearer it becomes. This is the first step toward effective communication. Many communications fail because of inadequate planning. Good planning must consider the goals and attitudes of those who will receive the communication and those who will be affected by it.
2. **Examine the true purpose of each communication**—Before you communicate, ask yourself what you really want to accomplish with your message—obtain information, initiate action, change another person's attitude? Identify your most important goal and then adapt your language, tone, and total approach to serve that specific objective. Don't try to accomplish too much with each communication. The sharper the focus of your message, the greater its chances of success.
3. **Consider the total physical and human setting whenever you communicate**—Meaning and intent are conveyed by more than words alone. Many other factors influence the overall impact of a communication, and managers must be sensitive to the total setting in which they communicate. Consider, for example, your sense of timing, or the circumstances under which you make an announcement or render a decision; the physical setting; whether you communicate in private or otherwise, for example, the social climate that pervades work relationships within your company or department and sets the tone of its communications; and custom and practice, or the degree to which your communication conforms to, or departs from, the expectations of your audience. Be constantly aware of the total setting in which you communicate. Like all living things, communication must be capable of adapting to its environment.

4. **Consult with others, when appropriate, in planning communications**—Frequently, it is desirable or necessary to seek the participation of others in planning a communication or in developing the facts on which to base the communication. Such consultation often lends additional insight and objectivity to your message. Those who have helped you plan your communication will give it their active support.

5. **Be mindful of the overtones while you communicate rather than merely the basic content of your message**—Your tone of voice, your expression, and your apparent receptiveness to the responses of others have a significant effect on those you wish to reach. Frequently overlooked, these subtleties of communication often affect a listener's reaction to a message even more than its basic content. Similarly, your choice of language—particularly your awareness of the fine shades of meaning and emotion in the words you use—predetermines, in large part, the reactions of your listeners.

6. **Take the opportunity, when it arises, to convey something of help or value to the receiver**—Consideration of the other person's interests and needs—trying to look at things from the other person's point of view—frequently points out opportunities to convey something of immediate benefit or long-range value to the other person. Subordinates are most responsive to managers whose messages take the subordinates' interests into account.

7. **Follow up your communication**—Your best efforts at communication may be wasted, and you may never know whether you have succeeded in expressing your true meaning and intent, if you do not follow up and evaluate how well your message was received. You can do this by asking questions, encouraging the receiver to express his or her reactions, following up on contacts, and subsequently reviewing performance. Make certain that you get feedback for every important communication so that complete understanding and appropriate action result.

8. **Communicate for tomorrow as well as today**—Even though communications may be aimed primarily at meeting the demands of an immediate situation, they must be planned with the past in mind if they are to be viewed as consistent by the receiver. Most important, however, communications must be consistent with long-range interests and goals. For example, it is not easy to communicate frankly on matters such as poor performance or the shortcomings of a loyal subordinate, but postponing disagreeable communications makes these matters more difficult in the long run and is actually unfair to your subordinates and your company.

9. **Be sure your actions support your communications**—In the final analysis, the most persuasive kind of communication is not what you say but what you do. When your actions or attitudes contradict your words, others tend to discount what you have said. For every manager, good supervisory practices—such as clear assignment of responsibility and authority, fair rewards for effort, and sound policy enforcement—communicate more than all the gifts of oratory.

10. **Last, but by no means least, seek not only to be understood, but also to understand—be a good listener**—When you start talking, you often cease to listen, or at least to be attuned to the other person's unspoken reactions and attitudes. Even more serious is the occasional inattentiveness you may be guilty of when others are attempting to communicate with you. Listening is one of the most important, most difficult, and most neglected skills in communication. It demands that you concentrate not only on the explicit meanings that another person is expressing but also on the implicit meanings, unspoken words, and undertones that may be far more significant.

Verbal and Nonverbal Interpersonal Communication   Interpersonal communication is generally divided into two types: verbal and nonverbal. Up to this point, this chapter has emphasized **verbal communication**—communication that uses either spoken or written words to share information with others.

Nonverbal communication is sharing information without using words to encode thoughts. Factors commonly used to encode thoughts in nonverbal communication are gestures, vocal tones, and facial expressions.[33] In most interpersonal communication, however, verbal and nonverbal communications are not mutually exclusive. Instead, the destination's interpretation of a message is generally based both on the words contained in the message and on nonverbal factors such as the source's gestures and facial expressions.

STEPS FOR SUCCESS

Crafting an Elevator Speech

The idea behind an *elevator speech* is that, if you were on an elevator in a high-rise building and someone introduced him- or herself to you, what would you say about yourself before the elevator reached the top of the building? Developing an elevator speech is essential when you are networking at events such as job fairs or professional meetings. Being able to describe who you are concisely is key. Here are some suggestions:

- Your introduction should be less than one minute. Anything over one minute may cause some to lose interest.

- Highlight only the essentials. Mention your name, where you work, your college and major, and why you are qualified for the job (or are interested in networking with the other person).
- Make eye contact. During your elevator speech, be sure to maintain appropriate eye contact.
- Give a firm handshake. Either at the beginning or end of your elevator speech, shake the other person's hand in a firm, professional manner.
- Practice. The best elevator speeches do not sound rehearsed, but they are polished.

The Importance of Nonverbal Communication   In an interpersonal communication situation in which both verbal and nonverbal factors are present, nonverbal factors may have more influence on the total effect of the message.[34] Over two decades ago, Albert Mehrabian developed the following formula to indicate the relative contributions of verbal and nonverbal factors to the total effect of a message: total message impact $= 0.07$ words $+ 0.38$ vocal tones $+ 0.55$ facial expressions. Other nonverbal factors besides vocal tones that can influence the effect of a verbal message are facial expressions, gestures, gender, and dress. Managers who are aware of this great potential influence of nonverbal factors on the effect of their communications will use nonverbal message components to complement their verbal message components whenever possible.[35]

Nonverbal messages can also be used to add meaning to verbal messages. For instance, one may nod one's head or change the tone of one's voice to show either agreement or disagreement.

Managers must be especially careful when they are communicating that verbal and nonverbal factors do not present contradictory messages. For example, if the words of a message express approval while the nonverbal factors express disapproval, the result will be message ambiguity that leaves the destination frustrated.

Managers who are able to communicate successfully through a blend of verbal and nonverbal communication are critical to the success of virtually every organization. In fact, the Darden Graduate School of Business at the University of Virginia commissioned a recent survey of corporate recruiters across the United States, and the survey revealed that the skill most organizations seek in prospective employees is facility at verbal and nonverbal communication.

Interpersonal Communication in Organizations

14-4 Hints for communicating in organizations

To be effective communicators, managers must understand not only general interpersonal communication concepts but also the characteristics of interpersonal communication within organizations, or **organizational communication**. Organizational communication relates directly to the goals, functions, and structure of human organizations.[36] To a large extent, organizational success is determined by the effectiveness of organizational communication.[37]

Although organizational communication was frequently referred to by early management writers, the topic did not receive systematic study and attention until after World War II. From World War II through the 1950s, the discipline of organizational communication made significant advances in areas such as mathematical communication theory and behavioral communication theory, and the emphasis on organizational communication has grown stronger in colleges of business throughout the nation since the 1970s.[38] The following sections focus on three fundamental organizational communication topics: (1) formal organizational communication, (2) informal organizational communication, and (3) the encouragement of formal organizational communication.

Formal Organizational Communication

In general, organizational communication that follows the lines of the organization chart is called **formal organizational communication**.[39] As discussed in Chapter 10, the organization chart depicts relationships among people and jobs and shows the formal channels of communication among them.

Types of Formal Organizational Communication   The three basic types of formal organizational communication are downward, upward, and lateral.

1. **Downward organizational communication** is communication that flows from any point on an organization chart downward to another point on the organization chart. This type of formal organizational communication is associated primarily with the direction and control of employees. Job-related information that focuses on what activities are required, when they should be performed, and how they should be coordinated with other activities within the organization must be transmitted to employees. This downward communication typically includes a statement of organizational philosophy, management system objectives, position descriptions, and other written information relating to the importance, rationale, and interrelationships of various departments.

   Downward communication thus refers to the messages that management delivers to employees. Such communication can have a significant impact on an organization's productivity and hence its profitability. Thanks to technological advances, many organizations are able to leverage technology to enhance the communication that flows from management to the workforce. Consider, for example, Ericsson, a leading manufacturer of telecommunication equipment and a service provider. With a geographically dispersed workforce, Ericsson leadership sought an efficient way to communicate company news quickly and uniformly throughout the organization. Ericsson turned to audio podcasting as a way to deliver up-to-the-minute information to its over 75,000 employees in the field. Podcasts have helped the company boost the effectiveness of its salesforce.[40]

2. **Upward organizational communication** is communication that flows from any point on an organization chart upward to another point on the organization chart.[41] This type of organizational communication contains primarily the information managers need in order to evaluate the organizational area for which they are responsible and to determine whether something is going wrong within it. Techniques that managers commonly use to encourage upward organizational communication are informal discussions with employees, attitude surveys, the development and use of grievance procedures, suggestion systems, and an open-door policy that invites employees to come in whenever they would like to talk to management.[42] Organizational modifications that are based on the feedback provided by upward organizational communication enable a company to be more successful in the future.

3. **Lateral organizational communication** is communication that flows from any point on an organization chart horizontally to another point on the organization chart. Communication that flows across the organization usually focuses on coordinating the activities of various departments and developing new plans for future operating periods. Within the organization, all departments are in communication with all other departments. Only through lateral communication can these departmental relationships be coordinated well enough to enhance the attainment of management system objectives.

Patterns of Formal Organizational Communication   By its very nature, organizational communication creates patterns of communication among organization members. These patterns evolve from the repeated occurrence of various serial transmissions of information. According to Haney, a **serial transmission** involves passing information from one individual to another in a series. It occurs under the following circumstances:[43]

Figure 14.7

Comparison of three patterns of organizational communication based on the variables of speed, accuracy, organization, emergence of leader, and morale

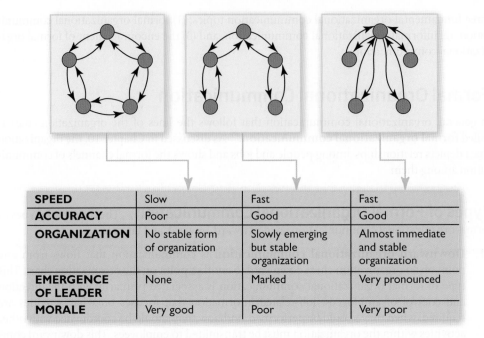

SPEED	Slow	Fast	Fast
ACCURACY	Poor	Good	Good
ORGANIZATION	No stable form of organization	Slowly emerging but stable organization	Almost immediate and stable organization
EMERGENCE OF LEADER	None	Marked	Very pronounced
MORALE	Very good	Poor	Very poor

A communicates a message to B, B then communicates A's message (or rather his or her interpretation of A's message) to C, C then communicates his or her interpretation of B's interpretation of A's message to D, and so on. The originator and the ultimate recipient of the message are separated by middle people.

One obvious weakness of a serial transmission is that messages tend to become distorted as the length of the series increases. Research has shown that message details may be omitted, altered, or added in a serial transmission.

The potential inaccuracy of transmitted messages is not the only weakness of serial transmissions. A classic article by Alex Bavelas and Dermot Barrett makes the case that serial transmissions can also influence morale, the emergence of a leader, the degree to which individuals involved in the transmissions are organized, and these individuals' efficiency.[44] Three basic organizational communication patterns and their corresponding effects on the variables just mentioned are shown in **Figure 14.7**.

MyLab Management Watch It

If your instructor has assigned this activity, go to www.pearson.com/mylab/management to complete the video exercise.

Informal Organizational Communication

Informal organizational communication does not follow the lines of the organization chart.[45] Instead, this type of communication typically follows the pattern of personal relationships among organization members: One friend communicates with another friend, regardless of their relative positions on the organization chart. Informal organizational communication networks generally exist because organization members have a desire for information that is not furnished through formal organizational communication.[46] In times of economic downturn, for example, informal communication tends to increase because organization members are scavenging for information from almost anyone regarding how well the organization is doing and if job cutbacks seem imminent.[47]

To manage informal organizational communication appropriately, managers must strive to understand how this informal network operates in their organizations. For example, at Steelcase in Grand Rapids, Michigan, management conducted a study to better understand the informal communication that went on within the company. The study yielded valuable information: For instance, at Steelcase the days of standing around the water cooler to exchange the latest organizational gossip or company news may be over. Only 1 percent of Steelcase employees go to the cooler to get something besides water. At Steelcase, informal communication conversations are more likely to take place in the office kitchen, at a coworker's desk, or through e-mail.[48]

Patterns of Informal Organizational Communication
The informal organizational communication network, or **grapevine**, has three main characteristics:

1. It springs up and is used irregularly within the organization.
2. It is not controlled by top executives, who may not even be able to influence it.
3. It exists largely to serve the self-interests of the people within it.

Understanding the grapevine is a prerequisite for a complete understanding of organizational communication. It has been estimated that 70 percent of all communication in organizations flows along the organizational grapevine. Not only do grapevines carry great amounts of communication, but they also carry it at rapid speeds. Employees commonly cite the company grapevine as the most reliable and credible source of information about company events.[49]

Like formal organizational communication, informal organizational communication uses serial transmissions. The difference is that it is more difficult for managers to identify the organization members involved in these informal transmissions than it is for managers to identify the members of the formal communication network. A classic article by Keith Davis that appeared in the *Harvard Business Review* has been a significant help to managers in understanding how organizational grapevines spring up and operate. **Figure 14.8** sketches the four most common grapevine patterns as outlined by Davis. These pattern are as follows:[50]

1. **The single-strand grapevine**—A tells B, who tells C, who tells D, and so on. This type of grapevine tends to distort messages more than any other.
2. **The gossip grapevine**—A informs everyone else on the grapevine.
3. **The probability grapevine**—A communicates randomly—for example, to F and D. F and D then continue to inform other grapevine members in the same way.
4. **The cluster grapevine**—A selects and tells C, D, and F. F selects and tells I and B, and B selects and tells J. Information in this grapevine travels only to selected individuals.

DEALING WITH GRAPEVINES

Clearly, grapevines are a factor that managers must deal with because grapevines can, and often do, generate rumors that are detrimental to organizational success. Exactly how individual managers should deal with the grapevine, of course, depends on the specific organizational situation in which they find themselves. For example, managers can use grapevines advantageously to maximize information flow to employees. When employees have what they view as sufficient organizational information, their sense of belonging to the organization and their level of productivity seem to increase. Some writers even argue that managers should encourage the development of grapevines and strive to become grapevine members so that they can gain feedback that could be valuable in improving the organization.[51]

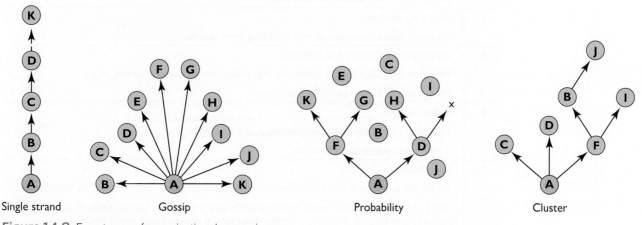

Figure 14.8 Four types of organizational grapevines

Encouraging Organizational Communication

14-5   Useful ideas for encouraging organizational communication

Because an organization acts only in the way its organizational communication directs it to act, organizational communication is often called the *nervous system of the organization*. Formal organizational communication is generally the more important type of communication within an organization, so managers should encourage its free flow.

One strategy for promoting formal organizational communication is to listen attentively to messages that come through formal channels. Listening shows organization members that the manager is interested in what subordinates have to say and encourages them to use formal communication channels in subsequent situations. **Table 14.2** presents some general guidelines for being a good listener.

The United Kingdom segment of McDonald's offers a useful example of how to increase listening within a company. When faced with meeting a number of daunting organizational challenges, U.K. CEO Peter Beresford instituted a program called Listening Campaign. Under the program, Beresford and his staff had face-to-face meetings with various stakeholder groups, including staff members, customers, and investors. The purpose was to listen to stakeholders and gather input regarding the challenges Beresford faced. According to Beresford, the success of Listening Campaign was undeniable. Through listening, he achieved numerous benefits, including building more effective work teams, identifying organizational problems and their solutions, and implementing sound problem solutions.[52]

TABLE 14.2   Ten Commandments for Being a Good Listener

1.	*Stop talking!*
	You cannot listen if you are talking.
	Polonius (*Hamlet*): "Give every man thine ear, but few thy voice."
2.	*Put the talker at ease.*
	Help the talker feel free to talk.
	This is often called establishing a permissive environment.
3.	*Show the talker that you want to listen.*
	Look and act interested. Do not read your e-mail while he or she talks.
	Listen to understand rather than to oppose.
4.	*Remove distractions.*
	Do not doodle, tap, or shuffle papers.
	Will it be quieter if you shut the door?
5.	*Empathize with the talker.*
	Try to put yourself in the talker's place so that you can see his or her point of view.
6.	*Be patient.*
	Allow plenty of time. Do not interrupt the talker.
	Do not head for the door or walk away.
7.	*Hold your temper.*
	An angry person gets the wrong meaning from words.
8.	*Go easy on argument and criticism.*
	This puts the talker on the defensive. He or she may "clam up" or get angry.
	Do not argue: Even if you win, you *lose*.
9.	*Ask questions.*
	This encourages the talker and shows you are listening.
	It helps to develop points further.
10.	*Stop talking!*
	This is the first and the last commandment because all other commandments depend on it.
	You just can't do a good job of listening while you are talking. Nature gave us two ears but only one tongue, which is a gentle hint that we should listen more than we talk.

Some other strategies to encourage the flow of formal organizational communication are as follows:

- Support the flow of clear and concise statements through formal communication channels. Receiving an ambiguous message through a formal organizational communication channel can discourage employees from using that channel again.
- Ensure that all organization members have free access to formal communication channels. Obviously, organization members cannot communicate formally within the organization if they don't have access to the formal communication network.
- Assign specific communication responsibilities to the staff personnel who could be of enormous help to line personnel in spreading important information throughout the organization.
- Make sure that the leaders sending messages are trusted by the workforce. A recent study reported than less than 40 percent of employees have trust or confidence in their senior leadership.[53]

CHALLENGE CASE SUMMARY

One of Evernote CEO Phil Libin's primary responsibilities is *influencing*—guiding the activities of Evernote employees to enhance the accomplishment of organizational objectives. Libin could perform this function by *leading* individuals such as division managers or software engineers, *motivating* them to do better jobs, working well with various *groups* of employees, *encouraging* creativity and innovation, and *communicating* successfully with employees.

Of all these influencing activities, however, communicating should be especially important to Libin. Communication is the main tool through which Libin and his leadership team should, at least to some extent, accomplish their duties. As an example in the Challenge Case, his announcements at weekly all-employee meetings contribute to his goal of ensuring that employees understand how their work contributes to the company's larger vision. Almost any impact (planning, organizing, or controlling) Libin plans to exert on Evernote will require him to communicate with other Evernote employees. In essence, Libin must be a good communicator if he is to be a successful manager at Evernote.

In discussing Phil Libin's ability to communicate, we are actually discussing his ability to share ideas with other Evernote employees. For Libin to be a successful communicator, he must concentrate on the three essential elements of the communication process. The first element is the source—the individual who wishes to share information with another. For example, when Libin is sharing the company's vision with employees, he is the source. The second element is the signal—the message transmitted by Libin. The third element is the destination—in this example, the Evernote employees with whom Libin wishes to share information. Libin should communicate with Evernote employees by determining what information he wants to share, encoding the information, and then transmitting the message. The employees will then interpret the message and respond accordingly. Libin's communication is successful if subordinates interpret messages as he intends.

If Libin is to be a successful communicator, he must minimize the impact of numerous communication barriers, including:

1. Evernote employees needing to have more information and more complex information to do their jobs
2. Message interference
3. Libin's view of the destination as well as the destination's view of Libin
4. The perceptual process of the people involved in the communication attempt
5. Words with multiple meanings

The employees' reactions to Libin's messages can provide him with perhaps his most useful tool for making communication successful—feedback. When feedback does not seem appropriate, Libin should transmit another message to clarify the meaning of his first message. He must be alert to both verbal and nonverbal feedback. Over time, if feedback indicates that Libin is a relatively unsuccessful communicator, he should analyze the situation carefully to improve his communication effectiveness. He might find, for instance, that he is using vocabulary that is generally inappropriate for certain employees or that he is not following one or more of the 10 commandments of good communication.

In addition, Libin must remember that he can communicate without using words. His facial expressions, gestures, and even the tone of his voice convey meaning to people. Most of Libin's communication situations involve both verbal and nonverbal messages to Evernote employees. Because the impact of a message may be generated mostly by its nonverbal components, Libin must be certain that his nonverbal messages complement his verbal messages. For example, with his use of a robot to visit employees' work areas, as mentioned in the Challenge Case, Libin conveys the message that he wants employees to interact with him even when he is away from the office.

As CEO of Evernote, Phil Libin must strive to understand the intricacies of organizational communication—that is, interpersonal communication as it takes place within the organization. The success of organizational communication at Evernote is an important factor in determining the company's level of success. Libin can communicate with his people in two basic ways: formally and informally.

In general, Libin's formal communication should follow the lines on the organization chart. Libin can communicate downward to, for example, divisional managers or upward to, for example, Evernote's board of directors. Libin's downward communication will commonly focus on the company's vision and the activities that subordinates are performing. His upward communication will usually illustrate how the company is performing. Because Libin is CEO and has no one else at the same level within the organization, he would not communicate laterally. He should take steps, however, to ensure that lateral communication does occur at other organizational levels in order to enhance planning and coordination at Evernote.

It is certain that an extensive grapevine exists at Evernote. Although the company grapevine must be dealt with, Libin may not be able to influence it significantly. Evernote employees, like employees at any other company, typically are involved in grapevines for self-interest and because the formal organization has not furnished them with the information they believe they need.

By developing various social relationships, Libin could conceivably become part of the grapevine and obtain valuable feedback from it. Also, because grapevines generate rumors that could have a detrimental effect on Evernote's success, Libin should try to ensure that personnel are given, through formal organization communication, all the information they need to do their jobs well, thereby reducing the need for a grapevine.

Because formal organizational communication is vitally important to Evernote, Libin should try to encourage its flow as much as possible. By listening intently to messages that come to him over formal channels, supporting the flow of clear messages, and making sure that all Evernote employees have access to these channels, Libin can make sure that Evernote's communication is the best it can be.

MyLab Management Assessing Your Management Skill

If your instructor has assigned this activity, go to www.pearson.com/mylab/management to complete the exercise related to the Challenge Case.

DEVELOPING COMMUNICATION SKILL

This section is specially designed to help you develop communication skills. An individual's communication skill is based on an understanding of the concepts and the ability to apply those concepts. The following activities will help to enhance your communication skills in various management situations.

Class Preparation and Personal Study

To help you prepare for class, perform the activities outlined in this section. Performing these activities will help you enhance your classroom performance significantly.

Reflecting on Target Skill

On page 334, this chapter opens by presenting a target management skill along with a list of related objectives outlining knowledge and understanding that you should aim to acquire related to that skill. Review this target skill and the list of objectives to make sure that you've acquired all pertinent information in the chapter. If you do not feel that you've reached a particular objective(s), study related chapter coverage until you do.

Know Key Terms

Understanding the following key terms is critical to your preparing for class. Define each of these terms. Refer to the page(s) referenced after a term to check your definition or to gain further insight regarding the term.

influencing **336**
emotional intelligence **338**
communication **339**
source/encoder **340**
message **340**
signal **340**
decoder/destination **340**
successful communication **340**
unsuccessful communication **341**
communication macrobarrier **341**
communication microbarrier **342**
message interference **342**
perception **343**
feedback **344**
verbal communication **345**
nonverbal communication **345**
organizational communication **346**
formal organizational communication **347**
serial transmission **347**
informal organizational communication **348**
grapevine **349**

Know How Management Concepts Relate

This section comprises activities that will sharpen your understanding of communication concepts. Answer these essay questions as completely as possible.

14-1 Using examples, list and explain common macrobarriers.

14-2 Distinguish between the three main types of formal organizational communication.

14-3 Draw three types of organizational grapevines and explain how communication effectiveness might be affected by each type.

MyLab Management
Personal Inventory Assessment

Go to www.pearson.com/mylab/management to complete the Personal Inventory Assessment related to this chapter.

 PERSONAL INVENTORY ASSESSMENT

Management Skills Exercises

Learning activities in this section are aimed at helping you develop communication skills.

MyLab Management
Discussion Questions

Go to www.pearson.com/mylab/management to complete the problems marked with this icon ✪.

✪ Cases

How Evernote's Phil Libin Keeps Communication Flowing

The Challenge Case "How Evernote's Phil Libin Keeps Communication Flowing" (p. 335) and its related Challenge Case Summary were written to help you better understand the management concepts contained in this chapter. Answer the following discussion questions about the Challenge Case to see how your understanding of influencing and communication can be applied in a company like Evernote.

14-4 List three problems that could have resulted at Evernote if Libin had been a poor communicator.

14-5 Explain how the problems you listed in number 14-4 could have been caused by Libin's inability to communicate.

14-6 Assuming that Libin is a good communicator, discuss three ways he is positively affecting Evernote because of his communication expertise.

Houston Zoo Improves Internal Communication

Read the case and answer the questions that follow. Studying this case will help you better understand how concepts relating to communication can be applied in an organization such as Houston Zoo.

The Houston Zoo is a large facility in Southeast Texas with nearly 2.5 million visitors each year, and they come to see over 6,000 animals. It takes a large employee base to staff an operation like this—over 400 such associates. They ensure the well-being of the animals, but they also make certain that guests have a safe and fun experience. Communication in an environment like this is vital.

Recently, Houston Zoo enhanced its internal communication processes through an advanced intranet system that permits employees to share data, find the information they need to perform their jobs, and engage in simple and complex tasks. Everything from medical guides for veterinarians to how to fill out a human resource benefit form is on the new intranet system. But this was not always the case. According to Houston Zoo's web administrator, Kara Masharani, "Staff spent a lot of time telling each other how to accomplish a simple task like getting a new name badge, where stuff was stored or which version of a file or form was the most current. We needed a better and faster way for people to get to that information."

When the new intranet system, nicknamed The Watering Hole, was first launched, it was kept fairly simple. "We started by getting together 12 people from different departments," said Masharani, "including zookeepers, finance, and purchasing, and asked them what they needed from the new platform. We then figured out 20 things that were most greatly needed to be easily accessible and mapped out the site structure accordingly."

Today, The Watering Hole has become more expansive, covering numerous internal communication activities. And employees are readily utilizing the site. "Almost all our staff sign-in to the intranet every day," Masharani said. "Even staff who work out in the grounds will visit a PC for a few minutes to access The Watering Hole for the latest information and news."

Associates have found the intranet system extremely helpful for not only communicating internally but also serving guests at the zoo. Customer service has improved because employees can easily find and access information that serves guests efficiently and effectively. One aspect

that has been particularly helpful is the installation of several "I want to . . . " tabs. This saves a significant amount of time because an employee can easily type in to the prompt something along the lines of "I want to . . . reserve a meeting room." Everything that is needed to do this task is then available to the associate. According to Masharani, "You can click to do routine tasks, from reserving a cart for a visitor, to ordering new business cards, requesting uniforms, or logging a support ticket with the IT team."

Keeping the hundreds of employees up to date on events at the zoo is also important. The Watering Hole facilitates the dissemination of information among the staff members. "Our staff meetings are really fun, and there's often interesting news, like an animal birth announcement or a new species arriving at the zoo. The only problem," Masharani said, "is that not everyone can attend, either because it's their day off, or because they're out working on site." With The Watering Hole, associates can stay abreast of the latest news. "It's just one more way that the technology brings us all together and makes us feel part of the same team," she said.[54]

Questions

14-7 Using terms from this chapter, assess Houston Zoo's internal communication system called The Watering Hole. What are its strengths? What are its weaknesses?

14-8 What macrobarriers and microbarriers do you think might exist for The Watering Hole?

14-9 Which type or types of formal organizational communication are embodied by The Watering Hole? Explain.

14-10 What advice would you give to Kara Masharani to improve The Watering Hole? Why?

Experiential Exercises

Developing Nonverbal Communication Skills

Directions. Read the following scenario and then perform the listed activities. Your instructor may wish you to perform the activities as an individual or within groups. Follow all of your instructor's directions carefully.

The purpose of this exercise is to develop your nonverbal communication skills. Apply yourself as much as possible. The more you focus on the activity, the greater your chances of developing your skill will be.

Procedure

1. Instructors need to divide the class into groups of approximately four students each.
2. Each group is then given 10 minutes to complete the following task via a group discussion: *List as many advantages and disadvantages as you can about the impact of globalized markets on your country's business at home and overseas.*
3. Before discussions begin, each group will be given approximately five minutes so that *members can work individually* to (a) list two feelings they would like to

project during the group discussion and (b) list corresponding nonverbal actions they will use to express those feelings. For example, one feeling might be anger, and the related nonverbal action could be scowling. Individuals should NOT share their work with other group members.

4. Once members have finished their individual work in No. 3, the instructor will signal for a group discussion to begin.

5. After the discussion, the instructor should allow each group about five minutes so that individuals can talk about what feelings they think other individuals were trying to communicate. All should keep track of how many times their nonverbal messages are successful in communicating their intended feelings.

6. The instructor will open the discussion about the exercise by asking questions such as the following:

   a. Were you successful in communicating nonverbally? Why?

   b. Is it easy for you to communicate nonverbally? Why?

   c. What did you learn from this exercise about increasing the managerial skill of communicating nonverbally?

You and Your Career

You probably don't go anywhere without your smartphone. On it, you keep up with friends and family through social media, play games, consult your calendar, wake up to its alarm clock, get directions, and so on. But do older generations use their phones in the same manner?

Write a short description of how each generation utilizes smartphones. Start with yours. Then, examine those who are in their mid-20s to 35 years of age, 35 to 50, and 50 and older. How would you characterize each generation's use of smartphones as a means of communication? Is one generation more likely to call someone or send a text? Also, evaluate the best approaches for each generation to communicate with the others. Is your grandfather more likely to tag you in a photograph on Facebook, or would it be your mother? Think about how each generation views the utilization of a cell phone as a communication device.

Building Your Management Skills Portfolio

Your Management Skills Portfolio is a collection of activities specially designed to demonstrate your management knowledge and skill. Be sure to save your work. Taking your printed portfolio to an employment interview could prove helpful.

The portfolio activity for this chapter is about improving the communication processes in Abu Dhabi Health Services Company. Study this information and complete the exercises that follow.

Hospitals in Dubai are incredibly successful at attracting medical tourists—in 2016, they carried out procedures on nearly 330,000 overseas patients. The most common procedures were for orthopedics, plastic surgery, dentistry, and fertility treatments. Dubai hopes that the number of annual overseas medical visitors will reach 500,000 by 2020.

Judging by the nature of complaints and the results of surveys, one of the main criticisms of healthcare in Dubai is poor communication, which accounted for some 85 percent of all complaints. In order to remove this potential barrier to the expansion of the industry, all hospitals and clinics operating under the Abu Dhabi Health Services Company introduced a patient portal that gives patients immediate access to care updates.

Assume that you have the primary responsibility for communications at the company, and answer the following questions:

14-11 What three goals would you set for building the new communications environment at Abu Dhabi Health Services Company?

_____

_____

_____

14-12 Explain what each goal would contribute toward in establishing a new environment that supports reaching organizational goals.

_____

_____

_____

14-13 List a primary step you would take in trying to achieve each goal.

_____

_____

_____

14-14 How long do you think it would take to establish the new communication environment at Abu Dhabi Health Services Company? Why?

_____

_____

_____

MyLab Management
Writing Assignments

If your instructor has assigned this activity, go to www.pearson.com/mylab/management for the following assisted-graded writing assignments:

Assisted-Grading Questions

14-15 How can managers encourage the flow of formal communication in organizations?

14-16 What is emotional intelligence? How does it relate to influencing people in organizations?

Endnotes

1. Adam Bryant, "The Phones Are Out, but the Robot Is In," *New York Times*, April 7, 2012, http://www.nytimes.com.

2. Ibid.; Arik Hesseldahl, "Seven Questions for Evernote CEO Phil Libin," *All Things D*, December 1, 2013, http://allthingsd.com; Jennifer Wang, "The Empowering Force," *Entrepreneur* (March 2013): 60; Chris O'Brien, "How I Made It: Evernote CEO Phil Libin," *Los Angeles Times*, August 2, 2013, http://articles.latimes.com; Ryan Tate, "Evernote Wants to Become the Nike for Your Brain: 10 Questions with CEO Phil Libin," *Wired*, July 29, 2013, http://www.wired.com; Casey Newton, "A Backpack to Remember: Can Evernote Become a Lifestyle Company?," *The Verge*, September 2013, http://www.theverge.com; Evernote, "About Us," http://evernote.com/corp, accessed March 25, 2014.

3. For an article describing why some managers prefer certain influence tactics, see H. Steensma, "Why Managers Prefer Some Influence Tactics to Other Tactics: A Net Utility Explanation," *Journal of Occupational and Organizational Psychology* 80 (2007): 355.

4. Writankar Mukherjee, "Five Ways to Master the Art of Influencing People," *The Economic Times* (online), July 16, 2011.

5. For an article describing the most effective influencing tactics, see Joyce Leong, Michael Bond, and Ping Ping Fu, "Perceived Effectiveness of Influence Strategies among Hong Kong Managers," *Asia Pacific Journal of Management* 24 (2007): 75–97.

6. Daniel Goleman, "Leadership That Gets Results," *Harvard Business Review* (March–April 2000): 78–90; Bano Fakhra Batool, "Emotional Intelligence and Effective Leadership," *Journal of Business Studies Quarterly* 4, no. 3 (March 2013): 84–94.

7. Joshua Freedman, "The Business Case for Emotional Intelligence," academia.edu, October 1, 2010 (David C. McClelland, "Identifying Competencies with Behavioural Event Interviews," *Psychological Science*, 9[5] 331–340, 1998); Steve Crabtree, "Worldwide, 13% of Employees Are Engaged at Work," Gallup, October 8, 2013, www.gallup.com/poll/165269/worldwide-employees-engaged-work.aspx; Joshua Freedman and Carina Fiedeldey-Van Dijk, Ph.D., 2003, "Speaking Out: What Motivates Employees to Be More Productive," 2003, www.6seconds.org and www.epsyconsultancy.com/resources/Speaking%20Out-productivity.pdf.

8. Joseph Rode et al., "Emotional Intelligence and Individual Performance: Evidence of Direct and Moderated Effects," *Journal of Organizational Behavior* 28 (2007): 399–421.

9. Nick Tasler and Travis Bradberry, "Emotional Intelligence: Skills Worth Learning," *Bloomberg Businessweek*, March 27, 2009, http://www.businessweek.com.

10. "Why Emotional Intelligence Matters at Work," *Work & Family Life* 17, no. 4 (April 2003): 4.

11. Kristi Casey Sanders, "What's Your EQ?," PlanYourMeetings.com, August 23, 2009.

12. For more on positive psychological capital, see James B. Avey, Fred Luthans, and Carolyn M. Youssef, "The Additive Value of Positive Psychological Capital in Predicting Work Attitudes and Behaviors," *Journal of Management* 36, no. 2 (March 2010): 430–452.

13. For discussion of the importance of communication, see Terrence Coan, "Communication: The Key to Success," *Information Management Journal* (May/June 2002): 1.

14. For discussion of communication techniques that are valuable for building organizational commitment, see Mary Bambacas and Maraget Patrickson, "Interpersonal Communication Skills That Enhance Organizational Commitment," *Journal of Communication Management* 12, no. 1 (2008): 51–72. For a discussion of communication techniques that are useful in selling situations, see "The Elements of Effective Communication," *Agency Sales* 30, no. 12 (December 2000): 45–46.

15. For an article describing the most important aspects of effective communication, see Donald English, Edgar Manton, and Janet Walker, "Human Resource Managers' Perception of Selected Communication Competencies," *Education* 127 (2007): 410–419; Kuang-Peng Hung and Chung-Kuang Lin, "More Communication Is Not Always Better? The Interplay between Effective Communication and Interpersonal Conflict in Influencing Satisfaction," *Industrial Marketing Management* 42, no. 8 (November 2013): 1223.

16. This section is based on the following classic article on interpersonal communication: Wilbur Schramm, "How Communication Works," in Wilbur Schramm, ed., *The Process and Effects of Mass Communication* (Urbana: University of Illinois Press, 1954), 3–10. For an innovative assignment on communication, see Karl L. Smart and Richard Featheringham, "Developing Effective Interpersonal Communication and Discussion Skills," *Business Communication Quarterly* 69 (2006): 276–283.

17. For more information regarding the elements of interpersonal communication, see Phyl Johnson, "Handbook of Interpersonal Communication," *Organization Studies* 24 (2003): 989.

18. David S. Brown, "Barriers to Successful Communication: Part I, Macrobarriers," *Management Review* (December 1975): 24–29. For an interesting discussion of culture and language as macrobarriers, see Vesa Peltokorpi and Lisbeth Clausen, "Linguistic and Cultural Barriers to Intercultural Communication in Foreign Subsidiaries," *Asian Business & Management* 10, no. 4 (November 2011): 509–528.

19. James K. Weekly and Raj Aggarwal, *International Business: Operating in the Global Economy* (New York: Dryden Press, 1987).

20. Michael D. Shear, "White House Revamps Communication Strategy," *Washington Post*, February 15, 2010, http://www.washingtonpost.com. See also "Nissan Motor Company Strengthens Brand Power in New Multi-Year Agreement with Omnicom Group: Agreement Provides Marketing Communications Strategy across Company's Global Footprint," *PR Newswire* [New York], October 3, 2013.

21. "Tips for Effective Cross-Cultural Communication," http://meetingsimagined.com/tips-trends/tips-effective-cross-cultural-communication.

22. For an interesting case study describing communication skills within the global arena, see Sabine Jaccaud and Bill Quirke, "Structuring Global Communication to Improve Efficiency," *Strategic Communication Management* 10 (2006): 18–21.

23. Davis S. Brown, "Barriers to Successful Communication: Part II, Microbarriers," *Management Review* (January 1976): 15–21. For review of skills useful in overcoming these microbarriers, see Isa N. Engleberg, Susan M. Ward, Lynn M. Disbrow, James A. Katt, Scott A. Myers, and Patricia O'Keefe, "The Development of a Set of Core Communication Competencies for Introductory Communication Courses," *Journal of Communication Education* 66, no. 1 (2017): 1–18.

24. Sally Bulkley Pancrazio and James J. Pancrazio, "Better Communication for Managers," *Supervisory Management* (June 1981): 31–37. For discussion of the role of situational awareness in becoming a more effective communicator, see Scott Titsworth, "Improving Situational Awareness for Instructional Communication Research: A Forum Response," *Communication Education* 66, no. 1 (2017): 122–125.

25. This figure is based on Loriann Roberson and Carol T. Kulik, "Stereotype Threat at Work," *Academy of Management Perspectives* 21, no. 2 (May 2007): 28–29.

26. Kris Dunn, "The Five Biggest Lies in HR," *Workforce Management*, March 2010, http://www.workforce.com.

27. Lydia Strong, "Do You Know How to Listen?," in M. Joseph Dooher and Vivienne Marquis, eds., *Effective Communications on the Job* (New York: American Management Association, 1956), 28. For an illustration of how refusing to listen may cause everyday problems to persist, see "Would Listening to the Other Be So Bad?," *The Times of Israel* (2017, May 3).

28. Robert E. Callahan, C. Patrick Fleenor, and Harry R. Knudson, *Understanding Organizational Behavior: A Managerial Viewpoint* (Columbus, OH: Charles E. Merrill, 1986). For practical insights on how to give feedback to millennials, see E. Anderson, A. A. Buchko, and K. J. Buchko, "Giving Negative Feedback to Millennials," *Management Research Review* 39, no. 6, (2016): 692–705.

29. For more on nonverbal issues, see Paul Preston, "Nonverbal Communication: Do You Really Say What You Mean?," *Journal of Healthcare Management* 50, no. 2 (March/April 2005): 83–86.

30. For a study demonstrating the importance of feedback format, see L. Atwater and J. Brett, "Feedback Format: Does It Influence Manager's Reactions to Feedback?," *Journal of Occupational and Organizational Psychology* 79 (2006): 517.

31. B&H, "Focus at B&H: The Customer's Experience," http://www.bhphotovideo.com/find/HelpCenter/AboutUs.jsp, accessed May

21, 2012; B&H, "Help Center," http://www.bhphotovideo.com/find/ HelpCenter/NYSuperStore08.jsp, accessed May 21, 2012; Paul Kerr, "Communication That Resonates," February 2012, http://www.pur due.edu/hr/LeadingEdition/Ledi_0212_communication.html, accessed May 21, 2012.

32. Reprinted by permission of the publisher from "Ten Command-ments of Good Communication," by American Management Asso-ciation AMA-COM et al., from Management Review (October 1955). © 1955 American Management Association, Inc. All rights reserved. For discussion of employability and communication skill, see S. Jeswani, "Assessment of Employability Skills among Fresh Engineering Graduates: A Structural Equation Modeling Approach," *IUP Journal of Soft Skills* 10, no. 2 (2016): 7–43.

33. Ted Pollock, "Mind Your Own Business," *Supervision* (May 1994): 24–26; Joseph R. Bainbridge, "Joint Communication: Verbal and Nonverbal," *Army Logistician* 30, no. 4 (July/August): 40–42. For a lit-erature review focusing on the role of nonverbal communication in the social organizational world, see S. Bonaccio, J. O'Reilly, S. L. O'Sullivan, and F. Chiocchio, "Nonverbal Behavior and Communi-cation in the Workplace: A Review and an Agenda for Research," *Journal of Management* 42, no. 5 (2016): 1044–1074.

34. Paul Preston, "Nonverbal Communication: Do You Really Say What You Mean?," *Journal of Healthcare Management* 50 (2005): 83–86.

35. For discussion exploring the role of gestures in improving problem-solving, see S. C. Lozano and B. Tversky, "Communicative Gestures Facilitate Problem Solving for Both Communicators and Recipi-ents," *Journal of Memory and Language* 92 (2107): 359.

36. For a definition of communication versus organizational communi-cation and a thorough review of related scholarship, see J. Key-ton, "Communication in Organizations," *Annual Review of Organizational Psychology and Organizational Behavior* 4 (2107): 501–526.

37. For an article that describes how employees perceive different types of organizational communication, see Zinta S. Byrne and Elaine LeMay, "Different Media for Organizational Communication: Perceptions of Quality and Satisfaction," *Journal of Business and Psychology* 21 (2006): 149–173.

38. Kenneth R. Van Voorhis, "Organizational Communication: Advances Made during the Period from World War II through the 1950s," *Journal of Business Communication* 11 (1974): 11–18.

39. Samuel C. Certo, *Supervision: Concepts and Skill-Building* (New York: McGraw-Hill, 2013), 278.

40. Company website, "Boost Sales Effectiveness via Internet Podcast-ing," http://www.mobilecastmedia.com, accessed May 19, 2010.

41. For a discussion of upward organizational communication and organizational change, see G. Tanner and K. Otto, Superior-Subordinate Communication during Organizational Change: Under Which Conditions Does High-Quality Communication Become Important?," *The International Journal of Human Resource Man-agement* 27, no. 19 (2106): 2183.

42. For an article stressing the importance of upward and downward communication for managers, see W. H. Weiss, "Communications: Key to Successful Supervision," *Supervision* 59, no. 9 (September 1998): 12–14.

43. William V. Haney, "Serial Communication of Information in Organi-zations," in Sidney Mailick and Edward H. Van Ness, eds., *Concepts and Issues in Administrative Behavior* (Englewood Cliffs, NJ: Prentice Hall, 1962), 150. For a discussion involving implications of off-site patterns of communication, see Robert M. Egan, Wendy Miles, John R. Birstler, and Margaret Klayton-Mi, "Can the Rift between Allison and Penny Be Mended?," *Harvard Business Review* 76, no. 4 (July/August 1998): 28–35.

44. Alex Bavelas and Dermot Barrett, "An Experimental Approach to Organizational Communication," *Personnel* 27 (1951): 366–371.

45. Polly LaBarre, "The Other Network," *Industry Week* (September 19, 1994): 33–36.

46. For an article describing how to assess the existence of informal orga-nizational communication, see R. Guimera, L. Danon, A. Diaz-Guilera, F. Giralt, and A. Arenas, "The Real Communication Network behind the Formal Chart: Community Structure in Organizations," *Journal of Economic Behavior and Organization* 61 (2006): 653–667.

47. "Recession Ripening the Office Grapevine? Three Communication Tips to Keep Employees on Track," *Business Management Daily*, August 13, 2009, http://www.businessmanagementdaily.com.

48. "Steelcase Workplace Index Survey Examines 'Water Cooler' Con-versations at Work: Study Confirms Gossip Is Here to Stay, Which May Benefit Employers," *PR Newswire*, August 9, 2007.

49. George de Mare, "Communicating: The Key to Establishing Good Working Relationships," *Price Waterhouse Review* 33 (1989): 30–37; Stanley J. Modic, "Grapevine Rated Most Believable," *Industry Week* (May 15, 1989): 11, 14.

50. Keith Davis, "Management Communication and the Grapevine," *Harvard Business Review* (January/February 1953): 43–49. For a recent study on the impact of grapevine gossip on organizations, see A. M. O. Agba, F. O. Eteng, and T. C. Titus, "Effect of Workplace Gossip on Work Relations and Organizational Performance," *Kuwait Chapter of the Arabian Journal of Business and Management Review* 6, no. 6 (2017): 31–42.

51. Linda McCallister, "The Interpersonal Side of Internal Communica-tions," *Public Relations Journal* (February 1981): 20–23. See also Joseph M. Putti, Samuel Aryee, and Joseph Phua, "Communication Relationship Satisfaction and Organizational Commitment," *Group and Organizational Studies* 15 (March 1990): 44–52.

52. Ali Carruthers, "Listening to Company Stakeholders at McDonald's Restaurants," *The Business Communicator* 6, no. 4 (September 2005): 8–9.

53. D. Keith Denton, "Creating Trust," *Organization Development Journal*, December 1, 2009, http://findarticles.com.

54. "Houston Zoo Focuses on Animal and Visitor Care with Interact," Interact company website, https://www.interact-intranet.com/customers/houston-zoo/.

15 Leadership

TARGET SKILL

 Leadership Skill: the ability to direct the behavior of others toward the accomplishment of objectives

LEADERSHIP SKILL AND YOUR CAREER

Leadership skill can be of great value to you in enhancing your management career. For example, this skill can help you direct people so that they become more truly committed to performing their jobs to the best of their ability. Building this commitment helps workers become more productive in their jobs, contributes more significantly to organizational success, builds your image as a competent manager, makes you more valuable to your organization, and supports your promotions as you build your career.

OBJECTIVES

To help build my _leadership skill_, when studying this chapter, I will attempt to acquire:

15-1 A working definition of _leadership_

15-2 An understanding of early approaches to leadership

15-3 An appreciation for more recent approaches to leadership

15-4 Insights into how leaders should make decisions

15-5 Hints on how leaders change organizations

15-6 An understanding of how leaders should coach

15-7 An appreciation for emerging leadership concepts

MyLab Management Chapter Warm Up

If your instructor has assigned this activity, go to www.pearson.com/mylab/management to complete the chapter warm up.

CHALLENGE CASE

Bain & Company's CEO, Bob Bechek, Leads the Team

Bain & Company is a management consulting firm based in Boston, Massachusetts, that helps organizations around the world with management issues. With 7,000 employees and over $2 billion in revenue, the company is a powerhouse among consulting firms. The CEO of Bain, Bob Bechek, began his career at the company 30 years ago as an intern and worked his way to the top of the organization.

In 2016, Bechek was named the "best liked CEO" in America by glassdoor.com. The honor was based on hundreds of anonymous ratings, and he has a 99 percent approval rating.[1] But how did he get to this point? How does a leader like Bechek become so popular among his employees?

When he assumed the internship role with Bain, he was seeking an experience grounded in a solid organizational culture. "What attracted me to Bain," said Bechek, "was that I felt like I found a hot firm that was focused entirely and passionately on results or impact, rather than reports and did so within an extraordinarily people-oriented culture that I thought would be very good for me, given my particular nature."

Even before his internship, he held quite a number of jobs. This provided him with a unique experience that is helpful for someone in the management consulting industry because he has a familiarity with a variety of industries. As he recalled, "I was a kid who had more odd jobs than a lot of people going back to when I was a boy—from home construction to a steel factory UAW [United Automobile Workers] job. I was a technician in a nuclear reactor facility. I delivered pizzas and newspapers and mowed lawns. I was on a shopping center maintenance crew." This myriad of experiences prepared him for his job at Bain. The company has offices in 36 countries, so an understanding of how all types of businesses carry out operations is important.

After his internship, Bechek moved up through the ranks, eventually becoming an executive with the firm as the co-head of Bain's Global Telecom, Media, and Technology practice. Then he became the leader of Bain's entire northeast region and finally, in 2012, became the CEO. On a personal level, he has understood the value of modesty and realizing that there is always much to learn. His goal has been to lead by the example he sets for all the associates of the organization.

As the CEO of Bain & Company today, overseeing 7,000 employees, Bechek puts a priority on effective leadership

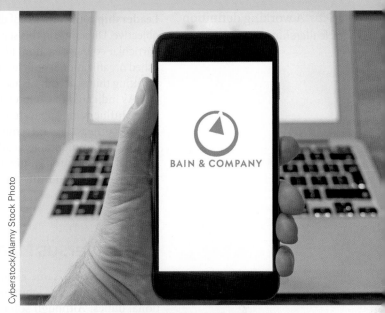

Cyberstock/Alamy Stock Photo

Bain & Company is one of the "big three" management consulting firms. Based in Boston, the organization provides consultation to businesses, nonprofits, and government agencies.

through informal means. "I think the reality of power and influence and getting things done is overwhelmingly about informal authority nowadays," he said. "Even in my current role, the vast majority of what I do is exerted through informal and not formal authority. If you're trying to get people galvanized around a particular course of action—or to feel inspired about what we're trying to do or feel appreciated, motivated, and valued—that has almost nothing to do with formal authority."[2]

Clearly, Bechek's leadership abilities facilitate his management of a worldwide organization, but his understanding of authority and what prompts others to follow him is how he has helped grow the firm and become the most-liked CEO in the country.

THE LEADERSHIP CHALLENGE

The Challenge Case reviews the leadership of Bob Bechek, CEO of Bain & Company. The information in the chapter would be helpful to an individual such as Bechek as the basis for developing a useful leadership strategy to achieve success. The chapter discusses how to define leadership, the difference between a leader and a manager, the trait approach to leadership, the situational approach to leadership, leadership today, and current topics in leadership.

Defining Leadership

15-1   A working definition of *leadership*

Leadership is the process of directing the behavior of others toward the accomplishment of an objective. Directing, in this sense, means causing individuals to act in a certain way or to follow a particular course of action. Ideally, this course is perfectly consistent with factors such as established organizational policies, procedures, and job descriptions. The central theme of leadership is getting things accomplished through people.[3]

As indicated in Chapter 14, leadership is one of the four main interdependent activities of the influencing subsystem and is accomplished, at least to some extent, by communicating with others. It is extremely important that managers have a thorough understanding of what leadership entails. Leadership has always been considered a prerequisite for organizational success; today, given the increased capability afforded by enhanced communication technology and the rise of international business, leadership is more important than ever before.[4]

Leader versus Manager

Leading is not the same as managing. Many executives fail to grasp the difference between the two and therefore labor under a misapprehension about how to carry out their organizational duties. Although some managers are leaders and some leaders are managers, leading and managing are not identical activities.[5] According to Theodore Levitt, management consists of:

> the rational assessment of a situation and the systematic selection of goals and purposes (what is to be done); the systematic development of strategies to achieve these goals; the marshalling of the required resources; the rational design, organization, direction, and control of the activities required to attain the selected purposes; and, finally, the motivating and rewarding of people to do the work.[6]

Leadership, as one of the four primary activities of the influencing function, is a subset of management. Managing is much broader in scope than is leading and focuses on nonbehavioral as well as behavioral issues. In contrast, leading emphasizes mainly behavioral issues. **Figure 15.1** makes the point that, although not all managers are leaders, the most effective managers over the long term are leaders.

Merely possessing management skills is no longer sufficient for success as an executive in the business world. Modern executives need to understand the difference between managing and leading and know how to combine the two roles to achieve organizational success. A manager makes sure that a job gets done, and a leader cares about and focuses on the people who do the job. Combining management and leadership, therefore, requires demonstrating a calculated and logical focus on organizational processes (management) along with a genuine concern for workers as people (leadership).[7]

Figure 15.1

The most effective managers over the long term are also leaders

Early Approaches to Leadership

The Trait Approach to Leadership

15-2 An understanding of early approaches to leadership

The **trait approach to leadership** is based on early leadership research that assumed a good leader is born, not made. Primarily, this research attempted to describe successful leaders as precisely as possible. The reasoning was that if a complete profile of the traits of a successful leader could be drawn, it would be fairly easy to identify the individuals who should and should not be placed in leadership positions.[8]

Many of the early studies that attempted to summarize the traits of successful leaders were documented. One of these summaries concluded that successful leaders tend to possess the following characteristics:[9]

1. Intelligence, including judgment and verbal ability
2. Past achievement in scholarship and athletics
3. Emotional maturity and stability
4. Dependability, persistence, and a drive for continuing achievement
5. The skill to participate socially and adapt to various groups
6. A desire for status and socioeconomic position

Evaluations of these trait studies have concluded, however, that their findings are inconsistent. One researcher said that 50 years of study have failed to produce one personality trait or set of qualities that can be used consistently to differentiate leaders from nonleaders.[10]

Still, researchers continue to examine the issue. A recent study by Frank Walter and Helka Bruch analyzes the phenomenon of the charismatic leader and identifies some traits inherent in such leaders.[11] Thus far, however, research has failed to articulate definitively a trait or combination of traits that indicate an individual will be a successful leader. Leadership is apparently a much more complex issue.

Contemporary management writers and practitioners generally agree that leadership ability cannot be explained by an individual's traits or inherited characteristics. They believe, rather, that individuals can be trained to be good leaders. In other words, leaders are made, not born.[12] That is why thousands of employees each year are sent to leadership training programs.[13]

Companies are finding that the benefits of building leadership talent include not only enhancing company success but also gaining an advantage in attracting the best college graduates as new hires.

Behavioral Approaches to Leadership

The failure to identify predictive leadership traits led researchers in this area to turn to other variables to explain leadership success. Rather than looking at traits leaders should possess, the behavioral approach looked at what good leaders do. Are they concerned with getting a task done, for instance, or do they concentrate on keeping their followers happy and maintaining high morale?

Two major studies were conducted to identify leadership behavior, one by the Bureau of Business Research at Ohio State University (referred to as the OSU studies), and the other by the University of Michigan (referred to as the Michigan studies).

The OSU Studies   The OSU studies concluded that leaders exhibit two main types of behavior:

- **Structure behavior** is any leadership activity that delineates the relationship between the leader and the leader's followers or establishes well-defined procedures that the followers should adhere to in performing their jobs. Overall, structure behavior limits the self-guidance of followers in the performance of their tasks, and although it can be relatively firm, it is never rude or malicious.

    Structure behavior can be useful to leaders as a means of minimizing follower activity that does not significantly contribute to organizational goal attainment. Leaders must be careful, however, not to go overboard and discourage follower activity that *will* contribute to organizational goal attainment.

Figure 15.2

Four fundamental leadership styles based on structure behavior and consideration behavior

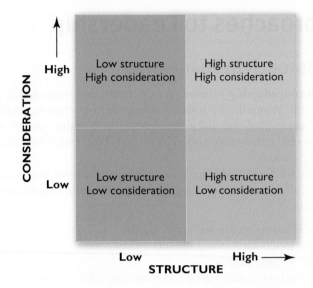

- **Consideration behavior** is leadership behavior that reflects friendship, mutual trust, respect, and warmth in the relationship between leader and followers. This type of behavior generally aims to develop and maintain a good relationship between the leader and the followers.

Research by consulting firm Lore International Institute reveals that, to succeed in the workplace, it's important for leaders to demonstrate trustworthiness, honesty, and an ability to collaborate. According to the findings, leaders can "kill" trust between themselves and workers by being (1) *credit hogs* and taking credit for the good ideas of others, (2) *lone rangers* and working mostly by themselves and not closely with other workers, (3) *egomaniacs* and believing that success will come only through the efforts of management as opposed to those of workers, or (4) *mules* and being stubborn and inflexible.[14]

The OSU studies resulted in a model that depicts four fundamental leadership styles. A **leadership style** is the behavior a leader exhibits while guiding organization members in appropriate directions.[15] Each of the four leadership styles depicted in **Figure 15.2** is a different combination of structure behavior and consideration behavior. For example, the high-structure/ low-consideration leadership style emphasizes structure behavior and deemphasizes consideration behavior.

The OSU studies made a significant contribution to our understanding of leadership, and the central ideas generated by these studies still serve as the basis for modern leadership thought and research.[16]

The Michigan Studies

About the same time the OSU leadership studies were being carried out, researchers at the University of Michigan, led by Rensis Likert, were also conducting a series of historically significant leadership studies.[17] After analyzing information based on interviews with leaders and followers (i.e., managers and subordinates), the Michigan studies pinpointed two basic types of leader behavior: job-centered behavior and employee-centered behavior.

Job-centered behavior is leader behavior that focuses primarily on the work that a subordinate is doing. The job-centered leader is interested in the job that a subordinate is doing and in how well the subordinate is performing that job.

Employee-centered behavior is leader behavior that focuses primarily on subordinates as people. The employee-centered leader is attentive to the personal needs of subordinates and is interested in building cooperative work teams that are satisfying to subordinates and advantageous for the organization. Considerable research has been focused on this relationship and its outcomes, which are sometimes referred to as the *Pygmalion effect*, a phenomenon in which the more leaders believe their subordinates can achieve, the more the subordinates *do* achieve.[18]

The results of the OSU studies and the Michigan studies are similar. Both research efforts indicate two primary dimensions of leader behavior: a work dimension (structure behavior/job-centered behavior) and a people dimension (consideration behavior/employee-centered behavior). The following sections focus on determining which of these two primary dimensions of leader behavior is more advisable for a manager to adopt.

Effectiveness of Various Leadership Styles

An early investigation of high school superintendents concluded that desirable leadership behavior is associated with strong leader emphasis on both structure and consideration and that undesirable leadership behavior is associated with weak leader emphasis on both dimensions. Similarly, the managerial grid described in Chapter 13 implies that the most effective leadership style is characterized by a high level of consideration and an effective structure. Results of a more recent study indicate that subordinates always prefer a high level of consideration.[19]

Comparing Styles

One should be cautious, however, about concluding that any single leadership style is more effective than any other. Leadership situations are so varied that pronouncing one leadership style as the most effective is an oversimplification. In fact, a successful leadership style for managers in one situation may prove ineffective in another situation. Recognizing the need to link leadership styles to appropriate situations, A. K. Korman noted, in a classic article, that a worthwhile contribution to leadership literature would be a rationale for systematically linking appropriate styles with various situations in order to ensure effective leadership.[20] The life cycle theory of leadership, which is covered in the next section, provides such a rationale.

More Recent Approaches to Leadership

Leadership studies have shifted emphasis from the trait approach to the situational approach, which suggests that leadership style must be appropriately matched to the situation that the leader faces. The more modern **situational approach to leadership** is based on the assumption that each instance of leadership is different and therefore requires a unique combination of leaders, followers, and leadership situations.[21]

15-3 An appreciation for more recent approaches to leadership

This interaction is commonly expressed in formula form: $SL = f(L, F, S)$, where SL is *successful leadership*; f stands for *function of*; and L, F, and S are, respectively, the *leader*, the *follower*, and the *situation*.[22] Translated, this formula says that successful leadership is a function of a leader, a follower, and a situation that are appropriate for one another.

TIPS FOR MANAGING AROUND THE GLOBE

Adapting Your Leadership Style in Other Cultures

As you progress through your career, you will encounter many people from different cultures, and being an effective leader means understanding these cultures as well as being open-minded about them. There are several ideas to keep in mind when leading those from a different part of the world than you come from.

First, simply be aware of cultural sensitivity. If you have someone working for you, realize that he or she may have traveled a great distance for the position. Perhaps the employee uprooted his or her family to move for the job or, worse, left the family behind until he or she could save up enough money to immigrate.

Second, try to acquire cultural knowledge. Learn about other cultures and what it means to lead someone from a culture different than your own. Understand that someone from Asia may hold the belief that negotiating or asking for additional money is disrespectful to authority. Another example is that most Germans prefer to keep things professional and businesslike at work, with very little joking or telling long stories about non-work-related activities. Finally, don't avoid other cultures. Avoid falling into the trap of hiring people only like yourself. By bringing others onto the team, you will be expanding the possibilities of success in any organization you lead.[23]

The Life Cycle Theory of Leadership

The **life cycle theory of leadership** is a rationale for linking leadership styles with various situations to ensure effective leadership. This theory posits essentially the same two types of leadership behavior as the OSU leadership studies do, but it calls them "task" and "relationships" rather than, respectively, "structure" and "consideration."

The life cycle theory is based on the relationship among follower maturity, leader task behavior, and leader relationship behavior. In general terms, according to this theory, leadership style should reflect the maturity level of the followers. *Maturity* is defined as the ability of followers to perform their jobs independently, to assume additional responsibilities, and to desire to achieve success. The more of each of these characteristics that followers possess, the more mature they are said to be. (Maturity here is not necessarily linked to chronological age.)

Figure 15.3 illustrates the life cycle theory of leadership model. The curved line indicates the maturity level of the followers: Maturity level increases as the maturity curve runs from right to left. In more specific terms, the theory indicates that effective leadership behavior should shift as follows:[24] (1) high-task/low-relationship behavior to (2) high-task/high-relationship behavior to (3) high-relationship/low-task behavior to (4) low-task/low-relationship behavior, as one's followers progress from immaturity to maturity. In sum, a manager's leadership style will be effective only if it is appropriate for the maturity level of the followers.

Some exceptions apply to the general philosophy of the life cycle theory. For example, if there is a short-term deadline to meet, a leader may find it necessary to accelerate production through a high-task/low-relationship style rather than through a low-task/low-relationship style, even if the followers are mature. A high-task/low-relationship leadership style carried out over the long term with such followers, though, would typically result in a poor working relationship between leader and subordinates.

Applying Life Cycle Theory
Following is an example of how the life cycle theory applies to a leadership situation:

- A man has just been hired as a salesperson in a men's clothing store. At first, this individual is extremely immature—that is, unable to solve task-related problems independently. According to the life cycle theory, the appropriate style for leading this salesperson at his level of maturity is high-task/low-relationship—that is, the leader should tell the salesperson exactly what should be done and how to do it. The salesperson should be shown how to make change and charge sales and how to handle merchandise returns. The leader should also begin laying the groundwork for developing a personal relationship with the salesperson. Too much relationship behavior at this point should be avoided, however, because it can easily be misinterpreted as permissiveness.

Figure 15.3

The life cycle theory of leadership model

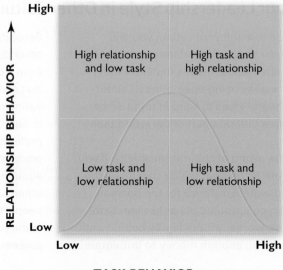

- As time passes and the salesperson gains some job-related maturity, the appropriate style for leading him would be high-task/high-relationship. Although the salesperson's maturity has increased somewhat, the leader still needs to watch him closely because he requires guidance and direction at times. The main difference between this leadership style and the first one is the amount of relationship behavior displayed by the leader. Building on the groundwork laid during the period of the first leadership style, the leader can now start to encourage an atmosphere of mutual trust, respect, and friendliness between the salesperson and her.

- As more time passes and the salesperson's maturity level increases still further, the appropriate style for leading this individual will become high relationship/low task. The leader can now deemphasize task behavior because the salesperson is of above-average maturity in his job and is capable of independently solving most job-related problems. The leader would continue to develop a relationship with her follower.

- Once the salesperson's maturity level reaches its maximum, the appropriate style for leading him is low task/low relationship. Again, the leader deemphasizes task behavior because the follower is thoroughly familiar with the job. Now, however, the leader can also deemphasize relationship behavior because she has fully established a good working relationship with the follower. At this point, task behavior is seldom needed, and relationship behavior is used primarily to nurture the good working rapport that has developed between the leader and the follower. The salesperson, then, is left to do his job without close supervision, knowing that he has a positive working relationship with a leader who can be approached for guidance whenever necessary.

The life cycle approach more than likely owes its acceptance to its intuitive appeal. Although at first glance it appears to be a useful leadership concept, managers should bear in mind that little scientific investigation has been conducted to verify its worth, and therefore it should be applied with caution.[25]

Fiedler's Contingency Theory

Situational theories of leadership such as the life cycle theory are based on the concept of **leader flexibility**—the idea that successful leaders must change their leadership styles as they encounter different situations. Can any leader be so flexible as to span all major leadership styles? The answer to this question is that some leaders can be that flexible, and some cannot.

Unfortunately, numerous obstacles get in the way of leader flexibility. One obstacle is that a leadership style is sometimes so ingrained in a leader that it takes years for the leader's style to even approach flexibility. Another obstacle is that some leaders have experienced such success in a basically static situation that they believe developing a flexible style is unnecessary. Yet another obstacle is the widely held notion that, in order for leaders to be considered successful in a new role, they need to generate "quick wins." This focus on making a significant contribution to the organization soon after assuming the leadership role actually impedes a leader's ability to be flexible and exhibit his or her true style.[26]

Changing the Organization to Fit the Leader
One strategy, proposed by Fred Fiedler, for overcoming these obstacles is changing the organizational situation to fit the leader's style rather than changing the leader's style to fit the organizational situation.[27] Applying this idea to the life cycle theory of leadership, an organization may find it easier to shift leaders to situations appropriate for their leadership styles than to expect those leaders to change styles as situations change. After all, it would probably take three to five years to train a manager to use a concept such as life cycle theory effectively, whereas changing the situation that the leader faces can be done quickly simply by exercising organizational authority.

According to Fiedler's **contingency theory of leadership**, leader–member relations,[28] task structure, and the position power of the leader are the three primary factors that should be considered when moving leaders into situations appropriate for their leadership styles:

- **Leader–member relations** is the degree to which the leader feels accepted by the followers.
- **Task structure** is the degree to which the goals—the work to be done—and other situational factors are outlined clearly.
- **Position power** is determined by the extent to which the leader has control over the rewards and punishments that followers receive.

TABLE 15.1 **Eight Combinations, or Octants, of Three Factors: Leader–Member Relations, Task Structure, and Leader Position Power**

Octant	Leader–Member Relations	Task Structure	Leader Position Power
I	Good	High	Strong
II	Good	High	Weak
III	Good	Weak	Strong
IV	Good	Weak	Weak
V	Moderately poor	High	Strong
VI	Moderately poor	High	Weak
VII	Moderately poor	Weak	Strong
VIII	Moderately poor	Weak	Weak

How these three factors can be arranged in eight different combinations, called *octants*, is presented in **Table 15.1**.

Figure 15.4 shows how effective leadership varies among the eight octants. From an organizational viewpoint, this figure implies that management should attempt to match permissive, passive, and considerate leaders with situations reflecting the middle of the continuum, containing the octants 4, 5, 6, and 7. It also implies that management should try to match controlling, active, and structuring leaders with the extremes of this continuum.

Fiedler suggests the following actions that can be taken to modify the leadership situation:[29]

1. In some organizations, we can change the individual's task assignment. We may assign to one leader the structured tasks that have implicit or explicit instructions telling him what to do and how to do it, and we may assign to another the tasks that are nebulous and vague. The former are the typical production tasks; the latter are exemplified by committee work, by the development of policy, and by tasks that require creativity.

2. We can change the leader's position power. We not only can give him a higher rank and corresponding recognition, but we can also modify his position power by giving him subordinates who are equal to him in rank and prestige or subordinates who are two or three ranks below him. We can give him subordinates who are experts in their specialties or subordinates who depend on the leader for guidance and instruction. The leader can give the

Figure 15.4

How effective leadership style varies with Fiedler's eight octants

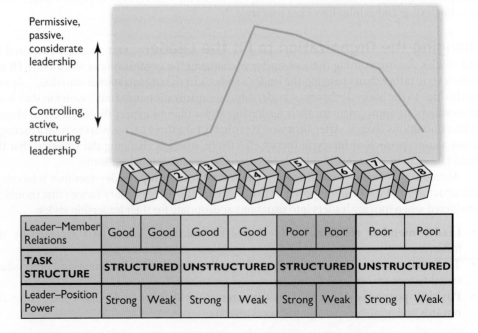

Leader–Member Relations	Good	Good	Good	Good	Poor	Poor	Poor	Poor
TASK STRUCTURE	**STRUCTURED**		**UNSTRUCTURED**		**STRUCTURED**		**UNSTRUCTURED**	
Leader–Position Power	Strong	Weak	Strong	Weak	Strong	Weak	Strong	Weak

final say in all decisions affecting his group, or we can require that he make decisions in consultation with his subordinates, or even that he obtain their concurrence. We can channel all directives, communications, and information about organizational plans through the leader alone, giving him expert power, or we can provide these communications concurrently to all his subordinates.

3. We can change the leader–member relations in this group. The leader can work with groups whose members are very similar to him in attitude, opinion, technical background, race, and cultural background, or we can assign him subordinates with whom he differs in any one or several of these important aspects. Finally, we can assign the leader to a group in which the members have a tradition of getting along well with their supervisors or to a group that has a history and tradition of conflict.

Fiedler's work certainly helps destroy the myths about one best leadership style and that leaders are born, not made. In addition, his work supports the theory that almost every manager in an organization can be a successful leader if she or he is placed in a situation appropriate to that person's leadership style. This matching of leadership style to the situation, of course, assumes that someone in the organization has the ability to assess the characteristics of the organization's leaders and other important organizational variables and then to bring the two together accordingly.

Fiedler's model, like all theoretical models, also has its limitations; even though it may not provide concrete answers, it does emphasize the importance of situational variables in determining leadership effectiveness. As noted earlier, it may actually be easier to change the leadership situation or move the leader to a more favorable situation than to try to change the leader's style.[30]

The Path-Goal Theory of Leadership

The **path–goal theory of leadership** suggests that the primary activities of a leader are to make desirable and achievable rewards available to organization members who attain organizational goals and to clarify the kinds of behavior that must be performed to earn those rewards.[31] The leader outlines the goals that followers should aim for and clarifies the path that followers should take to achieve those goals and earn the rewards contingent on doing so.[32] Overall, the path–goal theory maintains that managers can facilitate job performance by showing employees how their performance directly affects their receiving desired rewards.

Ursula Burns, CEO of Xerox, has called herself "chief storyteller"—someone who offers a compelling description of where the company is headed and what it can achieve. This is an example of achievement behavior in the path–goal theory of leadership.

Leadership Behavior According to the path–goal theory of leadership, leaders exhibit four primary types of behavior:

1. **Directive behavior**—Directive behavior is aimed at telling followers what to do and how to do it. The leader indicates what performance goals exist and precisely what must be done to achieve them.
2. **Supportive behavior**—Supportive behavior is aimed at being friendly with followers and showing interest in them as human beings. Through supportive behavior, the leader demonstrates sensitivity to the personal needs of followers.
3. **Participative behavior**—Participative behavior is aimed at seeking suggestions from followers regarding business operations to the extent that followers are involved in making important organizational decisions. Followers often help determine the rewards that will be available to them in the organization and what they must do to earn those rewards.
4. **Achievement behavior**—Achievement behavior is aimed at setting challenging goals for followers to reach and expressing and demonstrating confidence that they will measure up to the challenge. This leader behavior focuses on making goals difficult enough that employees will find achieving them challenging, but not so difficult that employees will view them as impossible and give up trying to achieve them.

Adapting Behavior to Situations As with other situational theories of leadership, the path–goal theory proposes that leaders will be successful if they appropriately match these four types of behavior to the situations they face. For example, if inexperienced followers do not have a thorough understanding of a job, a manager may appropriately use more directive behavior to develop this understanding and ensure

Ivan Nickolov/INB WENN Photos/Newscom

that serious job-related problems are avoided. For more experienced followers, who have a more complete understanding of a job, directive behavior would probably be inappropriate and might create interpersonal problems between leader and followers.

If jobs are highly structured, with little room for employee interpretation of how the work should be done, directive behavior is less appropriate than when much room is provided for employees to determine how the work gets done. When followers are deriving much personal satisfaction and encouragement from work and enjoy the support of other members of their work group, supportive behavior by the leader is not as important as it is when followers are gaining little or no satisfaction from their work or from personal relationships in the work group.

The primary focus of the path–goal theory of leadership is on how leaders can increase employee effort and productivity by clarifying performance goals and the path to be taken to achieve those goals. This theory of leadership has gained increasing acceptance in recent years. In fact, research suggests that the path–goal theory is highly promising for enhancing employee commitment to achieving organizational goals and thereby increasing the probability that organizations will be successful. It should be pointed out, however, that the research done on this model has been conducted mostly on its parts rather than on the complete model.[33]

A Special Situation: How Leaders Make Decisions

15-4 Insights into how leaders should make decisions

The Tannenbaum and Schmidt Leadership Continuum

Because one of the most important tasks of a leader is making sound decisions, all practical and legitimate leadership thinking emphasizes decision making. Tannenbaum and Schmidt, who wrote one of the first and perhaps most-often-quoted articles on the situational approach to leadership, discuss situations in which a leader makes decisions.[34] **Figure 15.5** presents their model of leadership behavior.

This model is actually a continuum, or range, of leadership behavior available to managers when they are making decisions. Note that each type of decision-making behavior depicted in the figure has both a corresponding degree of authority used by the manager and a related amount of freedom available to subordinates. Management behavior, at the extreme left of the model, characterizes the leader who makes decisions by maintaining high levels of control and allowing

Figure 15.5 Continuum of leadership behavior that emphasizes decision making

subordinates little freedom. Behavior at the extreme right characterizes the leader who makes decisions by exercising little control and allowing subordinates much freedom and self-direction. Behavior between the extremes reflects gradations in leadership from autocratic to democratic.

Managers displaying leadership behavior toward the right side of the model are more democratic and are called *subordinate-centered* leaders. Those displaying leadership behavior toward the left side of the model are more autocratic and are called *boss-centered* leaders.

Each type of leadership behavior in this model is explained in more detail in the following list:

1. **The manager makes the decision and announces it**—This behavior is characterized by the manager (a) identifying a problem, (b) analyzing various alternatives available to solve it, (c) choosing the alternative that will be used to solve it, and (d) requiring followers to implement the chosen alternative. The manager may or may not use coercion, but the followers have no opportunity to participate directly in the decision-making process.

2. **The manager "sells" the decision**—The manager identifies the problem and independently arrives at a decision. Rather than announce the decision to subordinates for implementation, however, the manager tries to persuade subordinates to accept the decision.

3. **The manager presents ideas and invites questions**—Here, the manager makes the decision and attempts to gain acceptance through persuasion. One additional step is taken, however: Subordinates are invited to ask questions about the decision.

4. **The manager presents a tentative decision that is subject to change**—The manager allows subordinates to have some part in the decision-making process but retains the responsibility for identifying and diagnosing the problem. The manager then arrives at a tentative decision that is subject to change on the basis of subordinate input. The final decision is made by the manager.

5. **The manager presents the problem, gets suggestions, and then makes the decision**— This leadership activity is the first of those described thus far that allows subordinates the opportunity to offer solutions before the manager does. The manager, however, is still the one who identifies the problem.

6. **The manager defines the limits and asks the group to make a decision**—In this type of leadership behavior, the manager first defines the problem and sets the boundaries within which a decision must be made. The manager then enters into a partnership with subordinates to arrive at an appropriate decision. The danger here is that if the group of subordinates does not perceive that the manager genuinely desires a serious group decision-making effort, it will tend to arrive at conclusions that reflect what it thinks the manager wants rather than what the group actually wants and believes is feasible.

7. **The manager permits the group to make decisions within prescribed limits**—Here, the manager becomes an equal member of a problem-solving group. The entire group identifies and assesses the problem, develops possible solutions, and chooses an alternative to be implemented. Everyone within the group understands that the group's decision will be implemented.

Determining How to Make Decisions as a Leader The true value of the model developed by Tannenbaum and Schmidt lies in its use for making practical and desirable decisions. According to these authors, the three primary factors, or forces, that influence a manager's determination of which leadership behavior to use in making decisions are as follows:

1. **Forces in the Manager**—Managers should be aware of four forces within themselves that influence their determination of how to make decisions as a leader. The first force is the manager's values, such as the relative importance to the manager of organizational efficiency, personal growth, the growth of subordinates, and company profits. For example, a manager who values subordinate growth highly will probably want to give group members the valuable experience of making a decision even though he or she could make the decision much more quickly and efficiently alone.

   The second influencing force is level of confidence in subordinates. In general, the more confidence a manager has in his or her subordinates, the more likely it is that the manager's decision-making style will be democratic, or subordinate-centered. The reverse is also true: The less confidence a manager has in subordinates, the more likely it is that the manager's decision-making style will be autocratic, or boss-centered.

The third influencing force within the manager is personal leadership strengths. Some managers are more effective at issuing orders than leading group discussions, and vice versa. Managers must be able to recognize their own leadership strengths and capitalize on them.

The fourth influencing force within the manager is tolerance for ambiguity. The move from a boss-centered style to a subordinate-centered style means some loss of certainty about how problems will be solved. A manager who is disturbed by this loss of certainty will find it extremely difficult to be successful as a subordinate-centered leader.

2. **Forces in Subordinates**—A manager also should be aware of forces within subordinates that influence the manager's determination of how to make decisions as a leader.[35] To lead successfully, the manager needs to keep in mind that subordinates are both somewhat different and somewhat alike and that any cookbook approach to leading all subordinates is therefore impossible. Generally speaking, however, managers can increase their leadership success by allowing subordinates more freedom in making decisions when:

   • The subordinates have a relatively high need for independence (people differ greatly in the amount of direction they desire).
   • They have a readiness to assume responsibility for decision making (some see additional responsibility as a tribute to their abilities; others see it as someone above them "passing the buck").
   • They have a relatively high tolerance for ambiguity (some employees prefer to be given clear-cut directives; others crave a greater degree of freedom).
   • They are interested in the problem and believe solving it is important.
   • They understand and identify with the organization's goals.
   • They have the necessary knowledge and experience to deal with the problem.
   • They have learned to expect to share in decision making (people who have come to expect strong leadership and then are suddenly told to participate more fully in decision making are often upset by this new experience; conversely, people who have enjoyed a considerable amount of freedom usually resent the boss who assumes full decision-making powers).

   If subordinates do not have these characteristics, the manager should probably assume a more autocratic, or boss-centered, approach to making decisions.

3. **Forces in the Situation**—The last group of forces that influence a manager's determination of how to make decisions as a leader are forces in the leadership situation. The first such situational force is the type of organization in which the leader works. Organizational factors, including the size of working groups and their geographic distribution, are especially important influences on leadership style. Extremely large work groups or wide geographic separations of work groups, for example, could make a subordinate-centered leadership style impractical.

   The second situational force is the effectiveness of a group. To gauge this force, managers should evaluate issues such as the experience of group members in working together and the degree of confidence they have in their abilities to solve problems as a group. As a general rule, managers should assign decision-making responsibilities only to effective work groups.

   The third situational force is the problem to be solved. Before deciding to act as a subordinate-centered leader, a manager should be sure the group has the expertise necessary to make a decision about the problem in question. If it does not, the manager should move toward more boss-centered leadership.

   The fourth situational force is the time available to make a decision. As a general guideline, the less time available, the more impractical it is to assign decision making to a group because a group typically takes more time than an individual to reach a decision.

As the situational approach to leadership implies, managers will be successful decision makers only if the method they use to make decisions appropriately reflects the leader, the followers, and the situation.

MyLab Management Watch It

If your instructor has assigned this activity, go to www.pearson.com/mylab/management to complete the video exercise.

Determining How to Make Decisions as a Leader: An Update Tannenbaum and Schmidt's 1957 article on leadership decision making was so widely accepted that the two authors were invited by *Harvard Business Review* in the 1970s to update their original work.[36] In this update, they warn that in modern organizations, the relationship among forces within the manager, subordinates, and situation has become more complex and more interrelated since the 1950s, which obviously makes it harder for managers to determine how to lead.

The update also points out that new organizational environments have to be considered when determining how to lead. For example, factors such as affirmative action and pollution control—which hardly figured into managers' decision making in the 1950s—have become significant influences on the decision making of leaders since the 1970s.

The Vroom-Yetton-Jago Model

Another major decision-focused theory of leadership that has gained widespread attention was first developed in 1973 and then refined and expanded in 1988.[37] This theory, which we will call the **Vroom–Yetton–Jago (VYJ) model of leadership** after its three major contributors, focuses on how much participation to allow subordinates in the decision-making process. The VYJ model is built on two important premises:

1. Organizational decisions should be of high quality (should have a beneficial impact on performance).
2. Subordinates should accept and be committed to organizational decisions that are made.

Decision Styles The VYJ model suggests five different decision styles or ways that leaders make decisions. These styles range from autocratic (the leader makes the decision) to consultative (the leader makes the decision after interacting with the followers) to group-focused (the manager meets with the group, and the group makes the decision). All five decision styles within the VYJ model are described in **Figure 15.6**.

Using the Model The VYJ model, presented in **Figure 15.7**, is a method for determining when a leader should use which decision style. As you can see, the model is a type of decision tree. To determine which decision style to use in a particular situation, the leader starts at the left of the decision tree by stating the organizational problem being addressed. Then the leader asks a series of questions about the problem as determined by the structure of the decision tree until he or she arrives at the decision style appropriate for the situation at the far right of the model.

Consider, for example, the bottom path of the decision tree. After stating an organizational problem, the leader determines that a decision related to that problem has a low-quality requirement, that it is important for subordinates be committed to the decision, and that it is uncertain whether a decision made solely by the leader will be committed to by subordinates. In this

DECISION STYLE	DEFINITION
AI	Manager makes the decision alone.
AII	Manager asks for information from subordinates but makes the decision alone. Subordinates may or may not be informed about what the situation is.
CI	Manager shares the situation with individual subordinates and asks for information and evaluation. Subordinates do not meet as a group, and the manager alone makes the decision.
CII	Manager and subordinates meet as a group to discuss the situation, but the manager makes the decision.
GII	Manager and subordinates meet as a group to discuss the situation, and the group makes the decision.
A = autocratic; C = consultative; G = group	

Figure 15.6

The five decision styles available to a leader according to the Vroom–Yetton–Jago model

QR	Quality Requirement:	*How important is the technical quality of this decision?*
CR	Commitment Requirement:	*How important is subordinate commitment to the decision?*
LI	Leader's Information:	*Do you have sufficient information to make a high-quality decision?*
ST	Problem Structure:	*Is the problem well structured?*
CP	Commitment Probability:	*If you were to make the decision by yourself, is it reasonably certain that your subordinate(s) would be committed to the decision?*
GC	Goal Congruence:	*Do subordinates share the organizational goals to be attained in solving this problem?*
CO	Subordinate Conflict:	*Is conflict among subordinates over the preferred solution likely?*
SI	Subordinate Information:	*Do subordinates have sufficient information to make a high-quality decision?*

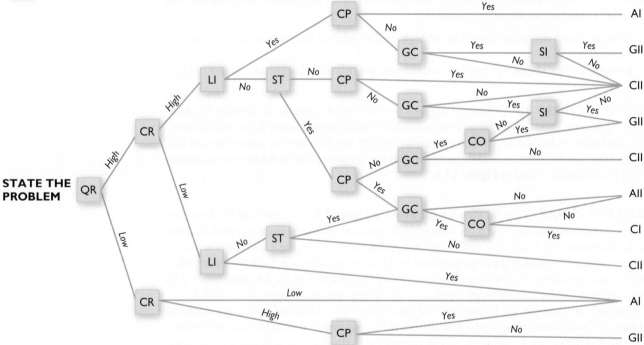

Figure 15.7 The Vroom–Yetton–Jago model

situation, the model suggests that the leader use the GII decision—that is, the leader should meet with the group to discuss the situation and then allow the group to make the decision.

The VYJ model seems promising. Research on an earlier version of this model yielded some evidence that managerial decisions consistent with the model are more successful than are managerial decisions inconsistent with the model.[38] The model is rather complex, however, and therefore is difficult for practicing managers to apply.[39]

Leaders Changing Organizations

15-5 Hints on how leaders change organizations

Transformational leadership is leadership that inspires organizational success by profoundly affecting followers' beliefs in what an organization should be as well as their values, such as justice and integrity.[40] This style of leadership creates a sense of duty within an organization, encourages new ways of handling problems, and promotes learning for all organization members.[41] Transformational leadership is closely related to concepts such as charismatic leadership and inspirational leadership.

Bennett Cohen and Jerry Greenfield, cofounders of the iconic Ben & Jerry's ice cream brand, are examples of transformational leaders. From the outset, profitability was only one of their goals. They were equally interested in creating an enterprise that operated in environmentally responsible ways and gave back to the communities in which it did business. According to Greenfield, "We measured our success not just by how much money we made, but by how much we contributed to the community."[42]

Perhaps transformational leadership is receiving more attention nowadays because of the dramatic changes many organizations are going through and the critical importance of transformational leadership in successfully "transforming" or changing organizations. In fact, recent studies have found evidence linking certain traits—hope, optimism, and resiliency—to the success of transformational leaders.[43]

The Tasks of Transformational Leaders

Transformational leaders perform several important tasks. First, they raise followers' awareness of organizational issues and their consequences. Organization members must understand an organization's high-priority issues and what will happen if those issues are not successfully resolved. Second, transformational leaders create a vision of what the organization should be, build commitment to that vision throughout the organization, and facilitate organizational changes that support the vision. In sum, transformational leadership is consistent with the strategy developed through an organization's strategic management process.[44]

Managers of the future will continue to face the challenge of significantly changing their organizations, primarily because of the accelerating trend toward positioning organizations to be more competitive in a global business environment. Therefore, transformational leadership will probably get increasing attention in the leadership literature. Although the practical appeal of and interest in this style of leadership are strong, more research is needed to develop insights into how managers can become successful transformational leaders.

Leaders Coaching Others

Coaching is leadership that instructs followers on how to meet the specific organizational challenges they face.[45] Operating like an athletic coach, the coaching leader identifies inappropriate behavior in followers and suggests how they might correct that behavior.[46] The increasing use of teams has elevated the importance of coaching in today's organizations, and recent research has begun to identify the leader's role in fostering a team's success.[47] Characteristics of an effective coach are presented in **Table 15.2**.

15-6   An understanding of how leaders should coach

STEPS FOR SUCCESS

Tips for Establishing a Coaching Program

Organizations that desire to establish a successful coaching program for employees understand that an effective program requires time and support from every level. Here are some suggestions for instituting a coaching program:[48]

- Encourage all employees to seek out a coach. Any associate can coach anyone else.
- Set the example. As the leader, find a coach and encourage other leaders to do the same.
- Remind employees that coaching is important and not to focus on a "good match" or "chemistry."

- Have only one coach at a time. This ensures that an individual is receiving full attention from the coach.
- Meet regularly. Coaching pairs should meet for about an hour every two to three weeks.
- Seek out a new coach. Once the coaching process comes to a close, immediately find a new coach.
- Provide training on how to be an effective coach. Make certain all associates have the skills, perspectives, and approaches to be a good coach.

TABLE 15.2   **Characteristics of an Effective Coach**

Trait, Attitude, or Behavior	Action Plan for Improvement
1. Empathy (putting self in other person's shoes)	*Sample:* Will listen and try to understand person's point of view. *Your own:*
2. Listening skill	*Sample:* Will concentrate extra hard on listening. *Your own:*
3. Insight into people (ability to size them up)	*Sample:* Will jot down observations about people on first meeting, then verify in the future. *Your own:*
4. Diplomacy and tact	*Sample:* Will study book of etiquette. *Your own:*
5. Patience toward people	*Sample:* Will practice staying calm when someone makes a mistake. *Your own:*
6. Concern for welfare of people	*Sample:* When interacting with another person, will ask myself, "How can this person's interests best be served?" *Your own:*
7. Minimum hostility toward people	*Sample:* Will often ask myself, "Why am I angry at this person?" *Your own:*
8. Self-confidence and emotional stability	*Sample:* Will attempt to have at least one personal success each week. *Your own:*
9. Noncompetitiveness with team members	*Sample:* Will keep reminding myself that all boats rise with the same tide. *Your own:*
10. Enthusiasm for people	*Sample:* Will search for the good in each person. *Your own:*

Coaching Behavior

A successful coaching leader is characterized by many different kinds of behavior, including the following:

- **Listens closely**—The coaching leader tries to discover the facts in what is said and the feelings and emotions behind what is said. Such a leader is careful to listen and not fall into the trap of immediately rebutting statements made by followers.
- **Gives emotional support**—The coaching leader gives followers personal encouragement.[49] Such encouragement should constantly be aimed at motivating them to do their best to meet the high demands of successful organizations.
- **Shows by example what constitutes appropriate behavior**—The coaching leader shows followers, for instance, how to handle an employee problem or a production glitch. By demonstrating expertise, the coaching leader earns the trust and respect of followers.

Each of the above leadership concepts focuses on a different but critical situation that leaders face: making decisions, changing organizations, and coaching others. Each concept has received notable attention in recent management literature.

Leaders should not choose one of these concepts as the prime determinant of how they lead. Instead, leaders should internalize all of these concepts so that they can make better decisions, change organizations, and coach others as related leadership challenges arise.

Leadership: Emerging Concepts for Modern Times

15-7 An appreciation for emerging leadership concepts

Leaders in today's organizations have been confronting many situations rarely encountered by organizational leaders of the past.[50] Never before have managers faced such tremendous aftershocks of economic hard times as well as ethical meltdowns of companies like Enron,

WorldCom, and Adelphia. Today's leaders are often called upon to make unprecedented, massive personnel cuts in order to eliminate unnecessary levels of organizations and thereby lower labor expenses, to create work teams to enhance organizational decision making and workflow, to reengineer work so that organization members will be more efficient and effective, and to initiate programs designed to improve the overall quality of organizational functioning.

Naturally, leadership approaches are emerging to handle these new, nontraditional situations. Overall, these emerging approaches emphasize leaders concentrating on getting employees involved in the organization and giving them the freedom to use their abilities as they think best. These emerging leadership approaches depend mostly on a great amount of trust between managers and employees.[51] **Figure 15.8** contrasts the "soul" of emerging leadership approaches with the "mind" of the manager. The following sections discuss servant leadership, Level 5 leadership, and authentic leadership as examples of leadership approaches that focus on more modern problems and the situations facing managers today.

Servant Leadership

Servant leadership is an approach to leading in which leaders view their primary role as helping followers in their quests to satisfy personal needs, aspirations, and interests.[52] Servant leaders see pursuit of their own personal needs, aspirations, and interests as secondary to their followers' pursuits of these factors.[53] Overall, servant leaders place high value on service to others over their own self-interests[54] and see their main responsibility as caring for the human resources of the organizations.[55] Servant leaders maintain that human resources are the most valuable resources in organizations and constantly strive to transform their followers into wiser and more autonomous individuals. Logically, the result of wiser and more autonomous followers is more successful organizations.

Some industry observers would characterize Tony Hsieh as a servant leader because his focus on building organizations emphasizes helping followers to be more effective in fulfilling their personal needs, aspirations, and interests. Hsieh, the CEO of Zappos.com, a leading online retailer, believes a healthy work environment is the most important attribute of a successful business. Early in his career, Hsieh built a successful company, but as it grew, he found it increasingly difficult to enjoy his work. The problem, he determined, was that employees were not engaged or truly interested in their work. As a result, Hsieh became progressively more dissatisfied with his own company. In his next company, Zappos.com, Hsieh focused on building a work environment that made employees feel so good about their careers and their daily contributions that they were delighted to come to work.[56]

Servant leaders possess several distinctive characteristics that, when taken together, better enable these leaders to help followers pursue their needs, aspirations, and interests.[57] Listed here are a few of the more notable of these servant leader characteristics:[58]

. . . **good listeners.** Listening is a critical characteristic of servant leaders. The ability to listen carefully to follower comments, for example, helps the servant leader more accurately define the critical factors of follower needs, aspirations, and interests and thereby more

European pressphoto agency b.v./Alamy Stock Photo

San Antonio Spurs' coach, Gregg Popovich, demonstrates some of his effective coaching skills by his patience and appropriate behavior on the basketball court sidelines.

LEADER	MANAGER
SOUL	**MIND**
Visionary	Rational
Passionate	Consultative
Creative	Persistent
Flexible	Problem-solving
Inspirational	Tough-minded
Innovative	Analytical
Courageous	Structured
Imaginative	Deliberate
Experimental	Authoritative
Independent	Stabilizing

Figure 15.8

Characteristics of the emerging leader versus characteristics of the manager effectively assist followers in their quests to achieve these factors. Without such an accurate definition, the servant leader's task of helping followers achieve these factors would be virtually hopeless. Overall, listening provides servant leaders with the feedback they can use to better serve their followers.

... **persuasive.** Seldom do servant leaders use their authority to mandate that their followers take certain actions. Instead, servant leaders focus on convincing followers of activity that should be performed. Such persuasive ability enables servant leaders to ensure that followers act appropriately but without creating the resentment between leader and followers that typically develops when a leader mandates activity without accepting follower input.

... **aware of their surroundings.** Servant leaders are keenly aware of organizational surroundings. As such, servant leaders know what factors might create barriers in followers' quests to pursue their needs, interests, and aspirations and take action to eliminate those barriers. Servant leaders help followers deal with such barriers by furnishing critical ideas and information regarding formidable organizational challenges.[59]

... **empathetic.** Empathy is the intellectual identification with the feelings, thoughts, or attitudes of another. Being empathetic helps servant leaders to relate better to followers when helping them solve problems. Servant leaders understand the situations in which followers find themselves and are thereby better equipped to assist them in their pursuit of interests, aspirations, and needs.

... **stewards.** A steward is defined as an individual who is entrusted with managing the affairs of another. Overall, servant leaders see themselves as being entrusted with managing the human assets of an organization and with the responsibility to help organization members maximize their potentials. Servant leaders are committed to developing the human assets that are instrumental in achieving organizational success.

Undeniably, servant leadership has gained increasing and significant popularity in recent decades. The notion of servant leadership, however, is not new. Servant leadership was first introduced by Christianity's founder, Jesus Christ, and has been practiced by monarchs for more than 1,000 years.[60] Some of the growing popularity of the servant leadership concept can probably be attributed to the intuitive attractiveness of the concept.[61] For example, some management theorists believe that servant leadership's focus on empowerment, sense of community, and sharing of authority suggests that servant leadership is likely a theory with significant potential for enhancing organizational success.[62]

Recent research has analyzed the relationship between servant leadership and personality characteristics.[63] For example, one study assessed whether a relationship between one's ability to be a servant leader and personality traits such as agreeableness could be identified.[64] Agreeableness has been defined in this context as someone who is altruistic, generous, and eager to help others. The results of this study indicated that the managers who were rated by their employees as servant leaders were also highly agreeable people. In addition, servant leaders demonstrated admirable values such as empathy, integrity, and competence. Although some research has been done in this area, additional research aimed at defining the worth of servant leadership theory to practicing managers more precisely is advisable.

Level 5 Leadership

In 2001, Jim Collins wrote a book called *Good to Great*. The book quickly gained both attention and notoriety.[65] Its purpose was to report the results of a five-year study conducted by Collins in which he studied 1,435 *Fortune* 500 companies. The study focused on answering two questions: Can an organization become great? If so, how? Greatness was defined as a company being able to average a cumulative stock return that was 6.9 times higher than that of the general stock market for 15 years.[66] Of all the companies studied, only 11 were able to achieve greatness.

So how did these companies achieve greatness? Collins concluded that the one thing all 11 companies had in common was Level 5 leaders. **Level 5 leadership** is an approach to leadership that blends personal humility with an intense will to build long-range organizational success.

PRACTICAL CHALLENGE: LEADING FOR GREATNESS

The 30% Club Is Now in Hong Kong

The 30% Club in Hong Kong is an outreach arm of the Women's Foundation, a not-for-profit organization established in 2004 with the aim of improving the lives of women and girls in Hong Kong. This is achieved mainly through education, advocacy, and community programs. The 30% Club aims to raise awareness about the benefits of gender diversity at the top management level, encourage debate and discussion on the subject, and actively support initiatives to bring women into executive and non-executive roles. The 30% Club was originally launched in the United Kingdom in 2010, and the Hong Kong branch joined the global initiative with the goal of increasing the number of women on Hong Kong's corporate boards. In 2017, the Hong Kong branch was able to announce that the number of women on the boards of Hang Seng Index companies had increased from 11.1 percent in 2016 to 13.3 percent. The new Hong Kong targets are 20 percent by 2020 and, importantly, no zero percent in any company by the end of 2018. Meanwhile, in the United Kingdom, 27 percent of FTSE100 boards are female.[67]

Basically, **personal humility** means being modest or unassuming when it comes to citing personal accomplishments. Such leaders do not seek public praise and never boast. Instead, Level 5 leaders have a tendency to give credit to others when things go right and to blame themselves when things go wrong. These leaders are not egocentric and are even seen as shy at times. Such leaders do not try to gain the personal notoriety or celebrity that might accrue to them because of the positions they hold. In short, these leaders are ambitious about achieving company success, not individual success.

Professional will is a strong and unwavering commitment to do whatever is necessary to build long-term company success. Level 5 leaders set the standards for maintaining this long-term company success. They know what is necessary to meet such standards and are resolute in doing what is necessary, no matter how difficult.[68]

According to Collins's research, Level 5 leaders are catalysts for spurring organizations toward achieving greatness. As **Figure 15.9** shows, research pinpoints four other levels of leadership. Although Level 5 is the most effective level in spurring an organization from good to great performance, leaders at the other four levels can produce high levels of success—but not high enough to achieve greatness as defined by Collins's study.

Authentic Leadership

Authentic leadership is leadership conducted by leaders who are deeply aware of their own and others' moral perspectives and who are confident, hopeful, optimistic, resilient, and of high moral character.[69] Authentic leaders are clear on their personal moral beliefs and values, make them known to others, and use them as the basis for action.[70]

Authentic leaders also have moral courage. **Moral courage** is the strength to take actions that are consistent with moral beliefs despite pressures, either inside or outside the organization, to do otherwise. Much has been written about leaders bowing to pressures to make profits in the short run and taking action that is inconsistent with their moral beliefs. Moral courage enables leaders to stand up for their moral beliefs, disregard pressures to do otherwise, and take actions consistent with those beliefs.[71]

It is reasonable to question the validity of the authentic leadership concept simply because it is relatively new and, as a result, does not have a large body of research exploring its merits. However, do not overlook the potentially positive impact of authentic leadership on organizational success. For example, one report indicates that authentic leadership is a worthwhile vehicle for creating healthy work environments for practicing nurses as well as other groups throughout the health-care industry.[72]

Figure 15.9
Level 5 hierarchy

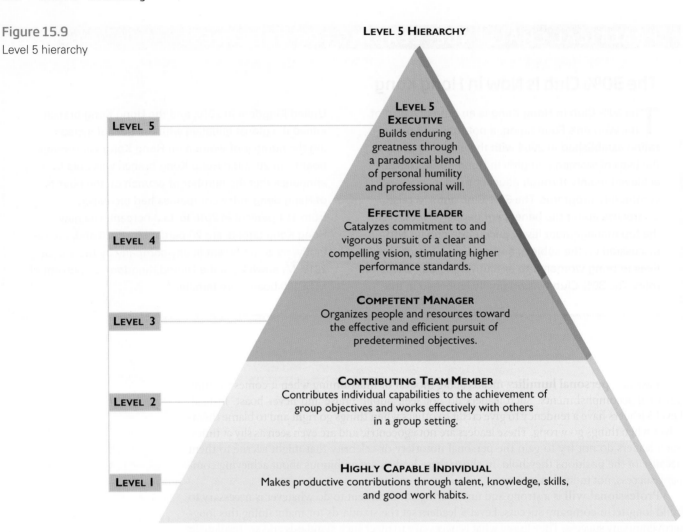

LEVEL 5 HIERARCHY

LEVEL 5

LEVEL 5 EXECUTIVE
Builds enduring greatness through a paradoxical blend of personal humility and professional will.

LEVEL 4

EFFECTIVE LEADER
Catalyzes commitment to and vigorous pursuit of a clear and compelling vision, stimulating higher performance standards.

LEVEL 3

COMPETENT MANAGER
Organizes people and resources toward the effective and efficient pursuit of predetermined objectives.

LEVEL 2

CONTRIBUTING TEAM MEMBER
Contributes individual capabilities to the achievement of group objectives and works effectively with others in a group setting.

LEVEL 1

HIGHLY CAPABLE INDIVIDUAL
Makes productive contributions through talent, knowledge, skills, and good work habits.

CHALLENGE CASE SUMMARY

As noted in the chapter discussion, managers such as Bob Bechek, CEO of Bain & Company, should understand that leadership activities involve directing the behavior of organization members so that the company will achieve success. Managers also should understand that leading and managing are not the same thing. Managing involves planning, organizing, influencing, and controlling, whereas leading is performing an activity that is part of the influencing function of management. To maximize long-term success, managers should strive to be both managers and leaders.

In assessing their leadership abilities, managers such as Bechek should not fall into the trap of trying to increase leadership success by changing personal traits or attitudes to mirror those of successful leaders they

might know. Studies based on the trait approach to leadership indicate that merely changing their characteristics will not guarantee leadership success.

Such managers should see behavioral approaches to leadership as being much more useful than the trait approach. The OSU leadership studies furnish a manager with insights on leadership behavior in general situations. According to these studies, managers can exhibit two general types of leadership behavior: structure and consideration. Managers are using structure behavior when they tell personnel what to do—for example, when managers tell them exactly how to do a particular project. In contrast, they are using consideration behavior when they attempt to develop a kinder rapport with their employees by discussing their concerns and developing friendships with them.

Of course, depending on how much managers emphasize these two behaviors, their leadership styles can reflect a combination of structure and consideration ranging from high structure/low consideration to low structure/high consideration. For example, if managers stress giving orders to employees and deemphasize developing relationships with them, they are exhibiting high structure/low consideration. If they emphasize a good rapport with their employees and allow them to function mostly independently, their leadership styles would be termed low structure/high consideration.

The situational approach to leadership affords more insights than does the trait approach on how managers like Bechek can help their companies achieve success. The situational approach suggests that successful leadership is determined by the appropriateness of a combination of three factors: (1) the manager as a leader, (2) the manager's employees as followers, and (3) the situations within the company the manager faces. Each of these factors plays a significant role in determining whether managers are successful leaders.

Although no single leadership style is more effective than any other in all situations, the life cycle theory of leadership provides managers with a strategy for using various styles in various situations. According to this theory, managers should make their style consistent primarily with the maturity levels of the organization members they are leading. As followers progress from immaturity to maturity, managers' leadership styles should shift systematically from (1) high-task/low-relationship behavior to (2) high-task/high-relationship behavior to (3) high-relationship/low-task behavior to (4) low-task/low-relationship behavior.

The life cycle theory also says that managers should be flexible enough to behave according to the situations they encounter at their organizations. If managers find it extremely difficult to be flexible, however, they should attempt to structure their situations in order to make them appropriate for their style. As suggested by Fiedler, if a manager's leadership style is high task in nature, he or she generally will be a more successful leader in situations best described by octants 1, 2, 3, and 8 in Table 15.1 and in Figure 15.4. If a manager's leadership style is more relationship oriented, however, he or she will probably be a more successful leader in situations representative of octants 4, 5, 6, and 7. Overall, Fiedler's work provides managers with insights on how to change situations so that they will be appropriate for their own leadership styles.

The path–goal theory of leadership suggests that in leading, managers should clarify what rewards are available to followers in the organization and how those rewards can be earned, and eliminate barriers that could prohibit followers from earning the rewards. Managers can use directive behavior, supportive behavior, participative behavior, and achievement behavior in implementing the path–goal theory.

One of the most important activities managers perform as leaders is making decisions. They can make decisions in any number of ways, ranging from authoritarian to democratic. In trying to decide exactly how to make decisions as leaders, managers should consider forces in themselves as managers, forces in their subordinates, and forces in the specific organizational situations they face. Forces within managers include their own ideas about how to lead and their levels of confidence in the employees they are leading. If managers believe that they are more knowledgeable than their staff about achieving acquisition success, they will likely make boss-centered decisions about what steps to take to create acquisition success. Forces within subordinates, such as the need for independence, the readiness to assume responsibility, and the knowledge of and interest in the issues to be decided, also affect managers' decisions as leaders. If a manager's staff members are relatively independent and responsible and if they feel strongly about acquisition success and how it should be achieved, then the manager would be more inclined to allow his or her employees more freedom in deciding how to achieve that acquisition success.

Forces within the company include the number of people making decisions and the problem to be solved. For example, if a manager's staff is small, he or she will be more likely to use a democratic decision-making style, allowing his or her employees to become involved in decisions such as how to best achieve acquisition success. Managers will also be likely to use a subordinate-centered leadership style if their employees are knowledgeable about what makes a company successful. The VYJ model says that managers should try to make decisions so that the quality of decisions is enhanced and followers are committed to the decisions. Managers can try to ensure that such decisions are made by matching their decision-making style (autocratic, consultative, or group) to the particular situation they face.

If Bechek became the leader of a different organization, he might become a transformational leader, one who inspires followers to focus seriously on achieving organizational objectives. As a transformational leader, Bechek would encourage new ideas, create a sense of duty, and encourage employees to learn and grow. As this hypothetical company experienced significant growth, the importance of its transformational leader would increase.

Other popular leadership styles also offer managers such as Bechek insights about how to be a successful leader. As a coaching leader, Bechek would focus on instructing followers how to meet the special challenges they face, such as expansion through global acquisition. In the role of coaching leader, he would listen closely, give emotional support, and show by example what should be done. As a servant leader, Bechek would help followers satisfy their personal needs, aspirations, and interests. Skills like being a good listener, being persuasive, and being aware of his surroundings would help Bechek become a successful servant leader. As a Level 5 leader, Bechek would display humility and a strong will to achieve company objectives. Last, to enhance his success at Bain & Company, Bechek should focus on being an authentic leader. Authentic leaders possess high moral courage: the strength to take action consistent with moral beliefs despite pressure to do otherwise.

Overall, managers must keep in mind that these leadership approaches are aimed at getting people involved in an organization and giving them the freedom to use their abilities as they think best. Certainly, leaders are always free to choose bits and pieces from any of these approaches in order to craft a personal leadership style that best fits their personal needs. However, leaders must always keep in mind that, regardless of the type of leaders they are, they must earn and maintain the trust of their followers if they are to be successful in the long run.

MyLab Management Assessing Your Management Skill

If your instructor has assigned this activity, go to www.pearson.com/mylab/management to complete the exercise related to the Challenge Case.

DEVELOPING LEADERSHIP SKILL

This section is specially designed to help you develop leadership skills. An individual's leadership skill is based on an understanding of the concepts and the ability to apply those concepts. The following activities will help to enhance your leadership skills in various organizational situations.

Class Preparation and Personal Study

To help you to prepare for class, perform the activities outlined in this section. Performing these activities will help you enhance your classroom performance significantly.

Reflecting on Target Skill

On page 358, this chapter opens by presenting a target management skill along with a list of related objectives outlining knowledge and understanding that you should aim to acquire related to that skill. Review this target skill and the list of objectives to make sure that you've acquired all pertinent information within the chapter. If you do not feel that you've reached a particular objective(s), study related chapter coverage until you do.

Know Key Terms

Understanding the following key terms is critical to your preparing for class. Define each of these terms. Refer to the page(s) referenced after a term to check your definition or to gain further insight regarding the term.

leadership **360**
trait approach to leadership **361**
structure behavior **361**

consideration behavior **362**
leadership style **362**
job-centered behavior **362**
employee-centered behavior **362**
situational approach to leadership **363**
life cycle theory of leadership **364**
leader flexibility **365**
contingency theory of leadership **365**
leader–member relations **365**
task structure **365**
position power **365**
path–goal theory of leadership **367**
directive behavior **367**
supportive behavior **367**
participative behavior **367**
achievement behavior **367**
Vroom–Yetton–Jago (VYJ) model of leadership **371**
transformational leadership **372**
coaching **373**
servant leadership **375**

Know How Management Concepts Relate

This section comprises activities that will further sharpen your understanding of management concepts. Answer essay questions as completely as possible.

15-1 Is it important for you as a manager to understand the difference between leadership and management? Explain fully.

15-2 The Michigan studies identified two basic types of leader behavior. What are these two types and their characteristics? Would they be useful to you as a manager?

15-3 Explain how you would use the Vroom–Yetton–Jago (VYJ) model of leadership to choose decision styles.

MyLab Management
Personal Inventory Assessment

Go to www.pearson.com/mylab/management to complete the Personal Inventory Assessment related to this chapter.

Management Skills Exercises

Learning activities in this section are aimed at helping you develop leadership skills.

MyLab Management
Discussion Questions

Go to www.pearson.com/mylab/management to complete the problems marked with this icon .

✪ Cases

Bain & Company's CEO, Bob Bechek, Leads the Team

The Challenge Case "Bain & Company's CEO, Bob Bechek, Leads the Team" (p. 359) and its related Challenge Case Summary were written to help you understand the management concepts contained in this chapter. Answer the following discussion questions about the Challenge Case to further enrich your understanding of chapter content.

15-4 Based on what you read, which type of leadership style is most closely associated with Bechek? Explain.

15-5 Do you feel that Bechek should use more of a boss-centered or a subordinate-centered leadership style at Bain & Company? Why?

15-6 If Bechek decided to use a transformational leadership style, what would you suggest he do in order to utilize this approach? Be specific.

Jeff Bezos Is the Force of Nature behind Amazon

Read the case and answer the questions that follow. Studying this case will help you better understand how concepts relating to leadership can be applied in a company such as Amazon.

Jeff Bezos is a giant in management. *Forbes* magazine recently named him its top CEO based on the performance of the company he founded, online retailer Amazon. Bezos started Amazon a few years after earning a degree in computer science and electrical engineering. Not satisfied with applying his analytic skills to finance, he started an online bookstore, incorporating the business in 1994 and launching the website in 1995. Today, Amazon is a retailing monster, with more than 20 million products and revenues of $48 billion. It is also a company built on 14 leadership principles that reflect the character of the company's founder.

Topmost in Bezos's mind as a business leader is his passion for pleasing customers. In a famous gesture, Bezos requires that in meetings, an empty chair be placed at the table to represent the customer, the invisible presence everyone must be most concerned about. Even if a service that delights customers costs money—say, sturdier boxes that customers can reuse—Bezos will forge ahead. He even has a publicly available e-mail address, jeff@amazon.com, so that he can learn directly what customers love and hate. When he receives a complaint, he is apt to forward it to Amazon managers, adding as his only comment a question mark, implicitly demanding an investigation and explanation. Employees know they have just a few hours to resolve the problem and report their solution.

In addition, Bezos insists that decisions be firmly grounded in data. At weekly meetings, managers must evaluate their performance based strictly on data related to the company's 500 quantitative goals, 80 percent of which are related to customer satisfaction. Because the data will inevitably point to the best answer, Bezos does not shy from confrontation in decision making. He expects employees to argue their positions, on the assumption that the best ideas will become evident. As one of Amazon's leadership principles state, "Leaders have conviction and are tenacious. They do not compromise for the sake of social cohesion." Therefore, the employees who succeed at Amazon are the ones who thrive on conflict.

Another of Bezos's values, frugality, partly derives from Amazon's start-up experience. The company was not profitable for years, and many observers doubted it would survive, with its strategy of charging prices below costs. Survival required limiting any expenses not connected to making customers happy. In contrast to tech companies that keep employees happy with fun amenities, Amazon gives employees desks made out of doors and charges them for snacks. However, the basis for forcing employees to be frugal is not just to help the company earn a profit; it is also to enable the company to continue pleasing customers with the best prices.

Bezos is notoriously demanding. If employees let customers down or fail to live up to his high standards, he is blunt—even rude—in his assessment (reported comments include "Are you lazy or just incompetent?" and "If I hear that idea again, I'm gonna have to kill myself"). If his harsh comments hurt employees' feelings, well, that is not a major concern of his because the goal is to make *customers* happy. However, employees observe that when Bezos says an idea is bad, his own idea almost always is the better one, even in functions outside his expertise. The demands he places on others inspire them to improve, innovate, and make a difference continually.

Under Bezos's leadership, Amazon has continued to grow and eat into one product category after another. Most remarkably, that growth is not at the cost of great service. In the University of Michigan's American Customer Satisfaction Index, Amazon lands in the top spot for retailing year after year.[73]

Questions

15-7 Which theory of leadership do you think best describes Jeff Bezos's contribution to Amazon's performance? Describe how it applies.

15-8 Does Bezos create an environment in which you could contribute effectively as a manager? Explain.

15-9 Do you think Bezos is a better leader or a better manager? Explain.

Experiential Exercises

Making a Decision

Directions. Read the following scenario and then perform the listed activities. Your instructor may want you to perform the activities as an individual or in a group. Follow all of your instructor's directions carefully.

Assume you are the president of an online retailer specializing in toner cartridges for office printers and copiers. The business has been successful since it was founded nine years ago, with revenues approaching $10 million. You have about 300 employees, and the company has increased sales by about 10 percent each year. Though your customers are located throughout the United States, there is a lot of competition in the toner industry, and you would like to see your firm grow more dramatically.

Coincidentally, a rival firm has contacted you about a possible sale of the business. The rival's president is 70 years old, about to retire, and has offered his business to you for the sum of $4 million. Though you have only about $1 million in cash reserves, you are confident that you will be able to secure a bank loan for the $3 million balance (which will obviously increase the firm's long-term debt). Unfortunately, you have to make a quick decision because the rival business

has given you only one week to respond before its president approaches another company about a possible acquisition.

Your team of upper-level managers is experienced and knowledgeable, but none of them have been with your company for more than two years. Some of them, particularly the vice president of sales, would probably be against the acquisition because she is convinced that she can drive sales even greater than what the company has been experiencing. She has been a strong proponent of sales promotions, and she often says in meetings, "We will bankrupt our competition!" You know the industry, and you are very familiar with the rival company. You feel that the acquisition would help grow your company faster than through just incremental increases in sales. The challenge before you is whether or not to acquire the rival company on your own or invite input from your executive team and have them help make the decision.

Learning Activity

15-10 How would you make the decision regarding whether or not to make the acquisition?
   a. Simply make the decision and announce it.
   b. Make the decision but try to convince others it's best.
   c. Present a tentative decision subject to change based on input.
   d. Present the dilemma and ask for input before making the decision.
   e. Allow the executive team (all of the vice presidents) to make the decision.

15-11 Explain your answer to question 15-10. Be sure to focus on why you chose the option you did as well as why you did not choose the other options.

_____

_____

_____

_____

15-12 As a leader, would you find making this decision challenging? Why or why not?

_____

_____

_____

_____

15-13 Ultimately, what would you decide? Whether you make the decision on your own or invite input, would the acquisition of the rival firm be made? Why or why not?

_____

_____

_____

_____

You and Your Career[74]

You have just graduated from college and are interested in a career in government. In looking for your first job, you find out that the city manager's office of the City of

Sacramento, California, has recently begun to recognize the significant retirement projections among its baby boomer employees. According to the city manager, to deal with the impending retirements, Sacramento's city government will start designing and offering leadership development programs to its employees. The programs will focus on helping young leaders understand how various parts of city government operate as well as helping them develop a broad network of relationships within city government as a whole.

Would this information about Sacramento's city government raise or lower your interest in working there? Explain. How would you find out if other potential employers offer similar programs? Name another topic you would like to see covered in Sacramento's leadership development program and explain its significance.

Building Your Management Skills Portfolio

Your Management Skills Portfolio is a collection of activities specially designed to demonstrate your management knowledge and skill. Be sure to save your work. Taking your printed portfolio to an employment interview could be helpful in obtaining a job.

The portfolio activity for this chapter is Leadership Skill in a Special Situation. Study the following information and complete the exercises that follow.[75]

On April 5, 2010, there was an explosion at the Upper Big Branch mine in West Virginia. Of the 31 miners at the site, 29 were killed. The Upper Big Branch mine is owned by Massey Energy and the CEO, Don Blankenship, was charged with one misdemeanor count of conspiracy to violate federal safety regulations. In 2016, he was sentenced to one year in jail (he had originally faced a possible 30-year sentence).

The court case was significant. Is the CEO liable for a disaster that results in the deaths of employees? In this particular case, Blankenship was found guilty of conspiring to violate certain mine safety and health standards. However, his sentence sends a message that the leader of an organization is ultimately responsible for events under his or her watch.

For five years prior to the explosion, the Mine Safety and Health Administration cited Massey Energy over 1,300 times for safety violations. In the two months before the explosion, the mine had to be evacuated three times due to high levels of methane gas. In addition, the agency fined the company almost $2 million during this same time period. Clearly, safety regulations are important—especially in the mining industry—but inspections, training, safety equipment, and so on are all time-consuming and expensive. In one memo sent by Blankenship to superintendents of his mines, he reminded them that the focus of the company is to mine coal, saying, "If any of you have been asked . . . to do anything other than run coal . . . you need to ignore them and run coal. This memo is necessary only because we seem not to understand that coal pays the bills."

During the trial, it was stated that Blankenship impeded mine inspections by getting advanced notice of an inspection so that employees could conceal any safety violations. In addition, whenever citations were issued by the inspectors, Massey Energy avoided having the mine closed by using appeals processes to tie the cases up in courts for extended periods of time.

Activity 1

Circle the option that best reflects your opinion about Don Blankenship's leadership situation at Massey Energy. Don Blankenship should have been held responsible for the mining disaster at Upper Big Branch mine.

1. Definitely
2. Possibly
3. Definitely not

Activity 2

Now that you have expressed your opinion about Don Blankenship's role in the mine disaster, explain this opinion below in 50 words or fewer.

_____

_____

_____

Activity 3

Conduct an online search about Don Blankenship, Massey Energy, and the Upper Big Branch mine disaster. Based on your research, how would you characterize Blankenship's leadership style? Be specific.

_____

_____

_____

Activity 4

In general, should the president of a company be held liable for events at the firm, even if the president was not actually present or involved in the event? For example, should the president be held responsible for a customer who dies while using one of the company's products incorrectly? Or should the president be liable for an employee who commits sexual harassment in the workplace? Explain your response.

_____

_____

_____

MyLab Management
Writing Assignments

If your instructor has assigned this activity, go to www.pearson.com/mylab/management for the following assisted-graded writing assignments:

Assisted-Grading Questions

15-14 What is the difference between the "situational approach" and the "trait approach" to leadership? Which approach seems to have more relevance to you as a manager? Explain.

15-15 Given all that you've learned in this chapter, what kind of leader will you try to be as a manager? Explain.

Endnotes

1. Emma Ockerman, "These Are the Best-Liked CEOs in the Country," Time.com (June 9, 2016).
2. Jeff Schmitt, "Executive Q&A: Bain's Bob Bechek," Poets & Quants, April 30, 2016, http://poetsandquants.com/2016/04/30/executive-qa-bain-companys-bob-bechek/.
3. Elise Goldman, "The Significance of Leadership Style," *Educational Leadership* 55, no. 7 (April 1998): 20–22. For a worthwhile look at the importance of instilling leadership in all members of a corporation, see Scott Payne, "Corporate Training Trend: Building Leadership," *Grand Rapids Business Journal*, November 13, 2000, B2; see also Dusya Vera and Mary Crossan, "Strategic Leadership and Organizational Learning," *Academy of Management Review* 29 (2004): 222.
4. David Nadler and Michael L. Tushman, "Beyond the Charismatic Leader: Leadership and Organizational Change," *California Management Review* 32 (Winter 1990): 77–97; This discussion underscores the importance of leadership in health services: M. Chan, D. de Camps Meschino, D. Dath, J. Busari, J. D. Bohnen, L. M. Samson, . . . M. Sánchez-Mendiola, "Collaborating Internationally on Physician Leadership Development: Why Now?," *Leadership in Health Services* 29, no. 3 (2016): 231–239.
5. Abraham Zaleznik, "Executives and Organizations: Real Work," *Harvard Business Review* (January/February 1989): 57–64; C. Chiu, P. Balkundi, and F. J. Weinberg, "When Managers Become Leaders: The Role of Manager Network Centralities, Social Power, and Followers' Perception of Leadership," *The Leadership Quarterly* 28, no. 2 (2017): 334–348.
6. Theodore Levitt, "Management and the Post-Industrial Society," *Public Interest* (Summer 1976): 73.
7. Patrick L. Townsend and Joan E. Gebhardt, "We Have Lots of Managers . . . We Need Leaders," *Journal for Quality and Participation* (September 1989): 18–20; Craig Hickman, "The Winning Mix: Mind of a Manager, Soul of a Leader," *Canadian Business* 63 (February 1990): 69–72. For a discussion of how successful executives place more importance and emphasis on leadership than on management, see Michael E. McGrath, "The Eight Qualities of Success," *Electronic Business* 24, no. 4 (April 1998): 9–10.
8. For a study assessing the validity of traits theory, see Dean Gehring, "Applying Traits Theory of Leadership to Project Management," *Project Management Journal* 38 (2007): 44–55.
9. Ralph M. Stogdill, "Personal Factors Associated with Leadership: A Survey of the Literature," *Journal of Psychology* 25 (January 1948): 35–64.
10. Cecil A. Gibb, "Leadership," in Gardner Lindzey, ed., *Handbook of Social Psychology* (Reading, MA: Addison-Wesley, 1954).
11. Frank Walter and Helka Bruch, "An Affective Events Model of Charismatic Leadership Behavior: A Review, Theoretical Integration, and Research Agenda," *Journal of Management* 35, no. 6 (December 2009): 1428–1452.
12. Valerie Sessa, "Creating Leaderful Organizations: How to Bring Out Leadership in Everyone," *Personnel Psychology* 56 (2003): 762.
13. J. Oliver Crom, "What's New in Leadership?," *Executive Excellence* 7 (January 1990): 15–16.
14. Charles S. Lauer, "In Each Other We Trust," *Modern Healthcare* 37, no. 37 (September 17, 2007): 20.
15. For an interesting discussion on the relationship between leadership and employee retention, see Pamela Ribelin, "Retention Reflects Leadership Style," *Nursing Management* 34 (2003): 18.
16. Vishwanath V. Baba and Merle E. Ace, "Serendipity in Leadership: Initiating Structure and Consideration in the Classroom," *Human Relations* 42 (June 1989): 509–525. For a further discussion of leadership style, see Maria Guzzo, "People to Watch: Mike Parton—Classic Leadership Style," *Pittsburgh Business Times Journal* (June 23, 2000): 14.
17. Rensis Likert, *New Patterns of Management* (New York: McGraw-Hill, 1961). For more on the work of Likert, see P. F. Sorensen, T. Yaeger, and R. Narel, "The New Golden Age of Organization Development Research and Knowledge," *Organization Development Journal* 35, no. 1 (2017): 47–55.
18. Xander M. Bezuijen, Peter T. van den Berg, Karen van Dam, and Hank Thierry, "Pygmalion and Employee Learning: The Role of Leader Behaviors," *Journal of Management* 35, no. 5 (October 2009): 1248–1267.
19. Harvey A. Hornstein, Madeline E. Heilman, Edward Mone, and Ross Tartell, "Responding to Contingent Leadership Behavior," *Organizational Dynamics* 15 (Spring 1987): 56–65.
20. A. K. Korman, "'Consideration,' 'Initiating Structure,' and Organizational Criteria—A Review," *Personnel Psychology* 19 (Winter 1966): 349–361. See also Rick Roskin, "Management Style and Achievement: A Model Synthesis," *Management Decision* 27 (1989): 17–22.
21. For an interesting application of the situational leadership model, see R. Vecchko, R. Bullie, and D. Brazil, "The Utility of Situational Leadership Theory: A Replication in a Military Setting," *Small Group Research* 37 (2006): 407.
22. For a discussion of a leader in a military situation, see Sherrill Tapsell, "Managing for Peace," *Management* 45, no. 5 (June 1998): 32–37.
23. Christie Samson, "3 Leadership Traits of an Effective Cross-Cultural Leader," March 30, 2015, http://paulsohn.org/3-leadership-traits-of-an-effective-cross-cultural-leader/.
24. P. Hersey and K. H. Blanchard, "Life Cycle Theory of Leadership," *Training and Development Journal* (May 1969): 26–34.
25. Mary J. Keenan, Joseph B. Hurst, Robert S. Dennis, and Glenna Frey, "Situational Leadership for Collaboration in Health Care Settings," *Health Care Supervisor* 8 (April 1990): 19–25. See also Jane R. Goodson, Gail W. McGee, and James F. Cashman, "Situational Leadership Theory: A Test of Leadership Prescriptions," *Group and Organizational Studies* 14 (December 1989): 446–461.
26. Mark E. Van Buren and Todd Safferstone, "The Quick Wins Paradox," *Harvard Business Review*, January 2009, http://hbr.org.
27. Fred E. Fiedler, "Engineer the Job to Fit the Manager," *Harvard Business Review* (September/October 1965): 115–122.
28. For an interesting look at how different types of leaders and followers perform at different types of tasks, see R. Miller, J. Butler, and C. Cosentino, "Followership Effectiveness: An Extension of Fiedler's Contingency Model," *Leadership and Organization Development* 25 (2004): 362.
29. F. E. Fiedler, *A Theory of Leadership Effectiveness* (New York: McGraw-Hill, 1967), 255–256. © 1967 by McGraw-Hill, Inc. Used with permission of McGraw-Hill Company.
30. L. H. Peters, D. D. Harike, and J. T. Pohlmann, "Fiedler's Contingency Theory of Leadership: An Application of the Meta-Analysis Procedures of Schmidt and Hunter," *Psychological Bulletin* 97 (1985): 224–285.
31. Robert J. House and Terence R. Mitchell, "Path–Goal Theory of Leadership," *Journal of Contemporary Business* (Autumn 1974): 81–98; Gary A. Yukl, *Leadership in Organizations*, 8th ed. (Upper Saddle River, NJ: Prentice Hall, 2012).
32. For a recent article on the path–goal theory, see Sikandar Hayyat Malik, Shamsa Aziz, and Hamid Hassan, "Leadership Behavior and Acceptance of Leaders by Subordinates: Application of Path Goal Theory in Telecom Sector," *International Journal of Trade, Economics and Finance* 5, no. 2 (April 2014): 170–175.
33. For a worthwhile review of the path–goal theory of leadership, see Gary A. Yukl, *Leadership in Organizations*, 8th ed. (Upper Saddle River, NJ: Prentice Hall, 2012).
34. Robert Tannenbaum and Warren H. Schmidt, "How to Choose a Leadership Pattern," *Harvard Business Review* (March/April 1957): 95–101.
35. William E. Zierden, "Leading through the Follower's Point of View," *Organizational Dynamics* (Spring 1980): 27–46. See also Robert Tannenbaum and Warren H. Schmidt, "How to Choose a Leadership Pattern," *Harvard Business Review* (March/April 1957): 95–101.
36. Robert Tannenbaum and Warren H. Schmidt, "How to Choose a Leadership Pattern," *Harvard Business Review* (May/June 1973): 162–180.
37. Victor H. Vroom and Arthur G. Jago, *The New Leadership* (Upper Saddle River, NJ: Prentice Hall, 1988).
38. Gary A. Yukl, *Leadership in Organizations*, 2nd ed. (Upper Saddle River, NJ: Prentice Hall, 1989).
39. For an application of the Vroom–Yetton–Jago model, see "The Behaviour of Managers in Austria and the Czech Republic: An Intercultural Comparison Based on the Vroom/Yetton Model of Leadership and Decision Making," *Journal of East European Management Studies* 9 (2004): 411–430.

40. Karl W. Kuhnert and Philip Lewis, "Transactional and Transformational Leadership: A Constructive/Developmental Analysis," *Academy of Management Review* (October 1987): 648–657; S. A. Fischer, "Transformational Leadership in Nursing: A Concept Analysis," *Journal of Advanced Nursing* 72, no. 11 (2016): 2644–2653.

41. For an article describing the effects of this type of leadership, see J. Schaubroeck, S. Lam, and S. Cha, "Embracing Transformational Leadership: Team Values and the Impact of Leader Behavior on Team Performance," *Journal of Applied Psychology* 92 (2007): 1020.

42. Lauren Folino, "The Great Leaders Series: Ben Cohen and Jerry Greenfield, Co-Founders of Ben & Jerry's Homemade," *Inc.*, February 18, 2010, http://www.inc.com.

43. Suzanne J. Peterson, Fred O. Walumbwa, Kristin Byron, and Jason Myrowitz, "CEO Positive Psychological Traits, Transformational Leadership, and Firm Performance in High-Technology Start-Up and Established Firms," *Journal of Management* 35, no. 2 (March 2009): 348–368.

44. Bernard M. Bass, *Leadership and Performance Beyond Expectations* (New York: Free Press, 1985).

45. For an in-depth look at the positive effects of coaching on employee productivity, see Bill Blades, "Great Coaching Can Increase Revenue," *Arizona Business Gazette*, January 18, 2001, 5.

46. For practical tips on developing this style of leadership, see M. Wakefield, "New Views on Leadership Coaching," *Journal for Quality and Participation* 29 (2006): 9–14.

47. Frederick P. Morgeson, D. Scott DeRue, and Elizabeth P. Karam, "Leadership in Teams: A Functional Approach to Understanding Leadership Structures and Processes," *Journal of Management* 36, no. 1 (January 2010): 5–39.

48. Gregg Thompson, "7 Ways to Create a Coaching Culture," *Chief Learning Officer* 16, no. 5 (June 2017): 66.

49. Jennifer Shrader, "Gulley: Empathy Most Important Part of Leadership," *McClatchy–Tribune Business News* [Washington], October 9, 2013.

50. To learn how some managers are reacting to more recent challenges, see Jaclyn Fierman, "Winning Ideas from Maverick Managers," *Fortune* (February 6, 1995): 66–80. For a fresh approach to leadership that managers are taking, see George Fraser, "The Slight Edge: Valuing and Managing Diversity," *Vital Speeches of the Day* 64, no. 8 (February 1, 1998): 235–240.

51. Holly H. Brower, Scott W. Lester, M. Audrey Korsgaard, and Brian R. Dineen, "A Closer Look at Trust between Managers and Subordinates: Understanding the Effects of Both Trusting and Being Trusted on Subordinate Outcomes," *Journal of Management* 35, no. 2 (March 2009): 327–347.

52. Robert K. Greenleaf, *Servant Leadership: A Journey into the Nature of Legitimate Power and Greatness* (Mahwah, NJ: Paulist Press, 1977); M. F. Coetzer, M. Bussin, and M. Geldenhuys, "The Functions of a Servant Leader," *Administrative Sciences* 7, no. 1 (2017): 5.

53. To learn how servant leadership is associated with trust, see E. Joseph and B. Winston, "A Correlation of Servant Leadership, Leader Trust, and Organizational Trust," *Leadership and Organization Development Journal* 26 (2005): 6–23.

54. Max E. Douglas, "Servant Leadership: An Emerging Supervisory Model," *SuperVision* 64, no. 2 (February 2003): 6–9; Bright Mahembe and Amos S. Engelbrecht, "The Relationship between Servant Leadership, Affective Team Commitment and Team Effectiveness," *SA Journal of Human Resource Management* 11, no. 1 (2013): 1–10.

55. Sen Sendjaya and James C. Sarros, "Servant Leadership: Its Origin, Development, and Application in Organizations," *Journal of Leadership and Organizational Studies* 9, no. 2 (Fall 2002): 57–64.

56. "On a Scale of 1 to 10, How Weird Are You?," *New York Times*, January 10, 2010, http://www.nytimes.com.

57. For a look at the personality characteristics of servant leaders, see R. Washington, C. Sutton, and H. Field, "Individual Differences in Servant Leadership: The Roles of Values and Personality," *Leadership and Organization Development Journal* 27 (2006): 700–716.

58. Ron Rowe, "Leaders as Servants," *New Zealand Management* 50, no. 1 (February 2003): 24–25.

59. Reylito A. H. Elbo, "In the Workplace," *BusinessWorld* (September 4, 2002): 1.

60. Keshavan Nair, *A Higher Standard of Leadership: Lessons from the Life of Gandhi* (San Francisco, CA: Berrett-Koehler, 1994).

61. Robert F. Russell and A. Gregory Stone, "A Review of Servant Leadership Attributes: Developing a Practical Model," *Leadership and Organization Development Journal* 23, no. 3: 145–157.

62. Bernard M. Bass, "The Future of Leadership in Learning Organizations," *Journal of Leadership Studies* 7, no. 3 (2000): 18–40.

63. See R. Washington, C. Sutton, and H. Field, "Individual Differences in Servant Leadership: The Roles of Values and Personality," *Leadership and Organization Development Journal* 27 (2006): 700–716.

64. Ibid., 700.

65. Jim Collins, *Good to Great: Why Some Companies Make the Leap . . . and Others Don't* (New York: HarperCollins, 2001).

66. Jim Collins, "Level 5 Leadership: The Triumph of Humility and Fierce Resolve (HBR Classic)," *Harvard Business Review* (July 1, 2005).

67. Paul J. Davies, "HK Backs 'Women on Company Boards' Drive," *The Financial Times*, March 11, 2013, http://30percentclub.org.hk/.

68. Collins, *Good to Great*: 20.

69. Fred Luthans, Steve Norman, and Larry Hughes, "Authentic Leadership: A New Approach for a New Time," in Ronald J. Burke and Cary L. Cooper, *Inspiring Leaders* (New York: Routledge, 2006), 84–104; Dana Yagil and Hana Medler-Liraz, "Feel Free, Be Yourself: Authentic Leadership, Emotional Expression, and Employee Authenticity," *Journal of Leadership & Organizational Studies* 21, no. 1 (February 2014): 59.

70. Bruce J. Avolio and William L. Gardner, "Authentic Leadership Development: Getting to the Root of Positive Forms of Leadership," *Leadership Quarterly* 16 (2005): 315–338; M. G. Ehret, "Common Leadership Strategies and Practices among Authentic Senior Leaders," *PsycINFO*.

71. Douglas R. May, Adrian Y. L. Chan, Timothy D. Hodges, and Bruce J. Avolio, "Developing the Moral Component of Authentic Leadership," *Organizational Dynamics* 32, no. 3 (2003): 247–260.

72. Maria R. Shirey, "Authentic Leaders Creating Healthy Work Environments for Nursing Practice," *American Journal of Critical Care* 15, no. 3 (May 2006): 256–267.

73. Brad Stone, "The Secrets of Bezos: How Amazon Became the Everything Store," *Bloomberg Businessweek*, October 10, 2013, http://www.businessweek.com; George Anders, "Jeff Bezos Reveals His No. 1 Leadership Secret," *Forbes*, April 4, 2014, http://www.forbes.com; Adam Auriemma, "Bezos as Boss: How the Amazon CEO Rules," *Wall Street Journal*, February 12, 2014, http://blogs.wsj.com; Amazon, "Leadership Principles," http://www.amazon.com, accessed April 3, 2014.

74. Brian W. T. Moffitt, "City Management Institute: A Blueprint for Leadership Succession," *Government Finance Review* 23, no. 4 (August 2007): 55–59.

75. This material is based on Sandy Says, "Letters from Don Blankenship," *EHS Today* 10, no. 6 (June 2017): 4.

16

Motivation

TARGET SKILL

Motivation Skill: the ability to create organizational situations in which individuals performing organizational activities are simultaneously satisfying personal needs and helping the organization attain its goals

MOTIVATION SKILL AND YOUR CAREER

Motivation skill can be of great value to you in enhancing your management career. For example, this skill can help you to build the dedication of organization members so that they focus on their work. Building this dedication helps workers become more productive, contributes more significantly to organizational success, builds your image as a competent manager, makes you more valuable to your organization, and supports your promotions as you build your career.

OBJECTIVES

To help build my *motivation skill*, when studying this chapter, I will attempt to acquire:

16-1 A useful definition of *motivation*

16-2 Insights about the process theories of motivation

16-3 Practical ideas related to the content theories of motivation

16-4 An understanding of the importance of motivating organization members

16-5 Insights about specific strategies for motivating organization members

---

MyLab Management Chapter Warm Up

If your instructor has assigned this activity, go to www.pearson.com/mylab/management to complete the chapter warm up.

CHALLENGE CASE

How Disney Motivates Its Employees

At one point in his career at Walt Disney Company, Lee Cockerell was the executive vice president of operations. This meant he oversaw over 40,000 associates at four theme parks; three water parks; 20 resorts; five golf courses; and several sports complexes, entertainment venues, and retail stores. Managing that many individuals requires solid leadership and the ability to motivate employees at all levels of the organization.

Cockerell states that the essence of effective management can be found in a handful of tenets that he has discovered throughout his career. First, managers should realize that every team member is important. "A truly inclusive leader," Cockerell said, "creates an open, friendly, collaborative environment. The reason is simple: When everyone matters and everyone knows they matter, employees are happy to come to work, and to give you all their energy, creativity, and loyalty." Conversely, if associates do not feel included, they tend to perform poorly.

Second, he points out that employees are the brand of the organization. According to Cockerell, "the term *brand* usually conjures up a logo or a slogan. In reality, your people are your brand. No matter how good your products and services are, you can't achieve true excellence unless you attract great people, develop great people, and keep great people." Once a manager learns this, the actual process of managing becomes easier. It may take a longer period of time to hire the right people, but ultimately it's worth it.

Third, Cockerell puts an emphasis on training. "Great leaders give their people effective, thorough, consistent training," he said, "along with ample opportunities to keep on learning." It's not just on-the-job training, but also training in the organization's culture, understanding the values of the company as well as the mission statement, and having a firm grasp of customer service. "Don't just teach them how to do their jobs," Cockerell added, "instill in them a higher sense of purpose. That's what motivates them to truly excel."

Fourth, the manager is responsible for finding and eliminating anything that gets in the way of employees' ability to do their jobs. Whether it is easy-to-understand processes or being a good problem solver, successful managers are always looking for employee impediments. "Effective processes make routine things run smoothly," Cockerell said, "which frees employees to do the extra things that turn a good business into a great business.

Walt Disney Company is a worldwide media and entertainment business with subsidiaries such as theme parks, resorts, the ABC television network, ESPN, Pixar Animation Studios, Marvel Studios, and LucasFilm.

Ineffective processes, on the other hand, create hassles, and hassles lead to alienated customers and frustrated employees."

Finally, Cockerell insists that managers should be the embodiment of a great leader in order to keep associates motivated. "Like it or not," he said, "leaders are being watched, evaluated, and emulated, so they have to behave like impeccable professionals at all times. True professionals are not only competent, they personify integrity, dignity, and reliability every minute of their working lives." For this reason, Cockerell says that it is important to develop character and know one's values. "Great leaders," he said, "know what they stand for, and they communicate their values to their people. They are always prepared to do the right thing."[1]

THE MOTIVATION CHALLENGE

Lee Cockerell, executive vice president of operations for Walt Disney Company, focuses on basic principles that motivate employees. According to the Challenge Case, Cockerell motivates employees by ensuring that every employee is important, making certain they are part of the brand, providing training, removing hassles, and setting the example for all associates to follow. The material in this chapter provides insights into why managers such as Cockerell should focus on motivating workers and how managers might do so. Major topics in this chapter are the motivation process and motivating organization members.

To be successful in working with subordinates, managers need to acquire a thorough understanding of the motivation process. To that end, the definition of motivation, various motivation models, and theories of people's needs are the main discussion topics in this chapter.

Defining Motivation

16-1 A useful definition of *motivation*

Motivation is the inner state that causes an individual to behave in a way that ensures the accomplishment of some goal.[2] In other words, motivation explains why people act as they do.[3] The better a manager understands organization members' behavior, the more that manager will be able to influence subordinates' behavior to make it work toward the accomplishment of organizational objectives. Because productivity is a result of the behavior of organization members, motivating organization members is the key to reaching organizational goals.[4]

Several motivation theories have been proposed over the years. Most of these theories can be categorized into two basic types: process theories and content theories. A **process theory of motivation** is an explanation of motivation that emphasizes how individuals are motivated. Process theories focus essentially on the steps that occur when an individual is motivated. A **content theory of motivation** is an explanation of motivation that emphasizes people's internal characteristics. Content theories focus on understanding what needs people have and how those needs can be satisfied. For years, industrial and organizational (I/O) psychologists have worked to integrate the many theories of motivation and identify where each has an effect in the motivation process.[5]

The following sections discuss important process and content theories of motivation and establish a relationship between them that should prove useful to managers in motivating organization members.

Process Theories of Motivation

16-2 Insights about the process theories of motivation

Four important theories describe how motivation occurs:

1. Needs-goal theory
2. Vroom expectancy theory
3. Equity theory
4. Porter–Lawler theory

These theories build on one another to furnish a description of the motivation process that begins at a relatively simple and easily understood level and culminates at a somewhat more intricate and realistic level.

The Needs-Goal Theory of Motivation

The **needs-goal theory** of motivation, diagrammed in **Figure 16.1**, is the most fundamental of the motivation theories discussed in this chapter. As the figure indicates, motivation begins with an individual feeling a need. This need is then transformed into behavior directed at supporting, or allowing, the performance of goal behavior to reduce the felt need. Theoretically, goal-supportive behavior and goal behavior continue until the felt need has been significantly reduced.

When an individual feels hunger, for example, this need is typically first transformed into behavior directed at supporting the performance of the goal behavior of eating. This supportive behavior could include activities such as buying, cooking, and serving food. The goal-supportive behaviors and the goal behavior itself—eating—generally continue until the individual's hunger substantially subsides. When the individual experiences hunger again, however, the entire cycle is repeated.

Figure 16.1
The needs-goal theory of motivation

Washington Nationals pitcher Ron Villone provides an example of the needs-goal theory of motivation. When Villone was with the New York Yankees, he heard an interesting statistic: If his team made the playoffs that year, they would be the only team to have reached the post-season both that year and the preceding year. Instead of relishing the glory, Villone immediately started thinking about the playoff team he would face, the strengths and weaknesses of its hitters, and how he might pitch to each one's weakness. Villone was thus demonstrating a strong need to perform well as a pitcher. Because of this need, he started performing goal-supportive activities that included planning how to pitch to each hitter. Once in a game situation, Villone's goal behavior—that is, how players would hit his pitches—would be the feedback that determined whether he satisfied his felt need.

Goal setting can play a prominent role in influencing motivation. For more than 30 years, researchers have provided evidence suggesting that, compared to individuals who don't set goals, individuals who set goals have an easier time focusing on activities relevant to those goals and avoiding distractions that prevent them from reaching those goals.

A team of researchers examined the role of goal setting while studying the performance of undergraduate students struggling with their grades. This is an important context to study because almost 25 percent of students who start undergraduate programs never graduate. The researchers recruited 85 students who were struggling with their grades. Over the course of a semester, half of those students went through a goal-setting program, which helped them identify personal goals and derive strategies for reaching those goals. The other students were placed in a control group and did not participate in this goal-setting program (these students were instead asked to complete a number of tasks that were unrelated to goal setting).

After approximately 16 weeks, the researchers examined the performance of the students in both groups. Do you think that there was a difference between the two groups of students? Why or why not?[6]

The Role of Individual Needs

If managers are to have any success in motivating employees, they must understand the personal needs of those employees. When managers offer rewards that are not relevant to employees' personal needs, the employees will not be motivated. For example, if a top executive is already extremely well paid, more money is not likely to be an effective motivator. What is required is a more meaningful incentive—perhaps a higher-level title or an offer of partnership in the firm. Managers must be familiar with the needs their employees have and offer them rewards that can satisfy those needs.[7]

The Vroom Expectancy Theory of Motivation

In reality, the motivation process is more complex than presumed by the needs-goal theory. The **Vroom expectancy theory** of motivation encompasses some of these complexities.[8] Like the needs-goal theory, the Vroom expectancy theory is based on the premise that felt needs cause human behavior. However, the Vroom theory also addresses the issue of **motivation strength**—an individual's degree of desire to perform a behavior. As this desire increases or decreases, motivation strength fluctuates correspondingly.

Motivation and Perceptions

Vroom's expectancy theory is shown in equation form in **Figure 16.2**. According to this equation, motivation strength is determined by the perceived value of the result of performing a behavior and the perceived probability that the

Figure 16.2

Vroom's expectancy theory of motivation in equation form

$$\underset{\text{strength}}{\text{Motivation}} = \underset{\text{of performing behavior}}{\text{Perceived value of result}} \times \underset{\text{result will materialize}}{\text{Perceived probability that}}$$

behavior performed will cause the result to materialize. As both of these factors increase, so does motivation strength, or the desire to perform the behavior. People tend to perform behaviors that maximize their personal rewards over the long term.

To see how Vroom's theory applies to human behavior, suppose a college student has been offered a summer job painting three houses at the rate of $200 per house. If we assume that the student needs money, her motivation strength, or desire, to paint the houses will be determined by two major factors: her perception of the value of $600 and her perception of the probability that she can actually paint the houses satisfactorily and receive the $600. As the student's perceived value of the $600 reward and perceived probability that she can paint the houses increase, the student's motivation strength to paint the houses will also increase.

Equity Theory of Motivation

Equity theory, the work of J. Stacy Adams, looks at an individual's perceived fairness of an employment situation and finds that perceived inequities can lead to changes in behavior. Adams found that when individuals believe they have been treated unfairly in comparison with their coworkers, they will react in one of the following ways to try to right the inequity:[9]

1. Some will change their work outputs to better match the rewards they are receiving. If they believe they are being paid too little, they will decrease their work outputs; if they believe they are being paid more than their coworkers, they will increase their work outputs to match their rewards.

2. Some will try to change the compensation they receive for their work by asking for a raise or by taking legal action.

3. If attempts to change the actual inequality are unsuccessful, some will try to change their own perceptions of the inequality. They may do this by distorting the status of their jobs or by rationalizing away the inequity.

4. Some will leave the situation rather than try to change it. People who feel they are being treated unfairly on the job may decide to quit that job rather than endure the inequity.

Perceptions of inequities can arise in any number of management situations—among them, work assignments, promotions, ratings reports, and office assignments—but they occur most often in the area of pay. However, all of these issues are emotionally charged because they all pertain to people's feelings of self-worth. What is a minor inequity in the mind of a manager can loom as extremely important in the mind of an employee. Therefore, effective managers strive to deal with equity issues because the steps workers are prone to take to balance the scales are often far from beneficial to the organization.

For example, after American Airlines employees and union workers took pay cuts and made other concessions worth more than $1.6 million, they learned that American had awarded bonuses totaling $21 million to company executives. Representatives of the Transport Workers Union soon presented American Airlines Chief Executive Gerard J. Arpey with a petition bearing 17,000 signatures protesting the company's executive compensation practices. The perceived inequity between the concessions made by nonmanagers and the bonuses awarded to managers is the kind of issue that can lead to business disruptions like work slowdowns and strikes.[10]

The Porter–Lawler Theory of Motivation

Porter and Lawler developed a motivation theory that provides a more complete description of the motivation process than do either the needs-goal theory or the Vroom expectancy theory.[11] Still, the **Porter–Lawler theory** of motivation (see **Figure 16.3**) is consistent with those two theories in that it accepts the premises that felt needs cause human behavior and that the effort expended to accomplish a task is determined by the perceived value of the rewards that will result from finishing the task and the probability that those rewards will materialize.

In addition, the Porter–Lawler motivation theory stresses three other characteristics of the motivation process:

1. The perceived value of a reward is determined by both intrinsic and extrinsic rewards that result in need satisfaction when a task is accomplished. An **intrinsic reward** comes directly from performing the task, whereas an **extrinsic reward** is extraneous to the task.[12] For example, when a manager counsels a subordinate about a personal problem, the manager may get an intrinsic reward in the form of personal satisfaction at helping another individual. In addition to this intrinsic reward, however, the manager receives an extrinsic reward in the form of the overall salary the manager is paid.[13]
2. The extent to which an individual effectively accomplishes a task is determined primarily by two variables: the individual's perception of what is required to perform the task and the individual's ability to perform the task. Effectiveness at accomplishing a task increases as the perception of what is required to perform the task becomes more accurate and the ability to perform the task increases.
3. The perceived fairness of rewards influences the amount of satisfaction produced by those rewards. The more equitable an individual perceives the rewards to be, the greater the satisfaction the individual will experience as a result of receiving the rewards.

Content Theories of Motivation: Human Needs

The motivation theories discussed thus far imply that an understanding of motivation is based on an understanding of human needs. Some evidence indicates that most people have strong needs for self-respect, respect from others, promotion, and psychological growth.[14] Although identifying all human needs is impossible, several theories have been developed to help managers better understand these needs:

16-3 Practical ideas related to the content theories of motivation

1. Maslow's hierarchy of needs
2. Alderfer's ERG theory
3. Argyris's maturity-immaturity continuum
4. McClelland's acquired needs theory

Figure 16.3 The Porter–Lawler theory of motivation

Maslow's Hierarchy of Needs

Perhaps the most widely accepted description of human needs is the hierarchy of needs concept developed by Abraham Maslow.[15] Maslow states that human beings possess the five basic needs described here and theorizes that these five basic needs can be arranged in a hierarchy of importance—the order in which individuals generally strive to satisfy them.[16] The needs and their relative positions in the hierarchy of importance are shown in **Figure 16.4**.

- The **physiological need** relates to the normal functioning of the body. Physiological needs include the desires for water, food, rest, sex, and air. Until these needs are met, a significant portion of an individual's behavior will be aimed at satisfying them. Once the needs are satisfied, however, behavior is aimed at satisfying the needs on the next level of Maslow's hierarchy.
- The **security or safety need** relates to an individual's desire to be free from harm, including both bodily and economic disaster. Traditionally, management has best helped employees satisfy their physiological and security needs by providing adequate wages or salaries, which employees use to purchase things such as food and housing.
- The **social need** includes the desire for love, companionship, and friendship. Social needs reflect a person's desire to be accepted by others. As they are satisfied, behavior shifts to satisfying esteem needs.
- The **esteem need** is concerned with the desire for respect. Esteem needs are generally divided into two categories: self-respect and respect from others. Once esteem needs are satisfied, the individual moves to the pinnacle of the hierarchy and emphasizes satisfying self-actualization needs.
- The **self-actualization need** refers to the desire to maximize whatever potential an individual possesses. For example, in the nonprofit setting of a public high school, a principal who seeks to satisfy self-actualization needs would strive to become the best principal possible. Self-actualization needs occupy the highest level of Maslow's hierarchy.[17]

The traditional concerns about Maslow's hierarchy are that it has no research base, that it may not accurately reflect basic human needs, and that it is questionable whether human needs can be neatly arranged in such a hierarchy. Nevertheless, Maslow's hierarchy is probably the most popular conceptualization of human needs to date, and it continues to be positively discussed in management literature.[18] Still, the concerns expressed about it should remind managers to look upon Maslow's hierarchy more as a subjective statement than as an objective description of human needs.[19]

Alderfer's ERG Theory

Clayton Alderfer responded to some of the criticisms of Maslow's work by conducting his own study of human needs.[20] He identified three basic categories of needs:

1. **Existence need**—the need for physical well-being
2. **Relatedness need**—the need for satisfying interpersonal relationships
3. **Growth need**—the need for continuing personal growth and development

Figure 16.4
Maslow's hierarchy of needs

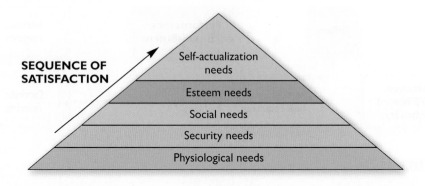

PRACTICAL CHALLENGE: DEVELOPING REWARDS

Excellence in Motion–Jaguar Land Rover Graduate Rewards

Maslow's and Alderfer's models suggest that employees strive to meet different needs at different times. In engineering industries, this becomes a vital tool in ensuring that qualified graduates are recruited. To attract the ideal candidates, a special set of incentives needs to be offered. Managers at Jaguar Land Rover, a Tata subsidiary with British heritage, are acutely aware of this, and having been in the market since the 1930s, they understand that they need to be able to attract the very best engineers from around the world to stay at the forefront of development. For this reason, not only does the management offer extensive learning opportunities, but it also offers fresh recruits a competitive pay of $38,000 with a bonus of $2,600. The recruits are assigned to an individual (known as a "buddy") who was a part of the program the year before to help them settle in with the company. The new candidates are immediately shown the ropes and are a part of an intensive induction program. From day one, they are made aware of the high-quality engineering work expected from them, and most importantly, what the end results of their efforts should be.[21]

The first letters of these three needs form the acronym ERG, which is how the theory is now known.

Alderfer's ERG theory is similar to Maslow's theory except in three major respects. First, Alderfer identified only three orders of human needs, compared to Maslow's five orders. Second, in contrast to Maslow, Alderfer found that people sometimes activate their higher-level needs before they have completely satisfied all of their lower-level needs. Third, Alderfer concluded that movement in his hierarchy of human needs is not always upward. For instance—and this is reflected in his frustration-regression principle—he found that a worker frustrated by his failure to satisfy an upper-level need might regress by trying to fulfill an already satisfied lower-level need.

Alderfer's work, in conjunction with Maslow's, has implications for management. Employees frustrated by work that fails to provide opportunities for growth or development on the job might concentrate their energies on trying to make more money, thus regressing to a lower level of needs. To counteract such regression, management might use job enrichment strategies designed to help people meet their higher-order needs.

Argyris's Maturity-Immaturity Continuum

Argyris's maturity-immaturity continuum also furnishes insights into human needs.[22] This continuum concept focuses on the personal and natural development of people to explain human needs. According to Chris Argyris, as people naturally progress from immaturity to maturity, they move:

1. From a state of passivity as an infant to a state of increasing activity as an adult
2. From a state of dependence on others as an infant to a state of relative independence as an adult
3. From being capable of behaving in only a few ways as an infant to being capable of behaving in many different ways as an adult
4. From having erratic, casual, shallow, and quickly dropped interests as an infant to having deeper, more lasting interests as an adult
5. From having a short-time perspective as an infant to having a much longer-time perspective as an adult
6. From being in a subordinate position as an infant to aspiring to occupy an equal or superordinate position as an adult
7. From a lack of self-awareness as an infant to awareness and control over self as an adult

According to Argyris's continuum, then, as individuals mature, they have increasing needs for more activity, enjoy a state of relative independence, behave in many different ways, have deeper and more lasting interests, are capable of considering a relatively long-time perspective, occupy an equal position vis-à-vis other mature individuals, and have more awareness of

Michaeljung/Fotolia

Argyris's continuum sees needs shifting as people become more mature. What changes in your needs do you observe as you become more independent, gain self-control, and develop a longer-term perspective?

themselves and control over their own destinies. Note that, unlike Maslow's needs, Argyris's needs are not arranged in a hierarchy. Like Maslow's hierarchy, however, Argyris's continuum is primarily a subjective explanation of human needs.

McClelland's Acquired Needs Theory

Another theory about human needs, called **McClelland's acquired needs theory**, focuses on the needs that people acquire through their life experiences. This theory, formulated by David C. McClelland in the 1960s, emphasizes three of the many needs human beings develop in their lifetimes:

1. **Need for achievement (nAch)**—the desire to do something better or more efficiently than it has ever been done before
2. **Need for power (nPower)**—the desire to control, influence, or be responsible for others
3. **Need for affiliation (nAff)**—the desire to maintain close, friendly, personal relationships

The individual's early life experiences determine which of these needs will be highly developed and therefore will dominate the personality.

Bob Crane, entrepreneurial founder of C. Crane, is an example of an individual motivated by the need for achievement. Crane's dream is to save the world energy, and he works to achieve that dream by inventing energy-saving devices that are better and more efficient than any previous devices. His latest product, the GeoBulb, is an LED lightbulb that uses half the energy of a fluorescent bulb, contains no lead or mercury, and will last 30,000 hours or up to 10 years. Crane's not in it for the money. As he puts it, "It's 100% altruistic, and we hope that we'll get paid in time." Although the company hasn't made Crane a wealthy man, he says working toward his goal makes him happy.[23]

McClelland's studies of these three acquired human needs have significant implications for management.

Need for Achievement

McClelland claims that, in some businesspeople, the need to achieve is so strong that it is more motivating than the quest for profits. To maximize their satisfaction, individuals with significant achievement needs set goals for themselves that are challenging yet achievable. Although such people are willing to assume risk, they assess it carefully because they do not want to fail. Therefore, they will avoid tasks that involve too much risk. People with a small need for achievement, on the other hand, generally avoid challenges, responsibilities, and risk.

Need for Power

People with a significant need for power are greatly motivated to influence others and to assume responsibility for subordinates' behavior. They are likely to seek advancement and to take on work activities that have increasing amounts of responsibility in order to earn that advancement. Power-oriented managers are comfortable in competitive situations and enjoy their decision-making roles.

Need for Affiliation

Managers with a significant need for affiliation have a cooperative, team-centered managerial style. They prefer to influence subordinates to complete their tasks through team efforts. The danger is that managers with a significant need for affiliation can lose their effectiveness if this need for social approval and friendship interferes with their willingness to make managerial decisions.[24]

Importance of Motivating Organization Members

16-4 An understanding of the importance of motivating organization members

People are motivated to perform behavior that satisfies their personal needs. Therefore, from a managerial viewpoint, motivation is the process of furnishing organization members with the opportunities to satisfy their needs by performing productive behavior within the organization.

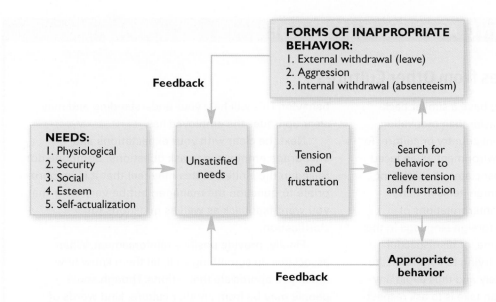

Figure 16.5
Unsatisfied needs of
organization members resulting
in either appropriate or
inappropriate behavior

In reality, managers do not motivate people. Rather, they create environments in which organization members motivate themselves.[25]

As discussed in Chapter 14, motivation is one of the four primary interrelated activities of the influencing function performed by managers to guide the behavior of organization members toward the attainment of organizational objectives. **Figure 16.5** makes the point that unsatisfied needs can lead organization members to perform either appropriate or inappropriate behavior. Successful managers minimize inappropriate behavior and maximize appropriate behavior among subordinates, thus raising the probability that productivity will increase and lowering the probability that it will decrease.

Strategies for Motivating Organization Members

Managers have various strategies at their disposal for motivating organization members. Each strategy is aimed at satisfying subordinates' needs (consistent with the descriptions of human needs in Maslow's hierarchy, Alderfer's ERG theory, Argyris's maturity-immaturity continuum, and McClelland's acquired needs theory) through appropriate organizational behavior. These managerial motivation strategies are as follows:

16-5   Insights about specific strategies for motivating organization members

1. Managerial communication
2. Theory X and Theory Y
3. Job design
4. Behavior modification
5. Likert's management systems
6. Monetary incentives
7. Nonmonetary incentives

These strategies are discussed in the sections that follow. Throughout the discussion, it is important to remember that no single strategy will always be more effective for a manager than any other. Most managers find that some combination of these strategies is most effective in the organization setting.

Managerial Communication

Perhaps the most basic motivation strategy that managers can use is to communicate well with organization members. Effective manager–subordinate communication can satisfy basic human needs such as recognition, a sense of belonging, and security. For example, a simple managerial action such as attempting to become better acquainted with subordinates can contribute

TIPS FOR MANAGING AROUND THE GLOBE

Motivating Employees from Other Cultures

Motivating employees who have a similar background to you is much easier than motivating those who come from a different country or culture. To maintain a positive working environment when faced with attempting to motivate associates of a different culture, it's important to keep three items in mind.

First, be cognizant of your interpretations of behavior. A person speaking a foreign language in the office is not necessarily lazy, rude, or disrespectful. That individual may simply be trying to communicate an important message accurately and thus avoid any ambiguity. The best step you can take is to ask respectfully why an employee is engaging in a certain behavior. This will help your understanding and may clear up issues the employee has.

Next, be clear with your expectations and encourage employees to ask questions. Someone not raised in the United States may feel that it is inappropriate to question the manager, but be very clear that you want feedback as well as questions for clarification.

Finally, provide positive reinforcement. When associates do something well, let them know how much you appreciate their efforts. Though some people may be from another culture, kind words of praise are always appreciated.[26]

substantially to the satisfaction of each of these three needs. A message praising a subordinate for a job well done can help satisfy the subordinate's recognition and security needs.

As a general rule, managers should strive to communicate often with other organization members, not only because communication is the primary means of conducting organizational activities but also because communication is a basic tool for satisfying the human needs of organization members.[27]

Theory X and Theory Y

Another motivation strategy involves managers' assumptions about human nature. Douglas McGregor identified two sets of assumptions: **Theory X** involves negative assumptions about people that McGregor believes managers often use as the basis for dealing with their subordinates (e.g., the average person has an inherent dislike of work and will avoid it whenever he or she can). **Theory Y** represents positive assumptions about people that McGregor believes managers should strive to use (e.g., people will exercise self-direction and self-control in meeting their objectives).[28]

The Theory X/Theory Y debate should resonate for managers across many work settings.[29] McGregor implies that managers who use Theory X assumptions are "bad" and that those who use Theory Y assumptions are "good."[30] William Reddin, however, argues that production might be increased by using *either* Theory X *or* Theory Y assumptions, depending on the situation the manager faces: "Is there not a strong argument for the position that any theory may have desirable outcomes if appropriately used?" The problem is that McGregor considered only the ineffective application of Theory X and the effective application of Theory Y. Reddin thus proposes a **Theory Z**—an effectiveness dimension that implies that managers who use either Theory X or Theory Y assumptions when dealing with people can be successful, depending on their situation.[31]

The basic rationale for using Theory Y rather than Theory X in most situations is that managerial activities that reflect Theory Y assumptions generally are more successful in satisfying the human needs of most organization members than are managerial activities that reflect Theory X assumptions. Therefore, activities based on Theory Y assumptions are more apt to motivate organization members than are activities based on Theory X assumptions.[32]

Job Design
A third strategy that managers can use to motivate organization members involves designing the jobs that organization members perform. The following sections discuss earlier and more recent job design strategies.

EARLIER JOB DESIGN STRATEGIES

A movement has long existed in American business to make jobs simpler and more specialized to increase worker productivity. The idea behind this movement is to make workers more productive by enabling them to be more efficient. Perhaps the best example of a job design inspired by this movement is the automobile assembly line. The negative result of work simplification and specialization, however, is job boredom. As jobs become simpler and more specialized, they typically become more boring and less satisfying to workers, and thus productivity suffers.

JOB ROTATION

The first major attempt to overcome job boredom was **job rotation**—moving workers from job to job rather than requiring them to perform only one simple and specialized job over the long term.[33] For example, a gardener would do more than just mow lawns; he might also trim bushes, rake grass, and sweep sidewalks.

Although job rotation programs have been known to increase organizational profitability, most of them are ineffective as motivation strategies because, over time, people become bored with all the jobs they are rotated into.[34] Job rotation programs are often effective, however, for achieving other organizational objectives, such as training, because they give individuals an overview of how the various units of the organization function. Job rotation can also be an effective procedure for reducing absenteeism—a significant problem in some organizations.[35]

JOB ENLARGEMENT

Another strategy developed to overcome the boredom of doing very simple and specialized jobs is **job enlargement**, or increasing the number of operations an individual performs in order to enhance the individual's satisfaction with work. According to the job enlargement concept, the gardener's job would become more satisfying as activities such as trimming bushes, raking grass, and sweeping sidewalks were added to his initial activity of mowing grass. Although some research supports the contention that job enlargement does make jobs more satisfying, other research does not.[36] Still, job enlargement programs are more successful at increasing job satisfaction than are job rotation programs.

A number of other job design strategies have evolved since the development of job rotation and job enlargement programs. Two of these more recent strategies are job enrichment and flextime.

JOB ENRICHMENT

Frederick Herzberg concluded from his research that the degrees of satisfaction and dissatisfaction that organization members feel as a result of performing a job are two different variables determined by two different sets of items.[37] The items that influence the degree of job dissatisfaction are called **hygiene, or maintenance, factors**, whereas those that influence the degree of job satisfaction are called **motivating factors (motivators)**. Hygiene factors relate to the work environment, and motivating factors relate to the work itself. The items that make up Herzberg's hygiene and motivating factors are presented in **Table 16.1**.

Herzberg believes that when the hygiene factors of a particular job situation are undesirable, organization members will become dissatisfied. Making these factors more desirable—for

TABLE 16.1   **Herzberg's Hygiene Factors and Motivators**

Dissatisfaction: Hygiene or Maintenance Factors	Satisfaction: Motivating Factors
1. Company policy and administration	1. Opportunity for achievement
2. Supervision	2. Opportunity for recognition
3. Relationship with supervisor	3. Work itself
4. Relationship with peers	4. Responsibility
5. Working conditions	5. Working conditions
6. Salary	6. Personal growth
7. Relationship with subordinates	

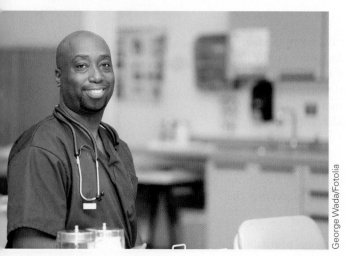

Many nurses are strongly motivated by a sense of purpose—that they are contributing to people's health and well-being.

example, by increasing salary—will rarely motivate people to do a better job, but it will keep them from becoming dissatisfied. In contrast, when the motivating factors of a particular job situation are compelling, employees usually are motivated to do a better job. People tend to be more motivated and productive as more motivators are built into their job situations. During periods of economic recession or high unemployment, many workers are dissatisfied, either because they are doing the work of several people as the result of layoffs in their organization or because they feel "trapped" by a boring job they cannot afford to leave because of the difficulty of finding a new one.[38]

The process of incorporating motivators into a job situation is called **job enrichment**.[39] Early reports indicated that companies such as Texas Instruments and Volvo had notable success in motivating organization members through job enrichment programs. More recent reports continue to support the value of job enrichment, but they indicate that a job enrichment program must be carefully designed and administered for it to be successful.[40]

Many management theorists espouse views that seem consistent with Herzberg's hygiene factor–motivator concept. David Pink, for example, believes that pay in itself is not a motivator. Instead, Pink claims that motivation comes from three different sources: autonomy (the ability to direct one's own life), mastery (continuous improvement at something that an individual considers important), and purpose (to contribute to something larger than oneself).[41]

Job Enrichment and Productivity   Herzberg's overall conclusions are that the most productive organization members are those involved in work situations that have both desirable hygiene and motivating factors. The needs in Maslow's hierarchy that desirable hygiene factors and motivating factors generally satisfy are shown in **Figure 16.6**. Esteem needs can be satisfied by both types of factors. An example of esteem needs satisfied by a hygiene factor is a private parking space—a status symbol and a working condition indicating the employee's importance to the organization. An example of esteem needs satisfied by a motivating factor is an award given for outstanding performance—a public recognition of a job well done that displays the employee's value to the organization.

FLEXTIME

Another more recent job design strategy for motivating organization members is based on a concept called *flextime*.[42] Perhaps the most common traditional characteristic of work in the United States is that jobs are performed within a fixed, eight-hour workday. However, this tradition has recently been challenged. Faced with motivation problems and excessive absenteeism, many managers have turned to scheduling innovations as a possible solution.[43]

The main purpose of these scheduling innovations is not to reduce the total number of work hours but rather to give workers greater flexibility in scheduling their work hours. The main thrust of **flextime**, or a flexible working hours program, is that it allows workers to

Figure 16.6

Needs in Maslow's hierarchy of needs that desirable hygiene and motivating factors generally satisfy

TABLE 16.2   **Advantages and Disadvantages of Using Flextime Programs**

Advantages	Disadvantages
Improved employee attitude and morale	Lack of supervision during some hours of work
Accommodation of working parents	Key people unavailable at certain times
Decreased tardiness	Understaffing at times
Fewer commuting problems—workers can avoid congested streets and highways	Problem of accommodating employees whose output is the input for other employees
Accommodation of those who wish to arrive at work before normal workday interruptions begin	Employee abuse of flextime program
	Difficulty in planning work schedules
Increased production	Problem of keeping track of hours worked or accumulated
Facilitation of employees' scheduling of medical, dental, and other types of appointments	
Accommodation of leisure-time activities of employees	Inability to schedule meetings at convenient times
Decreased absenteeism	Inability to coordinate projects
Decreased turnover	

complete their jobs within a workweek of a normal number of hours that they schedule themselves.[44] The choices of starting and finishing times can be as flexible as the organizational situation allows. To ensure that flexibility does not become counterproductive within the organization, however, many flextime programs stipulate a core period of the day during which all employees must be on the job.

Advantages of Flextime

Various kinds of organizational studies have indicated that flextime programs have some positive organizational effects. Douglas Fleuter reported, for example, that flextime contributes to greater job satisfaction, which typically results in greater productivity. Other researchers conclude that flextime programs can result in higher levels of motivation in workers. Organization members generally consider flextime programs desirable, and when recruiting qualified new employees, organizations that have such programs can usually compete better with organizations that don't offer flextime. (The advantages and disadvantages of flextime programs appear in **Table 16.2**.) Although many well-known companies, such as Scott Paper, Sun Oil, and Samsonite, have adopted flextime programs,[45] more research is needed before flextime's true worth can be assessed conclusively.

Behavior Modification

A fourth strategy that managers can use to motivate organization members is based on a concept known as behavior modification. As stated by B. F. Skinner, the Harvard psychologist considered by many to be the father of behavioral psychology, **behavior modification** focuses on encouraging appropriate behavior by controlling the consequences of that behavior.[46] According to the law of effect, behavior that is rewarded tends to be repeated, whereas behavior that is punished tends to be eliminated.

Although behavior modification programs typically involve the administration of both rewards and punishments, rewards are generally emphasized because they are more effective than punishments in influencing behavior. Obviously, the main theme of behavior modification is not new.

Reinforcement

Behavior modification theory asserts that if managers want to modify subordinates' behavior, they must ensure that appropriate consequences occur as a result of that behavior. **Positive reinforcement** is a reward that consists of a desirable consequence of behavior, and **negative reinforcement** is a reward that consists of the elimination of an undesirable consequence of behavior.[47]

If arriving at work on time is positively reinforced, or rewarded, the probability increases that a worker will arrive on time more often.[48] If arriving late for work causes a worker to experience some undesirable outcome, such as a verbal reprimand, that worker will be negatively reinforced when this outcome is eliminated by on-time arrival. According to behavior modification theory, positive reinforcement and negative reinforcement are both rewards that increase the likelihood that a behavior will continue.

Punishment

Punishment is the presentation of an undesirable behavior consequence or the removal of a desirable behavior consequence that decreases the likelihood the behavior will continue. To use our earlier example, a manager could punish employees for arriving late for work by exposing them to some undesirable consequence, such as verbal reprimand, or by removing a desirable consequence, such as their wages for the amount of time they are late.[49] Although punishment would probably quickly convince most workers to come to work on time, it might also have undesirable side effects, such as high absenteeism and turnover, if it is emphasized over the long term.[50]

MyLab Management Watch It

If your instructor has assigned this activity, go to www.pearson.com/mylab/management to complete the video exercise.

Applying Behavior Modification

Behavior modification programs have been applied both successfully and unsuccessfully in a number of organizations. Management at Emery Worldwide, for example, found that an effective feedback system is crucial to making a behavior modification program successful.[51] This feedback system should be aimed at keeping employees informed of the relationship between various behaviors and their consequences.

Other ingredients of successful behavior modification programs include the following:[52]

1. Giving different kinds of rewards to different workers according to the quality of their performances
2. Telling workers that what they are doing is wrong
3. Punishing workers privately to avoid embarrassing them in front of others
4. Always giving rewards and punishments that are earned to emphasize that management is serious about its behavior modification efforts

The behavior modification concept is also applied to cost control in organizations, with the objective of encouraging employees to be more cost conscious. Under this type of behavior modification program, employees are compensated in a manner that rewards cost control and cost reduction and penalizes cost acceleration.[53]

Managers have added a component to the behavior modification process that identifies the role of cognition in workplace behavior.[54] More specifically, when tackling problems such as an inappropriate corporate culture, managers may recognize a need to change the way employees think about the corporate culture in addition to the way they behave. Cognitive behavior modification programs are best implemented by an outside expert consultant who can identify negative cognitive and behavioral processes. Even though these programs have demonstrated much promise, however, further empirical analysis is necessary to solidify their place in the corporate environment.

Likert's Management Systems

Another strategy that managers can use to motivate organization members is based on the work of Rensis Likert, a noted management scholar.[55] After studying several types and sizes of organizations, Likert concluded that management styles in organizations can be categorized into the following systems:

- **System 1**—This style of management is characterized by a lack of confidence or trust in subordinates. Subordinates do not feel free to discuss their jobs with superiors and are motivated by fear, threats, punishments, and occasional rewards. Information flow in the organization is directed primarily downward; upward communication is viewed with great suspicion. The bulk of all decision making is done at the top of the organization.

Tips for Disciplining Employees Effectively

When employees do something wrong, such as repeatedly arriving to work late or failing to perform their jobs satisfactorily, the manager must sit down and discuss the situation. Here are some tips for making your employee counseling session productive:[56]

- Focus on the behavior, not the person. Your attention should be on removing the bad behavior and not making the discussion a personal vendetta against the associate.
- Clarify the right way to behave. Avoid just saying the employee did not do something correctly; show him or her the proper behavior.
- Stay positive. Don't say that the employee is "stupid" or "can never do anything right."
- Have the conversation in private. Disciplining an employee publicly is embarrassing and can have a negative impact on morale for the other associates.
- End on a good note. Remind the employee how much you appreciate his or her work and that you hope both of you can put the incident behind you.

- **System 2**—This style of management is characterized by a condescending, master-to-servant style of confidence and trust in subordinates. Subordinates do not feel free to discuss their jobs with superiors and are motivated by rewards and actual or potential punishments. Information flows mostly downward; upward communication may or may not be viewed with suspicion. Although policies are made primarily at the top of the organization, decisions within a prescribed framework are made at lower levels.
- **System 3**—This style of management is characterized by substantial, though not complete, confidence in subordinates. Subordinates feel fairly free to discuss their jobs with superiors and are motivated by rewards, occasional punishments, and some involvement. Information flows both upward and downward in the organization. Upward communication is often accepted, though at times it may be viewed with suspicion. Although broad policies and general decisions are made at the top of the organization, more specific decisions are made at lower levels.
- **System 4**—This style of management is characterized by complete trust and confidence in subordinates. Subordinates feel completely free to discuss their jobs with superiors and are motivated by factors such as economic rewards, which are based on a compensation system developed through employee participation and involvement in goal setting. Information flows upward, downward, and horizontally. Upward communication is generally accepted—but even when it is not, employees' questions are answered candidly. Decision making is spread widely throughout the organization and is well coordinated.

Styles, Systems, and Productivity   Likert has suggested that as management style moves from system 1 to system 4, the human needs of individuals within the organization tend to be satisfied more effectively over the long term. Thus, an organization that moves toward system 4 tends to become more productive over the long term.

Figure 16.7 illustrates the comparative long- and short-term effects of both system 1 and system 4 on organizational production. Managers may increase production in the short term by using a system 1 management style because motivation by fear, threat, and punishment is generally effective in the short run. Over the long run, however, this style usually causes production to decrease, primarily because of the long-term dissatisfaction of organization members' needs and the poor working relationships between managers and subordinates.

Conversely, managers who initiate a system 4 management style will probably face some decline in production initially but will see an increase in production over the long term. The short-term decline occurs because organization members must adapt to the new system that management is implementing. The production increase over the long term materializes as a

Figure 16.7

Comparative long-term and short-term effects of system 1 and system 4 on organizational production

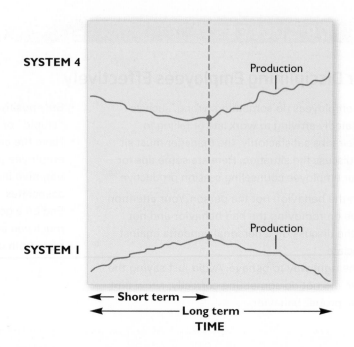

result of organization members' adjustment to the new system, greater satisfaction of their needs, and good working relationships that develop between managers and subordinates.

This long-term production increase under system 4 can also be related to decision-making differences in the two management systems. Because the decisions reached in system 4 are more likely to be understood thoroughly by organization members than are decisions reached in system 1, decision implementation is more likely to be efficient and effective in system 4 than in system 1.

Monetary Incentives

A number of firms make a wide range of money-based compensation programs available to their employees as a form of motivation. For instance, employee stock ownership plans (ESOPs) motivate employees to boost production by offering them shares of company stock as a benefit. Managers are commonly given stock bonuses as an incentive to think more like an owner and ultimately do a better job of building a successful organization. Other incentive plans include lump-sum bonuses—one-time cash payments—and gain sharing, a plan under which members of a team receive a bonus when their team exceeds a goal. All of these plans link pay closely to performance.[57] Many organizations have found that, by putting more of their employees' pay at risk, they can peg more of their total wage costs to sales, which makes expenses more controllable in a downturn.[58] Whatever approach a monetary incentive program takes, it is important that it be accompanied by communication to all employees, describing the organization's business goals and explaining how employees' behavior contributes to accomplishing those goals.[59]

Comarco CEO Sam Inman found an innovative way to use monetary incentives to inspire motivation among his employees: He eliminated the annual review and automatic pay raises. Instead, Inman now distributes awards and raises on a random basis, after an employee has achieved a goal or delivered a project. Employees of Comarco, the maker of universal charge adapters, have also received on-the-spot rewards like gift certificates, plane tickets, and vacations for jobs well done.[60]

Nonmonetary Incentives

A firm can also use nonmonetary means to keep its employees committed and motivated. For instance, some companies have a policy of promoting from within. They go through an elaborate process of advertising jobs internally before going outside the company to fill vacancies. Another nonmonetary incentive emphasizes quality, on the theory that most workers are unhappy when they know their work goes toward producing a shoddy product.[61]

CHALLENGE CASE SUMMARY

Motivation is an inner state that causes individuals to act in certain ways that ensure the accomplishment of a goal. Lee Cockerell seems to have a thorough understanding of the motivation process. He focuses on influencing the behavior of his employees in order to enhance the success of Walt Disney Company. Cockerell encourages employees to be enthusiastic and committed to extraordinary customer service. His focus on motivation is a valuable tool in maintaining Disney's image.

To motivate employees at Disney, Cockerell must keep five principles of human motivation clearly in mind: (1) Felt needs cause behavior aimed at reducing those needs. (2) The degree of desire to perform a particular behavior is determined by an individual's perceived value of the result of performing the behavior and the perceived probability that the behavior will cause the result to materialize. (3) The perceived value of the reward for a particular behavior is determined by both intrinsic and extrinsic rewards that result in need satisfaction when the behavior is accomplished. (4) Individuals can accomplish a task effectively only if they understand what the task requires and have the ability to perform the task. (5) The perceived fairness of a reward influences the degree of satisfaction generated when the reward is received.

Cockerell undoubtedly understands the basic motivation principle that felt needs cause behavior. Before managers can have maximum impact on employees' motivation, they must meet the more complex challenge of being thoroughly familiar with the various individual human needs of their employees. According to Maslow, people generally possess physiological needs, security needs, social needs, esteem needs, and self-actualization needs arranged in a hierarchy of importance. Argyris suggests that as people mature, they have increasing needs for activity, independence, flexibility, deeper interests, analyses of longer-time perspectives, a position of equality with other mature individuals, and control over personal destinies. McClelland believes that the need for achievement—the desire to do something better or more efficiently than it has been done before—is a powerful human need. At Disney, compensation and benefits can enable employees to meet their physiological and security needs as well as their needs for independence. The focus on customer service can target social and esteem needs and can even contribute to a sense of achievement. Disney's diversity policies can satisfy esteem needs and address the desire for a position of equality.

Once a manager understands that felt needs cause behavior and is aware of people's different types of needs, he or she is ready to apply this information to motivating employees. From Cockerell's viewpoint, motivating employees means furnishing them with opportunities to satisfy their human needs by performing their jobs. This notion is especially important because successful motivation tends to increase employee productivity. If Cockerell does not furnish his employees with opportunities to satisfy their human needs while working, low morale will probably eventually develop. Signs of this low morale might be only a few employees initiating creative approaches to customer service, people avoiding the confrontation of tough situations, and employees resisting innovation.

What does the preceding information recommend that Cockerell actually do to motivate employees? Manager–employee communication can help satisfy employee needs for recognition, belonging, and security. Another of Cockerell's strategies might be based on McGregor's Theory X and Theory Y concepts. In following these concepts, Cockerell should assume that work is as natural as play; employees can be self-directed in accomplishing goals; granting rewards encourages the achievement of objectives; employees seek and accept responsibility; and most employees are creative, ingenious, and imaginative. By adopting these assumptions, Cockerell can be more inclined to allow employees more freedom in the workplace and thereby open up many opportunities for employees to satisfy many of the needs defined by Maslow, Argyris, and McClelland.

Cockerell could use two major job design strategies to motivate his employees at Disney. With job enrichment, Cockerell can incorporate into jobs motivating factors such as opportunities for achievement, recognition, and personal growth. Giving employees the latitude to go beyond standard procedures in resolving customer problems, and then publicly acknowledging their successes, is one way that Cockerell enriches jobs at Disney. For maximum success, however, employees need to have positive attitudes toward the hygiene factors at the company, including company policy and administration, supervision, salary, and working conditions.

The second job design strategy that Cockerell can use to motivate his employees is flextime. With flextime, Disney employees could have some freedom in scheduling the beginning and ending of their workdays. However, flextime may be limited by organizational factors such as the urgency of a particular project or the availability of employees at times when customers are present, such as at the entertainment parks or golf courses.

Cockerell can apply behavior modification to his situation at Disney by rewarding appropriate employee behavior and punishing inappropriate employee behavior. Punishment has to be used carefully, however. If used continually, the working relationship between Cockerell and his employees could be destroyed. For the behavior modification program to succeed, Cockerell has to furnish employees with feedback on which behaviors are appropriate and which are inappropriate, give workers different rewards depending on the quality of their performance, tell workers what they are doing wrong, punish workers only in private, and consistently give rewards and punishments when earned.

To use Likert's system 4 management style to motivate employees over the long term, Cockerell has to demonstrate complete confidence in his workers and encourage them to feel completely free to discuss problems with him. In addition, communication among the managers and employees at Disney has to flow freely in all directions within the organizational structure, with upward communication discussed candidly. Cockerell's decision-making process under system 4 has to involve many employees. Cockerell can use the principle of supportive relationships as the basis for his system 4 management style.

No single strategy mentioned in this chapter for motivating organization members will necessarily be more valuable to managers such as Cockerell than any of the other mentioned strategies. In reality, Cockerell will probably find that a combination of all these strategies is most useful in motivating his employees to maintain Disney's reputation as a top provider of high-quality customer service.

MyLab Management Assessing Your Management Skill

If your instructor has assigned this activity, go to www.pearson.com/mylab/management to complete the exercise related to the Challenge Case.

DEVELOPING MOTIVATION SKILL

This section is specially designed to help you develop motivation skills. An individual's motivation skill is based on an understanding of the concepts and the ability to apply those concepts. The following activities will help to enhance your motivation skills in various organizational situations.

Class Preparation and Personal Study

To help you prepare for class, perform the activities outlined in this section. Performing these activities will help you enhance your classroom performance significantly.

Reflecting on Target Skill

On page 386, this chapter opens by presenting a target management skill along with a list of related objectives outlining knowledge and understanding that you should aim to acquire related to that skill. Review this target skill and the list of objectives to make sure that you've acquired all pertinent information within the chapter. If you do not feel that you've reached a particular objective(s), study related chapter coverage until you do.

Know Key Terms

Understanding the following key terms is critical to your preparing for class. Define each of these terms. Refer to the page(s) referenced after a term to check your definition or to gain further insight regarding the term.

motivation **388**
process theory of motivation **388**
content theory of motivation **388**
needs-goal theory **388**

Know How Management Concepts Relate

This section comprises activities that will further sharpen your understanding of management concepts. Answer essay questions as completely as possible.

16-1 Vroom's expectancy theory is more complex than the needs-goal theory. What are the main points of Vroom's motivation theory?

16-2 Early versions of job design strategies tended to focus on making jobs easier to help make people more productive. How is job design used today? Which of the four do you think is the most effective?

MyLab Management
Personal Inventory Assessment

Go to www.pearson.com/mylab/management to complete the Personal Inventory Assessment related to this chapter.

Management Skills Exercises

Learning activities in this section are aimed at helping you develop motivation skills.

MyLab Management
Discussion Questions

Go to www.pearson.com/mylab/management to complete the problems marked with this icon ⭐.

✪ Cases

How Disney Motivates Its Employees

The Challenge Case "How Disney Motivates Its Employees" (p. 387) and its related Challenge Case Summary were written to help you understand the management concepts contained in this chapter. Answer the following discussion questions about the Challenge Case to further enrich your understanding of chapter content.

16-3 Do you think it would be unusual for a manager such as Lee Cockerell to spend a significant portion of his time motivating his employees? Explain.

16-4 Which of the needs on Maslow's hierarchy of needs could delivering exceptional customer service at Disney satisfy? Why?

16-5 Is it possible for Cockerell's efforts to succeed in motivating workers yet be detrimental to organizational success? Explain.

Motivation at United Way

Read the case and answer the questions that follow. Studying this case will help you better understand how concepts relating to motivation can be applied in an organization such as the United Way.

The United Way is a nonprofit organization that has been around since 1887. Founded to help charities raise funds, the United Way also provides grants and coordinates emergency relief services. It is one of the largest nonprofit agencies in the United States, with about 1,300 local organizations and a reach covering 46 countries.[62]

In a difficult economic climate, nonprofits such as the United Way—as well as the charities they support—have found themselves in a trying situation. Donations to all kinds of charitable organizations have dropped precipitously. As people have less discretionary money available, they use what they have for their own needs and, therefore, give less to charities. At the same time, more people desperately need assistance from others to make ends meet. In a recent year, the United Way experienced a 68 percent increase in the number of requests for basic needs.[63] This is a clear indication that individuals and families have been hit hard by the recession. With this increase in need and a decrease in donations, the organization is experiencing an incredible strain.

So how does a manager motivate employees and volunteers during tough economic environments?

Keeping a large staff of full-time employees as well as tens of thousands of volunteers motivated is not an easy task even in the best of times. For an organization that relies on the passion and dedication of those associated with it, motivation becomes even more challenging when financial incentives are out of the question. So the United Way had to find the means to motivate its staff in a way that was also financially responsible. What it discovered was that training employees and volunteers could be a key method of enriching professional lives. With 9,300 employees and countless volunteers, tackling this effectively is challenging but vital. Heidi Kotzian, director of marketing and national events at the United Way, said the organization "will succeed only if our staff has the tools and knowledge they need to effect change."[64] Thus, training not only keeps people associated with the organization excited about their roles within the United Way but also facilitates ongoing organizational performance.

Traditionally, training and development of employees is an area of an organization's budget that gets slashed in economic downturns. Broad-stroked budget cuts are the norm when both nonprofit and for-profit entities attempt to keep costs to a minimum. Often, training is seen as a luxury expense and is put on the back burner until the economic situation improves.

But the United Way is taking a different approach by stepping up its training efforts. Working with the marketing team, the training function was revamped and treated like a "brand"—something that could be readily recognized by employees and even eagerly sought out by those same employees. A catalog consisting of 34 pages of training opportunities is marketed to every employee in the organization.

Feedback from employee participants in various training sessions provides continuous improvement. The organization can determine what works and what doesn't. It also collects data on what training and development skills employees desire to learn. This is important because meeting the needs of the staff is vital for maintaining motivation. For volunteers who do not receive a salary or wage but devote sometimes countless hours of their time, maintaining a high degree of motivation is essential.

For Kotzian, the results speak for themselves. The organization has seen increased efficiencies and also more teamwork and improved communication. "We have seen a boost internally," she said, "from those recognizing the benefits of reaching local United Way staff through learning courses and events."[65]

Questions

16-6   Which theory of motivation do you think is most applicable in describing the United Way's use of training? Explain.

16-7   With a very limited budget, what other nonmonetary incentives can you identify to maintain employees' commitment to the United Way?

16-8   Thinking solely about the United Way's volunteers, how would you motivate them, given that they are unpaid but still have a strong dedication to the work they do?

Experiential Exercises

Analyzing Study Results

Directions. Read the following scenario and then perform the listed activities. Your instructor may want you to perform the activities as an individual or in a group. Follow all of your instructor's directions carefully.

You are part of a special task force established by the human resources department of a farm equipment manufacturing company in the Midwest. The company has 2,200 employees, 405 of whom are managers at various organizational levels. Your task force's assignment is to analyze the results of a survey recently completed by managers within the company and to recommend whatever action, if any, might be necessary, given your opinions about the survey results.

The following chart summarizes the results of the survey, which concerned managers' beliefs about the amount of information they receive from others in the company regarding how well they are doing their jobs, their job duties, organizational policies, pay and benefits, and how technology changes within the company affect their jobs. According to survey results, managers believe they need more information in all areas to do their jobs properly.

Activity

Your instructor will divide your class into small groups and appoint a discussion leader for each group. Assume the role of the task force and answer the following questions. After discussion has completed, your instructor will lead the class in a discussion regarding the opinions of all groups.

16-9   Do you believe the results are having a negative effect within the company on the level of managers' commitment to attaining organizational success? Explain.

16-10   Given the survey results and Maslow's hierarchy of needs, discuss the extent to which you believe managers' personal needs are being met within the organization.

16-11   Given your thoughts about questions 16-9 and 16-10, what action (if any) would you recommend be taken to improve the level of organizational success? Explain, and be as specific as possible.

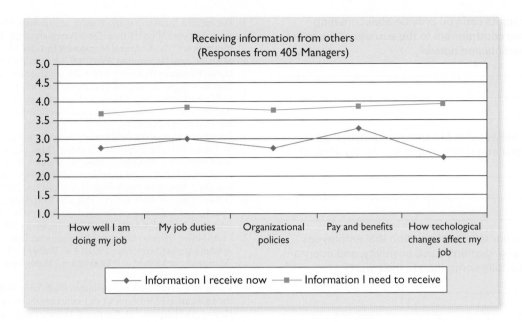

You and Your Career

Throughout this chapter, you learned about theories of motivation and incentives. When you start your career as a manager, it will be important that you have a firm understanding of these concepts so that you can motivate others effectively. But how much of the task of motivating is the responsibility of the manager and how much belongs to the employee? Think about motivation in its broadest sense and consider how much responsibility the employee bears in ensuring that he or she is motivated.

16-12 What percentage of motivation is the responsibility of the manager? For the employee? Explain how you arrived at these percentages.

16-13 Are there some people who cannot be motivated? If so, does that mean the manager should do nothing for these individuals? Explain.

16-14 If you were working for an ineffective manager who did not know how to motivate, what steps would you take to become self-motivated?

16-15 Beyond what you said in question 16-14, what motivates you? Why?

Building Your Management Skills Portfolio

Your Management Skills Portfolio is a collection of activities specially designed to demonstrate your management knowledge and skill. Be sure to save your work. Taking your printed portfolio to an employment interview could prove helpful.

The portfolio activity for this chapter is employee engagement and motivation. Study this information and complete the exercises that follow.

Regardless of the nature of a business or organization or where it might be located, engaged and motivated employees are essential. If employees actually care about their job and their role in the organization, it will be more effective, efficient, and profitable.

In 2017, the analytics company Gallup carried out a global survey on employee engagement. This "State of the Global Workplace" report covered 155 countries. One of the countries that showed some cause for concern in the report was the UAE, where some 85 percent of the working population claimed that they were "not engaged" or "actively disengaged" in their work. This means that the vast majority of the UAE workforce was not as productive or committed as employers would have hoped.

The UAE showed results that were higher than many in Europe, the Far East, other parts of the Middle East, and North Africa. You have been contacted by the CEO of a major chain of hotels and restaurants across the Middle East. She is particularly concerned because the chain is most dominant and headquartered in the UAE. She has also been aware for some time that the profitability of some of the operations has not been as high as her advisors had forecasted. She could find no reason for the poor results but now believes that employee engagement and motivation are the answer.

It is her intention to create a happier and therefore more motivated and productive workforce. She wants to accelerate the transformation of workplace culture and expects you to provide her with further information and a road map to achieve this aim. She wants a high-development, high-performance organization.

16-16 What role do you think the individual needs of people play in building a successful company?

_____

_____

_____

16-17 What insights can you provide about creating employee commitment to the success of the chain of restaurants and hotels?

_____

_____

_____

16-18 Do you believe that Millennial employees are a particular challenge? Why might this be significant?

_____

_____

_____

16-19 What is your take on the notion that employees require engagement, trust, positivity, and integration to be fully committed to their work?

_____

_____

_____

16-20 What management style would you use in the business? Discuss its short- and long-term implications for production levels.

_____

_____

_____

MyLab Management
Writing Assignments

If your instructor has assigned this activity, go to www.pearson.com/mylab/management for the following assisted-graded writing assignments:

Assisted-Grading Questions

16-21 Write out the equation for the expectancy theory of motivation. How can you use this equation to improve your motivation skill? Be specific.

16-22 Is Maslow's hierarchy of needs useful to managers? Why?

16-23 Which strategy for motivating organization members presented in the chapter would you find easiest to implement? Why? Which would you find most difficult to use? Why?

Endnotes

1. Lee Cockerell, "Creating Leadership Magic," _Leader to Leader_ (Summer 2009): 31–36.
2. Kaylene C. Williams and Caroline C. Williams, "Five Key Ingredients for Improving Student Motivation," _Research in Higher Education Journal_ 12 (August 2011): 1–23; Carole L. Jurkiewicz, Tom K. Massey, Jr., and Roger G. Brown, "Motivation in Public and Private Organizations: A Comparative Study," _Public Productivity & Management Review_ 21, no. 3 (March 1998): 230–250.
3. For a useful discussion of motivation, see Thomas Wright, "What Every Manager Should Know: Does Personality Help Drive Employee Motivation?," _The Academy of Management Executive_ 17 (2003): 131.
4. Mike DeLuca, "Motivating Your Staff Is Key to Your Success," _Restaurant Hospitality_ (February 1995): 20; see also Sanford De Voe and Sheena Ivengar, "Managers' Theories of Subordinates: A Cross-Cultural Examination of Manager Perceptions of Motivation and Appraisal of Performance," _Organizational Behavior and Human Decision Processes_ 93 (2004): 47.
5. For an overview of the field known as work motivation, see James M. Diefendorff and Megan M. Chandler, "Maintaining, Expanding, and Contracting the Organization," in Sheldon Zedeck, ed., _APA Handbook of Industrial and Organizational Psychology_, vol. 3. (Washington, D.C.: American Psychological Association, 2011), 65–135.
6. D. Morisano, J. B. Hirsch, R. O. Phil, and B. M. Shore, "Setting, Elaborating, and Reflecting on Personal Goals Improves Academic Performance," _Journal of Applied Psychology_ 95, no. 2 (2010): 255–264.
7. Craig Miller, "How to Construct Programs for Teams," _Reward & Recognition_ (August/September 1991): 4–6; Walter F. Charsley, "Management, Morale, and Motivation," _Management World_ 17 (July/August 1988): 27–28.
8. Victor H. Vroom, _Work and Motivation_ (New York: Wiley, 1964); for the application of Vroom's work to the construction industry, see Hassan Ali Halepota, "Motivational Theories and Their Application in Construction: A Publication of the American Association of Cost Engineers," _Cost Engineering_ 47, no. 3 (March 2005): 14–18.
9. J. Stacy Adams, "Towards an Understanding of Inequity," _Journal of Abnormal and Social Psychology_ 67 (1963): 422–436. For the possible effects of equity theory in China, see Yujun Lian, Zhi Su, and Yuedong Gu, "Evaluating the Effects of Equity Incentives Using PSM: Evidence from China," _Frontiers of Business Research in China_ 5, no. 2 (June 2011): 266–290. For a rationale linking expectancy and equity theories, see Joseph W. Harder, "Equity Theory versus Expectancy Theory: The Case of Major League Baseball Free Agents," _Journal of Applied Psychology_ (June 1991): 458–464.
10. Eric O'Keefe, "Executive Pay Proposals Rejected at AMR," _New York Times_, May 17, 2007, C5.
11. L. W. Porter and E. E. Lawler, _Managerial Attitudes and Performance_ (Homewood, IL: Richard D. Irwin, 1968). For more information on intrinsic and extrinsic rewards, see Pat Buhler, "Rewards in the Organization," _Supervision_ 50 (January 1989): 5–7.
12. Eunmi Chang, "Composite Effects of Extrinsic Motivation on Work Effort: A Case of Korean Employees," _Journal of World Business_ 38 (2003): 70.
13. For a study that assesses the effectiveness of intrinsic and extrinsic rewards, see R. C. Mahaney and A. Lederer, "The Effect of Intrinsic and Extrinsic Rewards for Developers on Information Systems Project Success," _Project Management Journal_ 37 (2006): 42–54.
14. Eric G. Flamholtz and Yvonne Randle, "The Inner Game of Management," _Management Review_ 77 (April 1988): 24–30.
15. Abraham Maslow, _Motivation and Personality_, 2nd ed. (New York: Harper & Row, 1970). For a more recent discussion of the value of Maslow's ideas, see Edward Hoffman, "Abraham Maslow: Father of Enlightened Management," _Training_ 25 (September 1988): 79–82.
16. "Maslow's Hierarchy of Needs Revisited," _Nursing Forum_ 38 (2003): 3.
17. For a discussion of an empowerment tool that managers can use to help employees satisfy their esteem and self-actualization needs, see Chris Argyris, "Empowerment: The Emperor's New Clothes," _Harvard Business Review_ 76, no. 3 (May/June 1998): 98–105.
18. For critiques of Maslow, see Jack W. Duncan, _Essentials of Management_ (Hinsdale, IL: Dryden Press, 1975), 105; Edward Hoffman, "Abraham Maslow: Father of Enlightened Management," _Training_ 25 (September 1988): 79–82; Dale L. Mort, "Lead Your Team to the Top," _Security Management_ 32 (January 1988): 43–45.
19. For information about Maslow's revised hierarchy of needs, see M. Koltko-Rivera, "Rediscovering the Later Version of Maslow's Hierarchy of Needs: Self-Transcendence and Opportunities for Theory, Research, and Unification," _Review of General Psychology_ 10 (2006): 302–317.
20. Clayton Alderfer, _Existence, Relatedness, and Growth_ (New York: Free Press, 1972). For a reconstruction of Maslow's hierarchy, see Francis Heylighen, "A Cognitive-Systemic Reconstruction of Maslow's Theory of Self-Actualization," _Behavioral Science_ (January 1992): 39–58.

21. Jaguar Land Rover website, Careers, http://www
.jaguarlandrovercareers.com/jlr-roles/graduate/; Russell Youll,
"Jaguar Land Rover Received Almost 40 Applications for Every
Graduate Job This Year," *Coventry Telegraph*, July 8, 2014.

22. Chris Argyris, *Personality and Organization* (New York: Harper &
Bros., 1957). See also Charles R. Davis, "The Primacy of Self-
Development in Chris Argyris's Writings," *International Journal of
Public Administration* 10 (September 1987): 177–207.

23. Karen E. Klein, "Where an Inventor-Entrepreneur Finds Motivation," *Bloomberg Businessweek*, August 4, 2009, http://www.business
week.com.

24. David C. McClelland and David G. Winter, *Motivating Economic
Achievement* (New York: Free Press, 1969). See also Lawrence Holp,
"Achievement Motivation and Kaizen," *Training and Development Jour-
nal* 43 (October 1989): 53–63; D. C. McClelland and David H. Burn-
ham, "Power Is the Great Motivator," *Harvard Business Review*
(January/February 1995): 126–139.

25. Michael Sanson, "Fired Up!," *Restaurant Hospitality* (February 1995):
53–64.

26. Sondra Theiderman, "Motivating Employees from Other Cultures,"
accessed July 27, 2017, https://www.monster.com/career-advice/
article/motivating-employees-from-other-cultures.

27. For an empirical investigation of the importance of a manager's
ability to communicate effectively, see D. English, E. Manton, and J.
Walker, "Human Resource Managers' Perception of Selected Communication Competencies," *Education* 127 (2007): 410–418.

28. Douglas McGregor, *The Human Side of Enterprise* (New York:
McGraw-Hill, 1960). For discussion of how Theory X and Theory Y
assumptions held by managers can influence their views on how
others should participate in making decisions, see Travis L. Russ,
"Theory X/Y Assumptions as Predictors of Managers' Propensity
for Participative Decision Making," *Management Decision* 49, no. 5
(2011): 823–836; see also Travis L. Russ, "The Relationship between
Theory X/Y: Assumptions and Communication Apprehension,"
Leadership & Organization Development Journal 34, no. 3 (2013):
238–249.

29. Elizabeth A. Fisher, "Motivation and Leadership in Social Work
Management: A Review of Theories and Related Studies," *Administration in Social Work* 33, no. 4 (October–December 2009): 347–367.

30. For more information about McGregor's Theory Y, see C. Carson,
"A Historical View of Douglas McGregor's Theory Y," *Management
Decision* 43 (2005): 450–462.

31. For more information about applying Theory Z in the workplace,
see Richard Daft, "Theory Z: Opening the Corporate Door for Participative Management," *Academy of Management Executive* 18 (2004):
117.

32. For more information about the possible usefulness of Theory X,
see Michael Bobic and William Davis, "A Kind Word for Theory X:
Or Why So Many Newfangled Management Techniques Quickly
Fail," *Journal of Public Administration Research and Theory* 13 (2003):
239.

33. For more information on reducing boredom in the workplace, see
Z. Bhadury and Z. Radovilsky, "Job Rotation Using the Multi-
Period Assignment Model," *International Journal of Production Research*
44 (2006): 4431.

34. For a comprehensive review of job design literature see G. R. Oldham and Y. Fried, "Job Design Research and Theory: Past, Present
and Future," *Organizational Behavior and Human Decision Processes* 136
(2016): 20; see also Wipawee Tharmmaphornphilas and Bryan A.
Norman, "A Quantitative Method for Determining Proper Job Rotation Intervals," *Annals of Operations Research* 128 (2004): 251.

35. Julia Weichel, Sanjin Stanic, José Alonso Enriquez Diaz, and Ekke-
hart Frieling, "Job Rotation—Implications for Old and Impaired
Assembly Line Workers," *Occupational Ergonomics* 9, no. 2 (June
2010): 67–74.

36. L. E. Davis and E. S. Valfer, "Intervening Responses to Changes in
Supervisor Job Designs," *Occupational Psychology* (July 1965):
171–190.

37. This section is based on Frederick Herzberg, "One More Time: How
Do You Motivate Employees?," *Harvard Business Review* (January/
February 1968): 53–62. See also Deborah B. Smith and Joel Shields,
"Factors Related to Social Service Workers' Job Satisfaction:

38. Katina W. Thompson, "Underemployment Perceptions, Job Attitudes, and Outcomes: An Equity Theory Perspective," *Academy of
Management Proceedings* (2009): 1–6.

39. For an understanding of how job enrichment relates to other workplace factors, see L. Lapierre, R. Hackett, and S. Taggar, "A Test of
the Links between Family Interference with Work, Job Enrichment,
and Leader-Member Exchange," *Applied Psychology* 55 (2006): 489.

40. Scott M. Meyers, "Who Are Your Motivated Workers?," *Harvard
Business Review* (January/February 1964): 73–88; J. Barton Cunning-
ham and Ted Eberle, "A Guide to Job Enrichment and Redesign,"
Personnel 67 (February 1990): 56–61.

41. Ray B. Williams, "How to Motivate Employees: What Managers
Need to Know," *Psychology Today*, February 13, 2010, http://www
.psychologytoday.com.

42. For an analysis of the strengths of implementing flextime in the
workplace, see J. Haar, "Exploring the Benefits and Use of Flextime: Similarities and Differences," *Qualitative Research in Accounting and Management* 4 (2007): 69; see also Kalpana Solanki,
"Association of Job Satisfaction, Productivity, Motivation, Stress
Levels with Flextime," *Journal of Organisation and Human Behaviour*
2, no. 2 (2013): 1–10.

43. A. Okulicz-Kozaryn and L. Golden, "Happiness Is Flextime," *Applied
Research in Quality of Life* (2017), doi:http://dx.doi.org/10.1007/
s11482-017-9525-8.

44. D. A. Bratton, "Moving Away from Nine to Five," *Canadian Business
Review* 13 (Spring 1986): 15–17.

45. Douglas L. Fleuter, "Flextime—A Social Phenomenon," *Personnel
Journal* (June 1975): 318–319; Jill Kanin-Lovers, "Meeting the
Challenge of Workforce, 2000," *Journal of Compensation and Benefits* 5
(January/February 1990): 233–236.

46. B. F. Skinner, *Contingencies of Reinforcement* (New York: Appleton-
Century-Crofts, 1969); To see how behavior modification can relate
to a business model, see "Amazon's Business Model? Behavior
Modification," *Market Talk Dow Jones Institutional News*, New York
(February 7, 2017).

47. For an interesting discussion of accounting as a means of reward-
ing employees, see Mahmoud Ezzamel and Hugh Willmott,
"Accounting, Remuneration, and Employee Motivation in the
New Organization," *Accounting and Business Research* 28, no. 2
(Spring 1998): 97–110.

48. For further information about the use of positive reinforcement in
the workplace, see D. Wiegand and S. Geller, "Connecting Positive
Psychology and Organizational Behavior Management:
Achievement Motivation and the Power of Positive Reinforcement,"
Journal of Organizational Behavior Management 24 (2004/2005): 3.

49. P. M. Padakoff, "Relationships between Leader Reward and Punishment Behavior and Group Process and Productivity," *Journal of Management* 11 (Spring 1985): 55–73.

50. For an understanding of the potential repercussions of excessive
punishment, see Steven Schepman and Lynn Richmond, "Employee
Expectations and Motivation: An Application from the Learned
Helplessness Paradigm," *Journal of American Academy of Business* 3
(2003): 405.

51. "New Tool: Reinforcement for Good Work," *Psychology Today* (April
1972): 68–69.

52. W. Clay Hamner and Ellen P. Hamner, "Behavior Modification on
the Bottom Line," *Organizational Dynamics* 4 (Spring 1976): 6–8.

53. James K. Hickel, "Paying Employees to Control Costs," *Human
Resources Professional* (January/February 1995): 21–24.

54. For more information about cognitive-behavior modification, see D.
Boan, "Cognitive-Behavior Modification and Organizational Culture,"
Consulting Psychology Journal: Practice and Research 58 (2006): 51–61.

55. Rensis Likert, *New Patterns of Management* (New York: McGraw-Hill,
1961). For an interesting discussion of the worth of Likert's ideas,
see Marvin R. Weisbord, "For More Productive Workplaces," *Journal
of Management Consulting* 4 (1988): 7–14. The following descriptions
are based on the table of organizational and performance characteristics of different management systems in Rensis Likert, *The
Human Organization* (New York: McGraw-Hill, 1967), 4–10.

Revisiting Herzberg's Motivation to Work," *Administration in Social
Work* 37, no. 2 (2013): 189.

56. Gerry Ennis, "What's It Going to Take to Get Him to Do It Right?," *Supervision* 78, no. 1 (January 2017): 16–19.

57. For an empirical investigation of the effectiveness of monetary incentives, see H. McGee, A. Dickinson, B. Huitema, and K. Culig, "The Effects of Individual and Group Monetary Incentives on High Performance," *Performance Improvement Quarterly* 19 (2006): 107–130.

58. For a discussion questioning the limitations of monetary incentives, see C. Maier, H. Woratschek, T. Ströbel, and B. Popp, "Is It Really All about Money? A Study on Incentives in Elite Team Sports," *European Sport Management Quarterly* 16, no. 5 (2016): 592–612.

59. "Create a Successful Incentive Program," *Journal of Financial Planning* (May/June 2010): 12–13.

60. Jena McGregor, "Will Ending Annual Reviews Make You More Like a Startup?," *BusinessWeek*, August 28, 2009, http://www.business-week.com.

61. For an illustration outlining how monetary and nonmonetary incentives should suit the situation, see "Creating Incentives That Are Fit to Purpose," *Gulf News* (January 22, 2017).

62. Gordon Johnson, "Marketing Learning the United Way," *Chief Learning Officer* 9, no. 5 (2010): 42–47; www.unitedway.org.

63. Dan Kadlec, "The Nonprofit Squeeze," *Time* 173, no. 12 (2009): 49–50.

64. See endnote 62.

65. See endnote 62.

Groups and Teams

TARGET SKILL

 Team Skill: the ability to manage a collection of people so that they influence one another toward the accomplishment of an organizational objective(s)

TEAM SKILL AND YOUR CAREER

Team skill can be of great value in enhancing your management career. For example, this skill can help you to build a collection of department members as a working unit that reaches department goals more successfully together than if doing their jobs primarily as individuals. Building such collections of people enables workers to contribute more significantly to organizational success, enhances your image as a competent manager, makes you more valuable to your organization, and supports your promotions as you build your career.

OBJECTIVES

To help build my *team skill*, when studying this chapter, I will attempt to acquire:

17-1 A definition of the term *group* as used in the context of management

17-2 A thorough understanding of the different kinds of groups that exist in organizations

17-3 Knowledge of how to manage work groups

17-4 An understanding of how the term *team* is used in the context of organizations

17-5 Insights about the stages of team development

17-6 Knowledge regarding the relationship between collaboration and effective teams

---

MyLab Management Chapter Warm Up

If your instructor has assigned this activity, go to www.pearson.com/mylab/management to complete the chapter warm up.

Better Teamwork Makes Numerica Credit Union a Winner

When Carla Altepeter took the position of chief executive officer of Numerica Credit Union, she saw some significant problems. At Numerica—which serves borrowers and savers in a region that includes Spokane, Washington, and northern Idaho—employees below the top-management level did not understand the organization's goals or have a voice in decision making. This lack of communication isolated individuals, and they did not function as a team. Projects then fell behind as the individual charged with project management struggled to keep track of all the work. In addition, employees directed their energy toward fixing problems rather than pleasing customers. These problems ultimately showed up in Numerica's business performance: Its growth lagged behind that of its competitors.

Altepeter decided that Numerica's employees needed to be better connected with the information that would help them collaborate on achieving shared goals. She brought in a software company to set up a system called Connections Online (COL). With COL, every employee can look up the credit union's strategy and see all the goals aimed at carrying out that strategy. They can see what projects are under way, who is working on them, and what the status is. Besides making project management more efficient, the COL system shows employees how each of them functions as part of something bigger.

The COL system has been especially helpful for projects that span the credit union's different departments. In a single year, Numerica could be carrying out more than a dozen projects that bring together employees from different departments and levels of the organization. For example, the credit union's facilities team recently coordinated a project to remodel one of Numerica's branches. Altepeter notes that collaboration across departments can take extra time but results in higher-quality outcomes. In the case of the branch remodeling, use of the COL system helped the team finish on time and under budget because, from the beginning, everyone involved understood the project's scope and goals.

Reward programs also help Numerica meet its goals for improving how employees collaborate. Along with their pay and benefits, employees can earn rewards for behavior that supports the credit union's values and performance. A recognition program called STAR (which stands for Service, Teamwork, Accountability, and

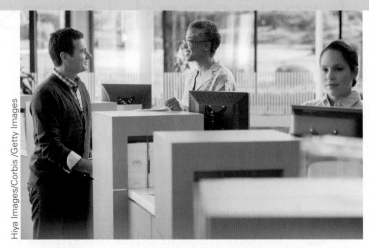

Hiya Images/Corbis /Getty Images

Numerica successfully remodeled a branch location by collaborating together across departments. Collaboration can take extra time but usually results in higher-quality outcomes.

Reflect, learn, and grow) acknowledges employees who do what the company refers to as good deeds.

All this attention to how employees work together has paid off for Numerica. In the two years after Altepeter became CEO, the credit union saw its loans to customers jump by 21 percent the first year and by another 19 percent the following year. Return on assets (a basic measure of financial performance for a credit union) also was exceeding goals. Out of the 16 performance measures Altepeter has been tracking, she recently noted that nine are significantly exceeding their goals, and only one is falling short.[1]

THE TEAM CHALLENGE

The Challenge Case highlights the important role that teams play in the success of Numerica Credit Union. The material in this chapter should help managers, such as those at Numerica, gain insights about how to manage teams successfully. This chapter (1) defines groups, (2) discusses the kinds of groups that exist in organizations, (3) explains what steps managers should take to manage groups appropriately, and (4) explains team management.

The previous chapters in Part 5 dealt with three primary activities of the influencing function: communication, leadership, and motivation. This chapter focuses on managing teams, the last major influencing activity to be discussed in this text. As with the other three activities, managing teams requires guiding the behavior of organization members in ways that increase the probability of reaching organizational objectives.

Groups

To deal with groups appropriately, managers must have a thorough understanding of the nature of groups in organizations.[2] As used in management-related discussions, a **group** is not simply a gathering of people. Rather, it is "any number of people who (1) interact with one another, (2) are psychologically aware of one another, and (3) perceive themselves to be a group."[3] Groups are characterized by frequent communication among members over time and by a small enough size to permit each member to communicate with all other members on a face-to-face basis. As a result of this communication, each group member influences and is influenced by all other group members.

The study of groups should be important to managers because the most common ingredient of all organizations is people, and the most common technique for accomplishing work through people is dividing them into work groups. In a classic article, Cartwright and Lippitt list four additional reasons why managers should study groups:[4]

1. Groups exist in all kinds of organizations.
2. Groups inevitably form in all facets of organizational existence.
3. Groups can cause either desirable or undesirable consequences within the organization.
4. An understanding of groups can help managers increase the probability that the groups with which they work will cause desirable consequences within the organization.[5]

17-1 A definition of the term *group* as used in the context of management

Kinds of Groups in Organizations

Organizational groups are typically divided into two basic types: formal and informal.

Formal Groups

A **formal group** is a group that exists within an organization by virtue of management decree to perform tasks that enhance the attainment of organizational objectives.[6] **Figure 17.1** is an organization chart showing a formal group. Placing organization members in areas such as marketing departments, human resource departments, and production departments is an example of establishing formal groups.

Actually, organizations are made up of a number of formal groups that exist at various organizational levels. The coordination of and communication among these groups is the responsibility of managers, or supervisors, commonly called "linking pins."

Formal groups are also clearly defined and structured. The next sections discuss the basic kinds of formal groups, examples of formal groups as they exist in organizations, and the four stages of formal group development.

17-2 A thorough understanding of the different kinds of groups that exist in organizations

Kinds of Formal Groups
Formal groups are commonly divided into command groups and task groups. A **command group** is a formal group that is outlined in the chain of command on an organization chart. Command groups typically handle routine organizational activities.

Figure 17.1 A formal group

A **task group** is a formal group of organization members who interact with one another to accomplish most of the organization's nonroutine tasks. Although task groups are usually made up of members of the same organizational level, they can consist of people from different levels in the organizational hierarchy.[7] For example, a manager might establish a task group to consider the feasibility of manufacturing a new product and include representatives from various levels of organizational areas such as production, market research, and sales.[8]

Examples of Formal Groups

Two formal groups that are often established in organizations are committees and work teams. Committees are the more traditional formal group; work teams have only recently gained acceptance and support in U.S. organizations. The part of this text dealing with the managerial function of organizing emphasized command groups; however, the examples here emphasize task groups.

Committees

A **committee** is a group of individuals charged with performing a type of specific activity and is usually classified as a task group. From a managerial viewpoint, committees are established for four major reasons:[9]

1. To allow organization members to exchange ideas
2. To generate suggestions and recommendations that can be offered to other organizational units
3. To develop new ideas for solving existing organizational problems
4. To assist in the development of organizational policies

Committees exist in almost all organizations and at all organizational levels. As **Figure 17.2** suggests, however, the larger the organization, the greater the probability that it will use committees regularly. The following two sections discuss why managers should use committees and what makes a committee successful.

WHY MANAGERS SHOULD USE COMMITTEES

Managers generally agree that committees have several uses in organizations:

*   Committees can improve the quality of decision making. As more people become involved in making a decision, the strengths and weaknesses of various alternatives tend to be discussed in greater detail, and the chances of reaching a higher-quality decision increase.
*   Committees encourage the expression of honest opinions. Committee members feel protected enough to say what they really think because the group output of a committee cannot be associated with any one member of that group.
*   Committees also tend to increase organization members' participation in decision making and thereby enhance the chances of widespread support of decisions. Another result of this increased participation is that committee members satisfy their social or self-esteem needs through committee work.

Figure 17.2

Percentage of companies that have committees, by size of company

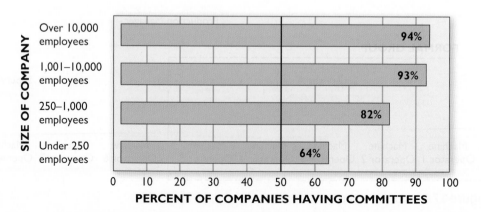

- Finally, committees ensure the representation of important groups in the decision-making process. Managers must choose committee members wisely, however, in order to achieve appropriate representation; if a committee does not adequately represent various interest groups, any decision it comes to may well be counter to the interests of an important organizational group.

Committees are often used to recruit new organization members. Consider, for example, the case of Red Robin Gourmet Burgers, a national chain of casual dining restaurants. Two activist investor groups that own nearly 8 percent of Red Robin stock filed a complaint with the Securities and Exchange Commission over the performances of the board and the company's chief executive. The company later announced several changes to its board structure. In addition, the board of directors agreed to form a search committee to identify a new chief executive. The search committee consisted of the board chair and three new directors approved by the investor groups.[10]

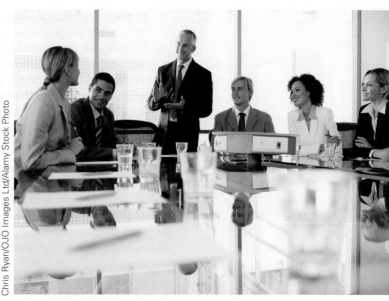

A successful committee has clear goals and authority, along with a size of about 5 to 10 members.

Although executives vary somewhat in their enthusiasm about using committees in organizations, a study reported by McLeod and Jones concludes that most executives favor using committees. The executives who took part in this study said they got significantly more information from organizational sources other than committees but found the information from committees to be more valuable than the information from any other source. Nevertheless, some top executives express only qualified support for using committees as work groups, and others have negative feelings toward committees. Still, the executives who feel positively about committees or who display qualified acceptance of them in general outnumber those who look upon committees negatively.

WHAT MAKES COMMITTEES SUCCESSFUL

Although committees have become an accepted management tool, managerial action taken to establish and run them is a major variable in determining their degree of success.

Procedural Steps   Several procedural steps can be taken to increase the probability that a committee will be successful:[11]

- The committee's goals should be clearly defined, preferably in writing, to focus the committee's activities and reduce the time members devote to discussing just what it is the committee is supposed to be doing.
- The committee's authority should be specified. Is it merely to investigate, advise, and recommend, or is it authorized to implement its decisions?
- The optimum size of the committee should be determined. With fewer than 5 members, the advantages of group work may be diminished. With more than 10 or 15 members, the committee may become unwieldy. Although the optimal size varies with the circumstances, the ideal number of committee members for most tasks seems to be from 5 to 10.
- A chairperson should be selected on the basis of his or her ability to run an efficient meeting—that is, the ability to keep committee members from getting bogged down in irrelevancies and to see to it that the necessary paperwork gets done.
- Appointing a permanent secretary to handle communications is often useful.
- The agenda and all supporting material for the meeting should be distributed before the meeting takes place. When members have a chance to study each item beforehand, they are likely to stick to the point and be prepared to make informed contributions.
- Meetings should start on time, and their ending time should be announced at the outset.

People-Oriented Guidelines   In addition to these procedural steps, managers can follow a number of more people-oriented guidelines to increase the probability that a committee will succeed. In particular, a manager can raise the quality of committee discussions by doing the following:[12]

- **Rephrasing ideas already expressed**—This rephrasing ensures that the manager as well as the other people on the committee clearly understand what has been said.
- **Bringing all members into active participation**—Every committee member is a potential source of useful information, so the manager should serve as a catalyst to spark individual participation whenever appropriate.
- **Stimulating further thought by members**—The manager should encourage committee members to think ideas through carefully and thoroughly because only this type of analysis will generate high-quality committee output.

Groupthink   Managers should also help the committee avoid a phenomenon called "groupthink." **Groupthink** is the mode of thinking that group members engage in when the desire for agreement so dominates the group that it overrides the need to appraise alternative solutions realistically.[13] Groups tend to slip into groupthink when their members become overly concerned about being too harsh when critiquing one another's ideas and lose their objectivity.[14] Such groups tend to seek complete support on every issue in order to avoid conflicts that might endanger the "we-feeling" atmosphere.[15]

Groupthink, a term initially established by Irving Janis, occurs in five stages. The first stage, antecedents, describes what precursors are associated with the development of groupthink. For example, a group with a high level of cohesiveness is likely to be susceptible to groupthink. The second stage, concurrence seeking, occurs when a group member agrees with the entire group's position even though the group member privately opposes the entire group's position. The third stage, symptoms of groupthink, occurs as group members feel pressured to conform and censor their own ideas. The fourth stage, decision-making defects, occurs when group members fail to make effective decisions. An example of decision-making defects involves a group not collecting the needed information to make an effective decision. The fifth stage, poor decision outcomes, occurs when the group performs poorly.

Often, managers subconsciously rely on the people they know best as a sounding board for decision making and look to their own small group of friends or colleagues in the workplace to help them analyze situations. Their regular interaction with this informal network may bias their thinking and create its own type of groupthink. Managers must be aware of how this phenomenon can affect their decisions. Specifically, they need to recognize the different types and stages of groupthink so that they can identify them and rectify them objectively in the workplace.[16]

MyLab Management Watch It

If your instructor has assigned this activity, go to www.pearson.com/mylab/management to complete the video exercise.

Work Teams   A **work team** is another example of a task group used in organizations. Contemporary work teams in the United States evolved from the problem-solving teams—based on Japanese-style quality circles—that were widely adopted in the 1970s.[17] Problem-solving teams consist of 5 to 12 volunteer members from different areas of the department who meet weekly to discuss ways to improve quality and efficiency.

SPECIAL-PURPOSE AND SELF-MANAGED TEAMS

Special-purpose teams evolved in the early to middle 1980s from problem-solving teams. The typical special-purpose team consists of workers and union representatives meeting together to collaborate on operational decisions at all levels. The aim is to create an atmosphere conducive to quality and productivity improvements.

Special-purpose teams laid the foundation for the self-managed work teams that arose in the 1990s, and it is these teams that appear to be the wave of the future. Self-managed teams consist of 5 to 15 employees who work together to produce an entire product. Members learn all the tasks required to produce the product and rotate from job to job. Self-managed teams even take over managerial duties such as scheduling work and vacations and ordering materials. Because these work teams give employees so much control over their jobs, they represent a fundamental change in how work is organized. (Self-managed teams will be discussed in some detail later in this chapter.)

Employing work teams allows a firm to draw on the talents and creativity of all its employees, not just a few maverick inventors or top executives, to make important decisions. As product quality becomes more and more important in the business world, companies will need to rely more and more on the team approach to stay competitive. Consider the situation at Yellow Freight Systems, a shipping company whose management was intent on giving its customers excellent service. To address this concern, management established a work team made up of employees from many different parts of the company, including marketing, sales, operations, and human resources. The overall task of the work team was to run the excellence-in-service campaign that management had initiated.[18]

Stages of Formal Group Development

Another requirement for successfully managing formal groups is understanding the stages of formal group development. In a classic book, Bernard Bass suggested that group development is a four-stage process that unfolds as the group learns how to use its resources.[19] Although these stages may not occur sequentially, for the purpose of clarity, the discussion that follows will assume that they do.

The Acceptance Stage

It is common for members of a new group to mistrust one another somewhat initially. The acceptance stage is reached only after this initial mistrust dwindles and the group has been transformed into one characterized by mutual trust and acceptance.

The Communication and Decision-Making Stage

Once they have passed through the acceptance stage, group members are better able to communicate frankly with one another. This frank communication provides the basis for establishing and using an effective group decision-making mechanism.

The Group Solidarity Stage

Group solidarity comes naturally as the mutual acceptance of group members increases and as communication and decision making continue within the group. At this stage, members become more involved in group activities and cooperate rather than compete with one another. In addition, members find belonging to the group extremely satisfying and are committed to enhancing the group's overall success.

The Group Control Stage

A natural result of group solidarity is group control. In this stage, group members attempt to maximize the group's success by matching individual abilities with group activities and by assisting one another. Flexibility and informality usually characterize this stage.

As a group passes through each of these four stages, it generally becomes more mature and effective—and therefore more productive. The group that reaches maximum maturity and effectiveness is characterized by the following traits in its members:

- **Members function as a unit**—The group works as a team. Members do not disturb one another to the point of interfering with their collaboration.
- **Members participate effectively in group effort**—Members work hard when there is something to do. They seldom loaf, even when they have the opportunity to do so.
- **Members are oriented toward a single goal**—Group members work for the common purpose; they do not waste group resources by moving in different directions.
- **Members have the equipment, tools, and skills necessary to attain the group's goals**—Members are taught the various parts of their jobs by experts and strive to acquire whatever resources they need to attain group objectives.
- **Members ask and receive suggestions, opinions, and information from one another**—A member who is uncertain about something stops working and asks another member for information. Group members generally talk to one another openly and frequently.

Leading Group Development

Whether you are a manager or the nonmanager leader of a group, you can help the group progress toward greater maturity. Here are some ideas from several business writers for doing so:[20]

- Give the group meaningful goals. Employees will be more committed to the group if they see that it does something important.
- Provide the group with the resources it needs to achieve its goals.
- Cross-train employees—that is, teach them to carry out tasks and make decisions related to more than a single, specialized job. This gives group members a broader perspective on the company's goals, a better understanding of its customers or products, and a greater ability to understand their coworkers in the group.
- Encourage disagreement as long as it is respectful and the team unites to implement its decisions.
- Be a role model for contributing to the group, treating others respectfully, and especially listening to other people's ideas.

Informal Groups

Informal groups, the second major kind of group that can exist within an organization, are groups that develop naturally as people interact. An **informal group** is defined as a collection of individuals whose common work experiences result in the development of a system of interpersonal relations that extend beyond those established by management.[21]

As **Figure 17.3** shows, informal group structures can deviate significantly from formal group structures. As is true of Supervisor A in the figure, an organization member can belong to more than one informal group at the same time. In contrast to formal groups, informal groups are not highly structured in procedure and, although generally they are not formally recognized by management, some organizations have seen the value of integrating informal groups into their corporate structure.[22]

The next sections discuss the following subjects:

1. The various kinds of informal groups that exist in organizations
2. The benefits people usually reap from belonging to informal groups

Figure 17.3 Three informal groups that deviate significantly from formal groups within the organization

Kinds of Informal Groups Informal groups are divided into two general types: interest groups and friendship groups. An **interest group** is an informal group that gains and maintains membership primarily because of a common concern that members have about a specific issue. An example is a group of workers pressing management for better pay or working conditions. Once the interest or concern that instigated the formation of the informal group has been eliminated, the group will probably disband.

As its name implies, a **friendship group** is an informal group that forms in organizations because of the personal affiliation members have with one another. Personal factors such as recreational interests, race, gender, and religion serve as foundations for friendship groups. As with interest groups, the membership of friendship groups tends to change over time. In this case, however, membership changes as friendships dissolve or new friendships are made.

Benefits of Informal Group Membership Informal groups tend to develop in organizations because of various benefits the group members obtain from belonging to the group:[23]

1. Perpetuation of social and cultural values that group members consider important
2. Status and social satisfaction that people might not enjoy without group membership
3. Increased ease of communication among group members
4. Increased desirability of the overall work environment

These benefits may be one reason that employees who are on fixed shifts or who continually work with the same groups tend to be more satisfied with their work than are employees whose shifts are continually changing.

Andersen Ross/Blend Images/Alamy Stock Photo

Workers who interact on the job often discover common interests that encourage the establishment of an informal group.

Managing Work Groups

To manage work groups effectively, managers must simultaneously consider the effects of both formal and informal group factors on organizational productivity. This consideration requires two steps:

1. Determining group existence
2. Understanding the evolution of informal groups

17-3 Knowledge of how to manage work groups

Determining Group Existence

The most important step managers need to take when managing work groups is to determine who the groups' members are and what informal groups exist within the organization.

Sociometry is an analytical tool that managers can use to make these determinations. They can also use sociometry to get information about the internal workings of an informal group, including the identity of the group leader, the relative status of group members, and the group's communication networks.[24] This information on informal groups, combined with an understanding of the established formal groups shown on the organization chart, will give managers a complete picture of the organization's group structure.

Sociometric Analysis The procedure for performing a sociometric analysis in an organization is quite basic: Various organization members simply are asked, through either an interview or a questionnaire, to name several other organization members with whom they like to spend free time. A **sociogram** is then constructed to summarize the informal relationships among group members. Sociograms are diagrams that visually link individuals within the population queried according to the number of times they were chosen and whether the choice was reciprocated.

Applying the Sociogram Model   **Figure 17.4** shows two sample sociograms based on a classic study of two groups of boys in a summer camp—the Bulldogs and the Red Devils. An analysis of these sociograms leads to several interesting conclusions. First, more boys within the Bulldogs than within the Red Devils were chosen as being desirable to spend time with. The implication is that the Bulldogs are a closer-knit informal group than the Red Devils. Second, the greater the number of times an individual was chosen, the more likely it is that the individual is the group leader. Thus, individuals C and E in Figure 17.4 are probably Bulldog leaders, and individuals L and S are probably Red Devil leaders. Third, communication between L and most other Red Devil members is likely to occur directly, whereas communication between C and other Bulldogs is likely to pass through other group members.

Sociometric analysis can give managers many useful insights concerning the informal groups within their organization. Managers who do not want to perform a formal sociometric analysis can at least casually gather information on what form a sociogram might take in a particular situation. They can pick up this information through ordinary conversations with other organization members as well as through observations of how various organization members interact with one another.

Understanding the Evolution of Informal Groups

As we have seen, the first prerequisite for managing groups effectively is knowing what groups exist within an organization and what characterizes the membership of those groups. The second prerequisite is understanding how informal groups evolve. This understanding will give managers some insights on how to encourage the development of appropriate informal groups—that is, groups that support the attainment of organizational objectives and whose members maintain good relationships with formal work groups.

Figure 17.4 Sample sociograms

Figure 17.5
Homans's ideas on how informal groups develop

The Homans Model

Perhaps the most widely accepted framework for explaining the evolution of informal groups was developed by George Homans.[25] **Figure 17.5** broadly summarizes his theory. According to Homans, the informal group is established to provide satisfaction and growth for its members. At the same time, the sentiments, interactions, and activities that emerge within an informal group result from the sentiments, interactions, and activities that already exist within a formal group. Given these two premises, it follows that feedback on the functioning of the informal group can give managers ideas about how to modify the formal group in order to increase the probability that informal group members will achieve the satisfaction and growth they desire. The ultimate consequence will be reinforcing the solidarity and productiveness of the formal group—to the advantage of the organization.

Applying the Homans Model

To see what Homans's concept involves, suppose that 12 factory workers are members of a formal work group that manufactures toasters. According to Homans, as these workers interact to assemble toasters, they might discover common personal interests that encourage the evolution of one or more informal groups that would maximize the satisfaction and growth of their members. Once established, these informal groups will probably resist changes in the formal work group that threaten the satisfaction and growth of the informal groups' members. On the other hand, modifications in the formal work group that enhance the satisfaction and growth of the informal groups' members will tend to be welcomed.

Teams

The preceding sections of this chapter discussed groups—what they are, what kinds exist in organizations, and how such groups should be managed. This section focuses on a special type of group: teams. It covers the following topics:

1. Differences between groups and teams
2. Types of teams that exist in organizations
3. Stages of development that teams go through
4. What constitutes an effective team
5. Relationship between trust and team effectiveness
6. Relationship between collaboration and effective teams

17-4   An understanding of how the term *team* is used in the context of organizations

Groups versus Teams

The terms *group* and *team* are not synonymous. As we have seen, a group consists of any number of people who interact with one another, are psychologically aware of one another, and think of themselves as a group. A **team** is a group whose members influence one another toward the accomplishment of an organizational objective(s).

Not all groups in organizations are teams, but all teams are groups. A group qualifies as a team only if its members focus on helping one another accomplish organizational objectives.[26] In today's quickly changing business environment, teams have emerged as a requirement for success.[27] Therefore, good managers constantly try to help groups become teams.

A team-building exercise is a training tool for helping transform a group into a team. For Ken Keller, the owner of Renaissance Executive Forums, it meant taking his group to a

Sonoma, California, vineyard; dividing people into teams; and challenging them to create their own wine. Team members had to collaborate to come up with a wine from the basic ingredients provided and then design a label and a marketing strategy. Keller says team-building exercises work because they require a group to focus on an unfamiliar task and work together to achieve a goal.[28]

The questions of how teams plan, set goals, and make decisions continue to be the subjects of much field research.[29] The following part of the chapter provides insights on how managers can facilitate the evolution of groups into teams.

Types of Teams in Organizations

Organizational teams take many different forms. The following sections discuss three types of teams commonly found in today's organizations: problem-solving teams, self-managed teams, and cross-functional teams.

Problem-Solving Teams

Problem-Solving Teams   Management confronts many different organizational problems daily. Examples are production systems that are not manufacturing products at the desired levels of quality, workers who appear to be listless and uninvolved, and managers who are basing their decisions on inaccurate information.

For assistance in solving such formidable problems, management commonly establishes special teams. A team set up to help eliminate a specified problem within the organization is called a **problem-solving team**.[30] The typical problem-solving team has 5 to 12 members and is formed to discuss ways to improve quality in all phases of the organization, to make organizational processes more efficient, or to improve the overall work environment.[31]

After the problem-solving team reaches a consensus, it makes recommendations to management about how to deal with the specified problem. Management may respond to the team's recommendations by implementing them in their entirety, by modifying and then implementing them, or by requesting further information to assess them. Once the problem that management asked the problem-solving team to address has been solved, the team is generally disbanded.

PRACTICAL CHALLENGE: SOLVING PROBLEMS AS A TEAM

Malaysian Team Synergy and Problem Solving

According to the Malaysia Productivity Corporation, set up in 1962 as a joint project between the United Nations Special Fund and the Federal Government, productive teams need to have synergy to be capable of solving problems.

Malaysia has gradually shifted toward an innovation-led economy. As such, it needs highly productive teams to keep up with the development of the economy. A team with synergy and the ability to solve problems will make full use of all of the information, skills, and experience that the team members have and can offer to the team. By positively sharing their skills to achieve a common goal, they can develop mutual trust and contribute to the success as a team, not as a group of individuals.

Petra Energy Berhad is a Malaysian oil and gas service company. It operates in a highly competitive market where the slightest delays in solving problems can cost millions of dollars a day. The workforce is led by a core team of professionals. Not only do they ensure that the strictest health, safety, and security measures are taken, but they also operate as a fully integrated, synergistic team to solve problems.[33]

Self-Managed Teams

The **self-managed team**, sometimes called a *self-managed work group* or a *self-directed team*, is a team that plans, organizes, influences, and controls its own work situation with only minimal intervention and direction from management.[32] This creative team design involves a highly integrated group of several skilled individuals who are cross-trained and have the responsibility and authority to perform a specified activity.

Activities typically carried out by management in a traditional work setting—creating work schedules, establishing work pace and breaks, developing vacation schedules, evaluating performance, determining the level of salary increases and rewards received by individual workers, and ordering materials to be used in the production process—are instead carried out by members of the self-managed team. Generally responsible for whole tasks as opposed to "parts" of a job, the self-managed team is an important way of structuring, managing, and rewarding work.[34] Because these teams require only minimum management attention, they free managers to pursue other management activities such as strategic planning.

Reports of successful self-managed work teams are plentiful.[35] These teams are growing in popularity because today's business environment seems to require such work teams to solve complex problems independently, because American workers have come to expect more freedom in the workplace, and because the speed of technological change demands that employees be able to adapt quickly. Recent studies seem to suggest that the collective behavior of a self-managed team can make it more effective than the individual efforts of its team members.[36]

Not all self-managed teams are successful, however. To ensure the success of a self-managed team, the manager should carefully select and properly train its members.[37]

Cross-Functional Teams

A **cross-functional team** is a work team composed of people from different functional areas of the organization—marketing, finance, human resources, and operations, for example—who are all focused on a specified objective.[38] Cross-functional teams may or may not be self-managed, although self-managed teams are generally cross-functional. Because cross-functional team members are from different departments within the organization, the team possesses the expertise to coordinate all the department activities within the organization that affect its own work.[39] Some examples of cross-functional teams are teams established to choose and implement new technologies throughout an organization, teams formed to improve marketing effectiveness within the organization, and teams established to control product costs.[40]

This section discussed three types of teams that exist in organizations: problem-solving, self-directed, and cross-functional. It should be noted here that managers can establish various combinations of these three types of teams. **Figure 17.6** illustrates some possible combinations that managers could create. For example, **a** in the figure represents a team that is problem-solving, self-directed, and cross-functional, and **b** represents one that is problem-solving but is neither cross-functional nor self-directed. Before establishing a team, managers should carefully study their own unique organizational situation and then set up the type of team that best suits that situation.

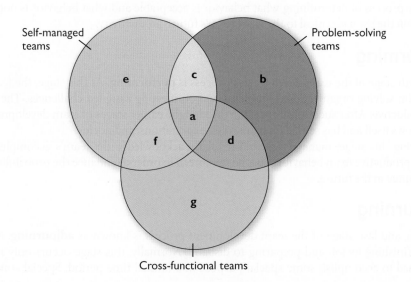

Figure 17.6

Possible team types based on various combinations of self-directed, problem-solving, and cross-functional teams

Stages of Team Development

17-5 Insights about the stages of team development

More and more modern managers are using work teams to accomplish organizational tasks. Simply establishing such a team, however, does not guarantee that it will be productive. In fact, managers should be patient when an established work team is not initially productive because teams generally need to pass through several developmental stages before they become productive. Managers must also understand this developmental process so that they can facilitate it. The following sections discuss the various stages a team usually must pass through before it becomes fully productive.[41]

Forming

Forming is the first stage of the team development process. During this stage, members of the newly formed team become oriented to the team and acquainted with one another. This period is also characterized by exploring issues related to the members' new job situations, such as what is expected of them, who has what kind of authority within the team, what kinds of people are team members, and what skills team members possess.

The forming stage of team development is usually characterized by uncertainty and stress. Recognizing that team members are struggling to adjust to their new work situations and to one another, managers should be tolerant of lengthy, informal discussions exploring team specifics and not regard these discussions as time wasters. The newly formed team must be allowed an exploratory period so that it will become truly productive.

Storming

After a team has formed, it begins to storm. **Storming**, the second stage of the team development process, is characterized by conflict and disagreement as team members become more assertive in clarifying their individual roles. During this stage, the team seems to lack unity because members are continually challenging the way the team functions.

To help the team progress beyond storming, managers should encourage team members to feel free to disagree with any team issues and to discuss their own views fully and honestly. Most of all, managers should urge team members to arrive at agreements that will help the team reach its objective(s).

Norming

When the storming stage ends, norming begins. **Norming**, the third stage of the team development process, is characterized by agreement among team members on roles, rules, and acceptable behavior while working on the team. Conflicts generated during the storming stage are resolved in this stage.

Managers should encourage teams that have entered the norming stage to progress toward developing team norms and values that will be instrumental in building a successful organization. The process of determining what behavior is acceptable and what behavior is not acceptable within the team is critical to the work team's future productivity.

Performing

The fourth stage of the team development process is **performing**. At this stage, the team fully focuses on solving organizational problems and on meeting assigned challenges. The team is now productive: After successfully passing through the earlier stages of team development, the team knows itself and has settled on team roles, expectations, and norms.

During this stage, managers should regularly acknowledge the team's accomplishments because productive team behavior must be reinforced in order to enhance the probability that it will continue in the future.

Adjourning

The fifth, and last, stage of the team development process is known as **adjourning**. Now the team is finishing its job and preparing to disband. Normally, this stage occurs only in teams established to accomplish some special purpose in a limited time period. Special committees and task groups are examples of such teams. During the adjourning stage, team members are generally disappointed that the team is being broken up because disbandment means the loss of personally satisfying relationships and/or an enjoyable work situation.

During this phase of team development, managers should recognize team members' disappointment and sense of loss as normal and assure them that other challenging and exciting organizational opportunities await them. It is important that management then do everything necessary to integrate these people into new teams or other areas of the organization.

Although some work teams do not pass through every one of the development stages just described, understanding the stages of forming, storming, norming, performing, and adjourning will give managers many useful insights into how to build productive work teams. Above all, managers must realize that new teams are different from mature teams and that they are responsible for building whatever team they are in charge of into a mature, productive work team.[42]

Team Effectiveness

Earlier in this chapter, teams were defined as groups of people who influence one another to reach organizational targets. It is easy to see why effective teams are critical to organizational success. Effective teams come up with innovative ideas, accomplish their goals, and adapt to change when necessary.[43] Their individual members are highly committed both to the team and to organizational goals. Such teams are highly valued by upper management and recognized and rewarded for their accomplishments.[44] Recent research suggests that a substantial amount of mutual trust within a team can have a positive effect on the team's performance and result in even more rewards from management.[45]

Figure 17.7 identifies the characteristics of an effective team. Note the figure's implications of the steps managers need to take to build effective work teams in organizations. *People-related steps* include the following:[46]

1. Trying to make the team's work satisfying
2. Developing mutual trust among team members and between the team and management

Figure 17.7

Factors contributing to team effectiveness

3. Building good communication—from management to the team as well as between team members
4. Minimizing unresolved conflicts and power struggles within the team
5. Dealing effectively with threats toward and within the team
6. Building the perception that the jobs of team members are secure

Organization-related steps that managers can take to build effective work teams include the following:

1. Building a stable overall organization or company structure that team members view as secure
2. Becoming involved in team events and demonstrating interest in team progress and functioning
3. Properly rewarding and recognizing teams for their accomplishments
4. Setting stable goals and priorities for the team

Finally, Figure 17.7 implies that managers can build effective work teams by taking six *task-related steps*:

1. Developing clear objectives, directions, and project plans for the team
2. Providing proper technical direction and leadership for the team
3. Establishing autonomy for the team and challenging work within the team
4. Appointing experienced and qualified team personnel
5. Encouraging team involvement
6. Building visibility within the organization for the team's work

Modern managers must focus on building the effectiveness of not only domestic teams but also global teams. In the past, the effectiveness of a global team depended chiefly on a company having staff and factories on the ground in various countries and corporate headquarters carefully and methodically coordinating their activities. Today, however, the challenge is much different. Globally dispersed teams must be built into highly effective, sometimes even self-managed teams. Because of the ever-changing and fast-moving nature of competition, workers spread around the globe must be able to communicate and collaborate instantly. Fortunately for modern managers, the Internet is available to enable such collaboration. Managers must remember, however, that the availability of the Internet does not guarantee that global teams will be effective. The appropriate use of the Internet by global teams, however, can be a significant contributor to their effectiveness.

Trust and Effective Teams

Probably the most fundamental ingredient of effective teams is trust. Trust is believing in the reliability, ability, and integrity of another. Unless team members trust one another, the team leader, and management, managers may well find that creating an effective work team is impossible.[47]

Today the concern is that management is not inspiring the kind of trust that is essential to team effectiveness. The lack of trust within a team is likely to discourage team members from contributing and participating in the growth of a creative, productive team.[48] In addition, subordinates' trust in their managers is critically low, and employee opinion polls indicate that it may well decline even further in the future. Without trust in its manager, it seems that a team would have only marginal interest in forging productive working relationships.

As an example of a manager communicating often with team members to build trust, consider Burberry president Angela Ahrendts. Burberry, the quintessential British fashion house, offers British fashion elegance throughout the world. Ahrendts has become known as a people-oriented manager and communicates often with members of her team. According to Stacey Cartwright, the company's chief financial officer, Ahrendts is collaborative, likes to gather her team around her, and seems energized by the debates within the team. Ahrendts obviously knows that such communication with her team will almost certainly help build trust within the team, which should significantly contribute to team—and company—success.[49]

TIPS FOR MANAGING AROUND THE GLOBE

Establishing Trust in International Teams

Trust plays a key role in the effectiveness of globally dispersed teams just as it does in teams at a single location. But developing trust can be difficult for a global team given employees' physical and cultural differences. A Swedish project manager of multinational teams had difficulty discerning whether individuals understood their assignments; she handled the problem by e-mailing summaries of every meeting to them. A Lebanese project manager was amazed to discover that several members of his team were meeting for weekly breakfasts. When he realized how much the time spent together strengthened their trust and ability to work together, he saw it as a wise investment.

Researchers have identified ways to establish trust in teams with an international membership.

First, team leaders should recognize that some ways in which teams develop, such as by getting acquainted and being assigned roles, may not naturally take place when coworkers are dispersed. Therefore, at the beginning, leaders should hold discussions to define roles, responsibilities, and norms, including expectations for when team members should be available. Team leaders should also ask members to describe their strengths and personal values so that leaders can learn how everyone can contribute to the team. Finally, team leaders should try to bring team members to the same location at least occasionally so that team members can build relationships face-to-face.[50]

Management urgently needs to focus on reversing this trend toward declining trust.[51] Managers can use a number of different strategies to build trust within groups.[52]

- **Communicate often to team members**—This is a fundamental strategy. Keeping team members informed of organizational news, explaining why certain decisions have been made, and sharing information about organizational operations are examples of how managers should communicate to team members.
- **Show respect for team members**—Managers need to show team members that they are highly valued. They can demonstrate their respect for team members by delegating tasks to them, listening intently to feedback from the group, and appropriately acting on that feedback.
- **Be fair to team members**—Team members must receive the rewards they have earned. Managers must therefore conduct fair performance appraisals and objectively allocate and distribute rewards. It should go without saying that showing favoritism in this area sows mistrust and resentment.
- **Be predictable**—Managers must be consistent in their actions. Team members should usually be able to forecast what decisions management will make before those decisions are made. In addition, managers must live up to the commitments made to team members. Managers whose decisions are inconsistent and who fail to live up to the commitments they've made will not be trusted by their teams.
- **Demonstrate competence**—To build team trust, managers must show team members that they are able to diagnose organizational problems and have the skill to implement solutions to those problems. Team members tend to trust managers they perceive as competent and distrust those they perceive as incompetent.

Collaboration and Effective Teams

Collaboration was introduced in Chapter 1 as the ability to work with others in accomplishing a task. As businesses become increasingly global and complex, managers are seeing that collaboration within work teams is a key factor in building team success. Data collected over the last two decades show that time spent by managers and employees in collaborative activities has

17-6 Knowledge regarding the relationship between collaboration and effective teams increased by 50 percent or more.[53] In fact, some management theorists see collaboration as such an important answer to meeting today's team challenges that they advocate appointing a chief collaboration officer (CCO) in organizations.

Advice for building collaboration within an organization includes appreciating that, although technology tools that better enable collaboration can be valuable,[54] collaboration is mostly a people issue.[55] Managers desiring to build a collaborative team environment must focus on tasks like helping team members to trust one another, develop positive personal relationships with one another, and avoid offensive body language. Only if managers are successful in helping team members in such ways will team members share thoughts honestly and openly, which is the prerequisite of collaboration.

CHALLENGE CASE SUMMARY

For managers to be able to manage work, they need to understand the definition of the term *group*, and they need to understand that several types of groups exist in organizations. A group at Numerica Credit Union or any other organization is any number of people who interact, who are psychologically aware of each other, and who perceive themselves as a group. An organization such as Numerica is made up of formal groups, the groups that appear on its organization chart, such as the marketing department. Managers of groups act as the "linking pins" among departments. The ability of Numerica managers to coordinate and communicate with these groups and their success in dealing with their own departments are certainly important factors in the future success of the organization as a whole.

At times, managers at Numerica, from Carla Altepeter on down, can form new groups to handle some of their less routine challenges. For example, management could form a task group by choosing two people from each of several departments and getting them together to plan and implement the remodeling of a company branch. As with any other organization, Numerica also has to consider informal groups (those that do not appear on the organization chart). More discussion on informal groups will follow later in this Challenge Case Summary.

Numerica management could decide to form a committee to achieve some specific goal. For example, a committee might be formed to investigate how to enhance the quality of service delivered to new credit union members, which could allow various departments to exchange quality improvement ideas and generate related suggestions for management to consider. Such a committee could improve Numerica decision making in general by encouraging honest feedback from employees about quality issues in the organization. It could also be used to

get fresh ideas about enhancing service quality and to encourage Numerica employees to participate more diligently in improving the quality of services offered by the credit union. This approach would help ensure that all appropriate departments are represented in important quality decisions so that when Numerica takes action to improve the quality of its new-member services, for example, every important angle would be considered, including service design, implementation, marketing, customer service, and so on.

In managing such a quality committee at Numerica, management should encourage the members to take certain steps to help the committee be successful because a poorly run committee wastes everyone's time. For example, the committee should develop a clear definition of its goals and the limits of its authority: Is it merely going to think of quality improvement ideas, or should it also take the initial steps toward implementing those ideas?

In addition, the quality committee should not have too few or too many members. Issues such as appointing a secretary to handle communications and appointing a chairperson who is people-oriented must be addressed. Such a committee needs someone who can rephrase ideas clearly to ensure that everyone understands the ideas and someone who can encourage members to participate and think about the issues while avoiding groupthink: Original ideas should be generated by the committee members, not a unanimous opinion that the members agree to just because they are trying to avoid conflict.

Managers in organizations such as Numerica must be patient and understand that it will take some time for a new group to develop into a productive working unit. The members of any new work group must start by trusting and accepting one another and then begin communicating and exchanging ideas. Once acceptance and communication increase, group solidarity and control come naturally. Then the group members will get involved, cooperate, and try to maximize the group's success.

With the quality committee that is being used as an example, Numerica management must be patient and let it mature before expecting maximum effectiveness and productivity. If given time to develop, the group will function as a unit, members will participate willingly and effectively, and the group will reach valuable decisions about what needs to be done to improve the quality of services that Numerica offers.

Issues regarding informal groups could affect the success of work groups at Numerica Credit Union. Employee groups form because of certain commonalities. For example, minority employees could get together as a group to increase the opportunities for their professional growth at Numerica. Employees also form friendship groups, which ease communication and provide feelings of satisfaction in a company. In general, such informal groups can improve the work environment for everyone involved, so it can be advantageous for management to encourage their development.

Perhaps Numerica management could accelerate the development of a quality committee into a productive unit by including individuals who already know and trust one another because of their membership in one or more informal groups at Numerica. For example, some members of the newly formed quality committee might know and trust one another immediately as a result of their belonging to the company's bowling or softball team. Under such circumstances, the trust developed among employees through past informal group affiliations could help the formal quality committee develop into a productive group more quickly.

For a company such as Numerica to be successful, managers must be able to consider how formal and informal groups affect organizational productivity, and they need to determine what informal groups exist, know who the group members are, and understand how these groups form. Armed with this information, Numerica managers can strive to make their work groups more effective.

One way management can get information about the groups at Numerica is to use sociometry. A questionnaire asking employees with whom they spend time can be designed, and a sociogram can then be constructed to summarize this information. Managers could also do a more casual analysis by simply talking to their employees and observing how they interact with one another.

Managers in an organization such as Numerica should try to understand how informal groups evolve and should be aware that an organization's formal structure influences how informal groups develop within it. For example, assume that in one department at Numerica, 15 people work on lending. Many of them are interested in sports, have become friends because of this common interest, and work well together as a result. If a manager needed to make some changes in this department, he or she should try to accommodate such informal friendship groups in order to keep these employees satisfied with their jobs. Only with very good reason should a manager of such a department damage the existence of the productive friendship group by transferring any group members out of the lending department.

Managers in an organization such as Numerica Credit Union should keep in mind the four major factors that influence work-group effectiveness. First, the size of the work group can be important to its productivity. For example, a 20-person quality committee would probably be too large and would hamper the group's effectiveness. Remember also, however, that managers should consider informal groups before making changes in group size. The quality committee could end up being less productive without one or more of its respected members than it would be if it were slightly too large.

Another important factor that influences work-group effectiveness is group cohesiveness; a more cohesive group tends to be more effective than a less cohesive group. Ways to increase the cohesiveness of a work group might include allowing members to take breaks together or rewarding informal group members for a job well done.

Group norms, or behaviors required within the informal group, are a third factor that affects the productivity of formal group behavior. Because these norms ultimately affect profitability, managers must be aware of them and understand how to influence them within the formal group structure. For example, assume that a smaller informal group of workers within Numerica's lending department normally maintains the quality of loans by focusing mainly on weeding out applicants with marginal credit ratings. Because of this quality norm, however, the informal group members are focusing too much on minimizing risk and not enough on providing great service. Management could try to improve this situation by giving bonuses to the group members who meet service as well as risk management goals. The combination of criteria for rewards would probably increase the formal group's productivity while encouraging a positive norm within the informal group.

Status within informal groups also affects work-group productivity. For example, if Numerica managers want to increase a group's productivity, they should try to encourage the informal group's leaders as well as the group's formal supervisor. Chances are that a targeted group will become more productive if its high-status members support that objective.

Collaboration is also an important consideration when establishing and maintaining effective teams. For Numerica's managers to build collaborative teams, they must focus on tasks like helping team members trust one another, develop positive personal relationships with one another, and avoid offensive body language. A prerequisite of collaboration is for team members to share their thoughts honestly and openly.

Overall, if the company wants to maximize work-group effectiveness, management must remember both the formal and informal dimensions of its work groups while considering the four main factors that influence work-group productivity.

MyLab Management Assessing Your Management Skill

If your instructor has assigned this activity, go to www.pearson.com/mylab/management to complete the exercise related to the Challenge Case.

DEVELOPING TEAM SKILL

This section is specially designed to help you develop team skills. An individual's team skill is based on an understanding of the concepts and the ability to apply those concepts. The following activities will help to enhance your team skills in various organizational situations.

Class Preparation and Personal Study

To help you prepare for class, perform the activities outlined in this section. Performing these activities will help you to enhance your classroom performance significantly.

Reflecting on Target Skill

On page 411, this chapter opens by presenting a target management skill along with a list of related objectives outlining knowledge and understanding that you should aim to acquire related to that skill. Review this target skill and the list of objectives to make sure that you've acquired all pertinent information within this chapter. If you do not feel that you've reached a particular objective(s), study related chapter coverage until you do.

Know Key Terms

Understanding the following key terms is critical to your preparing for class. Define each of these terms. Refer to the page(s) referenced after a term to check your definition or to gain further insight regarding the term.

Know How Management Concepts Relate

This section comprises activities that will sharpen your understanding of team concepts. Answer essay questions as completely as possible.

17-1 Why do organizations create committees to carry out specific tasks?

17-2 What are the four stages of the formal group development process identified by Bernard Bass? Explain each stage.

17-3 What signs would you look for that indicate a team in your organization is storming? As a manager, what would you do if the team was indeed storming? Why?

17-4 What do you have to know about trust and collaboration to build effective work teams?

MyLab Management
Personal Inventory Assessment

Go to www.pearson.com/mylab/management to complete the Personal Inventory Assessment related to this chapter.

  PERSONAL INVENTORY ASSESSMENT

Management Skills Exercises

Learning activities in this section are aimed at helping you develop team skills.

MyLab Management
Discussion Questions

Go to www.pearson.com/mylab/management to complete the problems marked with this icon ✪.

✪ Cases

Better Teamwork Makes Numerica Credit Union a Winner

The Challenge Case "Better Teamwork Makes Numerica Credit Union a Winner" (p. 412) and its related Challenge Case Summary were written to help you better understand the management concepts contained in this chapter. Answer the following discussion questions about the Challenge Case to better understand how concepts relating to groups and teams can be applied in a company such as Numerica.

17-5 Describe the characteristics of an effective work team at Numerica Credit Union.

17-6 As a manager at Numerica, what steps would you take to turn a work group into an effective team? Explain the importance of each step.

How Yum! Brands Fosters Team Spirit

Read the case and answer the questions that follow. Studying this case will help you better understand how concepts relating to team building can be applied in a company such as Yum! Brands.

A reporter for *Fortune* magazine recently said that David Novak "may be the business world's ultimate team builder."[56] Novak, chief executive officer of Yum! Brands, is credited with delivering extraordinary growth and profits in the tough business of fast-food restaurants. Yum! Brands has built its trio of restaurant brands—KFC, Pizza Hut, and Taco Bell—into the world's largest restaurant company measured in terms of number of locations.

Novak says the company's strength comes from the value it places on teamwork. He notes that, as a manager, he is driven to win, adding, "You can't win without people." In Novak's experience, success requires a team effort.

According to Novak, the origin of his focus on teams came when he was manager of bottling operations for PepsiCo, which then owned the restaurants that now make up Yum! Brands. Meeting with route salespeople, Novak asked a series of questions about their work, and they repeatedly pointed out one of their coworkers as the expert. The man was in tears, hearing for the first time, after decades of service, that he was so well respected. Novak determined that he would never let a person's contributions go unrecognized.

From Pepsi Bottling, Novak moved to the top position at KFC, which had been unprofitable for years. Novak realized that to replace the bitterness he saw between headquarters and owners of the franchise restaurants, he needed to change the company's spirit. His goal was to establish the qualities of a great team: people determined to win, to compete, and also to have some fun. From that vision came the idea for the Rubber Chicken Award. As Novak met with his managers and visited his restaurants, whenever he heard about someone doing great work, he would personally hand over a rubber chicken with a personal message of thanks.

The Rubber Chicken Award became the first example of what is now the most famous outward sign of team building at Yum! Brands: enthusiastic recognition of employee performance. Every restaurant division has its own version of the award, and every leader has developed a personal award. Each is delivered with a personal, handwritten message of appreciation. But these awards are just one facet of the team-driven culture. The company has stated its values in a written document called "How

We Win Together." These values assert that "everyone has the potential to make a difference" and that employees should engage in "take the hill teamwork," including open discussion aimed at smart actions. Also, managers participate in a leadership development program called Taking People with You. Despite the name, the program does not start with rewarding others but with knowing oneself— how one thinks about and treats others. As managers come to understand themselves better, they begin thinking about the most effective ways to communicate, lead, and recognize the performance of their team members.

Today, Novak acknowledges that the job of team building is a work in progress. In particular, he says, the company has not yet fully spread its culture of teamwork into every one if its 40,000 restaurants around the world. But as long as Novak is CEO, building teams will be his passion.[57]

Questions

17-7   Consider the salespeople David Novak managed for Pepsi Bottling. How would you decide whether to characterize these employees as a group or a team?

17-8   If you were in charge of managing a Yum! Brands restaurant division, how would you ensure that an effective team emerges? How would you help build trust among the employees who work together in your division?

17-9   What challenges do you think might exist in developing teamwork at franchise restaurants? How would you overcome those challenges?

Experiential Exercises

Planning Your Team Development Program

Directions. Your instructor will divide your class into small groups of about five and appoint a discussion leader for each group. Each group is to evaluate the Mountaintop Game that appears here as a team-building activity. Decide whether you would use the activity as a real manager trying to build a real team in your organization. You would be the instructor or the person actually administering the game. Be sure to explain why the group does or does not believe that the exercise would be useful. After all the groups have finished their discussions, the instructor will lead a discussion of the entire class focused on the conclusions of the small groups.

Mountaintop Game[58]

Objective:

For group members to work together for the good of the group

Group Size:

Eight to 15 is ideal.

Materials:

- A rope hanging from the ceiling (i.e., gym climbing rope)
- Rope or other boundary marker
- Two coffee cans or similar height blocks or cans
- One pole, stick, or piece of pipe about 1 inch in diameter

Procedure for Administering the Game:

Set up the pole so that is sits horizontally across the two coffee cans about 3 or 4 feet to one side of the rope. On the other side of the rope, use a different piece of rope to make a circle that the whole group can stand in. For an added challenge, make the circle small so the group must work together to stand in it without falling out of the boundary. This circle should be about 3 to 4 feet from the rope as well.

Tell a story that requires the group to get from a cliff to a mountaintop some distance away. Starting behind the "cliff" (pole) they must grab the climbing rope without stepping off the "cliff." Once they have the rope, they must swing across to the other side and land on the "mountain" (the rope circle). Only one person may go across at a time. If anyone steps out of the boundary, knocks the pole off the cans, or touches the ground, the group must start over. For safety reasons, the leader should stand near the climbing rope to catch anyone who falls.

Possible Questions for Leading Discussion after the Game:

1. How did the group think of a plan?
2. How did the order that you were in factor into the plan?
3. How did you ensure that your teammates were safe during this activity?
4. How would this activity have been different if there was a real cliff and a real mountaintop?
5. Would you trust your teammates if the situation were really life or death? Why or why not?
6. How can you build trust as a team?

Variations:

- Give group members things to carry with them to the mountain for an added challenge.
- Set up a low platform for the group to stand on in place of the circle.

You and Your Career

Most companies have five different functional areas: human resources, sales, marketing, operations, and accounting. Just about any job title you can think of will likely fall into one of these five business functions. Which functional area would you most like to represent on a cross-functional team? For example, if the company you work for was developing a new product or service, would you rather represent operations, where you are part of the initial development and testing? Or would you prefer to be in human resources, responsible for hiring new associates and getting them trained? Or perhaps you might like marketing or sales, where the goal is to attract customers and ultimately get them to buy the new product or service. Or are you a numbers person and would enjoy the accounting or finance side of the organization? Develop a scenario where a cross-functional team must be created, and discuss which functional area of the business you would like to represent. Explain why you chose that particular business function.

Building Your Management Skills Portfolio

Your Management Skills Portfolio is a collection of activities specially designed to demonstrate your management knowledge and skill. Be sure to save your work. Taking your printed portfolio to an employment interview could prove helpful.

The portfolio activity for this chapter is about using committees and teams in accomplishing Disability Plus's mission. Study this information and complete the exercises that follow.

Disability Plus has been operating for nearly 50 years. Its primary objective is to provide assistance and support to individuals with disabilities. Disability Plus aims to ensure that these individuals can maximize their potential and to become integrated members of the broader society. At any one time, the charity operates more than 20 training programs, day care programs, and other services for around 10,000 people. The charity operates on a budget of just under $30 million, which limits their ability at present to expand their operations.

EXHIBIT 1   Disability Plus Mission Statement

Vision

To ensure that all people, regardless of disability, are valued and included members of the community.

Mission

We aim to ensure that all clients have the opportunity to become self-reliant and independent. We aim to provide them with the means to develop their potential.

Values

Our clients and mission are indivisible and paramount. We stand for compassionate integrity and professionalism.

Mission Process

We believe that potential is unlocked in the following ways:

Through Excellence

All of our services and operations are focused on providing quality experiences and assistance to our clients.

Inclusivity and Acceptance

All our services have a common goal of encouraging inclusivity and acceptance of our clients by the wider community.

Technology

Where possible, the latest mobile technology is to be used to help unlock the potential of our clients and their supporters.

Training and Development

The value of training and development for our clients and our employees is essential for continual improvements.

Independence

Our aim is to encourage self-help and to provide the means and support essential to accomplish this goal.

Cross-Generational Support

Our aim is to provide support and services from cradle to grave.

Professionalism

We aim to attract and develop the very best employees to support our clients and their needs.

Learning Activity

Assume you are the president of Disability Plus and have decided to establish a charity-wide committee to monitor and ensure the accomplishment of the charity's mission. Answer the following questions to indicate how you would form this committee and mold it into an effective work team.

17-10 What would you tell your employees to explain why you are appointing this committee?

_____

_____

_____

17-11 List four procedures you will have the committee follow as it does the work. Be sure to explain the value of each procedure.

Procedure 1:

_____

_____

_____

Value of Procedure 1:

_____

_____

_____

Procedure 2:

_____

_____

_____

Value of Procedure 2:

_____

_____

_____

Procedure 3:

_____

_____

_____

Value of Procedure 3:

_____

_____

_____

Procedure 4:

_____

_____

_____

Value of Procedure 4:

_____

_____

_____

17-12 Outline what you would say to the committee to encourage it to function as a team rather than as a group.

_____

_____

_____

17-13 Would you make the committee aware of the stages of team development? Explain.

_____

_____

_____

17-14 How would you help the committee members develop trust in one another? Be as specific as possible.

_____

_____

_____

MyLab Management
Writing Assignments

If your instructor has assigned this activity, go to www.pearson.com/mylab/management for the following assisted-graded writing assignments:

Assisted-Graded Questions

17-15 What are the differences between formal and informal groups? Explain how you would manage each type of group to help an organization achieve success.

17-16 What is the role of trust in building effective teams? As a manager, how would you build trust within a team?

Endnotes

1. Michael Bartlett, "Numerica Topples Silos for Transparent Communication," *Credit Union Journal*, November 25, 2013, Business Insights: Global, http://bi.galegroup.com; Frank J. Diekmann, "CU Journal's Annual Best Practices Awards Help CUs Be Successful," *Credit Union Journal*, November 25, 2013, EBSCOhost, http://web.b.ebscohost.com; Numerica Credit Union, "Career Opportunities," https://www.numericacu.com, accessed April 10, 2014; Numerica Credit Union, "About Us," https://www.numericacu.com, accessed April 11, 2014.

2. For an article illustrating the role of groups in Web projects, see J. C. Fagan and J. A. Keach, "Managing Web Projects in Academic Libraries," *Library Leadership & Management (Online)* 25, no. 3 (2011): 1C–23C, 1CA–8CA.

3. Edgar H. Schein, *Organizational Psychology* (Upper Saddle River, NJ: Prentice Hall, 1965), 67; for additional thoughts by Schein, see J. G. Joos and D. A. Wren, "In His Own Words: A Conversation with Edgar Schein," *Journal of Applied Management and Entrepreneurship* 15, no. 2 (2010): 112–120.

4. Dorwin Cartwright and Ronald Lippitt, "Group Dynamics and the Individual," *International Journal of Group Psychotherapy* 7 (January 1957): 86–102. For results of a qualitative group dynamics study, see Hossan Chowdhury, Christopher Dixon, and David Brown, "Impact of Group Dynamics on Eservice Implementation: A Qualitative Analysis of Australian Public Sector Organisational Change," *Journal of Organizational Change Management* 26, no. 5 (2013): 853–873.

5. For insights into how to be more persuasive in dealing with people in groups, see "MIT Sloan Professor's Research Identifies Top Persuasive Words in Meetings," *Business Wire* [New York] (June 20, 2013).

6. Schein, *Organizational Psychology*, 182. For more discussion of Schein's work as it relates to groups and organization culture, see Anthony J. Evans, "Balancing Corporate Culture: Grid-Group and Austrian Economics," *Review of Austrian Economics* 26, no. 3 (September 2013): 297–309.

7. For information on the role of gender in task groups, see S. Hysom and C. Johnson, "Leadership Structures in Same-Sex Task Groups," *Sociological Perspectives* 49 (2006): 391–410.

8. For a study exploring diversity and task group processes, see Warren E. Watson, Lynn Johnson, and Deanna Meritt, "Team Orientation, Self-Orientation, and Diversity in Task Groups," *Group & Organization Management* 23, no. 2 (June 1998): 161–188.

9. To understand further the possible duties of a committee, see Stephanie Balzer, "Committee to Study $500M Civic Plaza Expansion," *Business Journal* 21, no. 39 (June 22, 2001): 7.

10. Paul Ziobro, "Red Robin Forming Committee to Find New CEO," *Wall Street Journal*, March 5, 2010, http://online.wsj.com.

11. Cyril O'Donnell, "Group Rules for Using Committees," *Management Review* 50 (October 1961): 63–67. For hints on how to run a successful committee, see Emily Davis, "Tips for a Successful Fundraising Committee," *Nonprofit World* 31, no. 6 (November/December 2013): 6–7.

12. These and other guidelines are discussed in "Applying Small-Group Behavior Dynamics to Improve Action-Team Performance," *Employment Relations Today* (Autumn 1991): 343–353.

13. For an analysis of the symptoms associated with groupthink, see D. Henningsen, M. Henningsen, J. Eden, and M. Cruz, "Examining the Symptoms of Groupthink and Retrospective Sensemaking," *Small Group Research* 37 (2006): 36–64.

14. Robert McMurry, "The Tyranny of Groupthink," *Harvard Business Review* 81 (2003): 120.

15. See Irving L. Janis, *Groupthink* (Boston: Houghton Mifflin, 1982). For added practical insights about groupthink, see Michael Bond, *The Power of Others: Peer Pressure, Groupthink, and How the People around Us Shape Everything We Do* (London: Oneworld Publications, 2015).

16. Rob Cross, Robert J. Thomas, and David A. Light, "How 'Who You Know' Affects What You Decide," *Sloan Review*, January 9, 2009, http://sloanreview.mit.edu.

17. For further information about independent work teams, see K. Roper and D. Phillips, "Integrating Self-Managed Work Teams into Project Management," *Journal of Facilities Management* 5 (2007): 22–36.

18. For suggestions on how to create a team, see "Teamwork Translates into High Performance," *HR Focus* 75, no. 7 (July 1998): 7; see also Sheila Webber and Richard Klimoski, "Crews: A Distinct Type of Work Team," *Journal of Business and Psychology* 18 (2004): 261.

19. Bernard Bass, *Organizational Psychology* (Boston: Allyn and Bacon, 1965), 197–198.

20. Peter Economy, "Five Ways to Build an Extraordinary Team Culture," *Inc.*, October 18, 2013, http://www.inc.com; Michael A. Olguin, "Build a Winning Team Dynamic," *Inc.*, February 5, 2013, http://www.inc.com; Robert Sutton, "How to Scale Up Your Team to Greatness," *Fortune*, April 10, 2014, http://management.fortune .cnn.com; Katherine Reynolds Lewis, "How to Lead a Team When You're Not the Boss," *Fortune*, April 10, 2014, http://money.cnn.com.

21. A. B. Zendeh and S. O. Hamed, "A Model for Identification of Informal Groups' Leaders," *International Journal of Organizational Leadership* 6, no. 2 (2017): 176–189.

22. Richard McDermott and Douglas Archibald, "Harnessing Your Staff's Informal Networks," *Harvard Business Review*, March 2010, http://hbr.org.

23. Keith Davis and John W. Newstrom, *Human Behavior at Work: Organizational Behavior* (New York: McGraw-Hill, 1985), 310–312.

24. For the importance of determining such information, see Dave Day, "New Supervisors and the Informal Group," *Supervisory Management* 34 (May 1989): 31–33. For discussion of sociometry applied to multiple team issues, see J. H. Gutiérrez, C. Astudillo, P. Ballesteros-Pérez, D. Mora-Melià, and A. Candia-Véjar, "The Multiple Team Formation Problem Using Sociometry," *Computers & Operations Research* 75 (2016): 150.

25. George Homans, *The Human Group* (New York: Routledge Publishing, 1968). For a study exploring the value of informal groups in organizations, see R. Gulatiand and P. Puranam, "Renewal through Reorganization: The Value of Inconsistencies between Formal and Informal Organization," *Organization Science* 20, no. 2 (2009): 422–440, 478–479.

26. For information regarding the role of culture in workplace teams, see M. Uday-Riley, "Eight Critical Steps to Improve Workplace Performance with Cross-Cultural Teams," *Performance Improvement* 45 (2006): 28.

27. William G. Dyer, *Teambuilding: Issues and Alternatives* (Reading, MA: Addison-Wesley, 1987), 4. See also Dawn R. Deeter-Schmelz and Rosemary Ramsey, "A Conceptualization of the Functions and Roles of Formalized Selling and Buying Teams," *Journal of Personal Selling & Sales Management* (Spring 1995): 47–60.

28. Nancy Mann Jackson, "Team-Building with a Purpose," *Entrepreneur*, April 17, 2009, http://www.entrepreneur.com.

29. For an interesting discussion of the role that planning plays in the relationship between team goal orientation and performance, see Anju Mehta, Hubert Feild, Achilles Armenakis, and Nikhil Mehta, "Team Goal Orientation and Team Performance: The Mediating Role of Team Planning," *Journal of Management* 35, no. 4 (August 2009): 1026–1046.

30. For a recent article describing effective team problem-solving techniques, see V. Tran and H. Latapie, "Developing Virtual Team Problem-Solving and Learning Capability Using the Case Method," *Business Review, Cambridge* 8 (2007): 27–33.

31. J. H. Shonk, *Team-Based Organizations* (Homewood, IL: Irwin, 1922).

32. For a study exploring the relationship between leadership and self-managed teams, see Vanessa Urch Druskat and Jane Wheeler, "Managing from the Boundary: The Effective Leadership of Self-Managing Work Teams," *Academy of Management Journal* 46 (2003): 435.

33. Malaysia Productivity Corporation, "Developing a Productive Team," March 28, 2013, www.mpc.gov.my/home/?kod1=k&kod2=news&item=000160&sstr_lang=en&t=0; Petra Energy Berhad, "Synergising Partnerships," Petra Energy Group, Corporate Brochure, December 12, 2014, www.petraenergy.com.my/1958-09-14_PETRA%20CoporateBrochure.pdf.

34. Jack L. Lederer and Carl R. Weinberg, "Equity-Based Pay: The Compensation Paradigm for the Re-Engineered Corporation," *Chief Executive* (April 1995): 36–39.

35. For insights into self-managed teams and project management, see K. O. Roper and D. R. Phillips, "Integrating Self-Managed Work Teams into Project Management," *Journal of Facilities Management* 5, no. 1 (2007): 220–36.

36. For a different perspective on the value of teams in inspiring collective behavior, see Michael J. Mauboussin, "When Individuals Don't Matter," *Harvard Business Review*, October 2009, http://www.hbr.org.

37. Sami M. Abbasi and Kenneth W. Hollman, "Self-Managed Teams: The Productivity Breakthrough of the 1990s," *Journal of Managerial Psychology* 9 (1994): 25–30.

38. For further information about the components of an effective cross-functional team, see Yvonne Athanasaw, "Team Characteristics and Team Member Knowledge, Skills, and Ability Relationships to the Effectiveness of Cross-Functional Teams in the Public Sector," *International Journal of Public Administration* 26 (2003): 1167.

39. For a recent article describing the role of positive feedback in cross-functional teams, see H. Peelle, "Appreciative Inquiry and Creative Problem Solving in Cross-Functional Teams," *Journal of Applied Behavioral Science* 42 (2006): 447–467.

40. For more information on cross-functional teams, see D. Michael, D. Hutt, Beth A. Walker, and Gary L. Frankwick, "Hurdle the Cross-Functional Barriers to Strategic Change," *Sloan Management Review* (Spring 1995): 22–30; John Teresko, "Reinventing the Future," *Industry Week* (April 17, 1995): 32–38; Margaret L. Gagne and Richard Discenza, "Target Costing," *Journal of Business & Industrial Marketing* 10 (1995): 16–22.

41. Bruce W. Tuckman and Mary Ann C. Jensen, "Stages of Small Group Development Revisited," *Group and Organizational Studies* 2 (1977): 419–427.

42. For an empirical analysis of how to develop an effective team, see E. Chong, "Role Balance and Team Development: A Study of Team Role Characteristics Underlying High and Low Performing Teams," *Journal of Behavioral and Applied Management* 8 (2007): 202–217.

43. For further information on team effectiveness and leadership, see S. Baker and D. Gerlowski, "Team Effectiveness and Leader-Follower Agreement: An Empirical Study," *Journal of American Academy of Business, Cambridge* 12 (2007): 15–23.

44. Hans J. Thamhain, "Managing Technologically Innovative Team Efforts toward New Product Success," *Journal of Product Innovation Management* (March 1990): 5–18.

45. Kurt T. Dirks and Daniel P. Skarlicki, "The Relationship between Being Perceived as Trustworthy by Coworkers and Individual Performance," *Journal of Management* 35, no. 1 (February 2009): 136–157.

46. For insights about motivation and teams, see Gerben van der Vegt, Ben Emans, and Evert van de Vliert, "Motivating Effects of Task and Outcome Independence in Work," *Group & Organization Management* 23, no. 2 (June 1998): 124–143.

47. Jerre L. Stead, "People Power: The Engine in Reengineering," *Executive Speeches* (April/May 1995): 28–32.

48. Liz Wiseman and Greg McKeown, "Bringing Out the Best in Your People," *Harvard Business Review* (May 2010): 117–121.

49. Company website, http://www.burberryplc.com, accessed June 24, 2010; Peter Gumbel, "Burberry's New Boss Doesn't Wear Plaid," *Fortune* (October 15, 2007): 124–130.

50. Shardul Phadnis and Chris Caplice, "Global Virtual Teams: How Are They Performing?," *Supply Chain Management Review* (July/August 2013): 8–9; Betsy Medvedovsky, "Fast Fusion," *PM Network* (July 2013): 24–25; Maureen Bridget Rabotin, "The Intricate Web Connecting Virtual Teams," *T + D* (April 2014): 32–35.

51. For information on building trust in the context of teams, see P. Greenberg, R. Greenberg, and Y. Antonucci, "Creating and Sustaining Trust in Virtual Teams," *Business Horizons* 50 (2007): 325.

52. Fernando Bartolome, "Nobody Trusts the Boss Completely—Now What?," *Harvard Business Review* (March/April 1989): 114–131.

53. Robb Cross, Reb Rebele, and Adam Grant, "Collaborative Overload," *Harvard Business Review* (January/February 2016): 74–79.

54. "Business News: Creativity 365 Empowers Teams to Collaborate Better with Enhanced Content Ecosystem," *Computer Weekly News* (2016): 119.

55. Carol Kinsey Goman, "8 Tips for Collaborative Leadership," Forbes.com, February 13, 2014, https://www.forbes.com/sites/carolkinseygoman/2014/02/13/8-tips-for-collaborative-leadership/#6bed1e8b5fd9.

56. Geoff Colvin, "Great Job!," *Fortune*, August 12, 2013, EBSCOhost, http://web.b.ebscohost.com.

57. Ibid.; Yum! Brands, "About Yum! Brands," http://www.yum.com/company, accessed April 10, 2014; Ladan Nikravan, "A Taste for Growth," *Chief Learning Officer* (December 2013): 34–35.

58. This exercise is from www.teambuildingportal.com.

59. Information for this exercise is based on www.floridahospital.com.

Building Organization Culture

TARGET SKILL

Organization Culture Skill: the ability to establish a set of shared values of organization members regarding the functioning and existence of their organization to enhance the probability of organizational success

ORGANIZATION CULTURE SKILL AND YOUR CAREER

Organization culture skill can be of great value to you in enhancing your management career. For example, this skill can help you to build teams in organizations that value issues like a high regard for innovation. Building this regard for innovation within teams helps workers to think of new and better ideas for doing their jobs, become more productive in their jobs, and contribute more significantly to organizational success. It also builds your image as a competent manager, makes you more valuable to your organization, and supports your promotions as you build your career.

OBJECTIVES

To help build my *organization culture skill*, when studying this chapter, I will attempt to acquire:

18-1 An understanding of the term *organization culture*

18-2 Knowledge about the functions of organization culture

18-3 An appreciation for various types of cultures that can exist in organizations

18-4 Thoughts about how to build a high-performance organization culture

18-5 Tactics for keeping an organization culture alive and well

MyLab Management Chapter Warm Up

If your instructor has assigned this activity, go to www.pearson.com/mylab/management to complete the chapter warm up.

CHALLENGE CASE

Zappos Doesn't Sell Shoes—It "Delivers WOW"

Given the multitude of ways in which consumers can buy shoes, how did Zappos grow from a struggling start-up into a billion-dollar company in less than a decade? Managers took on the goal of extraordinary service and made it the cornerstone of an entire way of doing business—in effect, a corporate *culture*.

The manager credited with making Zappos an icon of culture is CEO Tony Hsieh. Hsieh started as an investor in Zappos. As the company grew, founder Nick Swinmurn hired Hsieh as chief executive. The new CEO was determined to avoid repeating his earlier experience of building a company he did not enjoy working for.

Instead, Hsieh preaches and models his vision of "delivering WOW"—going so far beyond customers' expectations that they exclaim in surprise. Hsieh uses the same kind of approach with employees. He placed delivering WOW at the head of 10 corporate values, which also include "embrace and drive change," "create fun and a little weirdness," and "pursue growth and learning." In pursuit of this last value, the company set up a Zappos Family Library, from which employees can borrow books on ideas for strengthening the company's culture. Hsieh also hired David Vik to serve as a "coach" to develop talent and reinforce the culture.

Vik set up a throne in his office, and whenever an employee visits, he or she sits in the throne. This is Vik's way of indicating that he sees employees' potential for greatness. The throne is only one of many cultural symbols. Support for "fun and a little weirdness" is as diverse as a petting zoo, employee karaoke, and doughnut-eating contests. To build relationships and show that everyone is valued, a Face Game greets employees whenever they log into the computer system. The game presents a photo of an employee's face and asks for the person's name. It responds to whatever name is entered by providing information about that employee.

Maintaining this culture extends to leadership and goals. To amaze customers requires creative decisions. Hsieh's leadership style involves pointing out issues and letting employees develop their own solutions. He sees himself mainly as the keeper of the Zappos vision. The company also challenges employees to make at least one weekly improvement in how the company delivers on its core values.

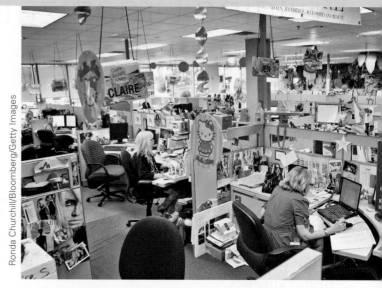

Ronda Churchill/Bloomberg/Getty Images

Zappos's corporate values include "embrace and drive change," "create fun and a little weirdness," and "pursue growth and learning." The fun-loving culture helps employees to feel valued.

Today, Zappos's vision has been rephrased slightly as "delivering happiness." If that sounds less exciting than "delivering WOW," it may represent the challenge of maintaining such a distinct culture. Vik notes that companies lose their positive culture when they stop talking about who they are and begin letting their cultural values become diluted. Zappos was purchased in 2009 by Amazon, which promised to let Hsieh continue running the business in his distinctive way. It remains to be seen whether he can maintain the fun-loving Zappos culture as part of Amazon, although at least Amazon shares Hsieh's single-minded dedication to customer service.[1]

THE ORGANIZATION CULTURE CHALLENGE

The Challenge Case illustrates the organization culture challenges that Zappos must meet. The remaining material in this chapter explains corporate culture concepts and helps develop the corresponding corporate culture skill that you will need to meet such challenges throughout your career. After studying chapter concepts, read the Challenge Case Summary at the end of the chapter to help you relate chapter content to meeting corporate culture challenges at Zappos.

Fundamentals of Organization Culture

This first section is an introduction to the concept of organization culture. Major topics in this section focus on defining organization culture and discussing the importance of organization culture. Overall, this section explains what organization culture is and indicates why managing organization culture is a critical component of a manager's job.

18-1 An understanding of the term *organization culture*

Defining Organization Culture

Organization culture is a set of values that organization members share regarding the functioning and existence of their organization. The actual characteristics of a particular culture are often difficult to define. Even employees in the same organization may describe the organization's culture differently. In part, these different descriptions might reflect their individual experiences and the meanings ascribed to those experiences.[2]

Organization culture is not established all at once by a manager; rather, it develops slowly over time. Basically, organization culture can be thought of as the personality of the organization and a description of how the organization functions. As such, organization culture has dimensions such as organizational rituals, special language, norms, and habits. An organization's culture can be characterized by describing such dimensions. When managers understand the significance of all such dimensions, they can use the dimensions to develop an organization culture that is beneficial to the firm.[3]

At times, organization culture may seem to include an almost endless list of considerations, and managers can become frustrated trying to define their organization's cultures accurately. To help define a culture, research suggests that managers ask a few basic questions:[4]

1. Do people innovate and take risks?
2. Are people attentive to detail?
3. Are people focused on the outcomes of what they do?
4. Is the organization sensitive to people?
5. Do people function as a team?
6. Are people in the organization aggressive?
7. Are people focused on maintaining the status quo?

Although discussions regarding organization culture seem to assume that only one culture exists within an organization, in fact, many subcultures can exist within an organization. An **organization subculture** is a mini-culture within an organization that can reflect the values and beliefs of a specific segment of the organization that is formed along lines such as established departments or geographic regions. Managers must be aware of the subcultures that exist and know how to manage them because subcultures can negatively or positively affect management efforts, such as organizational planning.[5] In managing organization culture, managers sometimes have a tendency to manage only the **dominant organization culture**, the shared values about organizational functioning held by the majority of organization members.[6] In managing organization culture, it's normally advisable for managers to consider the characteristics and potential influence of the organization's dominant culture as well as those of the subcultures.

The Importance of Organization Culture

Understanding and managing organization culture have become extremely important issues in order for modern managers to achieve organizational success. According to Michael Porter, a professor at Harvard Business School, organization culture is such an important issue that managers should not only take it seriously as a sound idea but should also embed it into organizational strategy to help build a competitive advantage.[7] Many management writers believe that an important prerequisite to organizational success is a manager's thorough understanding of organization culture concepts. Only through such an understanding can a manager begin to have an impact on encouraging the behavior of organization members that will lead to organizational success.[8]

P&G's Worldwide Business Conduct Manual

Procter & Gamble (P&G) is a global consumer products company, manufacturing everything from deodorant to detergents. Because of its worldwide reach, it has tens of thousands of employees in many countries. No matter where they are located, P&G employees are expected to adhere to a handful of key values established by the company. These are presented in a manual that every P&G employee receives:

• Treat the company's assets as you would your own. As associates are working with expensive equipment and machinery, they are expected to maintain quality care for these assets.

• Behave with the company's long-term success in mind. It is important that employees engage in behaviors that are consistent with not only the core beliefs of P&G but also the ultimate profitability of the firm.

• Always do the right thing. When it comes to ethical business practices, the company wants associates to err always on the side of doing what is right.

• Operate within the letter and spirit of the law. All employees are expected to follow the laws of whatever country in which they operate.

The manual also includes sections on where and how to report violations as well as statements regarding harassment, discrimination, and substance abuse.[9]

Functions of Organization Culture

18-2   Knowledge about the functions of organization culture

What purpose does organization culture play in an organization? In general terms, organization culture influences the behavior of everyone within an organization and, if carefully crafted, can have a significant, positive impact on organizational success.[10] Organization culture influences the way people carry out organizational processes and can create immense pressure on organization members to act in ways consistent with the culture. As a result, organization culture should reflect the values that are conducive to organizational goal attainment.

In more specific terms, organization culture has a variety of functions within an organization. First, organization culture can enhance organizational productivity. Organization members often become more productive as organization culture increases the emphasis on factors such as rewarding performance and setting goals.[11] Second, organization culture can serve as a component of organizational strategy.[12] Following this line of reasoning, competitive advantage arises from complex combinations of tangible as well as intangible resources. One such intangible resource is a culture that enhances organizational success. Third, organization culture provides a rationale for staffing.[13] That is, management must make sure that new hires are appropriate for the organization's culture. The employment interview is an ideal opportunity for managers to assess whether applicants might fit the organization culture and for applicants to assess whether the organization culture is a good fit for their personal needs and aspirations. During the interview, employers look for clues to issues such as an applicant's work ethic and personality, while job seekers want to learn more about company culture issues, including the allocation of rewards and promotions. Last, organization culture can act as a guideline for making operational decisions. Given an explicit organization culture, organization members tend to make decisions that are consistent with the values embedded in that culture.

Overall, organization culture functions to influence organization members to act in ways that are consistent with the accepted values of the organization. To assist organization members in identifying these beliefs and values, many organizations establish a code of conduct. A **code of conduct** is a document that reflects the core values of an organization and suggests how organization members should act in relation to those values.

Once established, a code of conduct may sometimes need to be changed. For example, although a code of conduct was already in place at Austin, Texas–based Tocquigny, the interactive ad agency suffered an embarrassing lapse involving Twitter. An unhappy prospective client confronted the chief executive: He had read that her agency was also courting one of his competitors.

Hurriedly, Tocquigny amended the social media guidelines in its code of conduct to include an admonition about respecting the firm's confidential and proprietary information. The agency also established a measure of control by assigning to one person the responsibility for posting.[14]

Managers must remember, however, that simply possessing a code of conduct does not guarantee that the organization's members will follow that code. Overall, management must not only work to establish a code of conduct within the organization but also take steps to ensure that behavior that follows the code is rewarded.

Types of Organization Culture

Based on the preceding discussion, we see that organization culture is made up of several different factors. Needless to say, putting all these factors together into a meaningful rationale that describes a culture can be difficult and frustrating for managers.

Fortunately, a model developed by Cameron and Quinn called the Competing Values Framework presents a rationale that managers can use to categorize organization cultures.[15] The Competing Values Framework appears in **Figure 18.1**. According to the model, cultures differ with respect to two sets of opposite values. The first set of opposite values is organizational flexibility and discretion versus organizational stability, order, and control. The second set of opposite values is an internal organizational focus versus an external organizational focus. Depending on how a culture incorporates various combinations of the competing values represented by these two dimensions, cultures can be divided into four types:

1. *Clan Culture.* As shown in Figure 18.1, **clan culture** is an organization culture characterized by a strong internal focus with a high degree of flexibility and discretion. The *clan culture* derives its name from the fact that this organization culture seems much like that of a family. This culture includes activities that reflect shared values and goals, cohesion among organization members, teamwork, and organization commitment to employees.

   The culture at Southwest Airlines is often used as an example of a clan culture. The following excerpt of a recent Thanksgiving Day message from Southwest Airlines president Colleen Barrett shows the emphasis of the Southwest Airlines culture on internal focus, flexibility, shared values and goals, and a strong commitment to employees:

   > As a Company, we are blessed to have 33,000-plus Employees who continually amaze me with their ability to live the Southwest Way. In an industry where change doesn't happen gradually, it happens overnight—if you are lucky to have that much advance notice—our People adapt to change faster than a chameleon. Unlike chameleons, when Southwest Employees adapt, they never change their true colors. Their Warrior Spirit, Servant's Heart, and Fun-LUVing attitude are part of my Thanksgiving blessings.[16]

18-3 An appreciation for various types of cultures that can exist in organizations

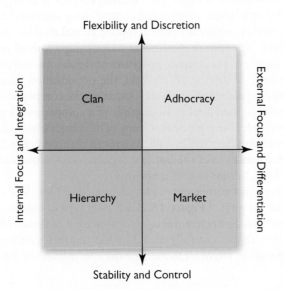

Figure 18.1
The Competing Values Framework depicts four different kinds of organization culture.[17]

In a clan culture, leaders are seen more as mentors and perhaps even parent figures than as bosses. However, as in any family, relationship issues can crop up, particularly involving mentoring.[18]

2. *Adhocracy Culture.* **Adhocracy culture** is an organization culture characterized by flexibility and discretion along with an external focus. As illustrated in Figure 18.1, an adhocracy is a culture reflecting an organization with a simple structure or a lack of structure. In essence, adhocracy is the opposite of bureaucracy. Within the adhocracy culture, one will find few rules or procedures. Instead, this culture is characterized by a creative workplace where people are entrepreneurial, taking risks to achieve success.

Google's organization culture has often been used as an example of an adhocracy culture. The following quote depicts the Google corporate culture as reflecting adhocracy characteristics:

> Though growing rapidly, Google still maintains a small company feel. At the Googleplex headquarters almost everyone eats in the Google café (known as "Charlie's Place"), sitting at whatever table has an opening and enjoying conversations with Googlers from all different departments. Topics range from the trivial to the technical, and whether the discussion is about computer games or encryption or ad serving software, it's not surprising to hear someone say, "That's a product I helped develop before I came to Google."

Google's emphasis on innovation and on its commitment to cost containment means that each employee is a hands-on contributor. There's little in the way of corporate hierarchy, and everyone wears several hats. For example, the international webmaster who creates Google's holiday logos spent a week translating the entire site into Korean. The chief operations engineer is also a licensed neurosurgeon. Because everyone realizes that he or she is an equally important part of Google's success, no one hesitates to skate over a corporate officer during roller hockey.[19]

3. *Hierarchy Culture.* Figure 18.1 shows that **hierarchy culture** is an organization culture characterized by an internal focus along with an emphasis on stability and control. The workplace with this type of culture is formal and structured. Leaders tend to focus on coordination and organization. Individuals within the workplace are concerned about efficiency, and formal rules and policies govern how people operate.

McDonald's restaurants are commonly given as an example of a hierarchy culture. The typical McDonald's restaurant has young employees with little significant experience and produces standardized products for customers. Restaurant success is built on efficient and quick food production. French fries are cooked for an established period, and hamburgers are topped with exact amounts of toppings like mustard and ketchup. Employees are thoroughly trained in the production rules, which cover all facets of restaurant operations, and management closely monitors employee behavior to make sure that the rules are executed precisely.

4. *Market Culture.* As indicated in Figure 18.1, **market culture** is an organization culture that reflects values that emphasize stability and control along with an external focus. An organization with a market culture is oriented toward all stakeholders in the market, not just customers. As such, this culture emphasizes relationships with all constituencies, including customers, suppliers, contractors, government regulators, and unions. Leaders in this culture tend to be hard-driving. In addition, the organization focuses on winning and emphasizes achieving ambitious goals and outpacing the competition.[20]

General Electric is often used as an example of a company with a market culture. The company operates under the premise that if any of its subsidiaries is not number one or two in market sales, the subsidiary will be sold. As a result of this premise, the company has sold more than 300 businesses over the last few decades. This organization culture is highly competitive and has a "results or else" mentality.

Research tells us that competent managers in each of these four organization cultures tend to act in different ways.[21] **Figure 18.2** lists each type of culture and shows the corresponding activities that competent managers within each of these cultures tend to emphasize. Studying this figure carefully will provide insights concerning how managers operating in each culture might act to increase the effectiveness of that culture.

CULTURE TYPE	ACTIVITIES MANAGERS TEND TO PERFORM
The Hierarchy Culture	... Make sure employees know exactly what is expected of them. ... Standardize policies and procedures so employees know exactly how to get work accomplished. ... Include in employee orientation a focus on tradition, values, and vision of the organization. ... Give employees regular feedback on how well they are performing jobs. ... Establish a monitoring system that shows how well employees are performing jobs.
The Market Culture	... Make sure everyone can name their three most critical customers. ... Accept only world-class quality in products and services. ... Give customers what they want the first time. ... Track how competitors are performing. ... Understand the keys to your competitors' success.
The Clan Culture	... Establish a clear goal for the work team. ... Establish specific work targets with deadlines that the team can accomplish. ... Empower others to perform. ... Coach and counsel employees. ... Celebrate the successes of work teams and individuals.
The Adhocracy Culture	... Hold people accountable for generating innovative ideas. ... Talk to people about their new ideas and what they expect the results of ideas could be. ... Reward those who come up with new ways to perform work. ... Establish vehicles for trying out new ideas. ... Make continuous improvement a feature of the workplace.

Figure 18.2
Four types of culture and the corresponding activities that managers can take to make them successful[22]

MyLab Management Watch It

If your instructor has assigned this activity, go to www.pearson.com/mylab/management to complete the video exercise.

Building a High-Performance Organization Culture

The development of culture within an organization is inevitable. In all organizations, culture can develop naturally over time as organization members interact with one another. Under these circumstances, the culture that develops may or may not facilitate or enhance organizational performance. On the other hand, the establishment and growth of a culture within an organization can be influenced by specific actions that management takes. Under these circumstances, the culture that develops will generally have a higher probability of encouraging effective performance within the organization than if the culture is left to develop naturally over time as organization members interact.

18-4 Thoughts about how to build a high-performance organization culture

Figure 18.3 summarizes the steps managers can take to help create an organization culture that yields high performance.[23] Each of the steps is discussed here:

1. *Lead as Champion.* Leaders in organizations must champion the organization climate. As such, leaders throughout the organization must explain repeatedly why the practices that help build organization culture are necessary and how such practices will benefit the organization. If the practices are new, leaders must convince organization members that the change is necessary.

2. *Link Work to Organizational Mission.* The purpose of an organizational mission is to clarify the purpose(s) of the organization. The mission statement helps employees understand why their organization exists. Helping employees understand how their work contributes

Figure 18.3

Steps that managers can take to build a high-performance organization culture

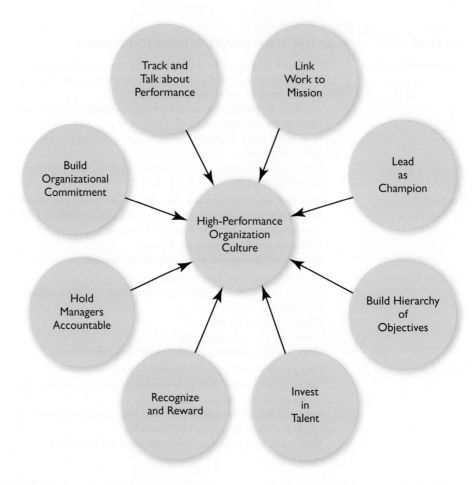

to accomplishing the organizational mission is critical. Such understanding emphasizes the great importance of employee efforts to the success of the organization and helps them develop a sense of pride in their jobs and the work they do. If employees understand how their efforts result in the accomplishment of the organizational mission, commitment to working hard so that the mission can be accomplished will normally follow.

3. *Track and Talk about Performance.* All organization members should constantly be thinking about their individual performance. What is excellent performance? How can performance be improved? Why is excellent performance necessary? Why should organization members strive to be outstanding performers? Performance, by managers and nonmanagers alike, should be defined and tracked to monitor how suitably individuals are performing. As performance is tracked, corrective action should be taken, if necessary, to foster performance improvement. Also, employees generally like to know how well the organization as a whole is performing. When organization members receive regular communication regarding the performance of the entire organization, they tend to stay focused on contributing to that performance.

4. *Build a Hierarchy of Objectives.* As discussed earlier, a hierarchy of objectives is a set of objectives wherein the overall objectives of the organization are divided into subobjectives for all sections and levels of the organization. As objectives at lower levels of the organization are accomplished, they contribute to the attainment of objectives at the next-higher level. Although defining objectives at lower levels may be difficult, the effort used to develop the hierarchy will be well spent. Even employees at the lowest organizational levels will generally be more focused on performance when they see the cascading set of objectives in the hierarchy of objectives. Throughout the organization, objectives should be challenging and have obvious rewards to be earned when the objectives are reached.

5. *Invest in Talent.* Certain employees will have more talent to perform a job than others. As such, these talented individuals have a greater capacity for performance. Talented employees generally demand higher wages in the labor market than others. Management must recognize

PRACTICAL CHALLENGE: BUILDING A HIGH-PERFORMANCE CULTURE

Xerox Emirates' Proactive Approach

Xerox has been around for over a hundred years. It operates in over 180 countries and has 140,000 employees. Xerox also functions in competitive and lucrative markets in the Middle East.

At the pinnacle of its business, Xerox Emirates claimed that it wanted to build a sustainable, high-performance culture. It does this by ensuring that it has an engaged and an aligned workforce through effective management practices coupled with training, rewards, coaching, and performance management.

Attracting the right kind of employee is always a challenge, and Xerox Emirates takes a proactive approach to, first, attract the right candidates, then to develop their skill set, and ultimately to retain the best people. Their HRM strategy is directly linked to the global strategic goals of the organization. These key goals or objectives include continuous improvement of business performance and the development of an organizational culture that supports and encourages innovation, quality improvements, and customer focus. This is done by encouraging managers to become better people-persons. Xerox wants a positive workforce with effective communication skills and employee engagement. Work–life balance is encouraged, as are ethical principles. Collectively, Xerox has created a high-performance culture that works.[24]

that, although talented employees may be more expensive to hire and retain, such employees are normally an effective means to achieve better organizational performance. In addition, managers must do whatever they can to retain talented employees once they are hired.

In addition to hiring individuals with the appropriate talent to improve organizational performance, management can invest in developing the talents of current employees. Through training, for example, management can focus on developing organization members' abilities in order to improve organizational performance. Organizations that invest in and maintain employees' work abilities send the message to all organization members that excellent performance is a top priority.

6. *Recognize and Reward.* Management needs to help employees *learn* to be high performers. As such, appropriate performance behavior needs to be reinforced or rewarded. Research tells us that reinforced behavior tends to be repeated: When management reinforces appropriate performance, appropriate performance tends to be repeated. Reinforcement can be monetary or nonmonetary. In certain instances, a simple, nonmonetary certificate in recognition of excellent performance can be as powerful a reinforcement as a monetary cash bonus. Recognition and reward practices within any organization should be evaluated periodically for possible improvement.

7. *Hold Managers Accountable.* The performance of managers should be tracked, with job-related progress being communicated to them both formally and informally. Maintaining this performance contributes to ensuring the success of a manager's area of responsibility, which in turn contributes to the performance and success of the organization as a whole. Managers should understand what is necessary for employees to be high performers and advise, coach, and counsel them about how to improve their performance and reach performance goals. Given the critical contribution that employee performance makes to organizational success, managers should be held accountable for supervising that performance.

8. *Build Organizational Commitment.* **Organizational commitment** can be defined as the dedication of organization members to uphold the values of the organization and to make worthwhile contributions to fulfilling the organizational purpose. Research indicates that one way to build organizational commitment is to maintain an organizational focus on providing excellent customer service. Such a focus seems to result in higher job satisfaction, which in turn seems to help build stronger organizational commitment.[25] Overall, this increased commitment to the organization seems to increase employees' desire to remain in the organization and to focus on providing quality goods and services. Foundation studies in this area indicate that organizational commitment serves as a "psychological bond" that influences individuals to act in ways that are consistent with the interests of the organization.[26]

Keeping Organization Culture Alive and Well

18-5 Tactics for keeping an organization culture alive and well

Given the critical contributions that organization culture makes to organizational success, managers must keep organization culture alive and well in their organizations. Important steps in this process include establishing a vision of organization culture, building and maintaining organization culture through artifacts, integrating new employees within organization culture, and maintaining the health of organization culture. Each of these steps is discussed in the following sections.

Establishing a Vision of Organization Culture

Managing organization culture usually begins by establishing a vision of what the culture of an organization should be. In essence, this vision becomes a target at which management aims. Without such a target, management will not have a benchmark for modifying and improving the organization culture over time.

Ethisphere magazine named Starbucks one of its World's Most Ethical Companies. A Starbucks manager claims treating employees right provides an environment where they treat others right, and ethical values include doing good both in the sense of providing communities with a gathering place and performing acts of community service.

Management should first reflect on what type of culture would be appropriate, given the organization's specific circumstances. Because of the complexity of circumstances in most modern organizations, most such cultures tend to be multidimensional. Managers should strive to establish the dimensions in their own culture that will best contribute to accomplishing the organizational mission. Dimensions commonly observed in modern organization cultures include focusing on quality, ethics, innovation, spirituality, diversity, and customers. Bear in mind that not all organization cultures contain all of these dimensions; instead, managers tend to decide which dimension(s) will best enhance organizational success and then take steps to include that dimension as a major feature of organization culture. Each of these dimensions is discussed here.

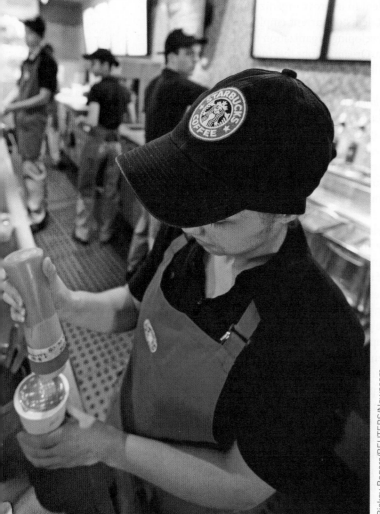

Rickey Rogers/REUTERS/Newscom

Quality Dimension   The **quality dimension of organization culture** is an element of organization culture that focuses on making sure a product, in the opinion of the customer, does what it is supposed to do. Organizations with such a culture tend to focus on communicating to customers their focus on quality and explaining how quality processes operate within the organization. Management generally hopes to benefit from such cultural emphasis by earning customer loyalty and repeat purchases because of customer satisfaction with products or services. An example of an organization with a strong quality dimension in its organization culture is KB Home, a home builder that operates mainly in 18 states in the southwestern and southeastern United States. KB Home uses its website to communicate to customers its focus on quality. At KB Home, the quality of the houses it produces is especially important: The company has a "100% Satisfied Pledge," which offers home buyers 10 quality construction checkpoints.

Ethics Dimension   The **ethics dimension of organization culture** is a facet of organization culture that focuses on making sure that an organization emphasizes not only what is good for the organization but also what is good for other human beings. Until recently, an ethics dimension has been unwisely ignored.[27]

Ethics training is arguably the most commonly used method for developing the ethics dimension of organization culture.[28] This training normally focuses on developing a common understanding throughout the organization of the role that ethics plays in organizational operations. However, ethics training does not guarantee that employees will choose the ethical behavior in every situation. Such training can start a useful dialogue, however, about correct and incorrect behavior in various organizational situations. In essence, ethics training is designed to give employees a usable framework for ethical reasoning that will help them make ethical choices in various organizational situations after training ends.

What can managers do to increase the probability that ethics training influences organization members to act ethically over time? First, after ethics training concludes, management can provide employees with a means for making ethical queries anonymously. Some organizations provide a hotline that employees can call to get advice about ethical dilemmas. Management can also try to make sure that organization members act ethically after ethics training concludes by establishing methods for reviewing the topics covered in ethics training. For example, a company can post updates to its intranet, publish brochures, and even use screen savers to remind employees about the issues covered in ethics training. Another tactic that management can use is to promote employees who behave ethically. Rewarding past ethical behavior is a powerful way to increase the probability that organization members will act ethically in the future.

Innovation Dimension The **innovation dimension of organization culture** is an aspect of organization culture that encourages the application of new ideas to improve organizational processes, products, or services. Innovation is a major source of organizational change and improvement. Once an innovation dimension is established, however, management cannot assume that it will continue to exist as time passes. An innovation dimension of organization culture can become significantly weakened or even disappear if it is not properly nurtured.

The 3M Company is known for producing thousands of imaginative products, which emerge from a culture widely regarded as innovative and creative. By its nature, invention is commonly a disorderly and inefficient process. Historically, 3M has allowed researchers to spend years testing products with little regard for the efficiency of the process.

Consider the invention of the Post-it note. The 3M inventor, Art Fry, fiddled with the idea for several years before the product went into full production in 1980. But then, management began making changes to the culture to emphasize efficiency. What the company didn't realize was that, in emphasizing efficiency, innovation was being squeezed out. Once 3M management realized that this innovation focus was being damaged, it took steps to somewhat deemphasize the focus on efficiency and to spend more on research and development in an effort to reinvigorate its culture of innovation, long considered to be the lifeblood of the company.[29]

Spirituality Dimension The **spirituality dimension of organization culture** is an aspect of organization culture that encourages organization members to integrate spiritual life and work life. A spiritual awakening seems to be occurring in the American workplace, and many managers are encouraging the development of this trend.[30] Managers seem to be doing so because of their belief that a spiritually humanistic work environment is beneficial for both employees and the organization. According to the logic of such managers, a spiritually reflective work environment will be personally satisfying to organization members, who will thereby become more productive and creative. On the other hand, such managers tend to believe that a workplace without a spiritual dimension will normally result in unsatisfied organization members, who will become frustrated and thereby consistently absent from the workplace.[31] Organization cultures that have a spiritual dimension typically do not focus on one specific type of spiritual belief or religion but instead emphasize the acceptance of whatever spiritual focus an organization member might possess. In emphasizing a spiritual focus, organizations create opportunities for spiritually based activities such as offering prayer, performing meditation, reading sacred texts, listening to worship music, and having objects in the workplace as reminders of one's spiritual beliefs.

Diversity Dimension The **diversity dimension of organization culture** is a component of organization culture that encourages the existence of basic human differences among organization members. Such differences can be in ethnicity, religion, physical ability, and/or sexual orientation. The diversity dimension is a mainstay of modern organization culture primarily because managers are eager to reap diversity-related advantages, such as an increased number of perspectives on how to solve problems and how to relate to diverse customers better.

Toyota's American division recently concluded that its corporate culture lacks diversity.[32] Organization members, as a group, were thought to be too homogeneous, thereby depriving management of the benefits of a diverse workforce. To solve this problem, Toyota is trying to make the population of organization members more diverse by hiring people from other industries and companies. These hirings, however, are being done carefully. Management does not want these new employees ruining its present and otherwise healthy corporate culture.

Customer Dimension   The **customer dimension of organization culture** is a facet of organization culture that focuses on catering to the needs of those individuals who buy the goods or services the organization produces. One recent survey indicates that 80 percent of executives believe they are doing an excellent job of serving customers, whereas only 8 percent of their customers agree.[33] Perhaps because of such survey results, along with the realization of the calamity that such results could cause in organizations, many managers are strengthening their organization culture's focus on customers.

Some organizations, however, are well known for their enduring commitment to customer satisfaction, have achieved much success because of it, and are expected to continue benefiting from it in the future. For example, many believe that Apple's success over the years is due primarily to its enduring commitment to knowing what customers want even before customers know it themselves. As another example, General Electric CEO Jeffrey Immelt has initiated "dreaming sessions" to brainstorm with key customers and develop a forward-looking view of customer needs.

Building and Maintaining Organization Culture through Artifacts

A **cultural artifact** is a dimension of an organization that helps to describe and reinforce the culture—or the beliefs, values, and norms—in which an artifact exists. As organization culture changes over time, cultural artifacts can also change because what the artifacts represent, how they appear, how they are used, and why they are used are no longer pertinent in the new culture. Several cultural artifacts commonly used by modern managers are discussed here.[34]

Values   At the heart of any organization's culture are its values. From a societal viewpoint, a **value** is a person's or social group's belief in which the person or the group has an emotional investment. In society, values can be "for" something, such as excellent health care for all of society, or "against" something, such as violence among society members. In organizations as well, values can be for things, such as hiring talented workers, rewarding excellent performance, and developing leadership skills, or against things, such as polluting the environment, discriminating in hiring practices, and maintaining the status quo.

Organizational values are reflected in organizational characteristics, including strategy, structure, and processes. Values are also reflected in the way leaders lead as well as in organizational rules, reward systems, policies, and procedures. More and more, modern managers are crafting values statements to communicate clearly cultural values held throughout the organization. A **values statement** is a formally drafted document that summarizes the primary values within the culture of a specific organization. A values statement gives managers the opportunity to communicate effectively and efficiently the values that drive the organization and thereby help increase the probability that appropriate values will influence organization member behavior. **Figure 18.4** contains a statement of values for Microsoft.

Social psychologist Michael O'Malley studies organization culture and, in his spare time, practices beekeeping. Indulging in his hobby has led O'Malley to study the habits of bees and, in his book *The Wisdom of Bees: What the Hive Can Teach Business about Leadership*, to apply those habits to management practices in building organizational values. For example, O'Malley says that older bees in the hive "mentor" younger bees. Culture is also important to the hive's overall productivity and well-being, and when colonies from two hives occasionally merge, an "enculturation" process ensures the success of the merger.[36]

Our Values

As a company, and as individuals, we value integrity, honesty, openness, personal excellence, constructive self-criticism, continual self-improvement, and mutual respect. We are committed to our customers and partners and have a passion for technology. We take on big challenges, and pride ourselves on seeing them through. We hold ourselves accountable to our customers, shareholders, partners, and employees by honoring our commitments, providing results, and striving for the highest quality.

Figure 18.4
Statement of Values for Microsoft[35]

Organizational Myths

An **organizational myth** is a popular belief or story that has become associated with a person or institution and illustrates an organization culture ideal. Myths are used to explain organizational beginnings or other events that are of great significance to the organization. Myths stimulate organization members to do a good job and provide the logic for actions taken. Some of the events reported in myths never actually happened, but they nevertheless serve as an inspirational foundation for behavior. Organizational myths are commonly perpetuated in organizations to enhance organization member pride in belonging and overall commitment to the organization.

One of the most famous myths in business history centers on Lee Iacocca and how he "saved" Chrysler Corporation from bankruptcy.[37] Iacocca took over as chair of Chrysler Corporation in 1979. At that time, Chrysler was in serious crisis. The company was losing money; had acquired unprofitable companies; and was producing low-quality products that necessitated huge, expensive product recalls. Iacocca took bold, nontraditional actions to save the company: He negotiated government backing of the company, took charismatic personal ads to the marketplace asking for customer support, and negotiated significant concessions with the United Auto Workers Union to dodge bankruptcy. Word began to spread quickly that Iacocca had single-handedly saved the company, which of course was not true. Many people were involved in saving Chrysler. However, the myth of Iacocca saving the company single-handedly helped create the Chrysler cultural value of trust and support for Chrysler leadership.

Organizational Sagas

An **organizational saga** is a narrative describing the adventures of a heroic individual or family significantly linked to an organization's past or present. In general, the purpose of a saga is to identify and perpetuate the organization's shared values. Organizational sagas usually reveal important historical facts such as early pioneers and products, past triumphs and failures, and the leaders who founded or transformed the company.

Mary Kay Ash was the founder of Mary Kay Cosmetics and one of the most successful entrepreneurs in the history of the United States. Information on the website of the company she founded describes a saga related to Mary Kay Cosmetic's company history. This information serves as an inspiration to all organization members because it lets them know that significant success is obtainable by all within the company through hard work, dedication, and self-confidence.

Managers at all levels can become involved in **organizational storytelling**, the act of passing along organizational myths and sagas to other organization members. From the example of Mary Kay Ash, it is obvious that modern managers can tell stories not only via word of mouth but also via the Internet.

Organizational Language

The language used in organizations often indicates the organization's shared values. Some companies reveal how they view the competition by repeatedly using phrases such as "Let's be number 1 in the marketplace" or how they feel about technology by repeatedly using phrases such as "Win through technology." Still other organizations repeatedly use the phrase "The customer is king" to emphasize how they feel about customer satisfaction. The language used at Walt Disney Companies reflects organizational values that are particularly noteworthy. At Walt Disney, rather than being called an employee, everyone is called a "member of the cast." This terminology emphasizes that, rather than simply

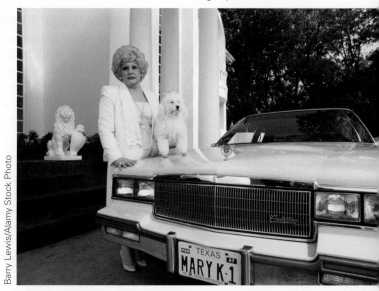

Mary Kay Cosmetics builds its company culture through inspirational stories, including that of founder Mary Kay Ash; organizational ceremonies; and rewards, including autos for top-selling representatives.

Barry Lewis/Alamy Stock Photo

STEPS FOR SUCCESS

Tips for Writing a Values Statement

A mission and vision statement is one of the first things a new business establishes. And though values of the firm are important, the values statement is often forgotten. However, it should be just as important as the mission and vision. Suggestions for crafting a values statement include the following:[38]

- Rather than asking what the company values, ask what the company believes.

- Determine values associated with finding solutions to problems.
- Establish values related to delivering exceptional service.
- Involve as many constituents as possible in the discussion.
- Weave the values into all forms of internal and external communication.

working, organization members should think of themselves as always being *on stage* and always needing to give customers the best *performance* possible. Many companies use slogans internally and externally through advertising to convey important organizational values. **Figure 18.5** presents several well-known slogans and the companies that use them to convey important organizational values.

Organizational Symbols

An **organizational symbol** is an object that has meaning beyond its intrinsic content. Symbols provide a road map indicating what is important in a particular organization. Some companies use impressive buildings to convey company strength. Other companies use logos, flags, and coats of arms to convey the importance they place on certain ideas or events. As examples, Prudential Life Insurance Company uses the Rock of Gibraltar to symbolize the company's dependability, strength, and unwavering commitment to its customers, and McDonald's uses the clown Ronald McDonald to symbolize the child-friendliness and fun available at McDonald's restaurants.

Organizational Ceremonies

An **organizational ceremony** is a formal activity conducted on important organizational occasions. Such occasions could include openings of new stores, anniversary dates of when employees were hired, and employee promotions. Perhaps one of the most well-known organizational ceremonies is the ceremony celebrating successful sales campaigns at Mary Kay Cosmetics. At the company's sales celebrations, everything—not just the decorations but also the sales prizes, including the automobiles awarded—has a significance.

Organizational Rewards

Rewards modify behavior in some way in most organizations.[39] Some rewards come from within the organization and can include compensation, satisfying work, and verbal recognition. Rewards can also come from outside the organization and can include comments from customers, competitors, and suppliers. Management should continually identify and reward those individuals who uphold the values of the organization. Rewarding people for engaging in behavior that reflects the important values of the organization culture is critical in increasing the probability of organizational success.

Figure 18.5

Well-known companies, their slogans, and the values these slogans reflect.

COMPANY	SLOGAN	VALUE REFLECTED
Maytag	"The dependability people"	Maytag products are durable.
Petland	"Petland Pets Make Life Better!"	Petland pets improve lives.
Allstate Insurance Co.	"You're In Good Hands With Allstate"	Allstate takes care of its customers.
Staples	"That was easy"	Staples solves problems easily.
Wal-Mart	"Always low prices. Always."	Wal-Mart has low prices every day.

Integrating New Employees into the Organization Culture

The previous section discussed how to keep organization culture alive and well through the use of cultural artifacts. This section focuses on how to keep organization culture alive and well by appropriately integrating newly hired organization members into the existing organization culture.

Organizational socialization is the process by which management can appropriately integrate new employees into the organization's culture.[40] As the U.S. economy improves, it is likely that employers will need to integrate more new employees. During periods of uncertainty and layoffs, employees who still have jobs tend to "stay put" even if they are dissatisfied with their positions. As the economy improves, however, those same employees will begin to leave their jobs, thus requiring employers to recruit new employees.[41] **Figure 18.6** presents the recommended steps for a socialization process and how the steps relate to one another. The following material discusses the process as a whole as well as each step in more detail.

As shown in Figure 18.6 , the organizational socialization process can begin with careful planning of the organization's recruitment process. As part of this planning, management should determine what types of individual characteristics would best fit into the organization culture. Such characteristics might include an individual's determination to be successful in the job, commitment to personal ethics, and levels of self-confidence and competitiveness. After such best-fit characteristics have been determined, management should use the recruitment process to identify the individuals possessing those characteristics. Naturally, after management has made this identification, purposeful steps should be taken to hire those individuals.

Once individuals possessing the best-fit characteristics are hired, management should continue the socialization process (step 2) by carefully crafting meaningful experiences for them during the first four to six weeks of the new recruits' presence within the organization. In this situation, experiences are meaningful if they expose the new hires to the important organizational culture values and emphasize the importance of the new individuals' commitment to those values. Such values might include the importance of tackling challenging work, the openness to training for handling new situations, and the importance of functioning as a team member. Such initial experiences can also involve new recruits observing and practicing new jobs with input from established organization members.

Once the individuals with the appropriate personal characteristics have been hired and have taken part in meaningful activities during the first four to six weeks of their employment, management should continue with their socialization by exposing them to appropriate role models (step 3). Management should focus on pairing new recruits with role models who possess the characteristics that would be valuable for the new recruits to develop themselves. The role models should exemplify cultural values such as being productive, highly motivated, and loyal to the organization and having significant trust in management.[44]

As the next step in the organizational socialization process, management should help new recruits understand various facets of the organization's informal structure and how it

Figure 18.6 Possible steps of a socialization process

complements the formal structure. Helping new recruits become members of the informal groups that uphold important organizational values should be especially important to management. Likewise, ignoring the informal focus in the organizational socialization process could result in new recruits unknowingly aligning themselves with the less productive facets of the organization's informal structure and thereby limit the new recruits' contributions to organizational success.

In the final step of the organizational socialization process, management must evaluate the cultural fit of the new recruits. New recruits are generally considered new for about one year. During new recruits' first year in the organization, management must keep in mind that they will make mistakes and struggle to adapt to the organization culture. This struggle to fit in with the organizational culture can be frustrating for new recruits and lead to premature turnover if not handled sensitively by management. New recruits must be able to practice new tasks, at times employing trial and error, without fear of punishment or failure.

With more than 2,500 attorneys in its offices on four continents, Jones Day is one of the world's largest law firms. Like most large firms, it has a set of qualities it looks for when recruiting new lawyers. For example, candidates must not exhibit a sense of entitlement or appear too focused on personal success. Also, because of its collaborative culture, the firm rules out candidates who seem likely to compete with their colleagues or are too interested in their peers' performance. Jones Day also has what is called a "closed" compensation system, and even its partners are not privy to information about the salaries of their peers. Although this kind of secrecy may be highly unusual in other businesses, it seems to be accepted within the firm's culture. What's more, it doesn't appear to affect the firm's success adversely: Unlike many of its competitors, Jones Day did not lay off lawyers during the recent global recession.[43]

Management must also remember that not all recruits are suitable for the organization culture and that some recruits may need to be weeded out to make room for other new recruits who may be a better fit. This weeding out can take place by moving poor performers either out of the organization or to jobs with less critical roles. As this weeding-out process occurs, management should reflect on any possible mistakes made during the organizational socialization process of the recruits and think of ideas on how to improve the process so that such mistakes will not be made in the future.

Maintaining the Health of Organization Culture

Arguably, the most important step that management can take to maximize the success of an organization is to create a healthy culture within that organization. A **healthy organization culture** is one that facilitates the achievement of the organization's mission and objectives. An **unhealthy organization culture** is one that does not facilitate the achievement of the organization's mission and objectives.

Managers must continually analyze the symptoms or signs related to the health of the organization and take action to build and maintain a healthy organization culture. A *healthy organization culture* is usually people-oriented and includes the characteristics listed in **Figure 18.7**. A manager should keep the characteristics of a healthy organization climate in mind and focus on maintaining and building organization culture health whenever possible. For example, if managers believe that organization culture is healthy, they should take steps to improve this health wherever possible. Even though an organization culture might be considered healthy, increasing the cultural focus on risk taking or on excellence in job performance might make the culture even healthier. On the other hand, a manager might believe that his or her organization culture is unhealthy. In this case, the manager must determine what factors are making the organization culture unhealthy, take steps to eliminate those factors, and introduce ingredients into the culture that will make it healthy.

That was the strategy implemented by Jonathan Ciano when he became CEO of Uchumi Supermarkets in Kenya, Africa. Soon after joining the company, Ciano saw obvious signs that organization culture was unhealthy. Staff theft and unregulated procurement systems led to record debt and uncertainty regarding the company's sustainability. To change the unhealthy culture into a healthy one, the new CEO confronted the issues of theft and uncontrolled procurement and also initiated a culture in which employees are able to think for themselves on behalf of the company. As a result, Uchumi employees are now making independent judgments and decisions.[44]

If Ciano's steps to make organization culture healthier are successful, he will see signs such as organization members fixing mistakes rather than rationalizing them, and new ideas and information will start to flow freely within the company. On the other hand, if the organization culture does not become healthier, the CEO will see signs such as employees blaming others when mistakes occur.

1. **Openness and humility from top to bottom of the organization**
   Arrogance kills off learning and growth by blinding us to our own weaknesses. Strength comes out of receptivity and the willingness to learn from others.

2. **An environment of accountability and personal responsibility**
   Denial, blame, and excuses harden relationships and intensify conflict. Successful teams hold each other accountable and willingly accept personal responsibility.

3. **Freedom for risk-taking within appropriate limits**
   Both extremes—an excessive, reckless risk-taking and a stifling, fearful control—threaten any organization. Freedom to risk new ideas flourishes best within appropriate limits.

4. **A fierce commitment to "do it right"**
   Mediocrity is easy; excellence is hard work, and there are many temptations for shortcuts. A search for excellence always inspires both inside and outside an organization.

5. **A willingness to tolerate and learn from mistakes**
   Punishing honest mistakes stifles creativity. Learning from mistakes encourages healthy experimentation and converts negatives into positives.

6. **Unquestioned integrity and consistency**
   Dishonesty and inconsistency undermine trust. Organizations and relationships thrive on clarity, transparency, honesty, and reliable follow-through.

7. **A pursuit of collaboration, integration, and holistic thinking**
   Turf wars and narrow thinking are deadly. Drawing together the best ideas and practices, integrating the best people into collaborative teams, multiplies organizational strength.

8. **Courage and persistence in the face of difficulty**
   The playing field is not always level, or life fair, but healthy cultures remain both realistic about the challenges they face and unintimidated and undeterred by difficulty.

Figure 18.7
Eight characteristics of a healthy organization culture[45]

CHALLENGE CASE SUMMARY

For Tony Hsieh, the Zappos chief executive officer mentioned in the Challenge Case, maintaining a culture emphasizing customer service that exceeds expectations means that he must understand the fundamental concepts of organization culture. He must also realize that in building this focus, he is actually attempting to build shared values within Zappos so that organization members view "delivering WOW" as a critical organizational activity. Ultimately, building and maintaining such a customer service culture at Zappos could help the company stay popular and profitable in the demanding retail industry. This culture can serve useful and valuable functions at Zappos such as enhancing company productivity, becoming part of the company's strategy for success, and providing a rationale for adding new staff.

However, Hsieh's organization culture challenges extend beyond the issue of customer service. It may be worthwhile for Hsieh to determine what type of overall organization culture he would like to see at Zappos. Options include establishing a clan culture, an adhocracy culture, a hierarchy culture, or a market culture. In making this determination, Hsieh should consider the challenges facing Zappos and anticipate which culture or combination of cultures would best help Zappos meet these challenges.

For a retailer such as Zappos, maintaining customer loyalty is one of the greatest challenges. As Hsieh continues his efforts to ensure that Zappos stands out because of its exceptional service, he should continue maintaining an organization culture that encourages high performance. To create a high-performance culture, Hsieh must lead as a champion. That is, he must explain repeatedly why organization culture values such as delivering happiness, creating fun, and embracing change are critical for Zappos's success. He must also take steps to encourage organization members to act in ways that are consistent with the organization's cultural values. To create this high-performance culture, Hsieh should also focus on linking work to Zappos's mission, and recognize and reward individuals whose actions are consistent with the company's mission. In building a high-performance culture, Hsieh should take actions that include investing in outstanding talent, holding managers accountable for their actions, and increasing organization members' commitment to Zappos.

Besides establishing a customer service dimension of Zappos's organization culture, Hsieh must plan on keeping the culture alive and well, which actually starts with Hsieh envisioning exactly what the culture should be. Without such a vision, he will be unable to tweak the culture over time to keep it consistent with this vision. In addition to a customer dimension, Hsieh's vision of the culture could include a combination of dimensions focusing on areas such as quality, ethics, innovation, spirituality, and diversity.

Once the vision of Zappos's culture is complete in Hsieh's mind, the process of keeping that culture alive and well should probably focus on Hsieh choosing the artifacts he would like to use to establish and maintain the organization culture. Such artifacts already include a values statement outlining Zappos's key organization culture values. Other artifacts could be the development of organizational myths and sagas, which can be used to perpetuate cultural values; special language and ceremonies to bring key ingredients of Zappos's cultural values to life; and organization rewards that reinforce and encourage the behavior that is consistent with Zappos's organization culture.

Bringing new organization members into Zappos's culture is an important matter. Socializing new individuals into the culture will help ensure that the culture stays alive and well over the long run. Steps that Hsieh can take to socialize new organization members into Zappos's culture include carefully planning the company's recruitment process, providing meaningful experiences at Zappos once individuals are hired, exposing newcomers to appropriate Zappos role models, and weeding out organization members when they do not seem to be fitting well into the company's culture. Overall, Hsieh must focus on establishing a healthy organization culture at Zappos, a culture that facilitates the achievement of the company's goals.

MyLab Management Assessing Your Management Skill

If your instructor has assigned this activity, go to www.pearson.com/mylab/management to complete the exercise related to the Challenge Case.

DEVELOPING ORGANIZATION CULTURE SKILL

This section is specially designed to help you develop organization culture skills. An individual's organization culture skill is based on an understanding of the concepts and the ability to apply those concepts. The following activities will help to enhance your organization culture skills in various organizational situations.

Class Preparation and Personal Study

To help you prepare for class, perform the activities outlined in this section. Performing these activities will help you to enhance your classroom performance significantly.

Reflecting on Target Skill

On page 437, this chapter opens by presenting a target management skill along with a list of related objectives outlining knowledge and understanding that you should aim to acquire related to that skill. Review this target skill and the list of objectives to make sure that you've acquired all pertinent information within the chapter. If you do not feel that you've reached a

particular objective(s), study related chapter coverage until you do.

Know Key Terms

Understanding the following key terms is critical to your preparing for class. Define each of these terms. Refer to the page(s) referenced after a term to check your definition or to gain further insight regarding the term.

Know How Management Concepts Relate

This section comprises activities that will further sharpen your understanding of management concepts. Answer essay questions as completely as possible.

18-1 Organizational culture is often difficult to define, and some managers find it hard to identify all of its aspects. State and explain the questions used to define organizational culture.

18-2 Assume that you are a professor teaching a management course. What vision would you have for the course culture? List three artifacts you would use to establish and maintain this vision. Be sure to explain why you chose each artifact.

18-3 A culture will develop in an organization gradually as people interact. To ensure that the culture facilitates and enhances organizational performance, specific actions need to be taken by the management. What are these actions?

MyLab Management
Personal Inventory Assessment

Go to www.pearson.com/mylab/management to complete the Personal Inventory Assessment related to this chapter.

   PERSONAL INVENTORY ASSESSMENT

Management Skills Exercises

Learning activities in this section are aimed at helping you develop organization culture skills.

MyLab Management
Discussion Questions

Go to www.pearson.com/mylab/management to complete the problems marked with this icon ⭐.

⭐ Cases

Zappos Doesn't Sell Shoes–It "Delivers WOW"

The Challenge Case "Zappos Doesn't Sell Shoes—It 'Delivers WOW'" (p. 438) and its related Challenge Case Summary were written to help you better understand the management concepts contained in this chapter. Answer the following discussion questions about the Challenge Case to better understand how concepts relating to organization culture be applied in a company such as Zappos.

18-4 When Tony Hsieh came on board at Zappos, what first step would you have advised him to take to establish the customer-focused organization culture? Why is this the first step you would have recommended?

18-5 Based on the information provided, including Hsieh's vision for Zappos, which type of culture—a clan, market, hierarchy, or adhocracy culture—is the most appropriate for the company? Why?

18-6 Discuss how you would ensure that Zappos's organization culture remains a high-performance culture.

Testing the Health of Goldman Sachs's Culture

Read the case and answer the questions that follow. Studying this case will help you better understand how concepts relating to organization culture can be applied in a company such as Goldman Sachs.

When the real estate bubble, financial crisis, and major recession triggered waves of home foreclosures and lay-offs, many saw investment banks as the villains. Among the supposed bad guys was Goldman Sachs, which recently settled with the Securities and Exchange Commission for $550 million. However, defenders—including CEO Lloyd Blankfein—have pointed out that Goldman's strong culture enabled it to weather the storm and continue to lure great employees and prominent customers.

If Goldman's culture is so great, how did the firm get caught up in the financial collapse at all? One explanation is that several forces caused management to drift away from upholding its traditional values. The investment bank was founded more than 140 years ago. Growth during the 1970s prompted the firm to lay out in writing its principles for business conduct. Today, the 14 principles, starting with "Our clients' interests always come first," appear on Goldman's website and are handed out to all new employees. But for a time, Goldman struggled to compete while putting clients first. Deregulation brought more firms into investment banking, and larger banks were willing to take risks that Goldman had avoided taking. When those risks were profitable, Goldman looked bad if it did not play. In addition, growth itself was a challenge because taking on more clients meant being less selective in choosing those clients.

Nevertheless, Goldman has remained a desirable employer. The firm hires less than 3 percent of those who apply to be analysts or associates—jobs that involve working 70 or more hours per week. In addition, Goldman has landed a spot on *Fortune* magazine's list of great places to work every year since 1998, when the magazine started publishing the list. Because the rankings are based on feedback from employees, at least *some* employees must love Goldman. Their reasons could be the six- and seven-figure earnings common of jobs in the financial industry or perhaps perks such as the on-site health club and lectures by celebrities. But what employees consistently tell *Fortune* is that they primarily value the chance to be part of an elite team in a close-knit working community where their ideas are valued. They are also making major investment decisions that keep capitalism operating globally.

Artifacts of a prosperity-valuing culture abound at Goldman's headquarters in Manhattan. Like elegant attire, the building itself is a model of understated luxury, with no logo on the outside. Employees converge away from public view in the 11th-floor Sky Lobby, which features a beautiful coffee bar intended to promote informal communication. A spiral staircase leads from the Sky Lobby down a floor to the fitness center, which charges a monthly fee. The cafeteria not only is unsubsidized but also adjusts prices based on demand, just like the prices of financial securities are adjusted. Goldman assumes that its employees would rather take their compensation in dollars and decide what to buy—say, lunch at the cafeteria or in one of the restaurants the firm lured to the block.

As Goldman moves forward, it is trying to reinforce the healthiest aspects of its culture and to fix where it has drifted away from those aspects. In selecting employees, recruiters continue to focus on teamwork skills, such as flexibility and communication. At the same time, the firm has crafted additional rules for limiting risks and has rolled out a training program to help employees apply the values of making ethical, client-focused decisions.[46]

Questions

18-7 How would you define the organization culture of Goldman Sachs? Is it an environment where you would enjoy working?

18-8 Using the Competing Values Framework, what type of culture exists at Goldman Sachs? Explain your reasoning.

18-9 What advice would you give Goldman's management for maintaining a healthy culture, especially regarding the ethics and customer dimensions of its culture?

Experiential Exercises

Exploring the Values of New Recruits

Directions. Read the following scenario and then perform the listed activities. Your instructor may want you to perform the activities as an individual or in a group. Follow all of your instructor's directions carefully.

You are the head of the human resource department at a major real estate investment company that is involved in buying and selling commercial real estate around the world. You have a new job opening, and next week you will be going to the Kelly School of Business at Indiana University to interview graduating students who might fill this position. Today you are meeting with a small group of human resources personnel to develop a plan for discovering, during the job interviews, prospective job applicants' personal values. You and your team understand that discovering such values is an important part of the organizational socialization process.

Sales Executive Opening
Opening: Chicago Sales Executive
Company: Real Estate Sales Worldwide Number of Employees: 215 employees
Salary: USD 50,000/year
Benefits: Medical, dental, vision, 401(k), and vacation
Industry: Real estate
Location: Chicago, Illinois
Status: Full-time, entry-level employee
Career: No experience necessary
Education Required: Bachelor's degree
Expectations of Employee: Team-oriented individual will be successful in direct sales, possess time management skills, contribute to overall marketing plan, provide innovative ideas, and increase sales volume in slow periods.
Essential Job Duties Include: Soliciting new real estate buyers in the local market, following furnished sales leads, designing and executing strategies to meet sales goals, analyzing market trends, attending networking events, attending trade shows, scheduling property tours with customers, making sales presentations, and scheduling meetings with customers.

Directions. Your instructor will divide your class into small groups and designate who will be the head of human resources. This individual will lead the group in developing its plan. Later in the class, your instructor might ask someone from each group *actually to conduct* the planned employment interview with someone outside the group. This interview might be recorded and replayed in class for special discussion and learning opportunities.

You and Your Career

You are looking for a job and see an opening that piques your interest. You like the position and are qualified for it. In preparing for your employment interview, you decide to ask three questions about the organization's culture that will be vital to you in assessing the likelihood of your career flourishing with the company. List the three questions that you believe would help you assess the degree of career success you might have with the company. Explain why you would ask each question.

_____

_____

_____

Building Your Management Skills Portfolio

Your Management Skills Portfolio is a collection of activities specially designed to demonstrate your management knowledge and skill. Be sure to save your work. Taking your printed portfolio to an employment interview could prove helpful.

The portfolio activity for this chapter is about organizational culture in the French multinational hotel chain Accor. Read the following case about the AccorHotels and perform the skills activities that follow.

AccorHotels has 250,000 employees working in around 4,000 hotels across the world. The corporation recognizes that it is their employees that bring the business to life. Employees are encouraged to ensure that all guests have a great experience, create long-standing relationships through courtesy and service, and be spontaneous and show initiative. AccorHotels call their employees "Heartists," an embodiment of superior hospitality, curiosity, and inventiveness, all of which comes from the heart. In 2016, AccorHotels initiated this cultural transformation founded on empowerment and autonomy. Guests are promised that they will feel welcomed and employees are promised that they will feel valued. Employees are encouraged to share knowledge and experience at every level.

Skills Activities

Assume that you are opening an Accor Hotel in your own town or city. The last part of your planning is to design and implement the organizational culture that you would like to have in your branch of the hotel. Perform the organizational culture planning tasks that follow.

18-10 Write a paragraph describing the type of organization culture you would like to establish at your AccorHotel. Be sure to include all of the values you want for the hotel.

_____

_____

_____

_____

18-11 List and discuss in detail five cultural artifacts you would use to implement and maintain the values included in your organizational culture vision.

Artifact 1:

_____

_____

_____

What organizational culture value does this artifact emphasize, and how?

_____

_____

_____

Artifact 2:

_____

_____

_____

What organizational culture value does this artifact emphasize, and how?

_____

_____

_____

Artifact 3:

_____

_____

_____

What organizational culture value does this artifact emphasize, and how?

_____

_____

_____

Artifact 4:

_____

_____

_____

What organizational culture value does this artifact emphasize, and how?

_____

_____

_____

_____

Artifact 5:

_____

_____

_____

_____

What organizational culture value does this artifact emphasize, and how?

_____

_____

_____

_____

MyLab Management
Writing Assignments

If your instructor has assigned this activity, go to www.pearson.com/mylab/management for the following assisted-graded writing assignments:

Assisted-Grading Questions

18-12 Define *organization culture* and explain why organization culture skill is valuable to managers.

18-13 How would you turn an unhealthy organization culture into a healthy one? Be as specific as possible.

Endnotes

1. John Koetsier, "Zappos' Culture Coach: How 'Squishy' Stuff Like Culture Took Us to a Billion Dollars in Revenue," *VentureBeat*, February 17, 2013, http://venturebeat.com; Katherine Duncan, "The Positive Influence," *Entrepreneur* (March 2013): 62; Jeffrey Hollender, "Lessons We Can All Learn from Zappos CEO Tony Hsieh," *Guardian*, March 14, 2013, http://www.theguardian.com; Zappos, "Zappos Family Core Values," http://about.zappos.com, accessed April 15, 2014; Zappos, "Zappos Blogs," http://blogs.zappos.com, accessed April 15, 2014; Bill Taylor, "Why Amazon Is Copying Zappos and Paying Employees to Quit," *Harvard Business Review*, April 14, 2014, http://blogs.hbr.org.

2. Maria A. Dixon and Debbie S. Dougherty, "Managing the Multiple Meanings of Organizational Culture in Interdisciplinary Collaboration and Consulting," *Journal of Business Communication* 47, no. 1 (January 2010): 3–19.

3. For notable research on the effects of organization culture on workplace performance, see Md. Zabid Abdul Rashid, Murali Sambasivan, and Juliana Johari, "The Influence of Corporate Culture and Organizational Commitment on Performance," *Journal of Management Development* 22 (2003): 708; see also Lynn Waters, "Cultivate Corporate Culture and Diversity," *Nursing Management* 35 (2004): 36.

4. J. Chatman and D. F. Caldwell, "People and Organizational Culture: A Profile Comparison Approach to Assessing Person-Organization Fit," *Academy of Management Journal* (September 1991): 487–516. For discussion of seven key drivers to good culture see J. Iraci, "Can Corporate Culture Be Measured?," *The RMA Journal* 99 no. 7 (2017): 11, 12–16.

5. Mary G. Locke and Lucy Guglielmino, "The Influence of Subcultures on Planned Change in a Community College," *Community College Review* 34, no. 2 (October 2006): 108–128.

6. For an interesting study exploring African American female executives and dominant culture organizations, see Patricia S. Parker, "Negotiating Identity in Raced and Gendered Workplace Interactions: The Use of Strategic Communication by African American Women Senior Executives within Dominant Culture Organizations," *Communication Quarterly* 50, no. 3/4 (Summer 2002): 251.

7. Stefan Stern, "Wake Up and Smell the Coffee on Your Corporate Culture," *Financial Times* (March 27, 2007): 12.

8. Victor S. L. Tan, "Transforming Your Organization," *New Straits Times* (June 16, 2007): 58.

9. "Worldwide Business Conduct Manual," Procter & Gamble, http://www.pg.com/translations/ww_business_manual_pdf/English_WWB_Conduct_Manual.pdf, accessed August 14, 2017.

10. B. C. Madu, "Organization Culture as Driver of Competitive Advantage," *Journal of Academic and Business Ethics* 5 (2012): 1–9. Organization culture is so important that some organizations appoint a vice president of corporate culture; see HDL, Inc., "Health Diagnostic Laboratory Names Scott Blackwell Vice President of Corporate Culture," *Lab Business Week* (2012): 16.

11. Mike Foster, "Be Positive!," *Construction Distribution* 10, no. 2 (October/November 2007): 80.

12. Julie Verity, "Understanding Success: Economics and Human Nature," *Business Strategy Series* 8, no. 5 (2007): 330.

13. "Finding the Right Fit: Nearly Half of Workers Have Misjudged an Employer's Culture," *PR Newswire* (May 23, 2007).

14. Douglas MacMillan, "A Twitter Code of Conduct," *BusinessWeek*, May 8, 2009, http://www.businessweek.com.

15. Kim S. Cameron and Robert E. Quinn, *Diagnosing and Changing Organizational Culture* (Reading, MA: Addison-Wesley, 1999). For discussion of the importance of organization culture in organizations adapting to changing environments, see D. P. Costanza, N. Blacksmith, M. R. Coats, J. B. Severt, and A. H. Decostanza, "The Effect of Adaptive Organizational Culture on Long-Term Survival," *Journal of Business and Psychology* 31, no. 3 (2016): 361–381.

16. Southwest.com, http://southwest.com/about_swa/?ref=abtsw_fgn, accessed November 26, 2007.

17. Cameron and Quinn, *Diagnosing and Changing Organizational Culture* 32.

18. For an interesting discussion of the problems that can arise in mentoring relationships, see Dawn E. Chandler, Lillian Eby, and Stacy McManus, "When Mentoring Goes Bad," *MIT Sloan Management Review*, May 24, 2010, http://sloanreview.mit.edu.

19. Google's corporate culture, www.google.com/corporate/culture.html, accessed November 26, 2007. To explore the significance of Google's corporate culture, see Antonio Ortega-Parra, and Miguel Ángel Sastre-Castillo, "Impact of Perceived Corporate Culture on Organizational Commitment," *Management Decision* 51, no. 5 (2013): 1071–1083.

20. The environment in most professional services firms fits the description of a market culture. For a discussion about how a consulting firm intentionally challenged a tenet of that culture by instituting planned, uninterrupted time off, see Leslie A. Perlow and Jessica L. Porter, "Making Time Off Predictable—and Required," *Harvard Business Review*, October 2009, http://hbr.org.

21. Cameron and Quinn, *Diagnosing and Changing Organizational Culture* 186–201; Yung-Ho Cho, Gyu-Chang Yu, Min-Kyu Joo, and Chris Rowley, "Changing Corporate Culture over Time in South Korea," *Asia Pacific Business Review* 20, no. 1 (2014): 9.

22. Cameron and Quinn, *Diagnosing and Changing Organizational Culture* 233–245.

23. Howard Risher, "Fostering a Performance-Driven Culture in the Public Sector," *Public Manager* 36, no. 3 (Fall 2007): 51–56; Kyle Ristig, "Corporate Culture and Performance," Allied Academies International Conference, Academy of Organizational Culture, Communications and Conflict, *Proceedings*18, no. 2 (2013): 25.

24. Xerox website, http://www.xerox.com/about-xerox/company-facts/enae.html; Xerox UAE Careers, http://www.xeroxcareers.com/en-ae/about-us/default.aspx.

25. Yi-Jen Chen, "Relationships among Service Orientation, Job Satisfaction, and Organizational Commitment in the International Tourist Hotel Industry," *Journal of American Academy of Business* 1, no. 2 (September 2007): 71.

26. For an interesting discussion of what employers can do to enhance job satisfaction among their employees, see Paul Fairlie, "10 Ways to Make Work More Meaningful," *Workforce Management*, February 2010, http://www.workforce.com.

27. Jacquelyn Smith, "America's Reputable Companies," *Forbes*, April 4, 2012, http://www.forbes.com/sites/jacquelynsmith/2012/04/04/americas-most-reputable-companies, accessed May 26, 2012.

28. The remainder of this section is based on Jean Thilmany, "Supporting Ethical Employees," *HR Magazine* 52, no. 9 (September 2007): 105.

29. Brian Hindo, "At 3M, a Struggle between Efficiency and Creativity; How CEO George Buckley Is Managing the Yin and Yang of Discipline and Imagination," *BusinessWeek* (June 11, 2007): 8.

30. Mathew L. Sheep, "Nurturing the Whole Person: The Ethics of Workplace Spirituality in a Society of Organizations," *Journal of Business Ethics* 66, no. 4 (2006): 357–375.

31. Jean-Claude Garcia-Zamor, "Workplace Spirituality and Organizational Performance," *Public Administration Review* 63, no. 3 (May/June 2003): 355.

32. Jeff Mortimer, "Help Wanted: New Blood, Ideas Must Fuel Inclusive, Expanding Corporate Culture," *Automotive News*, October 29, 2007, T184.

33. Betsy Morris, "New Rule: The Customer Is King," July 11, 2006, CNNMoney.com.

34. The following section draws heavily from M. Higgins, Craig Mcallaster, Samuel C. Certo, and James P. Gilbert, "Using Cultural Artifacts to Change and Perpetuate Strategy," *Journal of Change Management* 6, no. 4 (December 2006): 397–415.

35. http://www.microsoft.com/about/en/us/default.aspx, accessed December 1, 2010.

36. Michelle V. Rafter, "The Hive Mind at Work," *Workforce Management*, May 2010, http://www.workforce.com.

37. This coverage is based on discussion of Lee Iacocca and Chrysler in Harrison M. Trice and Janice M. Beyer, *The Cultures of Work Organizations* (Upper Saddle River, NJ: Prentice Hall, 1993), 271–272; and J. F. Coates, "My Ideal Client*," *Technological Forecasting and Social Change* 113 (2016): 79–81.

38. Ann Goldman, "How to Write a Values Statement That Really Means Something," http://www.frontrangesource.com/how-to-write-a-values-statement-that-really-means-something/, accessed August 14, 2017.

39. J. Kerr and J. W. Slocum, Jr., "Managing Corporate Culture through Reward Systems," *Academy of Management Executive* 19, no. 4 (2005): 130. See also R. Prouska, A. G. Psychogios, and Y. Rexhepi, "Rewarding Employees in Turbulent Economies for Improved Organizational Performance," *Personnel Review* 45, no. 6 (2016): 1259–1280.

40. This section is based largely on Catherine Filstad, "How Newcomers Use Role Models in Organizational Socialization," *Journal of Workplace Living* 16 (2004): 396–410. For useful discussion regarding organizational socialization in an international context see C. Fu, Y. Hsu, M. A. Shaffer, and H. Ren, "A Longitudinal Investigation of Self-Initiated Expatriate Organizational Socialization," *Personnel Review* 46, no. 2 (2017): 182–204.

41. Michael Stewart, "The Road to Recovery: Four Crucial Steps to Regain Employees' Trust," *Workforce Management*, June 2010, http://www.workforce.com.

42. For discussion of the importance of trust in corporate culture, see I. M. Millstein and H. J. Gregory, "Rebuilding Trust: The Corporate Governance Opportunity for 2012," *Corporate Governance Advisor* 20, no. 2 (2012): 8–12.

43. "That 'Unique' Organizational Culture at Jones Day: Actually Already the Prevailing Model in Social Media," *Law and More*, May 24, 2010, http://lawandmore.typepad.com; Elie Mystal, "New Recruits at Jones Day Better Make Great Pets," *Above the Law*, May 24, 2010, http://abovethelaw.com; Elie Mystal, "Jones Day: Secrecy Breeds Strength?," *Above the Law*, September 14, 2009, http://abovethelaw.com.

44. "Use of Corporate Culture to Spur Growth in a Firm," *Africa News* (October 16, 2007).

45. Developed by the Institute for Business, Technology, and Ethics (IBTE), www.customerfocusconsult.com/articles/articles_template.asp?ID=36. For discussion on the positive effect of humility as a component of organizational culture, see J. N. Hook, D. Boan, D. E. Davis, J. D. Aten, J. M. Ruiz, and T. Maryon, "Cultural Humility and Hospital Safety Culture," *Journal of Clinical Psychology in Medical Settings* 23, no. 4 (2016): 402–409.

46. Anne VanderMey, "Yes, Goldman Sachs Really Is a Great Place to Work," *Fortune*, January 16, 2014, http://money.cnn.com; Goldman Sachs, "Why Goldman Sachs? Our Culture," http://www.goldmansachs.com, accessed April 15, 2014; Goldman Sachs, "Who We Are," http://www.goldmansachs.com, accessed April 15, 2014; Peter Lattman, "An Ex-Trader, Now a Sociologist, Looks at the Changes in Goldman," *New York Times*, September 30, 2013, http://dealbook.nytimes.com; HBR Ideacast, "How Goldman Sachs Drifted," *Harvard Business Review*, October 3, 2013, http://blogs.hbr.org.

19 Controlling, Information, and Technology

TARGET SKILL

Controlling Skill: the ability to use information and technology to ensure that an event occurs as it was planned to occur

CONTROLLING SKILL AND YOUR CAREER

Controlling skill will be of great value to you in enhancing your career. This skill will help you use information and technology to ensure that events occur as you planned. This ability contributes to organizational success, builds your image as a competent manager, makes you valuable to your organization, and supports promotions as you build your career.

OBJECTIVES

To help build my *controlling skill*, when studying this chapter, I will attempt to acquire:

19-1 A definition of control

19-2 A thorough understanding of the controlling process

19-3 Insights into the relationship between power and control

19-4 An understanding of the role of information in the control process

19-5 An appreciation of the importance of an information system (IS) to an organization

MyLab Management Chapter Warm Up

If your instructor has assigned this activity, go to www.pearson.com/mylab/management to complete the chapter warm up.

CHALLENGE CASE

Domino's Goes High-Tech with Easy Order

Just a decade ago, Domino's was on the brink of disaster. In 2008, the firm had $1.7 billion in debt but only $1.4 billion in revenue. Stores were shutting down, and the stock price was less than $3 per share.

Fast-forward to today. The company now has over $2.7 billion in sales, significant profits for franchisees, and a stock price near $200 per share.[1] How did it do it? First, the company changed its recipe to improve taste. But second, it went high-tech, so high-tech that the company is now in the top 10 list of businesses with the most online transactions—right up there with Amazon and Apple.[2] The technology goal for Domino's was to create an ordering system that would allow customers to place an order in 17 seconds or less. That's a difficult objective given that Domino's has 34 million possible combinations of toppings, sauce, and crust. In addition, to make certain that these orders are correct, control processes had to be established.

Kevin Vasconi, chief information officer at Domino's, attributes the success of Domino's to its Easy Order system. Technology has enabled the worldwide pizza chain to go from near bankruptcy to one of the most successful restaurant success stories of the twenty-first century. And it all begins at the top of the firm. "That's why I took the job," said Vasconi. "What a great opportunity as a technologist to work for a company where the CEO is already convinced that technology can change the business."

The Easy Order system permits customers to order pizza in many different ways, such as via an app, voice, and television, and even sending a pizza emoji through Twitter. This revolutionary approach to ordering pizza has enabled the company to get the ordering process down to just 17 seconds and to monitor the accuracy of each order. For Easy Order to be effective, all the company's stores had to install the software and technological infrastructure. And though expensive, this step proved to be the key to the firm's success. "It was maybe the most important technology decision made in the last decade at Domino's," said Vasconi.

Kvitka Fabian/Shutterstock

With Domino's Easy Order technology, the company went from the brink of disaster to being on the top 10 list of businesses with the most online transactions.

No matter how customers utilize Easy Order—whether through a smartwatch, text message, smart TV, or social media—it's important that customers have a positive transaction. More than half of the orders Domino's receives now come from the firm's Internet and mobile presence. For that reason, Vasconi places a great deal of importance on customers' perceptions of their interaction with Easy Order. "We want that," said Vasconi, "to be the best experience."[3]

THE CONTROLLING AND TECHNOLOGY CHALLENGE

According to the Challenge Case, Domino's implemented the Easy Order system to improve the customer ordering process. This involves the management function called control, but it also involves technology. Control can help professionals at Domino's and other organizations improve operations. The following chapter material elaborates on the control function as a whole. Major topics in this chapter are fundamentals of controlling, power and control, information, and information systems.

The Fundamentals of Controlling

19-1 A definition of control

As the scale and complexity of modern organizations grow, so does the problem of control in organizations. Therefore, prospective managers need a working knowledge of the essentials of the controlling function.[4] The following sections provide a definition of control, a definition of the process of controlling, and a discussion of the various types of control that can be used in organizations.

Defining Control

Stated simply, **control** entails ensuring that an event occurs as it was planned to occur.[5] As implied by this definition, planning and control are nearly inseparable functions.[6] In fact, these two functions have been called the Siamese twins of management.[7]

According to Murphy's Law, anything that can go wrong will go wrong.[8] Murphy's Law is a lighthearted adage that makes the serious point that managers should continually control—that is, they should check to see that organizational activities and processes are going as planned. This law reminds managers to remain alert for possible problems because, even if a management system appears to be operating well, it might actually be eroding under the surface. Therefore, managers must always seek feedback on how the system is performing and make corrective changes whenever warranted.

Controlling is the process managers go through to control. According to Robert Mockler, controlling is

a systematic effort by business management to compare performance to predetermined standards, plans, or objectives to determine whether performance is in line with these standards and presumably to take any remedial action required to see that human and other corporate resources are being used in the most effective and efficient way possible in achieving corporate objectives.[9]

For example, production workers generally have daily production goals. At the end of each working day, the number of units produced by each worker is recorded so that weekly production levels can be determined. If these weekly totals are significantly below weekly goals, the supervisor must take corrective action to ensure that actual production levels equal planned production levels. On the other hand, if production goals are being met, the supervisor should allow work to continue as it has in the past.[10]

The following sections discuss the controlling subsystem and provide more details about the control process itself.

The Controlling Subsystem

As with the planning, organizing, and influencing functions described in earlier chapters, controlling can be viewed as a subsystem of the overall management system. The purpose of this subsystem is to help managers enhance the success of the overall management system through effective controlling. **Figure 19.1** shows the specific components of the controlling subsystem.

The Controlling Process

19-2 A thorough understanding of the controlling process

As **Figure 19.2** illustrates, the controlling process has three main steps:

1. Measuring performance
2. Comparing measured performance to standards
3. Taking corrective action

Measuring Performance

Before managers can determine what must be done to make an organization more effective and efficient, they must measure current organizational performance.[11] Before they can take such a measurement, however, they must establish some unit of measure that gauges performance and observe the quantity of this unit as generated by the employee whose performance is being measured.[12]

Figure 19.1

Specific components of the controlling subsystem

Objectives
The controller (or comptroller) is responsible for all accounting activities within the organization.

Functions

1. *General accounting*—Maintain the company's accounting books, accounting records, and forms.

   a. Prepare balance sheets, income statements, and other statements and reports
   b. Give the president interim reports on operations for the recent quarter and fiscal year to date
   c. Supervise the preparation and filing of reports to the Securities and Exchange Commission (SEC)

2. *Budgeting*—Prepare a budget outlining the company's future operations and cash requirements.

3. *Cost accounting*—Determine the cost to manufacture a product and prepare internal reports for management of the processing divisions.

   a. Develop standard costs
   b. Accumulate actual cost data
   c. Prepare reports that compare standard costs to actual costs and highlight unfavorable differences

4. *Performance reporting*—Identify individuals in the organization who control activities and prepare reports to show how well or how poorly they perform.

5. *Data processing*—Assist in the analysis and design of a computer-based information system. Frequently, the data-processing department is under the controller, and the controller is involved in management of that department as well as other communications equipment.

6. *Other duties*—Other duties that may be assigned to the controller by the president or by corporate bylaws include:

   a. Tax planning and reporting
   b. Service departments such as mailing, telephone, janitors, and filing
   c. Forecasting
   d. Corporate social relations and obligations

- *How to Measure.* A manager who wants to measure the performance of five janitors, for example, first must establish units of measure that represent janitorial performance—such as the number of floors swept, the number of windows washed, or the number of lightbulbs changed. After designating these units of measure, the manager has to determine the number of each of these units accomplished by each janitor. The process of determining both the units of measure and the number of units associated with each janitor furnishes the manager with a measure of janitorial performance.

- *What to Measure.* Managers must always keep in mind that a wide range of organizational activities can be measured as part of the control process. For example, the amounts and types of inventory on hand are commonly measured to control inventory, whereas the quality of goods and services being produced is commonly measured to control product quality. Performance measurements can also relate to various effects of production, such as the degree to which a particular manufacturing process pollutes the atmosphere.

The degree of difficulty in measuring various types of organizational performance, of course, is determined primarily by the activity being measured. For example, it is far more difficult to measure the performance of a highway maintenance worker than it is to measure the performance of a student enrolled in a college-level management course.

Comparing Measured Performance to Standards

Once managers have taken a measure of organizational performance, their next step in controlling is to compare this measure against some standard. A **standard** is the level of activity established to serve as a model for evaluating organizational performance.[13] The performance evaluated can be that of the organization as a whole or that of some individuals working within the organization.[14] Standards may involve past performance (e.g., a company's performance last

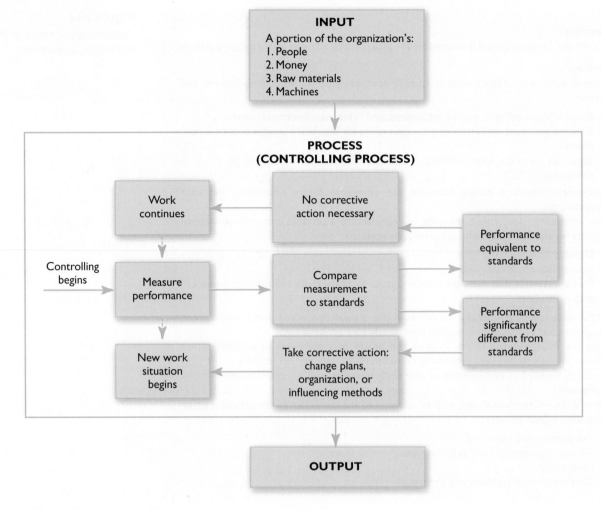

Figure 19.2 The controlling subsystem

year) or they may involve external parties (e.g., a competitor's performance or the performance of an entire industry).[15] In essence, standards are the yardsticks that determine whether organizational performance is adequate or inadequate.[16]

Studying operations at General Electric (GE) will give us some insights into the different kinds of standards managers can establish. GE has established the following standards:

1. **Profitability standards**—In general, these standards indicate how much money GE would like to make as profit over a given period—that is, its return on investment. GE is using computerized preventive maintenance more often on its equipment to help maintain profitability standards. Such maintenance programs have reduced labor costs and equipment downtime, and have thereby helped raise company profits.

2. **Market position standards**—These standards indicate the share of total sales in a particular market that GE would like to have relative to that of its competitors. GE market position standards were set by company chair John F. Welch, Jr., in 1988, when he announced that henceforth, any product his company offers must achieve the highest or second-highest market share compared to similar products offered by competitors or that product will be eliminated or sold to another firm.

3. **Productivity standards**—How much various segments of the organization should produce is the focus of these standards. Management at GE has found that one of the best ways to convince organization members to commit themselves to increasing company productivity is simply to treat them with dignity and make them feel part of the GE team.

4. **Product leadership standards**—GE intends to assume a leading position in product innovation in its field. Product leadership standards indicate what must be done to attain

such a position. Reflecting this interest in innovation, GE has pioneered the development of synthetic diamonds for industrial use. In fact, GE is considered the leader in this area, having recently discovered a method for making synthetic diamonds at a purity of 99.9 percent. In all probability, such diamonds will eventually be used as a component of super-high-speed computers.

5. **Personnel development standards**—Standards in this area include the type of training programs that GE personnel should undergo to expand their skill sets. GE's commitment to sophisticated training technology indicates the seriousness with which the company takes personnel development standards. Company training sessions are commonly supported by sophisticated technology, such as large-screen projection systems, computer-generated visual aids, combined video and computer presentations, and laser videos.

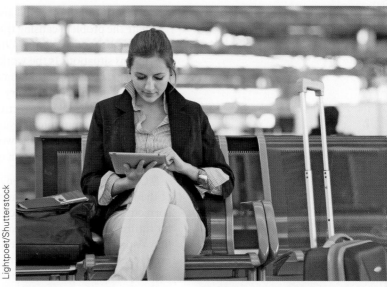

Lightpoet/Shutterstock

Performance standards for an airline would include on-time arrivals, wait times for service at the ticket counter, productivity, and customer satisfaction scores. Can you think of other standards that might apply?

6. **Employee attitudes standards**—These standards indicate what types of attitudes GE managers should strive to inculcate in GE employees. Like many other companies today, GE is trying to create in its employees positive attitudes toward product quality.

7. **Social responsibility standards**—GE recognizes its responsibility to make contributions to society. Standards in this area outline the levels and types of contributions that management believes GE should make. One recent activity that reflects GE's social responsibility standards is the renovation of San Diego's Vincent de Paul Joan Kroc center for the homeless, which was accomplished by work teams made up of GE employees. These teams painted, cleaned, and remodeled a building to create a better facility for some of San Diego's disadvantaged citizens.

8. **Standards reflecting the relative balance between short- and long-range goals**—These standards express the relative emphasis that should be placed on attaining various short- and long-range goals. GE recognizes that short-range goals exist to enhance the probability that long-range goals will be attained.

Successful managers pinpoint all the important areas of organizational performance and establish corresponding standards in each area.[17] Managers at American Airlines, for example, have set two specific standards for appropriate performance of its airport ticket offices: (1) At least 95 percent of the posted flight arrival times should be accurate, meaning that actual arrival times do not deviate more than 15 minutes from the posted times, and (2) at least 85 percent of customers coming to the airport ticket counter should not have to wait more than 5 minutes to be serviced.

Taking Corrective Action

After actual performance has been measured and compared with established performance standards, the next step in the controlling process is to take corrective action, if necessary. **Corrective action** is managerial activity aimed at bringing organizational performance up to the level of performance standards.[18] In other words, corrective action focuses on correcting the organizational mistakes that are hindering organizational performance. Before taking any corrective action, however, managers should make sure that the standards they are using were properly established and that their measurements of organizational performance are valid and reliable.[19]

- *Recognizing Problems.* At first glance, it seems a fairly simple proposition that a manager should take corrective action to eliminate a **problem**—that is, any factor within an organization that is a barrier to organizational goal attainment.[20] In practice, however, it often proves difficult to pinpoint the problem that is causing some undesirable organizational effect. Let us suppose that a performance measurement indicates that a certain worker is not adequately passing on critical information to fellow workers. If the manager is satisfied that the communication standards are appropriate and that the performance measurement information is both valid and reliable, the manager should take corrective action to eliminate the problem causing this substandard performance.

- *Recognizing Symptoms.* What exactly is the problem causing substandard communication in this situation? Is the worker is not communicating adequately simply because he or she doesn't want to communicate? Does the job make communication difficult? Does the worker need the necessary training to communicate in an appropriate manner? Before attempting to take corrective action, the manager must determine whether the worker's failure to communicate is a problem in itself or is a **symptom**—a sign that a problem exists.[21] For example, the worker's failure to communicate adequately could be a symptom of inappropriate job design or a cumbersome organizational structure.

Once the problem has been properly identified, corrective action can focus on one or more of the three primary management functions of planning, organizing, and influencing. That is, corrective action can include activities such as modifying past plans to make them more suitable for future organizational endeavors, making an existing organizational structure more suitable for existing plans and objectives, or restructuring an incentive program to ensure that efficient producers are rewarded more than inefficient producers. Note that because planning, organizing, and influencing are closely related, it is likely that the corrective action taken in one area will necessitate some corresponding action in one or both of the other two areas.

Many organizations use technology to help support their controlling activities. At discount retailer Stein Mart, for example, store managers use Oracle Retail, a suite of merchandising and planning tools, to help them minimize merchandising errors and take necessary corrective action. Stein Mart management recently purchased and implemented the Oracle system to help the company carry out its goals of delivering fresh merchandise to every store and gaining a thorough understanding of its unique customer base.[22]

MyLab Management Watch It

If your instructor has assigned this activity, go to www.pearson.com/mylab/management to complete the video exercise.

Power and Control

19-3 Insights into the relationship between power and control

To control successfully, managers must understand not only the control process but also how organization members relate to it. Up to this point, the chapter has emphasized the nonhuman variables of controlling. This section focuses on power, perhaps the most important human-related variable in the control process. The following sections present a definition of power, elaborate on the total power of managers, and list the steps managers can take to increase their power over other organization members.

A Definition of Power

Perhaps the two most-often-confused terms in management are *power* and *authority*. Authority was defined in Chapter 11 as the right to command or give orders. The extent to which an individual is able to influence others so that they respond to orders is called **power.**[23] The greater this ability, the more power an individual is said to have.

Power and control are closely related. To illustrate, after comparing actual performance with planned performance and determining that corrective action is necessary, a manager usually gives orders to implement this action. Although the orders are issued by virtue of the manager's organizational authority, they may or may not be followed precisely, depending on how much power the manager has over the individuals to whom the orders are addressed.

Business and management scholar and Stanford University professor Jeffrey Pfeffer claims that managers must learn how to wield power in order to advance their organization's agenda. In fact, he says, many highly competent professionals have floundered in management careers because they are uncomfortable with using power.[24] In the following sections, we describe the different types of power and the steps managers may take to increase their power.

Total Power of a Manager

The **total power** that a manager possesses is made up of two different kinds of power: position power and personal power. **Position power** is power derived from the organizational position that a manager holds.[25] In general, a manager moving from lower-level management to upper-level management accrues more position power. **Personal power** is power derived from a manager's relationships with others.[26]

Steps for Increasing Total Power

Managers can increase their total power by enhancing either their position power or their personal power, or both. Position power is generally enhanced by a move to a higher organizational position, but most managers have little personal control over when they will move up in an organization. Managers do have substantial control, however, over the amount of personal power they hold over other organization members. John P. Kotter stresses the importance of developing personal power:

> To be able to plan, organize, budget, staff, control, and evaluate, managers need some control over the many people on whom they are dependent. Trying to control others solely by directing them and on the basis of the power associated with one's position simply will not work—first, because managers are always dependent on some people over whom they have no formal authority, and second, because virtually no one in modern organizations will passively accept and completely obey a constant stream of orders from someone just because he or she is the "boss."[27]

To increase personal power, a manager should attempt to develop the following attitudes and beliefs in other organization members:[28]

1. **A sense of obligation toward the manager**—If a manager succeeds in developing this sense of obligation, other organization members will allow the manager to influence them to a certain extent. The basic strategy suggested for creating this sense of obligation is to do personal favors for people.
2. **A belief that the manager possesses a significant level of expertise within the organization**—In general, a manager's personal power increases as organization members perceive that the manager's level of expertise is significant. To raise perceptions of their expertise, managers must quietly make their notable achievements visible to others and create a successful track record and a solid professional reputation.

TIPS FOR MANAGING AROUND THE GLOBE

Australia: Cultural Differences in Management and Leadership

Effective use of power across cultures means successfully influencing others and using tactics that others consider appropriate. The Global Leadership & Organizational Behavior Effectiveness (Globe) Project 2014[29] examined the traits, exercise of power, and leadership styles of different cultures. For countries such as Australia, the disparity between non-Europeans in senior management and those in other work roles inevitably creates an imbalanced set of relationships.

Around 5 percent of senior business leaders in Australia do not have European roots, compared to 24 percent of the population. Australian managers from European backgrounds may look no different to those from the United States or from the United Kingdom, but the exercise of power and approach to leadership is subtly different; Australian managers are more egalitarian and favor individualism.

3. **A sense of identification with the manager**—The manager can strive to develop this identification by behaving in ways that other organization members respect and by espousing the goals, values, and ideals that the organization members commonly hold.[30] The following passage illustrates how a certain sales manager took steps to increase the degree to which his subordinates identified with him:

> One vice president of sales in a moderate-sized manufacturing company was reputed to be so much in control of his sales force that he could get them to respond to new and different marketing programs in a third of the time taken by the company's best competitors. His power over his employees was based primarily on their strong identification with him and what he stood for. Immigrating to the United States at age seventeen, this person worked his way up "from nothing." When made a sales manager in 1965, he began recruiting other young immigrants and sons of immigrants from his former country. When made vice president of sales in 1970, he continued to do so. In 1975, 85 percent of his sales force was made up of people whom he hired directly or who were hired by others he brought.[31]

4. **The perception that they are dependent on the manager**—The main strategy here is to convey clearly the amount of authority the manager has over organizational resources—not only those necessary for organization members to do their jobs but also those that organization members personally receive in forms such as salaries and bonuses. This strategy is aptly reflected in the managerial version of the Golden Rule: "He who has the gold makes the rules."

Making Controlling Successful

In addition to avoiding the potential barriers to successful controlling mentioned in the previous section, managers can perform certain activities to make the control process more effective. To increase the quality of the controlling subsystem, managers should make sure that controlling activities take all of the following factors into account.

Specific Organizational Activities Being Focused On

Managers should make sure that the various facets of the control process are appropriate to the control activity under consideration. For example, standards and measurements concerning a line worker's productivity are much different from standards and measurements concerning a vice president's productivity. Therefore, controlling ingredients related to the productivity of these individuals must be different if the control process is to be applied successfully.

Different Kinds of Organizational Goals

Control can be used for different purposes such as standardizing performance, protecting organizational assets from theft and waste, and standardizing product quality.[32] Managers should remember that the control process can be applied to many different facets of organizational life and that, if the organization will receive maximum benefit from controlling, each of these facets must be emphasized.

Timely Corrective Action

Some amount of time will necessarily elapse as managers gather control-related information, develop necessary reports based on this information, and decide what corrective action should be taken to eliminate a problem. However, managers should take the corrective action as promptly as possible and before the situation depicted by the gathered information changes. Unless corrective actions are timely, the organizational advantage of taking those actions may not materialize.

Communication of the Mechanics of the Control Process

Managers should also take steps to ensure that people know exactly what information is required for a particular control process, how that information is to be gathered and used to compile various reports, what the purposes of the various reports actually are, and what corrective actions are appropriate, given the information in those reports. The lesson here is simple: For control to be successful, all individuals involved in controlling must have a working knowledge of how the control process operates.[33]

Essentials of Information

As mentioned in the previous sections, *controlling* is the process of making things happen as planned. Of course, managers cannot make things happen as planned if they lack information on the manner in which various events in the organization occur. The remainder of this chapter discusses the fundamental principles of handling information in an organization by first presenting the essentials of information and then examining both information technology and information systems (ISs).

The process of developing information begins with gathering some type of facts or statistics, called **data.** Once gathered, data typically are analyzed. In general terms, **information** refers to details about a project or the set of conclusions derived from data analysis. In management terms, however, information refers to the set of conclusions derived from the analysis of data *that relate to the operation of an organization.* Before a project commences, it is important for team members to reach agreement on what the term *information* will mean to them. In this way, they will be assured of operating from a point of mutual understanding.[34]

As examples illustrating the relationship between data and information, managers gather data regarding pay rates that individuals receive within certain industries to collect information about how to develop competitive pay rates, data regarding hazardous-materials accidents to gain information about how to improve worker safety, and data regarding customer demographics to gain information about product demand in the future.[35] Large organizations often use information systems to help them spot market trends and respond quickly and efficiently.[36] In addition, many successful organizations are using the power of information systems to change the way they approach innovation.[37]

The information that managers receive heavily influences managerial decision making, which in turn determines the activities that will be performed within the organization, which ultimately determines the eventual success or failure of the organization. Some management writers consider information to be of such fundamental importance to the management process that they define *management* as the process of converting information into action through decision making.[38] The next sections discuss the factors that influence the value of information and how to evaluate information.

Factors Influencing the Value of Information

Some information is more valuable than other information.[39] The value of information is defined in terms of the benefit that can accrue to an organization through the use of that information.[40] The greater this benefit, the more valuable the information. Four primary factors determine the value of information:

1. Information appropriateness
2. Information quality
3. Information timeliness
4. Information quantity

In general, management should encourage the generation, distribution, and use of organizational information that is appropriate, of high quality, timely, and of sufficient quantity. Following this guideline will not necessarily guarantee that sound decisions are made, but it will ensure

19-4 An understanding of the role of information in the control process

Zappos strives for excellent customer service and relies on repeat business. Thus, call center employees are empowered to manage customer information and to act in ways that maximize customer satisfaction.

ZUMA Press, Inc./Alamy Stock Photo

that the resources necessary to make sound decisions are available.[41] Each of the factors that determines information value is discussed in more detail in the following paragraphs.

Information Appropriateness   **Information appropriateness** is defined in terms of how relevant the information is to the decision-making situation that the manager faces. If the information is quite relevant, then it is said to be appropriate. Generally, as the appropriateness of the information increases, so does the value of that information.

Figure 19.3 presents the characteristics of the information that is appropriate for the following common decision-making situations:[42]

1. Operational control
2. Management control
3. Strategic planning

Operational Control, Management Control, and Strategic Planning Decisions   *Operational control decisions* relate to ensuring that specific organizational tasks are carried out effectively and efficiently. *Management control decisions* relate to obtaining and effectively and efficiently using the organizational resources necessary to reach organizational objectives. *Strategic planning decisions* relate to determining organizational objectives and designating the corresponding actions necessary to reach those objectives.

As Figure 19.3 shows, the characteristics of appropriate information change as managers shift from making operational control decisions to making management control decisions, to making strategic planning decisions. Strategic planning decision makers need information that focuses on the relationship of the organization to its external environment, emphasizes the future, is wide in scope, and presents a broad view. The appropriate information for this type of decision is generally not completely current but tends to be more historical in nature. In addition, this information does not need to be completely accurate because strategic decisions tend to be characterized by some subjectivity and focus on areas that are difficult to measure, such as customer satisfaction.

The information appropriate for making operational control decisions has dramatically different characteristics from those of the information appropriate for making strategic planning decisions. Operational control decision makers need information that focuses, for the most part, on the internal organizational environment; emphasizes the performance history of the organization; and is well defined, narrow in scope, and detailed. In addition, the appropriate information for this type of decision is both extremely current and extremely accurate.

The information appropriate for making management control decisions generally has characteristics that fall somewhere between the extremes of appropriate operational control information and appropriate strategic planning information.

Figure 19.3

Characteristics of the information that is appropriate for decisions related to operational control, management control, and strategic planning

CHARACTERISTICS OF INFORMATION	OPERATIONAL CONTROL	MANAGEMENT CONTROL	STRATEGIC PLANNING
Source	Largely internal	⟶	External
Scope	Well defined, narrow	⟶	Very wide
Level of aggregation	Detailed	⟶	Aggregate
Time horizon	Historical	⟶	Future
Currency	Extremely current	⟶	Quite old/historical
Required accuracy	High	⟶	Low
Frequency of use	Very frequent	⟶	Infrequent

Information Quality

The second primary factor that determines the value of information is **information quality**—the degree to which information represents reality. The more closely information represents reality, the higher the quality and the greater the value of that information. In general, the higher the quality of information available to managers, the better equipped managers are to make appropriate decisions and the greater the probability that the organization will be successful over the long term.

Perhaps the most significant factor in producing poor-quality information is *data contamination*. Inaccurate data gathering can result in information that is of low quality and is thus a poor representation of reality.[43]

Information Timeliness

Information timeliness, the third primary factor that determines the value of information, is the extent to which the receipt of information allows decisions to be made and action to be taken so that the organization can gain some benefit from possessing the information. Information received by managers at the point when it can be used to the organization's advantage is said to be timely.

For example, a product may be selling poorly because its established market price is significantly higher than the price of competitive products. If management receives this information after the product has been discontinued, the information is not timely. If management receives it soon enough to be able to adjust the selling price of the product and thereby significantly increase sales, the information is timely.

Information Quantity

The fourth and final determinant of the value of information is **information quantity**—the amount of decision-related information that managers possess. Before making a decision, managers should assess the quantity of information they possess that relates to the decision being made. If this quantity is judged to be insufficient, more information should be gathered before managers make the decision. If the amount of information is judged to be as complete as necessary, managers can feel justified in making the decision.

Note that there is such a thing as *too* much information. According to Rick Feldcamp of Century Life of America, information overload—too much information to consider properly—can make managers afraid to make decisions and can result in important decisions going unmade. Information overload, commonly referred to as "paralysis by analysis," is generally considered the major cause of indecision in organizations.[44]

STEPS FOR SUCCESS

Getting a Handle on Big Data

The Internet and powerful computers let companies gather previously unimaginable amounts of data and analyze them to guide their decisions. This amount and type of data, known as big data, help managers make better-informed decisions. Raytheon and Harley-Davidson use computers in their factories to measure every detail of production activities. If a machine fails to turn a screw the correct number of times or the temperature in a painting booth varies from specifications, an error message triggers a correction. GE Aviation provides aircraft with sensors whose data, combined with historical data, help airlines schedule maintenance *before* parts fail.

However, working with this large volume of data poses challenges. An organization can overwhelm managers with a flood of unusable statistics. To make the most of big data, companies need a business goal for the information-analyzing project, not just a notion of sifting through data. Also, the information-analyzing project should deliver the information in a format that managers can understand. Presenting information in graphs, maps, meaningful colors, and other visual aids makes it more usable.[45]

Figure 19.4 Flowchart of main activities in evaluating information

Evaluating Information

Evaluating information is the process of determining whether the acquisition of specific information is justified. As with all evaluations of this kind, the primary concern of management should be to weigh the dollar value of the benefit gained from using some quantity of information against the cost of generating that information.

Identifying and Evaluating Data   According to the flowchart in **Figure 19.4**, the first major step in evaluating organizational information is to ascertain the value of that information by pinpointing the data to be analyzed and then determining the expected value or return to be gained from obtaining perfect information based on these data. Then this expected value is reduced by the amount of benefit that will not be realized because of the deficiencies and inaccuracies expected to appear in the information.

Evaluating the Cost of Data   Next, the expected value of the organizational information is compared with the expected cost of obtaining that information. If the expected cost does not exceed the expected value, the information should be gathered. If it does exceed the expected value, managers must either increase the information's expected value or decrease its expected cost before the information gathering can be justified. If neither of these objectives is possible, management cannot justify gathering the information.

The Information System (IS)

Technology consists of any type of equipment or process that organization members use in the performance of their work. This definition includes tools as old as a blacksmith's anvil and tools as new and innovative as virtual reality. This section discusses one segment of technology, **information technology (IT),** which is technology such as computers and telecommunication devices that focuses on the use of information in the performance of work.

19-5 An appreciation of the importance of an information system (IS) to an organization

An **information system (IS)** is a network of applications established within an organization to provide managers with the information that will assist them in decision making.[46] The following, more complete definition of an IS was developed by the Management Information System Committee of the Financial Executives Institute:

> A system designed to provide selected decision-oriented information needed by management to plan, control, and evaluate the activities of the corporation. It is designed within a framework that emphasizes profit planning, performance planning, and control at all levels. It contemplates the ultimate integration of required business information subsystems, both financial and nonfinancial, within the company.[47]

The typical IS is a formally established organizational network that gives managers continual access to vital information. For example, the IS normally provides managers with ongoing reports relevant to significant organizational activities such as sales, worker productivity, and labor turnover. Based on information they gain via an IS, managers make decisions that are aimed at improving organizational performance. Because the typical IS is characterized by computer usage, managers can use an IS to gain online access to company records and condensed information in the form of summaries and reports. Overall, the IS is a planned, systematic mechanism for providing managers with relevant information in a systematic fashion.[48]

The title of the specific organization member responsible for developing and maintaining an IS varies from organization to organization. In smaller organizations, a president or vice president may have this responsibility. In larger organizations, an individual with a title such as director of information systems or chief information officer (CIO) may be solely responsible for appropriately managing an entire IS department. The term *IS manager* is used in the sections that follow to indicate the person within an organization who has the primary responsibility for managing the IS. The term *IS personnel* is used to indicate the nonmanagement individuals within an organization who possess the primary responsibility for actually operating the IS. Examples of nonmanagement individuals are computer operators and computer programmers. The sections that follow describe an IS more fully and outline the steps that managers should take to establish an IS.

Describing the IS

The IS is perhaps best described by a summary of the steps necessary to operate it properly[49] and by a discussion of the different kinds of information that various managers need to make job-related decisions.

Operating the IS   IS personnel generally need to perform six sequential steps to operate an IS properly.[50] **Figure 19.5** summarizes the steps and indicates the order in which they are performed. The first step is to determine what information is needed within the organization, when it will be needed, and in what form it will be needed. Because the basic purpose of the IS is to assist management in making decisions, one way to begin determining management information needs is to analyze the following:

1. Decision areas in which management makes decisions
2. Specific decisions within these decision areas that management must actually make
3. Alternatives that must be evaluated in order to make these specific decisions

Figure 19.5

The six steps necessary to operate an IS properly, in order of their performance

STEP 1 — Determining information needs

STEP 2 — Determining and gathering appropriate data

STEP 3 — Summarizing data

STEP 4 — Analyzing data

STEP 5 — Transmitting information

STEP 6 — Using the information

For example, insights regarding what information management needs in a particular organization can be gleaned by understanding that management makes decisions in the area of plant and equipment; that a specific decision related to this area involves acquiring new equipment; and that two alternatives relating to this decision that must be evaluated are buying newly developed, high-technology equipment versus buying more standard equipment that has been around for some time in the industry.

PRACTICAL CHALLENGE: USING DATA FROM SOCIAL MEDIA

Big Data Scoring

Big Data Scoring, a European social media and big data scoring company, has been operating across Scandinavia and Central Europe since 2013. The company provides solutions to commercial banks, credit card providers, finance companies, and peer-to-peer lenders. Their processes—helping managers to detect, prevent, and remediate financial fraud and to calculate risks on large portfolios—have made individuals reconsider how they use social networks and whether they should be using them at all.

Among its many processes, Big Data Scoring analyzes data from Facebook to assess an individual's credit risk. It looks at the time spent by a user on the network along with the average educational level of the user's friends. According to Erki Kert, CEO of Big Data Scoring, people using Facebook for long periods of time every day are at greater risk than those who check in a few times a day.

It is unlikely that this form of credit scoring will take off in developed economies, as more conventional forms of credit checking have already been established and Big Data is not regulated by any national or independent authority. However, Kert maintains that the beneficiaries of their system are young individuals who don't have a personal financial history that can be used for credit scoring.[51]

The second major step in operating the IS is pinpointing and collecting data that will yield needed organizational information. This step is just as important as determining the information needs of the organization. If the collected data do not relate appropriately to the organization's information needs, it will be impossible to generate the needed information.

After information needs of the organization have been determined and appropriate data have been pinpointed and gathered, summarizing the data and analyzing the data are, respectively, the third and fourth steps that IS personnel generally should take to operate an IS properly. IS personnel find computer assistance to be the most beneficial in the performance of these two steps.

The fifth and sixth steps, respectively, are transmitting the information generated by the data analysis to the appropriate managers and getting those managers to use the information. The performance of these last two steps results in managerial decision making. Although each of the six steps is necessary for an IS to run properly, the time spent on performing each step will naturally vary from organization to organization.

Different Managers Need Different Kinds of Information   For maximum benefit, an IS must collect relevant data, transform that data into appropriate information, and transmit that information to the appropriate managers. However, appropriate information for one manager within an organization may not be appropriate information for another manager. Robert G. Murdick suggests that the degree of appropriateness of IS information for a manager depends on the activities for which the manager will use the information, the organizational objectives assigned to the manager, and the level of management at which the manager functions.[52] All of these factors are closely related. Murdick's thoughts on this matter are best summarized as shown in **Figure 19.6**. As you can see from this figure, the

Organizational Level	Type of Management	Manager's Organizational Objectives	Appropriate Information from IS	How IS Information Is Used
1. Top management	CEO, president, vice president	Survival of the firm, profit growth, accumulation and efficient use of resources	Environmental data and trends, summary reports of operations, exception reports of problems, forecasts	Corporate objectives, policies, constraints, decisions on strategic plans, decisions on control of the overall company
2. Middle management	Middle managers in such areas as marketing, production, and finance	Allocation of resources to assigned tasks, establishment of plans to meet operating objectives, control of operations	Summaries and exception reports of operating results, corporate objectives, policies, constraints, decisions on strategic plans, relevant actions and decisions of other middle managers	Operating plans and policies, exception reports, operating summaries, control procedures, decisions on resource allocations, actions and decisions related to other middle managers
3. First-line management	First-line managers whose work is closely related	Production of goods to meet marketing needs, supplying of budgets, estimates of resource requirements, movement and storage of materials	Summary reports of transactions, detailed reports of problems, operating plans and policies, control procedures, actions and decisions of related first-line managers	Exception reports, progress reports, resource requests, dispatch orders, cross-functional reports

Figure 19.6 Appropriate IS information under various sets of organizational circumstances

overall job situations of top managers, middle managers, and first-line managers are significantly different, so the kinds of information these managers need to perform their jobs satisfactorily are also significantly different.

Managing Information Systems

The effectiveness of an organization's IS depends largely on the ability of individuals within the organization to manage the IS properly. Three activities that improve IS effectiveness are managing user satisfaction, managing the IS workforce, and managing IS security. To the extent that employees are able to manage these activities, organizations will reap rewards in the form of IS effectiveness.

Different managers may require different kinds of information, and thus not all information systems are appropriate for all organizations. For example, for-profit firms gauge their success in terms of profitability: Do they make more money than they spend? Although nonprofits and government entities also track how their organizations use funds, they evaluate their performance using different criteria, such as how well their stakeholders are served. To support the operations of nonprofits and government agencies, Sage North America developed its MIP Fund Accounting financial management software. Sage's recent introduction of human resource (HR) modules that complement the software system enables users to automate their human resource activities with employee self-service, payroll, and tax-compliance capabilities.[53]

Managing User Satisfaction[54]

One of the most important determinants of IS effectiveness is the degree to which employees, or users, are satisfied with the IS. The degree of user satisfaction with the IS is determined by two main factors: (1) the quality of the IS and (2) the quality of the information. The quality of the IS refers to its ease of use. If a company's employees consider an IS easy to use, that IS would be labeled a high-quality IS. The quality of information, on the other hand, measures the degree to which the information produced by the IS is accurate and in a format required by the user. Taken together, then, users are satisfied with an IS when the IS is of high quality and provides high-quality information.

User satisfaction is important because of its direct influence on IS effectiveness. When users are satisfied with an IS, they will integrate the IS throughout their work routines and will become increasingly dependent on the IS. As users become increasingly dependent on the IS and increasingly integrate the IS into their routines, the IS becomes increasingly effective. These relationships are depicted in **Figure 19.7**.

Figure 19.7

A model of IS effectiveness

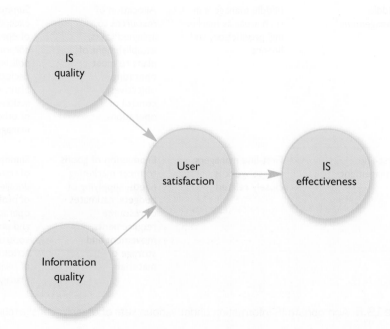

Managing the IS Workforce   During the economic and technological boom of the late 1990s, executives faced tremendous hurdles in terms of hiring and retaining IS employees.[55] Compared to other professionals during that period, IS professionals were considered more difficult to hire and retain because the economic and technological boom created a multitude of job prospects for IS professionals. Executives also found it quite expensive to replace the IS professionals who left; some estimates suggest that the cost of replacing an IS employee is 1 to 2.5 times his or her annual salary.[56]

In more recent years, almost two-thirds of leaders of technology firms report shortages of workers with IS skills.[57] As a result, companies have started to use workers in other countries to staff their IS departments—and many expect this trend to continue.[58] One survey indicated that almost half of firms outsource work to workers in other countries to reap the cost advantages.[59] Specifically, the cost of IS employees in other countries is much less than the cost of IS employees in the United States. This issue of lower costs partly explains why EDS, a Texas-based firm that offers its clients IT-based solutions, employs about 1,000 IS workers in India but expects this number to increase to nearly 20,000 in the near future.

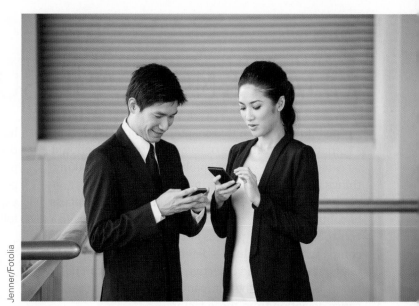
Jenner/Fotolia

The increasing use of mobile devices introduces a new security risk: Compared with the desktop and larger computers of the past, these devices are easily stolen, and if they contain private information that is not protected by strong passwords, thieves can steal private data as well as the hardware.

Despite the cost advantages associated with these overseas workers, this practice creates other problems, such as integrating domestic and nondomestic workforces, managing several languages and cultures, and defining global work expectations. In addition, U.S. firms might face a backlash from their U.S. customers who view the practice of outsourcing IS work to other countries as unpatriotic.

Managing IS Security   As corporations rely more heavily on information systems, they become more susceptible to security issues involving these systems. In particular, companies might lose valuable financial, employee, or customer data due to security breaches involving IS. In addition, companies become increasingly vulnerable to viruses, worms, and Trojan horses designed to paralyze information systems. As technology continues to change rapidly, it becomes more difficult for IS employees to prevent and eliminate these security threats.

In response to the increasing threat of security issues to information systems, private and public organizations around the world came together in 1992 to form the International Information Security Foundation. This committee produced a document known as the Generally Accepted System Security Principles (GASSP), which includes a set of best practices for IS managers.[60] The best practices listed within the GASSP provide a good starting point for managers when they are attempting to prevent security threats. **Table 19.1** provides an overview of some of the broad principles outlined in the GASSP.

TABLE 19.1   GASSP's Key Principles for Maintaining Information Security

Accountability principle	Organizations must clearly define and acknowledge information security accountability and responsibility.
Ethics principle	Organizations should use information and execute information security in an ethical manner.
Timeliness principle	Organizations should act in a timely manner to prevent or respond to breaches of and threats to information systems.
Assessment principle	Organizations should periodically assess the risks to information and information systems.
Equity principle	Management shall respect the rights of all employees when setting policy regarding security measures.

CHALLENGE CASE SUMMARY

The information in this chapter supports the notion that the efficient use of technology actually should be categorized as a control problem. Control is making things happen at Domino's in the way they were planned to happen. Going one step further, the process of controlling is the action that management takes to control. Ideally, this process at Domino's, as within any company, would include a determination of company plans, standards, and objectives so that steps can be taken to eliminate the company characteristics that cause deviation from these factors.

In theory, Domino's management should view controlling activities within the company as a subsystem of the organization's overall management system. For management to achieve organizational control, the controlling subsystem requires a portion of the people, money, and other resources available within the company.

The process portion of the controlling subsystem at Domino's involves three steps:

1. Measuring the performance levels of various selling units
2. Comparing these performance levels to predetermined performance standards for these units
3. Taking any corrective action necessary to make sure that actual performance levels are consistent with planned performance levels

Based on information in the Challenge Case, one area in which management should emphasize standards is with new technology, specifically the Easy Order system. Management has initiated this new process to ensure that customers can place an order quickly and also that the order is fulfilled correctly.

As the company gathers more information and considers potential corrective actions, management must be certain that each action is aimed at organizational problems rather than at symptoms of problems. For managers at Domino's to be successful in controlling, managers have to be aware not only of the intricacies of the control process itself but also of how to deal with people as they relate to the control process. With regard to people and control, managers must consider the amount of power they hold over organization members.

The total amount of power that Domino's management possesses comes from the positions they hold and from their personal relationships with other organization members. For example, the top managers already

have more position power than any other managers in the organization. Therefore, to increase their total power, the top managers would need to develop their personal power. Top management might attempt to expand their personal power by developing the following:

1. A sense of obligation in other organization members toward top managers
2. The belief in other organization members that top management has a significant level of task-related expertise
3. A sense of identification that other organization members have with top management
4. The perception in organization members that they are dependent on top management

Information at Domino's can be defined as conclusions derived from the analysis of data relating to the way in which the company operates. The case implies that managers at Domino's will be better able to make sound decisions, including better control decisions, because of the successful data handling achieved by its information system. One important factor in evaluating the overall worth of the information-handling system at Domino's would be the overall impact that the system has on the value of the information that company managers receive. A manager such as Kevin Vasconi must see that investing in reasonably priced technology can enhance the value of the information he receives and improve the appropriateness of his decisions. That is, investments in improving information system components can enhance the appropriateness, quality, timeliness, and quantity of information that Vasconi can use to make decisions. Vasconi must also believe and act on the notion that making investments in technology will significantly improve his decisions.

For a company such as Domino's to get maximum benefit from computer assistance, management must appropriately build each main ingredient of its information system (IS). The IS is the organizational network established to provide managers with the information that helps them make job-related decisions. Such a system would normally necessitate the use of several IS personnel who would help determine information needs at the company, help determine and collect appropriate Domino's data, summarize and analyze these data, transmit analyzed data to appropriate Domino's store managers, and generally help managers interpret received IS information.

To make sure managers receive appropriate information, IS personnel at Domino's must appreciate that different managers need different kinds of information. As an example, a top manager would normally need information that summarizes trends in consumer tastes, competitor moves, and productivity and costs related to various organizational units. Middle managers would need information that focuses more on specific operating units within the company, such as details regarding the performance of a specific store. Lower-level managers would normally need information about sales goals.

Assume that Vasconi has just decided to establish a new IS. Like any other company, Domino's would probably gain significantly by carefully planning the way in which its IS should be established. For example, perhaps the answers to the following questions, which might arise during the planning stage of the IS at Domino's, would be useful: Is an appropriate computer-based system being acquired and integrated? Does the company need new IS personnel, or will current personnel require further training to operate the new IS? Will managers need additional training to operate the new IS?

For the design and implementation stages of the new IS, Vasconi should seek answers to questions such as: How do we design the new IS based on managerial decision making? How can we ensure that the new IS, as designed and implemented, will actually be functional?

Vasconi, as well as IS personnel, should continually try to improve the new IS. All users of the IS should be aware of the symptoms of an inadequate IS and should constantly attempt to pinpoint and eliminate corresponding weaknesses. Suggestions for improving the new IS could include: (1) building additional cooperation between IS managers, IS personnel, and line managers; (2) stressing that the purpose of the IS is to provide managers with decision-related information; (3) using cost–benefit analysis to evaluate IS activities; and (4) ensuring that the IS operates in a people-conscious manner.

MyLab Management Assessing Your Management Skill

If your instructor has assigned this activity, go to www.pearson.com/mylab/management complete the exercise related to the Challenge Case.

DEVELOPING CONTROLLING SKILL

This section is specially designed to help you develop controlling skills. An individual's controlling skill is based on an understanding of the concepts and the ability to apply those concepts. The following activities will help to enhance your controlling skills in various organizational situations.

Class Preparation and Personal Study

To help you prepare for class, perform the activities outlined in this section. Performing these activities will help you enhance your classroom performance significantly.

Reflecting on Target Skill

On page 460, this chapter opens by presenting a target management skill along with related objectives outlining knowledge and understanding that you should aim to acquire related to that skill. Review this target skill and the list of objectives to make sure that you've acquired all pertinent information within the chapter. If you do not feel that you've reached a particular objective(s), study related chapter coverage until you do.

Know Key Terms

Understanding the following key terms is critical to your understanding of chapter material. Define each of these terms. Refer to the page(s) referenced after a term to check your definition or to gain further insight regarding the term.

Know How Management Concepts Relate

This section comprises activities that will further sharpen your understanding of management concepts. Answer essay questions as completely as possible.

19-1   With the help of examples, list and describe the differences between power and authority in management terms.

19-2   Information is vital to organizations. How are values and the benefits of that information judged by an organization?

19-3   Describe the six steps involved in information system performance.

Management Skills Exercises

Learning activities in this section are aimed at helping you develop controlling skills.

MyLab Management
Discussion Questions

Go to www.pearson.com/mylab/management to complete the problems marked with this icon ⭐.

⭐ Cases

Domino's Goes High-Tech with Easy Order

The Challenge Case "Domino's Goes High-Tech with Easy Order" (p. 461) and its related Challenge Case Summary were written to help you understand the management concepts contained in this chapter. Answer the following discussion questions about the Challenge Case to further enrich your understanding of chapter content.

19-4   Describe the importance of the Easy Order system at Domino's as it relates to the controlling process. What if Domino's had not implemented the Easy Order system?

19-5   The main steps of the controlling process are measuring performance, comparing performance to standards, and taking corrective action. Discuss the possible role of the Easy Order system at Domino's in each of these steps.

19-6   Discuss three challenges that the Easy Order system may experience, from customer problems to potential hacking from outside parties. How should Domino's handle each of these three challenges?

Metail Technology Improves Service and Reduces Returns

Read the case and answer the questions that follow. Studying this case will help you better understand how concepts relating to controlling through online technology can be applied in an organization such as Metail Technology.

Shopping online is clearly an easy and convenient way to purchase just about anything. But what about clothes? The problem is that clothing sizes vary between retailers, and styles, patterns, and colors are difficult to discern on a computer or mobile screen. What often happens is that customers order several sizes of one particular item they like, try those on, keep the one that fits, and return the rest. This becomes very costly for retailers.

To ameliorate this, one company has found a solution to help online retailers reduce costly returns and help customers find just what they're looking for the first time. The company is Metail, and it is changing how fashions are purchased online. Metail provides a revolutionary approach to clothes shopping by letting customers try on items virtually.

Customers can simply upload their important measurements like their height and weight, but also specific dimensions such as bra size or hip and waist circumferences. These data are then used to create a three-dimensional virtual model of the person. The shopper can even customize the digital mannequin further by specifying ethnicity or modifying the mannequin based on a person's unique shape.

Once the customer's avatar is created, the shopper can choose among the online retailer's items and "try on" the clothes. The customer can then view how the garment would appear based upon eight different angles of the mannequin. According to Jim Downing, chief technology officer for Metail, "That gives us one reference shape of how the garment would be, then at runtime we model the user's shape and have a physics simulation that we've fitted to the garment and digitized in order to model how the garment is going to change."

At Metail, they're modeling literally hundreds of garments per day for online retailers located around the world. At the moment, it costs retailers approximately $13 per garment to digitize it. However, cost controls are being put in place that should eventually see the price to retailers at around $4 per garment. In addition, at some point, Metail wants to develop technology that makes the mannequin more realistic and would be based on an actual photograph of the shopper. But this is an expensive endeavor and would require significant data storage. "The choreography," said Downing, "of data around the world to eventually get a picture of a person in clothes is considerable, even at our scale."

Still, Metail has helped retailers enhance the online shopping experience and also reduced very expensive returns. The emphasis on improving service is a significant draw to online retailers. According to Downing, "You can look to Amazon's success to see how far you can go with better service and better product information without anything too flashy." This is important because the simpler the interface is, the more likely customers are to have a positive shopping experience. "It's not that people are bad at following instructions," Downing added, "it's that they are bad at reading them at all."

As Metail changes the online clothes shopping landscape, it is important to recognize how far online retailing has come. Only a couple of years ago, the best an online customer could hope for were detailed photographs and text describing the garment; however, Metail is providing much more. "You can't engage fully with clothes online and you never will be able to, but there's a lot of mileage in being able to get closer than just a photo and some text," Downing said.[61]

Questions

19-7 How important is Metail's technology to online retailers? Explain.

19-8 How can Metail's virtual mannequins help online retailers with the controlling function of management?

19-9 What are the potential challenges or problems that may occur at an online retailer with Metail's virtual mannequin technology?

19-10 Does the concept of a virtual mannequin interest you? If two similar online clothing retailers offered items you like, but only one had the virtual mannequin, which would you be more likely to buy from? Why?

Experiential Exercises

Understanding the Controlling Process

Directions. Read the following scenario and then perform the listed activities. Your instructor may want you to perform the activities as an individual or within groups. Follow all of your instructor's directions carefully.

The controlling process consists of three steps: measure performance, compare measured performance to standards, and take corrective action. Apply this three-step process to your principles of management course. In other words, what are the standards that should be established to know that the course adequately met all expectations? Next, how would you measure performance, and is that performance based on what the instructor does or the students? Finally, what corrective actions would have to be taken if performance does not meet the standards?

You and Your Career

Two of the concepts covered in this chapter are information and technology. Think about your career after graduating from college. Specifically, imagine what the first one to three years will be like for you when you are no longer attending classes. What information will be important to you at that time? Also, what technology will be important to you? Be specific with your answers as you think about what aspects of information and technology will be most important in your career. In addition, what advances in both information and technology do you foresee? How will these advances affect your first three years after graduation?

Building Your Management Skills Portfolio

Your Management Skills Portfolio is a collection of activities specially designed to demonstrate your management knowledge and skill. Be sure to save your work. Taking your printed portfolio to an employment interview could prove helpful.

The portfolio activity for this chapter is about controlling at PT Kereta Api Indonesia (Kai). Study the following information and complete the exercises that follow.

Until 2009, PT Kereta Api Indonesia (KAI), Indonesia's state-owned railway company, had a reputation for underperformance and unreliability. The company saw an enormous improvement under the leadership of Ignatius Jonan.

For some time, KAI had posted significant losses due poor infrastructure, ageing rolling stock, and lack of available locomotives. Service quality was low, passenger safety poor, security inadequate, and many aspects of the business were in severe decline. In addition to these issues, Jonan faced low discipline and a low level of concern for the customer from the employees. He set out a four-point plan to tackle improvement in service quality, safety, comfort, and timeliness. By 2009, KAI had raised profits and performance was up across the network.

Assume that Jonan has contacted you to help him think of ways to improve the performance of those working for the company. His specific task for you involves making the controlling process relevant to the workers. In the following sections, answer the various questions as they pertain to KAI.

19-11 The first step in the controlling process involves measuring performance. If you were Ignatius Jonan, how would you measure the performance of the railway workers? Be specific.

_____

_____

_____

19-12 The second step in the controlling process entails comparing measured performance to standards.

   a. What types of standards would you develop to help assess the performance of these railway associates?

_____

_____

_____

   b. What information sources would you use to develop these standards?

_____

_____

_____

19-13 The final step in the controlling process involves taking corrective actions if necessary.

   a. What type of corrective actions would you take to help control the performance of the factory employees?

_____

_____

_____

   b. How would you determine whether corrective actions are necessary?

_____

_____

_____

MyLab Management
Writing Assignments

If your instructor has assigned this activity, go to www.pearson.com/mylab/management for the following assisted-graded writing assignments:

Assisted-Grading Questions

19-14 Define power and describe the determinants of an individual's power within an organization.

19-15 What are the determinants of information system effectiveness?

Endnotes

1. Google Finance, https://www.google.com/finance?q=NYSE%3ADPZ&ei=zM6NWfGZB8qgjAHrvJL4Dg, accessed August 11, 2017.
2. Domino's company website, "Fun Facts," https://biz.dominos.com/web/public/about-dominos/fun-facts, accessed August 11, 2017.
3. This case was based on Jonathan Maze, "How Domino's Became a Tech Company," *Nation's Restaurant News* 50 (April 18, 2016): 14–18.
4. For an illustration of the complexity of control in an international context, see Jean-François Hennart, "Control in Multinational Firms: The Role of Price and Hierarchy," *Management International Review* (Special Issue 1991): 71–96. See also "Defining Controls," *The Internal Auditor* 55, no. 3 (June 1998): 47.
5. For insights about control in the international arena, see John Volkmar, "Context and Control in Foreign Subsidiaries: Making a Case for the Host Country National Manager," *Journal of Leadership and Organizational Studies* 10 (2003): 93.
6. K. A. Merchant, "The Control Function of Management," *Sloan Management Review* 23 (Summer 1982): 43–55.
7. For a discussion relating planning and controlling to leadership, see Sushil K. Sharma and Savita Dakhane, "Effective Leadership: The Key to Success," *Employment News* 23, no. 10 (June 6–12, 1988): 1, 15.
8. For more discussion on Murphy's Law, see Grady W. Harris, "Living with Murphy's Law," *Research-Technology Management* (January/February 1994): 10–13.
9. Robert J. Mockler, ed., *Readings in Management Control* (New York: Appleton-Century-Crofts, 1970), 14.
10. For insights about the process that Delta Air Lines uses to control distribution costs, see Perry Flint, "Delta's 'Shot Heard' 'Round the World,'" *Air Transport World* (April 1995): 61–62.
11. Francis V. McCrory and Peter Gerstberger, "The New Math of Performance Measurement," *Journal of Business Strategy* (March/April 1991): 33–38; L. Bielski, "KPI: Your Metrics Should Tell a Story," *ABA Banking Journal* 99, no. 10 (2007): 66–68.
12. S. de Leeuwand and J. P. van den Berg, "Improving Operational Performance by Influencing Shopfloor Behavior via Performance Management Practices," *Journal of Operations Management* 29 (2011): 224–235. For more information about measuring employee performance, see A. J. Kinicki, K. J. L. Jacobson, S. J. Peterson, and G. E. Prussia, "Development and Validation of the Performance Management Behavior Questionnaire," *Personnel Psychology* 66 (2013): 1–45.
13. For discussion of quality-oriented performance standards, see Perry Rector and Brian Kleiner, "Performance Standards: Defining Quality Service in Community-Based Organizations," *Management Research News* 26 (2003): 161.
14. James M. Bright, "A Clear Picture," *Credit Union Management* (February 1995): 28–29.

15. P. Kuusela, T. Keil, and M. Maula, "Driven by Aspirations, but in What Direction? Performance Shortfalls, Slack Resources, and Resource-Consuming vs. Resource-Freeing Organizational Change," *Strategic Management Journal* 38 (2017): 1101–1120.

16. For a discussion of how standards are set, see James B. Dilworth, *Production and Operations Management: Manufacturing and Non-Manufacturing* (New York: Random House, 1986), 637–650. For more information on various facets of standards and standards setting, see Len Eglo, "Save Dollars on Maintenance Management," *Chemical Engineering* 97 (June 1990): 157–162.

17. For an example of a company surpassing performance standards, see Peter Nulty, "How to Live by Your Wits," *Fortune* (April 20, 1992): 19–20.

18. To better understand the importance of corrective action, see Zheng Gu, "Predicting Potential Failure, Taking Corrective Action Are Keys to Success," *Nation's Restaurant News* 33, no. 25 (June 21, 1999): 31–32.

19. For more about corrective action in developing countries, see Martin Brownbridge and Samuel Maimbo, "Can Prompt Corrective Action Rules Work in the Developing World?," *Journal of African Business* 4 (2003): 47.

20. For a review of other common problems in organizations, see Robert E. Quinn, Regina M. O'Neill, and Lynda St. Clair, *Pressing Problems in Modern Organizations (That Keep Us Up at Night): Transforming Agendas for Research and Practice* (New York: AMACOM, 1999).

21. For an illustration of the problem–symptom relationship, see Elizabeth Dougherty, "Waste Minimization: Reduce Wastes and Reap the Benefits," *R&D* 32 (April 1990): 62–68.

22. "Stein Mart Selects Oracle Retail Merchandising and Planning Applications," *Trading Markets*, April 22, 2010, http://www.tradingmarkets.com.

23. For an excellent review of research on power in organizations, see P. Fleming and A. Spicer, "Organizational Power in Management and Organization Science," *Academy of Management Annals* 8 (2014): 237–298.

24. Jeffrey Pfeffer, "Power Play," *Harvard Business Review* 88, no. 7/8 (July/August 2010): 84–92. See also B. L. Brescoll, "Who Takes the Floor and Why: Gender, Power, and Volubility in Organizations," *Administrative Science Quarterly* 56 (2012): 622–641.

25. For more information on how position power disparity influences group performance, see M. Tarakci, L. L. Greer, and P. J. F. Groenen, "When Does Paper Disparity Help or Hurt Group Performance?," *Journal of Applied Psychology* 101 (2016): 415–429.

26. See Amitai Etzioni, *A Comparative Analysis of Complex Organizations* (New York: Free Press, 1961), 4–6. See also N. Wellman, D. M. Mayer, M. Ong, and D. S. DeRue, "When Are Do-Gooders Treated Badly? Legitimate Power, Role Expectations, and Reactions to Moral Objection in Organizations," *Journal of Applied Psychology* 101 (2016): 793–814.

27. John P. Kotter, "Power, Dependence, and Effective Management," *Harvard Business Review* (July/August 1977): 128.

28. Ibid., 135–136.

29. GLOBE Project, "2014 Study," http://globeproject.com/study_2014; Dimitria Groutsis, Rae Cooper and Greg Whitwell, "Beyond the Pale: Cultural Diversity on ASX 100 Boards," University of Sydney, July 2018, http://sydney.edu.au/business/__data/assets/pdf_file/0010/368551/Beyond-the-Pale-Full-Report.pdf.

30. For a review of studies on employee identification, see E. Lee, T. Park, and B. Koo, "Identifying Organizational Identification as a Basis of Attitudes and Behaviors: A Meta-Analytic Review," *Psychological Bulletin* 141(2015): 1049–1080.

31. Kotter, "Power, Dependence, and Effective Management," 131.

32. W. Jerome III, *Executive Control: The Catalyst* (New York: Wiley, 1961), 31–34.

33. For an article emphasizing the importance of management understanding and being supportive of organizational control efforts, see Richard M. Morris III, "Management Support: An Underlying Premise," *Industrial Management* 31 (March/April 1989): 2–3.

34. The term *information* has been defined in various ways in academic and professional literature. For a classification of the various definitions, see Earl H. McKinney, Jr., "Information about Information: A Taxonomy of Views," *MIS Quarterly* 34, no. 2 (June 2010): 329–A5.

35. Garland R. Hadley and Mike C. Patterson, "Are Middle-Paying Jobs Really Declining?," *Oklahoma Business Bulletin* 56 (June 1988): 12–14; A. Essam Radwan and Jerome Fields, "Keeping Tabs on Toxic Spills," *Civil Engineering* 60 (April 1990): 70–72; Dean C. Minderman,

"Marketing: Desktop Demographics," *Credit Union Management* 13 (February 1990): 26.

36. Carol Davis and Edmund Haefele, "A Practical and Tested Infrastructure Design for Large Business Warehouse Systems," *Business Information Review* 27, no. 1 (2010): 43–55.

37. Michael S. Hopkins, "The Four Ways IT Is Revolutionizing Innovation," *Sloan Management Review* (Spring 2010): 51–56.

38. Henry Mintzberg, "The Myths of MIS," *California Management Review* (Fall 1972): 92–97; Jay W. Forrester, "Managerial Decision Making," in Martin Greenberger, ed., *Management and the Computer of the Future* (Cambridge, MA, and New York: MIT Press and Wiley, 1962), 37.

39. The following discussion is based largely on Robert H. Gregory and Richard L. Van Horn, "Value and Cost of Information," in J. Daniel Conger and Robert W. Knapp, eds., *Systems Analysis Techniques* (New York: Wiley, 1974), 473–489.

40. To better understand how information systems can improve the quality of an organization's information, see B. S. Butler and P. H. Gray, "Reliability, Mindfulness, and Information Systems," *MIS Quarterly* 30, no. 2 (2006): 211–224.

41. John T. Small and William B. Lee, "In Search of MIS," *MSU Business Topics* (Autumn 1975): 47–55.

42. G. Anthony Gorry and Michael S. Scott Morton, "A Framework for Management Information Systems," *Sloan Management Review* 13 (Fall 1971): 55–70.

43. Stephen L. Cohen, "Managing Human-Resource Data, Keeping Your Data Clean," *Training & Development Journal* 43 (August 1989): 50–54.

44. Michael A. Verespej, "Communications Technology: Slave or Master?," *Industry Week* (June 19, 1995): 48–55; John C. Scully, "Information Overload?," *Managers Magazine* (May 1995): 2. For more information on the importance of big data, see S. Erevelles, N. Fukawa, and L. Swayne, "Big Data Consumer Analytics and the Transformation of Marketing," *Journal of Business Research* 69 (2016): 897–904.

45. James R. Hagerty, "How Many Turns in a Screw? Big Data Knows," *Wall Street Journal*, May 15, 2013, http://online.wsj.com; Shira Ovide, "Big Data, Big Blunders," *Wall Street Journal*, March 8, 2013, http://online.wsj.com; Deborah Gage, "Pictures Make Sense of Big Data," *Wall Street Journal*, September 15, 2013, http://online.wsj.com; CIO Journal, "GE Launches Industrial Internet Analytics Platform," *Wall Street Journal*, June 18, 2013, http://blogs.wsj.com.

46. T. Mukhapadhyay and R. B. Cooper, "Impact of Management Information Systems on Decisions," *Omega* 20 (1992): 37–49.

47. Robert W. Holmes, "Twelve Areas to Investigate for Better MIS," *Financial Executive* (July 1970): 24.

48. Kenneth C. Laudon and Jane Price Laudon, *Management Information Systems: Organization and Technology* (New York: Macmillan, 1993), 38.

49. For an article discussing how a well-managed MIS promotes the usefulness of information, see Albert Lederer and Veronica Gardner, "Meeting Tomorrow's Business Demands through Strategic Information Systems Planning," *Information Strategy: The Executive's Journal* (Summer 1992): 20–27.

50. This section is based on Richard A. Johnson, R. Joseph Monsen, Henry P. Knowles, and Borge O. Saxberg, *Management Systems and Society: An Introduction* (Santa Monica, CA: Goodyear, 1976), 113–120; James Emery, "Information Technology in the 21st Century Enterprise," *MIS Quarterly* (December 1991): xxi–xxiii.

51. Benjamin Pimentel, "When Facebook Is Bad for One's Credit Rating," MarketWatch.com, March 13, 2014, http://www.marketwatch.com/story/when-facebook-is-bad-for-ones-credit-rating-2014-03-13?link=MW_latest_news; Peter Sayer, "Should Your Facebook Profile Influence Your Credit Score? Startups Say Yes," PCWorld, March 11, 2014, http://www.pcworld.com/article/2106920/startups-vie-to-evaluate-credit-risk-using-facebook-profiles.html; Wayne Rash, "CeBIT Code_n Exhibit Shows Why Useful Innovation Is the Best Kind," eWeek, March 13, 2013, http://www.eweek.com/cloud/cebit-coden-exhibit-shows-why-useful-innovation-is-the-best-kind.html; Big Data Scoring, http://www.bigdatascoring.com/home/about/.

52. Robert G. Murdick, "MIS for MBO," *Journal of Systems Management* (March 1977): 34–40.

53. "Sage North America Expands HR Management Software Choices for Nonprofit and Government Organizations," *Market Wire*, April 1, 2010, http://smart-grid.tmcnet.com.

54. The discussion is based on A. Rai, S. S. Lang, and R. B. Welker, "Assessing the Validity of IS Success Models: An Empirical Test and Theoretical Analysis," *Information Systems Research* 13, no. 1 (2002): 50–69.

55. For more information on the turnover of IS workers, see D. Joseph, K. Ng, C. Koh, and S. Ang, "Turnover of Information Technology Professionals: A Narrative Review, Meta-Analytic Structural Equation Modeling, and Model Development," *MIS Quarterly* 31, no. 3 (2007): 547–577.

56. C. O. Longenecker and J. A. Scazzero, "The Turnover and Retention of IT Managers in Rapidly Changing Organizations," *Information Systems Management* (Winter 2003): 58–63. See also J. B. Windeler and C. K. Riemenschneider, "The Influence of Ethnicity on Organizational Commitment and Merit Pay of IT Workers: The Role of Leader Support," *Information Systems Journal* 26 (2016): 157–190.

57. https://www.wsj.com/articles/what-tech-employees-want-1488856262j (accessed on July 17, 2017).

58. S. Overby, "The Future of Jobs and Innovation: Scenario One," *CIO*, December 15, 2003, www.cio.com. For information on the complexities involved with outsourcing information technology, see K. Han and S. Mithas, "Information Technology Outsourcing and Non-IT Operating Costs: An Empirical Investigation," *MIS Quarterly* 37 (2013): 315–331.

59. J. King, "IT's Global Itinerary," *Computerworld*, September 15, 2003, www.computerworld.com. To better understand how organizations can improve the transition for new employees, see S. S. Nifadkar and T. N. Bauer, "Breach of Belongingness: Newcomer Relationship Conflict, Information, and Task-Related Outcomes during Organizational Socialization," *Journal of Applied Psychology* 101, no. 1 (2016): 1–13.

60. M. R. Gramaila and I. Kim, "An Undergraduate Business Information Security Course and Laboratory," *Journal of Information Systems Education* 13, no. 3 (2003): 189–196.

61. This case is based on Clare McDonald, "Metail Fashions New Models to Improve the Online Clothes-Buying Experience," *Computer Weekly* (May 2, 2017): 10–13.

Production and Control

20

TARGET SKILL

 Production Skill: the ability to transform organizational resources into products

PRODUCTION SKILL AND YOUR CAREER

Production skill will be of great value to you in enhancing your career. This skill will help you to transform organizational resources into products that your organization can sell. This ability contributes to organizational success, builds your image as a competent manager, makes you valuable to your organization, and supports promotions as you build your career.

OBJECTIVES

To help build my *production skill*, when studying this chapter, I will attempt to acquire:

20-1 An understanding of production and productivity

20-2 An appreciation for the relationship between quality and productivity

20-3 Insights into the role of operations management concepts in the workplace

20-4 An understanding of how operations control procedures can be used to control production

20-5 Insights into operations control tools and how they evolve into a continual improvement approach to production management and control

---

MyLab Management Chapter Warm Up

If your instructor has assigned this activity, go to www.pearson.com/mylab/management to complete the chapter warm up.

CHALLENGE CASE

Tesla Production Will Be Fastest in History

It's a bold undertaking. Tesla—the electric car manufacturer with an almost cultlike following—will have the fastest ramp-up of production in automotive history. The Tesla Model 3 is the car that will become the standard for the firm as it attempts to go from high-end car company catering to the wealthy to mainstream car manufacturer.

In July 2017, Tesla rolled the first 30 Model 3s off the assembly line. As impressive as that sounds, it's taken the company 14 years to get to this point. The CEO, Elon Musk, promises that half a million will be made by the end of 2018, and by 2020, 1 million. No other car company has made automobiles this quickly. As a point of reference, in all of 2016, Tesla produced only 76,000 cars. To reach its goal, the company will need to produce more than that *each month* in the year 2020.

Priced at $35,000, the Model 3 has had a very successful preordering campaign. In just the first week that a customer could preorder the new model, over 325,000 reservations were made, with each order paying a $1,000 deposit. Keep in mind that these customers realized that they would not likely see the car they reserved for a year or two. But this is a testament to what Elon Musk has built. The various models introduced so far have been noted for their ultramodern look, reliable batteries, and surprising power.

With marketing underway, Tesla has had some difficult challenges with the production schedule. First, 2017 was a year with relatively low fuel prices, meaning that there was less demand for a car that runs on batteries and not on gasoline. Second, most states do not have the infrastructure for the volume of electric cars that Tesla wants to put on the road. Charging stations and service facilities will need to be built to keep the cars moving. In addition, Tesla experienced a public humiliation when the firm missed its production estimates of its Model S and Model X luxury models in 2017. The company blamed the production shortage on a shortfall of battery packs. The Insurance Institute for Highway Safety also failed to give a top safety

Alexandria Sage/Reuters

Tesla's Model 3 had 325,000 cars preordered in the first week it became available, with each customer placing $1,000 down to reserve the electric vehicle. The company plans to increase its production fivefold by 2020.

rating to the Model S. All these events hurt the company, causing its stock to fall from $370 to $310 during the year.

Despite these setbacks, a preorder of 325,000 cars is definitely putting Tesla back on the road map. Elon Musk is anticipating that demand will go even higher once the first cars are on the road and word-of-mouth gives the company positive reviews. And this is the reason Musk is planning on a fivefold increase in production: Higher demand means more cars sold. Being able to fulfill every order is the key to Tesla's success.[1]

THE PRODUCTION CHALLENGE

The Challenge Case describes the challenges Tesla is having in producing 1 million cars by the year 2020. Specifically, the production challenge of creating and meeting customer demand for the Model 3 is discussed. This chapter is designed to help managers in companies such as Tesla increase productivity.

Production and Productivity

To reach organizational goals, all managers must plan, organize, influence, and control in order to produce some type of goods or services. Naturally, these goods and services vary significantly from organization to organization. This section of the chapter defines production and productivity and discusses the relationship among quality, productivity, and automation.

20-1 An understanding of production and productivity

Defining Production

Production is the transformation of organizational resources into products. [2] In this definition, *organizational resources* are all the assets available to a manager to generate products, *transformation* is the set of steps necessary to change these resources into products, and *products* are various goods or services aimed at meeting human needs. Inputs at a manufacturing firm, for example, include raw materials, purchased parts, production workers, and even schedules. The transformation process encompasses the preparation of customer orders; the design of various products; the procurement of raw materials; and the production, assembly, and (perhaps) warehousing of products. Outputs, of course, consist of products appropriate for customer use.

"Production" occurs at service organizations as well. Inputs at a hospital, for instance, include ambulances; rooms; employees (doctors, nurses, administrators, receptionists); supplies (medicines, bandages, food); and (as at a manufacturer) funds, schedules, and records. The transformation process might begin with transporting patients to the facility and end with discharging them. In between, the hospital attends to patients' needs (nursing and feeding them, administering their medication, recording their progress). The output in this case is health care.

Productivity

Productivity is an important consideration when designing, evaluating, and improving modern production systems. [3] We can define **productivity** as the relationship between the total amount of goods or services being produced (output) and the organizational resources needed to produce them (input). This relationship is usually expressed by the following equation: [4]

$$\text{Productivity} = \frac{\text{outputs}}{\text{inputs}}$$

The higher the value of the ratio of outputs to inputs, the higher the productivity of the operation.

Managers should continually strive to improve their production processes. [5] As an example, Duke Energy committed to investing $1 billion over five years in smart-grid technology. The new technology promises to save energy, lower operating costs, and reduce the world's carbon footprint. Under the plan, Duke is replacing conventional electric meters with digital meters that allow remote meter reading, connections, and disconnections. [6]

It is no secret that over the past several years, workers in the United States have been among the world's most productive. [7] Some of the more traditional strategies for increasing productivity include improvements in the following areas: [8]

1. Effectiveness of the organizational workforce through training
2. The production process through automation
3. Product design to make products easier to assemble
4. The production facility by purchasing more modern equipment
5. The quality of the workers hired to fill open positions

Intel is an example of an organization that has taken steps to improve worker productivity by changing the way it designs offices. [9] Although Intel was initially credited with the popularization of cubicles, Intel executives have reconsidered the costs and benefits of cubicle arrangements, which block worker visibility while failing to reduce noise. Intel is now testing alternative office arrangements in several locations. One such arrangement involves providing large tables that employees can sit around in groups with notebook computers. Intel is hopeful that this arrangement will help to boost both morale and productivity.

Quality and Productivity

20-2 An appreciation for the relationship between quality and productivity

Quality can be defined as how well a product does what it is intended to do—how closely it satisfies the specifications to which it was built.[10] In a broad sense, quality is the degree of excellence on which products or services can be ranked on the basis of selected features or characteristics. Customers determine this ranking and also define quality in terms of appearance, performance, availability, flexibility, and reliability.[11] Product quality determines an organization's reputation.

MyLab Management Watch It

If your instructor has assigned this activity, go to www.pearson.com/mylab/management to complete the video exercise.

During the last decade or so, managerial thinking about the relationship between quality and productivity has changed drastically. Many earlier managers chose to achieve higher levels of productivity simply by producing a greater number of products given some fixed level of available resources. They saw no relationship between improving quality and increasing productivity. Quite the contrary: They viewed quality improvement as a controlling activity that took place toward the end of the production process and largely consisted of rejecting a number of finished products that were too obviously flawed to offer them to customers. Under this approach, quality improvement efforts were generally believed to *lower* productivity.

Focus on Continual Improvement

Management theorists have more recently discovered that concentrating on improving product quality throughout all phases of a production process actually improves the productivity of the manufacturing system.[12] U.S. companies were far behind the Japanese in making this discovery. As early as 1948, Japanese companies observed that continual improvements in product quality throughout the production process typically resulted in improved productivity. How does this improvement happen? According to Dr. W. Edwards Deming, a world-renowned quality expert, a serious and consistent focus on quality typically reduces nonproductive variables such as the reworking of products, production mistakes, delays and production snags, and inefficient use of time and materials.

Deming believed that, for continual improvement to become a way of life in an organization, managers need to understand their company and its operations. Most managers feel that they do know their company and its operations, but when they begin drawing flowcharts, they discover that their understanding of strategy, systems, and processes is far from complete. Deming recommended that managers question every aspect of an operation and involve workers in discussion before taking action to improve operations. He maintained that a manager who earnestly focuses on improving product quality throughout all phases of a production process will initiate a set of chain reactions that benefit not only the organization but also the society in which the organization exists.

Focus on Quality and Integrated Operations

Deming's flow diagram for improving product quality (see **Figure 20.1**) contains a complete set of organizational variables. It establishes the customer as part of the process and introduces the idea of continually refining the knowledge, design, and inputs of the process to increase customer satisfaction constantly. The diagram shows the operations process as an integrated whole, from the first input to the actual use of the finished product; thus, a problem at the beginning of the process will affect the entire process as well as the end product. Deming's diagram eliminates barriers between the company and the customer, between the customer and the suppliers, and between the company and its employees. Because the process is unified, the greater the harmony among all its components, the better the results will be.

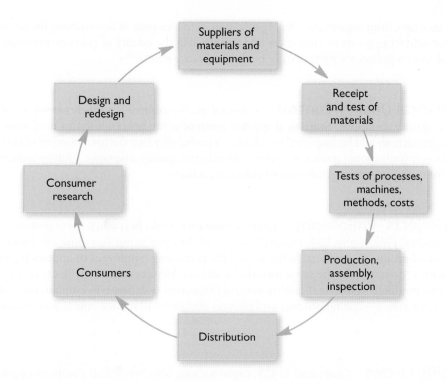

Figure 20.1

Deming's flow diagram for improving product quality

An organization's interpretation of quality is expressed in its strategies. If a company does not incorporate quality into its strategic plan, customers may look for other solutions.

Wal-Mart's continuous focus on "everyday low prices" has led some consumers to equate the retailer with low quality.[13] Because of these perceptions, Wal-Mart's sales growth decreased when some Wal-Mart customers started shopping at stores such as Target, which is associated with higher quality. The following sections elaborate on the relationship between quality and production by discussing quality assurance and quality circles as part of organizational strategy.

Quality Assurance   **Quality assurance** is an operations process involving a broad group of activities aimed at achieving an organization's quality objectives.[14] Quality assurance is a continuum of activities that starts when quality standards are set and ends when quality goods and services are delivered to the customer. Although the precise activities involved in quality

PRACTICAL CHALLENGE: CONTINUAL IMPROVEMENT

At Wisconsin Hospitals, Costs Fall as Quality Rises

More than a hundred Wisconsin hospitals have been working with the Wisconsin Hospital Association to improve outcomes for patients. Hospital administrators (managers) collaborate with doctors and employees to identify areas for improvement, such as decreasing the number of patients being readmitted because they experience problems after a hospital stay and decreasing the occurrence of infections associated with hospitalization. These teams develop safety checklists, improved procedures, and better methods for communication with patients. In the first year and a half of the program, readmissions have fallen by more than 20 percent, and bloodstream infections from central lines have fallen by 42 percent.

Continual improvement is also helping to lower costs. The 108 Wisconsin hospitals that are working with the association estimate that they have saved $45.6 million so far, mainly by preventing readmissions and reducing infections. Hospitals' reputations as well as their bottom lines are at stake: Since 2005, Medicare has been reporting quality measures online (at hospitalcompare.hhs.gov). More recently, the Wisconsin Hospital Association has been issuing bonuses and penalties based on hospitals' quality performance and readmission rates.[15]

assurance vary from organization to organization, activities such as determining the safest system for delivering goods to customers and maintaining the quality of parts or materials purchased from suppliers are parts of most quality assurance efforts.[16]

Statistical Quality Control

Statistical quality control is a much narrower concept than is quality assurance. **Statistical quality control** is the process used to determine how many products should be inspected to calculate a probability that the total number of products will meet organizational quality standards. An effective quality assurance strategy reduces the need for quality control and subsequent corrective actions.

"No Rejects" Philosophy

Quality assurance works best when management adopts a "no rejects" philosophy. Unfortunately, such a philosophy is not economically feasible for most mass-produced products. What *is* possible is training employees to approach production with a "do not make the same mistake" mind-set. Mistakes are costly because detecting defective products in the final quality control inspection is expensive. Emphasizing quality in the early stages—during product and process design—will reduce rejects and production costs.

Quality Circles

One trend in U.S. organizations is to involve all company employees in quality control by soliciting their ideas for judging and maintaining product quality. This trend developed from a successful Japanese control system known as *quality circles*. Although many U.S. corporations are now moving beyond the concept of the quality circle to that of the work team, as discussed in Chapter 17, many ideas generated from quality circles continue to be valid.[17]

A **quality circle** is a small group of workers who meet to discuss quality-related problems in a particular project and to communicate their solutions to these problems to management directly at a formal presentation session.[18] **Figure 20.2** shows the quality circle problem-solving process.

Most quality circles operate in a similar manner. The circle usually has fewer than eight members, and the circle leader is not necessarily the members' supervisor. Members may be workers on the project and/or outsiders. The focus is on operational problems rather than on interpersonal ones. The problems discussed in the quality circle may be assigned by management or uncovered by the group itself.

Automation

The preceding section discussed the relationship between quality and productivity in organizations. This section introduces the topic of automation, which shows signs of increasing organizational productivity in a revolutionary way.[19]

Automation is defined as the replacement of human effort by electromechanical devices in operations such as welding, materials handling, design, drafting, and decision making. It includes robots—mechanical devices built to perform repetitive tasks efficiently—and **robotics**, which is the study of the development and use of robots.

Over the past 20 years, a host of advanced manufacturing systems have been developed and implemented to support operations. Most of these automated systems combine hardware—industrial robots and computers—and software. The goals of automation include reduced inventories, higher productivity, and faster billing and product distribution cycles.

Amazon is an example of a company using automation to increase productivity. The company recently purchased Kiva Systems, a manufacturer of robots designed to improve warehouse productivity. When an order is placed, these robots search Amazon's warehouses for the

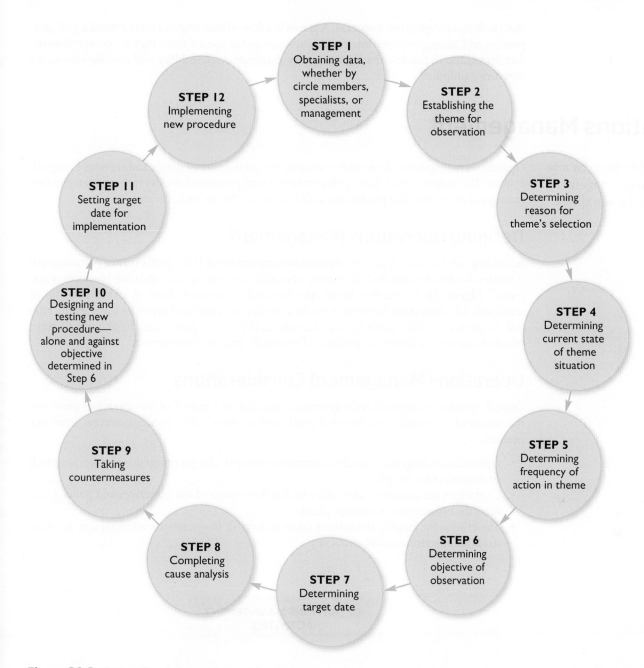

Figure 20.2 The quality circle problem-solving process

items purchased by the consumer and take the items to the Amazon employee tasked with ful-filling the order. These robots eliminate the need for employees to expend effort on retrieving the merchandise. Investors expect these robots to reduce order fulfillment costs by approxi-mately 30 percent, for a potential annual savings of nearly $1 billion for Amazon.[20]

Automation will have an important impact on the global workforce in the coming decades. A recent study suggests, for example, that almost 40 percent of jobs in the United States will be at high risk of automation by the early 2030s.[21] Industries facing particularly high risks of auto-mation include accommodation and food services, transportation, real estate rental and leasing, and retail trade.[22]

Strategies, Systems, and Processes

According to Kemper and Yehudai, an effective and efficient operations manager is skilled not only in management, production, and productivity but also in strategies, systems, and pro-cesses. A *strategy* is a plan of action. A *system* is a particular linking of organizational components that facilitates carrying out a process. A *process* is a flow of interrelated events toward a goal, purpose, or end. Strategies create interlocking systems and processes when they are comprehensive, functional, and dynamic—that is, when they designate responsibility and provide criteria for measuring output.[23]

Operations Management

20-3 Insights into the role of operations management concepts in the workplace

Operations management deals with managing the production of goods and services in organizations. The sections that follow define *operations management* and discuss various strategies that managers can use to make production activities more effective and efficient.

Defining Operations Management

According to Chase and Aquilano, **operations management** is the performance of managerial activities that involve selecting, designing, operating, controlling, and updating production systems.[24] **Figure 20.3** describes these activities and categorizes them as either periodic or continual. The distinction between periodic activities and continual activities involves the relative frequency of their performance: Periodic activities are performed from time to time, whereas continual activities are performed essentially without interruption.

Operations Management Considerations

Overall, *operations management* is the systematic direction and control of the operations processes that transform resources into finished goods and services.[25] This concept conveys three key notions:

- Operations management involves managers—people who get things done by working with or through other people.
- Operations management takes place within the context of the objectives and policies that drive the organization's strategic plans.
- The criteria for judging the actions taken as a result of operations management are standards for effectiveness and efficiency.

Figure 20.3 Major activities performed to manage production

Effectiveness is the degree to which managers attain organizational objectives: "doing the right things." **Efficiency** is the degree to which organizational resources contribute to productivity: "doing things right." A review of organizational performance based on these standards is essential to enhancing the success of any organization.[26]

A few years ago, a researcher studied how workers at a Domino's Pizza restaurant placed pepperoni on a pizza to keep it from sliding into the center when the pizza was put into the oven. Their technique was widely shared among Domino's franchises and helped ensure greater operational efficiency. The sharing of best practices is one way that an organization can ensure enhanced productivity.[27]

Operations strategies—capacity, location, product, process, layout, and human resource—are specific plans of action designed to ensure that resources are obtained and used effectively and efficiently. An operational strategy is implemented by people who get things done with and through people. The strategy is achieved in the context of the objectives and policies derived from the organization's strategic plan.

Capacity Strategy

Capacity strategy is a plan of action aimed at providing an organization with the right facilities to produce the needed output at the right time. The output capacity of the organization determines its ability to meet future demands for goods and services. *Insufficient capacity* results in a loss of sales, which in turn affects profits. *Excess capacity* results in higher production costs. A strategy that aims for *optimal capacity*, in which quantity and timing are in balance, provides an excellent basis for minimizing operating costs and maximizing profits.

Capacity flexibility enables a company to deliver its goods and services to its customers more quickly than its competitors do. This component of capacity strategy involves having flexible plants and processes, extensively trained employees, and easy and economical access to external capacity, such as suppliers.

Managers use capacity strategy to balance the costs of overcapacity and undercapacity. The difficulty of accurately forecasting long-term demand makes this balancing task risky. Modifying long-range capacity decisions while in production is both hard and costly. In a highly competitive environment, construction of a new high-tech facility might take longer than the life cycle of the product. Correcting overcapacity by closing a plant saddles management with high economic costs and even higher social costs—such as lost jobs, which devastate both employees and the community in which the plant operates—that will have a long-term, adverse effect on the firm.

The traditional concept of economies of scale led management to construct large plants that tried to do everything. The more modern concept of the focused facility has shown management that better performance can be achieved in specialized plants that concentrate on fewer tasks and are therefore smaller.

Five Steps in Capacity Decisions

Managers are more likely to make sound strategic capacity decisions if they adhere to the following five-step process:

1. Measure the capacity of currently available facilities.
2. Estimate future capacity needs on the basis of demand forecasts.
3. Compare future capacity needs and available capacity to determine whether capacity must be increased or decreased.
4. Identify ways to accommodate long-range capacity changes (expansion or reduction).
5. Select the best alternative based on quantitative and qualitative evaluations.

Location Strategy

Location strategy is a plan of action that provides an organization with a competitive location for its headquarters, manufacturing, services, and distribution activities.[28] A competitive location results in lower transportation and communication costs among the various facilities. These costs—which can run as high as 20 to 30 percent of a product's selling price—greatly affect the volume of sales and the amount of profit generated by the particular product. Many other quantitative and qualitative factors are important when formulating location strategy.

Factors in a Competitive Location   A successful location strategy requires a company to consider the following major factors in its location study:

- Nearness to market and distribution centers
- Nearness to vendors and resources
- Requirements of federal, state, and local governments
- The character of direct competition
- The degree of interaction with the rest of the corporation
- The quality and quantity of labor pools
- The environmental attractiveness of the area
- Taxes and financing requirements
- Existing and potential transportation
- The quality of utilities and services

The dynamic nature of these factors could make what is a competitive location today an undesirable location in five years.

Product Strategy   **Product strategy** is an operational plan of action outlining which goods and services an organization will produce and market.[29] Product strategy is the main component of an organization's operations strategy—in fact, it is the link between the operations strategy and the other functional strategies, especially marketing and research and development. In essence, product, marketing, and research and development strategies must fit together if management is to be able to build an effective overall operations strategy. A business's product and operations strategies should take into account the strengths and weaknesses of operations, which are primarily internal, as well as those of functional areas that are concerned more with external opportunities and threats.

Cooperation and coordination among its marketing, operations, and research and development departments from the inception of a new product are strongly beneficial to a company. At the very least, cooperation and coordination ensure a smooth transition from research and development to production because operations people will be able to contribute to the quality of the total product rather than merely attempting to improve the quality of its components. Even the most sophisticated product can be designed so that it is relatively simple to produce, thus reducing the number of units that must be scrapped or reworked during production as well as the need for highly trained and highly paid employees. All of these strategies lower production costs and thus increase a product's price competitiveness or profits, or both.

TIPS FOR MANAGING AROUND THE GLOBE

Choosing a Factory Location: Gothenburg Leads the Charge

The World Economic Forum calculates that by 2025, the global battery market for electric vehicles will be worth $100 billion. Despite many of the manufacturing plants being based outside of Europe, in China, South Korea, and the United States, Alelion Energy Systems chose Gothenburg as the location for Sweden's first mass-production-scale lithium-ion battery plant.

So why choose Gothenburg and why choose Sweden? According to Alelion, Sweden offered low-cost renewable energy, access to raw materials, and a large potential customer base. Alelion has seen orders increase by 400 percent from 2016 to 2018. The need to secure highly skilled Swedish engineers is therefore essential to keep pace with demand.

In the longer term, as the Gothenburg facility ramps up its production, Gothenburg as a port will provide another key locational and infrastructure advantage. Other businesses in allied markets have recognized the growing concentration of electro-mobility expertise in Gothenburg. Among those relocating to Gothenburg as a result are Volvo, Chalmers University of Technology, Scania, and the China Euro Vehicle Technology development center.[30]

Process Strategy

Process strategy is a plan of action outlining the means and methods that an organization will use to transform resources into goods and services. Materials, labor, information, equipment, and managerial skills are the resources that must be transformed. A competitive process strategy will ensure the most efficient and effective use of these organizational resources.

Types of Processes

All manufacturing processes may be grouped into three different types. The first type is the *continuous process*, a product-oriented, high-volume, low-variety process used, for example, in producing chemicals, beer, and petroleum products. The second type is the *repetitive process*, a product-oriented production process that uses modules to produce items in large lots. This mass-production or assembly-line process is characteristic of the auto and appliance industries. The third type of manufacturing process is used to produce small lots of custom-designed products such as furniture. This high-variety, low-volume system, commonly known as the *job-shop process*, includes the production of one-of-a-kind items as well as unit production. Spaceship and weapons systems production are considered job-shop activities. Organizations commonly employ more than one type of manufacturing process at the same time and in the same facility.

A continuous process such as the one shown here is an efficient way to produce in high volumes with low variety.

Process strategy is directly linked to product strategy. The decision to select a particular process strategy is often the result of external market opportunities or threats. The corporation decides what it wants to produce and then selects a process strategy to produce it. The product takes center stage, and the process becomes a function of the product.

The function of process strategy is to determine what equipment will be used, what maintenance will be necessary, and what level of automation will be most effective and efficient. The type of employees and the level of employee skills needed depend on the process strategy chosen.

Layout Strategy

Layout strategy is a plan of action that outlines the location and flow of all organizational resources around, into, and within production and service facilities. A cost-effective and cost-efficient layout strategy minimizes the expenses of processing, transporting, and storing materials throughout the production and service cycles.

Layout strategy—which is usually the last part of operations strategy to be formulated—is closely linked, either directly or indirectly, with all the other components of operations strategy: capacity, location, product, process, and human resources. It must target capacity and process requirements. It must satisfy the organization's product design, quality, and quantity requirements. It must target facility and location requirements. Finally, to be effective, the layout strategy must be compatible with the organization's established quality of work life.

A **layout** is the overall arrangement of equipment, work areas, service areas, and storage areas within a facility that produces goods or provides services.[31] Three basic types of layouts are used for manufacturing facilities:

1. A **product layout** is designed to accommodate high production volumes, highly specialized equipment, and narrow employee skills. It is appropriate for organizations that produce and service a limited number of different products. It is not appropriate for an organization that experiences constant or frequent changes of products.
2. A **process (functional) layout** is a layout pattern that groups together similar types of equipment. It is appropriate for organizations involved in a large number of different tasks. It best serves companies whose production volumes are low, whose equipment is multipurpose, and whose employees' skills are broad.

Figure 20.4
Three basic layout patterns

3. The **fixed-position layout** is one in which the product is stationary while resources flow. It is appropriate for organizations involved in a large number of different tasks that require low volumes, multipurpose equipment, and broad employee skills. A *group technology layout* is a product layout cell within a larger process layout. It benefits organizations that require both types of layouts.

Figure 20.4 illustrates the three basic layout patterns. Actually, most manufacturing facilities are a combination of two or more different types of layouts. Various techniques are available to assist management in designing an efficient and effective layout that meets the required specifications.

Human Resource Strategy

Human resources is the term used for individuals engaged in any of an organization's activities. Two human resource imperatives are as follows:

1. It is essential to optimize individual, group, and organizational effectiveness.
2. It is essential to enhance the quality of organizational life.

A **human resource strategy** is an operational plan to use an organization's human resources effectively and efficiently while maintaining or improving the quality of work life.[32] As discussed in Chapter 12, human resource management is about employees, who are the best means of enhancing organizational effectiveness. Whereas financial management attempts to increase organizational effectiveness through the allocation and conservation of financial resources, human resource management (personnel management) attempts to increase organizational effectiveness through factors such as the establishment of personnel policies, education and training, and procedures.

Chrysler Corporation recently adapted its human resource strategy after its acquisition by Italian automaker Fiat. Specifically, Chrysler hired 600 engineers—200 of them with a background in quality processes—to help fill the supply pipeline with vehicles. Working from a clean slate, Chrysler identified skilled designers who could adapt the Fiat platforms to cars and trucks to be marketed under brands such as Chrysler, Dodge, Jeep, and Ram.[33]

Operational Tools in Human Resource Strategy   Operations management attempts to increase organizational effectiveness by employing the methods used in the manufacturing and service processes. Human resources, one important factor of operations, must be compatible with operations tasks.

Labor force planning is the primary focus of the operations human resource strategy. It is an operational plan for hiring the right employees for a job and training them to be productive, which is a lengthy and costly process. A human resource strategy must be founded on fair treatment and trust, and the employee, not operations, must take center stage. However, the recent economic decline had a significant impact on the workforce, with widespread layoffs and many jobs moved offshore. As the economy continues to recover, the process of strategic workforce planning is more critical than ever and forces employers to revisit some of their conventional assumptions about hiring.[34]

Job design is an operational plan that determines who will do a specific job and how, and where the job will be done. The goal of job design is to facilitate productivity. Successful job design takes efficiency and behavior into account; it also guarantees that working conditions are safe and that the health of employees will not be jeopardized in the short or the long run. When executed effectively, job design sets the stage for a successful recruitment and retention program.[35]

Work methods analysis is an operational tool used to improve productivity and ensure the safety of workers. It can be performed for new or existing jobs. **Motion-study techniques** are another set of operational tools used to improve productivity.

Work measurement methods are operational tools used to establish labor standards. These standards are useful for planning, control, productivity improvements, costing and pricing, bidding, compensation, motivation, and financial incentives. In measuring organizational characteristics (e.g., pricing, quality), managers must ensure that their methods are compatible with the organization's objectives.[36]

Operations Control

Once a decision has been made to design an operational plan of action, resource allocations are considered. After management has decided on a functional operations strategy by using marketing and financial plans of action, it determines what specific tasks are necessary to accomplish functional objectives. This process is known as *operations control*.

Operations control is defined as making sure that operations activities are carried out as planned. The major components of operations control are just-in-time inventory control, maintenance control, cost control, budgetary control, ratio analysis, and materials control. Each of these components is discussed in detail in the following sections.

20-4 An understanding of how operations control procedures can be used to control production

Just-in-Time Inventory Control

Just-in-time (JIT) inventory control is a technique for reducing inventories to a minimum by arranging for production components to be delivered to the production facility "just in time" for them to be used.[37] The concept, developed primarily by the Toyota Motor Company of Japan, is also called "zero inventory" or *kanban*—the latter a Japanese term referring to purchasing raw materials by using a special ordering form.[38]

JIT is based on the management philosophy that products should be manufactured only when customers need them and only in the quantities customers require in order to minimize the amounts of raw materials and finished goods inventories that manufacturers keep on hand. It also emphasizes maintaining organizational operations by using only the resources that are absolutely necessary to meet customer demand.

Although the concept of JIT was developed primarily in Japan, its use has spread throughout the world. Several studies have demonstrated that manufacturing companies in the United States have decreased their inventories over time. More recently, other research finds that manufacturers in China, currently a hotbed of manufacturing used by companies around the world, are also reducing their inventories.[39]

Best Conditions for JIT

JIT works best in companies that manufacture relatively standardized products that experience consistent demand. Such companies can confidently order materials from suppliers and assemble products in small, continuous batches. The result is a smooth, consistent flow of purchased materials and assembled products, with little inventory buildup.

However, JIT is not the best choice for every organization. Companies that manufacture nonstandardized products that in turn experience sporadic or seasonal demand generally face more irregular purchases of raw materials from suppliers, more uneven production cycles, and greater accumulations of inventory.[40]

Advantages of JIT

When successfully implemented, JIT enhances organizational performance in several important ways. First, it reduces the unnecessary labor expenses generated by manufacturing products that are not sold. Second, it minimizes the tying up of monetary resources in purchases of production-related materials that do not result in timely sales. Third, it helps management hold down inventory expenses, particularly storage and handling costs. Better inventory management and control of labor costs, in fact, are the two most commonly cited benefits of JIT.

Characteristics of JIT

Experience indicates that successful JIT programs have certain common characteristics:[41]

1. **Closeness of suppliers**—Manufacturers using JIT find it beneficial to use raw materials suppliers who are based only a short distance from them. When a company is ordering smaller quantities of raw materials at a time, suppliers must sometimes be asked to make one or more deliveries per day. Short distances make multiple deliveries per day feasible. Nonetheless, relying on one large supplier may present disadvantages as well. For example, an earthquake once caused one of Toyota's piston suppliers to suspend its operations temporarily. Because the automaker practices JIT, the resulting shortage of pistons caused a delay in the delivery of about 55,000 vehicles.[42]
2. **High quality of materials purchased from suppliers**—Manufacturers using JIT find it especially difficult to overcome problems caused by defective materials. Because they keep their materials inventory small, defective materials purchased from a supplier may force them to discontinue the production process until another delivery from the supplier can be arranged. Such production slowdowns can be disadvantageous, causing late delivery to customers or lost sales.
3. **Well-organized receiving and handling of materials purchased from suppliers**—Companies using JIT must be able to receive and handle raw materials effectively and efficiently. Materials must be available for the production process where and when they are needed because if they are not, extra costs will be built into the production process.
4. **Strong management commitment**—Management must be strongly committed to the concept of JIT. The system takes time and effort to plan, install, and improve—and is therefore expensive to implement. Management must be willing to commit funds to initiate the JIT system and support it once it is functioning.

Maintenance Control

Maintenance control is aimed at keeping an organization's facility and equipment functioning at predetermined work levels. In the planning stage, managers must select a strategy that will direct personnel to fix equipment either before it malfunctions or after it malfunctions. The first strategy is referred to as a **pure-preventive maintenance policy**—machine adjustments, lubrication, cleaning, parts replacement, painting, and needed repairs and overhauls are done regularly, before facilities or machines malfunction. At the other end of the maintenance control continuum is the **pure-breakdown (repair) policy**, which decrees that facilities and equipment be fixed only after they malfunction.

Most organizations implement a maintenance strategy somewhere in the middle of the maintenance continuum. Management usually tries to select a level and frequency of maintenance that minimize the cost of both preventive maintenance and breakdowns (repair). Because no level of preventive maintenance can eliminate breakdowns altogether, repair will always be a necessary activity.

Whether management decides on a pure-preventive or a pure-breakdown policy, or on something in between, the prerequisite for a successful maintenance program is the availability of maintenance parts and supplies or replacement (standby) equipment. Some organizations choose to keep standby machines to protect themselves from the consequences of breakdowns. Plants that use special-purpose equipment are more likely to invest in standby equipment than are those that use general-purpose equipment.

Cost Control

Cost control is wide-ranging control aimed at keeping organizational costs at planned levels.[43] Because cost control relates to all organizational costs, it is involved in activities in all organizational areas, such as research and development, operations, marketing, and finance. If an organization is to be successful, costs in all organizational areas must be controlled. Cost control is therefore an important responsibility of all managers in an organization.

Operations activities are cost intensive—perhaps the most cost intensive of all organizational activities—so when significant cost savings are realized in organizations, they are generally realized at the operations level.

Operations managers are responsible for the overall control of the cost of goods or services sold. Producing goods and services at or below planned cost levels is their principal objective, so operations managers are commonly evaluated primarily on their cost control activities. When operations costs are consistently above planned levels, the organization may need to change its operations management.

Stages in Cost Control   The general cost control process has four stages:

1. Establishing standard or planned cost amounts
2. Measuring actual costs incurred
3. Comparing planned costs to incurred costs
4. Making changes to reduce actual costs to planned costs when necessary

When following these stages for specific operations cost control, the operations manager must first establish planned costs or cost standards for operations activities such as labor, materials, and overhead. Next, the operations manager must actually measure or calculate the costs incurred for these activities. Third, the operations manager must compare actual operations costs to planned operations costs and, fourth, take steps to reduce actual operations costs to planned levels if necessary.

Budgetary Control

As described in Chapter 7, a budget is a single-use financial plan that covers a specified length of time. An organization's **budget** is its financial plan outlining how funds in a given period will be obtained and spent.

In addition to being a financial plan, however, a budget can be the basis for *budgetary control*—that is, for ensuring that income and expenses occur as planned. As managers gather information on actual receipts and expenditures within an operating period, they may uncover significant deviations from budgeted amounts. If so, they should develop and implement a control strategy aimed at bringing actual performance in line with planned performance. This effort, of course, assumes that the plan contained in the budget is appropriate for the organization. The following sections discuss some potential pitfalls of budgets and human relations considerations that may make a budget inappropriate.

Potential Pitfalls of Budgets   To maximize the benefits of using budgets, managers must avoid several potential pitfalls, including the following:

1. **Placing too much emphasis on relatively insignificant organizational expenses**—In preparing and implementing a budget, managers should allocate more time for dealing with significant organizational expenses and less time for dealing with relatively insignificant organizational expenses. For example, the amount of time managers spend on developing and implementing a budget for labor costs typically should be much greater than the amount of time they spend on developing and implementing a budget for office supplies.

2. **Increasing budgeted expenses year after year without adequate information**—It does not necessarily follow that items contained in last year's budget should be increased this year. Perhaps the best-known method for overcoming this potential pitfall is zero-base budgeting.[44] **Zero-base budgeting** is a planning and budgeting process that requires managers to justify their entire budget request in detail rather than simply refer to budget amounts established in previous years.

    Some management theorists believe that zero-base budgeting is a better management tool than traditional budgeting—which simply starts with the budget amount established in the prior year—because it emphasizes focused identification and control of each budget item. It is unlikely, however, that this tool will be implemented successfully unless management adequately explains what zero-base budgeting is and how it is to be used in the organization. One of the earliest and most commonly cited successes in implementing a zero-base budgeting program took place in the Department of Agriculture's Office of Budget and Finance.

3. **Ignoring the fact that budgets must be changed periodically**—Managers should recognize that factors such as costs of materials, newly developed technology, and product demand change constantly and that budgets must be reviewed and modified periodically in response to those changes.

A special type of budget called a *variable budget* is sometimes used to determine automatically when such changes in budgets are needed. A **variable budget**, also known as a *flexible budget*, outlines the levels of resources to be allocated for each organizational activity according to the level of production within the organization. It follows, then, that a variable budget automatically indicates an increase in the amount of resources allocated for various organizational activities when production levels go up and a decrease when production goes down.

Human Relations Considerations in Using Budgets   Many managers believe that, although budgets are valuable planning and control tools, they can result in major human relations problems in an organization. A classic article by Chris Argyris, for example,

STEPS FOR SUCCESS

Controlling with a Budget

Advisers from the Small Business Administration and private-sector consultants agree that for a budget to be useful in operations control, managers must actively use budgets. Here are some ways to make budgetary controls effective:[45]

- Review the budget every month. In light of actual performance, decide whether revenue forecasts and budgeted expenses still seem realistic. Change any unrealistic numbers.
- For every line in the budget, be sure someone has the authority and responsibility to monitor that number and update performance data.

- Whenever unexpected changes occur, such as a big new client or a hike in the price of a key material, review the impact on expenses and earnings.
- Keep track of the budget's accuracy as well as the company's performance. If some numbers are frequently too high or too low, take that pattern into account for future budgeting.
- Share budget information with employees, and teach them how their actions affect the numbers. Tie rewards to meeting or beating the budgeted numbers.

shows how budgets can create pressures that unite workers against management, cause harmful conflict between management and factory workers, and create tensions that result in worker inefficiency and worker aggression against management.[46] If such problems are severe enough, a budget may result in more harm than good to an organization.[47]

Reducing Human Relations Problems   Several strategies have been suggested to minimize the human relations problems caused by budgets. The strategy recommended most often is to design and implement appropriate human relations training programs for finance personnel, accounting personnel, production supervisors, and all other key people involved in the formulation and use of budgets. These training programs should emphasize both the advantages and the disadvantages of applying pressure on people through budgets and the possible results of using budgets to imply that an organization member is a success or a failure at his or her job.

Ratio Analysis

Another type of control uses ratio analysis.[48] A *ratio* is a relationship between two numbers that is calculated by dividing one number into the other. **Ratio analysis** is the process of generating information that summarizes the financial position of an organization through the calculation of ratios based on various financial measures that appear on the organization's balance sheet and income statements.

The ratios available to managers for controlling organizations, shown in **Table 20.1**, can be divided into four categories:

1. Profitability ratios
2. Liquidity ratios
3. Activity ratios
4. Leverage ratios

Using Ratios to Control Organizations   Managers should use ratio analysis in three ways to control an organization:[49]

- **Managers should evaluate all ratios simultaneously.** This strategy ensures that managers will develop and implement a control strategy that is appropriate for the organization as a whole rather than a control strategy that suits only one phase or segment of the organization.
- **Managers should compare computed values for ratios in a specific organization with the values of industry averages for those ratios.** The values of industry averages for the ratios can be obtained from Dunn & Bradstreet; Robert Morris Associates, a national association of bank loan officers; the Federal Trade Commission (FTC); and the Securities and Exchange Commission (SEC). Managers increase the probability that they will formulate and implement appropriate control strategies when they compare their financial situations to those of competitors.
- **Managers' use of ratios should incorporate trend analysis.** Managers must remember that any set of ratio values is actually only a determination of the relationships that existed

TABLE 20.1   **Four Categories of Ratios**

Type	Example	Calculation	Interpretation
Profitability	Return on investment (ROI)	$\dfrac{\text{Profit after taxes}}{\text{Total assets}}$	Productivity of assets
Liquidity	Current ratio	$\dfrac{\text{Current assets}}{\text{Current liabilities}}$	Short-term solvency
Activity	Inventory turnover	$\dfrac{\text{Sales}}{\text{Inventory}}$	Efficiency of inventory management
Leverage	Debt ratio	$\dfrac{\text{Total debt}}{\text{Total assets}}$	How a company finances itself

in a specified time period (often a year). To employ ratio analysis to maximum advantage, they need to accumulate ratio values for several successive time periods in order to uncover specific organizational trends. Once these trends are revealed, managers can formulate and implement appropriate strategies for dealing with those trends.

Materials Control

Materials control is an operations control activity that determines the flow of materials from vendors through an operations system to customers. The achievement of desired levels of product cost, quality, availability, dependability, and flexibility heavily depends on the effective and efficient flow of materials. Materials management activities can be broadly organized into six groups or functions: purchasing, receiving, inventorying, floor controlling, trafficking, and shipping and distributing.

Procurement of Materials
Procurement involves the purchasing of materials, including raw materials, parts, subassemblies, and supplies. This procurement is the responsibility of the purchasing department, and the leaders of these departments are known as chief procurement officers (CPOs). Actually, purchases of production materials are largely automated and linked to a resources requirement planning system. Purchases of all other materials, however, are based on requisitions from users. The purchasing department's job does not end with the placement of an order; order follow-up is just as crucial. Given the nature of procurement, it should come as no surprise that surveys suggest that reducing purchasing costs remains the top priority of procurement managers.[50]

Receiving, Shipping, and Trafficking
Receiving activities include unloading, identifying, inspecting, reporting, and storing inbound shipments. Shipping and distribution activities are similar and may include preparing documents, packaging, labeling, loading, and directing outbound shipments to customers and to distribution centers. Shipping and receiving are sometimes organized as one unit.

A traffic manager's main responsibilities are selecting the transportation mode, coordinating the arrival and departure of shipments, and auditing freight bills.

Inventory and Shop-Floor Control
Inventory control activities ensure the continuous availability of purchased materials. Work-in-process and finished-goods inventories are inventory control subsystems. Inventory control specifies what, when, and how much to buy. Held inventories buffer the organization against a variety of uncertainties that can disrupt supply, but because holding inventory is costly, an optimal inventory control policy provides a predetermined level of certainty of supply at the lowest possible cost.

Shop-floor control activities include input/output control, scheduling, sequencing, routing, dispatching, and expediting.

Although many materials management activities can be programmed, the human factor is key to a competitive performance. Skilled and motivated employees are therefore crucial to successful materials control.

Operations Control Tools

20-5 Insights into operations control tools and how they evolve into a continual improvement approach to production management and control

In addition to understanding production, operations management, and operations control, managers need to be aware of various operations control tools that are useful in an operations facility. A **control tool** is a specific procedure or technique that presents pertinent organizational information in a way that helps managers and workers develop and implement an appropriate control strategy. That is, a control tool aids managers and workers in pinpointing the organizational strengths and weaknesses on which a useful control strategy must focus. This section discusses specific control tools for day-to-day operations as well as for longer-run operations.

Using Control Tools to Control Organizations

Continual improvement of operations is a practical, not a theoretical, managerial concern. It is, essentially, the development and use of better methods. Different types of organizations have different goals and strategies, but all organizations struggle daily to find better ways of doing things. This goal of continual improvement applies not just to money-making enterprises but also to organizations that have other missions. Because organizational leaders are continually changing systems and personal styles of management, everyone within the organization is continually learning to live with change.

Inspection

Traditionally, managers believed that if you wanted good-quality products, you hired many inspectors to make sure an operation was producing at the desired quality level. These inspectors examined and graded finished products or components, parts, or services at any stage of operation by measuring, tasting, touching, weighing, disassembling, destroying, and testing. The goal of inspection was to detect unacceptable quality levels before a bad product or service reached a customer. Whenever a lot of defects were found, management blamed the workers and hired more inspectors.

To Inspect or Not to Inspect Today, managers know that inspection cannot catch problems built into the system. The traditional inspection process does not result in improvement and does not guarantee quality. In fact, according to Deming, inspection is a limited, grossly overused, and often misused tool. He recommended that management stop relying on mass inspection to achieve quality and advocated instead either 100 percent inspection in those cases where defect-free work is impossible or no inspection at all where the level of defects is acceptably small.

Science photo/Fotolia

To prevent low-quality product from reaching the market, companies should have a solid quality assurance program in place.

Management by Exception

Management by exception is a control technique that allows only significant deviations between planned and actual performance to be brought to a manager's attention. Management by exception is based on the *exception principle*, a management principle that appeared in early management literature.[51] This principle recommends that subordinates handle all routine organizational matters, leaving managers free to deal with nonroutine, or exceptional, organizational issues.

Establishing Rules Some organizations rely on subordinates or managers to detect the significant deviations between standards and performance that signal exceptional issues. Other organizations establish rules to ensure that exceptional issues surface as a matter of normal operating procedure. Setting rules must be done carefully to ensure that all true deviations are brought to the manager's attention.

Two examples of rules based on the exception principle are the following:[52]

1. A department manager must immediately inform the plant manager if actual weekly labor costs exceed estimated weekly labor costs by more than 15 percent.
2. A department manager must immediately inform the plant manager if actual dollars spent plus estimated dollars to be spent on a special project exceed the funds approved for the project by more than 10 percent.

Although these two rules happen to focus on production-related expenditures, detecting and reporting significant rules deviations can be established in almost any organizational area.

If appropriately administered, the management-by-exception control technique ensures the best use of managers' time. Because only significant issues are brought to managers' attention, the possibility that managers will spend their valuable time working on relatively insignificant issues is automatically eliminated.

Of course, the significant issues brought to managers' attention could be organizational strengths as well as organizational weaknesses. Obviously, managers should try to reinforce the first and eliminate the second.

Management by Objectives

In management by objectives, which was discussed in Chapter 7, the manager assigns a specific set of objectives and action plans to workers and then rewards those workers on the basis of how close they come to reaching their goals. This control technique has been implemented in corporations that are intent on using an employee-participative means to improve productivity.

Break-Even Analysis

Another production-related control tool commonly used by managers is break-even analysis. **Break-even analysis** is the process of generating information that summarizes various levels of profit or loss associated with various levels of production. The next sections discuss three facets of this control tool: basic ingredients of break-even analysis, types of break-even analysis available to managers, and the relationship between break-even analysis and controlling.[53]

Basic Ingredients of Break-Even Analysis
Break-even analysis typically involves reflection, discussion, reasoning, and decision making relative to the following seven major aspects of production:

1. **Fixed costs**—A **fixed cost** is an expense incurred by the organization regardless of the number of products produced. Some examples are real estate taxes, upkeep to the exterior of a business building, and interest expenses on money borrowed to finance the purchase of equipment.
2. **Variable costs**—An expense that fluctuates with the number of products produced is a **variable cost**. Examples are costs of packaging a product, costs of materials needed to make the product, and costs associated with packing products to prepare them for shipping.
3. **Total cost**—The **total cost** is simply the sum of the fixed and the variable costs associated with production.
4. **Total revenue**—**Total revenue** is all sales dollars accumulated from selling manufactured products or services. Naturally, total revenue increases as more products are sold.
5. **Profit**—**Profit** is defined as the amount of total revenue that exceeds the total costs of producing the products sold.
6. **Loss**—**Loss** is the amount of the total costs of producing a product that exceeds the total revenue gained from selling the product.
7. **Break-even point**—The **break-even point** is the level of production at which the total revenue of an organization equals its total costs—that is, the point at which the organization is generating only enough revenue to cover its costs. The company is neither gaining a profit nor incurring a loss.

Types of Break-Even Analysis
Two somewhat different procedures can be used to determine the same break-even point for an organization: algebraic break-even analysis and graphic break-even analysis.

Algebraic Break-Even Analysis
The following simple formula is commonly used to determine the level of production at which an organization breaks even:

$$BE = \frac{FC}{P - VC}$$

TABLE 20.2 Fixed Costs and Variable Costs for a Book Publisher

Fixed Costs (Yearly Basis)		Variable Costs per Book Sold	
1. Real estate taxes on property	$ 1,000	1. Printing	$2.00
2. Interest on loan to purchase equipment	5,000	2. Artwork	1.00
3. Building maintenance	2,000	3. Sales commission	.50
4. Insurance	800	4. Author royalties	1.50
5. Salaried labor	80,000	5. Binding	1.00
Total fixed costs	$88,800	Total variable costs per book	$6.00

where

BE = the level of production at which the firm breaks even

FC = total fixed costs of production

P = price at which each individual unit is sold to customers

VC = variable costs associated with each product manufactured and sold

In using this formula to calculate a break-even point, two sequential steps must be followed. First, the variable costs associated with producing each unit must be subtracted from the price at which each unit will sell. The purpose of this calculation is to determine how much of the selling price of each unit sold can go toward covering total fixed costs incurred from producing all units. Second, the remainder calculated in the first step must be divided into total fixed costs. The purpose of this calculation is to determine how many units must be produced and sold to cover fixed costs. This number of units is the break-even point for the organization.

Say that a book publisher faces the fixed and variable costs per paperback book presented in **Table 20.2**. If the publisher wants to sell each book for $12, the break-even point could be calculated as follows:

$$BE = \frac{\$88,800}{\$12 - \$6}$$

$$BE = \frac{\$88,800}{\$6}$$

$$BE = 14,800 \text{ copies}$$

This calculation indicates that, if expenses and selling price remain stable, the book publisher will incur a loss if book sales are fewer than 14,800 copies, it will break even if book sales equal 14,800 copies, and it will make a profit if book sales exceed 14,800 copies.

Graphic Break-Even Analysis Graphic break-even analysis entails the construction of a graph showing all the critical elements in a break-even analysis. **Figure 20.5** is such a graph for the book publisher. Note that in a break-even graph, the total revenue line starts at zero.

Advantages of Using the Algebraic and Graphic Break-Even Methods

Both the algebraic and the graphic methods of break-even analysis for the book publisher result in the same break-even point—14,800 books produced and sold—but the processes used to arrive at this point are quite different.

Which break-even method managers should use is usually determined by the situation they face. For a manager who desires a quick yet accurate determination of a break-even point, the algebraic method generally suffices. For a manager who wants a more complete picture of the cumulative relationships among the break-even point, fixed costs, and escalating variable costs, the graphic break-even method is more useful. For example, the book publisher could quickly and easily see from Figure 20.5 the cumulative relationships of fixed costs, escalating variable costs, and potential profit and loss associated with various levels of production.

Control and Break-Even Analysis Break-even analysis is a useful control tool

because it helps managers understand the relationships among fixed costs, variable costs, total costs, and profit and loss within an organization. Once these relationships are understood,

Figure 20.5

Break-even analysis for a book publisher

* Note that drawing the variable costs line on top of the fixed costs line means that variable costs have been added to fixed costs. Therefore, the variable costs line also represents total costs.

managers can take steps to modify one or more of the variables to reduce the deviation between planned and actual profit levels.[54]

Increasing costs or decreasing selling prices has the overall effect of increasing the number of units an organization must produce and sell to break even. Conversely, the managerial strategy for decreasing the number of products an organization must produce and sell to break even entails lowering or stabilizing fixed and variable costs or increasing the selling price of each unit. The exact break-even control strategy that a particular manager should develop and implement is dictated primarily by that manager's specific organizational situation.

Other Broad Operations Control Tools

Some of the best-known and most commonly used operations control tools are discussed in the following sections. The primary purpose of these tools is to control the production of organizational goods and services.[55]

Decision Tree Analysis
Decision tree analysis, as you recall from Chapter 8, is a statistical and graphical, multiphased decision-making technique that contains a series of steps showing the sequence and interdependence of decisions. Decision trees allow a decision maker to deal with uncertain events by determining the relative expected value of each alternative course of action. The probabilities of different possible events are known, as are the monetary payoffs that would result from a particular alternative and a particular event. Decision trees are best suited to situations in which capacity decisions involve several capacity expansion alternatives and the selection of the alternative with the highest expected profit or the lowest expected cost is necessary.

Process Control
Statistical process control, known as **process control**, is a technique that assists in monitoring production processes. Production processes must be monitored continually to ensure that the quality of their output is acceptable. The earlier that one can detect a faulty production process, the better. If detection occurs late in the production process, the company may find parts that do not meet quality standards, and scrapping or reworking these units is a costly proposition. If a production process results in unstable performance or is completely out of control, corrective action must be taken. Process control can be implemented with the aid of graphical charts known as control charts.

Value Analysis

Value analysis is a cost control and cost reduction technique that helps managers control operations by focusing primarily on material costs. The goal of this analysis, which is performed by examining all the parts and materials and their functions, is to reduce costs by using cheaper components and materials so that product quality or appeal is not affected. Simplification of parts—which lowers production costs—is also a goal of value analysis. Value analysis can result not only in cost savings but also in an improved product.

Value analysis requires a team effort. This team, if not company-wide, should at least include personnel from operations, purchasing, engineering, and marketing.

Computer-Aided Design

Computer-aided design (CAD) systems include several automated design technologies. *Computer graphics* is used to design geometric specifications for parts, whereas *computer-aided engineering (CAE)* is employed to evaluate and perform engineering analyses on a part. CAD also includes technologies used in process design. CAD ensures the quality of a product by guaranteeing not only the quality of parts in the product but also the appropriateness of the product's design.

Computer-Aided Manufacturing

Computer-aided manufacturing (CAM) employs computers to plan and program equipment used in the production and inspection of manufactured items. Linking CAM and CAD processes through a computer is especially beneficial when production processes must be altered because, when CAD and CAM systems can share information easily, design changes can be implemented in a short period of time.

CHALLENGE CASE SUMMARY

Increasing productivity at Tesla, as described in the Challenge Case, is mainly a matter of integrating resources such as people, equipment, and materials to reduce cycle times. Tesla is attempting to increase its production capability to 1 million cars by the year 2020. This is significant because, in all of 2016, the firm produced only 76,000 units. It will be the fastest ramp-up of production in automotive history. Other ways to improve productivity at Tesla could include more effective training programs and more selective hiring decisions.

To maintain and improve product quality even as it improves efficiency, Tesla's management could establish a quality assurance program that continually monitors components and finished products to ensure that they are at acceptable levels. Quality circles could be established to involve employees in the effort to improve product and process quality. Automation also could improve the efficiency as well as the quality of manufacturing processes at Tesla.

As Tesla increases production, it will focus on operations management. Operations management is the systematic direction and control of the operations processes that transform resources into finished goods and services. Tesla will need new operations procedures to meet its production goal of 1 million cars. Once established, new operations procedures at Tesla must be continually monitored by management for both effectiveness ("doing the right things") and efficiency ("doing things right").

Factors that Tesla's management must consider when making operations decisions include *capacity strategy*, making sure that the company has appropriate resources to perform needed functions at appropriate times; *location strategy*, making sure that Tesla's resources are appropriately positioned for work when the work must be performed; *product strategy*, making sure that appropriate products are targeted and provided; *process strategy*, making sure that Tesla is employing appropriate steps in producing its products; *layout strategy*, making sure that the flow of raw materials and components is desirable; and *human resource strategy*, making sure that Tesla has employees who can make its products.

Operations control activities can help Tesla's management ensure that production is carried out as planned. *Just-in-time inventory control*, for example, would ensure that enough raw materials are in place and available just when they are needed for the next step in a production process. In contrast, putting money into large surpluses of tires, for example, would needlessly tie up company resources and reduce profitability. *Maintenance control* would ensure that the equipment needed to produce a product line is operating at a desirable level. *Cost control* would ensure that Tesla is not producing its products too expensively. *Budgetary control* would focus on acquiring company resources and using them to make products as stipulated by Tesla's financial plan.

Operations control at Tesla can also include ratio analysis, or determining relationships among various factors on Tesla's income statement and balance sheet to arrive at a good indication of the company's financial position. Through ratio analysis, Tesla's management could monitor factors such as inventory levels, production volume, and production costs to determine their overall impact on company profitability, liquidity, and leverage. To assess the impact on the financial condition of the company of producing various products at various locations, Tesla's management could track ratios over time to discern trends.

Finally, operations control at Tesla would need to include materials control to ensure that materials purchased from suppliers are flowing appropriately from vendors to manufacturing plants and are meeting production requirements. For example, the goal of monitoring the components provided by a contractor would be to ensure that these products are meeting the company's specifications and quality standards, as well as arriving on schedule and in the quantities ordered.

Several useful production control tools are available to Tesla's management to ensure that products are made efficiently and effectively. First, management can have products sampled and inspected to determine which, if any, should be improved and how to improve them. Second, Tesla can use management by exception to control product quality and costs. In this case, Tesla's workers would correct minor defects and bring only exceptional matters to management's attention. To use management by exception at Tesla successfully, it would be necessary to implement some carefully designed rules. One such rule might be that when 5 percent or more of components arrive late from a vendor, the inventory problem must be reported to a plant manager. The manager would then work with the vendor to resolve the delivery problem or find a more reliable vendor.

As an alternative, Tesla might prefer to use management by objectives to control efficiency. For example, management might set objectives for reducing cycle time and improving energy efficiency at the corporate level. Each business unit leader has objectives for improving cycle times and energy efficiency in the business unit. With management by objectives, each level of managers

and employees at Tesla should also have objectives to meet that contribute to those overall objectives. If the objectives are worthwhile and realistic, but some of Tesla's employees are still not reaching them consistently, then management would take steps to ensure that they are met.

Another control tool that Tesla's management might find highly useful is break-even analysis. Break-even analysis would furnish management with information about the various levels of profit or loss associated with various levels of revenue. To use this tool, Tesla would have to determine the total fixed costs necessary to operate each manufacturing facility, the price at which its products are sold, and the variable costs associated with making each type of product.

For example, if management wanted to determine how many Model 3s have to be sold before the company breaks even on making them, it could arrive at the break-even point algebraically by following three steps. First, all fixed costs attributable to making the Model 3—for example, rent for the factory where they are assembled—would be totaled. Second, all the variable costs of making the Model 3 would be totaled, and from this total, management would subtract the revenue from selling the Model 3. Variable costs include the pay for the workers who make the Model 3 as well as the costs of all raw materials and components purchased from contractors. Finally, the answer calculated in step 2 would be divided into the answer derived in step 1, and this figure would tell management how many Model 3s must be sold at the projected revenue level to break even.

An alternative way that Tesla's management could determine the break-even point would be by constructing a graph showing fixed costs, variable costs, and revenue per Model 3. Such a graph would probably give managers a more useful picture than the algebraic method would for formulating profit-oriented production plans for the product line and the facility.

Broader operations tools that are highly useful to managers exercising the control function include decision tree analysis, process control, value analysis, computer-aided design (CAD), and computer-aided manufacturing (CAM). Decision tree analysis, which supports complex decision making, could be a component of decision-making software such as the software that Tesla acquired for improving its production decisions. Process control and value analysis would be important for ensuring that Tesla is maintaining its quality standards and managing its materials costs. CAD is a basic tool that Tesla's engineers could use to design products that perform as intended, and it is likely to be linked to CAM in the locations where Tesla's processes are automated.

MyLab Management **Assessing Your Management Skill**
If your instructor has assigned this activity, go to www.pearson.com/mylab/management
to complete the exercise related to the Challenge Case.

DEVELOPING PRODUCTION SKILL

This section is specially designed to help you develop production skills. An individual's
production skill is based on an understanding of the concepts and the ability to apply
those concepts. The following activities will help to enhance your production skills in
various organizational situations.

Class Preparation and Personal Study

**To help you prepare for class, perform the activities outlined in this section. Performing
these activities will help you enhance your classroom performance significantly.**

Reflecting on Target Skill

On page 485, this chapter opens by presenting a target
management skill along with a list of related objectives
outlining knowledge and understanding that you should
aim to acquire related to that skill. Review this target skill
and the list of objectives to make sure that you've
acquired all pertinent information within the chapter. If
you do not feel that you've reached a particular
objective(s), study related chapter coverage until you do.

Know Key Terms

Understanding the following key terms is critical to your
preparing for class. Define each of these terms. Refer to
the page(s) referenced after a term to check your definition
or to gain further insight regarding the term.

Know How Management Concepts Relate

This section comprises activities that will sharpen your understanding of management concepts. Answer essay questions as completely as possible.

20-1. Explain how you can improve productivity in an organization.

20-2. Operations management involves the direction and control of processes. What are its key points?

20-3. Compare and contrast the following operations controls: maintenance control, cost control, budgetary control, and ratio analysis.

Management Skills Exercises

Learning activities in this section are aimed at helping you develop production skills.

MyLab Management
Discussion Questions

Go to www.pearson.com/mylab/management to complete the problems marked with this icon ⭐.

⭐ Cases

Tesla Production Will Be Fastest in History

The Challenge Case "Tesla Production Will Be Fastest in History" (p. 486) and its related Challenge Case Summary were written to help you understand the management concepts contained in this chapter. Answer the following discussion questions about the Challenge Case to further enrich your understanding of chapter content.

20-4 Why is Tesla attempting to increase production to 1 million units by 2020? From your knowledge of how products, and even cars, are manufactured, do you think the company will meet this goal? Why or why not?

20-5 List three concepts discussed in this chapter that could help Tesla's management increase productivity. Be sure to explain *how* each concept could help.

20-6 Which concept listed in question 20-5 do you think would have the greatest impact on increasing productivity? Explain fully.

Made in Belgium–DAF

Read the case and answer the questions that follow. Studying this case will help you better understand how concepts relating to just-in-time production can be applied in an organization such as DAF.

DAF Trucks is based in Oevel, in Westerlo, Belgium. It was established in 1966, and the size and facilities in the manufacturing plant have been developed gradually over the past 50 or so years with the aim of increasing production, efficiency, and responsiveness to customer needs. The company produced its 2 millionth axle in 2011 and its millionth cab in 2014. In 2015, the company completed the construction of a new cab paint shop, making it arguably the most technologically advanced facility of its kind in Europe and ensuring that production could be increased by 50 percent.

All of the cabs and axles are manufactured sequentially so that they can be delivered to the Eindhoven (Holland) assembly plant or to the UK-based Leyland Trucks facility exactly when they are needed and in the correct sequence to match customer orders. All of these companies are now owned by the US-based PACCAR corporation and use a common PACCAR Production System. This system recognizes that it is the employees on the production lines who know most about their job roles. The employees are encouraged to come up with ideas to complete tasks in a more intelligent and efficient manner.

DAF only ever produces cabs, axles, and finished trucks once they have been sold; in other words, they follow a build-to-order, just-in-time production strategy. When a customer confirms the order for a truck, DAF gives the customer a delivery date. This is to allow the customer to make all necessary preparations for the arrival of the truck on that date. DAF refers to this as delivery reliability. DAF needs to ensure that production runs smoothly and quickly, so this incorporates a short supply and production chain. The physical speed of the production is achieved by having a large number of small deliveries of components from suppliers and frequent deliveries of cabs to the truck assembly plants in Holland or the United Kingdom. This is achieved through methods such as EDI and direct-order entry.

The supply and production chain is also very flexible. Trucks are likely to have specific variations in design to match the exact requirements of the customer. Under normal manufacturing conditions, this could mean a huge inventory of parts and erratic and unpredictable production times. Using just-in-time processes, DAF is able to maintain low stock levels, minimize unnecessary handling, integrate suppliers into the processes, and maintain short administrative throughput times. At the same time, DAF is able optimize their deliveries into and out of facilities and encourage suppliers to produce standardized parts so that they can be switched if necessary without interrupting production.

Using these goals as the basis for all their production development, DAF is able to focus on continuous process improvement. The business is primarily concerned with developing and implementing increasingly more efficient systems in order to control the whole process from customer order to customer delivery.

DAF is keen to create partnerships along the whole manufacturing chain. They consider their suppliers to be real partners and look to them to come up with solutions to a range of supply- and quality-related problems. Thus, unless DAF can produce parts themselves at a lower cost, they can always rely on suppliers to produce them. In the spirit of standardization, DAF looks for suppliers who can deliver worldwide to other PACCAR businesses. They are interested in long-term relationships, and to this extent they involve suppliers at the earliest stages of new product designs. Each supplier enters a specific logistic agreement, and their performance is measured by DAF and the results reported back to the supplier.[56]

Questions

20-7 How would you evaluate DAF's layout strategy? Be specific.

20-8 What potential challenges do you see for DAF as it continues to scale up their production levels? How would you recommend overcoming these challenges?

20-9 If you were DAF, what other changes to the production would you try to implement?

Experiential Exercises

Calculating Break-Even Point

Directions. Read the following scenario and then perform the listed activities. Your instructor may want you to perform the activities as an individual or within groups. Follow all of your instructor's directions carefully.

Assume you own a small boutique fashion store that caters to both men and women who want the latest styles. The store has been open for only two months, but you realized that you did not determine exactly how many articles of clothing you must sell before you break even. After that point, you will begin to earn a profit. Using the information below, calculate the break-even point for the boutique. Each item of clothing sells for an average of $25.

Fixed Annual Costs	
Rent	$ 36,000
Interest on loan to purchase store equipment	$ 8,000
Insurance	$ 2,000
Salaried labor	$100,000
Variable Costs per Article of Clothing Sold	
Purchase price of the item	$ 10
Advertising	$ 2
Seasonal displays	$ 1
Maintenance and repairs	$ 1

You and Your Career

Already you may have held two or three jobs, perhaps even more. You probably have friends who work in other industries than you have. Think about these various types of jobs that you, your friends, and even family members have held. Describe the differences between a job that is in a production environment (such as manufacturing) and one that is service-oriented (such as sales). What characterizes these two types of work environments? After describing the differences, explain which you prefer.

Building Your Management Skills Portfolio

Your Management Skills Portfolio is a collection of activities specially designed to demonstrate your management knowledge and skill. Be sure to save your work. Taking your printed portfolio to an employment interview could be helpful in obtaining a job.

The portfolio activity for this chapter is Materials Control in a Manufacturer. Study the following information and complete the exercises that follow.

One of the concepts introduced in this chapter is materials control. It is an operations control activity that determines the flow of materials from vendors through an operations system to customers. Assume that you are the operations manager for a manufacturer that produces wooden picture frames in a variety of styles. The frames are sized from small desktop models to large, diploma-size frames. You have a good team of production workers, and they take pride in the products made at the plant.

Because you are responsible for the overall operations of the facility, you have decided to create a materials control audit to see how well the organization is performing its tasks, but you also need to establish a baseline so that comparisons can be made on improvements each quarter. What are some of the items you would examine in your audit? Pay particular attention to activities involved with the procurement of materials, receiving, shipping, trafficking, inventory, and shop-floor control. Review the section in the chapter to ensure you are familiar with each of these terms and concepts.

Develop the audit in the form of a formal report, detailing what would be examined for each of the major categories listed above.

_____

_____

_____

MyLab Management
Writing Assignments

If your instructor has assigned this activity, go to www.pearson.com/mylab/management for the following assisted-graded writing assignments:

Assisted-Grading Questions

20-10 Describe the advantages and disadvantages associated with just-in-time inventory control.

20-11 What is operations management?

Endnotes

1. This case was based on Michael Wayland, "High Noon," *Automotive News* 91 (July 10, 2017): 1.

2. James B. Dilworth, *Production and Operations Management: Manufacturing and Non-Manufacturing* (New York: Random House, 1986), 3.

3. For a better understanding of how employees' workspaces may influence their productivity, see K. H. Greenaway, H. A. Thai, S. A. Haslam, and S. C. Murphy, "Spaces That Signal Identity Improve Workplace Productivity," *Journal of Personnel Psychology* 15, no. 1 (2016): 35–43.

4. John W. Kendrick, *Understanding Productivity: An Introduction to the Dynamics of Productivity Change* (Baltimore, MD: Johns Hopkins University Press, 1977), 114.

5. E. Magnani, "The Productivity Slowdown, Sectoral Reallocations and the Growth of Atypical Employment Arrangements," *Journal of Productivity Analysis* 20 (2003): 121.

6. Raju Shanbhag, "Duke Energy Invests $1 Billion on Smart Grid Technology," *TMCnet*, February 25, 2010, http://www.tmcnet.com.

7. Justin Lahart, "Moment of Truth for U.S. Productivity Boom," *Wall Street Journal*, May 5, 2010, www.wsj.com, accessed July 6, 2010.

8. For an example of virtual offices created to increase worker productivity, see Michael K. Takagawa, "Turn Traditional Work Spaces into Virtual Offices," *Human Resources Professional* (March/April 1995): 11–14.

9. This example is based on D. Clark, "Theory & Practice: Why Silicon Valley Is Rethinking the Cubicle Office," *Wall Street Journal*, October 15, 2007, B9.

10. For more information regarding how quality control efforts can be customized, see D. Zhang, K. Linderman, and R. G. Schroeder, "Customizing Quality Management Practices: A Conceptual and Measurement Framework," *Decision Sciences* 45, no. 1 (2014): 81–114.

11. For more information on the interplay between product and service quality, see L. Xu, C. Blankson, and V. Prybutok, "Relative Contributions of Product and Service Quality in the Automobile Industry," *The Quality Management Journal* 24, no. 1 (2017): 21–36.

12. W. Edwards Deming, *Out of the Crisis* (Boston: MIT Centre for Advanced Engineering Study, 1986).

13. Gary McWilliams, "Wal-Mart Era Wanes amid Big Shifts in Retail; Rivals Find Strategies to Defeat Low Prices; World Has Changed," *Wall Street Journal*, October 3, 2007, A1.

14. John J. Dwyer, Jr., "Quality: Can You Prove It?," *Fleet Owner* (April 1995): 36.

15. Guy Boulton, "Report Touts Wisconsin Hospitals' Progress in Improving Patient Care," *Milwaukee Journal Sentinel*, January 26, 2014, http://www.jsonline.com; Dinesh Ramde, "Collaborative Effort Pays Off for Wisconsin Hospitals, Report Finds," *Wisconsin Rapids Tribune*, January 21, 2014, http://www.wisconsinrapidstribune.com; Wisconsin Hospital Association, "Wisconsin Hospitals Quality Improvement Efforts Reduce Health Care Costs by $46 Million," news release, January 21, 2014, http://www.wha.org/newsReleases .aspx; Centers for Medicare and Medicaid Services, Partnership for Patients, "About the Partnership," http://partnershipforpatients .cms.gov, accessed January 28, 2014.

16. "Key Ratings: Developing a Quality Assurance Framework for In-Service Training and Development," *Measuring Business Excellence* 7 (2003): 99.

17. Gerry Davidson, "Quality Circles Didn't Die—They Just Keep Improving," *CMA Magazine* (February 1995): 6.

18. M. Beyer, F. Gerlach, U. Flies, and R. Grol, "The Development of Quality Circles/Peer Review Groups as a Method of Quality Improvement in Europe: Results of a Survey in 26 European Countries," *Family Practice* 20 (2003): 443.

19. John Peter Koss, "Plant Robotics and Automation," *Beverage World* (April 1995): 108; Rob Spencer, "A Driving Force: Use of Robotics Remains Strong in Auto Industry," *Robotics World* 19, no. 1 (January/February 2001): 18–21. For more information on the limitations of automation, see R. Jelinek, "All Pain, No Gain? Why Adopting Sales Force Automation Tools Is Insufficient for Performance Improvement," *Business Horizons* 56 (2013): 635–642.

20. G. Bensinger, "Before Amazon's Drones Come the Robots," *Wall Street Journal*, December 8, 2013, http://online.wsj.com/news/

articles/SB10001424052702303330204579246012421712386?KEYWORDS=amazon+and+kiva, accessed February 24, 2014.

21. PWC's "UK Economic Outlook," http://www.pwc.co.uk/economic-services/ukeo/pwc-uk-economic-outlook-full-report-march-2017-v2.pdf, accessed August 2, 2017.

22. S. Nassauer, "Robots Are Replacing Workers Where You Shop," *Wall Street Journal*, https://www.wsj.com/articles/robots-are-replacing-workers-where-you-shop-1500456602, accessed August 2, 2017.

23. Robert E. Kemper and Joseph Yehudai, *Experiencing Operations Management: A Walk-Through* (Boston: PWS-Kent Publishing Company, 1991), 48.

24. Richard B. Chase and Nicholas J. Aquilano, *Production and Operations Management: A Life Cycle Approach* (Homewood, IL: Richard D. Irwin, 1981), 4.

25. Roger W. Schmenner, "Operations Management," *Business Horizons* 41, no. 3 (May/June 1998): 3–4; M. Rungtusanatham, T. Choi, D. Hollingworth, Z. Wu, and C. Forza, "Survey Research in Operations Management: Historical Analyses," *Journal of Operations Management* 21 (2003): 475.

26. To understand the challenges that stem from focusing solely on efficiency, see R. J. Schonberger and K. A. Brown, "Missing the Link in Competitive Manufacturing Research and Practice: Customer-Responsive Concurrent Production," *Journal of Operations Management* 49–51 (2017): 83–87.

27. Michelle V. Rafter, "Researcher Delivers a New Flavor of Management Courtesy of Domino's," *Workforce Management*, June 2010, http://www.workforce.com.

28. For an overview of location strategy, see A. Goerzen, C. G. Asmussen, and B. B. Nielsen, "Global Cities and Multinational Enterprise Location Strategy," *Journal of International Business Studies* 44 (2013): 427–450; M. Ketokivi, V. Turkulainen, T. Seppala, P. Rouvinen, and J. Ali-Yrkko, "Why Locate Manufacturing in a High-Cost Country? A Case Study of 35 Production Location Decisions," *Journal of Operations Management* 49–51 (2017): 20–30.

29. For a thorough discussion of product strategy, see Olav Sorenson, "Letting the Market Work for You: An Evolutionary Perspective on Product Strategy," *Strategic Management Journal* 21, no. 5 (May 2000): 577–592.

30. Business Sweden, "Charging Ahead in Gothenburg Alelion Opens Sweden's First Large-scale Lithium-Ion Battery Factory," https://www .business-sweden.se/en/Invest/news-and-downloads/investment-news/charging-ahead-in-gothenburg-alelion-opens-swedens-first-large-scale-lithium-ion-battery-factory/.

31. For an example of the kinds of layout issues that concern printers in Europe, see Jill Roth, "Molto Bene," *American Printer* (March 1994): 54–58.

32. For ways to ensure that human resource strategy is progressive, see Kevin Barksdale, "Why We Should Update HR Education," *Journal of Management Education* 22, no. 4 (August 1998): 526–530.

33. Bradford Wernle, "Chrysler Rushes to Hire as It Refills Product Pipeline," *Workforce Management*, January 13, 2010, http://www .workforce.com.

34. For two perspectives on labor force planning during a period of economic uncertainty, see John Zappe, "Dissatisfied Workers + Recovery = Workforce Planning," ERE.net, January 19, 2010, http://www.ere.net; Fay Hansen, "Strategic Workforce Planning in an Uncertain World," *Workforce Management*, July 2009, http://www .workforce.com.

35. For a step-by-step description of job design, see Rutgers University website, "How to Design a Job," http://uhr.rutgers.edu, accessed July 1, 2010. See also M. A. Huselid and B. E. Becker, "Bridging Micro and Macro Domains: Workforce Differentiation and Strategic Human Resource Management," *Journal of Management* 37: 421–428.

36. Sergio Sousa and Elaine E. Aspinwall, "Development of a Performance Measurement Framework for SMEs," *Total Quality Management & Business Excellence* 21, no. 5 (May 2010): 475–501.

37. For a review of JIT and lean production, see M. Holweg, "The Genealogy of Lean Production," *Journal of Operations Management* 25, no. 2 (2007): 420–437.

38. Lee J. Krajewski and Larry P. Ritzman, *Operations Management: Strategy and Analysis* (Reading, MA: Addison-Wesley, 1987), 573; Albert F. Celley, William H. Clegg, Arthur W. Smith, and Mark A.

Vonderembse, "Implementation of JIT in the United States," *Journal of Purchasing and Materials Management* (Winter 1987): 9–15. See also Y. Matsui, "An Empirical Analysis of Just-in-Time Production in Japanese Manufacturing Companies," *International Journal of Production Economics* 108 (2007): 153–164.

39. J. Shan and K. Zhu, "Inventory Management in China: An Empirical Study," *Production and Operations Management* (2012), doi: 10.1111/j.1937-5956.2012.01320.x.

40. Jeremy N. Smith, "What Comes after Just-in-Time?," *World Trade* 22, no. 4 (April 2009): 22–26. For a discussion of the costs associated with JIT, see C. Eroglu and C. Hofer, "Lean, Leaner, Too Lean? The Inventory-Performance Link Revisited," *Journal of Operations Management* 29: 356–369.

41. John D. Baxter, "Kanban Works Wonders, but Will It Work in U.S. Industry?," *Iron Age* (June 7, 1982): 44–48.

42. Amy Chozick, "Toyota Sticks by 'Just in Time' Strategy after Quake," *Wall Street Journal*, July 24, 2007, A2.

43. For discussion of cost control that focuses on corporate jets, see Mel Mandell, "Why Sharing Jets Is Cost Effective," *World Trade* 11, no. 7 (July 1998): 85.

44. George S. Minmier, "Zero-Base Budgeting: A New Budgeting Technique for Discretionary Costs," *Mid-South Quarterly Business Review* 14 (October 1976): 2–8.

45. Caron Beesley, "How to Build and Use a Business Budget That's Useful All Year Long," *Small Business Administration Community*, June 3, 2013, http://www.sba.gov; Eric Thomas, "Five Tips for 'Use It or Lose It' Budgets," *CIO Insight*, August 16, 2013, http://www.cioinsight.com; Frank Ross, "Confessions of a Budget Freak," *Landscape Management*, October 2013, EBSCOhost, http://web.ebscohost.com.

46. Chris Argyris, "Human Problems with Budgets," *Harvard Business Review* (January/February 1953): 108.

47. S. M. Clor-Proell, S. E. Kaplan, and C. A. Proell, "The Impact of Budget Goal Difficulty and Promotion Availability on Employee Fraud," *Journal of Business Ethics* 131 (2015): 773–790.

48. This section is based primarily on J. Fred Weston and Eugene F. Brigham, *Essentials of Managerial Finance*, 7th ed. (Hinsdale, IL: Dryden Press, 1985).

49. For an excellent discussion of ratio analysis and its alternatives, see W. Chen and L. McGinnis, "Reconciling Ratio Analysis and DEA as Performance Assessment Tools," *European Journal of Operational Research* 178, no. 1 (2007): 277–291.

50. The Deloitte Global CPO Survey 2016, www.deloitte.co.uk/cposurvey2016.

51. Lester R. Bittle, *Management by Exception* (New York: McGraw-Hill, 1964); Frederick W. Taylor, *Shop Management* (New York: Harper & Bros., 1911), 126–127.

52. These two rules are adapted from *Boardroom Reports* 5 (May 1976): 4.

53. For an interesting look at how entrepreneurs use break-even analysis, see A. Oe and H. Mitsuhashi, "Founders' Experiences for Start-ups' Fast Break-Even," *Journal of Business Research* 66 (2013): 2193–2201.

54. Robert J. Lambrix and Surenda S. Singhvi, "How to Set Volume-Sensitive ROI Targets," *Harvard Business Review* (March/April 1981): 174.

55. For a listing and discussion of quantitative tools and their appropriate uses, see Kemper and Yehudai, *Experiencing Operations Management*.

56. DAF Corporate, "Welcome to DAF Trucks," http://www.daf.com/en.

Appendix
Managing: History and Current Thinking

1

TARGET SKILL

Comprehensive Management Skill: the ability to apply collectively concepts from various major management approaches to perform a manager's job

COMPREHENSIVE MANAGEMENT SKILL AND YOUR CAREER

Comprehensive management skill can be of great value to you in enhancing your management career. This skill will help you to diagnose and solve problems from classical, behavioral, and management science perspectives. Such problem solving helps to rid the organization of unwanted barriers to goal attainment, contributes significantly to organizational success, builds your image as a problem solver, makes you more valuable to your organization, and supports your promotions as you build your career.

OBJECTIVES

To help build my *comprehensive management skill,* when studying this appendix, I will attempt to acquire:

A1-1 An understanding of the classical approach to management

A1-2 Knowledge about the behavioral approach to management

A1-3 Insights about the management science approach to management

A1-4 Information about the contingency approach to management

A1-5 An understanding of the system approach to management

A1-6 Knowledge about the learning organization approach to management

---

MyLab Management Chapter Warm Up

If your instructor has assigned this activity, go to www.pearson.com/mylab/management to complete the chapter warm up.

CHALLENGE CASE

How Management Innovation Keeps Ford Moving Ahead

Since Ford Motor Company's early years, innovative management has given the company a competitive edge. Ford introduced the Model T in 1908; it quickly became popular, but building it was expensive and slow. Because workers brought parts to a chassis remaining in one spot, it took more than 12 hours to put together each car. Henry Ford decided to set up the work differently: The chassis would be pulled along the floor to the parts and the workers. By 1914, improvements to the moving assembly line had trimmed the assembly time to 93 minutes per car.

But Ford saw more than a production process; he saw a new approach to managing workers. He used the efficiency gained from the assembly line to make working for the company more attractive so that workers would be less likely to quit. He more than doubled wages to $5 per day and shortened the nine-hour workday by an hour. He also set up training facilities where workers could learn to manage their money. Besides improving employee relations, these efforts made it possible for Ford's workers to become Ford customers as well.

Years later, the founder's son, Henry Ford II, also introduced management innovations. During World War II, the need to move people and materials around the world to win the war fueled the innovation of applying analytic methods to management problems. After the war, Ford brought the creators of the government's management information system to his company so that they could apply their methods there. These so-called whiz kids studied Ford's informal record-keeping systems and set up formal financial methods and controls to help the company function more efficiently.

Today, Ford technology has entered the twenty-first century. Under the leadership of Ford's previous CEO, Alan Mulally, Ford began using computer technology and analytic tools to predict consumer preferences and precisely schedule production to meet that demand. Mulally also demonstrated modern thinking in the way he managed people: He saw his role as creating an environment in which everyone focused on "moving the organization forward." Employees continue to be empowered to act when they see a problem. This still includes management negotiating with union representatives to find ways to make facilities work more efficiently rather than simply closing unprofitable operations. In this environment, employees can share in the organization's

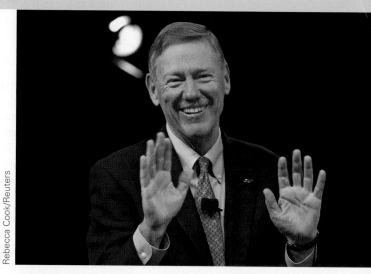

Rebecca Cook/Reuters

Ford focused on moving ahead under the leadership of previous CEO, Alan Mulally, by using twenty-first century technology and modern thinking in the management of its employees.

successes. Ford reported strong earnings for the year and announced that employees would receive a record profit-sharing payment of more than $8,000 each.[1]

THE COMPREHENSIVE MANAGEMENT SKILL CHALLENGE

The Challenge Case illustrates many different comprehensive management skill challenges that Ford Motor Company's management must strive to overcome. For Ford to be successful, management must collectively apply insights from the classical, behavioral, management science, contingency, systems, and learning organization approaches to managing. The remaining material in this appendix explains these approaches and helps you develop your comprehensive management skill. After studying appendix concepts, read the Challenge Case Summary at the end of the appendix to gain insights about using comprehensive management skill at Ford.

Chapter 1 focused primarily on defining *management*. This appendix presents various approaches to analyzing and reacting to management situations, each characterized by a different method of analysis and a different type of recommended action.

Over the years, a variety of different approaches to management have been developed, along with wide-ranging discussions of what each approach entails. In an attempt to simplify the discussion of the field of management without sacrificing significant information, Donnelly, Gibson, and Ivancevich combined the ideas of Koontz, O'Donnell, and Weihrich with those of Haynes and Massie and categorized three basic approaches to management:[2]

1. Classical approach
2. Behavioral approach
3. Management science approach

The following sections build on the work of Donnelly, Gibson, and Ivancevich in presenting the classical, behavioral, and management science approaches to analyzing the management task. The contingency approach is discussed as a fourth primary approach, whereas the system approach is presented as a recent trend in management thinking. The learning organization approach is continually evolving and is discussed as the newest way to analyze management.

The Classical Approach

A1-1 An understanding of the classical approach to management

The **classical approach to management** was the product of the first concentrated effort to develop a body of management thought. In fact, the management writers who participated in this effort are considered the pioneers of management study. The classical approach recommends that managers strive continually to increase organizational efficiency to increase production. Although the fundamentals of this approach were developed some time ago, contemporary managers are just as concerned as their predecessors were with finding the "one best way" to get the job done. As an illustration of this continuing concern, notable management theorists see striking similarities between the concepts of scientific management developed many years ago and the more current management philosophy of incorporating quality into all aspects of organizational operations.[3]

For discussion purposes, the classical approach to management can be broken down into two distinct areas. The first area, lower-level management analysis, consists primarily of the work of Frederick W. Taylor, Frank and Lillian Gilbreth, and Henry L. Gantt. These individuals studied mainly the jobs of workers at lower levels of an organization. The second area, comprehensive analysis of management, concerns the management function as a whole. The primary contributor to this area was Henri Fayol. **Figure A1.1** illustrates the two distinct areas in the classical approach.

Figure A1.1

Division of the classical approach to management into two areas and the major contributors to each area

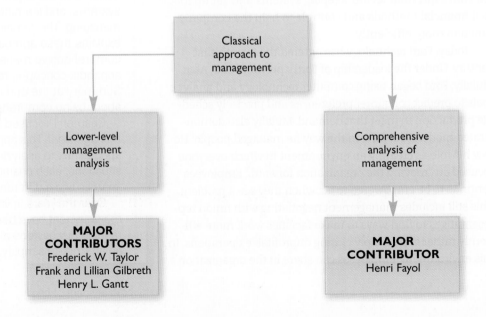

Lower-Level Management Analysis

Lower-level management analysis concentrates on the "one best way" to perform a task; that is, it investigates how a task situation can be structured to get the highest production from workers. The process of finding this "one best way" has become known as the *scientific method of management*, or simply **scientific management**. Although the techniques of scientific managers could conceivably be applied to management at all levels, the research, research applications, and illustrations relate mostly to lower-level managers. The work of Frederick W. Taylor, Frank and Lillian Gilbreth, and Henry L. Gantt is summarized in the sections that follow.

Frederick W. Taylor (1856–1915)

Because of the significance of his contributions, Frederick W. Taylor is commonly called the father of scientific management. His primary goal was to increase worker efficiency by scientifically designing jobs. His basic premise was that every job has one best way to be done and that this way should be discovered and put into operation.[4]

WORK AT BETHLEHEM STEEL CO.

Perhaps the best way to illustrate Taylor's scientific method and his management philosophy is to describe how he modified the job of employees whose sole responsibility was shoveling materials at Bethlehem Steel Company.[5] During the modification process, Taylor made the assumption that any worker's job could be reduced to a science. To construct the "science of shoveling," he obtained answers—through observation and experimentation—to the following questions:

1. Will a first-class worker do more work per day with a shovelful of 5, 10, 15, 20, 30, or 40 pounds?
2. What kinds of shovels work best with which materials?
3. How quickly can a shovel be pushed into a pile of materials and pulled out properly loaded?
4. How much time is required to swing a shovel backward and throw the load a given horizontal distance at a given height?

As Taylor formulated answers to these questions, he developed insights on how to increase the total amount of materials shoveled per day. He increased worker efficiency by matching shovel size with factors such as the size of the worker, the weight of the materials, and the height and distance the materials were to be thrown. By the end of the third year after Taylor's shoveling efficiency plan had been implemented, records at Bethlehem Steel showed that the total number of shovelers needed was reduced from about 600 to 140, the average number of tons shoveled per worker per day rose from 16 to 59, the average earnings per worker per day increased from $1.15 to $1.88, and the average cost of handling a long ton (2,240 pounds) dropped from $0.072 to $0.033—all in all, an impressive demonstration of the applicability of scientific management to the task of shoveling.[6]

Although Taylor's approach had a significant impact on productivity, his ideas were unpopular with unions and their workers, who feared that the reengineering of their jobs would ultimately lead to fewer workers being needed. In addition, the heightened emphasis on productivity led to a lessening of quality.[7]

However, managers continue to seek ways to improve organizational efficiency and productivity. For example, consulting firm Pace Productivity uses Taylor-like efficiency studies within its own organization. Using a Timecorder, the company's proprietary handheld electronic device, employees track their own time by pushing buttons associated with precoded work activities. When an employee presses a new button, time for the previous activity stops being recorded and time for the new activity begins being recorded. The Timecorder tracks how many times each activity occurs as well as how much time is cumulatively spent on each activity. Managers receive summary reports showing how many times work activities are performed and the time spent on the work activities, and suggesting, based on the results, ways to improve worker efficiency.

Frank Gilbreth (1868–1924) and Lillian Gilbreth (1878–1972)

The Gilbreths were also significant contributors to the scientific method. As a point of interest, the Gilbreths focused on "handicapped" as well as "nonhandicapped" workers.[8] Like other contributors to the scientific method, the Gilbreths subscribed to the idea of finding and then using the one best way to perform a job. The primary investigative tool in the Gilbreths' research was **motion study**, which consists of reducing each job to the most basic movements possible.

TABLE A1.1   **Sample Variables Considered in Analyzing Motions**

Worker Variables
1. Anatomy
2. Brawn
3. Contentment
4. Habits
5. Health

Environmental Variables
1. Work clothes
2. Heat
3. Materials quality
4. Tools
5. Lighting

Work Motion Requirements of Job
1. Acceleration requirements
2. Automation available
3. Inertia to overcome
4. Speed necessary
5. Combinations of motions required

Motion analysis is used today primarily to establish job performance standards. Each movement, or motion, that is used to do a job is studied to determine how much time the movement takes and how necessary it is to performing the job. Inefficient or unnecessary motions are pinpointed and eliminated.[9] In performing a motion study, the Gilbreths considered the work environment, the motion itself, and behavior variables concerning the worker. **Table A1.1** shows many factors from each of the categories that the Gilbreths analyzed.

Frank Gilbreth was born in Maine in 1868. After high school graduation, he qualified to enroll at the Massachusetts Institute of Technology but decided to work for a construction business in Boston instead.[10] He started as a bricklayer's apprentice and advanced to general superintendent. His experience as an apprentice bricklayer led him to do motion studies of bricklaying. He found that bricklayers could increase their output significantly by concentrating on performing some motions and eliminating others. **Table A1.2** shows a simplified portion of the results of one of Gilbreth's bricklaying motion studies. For each bricklaying motion, Gilbreth indicated whether it should be omitted for the sake of efficiency and why. He reduced the five motions per brick listed

PRACTICAL CHALLENGE: IMPROVING PRODUCTIVITY

Tracking Sensors Take Work Measurement to a New Level

Electronics technology can help improve productivity. Applying the sensor technology that tracks the location of a mobile phone, companies have asked their employees to wear sensors while working. Researchers combine the data with performance measures to learn what behaviors are associated with high productivity. At Bank of America, a study showed that the most productive workers interact often with their team members. Also, a statistical method called social network analysis can map out patterns of communication. The data show who the go-to employees are—and where people are lowering productivity by blocking the flow of information.

However, the gathering of detailed data about employee activities alarms some people. For example, a forklift driver in a Unified Grocers warehouse complained that he has felt that the company has treated him like a "human machine" ever since the company, in an effort to speed up work, began measuring his movements throughout the warehouse. Managers should thus consider workers' concerns. One way to address their concerns is to inform employees that only the patterns detected, not individual employee's actions, are reviewed. That was Bank of America's approach; it used the results to redesign its work areas, not to reward and punish individuals.[11]

TABLE A1.2   Partial Results for One of Frank Gilbreth's Bricklaying Motion Studies

Operation No.	The Wrong Way	The Right Way	Pick and Dip Method: The Exterior 4 Inches (Laying to the Line)
1	Step for mortar	Omit	On the scaffold, the inside edge of the mortar box should be plumb with the inside edge of the stock platform. On the floor, the inside edge of the mortar box should be 21 inches from the wall. Mortar boxes should never be more than 4 feet apart.
2	Reach for mortar	Reach for mortar	Do not bend any more than absolutely necessary to reach mortar with a straight arm.
3	Work up mortar	Omit	Provide mortar of the right consistency. Examine sand screen and keep it in repair so that no pebbles can get through. Keep tender on scaffold to temper up and keep mortar worked upright.
4	Step for brick	Omit	If tubs are kept 4 feet apart, no stepping for brick will be necessary on scaffold. On the floor, keep brick in a pile not nearer than 1 foot or more than 4 feet 6 inches from wall.
5	Reach for brick	Included in 2	Brick must be reached for at the same time that the mortar is reached for, and picked up at exactly the same time that the mortar is picked up. If it is not picked up at the same time, allowance must be made for operation.

under "The Wrong Way" to the one motion per brick listed under "The Right Way." Overall, Gilbreth's bricklaying motion studies resulted in reducing the number of motions necessary to lay a brick by approximately 70 percent, consequently tripling bricklaying production.

Lillian Gilbreth, who began as her husband's collaborator, earned two doctorates and was awarded numerous honorary degrees. After Frank's death, she continued his research while raising their 12 children and becoming the first woman professor at Purdue University. Lillian Gilbreth's work extended to applying the scientific method to the role of the homemaker and to the "handicapped."[12]

Much of the Gilbreths' work has broad application for how to design jobs today. However, the Gilbreths were also among the first to consider the employee as a productivity factor. For example, Frank Gilbreth recognized that, for motion studies to best impact jobs, managers need to communicate with employees about their jobs and develop their job-related skills.[13]

Henry L. Gantt (1861–1919)

The third major contributor to the scientific management approach was Henry L. Gantt. He, too, was interested in increasing worker efficiency. Gantt attributed unsatisfactory or ineffective tasks and piece rates (incentive pay for each product piece that an individual produces) primarily to the fact that these tasks and rates were set according to what had been done by workers in the past or to someone's *opinion* of what workers could do. According to Gantt, *exact scientific knowledge* of what a worker could do should be substituted for opinion. He considered task measurement and determination to be the role of scientific management.

Gantt's management philosophy is encapsulated in his statement that "the essential differences between the best system of today and those of the past are the manner in which tasks are 'scheduled' and the manner in which their performance is rewarded."[14] Using this rationale, he sought to improve systems or organizations through task-scheduling innovation and rewarding innovation.

SCHEDULING INNOVATION

The Gantt chart, the primary scheduling device that Gantt developed, is still the scheduling tool most commonly used by modern managers.[15] Basically, this chart provides managers with an easily understood summary of what work was scheduled for specific time periods, how much of this work has been completed, and by whom it was done.[16]

Special computer software, such as MacSchedule, has been developed to help today's managers apply the concept of the Gantt chart more efficiently and effectively.[17] MacSchedule allows managers to monitor easily complicated and detailed scheduling issues, such as the number of units planned for production during a specified period, when work is to begin and be completed, and the percentage of work that was actually completed during a specific period. (The Gantt chart is covered in much more detail in Chapter 7.)

REWARDING INNOVATION

Gantt was more aware of the human side of production than either Taylor or the Gilbreths were. He wrote that "the taskmaster (manager) of the past was practically a slave driver, whose principal function was to force workmen to do that which they had no desire to do, or interest in doing. The task setter of today under any reputable system of management is not a driver. When he asks the workmen to perform tasks, he makes it to their interest to accomplish them, and is careful not to ask what is impossible or unreasonable."[18]

In contrast to Taylor, who pioneered a piece-rate system under which workers were paid according to the amount they produced and who advocated the use of wage-incentive plans, Gantt developed a system wherein workers could earn a bonus in addition to the piece rate if they exceeded their daily production quota. Thus, Gantt believed in worker compensation that corresponds not only to production (through the piece-rate system) but also to overproduction (through the bonus system).

Comprehensive Analysis of Management

Whereas scientific managers emphasize job design when approaching the study of management, managers who embrace the comprehensive view—the second area of the classical approach—are concerned with the entire range of managerial performance.

Among the well-known contributors to the comprehensive view are Chester Barnard,[19] Alvin Brown, Henry Dennison, Luther Gulick and Lyndall Urwick, J. D. Mooney and A. C. Reiley, and Oliver Sheldon.[20] Perhaps the most notable contributor, however, was Henri Fayol. His book *General and Industrial Management* presents a management philosophy that still guides many managers today.[21]

Henri Fayol (1841–1925)   Because of his writings on the elements and general principles of management, Henri Fayol is usually regarded as the pioneer of administrative theory. The elements of management he outlined—planning, organizing, commanding, coordinating, and control—are still considered worthwhile divisions under which to study, analyze, and effect the management process.[22] (Note the close correspondence between Fayol's elements of management and the management functions discussed in Chapter 1—planning, organizing, influencing, controlling.)

The general principles of management suggested by Fayol, still considered useful in contemporary management practice, are presented here in the order developed by Fayol and are accompanied by corresponding defining themes:[23]

1. **Division of work**—Work should be divided among individuals and groups to ensure that effort and attention are focused on specific portions of the task. Fayol presented work specialization as the best way to use the human resources of an organization.
2. **Authority**—The concepts of authority and responsibility are closely related. Fayol defined *authority* as the right to give orders and the power to exact obedience. *Responsibility* involves being accountable and is therefore naturally associated with authority. Therefore, whoever assumes authority also assumes responsibility.
3. **Discipline**—A successful organization requires the common effort of all workers. Penalties should be applied judiciously to encourage this common effort.
4. **Unity of command**—Workers should receive orders from only one manager.
5. **Unity of direction**—The entire organization should be moving toward a common objective and in a common direction.
6. **Subordination of individual interests to the general interests**—The interests of one person should not take priority over the interests of the organization as a whole.
7. **Remuneration**—Many variables, such as cost of living, supply of qualified personnel, general business conditions, and success of the business, should be considered when determining a worker's rate of pay.

8. **Centralization**—Fayol defined *centralization* as lowering the importance of the subordinate role. *Decentralization* is increasing that importance. The degree to which centralization or decentralization should be adopted depends on the specific organization in which a manager is working.

9. **Scalar chain**—Managers in hierarchies are part of a chainlike authority scale. Each manager, from the first-line supervisor to the president, possesses certain amounts of authority. The president possesses the most authority; the first-line supervisor, the least. Lower-level managers should always keep upper-level managers informed of their work activities. The existence of a scalar chain and the adherence to it are necessary if an organization is to be successful.

10. **Order**—For the sake of efficiency and coordination, all materials and people related to a specific kind of work should be assigned to the same general location in the organization.

11. **Equity**—All employees should be treated as equally as possible.

12. **Stability of tenure of personnel**—Retaining productive employees should always be a high priority of management. Recruitment and selection costs, as well as increased product-reject rates, are usually associated with hiring new workers.

13. **Initiative**—Management should take steps to encourage worker initiative, which is defined as new or additional work activity undertaken through self-direction.

14. **Esprit de corps**—Management should encourage harmony and general good feelings among employees.[24]

These firefighters are working toward a common objective: to rescue the people from inside this car safely at an accident site.

Fayol's general principles of management cover a broad range of topics, but organizational efficiency, the correct handling of people, and appropriate management actions are the three general themes he stressed. With the writings of Fayol, the study of management as an immense, comprehensive activity began to receive more attention. Some modern management researchers seem to believe, however, that Fayol's work has not received as much acclaim as it deserves.[25]

Limitations of the Classical Approach

Contributors to the classical approach felt encouraged to write about their managerial experiences largely because of the success they enjoyed. Structuring work to be more efficient and defining the manager's role more precisely yielded significant improvements in productivity, which individuals such as Taylor and Fayol were quick to document.

However, the classical approach does not adequately incorporate human variables. People today do not seem to be as influenced by bonuses as people were in the nineteenth century. It is generally agreed that critical interpersonal areas, such as conflict, communication, leadership, and motivation, are shortchanged in the classical approach.

The Behavioral Approach

The **behavioral approach to management** emphasizes increasing production through an understanding of people. According to proponents of this approach, if managers understand their employees and adapt their organizations to those employees, organizational success will usually follow.

A1-2 Knowledge about the behavioral approach to management

The Hawthorne Studies

The behavioral approach is usually described as beginning with a series of studies conducted between 1924 and 1932 that investigated the behavior and attitudes of the workers at the Hawthorne (Chicago) Works of the Western Electric Company.[26] Accounts of the Hawthorne Studies are usually divided into two phases: the relay assembly test room experiments and the bank wiring observation room experiment. The following sections discuss both phases.

The Relay Assembly Test Room Experiments
The relay assembly test room experiments originally had a scientific management orientation. The experimenters believed that if they studied productivity long enough and under a large enough variety of working conditions (including variations in weather conditions, temperature, rest periods, work hours, and humidity), they would discover the working conditions that maximized production. The initial purpose of the relay assembly test room experiments was to determine the relationship between intensity of lighting and worker efficiency, as measured by worker output. Two groups of female employees were used as subjects. The light intensity for one group was varied, whereas the light intensity for the other group was held constant.

The results of the experiments surprised the researchers: No matter what conditions employees were exposed to, their production increased. Because the researchers found no consistent relationship between productivity and lighting intensity, they undertook an extensive interviewing campaign to determine why the subjects' production increased under all lighting conditions. The following are the main reasons, as formulated from the interviews:

1. The subjects found working in the test room enjoyable.
2. The new supervisory relationship during the experiment allowed the subjects to work freely, without fear.
3. The subjects realized that they were taking part in an important and interesting study.
4. The subjects seemed to become friendly as a group.

The experimenters concluded that human factors within organizations could significantly influence production. More research was needed, however, to evaluate the potential impact of this human component in organizations.

The Bank Wiring Observation Room Experiment
The purpose of the bank wiring observation room experiment was to analyze social relationships in a work group. Specifically, the study focused on the effect of group piecework incentives on a group of men who assembled terminal banks for use in telephone exchanges. The group piecework incentive system dictated that the harder the group worked as a whole, the more pay each member of the group would receive.

The experimenters believed that the study would show that the members of the work group would pressure one another to work harder so that each group member would receive more pay. To their surprise, the experimenters found the opposite: The work group pressured the faster workers to slow down their work rates. Instead of pressuring the men whose work rates would have decreased individual salaries, the group pressured the men whose work rates would have increased individual salaries. Evidently, the men were more interested in preserving work-group solidarity than in making more money. The researchers concluded that social groups in organizations could effectively exert enough pressure to influence individuals to disregard monetary incentives.[27]

Recognizing the Human Variable

Taken together, the series of studies conducted at the Hawthorne plant gave management thinkers a new direction for research. Obviously, after the studies showed that the human variable could either increase or decrease production dramatically, the human variable in the organization needed much more analysis. Managers began to realize that they needed to understand this influence so that they could maximize its positive effects and minimize its negative effects. This attempt to understand people is still a major force in today's organizational research.[28] The Hawthorne Studies results helped managers see that understanding what motivates employees is a crucial part of being a manager.[29] More current behavioral findings and their implications for management are discussed in greater detail in Chapters 14 through 18.

STEPS FOR SUCCESS

Understanding Employees

Learning to recognize and respect another person's point of view is an important skill in management—and in life. Management experts and researchers offer the following ideas for improving your ability to understand others:[30]

- Become a better listener. When another person is talking, set aside your thoughts about how you will respond. Instead, focus on understanding the speaker's words, tone, and other signals.
- Apply your listening skills to learn about the other person's assumptions and experiences. These will shape how that person understands your expectations and ideas. For example, when Mike Critelli was chief executive of Pitney Bowes, he inspired employees by identifying the "little gestures" they appreciated most.
- Read widely, especially good-quality writing. Recent research found that after subjects read passages from literary greats, they did a better job of interpreting facial expressions than before they had read the passages. This type of literature challenges readers to understand complex characters. Think of it as an empathy workout.

The Human Relations Movement

The Hawthorne Studies sparked the **human relations movement**, a people-oriented approach to management in which the interaction of people in organizations is studied to judge its impact on organizational success. The ultimate objective of this approach is to enhance organizational success by encouraging appropriate relationships among people. To put it simply, when management stimulates high productivity and worker commitment to the organization and its goals, human relations are said to be effective; when management supports low productivity and uncommitted workers, human relations are said to be ineffective. **Human relations skill** is defined as the ability to work with people in a way that enhances organizational success.

The human relations movement has made some important contributions to the study and practice of management. Advocates of this approach to management have continually stressed the need to use compassionate methods when managing people. Abraham Maslow, perhaps the best-known contributor to the human relations movement, believed that managers must understand the physiological, safety, social, esteem, and self-actualization needs of organization members. Douglas McGregor, another important contributor to the movement, emphasized a management philosophy built on the views that people can be self-directed, accept responsibility, and consider work to be as natural as play.[31] The ideas of both Maslow and McGregor are discussed thoroughly in Chapter 16. As a result of the tireless efforts of theorists such as Maslow and McGregor, modern managers better understand the human component in organizations and how to work with it appropriately to enhance organizational success.

SAS is dedicated to building a human-oriented work environment, which is consistent with the human relations movement. Leaders at SAS, the world's largest privately held software company, believe that employees represent the company's most significant asset. SAS works to maintain this asset by providing generous benefits like subsidized cafeterias and daycare; a free health clinic for employees and their families; and a recreation and fitness center that boasts a pool, a sauna, and massage facilities. By placing trust in its employees, SAS generates employee loyalty, productivity, and commitment. For 13 consecutive years, the company has been named one of *Fortune* magazine's "100 Best Companies to Work For."[32]

The Management Science Approach

Churchman, Ackoff, and Arnoff define the *management science*, or *operations research* (OR), approach as (1) an application of the scientific method to problems arising in the operation of a system and (2) the solution of these problems by solving mathematical equations representing the system.[33] The **management science approach** suggests that managers can best

A1-3 Insights about the management science approach to management

Diego Cervo/Shutterstock

Since World War II, large companies have used the management science approach to solve logistical or operational problems. Now, with advances in technology, companies of all sizes use this approach in their decision making.

improve their organizations by using the scientific method and mathematical techniques to solve operational problems.

The Beginning of the Management Science Approach

The management science, or operations research, approach can be traced to World War II, an era in which leading scientists were asked to help solve complex operational problems in the military.[34] The scientists were organized into teams that eventually became known as operations research (OR) groups. One OR group, for example, was asked to determine which gun sights would best stop German attacks on the British mainland. The term *management science* was actually coined by researchers in a UCLA–RAND academic complex featuring academic and industry researchers working together to solve operations problems.[35]

These early OR groups typically included physicists and other "hard" scientists who used the problem-solving method with which they had the most experience: the scientific method. The scientific method dictates that scientists:

1. Systematically *observe* the system whose behavior must be explained to solve the problem.
2. Use these specific observations to *construct* a generalized framework (a model) that is consistent with the specific observations and from which the consequences of changing the system can be predicted.
3. Use the model to *deduce* how the system will behave under conditions that have not been observed but that could be observed if the changes were made.
4. Finally, *test* the model by performing an experiment on the actual system to see whether the effects of the changes predicted using the model actually occur when the changes are made.[36]

The OR groups proved successful at using the scientific method to solve the military's operational problems.

Management Science Today

After World War II, America again became interested in manufacturing and selling products. The success of the OR groups in the military had been so obvious that managers were eager to try management science techniques in an industrial environment. After all, managers also have to deal with complicated operational problems.

By 1955, the management science approach to solving industrial problems had proved effective. Many people saw great promise in refining its techniques and analytical tools, and managers and universities pursued these refinements. By 1965, the management science approach was being used in many companies and applied to many diverse management problems, such as production scheduling, plant location, and product packaging.

In the 1980s, surveys indicated that management science techniques were used extensively in large, complex organizations. Smaller organizations, however, had not yet fully realized the benefits of using these techniques.

The widespread use of computers in the workplace and the introduction of the Internet have had a significant impact on organizations' use of management science techniques. In the twenty-first century, managers in organizations of all sizes now have ready access to a wealth of tools and other resources that enable them to apply the principles of management science to their companies easily. Not only has the introduction of technology transformed how businesses operate, but it also enables leaders to automate and organize their company's systems for greater consistency—*and* allows them to use the power of technology to aid in their decision making.[37]

Characteristics of Management Science Applications

Four primary characteristics are usually present in situations in which management science techniques are applied.[38] First, the management problems studied are so complicated that managers need help analyzing a large number of variables. Management science techniques increase the effectiveness of the managers' decision making in such a situation. Second, a management science application generally uses economic implications as guidelines for making a particular decision, perhaps because management science techniques are best suited for analyzing quantifiable factors such as sales, expenses, and units of production.

Third, the use of mathematical models to investigate a decision situation is typical in management science applications. Models constructed to represent reality are used to determine how the real-world situation might be improved. The fourth characteristic of a management science application is the use of computers. The great complexity of managerial problems and the sophisticated mathematical analysis that is required for problem-related information are two factors that make computers especially valuable to the management science analyst.

Today, managers use management science tools such as inventory control models, network models, and probability models to aid them in the decision-making process. Other parts of this text outline some of these models in greater detail and illustrate their applications to management decision making. Because management science thought is still evolving, increasingly sophisticated analytical techniques can be expected in the future.

The Contingency Approach

In simple terms, the **contingency approach to management** emphasizes that what managers do in practice depends on, or is contingent upon, a given set of circumstances—a situation.[39] In essence, this approach emphasizes if–then relationships: "If" this situational variable exists, "then" a manager probably would take this particular action. For example, if a manager has a group of inexperienced subordinates, then the contingency approach would recommend that he or she lead in a different fashion than if the subordinates were experienced.[40]

A1-4 Information about the contingency approach to management

In general, the contingency approach attempts to identify the conditions or situations in which various management methods have the best chance of success.[41] This approach is based on the premise that, although there probably is no one best way to solve a management problem in all organizations, there probably *is* one best way to solve any given management problem in any one organization. Perhaps the main challenges of using the contingency approach are the following:

1. Perceiving organizational situations as they actually exist
2. Choosing the management tactics best suited to those situations
3. Implementing those tactics competently

The notion of a contingency approach to management is not novel. It has become a popular discussion topic for contemporary management thinkers. The general consensus of their writings is that, if managers are to apply management concepts, principles, and techniques successfully, they must consider the realities of the specific organizational circumstances they face.[42]

MyLab Management Watch It

If your instructor has assigned this activity, go to www.pearson.com/mylab/management to complete the video exercise.

The System Approach

The **system approach to management** is based on general system theory. Ludwig von Bertalanffy, a scientist who worked mainly in physics and biology, is recognized as the founder of general system theory.[43] The main premise of the theory is that, to understand the operation of an entity fully, the entity must be viewed as a system. A **system** is a number of interdependent

A1-5 An understanding of the system approach to management parts functioning as a whole for some purpose. For example, according to general system theory, to understand fully the operations of the human body, one must understand the workings of its interdependent parts (ears, eyes, and brain). General system theory integrates the knowledge of various specialized fields so that the system as a whole can be better understood.

Types of Systems

According to von Bertalanffy, the two basic types of systems are closed systems and open systems. A **closed system** is not influenced by, and does not interact with, its environment. Such a system is mostly mechanical and has predetermined motions or activities that must be performed regardless of the environment. A clock is an example of a closed system. Regardless of its environment, a clock's wheels, gears, and other parts must function in a predetermined way if the clock as a whole is to exist and serve its purpose. The other type of system, the **open system**, is continually interacting with its environment. A plant is an example of an open system. Constant interactions with the environment influence the plant's state of existence and its future. In fact, the environment determines whether or not the plant will live.

Systems and "Wholeness"

The concept of "wholeness" is important in general system analysis. The system must be viewed as a whole and modifiable only through changes in its parts. Before one can modify the parts for the overall benefit of the system, however, one must have a thorough knowledge of how each part functions and the interrelationships among the parts. L. Thomas Hopkins suggested the following six guidelines for anyone conducting system analysis:[44]

1. The whole should be the main focus of analysis, with the parts receiving secondary attention.
2. Integration is the key variable in wholeness analysis. It is defined as the interrelatedness of the many parts within the whole.
3. Possible modifications in each part should be weighed in relation to possible effects on every other part.
4. Each part has some role to perform so that the whole can accomplish its purpose.
5. The nature of the part and its function is determined by its position in the whole.
6. All analysis starts with the existence of the whole. The parts and their interrelationships should then evolve to best suit the purpose of the whole.

Because the system approach to management is based on general system theory, analysis of the management situation as a system is stressed. The following sections present the parts of the management system and recommend information that can be used to analyze such a system.

The Management System

As with all systems, the **management system** is composed of a number of parts that function interdependently to achieve a purpose. The main parts of the management system are organizational input, organizational process, and organizational output. As discussed in Chapter 1, these parts consist of organizational resources, the production process, and finished goods, respectively. The parts represent a combination that exists to achieve organizational objectives, whatever they may be.

The management system is an open system—that is, one that interacts with its environment (see **Figure A1.2**). Environmental factors with which the management system interacts include the government, suppliers, customers, and competitors. Each of these factors represents a potential environmental influence that could significantly change the future of the management system.

Needless to say, tracking an environmental factor like customer opinion can be very time-consuming. The challenge of hotel managers, for example, who must track accurately what customers and others are saying about their hotels seems almost impossible to do. To help overcome this challenge, hotel managers can use a tool called ReviewPro to compile customer opinions. ReviewPro is a Web-based reputation management service for the hotel industry that organizes, tracks, and analyzes hotel reviews and other hotel-related comments on the Internet from a wide array of sites, including Facebook and Twitter. Overall, using a tool like ReviewPro helps hotel managers make better decisions about how to improve customer satisfaction.[45]

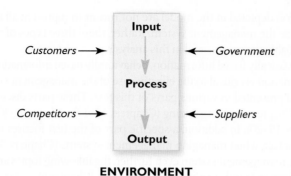

Figure A1.2
The open management system

The critical importance of managers knowing and understanding their customers is perhaps best illustrated by the constant struggle that supermarket managers face in knowing and understanding their customers. Supermarket managers fight for the business of a national population that is growing by less than 1 percent per year. Survival requires that they know their customers better than the competition does. That is why many food retailers conduct market research to uncover customer attitudes about different kinds of foods and stores. Armed with a thorough understanding of their customers that was gained from this type of research, they hope to win business from competitors who are not benefiting from the insights made possible by such research.[46]

Information for Management System Analysis

As noted earlier, general system theory supports the use of information from many specialized disciplines to better understand a system. Information from any discipline that can increase the understanding of management system operations enhances the success of that system. Although this statement is fairly sweeping, managers can get this wide-ranging information by using the first three approaches to management outlined in this appendix. Thus, the information used to discuss the management system in this text comes from three primary sources:

1. Classical approach to management
2. Behavioral approach to management
3. Management science approach to management

The use of these three sources of information to analyze the management system is referred to as **triangular management**. **Figure A1.3** presents the triangular management model. The three

Figure A1.3 The triangular management model

sources of information depicted in the model are not meant to represent all the information that can be used to analyze the management system. Rather, these three types of management-related information are probably the most useful in this analysis.

A synthesis of classically based information, behaviorally based information, and management science–based information is critical to the effective use of the management system. This information is integrated and presented in various parts of this text. These parts discuss management systems and planning (Chapters 7–9), organizing (Chapters 10–13), influencing (Chapters 14–18), and controlling (Chapters 19–20). In addition, a specific part of the text focuses on the modern challenges that managers face when managing management systems (Chapters 3–5). To deepen your understanding of the management system even further, the following topics are discussed in detail: entrepreneurship (Chapter 2) and creativity and innovation (Chapter 6).

Learning Organization: A New Approach?

A1-6 Knowledge about the learning organization approach to management

The preceding material in this appendix provides a history of management by discussing several different approaches to management. Each approach developed over a number of years and focused on the particular needs of the organizations at the time.

More recently, managers seem to be searching for new approaches to management.[47] Fueling this search is a range of issues modern managers face that their historical counterparts did not. These issues include a concern about the competitive decline of Western firms, the accelerating pace of technological change, the sophistication of customers, and the increasing emphasis on globalization.

A new approach to management that is evolving to handle this new range of issues can be called the *learning organization approach*. A **learning organization** is an organization that does well in creating, acquiring, and transferring knowledge and in modifying its behavior to reflect new knowledge.[48] Learning organizations emphasize systematic problem solving, experimenting with new ideas, learning from experience and past history, learning from the experiences of others, and transferring knowledge rapidly throughout the organization. Managers attempting to build a learning organization must create an environment conducive to learning and encourage the exchange of information among all organization members.[49] Honda, Corning, and General Electric are successful learning organizations.

The learning organization represents a specific, new *management paradigm*, or fundamental way of viewing and contemplating management. Peter Senge started serious discussions of learning organizations with his book *The Fifth Discipline: The Art & Practice of the Learning Organization*.[50] Senge, his colleagues at MIT, and many others have made significant progress in developing the learning organization concept. According to Senge, building a learning organization entails building five features within an organization:

1. **Systems thinking**—Every organization member understands his or her own job and how the jobs fit together to provide final products to the customer.
2. **Shared vision**—All organization members have a common view of the purpose of the organization and a sincere commitment to accomplish the purpose.
3. **Challenging of mental models**—Organization members routinely challenge the way business is done and the thought processes people use to solve organizational problems.
4. **Team learning**—Organization members work together, develop solutions to new problems together, and apply the solutions together. Working as teams rather than as individuals will help organizations gather collective force to achieve organizational goals.
5. **Personal mastery**—All organization members are committed to gaining a deep and rich understanding of their work. Such an understanding will help organizations successfully overcome important challenges that confront them.

Overall, managers attempting to build learning organizations face many different challenges. One such challenge involves ensuring that an organization changes as necessary. Changes in the external environment, like an increasingly global marketplace, rapid technological advances, and growing pressure to do more with less, all require managers to implement needed changes as they build their learning organizations.[51]

TIPS FOR MANAGING AROUND THE GLOBE

IBM's "Crowded" Learning Environment

IBM would meet most definitions of a learning organization. The global technology and consulting company relies on constant innovation to fulfill its mission to help clients build information systems that enable them to meet their goals. IBM relies on its 400,000 employees in over 170 countries to share their technology and business expertise to generate meaningful solutions.

Françoise LeGoues, who heads IBM's CIO Lab, devised an engaging way to encourage creativity and the transfer of knowledge across national borders. Her program, called iFundIT, invites information technology (IT) employees to submit ideas for improving IBM's internal activities. Every IT employee receives up to $2,000 to spend on any of the projects that seem promising. Following the example of crowdfunding websites such as Kickstarter and Indiegogo, any project that attracts a minimum level of funds ($25,000) is approved for development. Among more than 150 winning ideas are an app for using IBM's social media network to manage projects and a method for tracking how employees are using the company's apps.[52]

CHALLENGE CASE SUMMARY

As you learned in the Challenge Case at the beginning of this appendix, a large company such as Ford Motor Company is involved in many different kinds of activities. Managing such an enterprise is a complex process. Over the years, scientists and observers of management have proposed various ways to understand what managers can and should do to help their organizations achieve their goals. Considering this history of management theory can suggest practical ideas for how Ford's managers can help their company succeed in a challenging environment.

The classical approach to management recommends that managers continually strive to increase organizational efficiency and production, so it would likely have been of great use to CEO Alan Mulally in his quest to improve efficiency at Ford. At the lower level, scientific management seeks to identify the one best way to perform tasks as efficiently as possible. It may involve the selection of tools and the design of tasks that will allow workers to produce the maximum amount they can without sacrificing safety and quality. Applications of scientific management may include motion studies, scheduling charts, and rewards for innovation.

Another classical approach involves the comprehensive analysis of management, notably the work of Henri Fayol. Fayol defined the manager's job as a combination of planning, organizing, commanding, and controlling. He also specified many principles of effective management—for example, that work should be divided so that individuals can specialize and that authority should be delegated along with the responsibility for completing tasks.

Most modern organizations, including Ford, would be interested in the behavioral approach to management, which emphasizes increasing production through an understanding of people. It requires the application of human relations skill, or the ability to work with people in a way that enhances organizational success. This approach stresses the importance of treating people humanely and motivating them by setting up a rewarding work environment in which employees care about achieving work-related goals. For example, Douglas McGregor emphasized his finding that employees can be self-directed, accept responsibility, and consider work as natural as play.

The management science approach suggests that managers can best improve the organization by using the scientific method and mathematical techniques to solve operational problems by observing the system, constructing a model of it, deducing how the system will behave under new conditions, and testing the model with experiments. Today's widespread availability of computers makes management science techniques readily available. Popular applications include inventory control and probability models for decision making. Ford uses such methods to make complex decisions such as which features to include in the vehicles it manufactures each week and which new products to introduce.

The contingency approach to management emphasizes that what managers do in practice depends on the circumstances in which managers are acting. It reminds managers that they must consider practical realities when deciding how to act. At Ford, if Alan Mulally expected management and workers to be partners in operating plants efficiently, he had to consider practicalities such as costs and union members' willingness to change work rules. For example, *if* it is possible to operate profitably and *if* union representatives trust the process, *then* Mulally could move forward with his plan to assemble vehicles in the United States.

The system approach to management regards each organization as a system in which interdependent parts function as a whole. A business is an open system because it continually interacts with its environment. When managers such as Mulally want to make a change in their department or company, they need to consider the impact of the change on all parts of the system. A change in product design, for example, will affect the materials that need to be ordered, the way the product is produced, and customers' opinions of the product, among many other elements of the Ford "system."

A new approach to management is the learning organization approach. A learning organization excels at creating, acquiring, and transferring knowledge and in modifying behavior to reflect new knowledge. For Ford to be a learning organization, its management needs to build systems thinking, create a shared vision, challenge the organization's mental models, cultivate team learning, and get all employees committed to personal mastery of their work.

MyLab Management Assessing Your Management Skill

If your instructor has assigned this activity, go to www.pearson.com/mylab/management to complete the exercise related to the Challenge Case.

DEVELOPING COMPREHENSIVE MANAGEMENT SKILL

This section is specially designed to help you develop comprehensive management skills. An individual's comprehensive management skill is based on an understanding of the concepts and the ability to apply those concepts. The following activities will help to enhance your comprehensive management skills in various organizational situations.

Class Preparation and Personal Study

To help you prepare for class, perform the activities outlined in this section. Performing these activities will help you enhance your classroom performance significantly.

Reflecting on Target Skill

On page 514, this appendix opens by presenting a target management skill along with a list of related objectives outlining knowledge and understanding that you should aim to acquire related to that skill. Review this target skill and the list of objectives to make sure that you've acquired all pertinent information within the appendix. If you do not feel that you've reached a particular objective(s), study related appendix coverage until you do.

Know Key Terms

Understanding the following key terms is critical to your understanding of appendix material. Define each of these terms. Refer to the page(s) referenced after a term to check your definition or to gain further insight regarding the term.

classical approach to management **516**
scientific management **517**
motion study **517**
behavioral approach to management **521**

A1-2 How does Henri Fayol's contribution to management differ from the contributions of Frank and Lillian Gilbreth?

A1-3 Discuss the triangular management model as a tool for organizing how a manager should think about the management process.

Know How Management Concepts Relate

This section comprises activities that will further sharpen your understanding of management concepts. Answer these essay questions as completely as possible.

A1-1 How will you be able to use the classical approach to management in your job as a manager?

Management Skills Exercises

Learning activities in this section are aimed at helping you develop comprehensive management skills.

MyLab Management
Discussion Questions
Go to www.pearson.com/mylab/management to complete the problems marked with this icon ★.

★ Cases

How Management Innovation Keeps Ford Moving Ahead

The Challenge Case "How Management Innovation Keeps Ford Moving Ahead" (p. 515) and its related Challenge Case Summary were written to help you understand the management concepts contained in this appendix. Answer the following discussion questions about the introductory case to explore how fundamental management concepts can be applied to a company such as Ford Motor Company.

A1-4 Which of the approaches to management discussed in this appendix has each of Ford's CEOs (Henry Ford, Henry Ford II, and Alan Mulally) seemed to emphasize the *most* in his work as a manager? Explain.

A1-5 Which of the approaches to management discussed in this appendix has each of Ford's CEOs seemed to emphasize the *least* in his work as a manager? Explain.

A1-6 Mulally had a reputation as a successful manager at Ford. What advice would you give him and his successors so that they could become even more successful managers?

Managing UPS in an Internet Economy

Read the following case and answer the questions that follow. Studying this case will help you better understand how the history of an organization affects its current strategy. This case examines UPS.

By evolving along with shipping needs, UPS has come far from its 1907 origin as a Seattle messenger service run by a pair of teenagers with bicycles. Its evolution is reflected in its name changes: from American Messenger Company to Merchants Parcel Delivery, to United Parcel Service, to UPS. During that time, the company has shifted from running errands to placing delivery workers in stores, from serving just Seattle to acquiring other businesses and expanding its service to locations across the United States and around the world, from carrying single orders on bicycles to shipping by truck and air, and from providing transportation alone to helping companies plan the best ways to fulfill orders.

Today UPS is a multibillion-dollar global business with a reputation for highly efficient, reliable service. Maintaining those qualities while growing rapidly is difficult. UPS's managers tackle the challenge by using meticulous planning, advanced technology, and strict rules. Technology took on a prominent role at UPS in the 1990s when people began ordering products online, and sellers turned to UPS to deliver those orders. UPS then introduced its handheld computer, the Delivery Information Acquisition Device, which all drivers carry to transmit up-to-the-minute information about deliveries and to receive notices of changes in pickup schedules and traffic problems to avoid. Next, the company installed GPS sensors on delivery trucks to ensure that workers follow predetermined routes and schedules. UPS has recently begun rolling out a computer system that analyzes data and calculates the most efficient route for each driver on each day. Even a savings of just one mile per day, spread across all the drivers, would generate yearly savings of $50 million.

Work requirements also have a prominent role at UPS: Drivers must follow 340 rules to ensure that they deliver efficient, polite service, and the company expects them to use time and fuel efficiently without sacrificing customer service. However, the company does consider employee motivation. For example, the people behind UPS's new routing system involved drivers in the planning process.

This need for control was severely tested during the holiday shopping season of December 2013. Scott Abell, UPS's peak planning manager, and his team of 11 planners spent most of that year forecasting package volume and figuring out how to get packages to homes by Christmas Eve, even if bad weather disrupted transportation. (In 2004, for example, damage from an ice storm in Louisville, home of the central sorting facility, required that packages be loaded by hand. Abell and his team worked alongside the warehouse employees to get the job done.) Abell determined that UPS was prepared, but then several online retailers began offering next-day delivery on purchases made up until 11 p.m. on December 23. That promotion about doubled the number of packages that Abell's team had forecasted. Packages arrived in droves at the sorting facility—too many, in fact, to be accommodated inside the facility—and some Christmas gifts did not arrive on time after all.

These holiday shipping problems were costly. Between the extra resources needed to meet the demand and the refunds paid for the missed deadlines, UPS's costs outweighed the revenues from the extra deliveries. Managers are determined, however, to improve the company's planning and are looking at all options, including improved tracking systems, stricter terms for retailers, and an expansion of warehouse facilities.[53]

Questions

A1-7 Assume that you are a UPS manager responsible for a warehouse or for deliveries in a specific region. Based on the description of UPS, which of Henri Fayol's 14 principles of management would be most pertinent to you? Why?

A1-8 How can the system approach to management help Scott Abell in his role as peak planning manager?

A1-9 What do you imagine it was like to work at UPS in 1950? How do you think working conditions have changed at UPS since then?

Experiential Exercises

Analyzing The World's Fastest Workers

Directions. Read the following scenario and then perform the listed activities. Your instructor may wish you to perform the activities as an individual or within groups. Follow all of your instructor's directions carefully.

Use YouTube to find compilation videos featuring some of the world's fastest workers. These videos all provide examples of lower-level management analysis and concentrate on the "one best way" to perform a task. The focus is entirely on how a task situation can be structured to get the highest production from workers. The process of finding the "one best way" is now known as scientific management.

Activity 1: Compare the speed of one or more of the featured workers and consider how you would have performed the task. How are they similar? How are they different? Refer to specific behaviors in your comparison.

Activity 2: What tricks can you learn from the workers for improving your speed at carrying out a similar task?

Activity 3: What are the strengths and the limitations of a motion study that could be carried out on workers such as in these examples?

You and Your Career

Henri Fayol developed fourteen general principles of management, which are described in this appendix and are still useful today. Describe how your career will embody all fourteen of Fayol's principles. For example, with "division of work," how will you incorporate this into your first and succeeding managerial jobs? Be specific in your descriptions.

Building Your Management Skills Portfolio

Your Management Skills Portfolio is a collection of activities specially designed to demonstrate your management knowledge and skill. Be sure to save your work. Taking your printed portfolio to an employment interview could be helpful in obtaining a job.

The portfolio for this chapter is Comprehensive Management Skills. Read the following and perform the skills activities that follow.

Choose a company you are familiar with or one you would like to learn more about. Try to select a large one so that information about this firm can be readily found online. Ascertain the company's history, values, sales, and number of employees. In addition, try to locate recent objectives established by the company.

Activity 1

You have just been appointed as the new president of your selected company. To be successful in this position, you will need to apply insights from many different approaches to management as well as your comprehensive management skills. Answer the following questions to help you organize your thoughts about how to examine this company from a comprehensive management perspective.

1. Using the behavioral approach to management (managing by focusing on people), provide three areas that you would want to examine to determine how well employees get along with management.

   _____

   _____

   _____

2. Using the system approach to management (managing by viewing the organization as a whole), provide three areas that you would want to examine to determine how the major parts, divisions, or departments function together to achieve company goals.

   _____

   _____

   _____

3. Using the classical approach to management (managing by finding the "one best way" to do jobs), provide three areas that you would want to examine to determine if associates have the right tools to perform their jobs.

   _____

   _____

   _____

Activity 2

Based on the information you have gathered in Activity 1, explain how the triangular management model would help you organize your thoughts on enabling this company to maximize its success.

   _____

   _____

   _____

MyLab Management
Writing Assignments

If your instructor has assigned this activity, go to www.pearson.com/mylab/management for the following assisted-graded writing assignments:

Assisted-Grading Questions

A1-10. Discuss the primary limitations of the classical approach to management. Would this approach be more useful to managers today than it was to managers in the distant past? Explain.

A1-11. What is the "system approach" to management? How do the concepts of closed and open systems relate to this approach?

Endnotes

1. Ford Motor Company, "The Moving Assembly Line Debuted at the Highland Park Plant," Historic Sites, http://corporate.ford.com/our-company, accessed February 13, 2014; Ford Motor Company, "Henry Ford's $5-a-Day Revolution," Company Milestones, http://corporate.ford.com/our-company, accessed February 13, 2014; "The United Automobile Workers (UAW) and Ford Motor Company: Working Together," Company Milestones, http://corporate.ford.com/our-company, accessed February 13, 2014; "'Whiz Kids' Brought Financial Expertise and Modern Management to Ford Motor Company," Innovators, http://corporate.ford.com/our-company, accessed February 13, 2014; Julia King, "How Analytics Helped Ford Turn Its Fortunes," Computerworld, December 2, 2013, http://www.computerworld.com; Rik Kirkland, "Leading in the 21st Century: An Interview with Ford's Alan Mulally," McKinsey Quarterly, November 2013, http://www.mckinsey.com; Tom Perez, "Stronger Together: Labor and Management at Ford," Work in Progress (U.S. Department of Labor), http://social.dol.gov; Ben Klayman and Bernie Woodall, "Ford Posts Higher Profit but Faces Pressure in U.S.," Reuters, January 28, 2014, http://www.reuters.com.
2. James H. Donnelly, Jr., James L. Gibson, and John M. Ivancevich, Fundamentals of Management (Plano, TX: Business Publications, 1987), 6–8; Harold Koontz, Cyril O'Donnell, and Heinz Weihrich, Management, 8th ed. (New York: McGraw-Hill, 1984), 52–69; W. Warren Haynes and Joseph L. Massie, Management, 2nd ed. (Upper Saddle River, NJ: Prentice Hall, 1969), 4–13.
3. David W. Hays, "Quality Improvement and Its Origin in Scientific Management," Quality Progress (May 5, 1994): 89–90.
4. For an article describing how Taylor's work has given rise to other types of modern production research, see Betsi Harris Ehrlich, "Service with a Smile," Industrial Engineer 38, no. 8 (August 2006): 40–44.
5. Frederick W. Taylor, The Principles of Scientific Management (New York: Harper & Bros., 1947), 66–71; to see how Taylor's work is still relevant in modern times, see J. P. Vijai, G. S. R. Somayaji, R. J. R. Swamy, and P. Aital, "Relevance of F.W. Taylor's Principles to Modern Shop-Floor Practices," Benchmarking 24, no. 2 (2017): 445–466.
6. For more information on the work of Frederick Taylor, see Mary Godwyn and Jody Hoffer Gittell, "Fundamentals of Scientific Management," in Sociology of Organizations: Structures and Relationships (Thousand Oaks, CA: Pine Forge/Sage, 2012), 233–240; Hans Picard, "Quit Following Marx's Advice," ENR 246, no. 12 (March 26, 2001): 99.
7. "Date in Quality History," Quality Progress 43, no. 3 (March 2010): 14.
8. Franz T. Lohrke, "Motion Study for the Blinded: A Review of the Gilbreths' Work with the Visually Handicapped," International Journal of Public Administration 16 (1993): 667–668. For information illustrating how the career of Lillian Gilbreth has been an inspiration for women managers, see Thomas R. Miller and Mary A. Lemons, "Breaking the Glass Ceiling: Lessons from a Management Pioneer," S.A.M. Advanced Management Journal 63, no. 1 (Winter 1998): 4–9. For a critical biographical approach explaining the professional contributions of Frank Gilbreth see J. W. Gibson, J. Deem, J. E. Einstein, and J. H. Humphreys, "Applying a Critical Biography Perspective to the Work of Frank Gilbreth," Journal of Management History 22 no. 4 (2016): 413–436.
9. Edward A. Michaels, "Work Measurement," Small Business Reports 14 (March 1989): 55–63. For information regarding the application of time studies in a nursing home, see Greg Arling, Robert L. Kane, Christine Mueller, and Teresa Lewis, "Explaining Direct Care Resource Use of Nursing Home Residents: Findings from Time Studies in Four States," Health Services Research 42, no. 2 (April 2007): 827.
10. Dennis Karwatka, "Frank Gilbreth and Production Efficiency," Tech Directions 65, no. 6 (January 2006): 10.
11. Rachel Emma Silverman, "Tracking Sensors Invade the Workplace," Wall Street Journal, March 7, 2013, http://online.wsj.com; Alana Semuels, "Tracking Workers' Every Move Can Boost Productivity—and Stress," Los Angeles Times, April 8, 2013, http://articles.latimes.com; Martin Dewhurst, Bryan Hancock, and Diana Ellsworth, "Redesigning Knowledge Work," Harvard Business Review (January–February 2013): 60–64.
12. Fariss-Terry Mousa and David J. Lemak, "The Gilbreths' Quality System Stands the Test of Time," Journal of Management History 15, no. 2 (2009): 198–215.
13. Ibid.

14. Henry L. Gantt, *Industrial Leadership* (New Haven, CT: Yale University Press, 1916), 57. To see how Gantt's classic work has modern applications, see Y. Shiau, H. Chuang, C. Liu, and P. Yu, "Study on Constraint Time Construction Model for Replacement of Air Handling Unit in Department Stores," *Artificial Life and Robotics* 21, no. 3 (2016): 324–331.

15. For information on software that constructs Gantt charts, see Anonymous, *Fast Company* 182 (February 2014): 17–18, 20, 24, 26.

16. Marc Puich, "The Critical Path," *Biopharm International* 20, no. 3 (March 2007): 28, 30.

17. Doug Green and Denise Green, "MacSchedule Has Rich Features at Low Price," *InfoWorld* (July 12, 1993): 88.

18. Gantt, *Industrial Leadership*, 85.

19. Chester I. Barnard, *Organization and Management* (Cambridge, MA: Harvard University Press, 1952). Barnard's ideas are still used today as a rationale for carrying out organizational studies. See L. G. Keykanlu, M. S. Navakhi, and A. Batyari, "Investigating the Relationship between Organizational Culture and Employee Efficiency in Department of Natural Resources and Watershed," *Interdisciplinary Journal of Contemporary Research in Business* 5, no. 7 (2013): 376–383.

20. Alvin Brown, *Organization of Industry* (Upper Saddle River, NJ: Prentice Hall, 1947); Henry S. Dennison, *Organization Engineering* (New York: McGraw-Hill, 1931); Luther Gulick and Lyndall Urwick, eds., *Papers on the Science of Administration* (New York: Institute of Public Administration, 1937); J. D. Mooney and A. C. Reiley, *Onward Industry!* (New York: Harper & Bros., 1931); Oliver Sheldon, *The Philosophy of Management* (London: Sir Isaac Pitman and Sons, 1923).

21. Henri Fayol, *General and Industrial Management* (London: Sir Isaac Pitman and Sons, 1949). See also David Frederick, "Making Sense of Management I," *Credit Management* (December 2000): 34–35.

22. Charles A. Mowll, "Successful Management Based on Key Principles," *Healthcare Financial Management* 43 (June 1989): 122, 124; Carl A. Rodrigues, "Fayol's 14 Principles of Management Then and Now: A Framework for Managing Today's Organizations Effectively," *Management Decision* 39 (2001): 880–889.

23. Fayol, *General and Industrial Management*, 19–42. For an excellent discussion of the role of accountability and organization structure, see Elliott Jaques, "In Praise of Hierarchy," *Harvard Business Review* 68 (January/February 1990): 127–133. Fayol's work is still recommended today as the foundation for the logical way to manage. See Jennifer J. Stepniowski, "Be the Change," *Quality Progress* 46, no. 12 (December 2013): 66–67. For discussion linking authority as discussed by Fayol and a more modern notion of incentives, see M. Krakel, "Authority and Incentives in Organizations," *The Scandinavian Journal of Economics* 119, no 2 (2017): 295–311.

24. For an interesting discussion of how negative information doesn't always travel up the chain of command, see Jonathan Alter, "Failure to Launch: How Obama Fumbled HealthCare.gov," *Foreign Affairs* 93, no. 2 (March/April 2014): 39–50.

25. Lee D. Parker and Philip Ritson, "Fads, Stereotypes, and Management Gurus: Fayol and Follett Today," *Management Decision* 43, no. 10 (2005): 1335–1357.

26. For detailed summaries of these studies, see *Industrial Worker*, 2 vols. (Cambridge, MA: Harvard University Press, 1938); F. J. Roethlisberger and W. J. Dickson, *Management and the Worker* (Cambridge, MA: Harvard University Press, 1939). For a review of the Hawthorne Studies, see J. Muldoon, "The Hawthorne Studies: An Analysis of Critical Perspectives, 1936–1958," *Journal of Management History* 23, no. 1 (2017): 74–94.

27. Stephen Jones, "Worker Interdependence and Output: The Hawthorne Studies Reevaluated," *American Sociological Review* (April 1990): 176–190.

28. Jennifer Laabs, "Corporate Anthropologists," *Personnel Journal* (January 1992): 81–91; Samuel C. Certo, *Human Relations Today: Concepts and Skills* (Burr Ridge, IL: Irwin, 1995), 4; Scott Highhouse, "Well-Being: The Foundations of Hedonic Psychology," *Personnel Psychology* 54, no. 1 (Spring 2001): 204–206.

29. Michael Wilson, "The Psychology of Motivation and Employee Retention," *Maintenance Supplies* 50, no. 5 (July 2005): 48–49.

30. Mark Goulston and John Ullmen, "How to Really Understand Someone Else's Point of View," *Harvard Business Review*, April 22, 2013, http://blogs.hbr.org; Stephen R. Covey, "The Seven Habits of Highly Effective People: Habit 5, Seek First to Understand, Then to Be Understood," Stephen R. Covey website, https://www.stephen-covey.com, accessed February 13, 2014; Greg Toppo, "Want to Understand Others? Read Literary Fiction," *USA Today*, October 4, 2013, http://www.usatoday.com.

31. A. H. Reylito Elbo, "In the Workplace," *Business World* (2002): 1.

32. David A. Kaplan, "SAS: A New No. 1 Best Employer," CNNMoney.com, January 22, 2010, http://money.cnn.com.

33. C. West Churchman, Russell L. Ackoff, and E. Leonard Arnoff, *Introduction to Operations Research* (New York: Wiley, 1957), 18.

34. Hamdy A. Taha, *Operations Research: An Introduction* (New York: Macmillan, 1988), 1–2; see also Scott Shane and Karl Ulrich, "Technological Innovation, Product Development, and Entrepreneurship in Management Science," *Management Science* 2 (2004): 133–145.

35. Kalyan Singhal, Jaya Singhal, and Martin K Starr, "The Domain of Production and Operations Management and the Role of Elwood Buffa in Its Delineation," *Journal of Operations Management* 25, no. 2 (March 2007): 310. For a discussion of operations research in the health-care industry, see B. D. Bradley, T. Jung, T., Ananya Tandon-Vermassem Khoury, T. C. Y. Chan, and C. Yu-Ling, "Operations Research in Global Health: A Scoping Review with a Focus on the Themes of Health Equity and Impact," *Health Research Policy and Systems* 15 (2017), doi:http://dx.doi.org/10.1186/s12961-017-0187-7.

36. James R. Emshoff, *Analysis of Behavioral Systems* (New York: Macmillan, 1971), 10.

37. For a discussion of management science in the twenty-first century, see David R. Anderson, *An Introduction to Management Science: Quantitative Approaches to Decision Making* (Mason, OH: South-Western/Cengage Learning, 2012); Michael S. Hopkins, "Putting the Science in Management Science?," *MIT Sloan Management Review*, March 17, 2010. An interesting discussion of the issues related to establishing a health information technology system for the United States is found in David J. Bailer, "Guiding the Health Information Technology Agenda," *Health Affairs* 29, no. 4 (April 2010): 586–594.

38. The discussion concerning these characteristics is adapted from Donnelly, Gibson, and Ivancevich, *Fundamentals of Management*, 302–303; Efraim Turban and Jack R. Meredith, *Fundamentals of Management Science* (Plano, TX: Business Publications, 1981), 15–23.

39. For a practical application of the contingency approach to management, see Henri Barki, Suzanne Rivard, and Jean Talbot, "An Integrative Contingency Model of Software Project Risk Management," *Journal of Management Information Systems* 17, no. 4 (Spring 2001): 37–69.

40. For an application of the contingency approach to management in an information systems organization, see Narayan S. Umanath, "The Concept of Contingency beyond 'It Depends': Illustrations from IS Research Stream," *Information & Management* 40 (2003): 551–562.

41. Don Hellriegel, John W. Slocum, and Richard W. Woodman, *Organizational Behavior* (St. Paul, MN: West Publishing, 1986), 22.

42. J. W. Lorsch, "Organization Design: A Situational Perspective," *Organizational Dynamics* 6 (1977): 2–4; Louis W. Fry and Deborah A. Smith, "Congruence, Contingency, and Theory Building," *Academy of Management Review* (January 1987): 117–132.

43. For a more detailed development of von Bertalanffy's ideas, see "General System Theory: A New Approach to Unity of Science," *Human Biology* (December 1951): 302–361.

44. L. Thomas Hopkins, *Integration: Its Meaning and Application* (New York: Appleton-Century-Crofts, 1937), 36–49.

45. Company website, http://www.reviewpro.com, accessed April 15, 2010; Marina Zaliznyak, "Hotel Reputation Management Service ReviewPro Has Big International Plans," *TechCrunch*, January 5, 2010, http://eu.techcrunch.com.

46. Joe Schwartz, "Why They Buy," *American Demographics* 11 (March 1989): 40–41.

47. Ken Starkey, "What Can We Learn from the Learning Organization?," *Human Relations* 51, no. 4 (April 1998): 531–546.

48. David A. Garvin, "Building a Learning Organization," *Harvard Business Review* 74, no. 4 (July 1993): 78. For a more recent discussion of learning organizations, see Bente Elkjaer, "The Dance of Change: The Challenges of Sustaining Momentum in Learning Organizations," *Management Learning* 32, no. 1 (March 2000): 153–156.

49. For a study on the effectiveness of the learning organization approach, see Ashok Jashapara, "Cognition, Culture, and Competition: An Empirical Test of the Learning Organization," *The Learning Organization* 10 (2003): 31–50.

50. Peter Senge, *The Fifth Discipline: The Art & Practice of the Learning Organization* (New York: Doubleday/Currency, 1990). Used by permission of Doubleday, a division of Random House, Inc. For more background regarding implementing the learning organization philosophy, see H. Cierna, E. Sujová, P. Hbek, E. Horská, and Z. Kapsdorferová, "Learning Organization at Higher Education Institutions in the EU: Proposal for Implementing Philosophy of Learning Organization—Results from Research," *Quality and Quantity* 51, no. 3 (2017): 1305–1320.

51. Leonel Prieto, "Some Necessary Conditions and Constraints for Successful Learning Organizations," *Competition Forum* 7, no. 2 (2009): 513–520.

52. Ronald Alsop, "Sparking Innovation from the Bottom Up," *BBC Capital*, November 26, 2013, http://www.bbc.com; Ryan Hutton, "How IBM Bypasses Bureaucratic Purgatory," *Fortune*, December 5, 2013, EBSCOhost, http://web.b.ebscohost.com; IBM, "About IBM," http://www.ibm.com/ibm/us/en/, accessed February 13, 2014; IBM, "Background," IBM Newsroom, http://www.ibm.com/press, accessed February 13, 2014.

53. UPS, "About UPS: Company History," UPS Pressroom, http://www.pressroom.ups.com, accessed February 13, 2014; Steve Rosenbush, "UPS Says Automated Routing Will Transform Package Delivery," *Wall Street Journal*, October 28, 2013, http://blogs.wsj.com; Devin Leonard, "He'll Make Your Dreams Come True," *Bloomberg Businessweek*, December 23, 2013, EBSCOhost, http://web.b.ebscohost.com; Laura Stevens and Anna Prior, "UPS Unveils Plans to Improve Delivery Performance," *Wall Street Journal*, January 30, 2014, http://online.wsj.com; Devin Leonard, "D. Scott Davis, CEO, UPS," *Bloomberg Businessweek*, August 12, 2013, EBSCOhost, http://web.b.ebscohost.com; Jeff Berman, "UPS Reports a 2.8 Percent Gain in Q4 Revenue to $14.9 Billion," *Logistics Management*, January 30, 2014, http://www.logistics mgmt.com.

Glossary

Accountability refers to the management philosophy whereby individuals are held liable, or accountable, for how well they use their authority and live up to their responsibility of performing predetermined activities.

Achievement behavior is aimed at setting challenging goals for followers to reach and expressing and demonstrating confidence that they will measure up to the challenge.

Activity is a specified set of behavior within a project.

Adhocracy culture is an organizational culture characterized by flexibility and discretion along with an external focus.

Adjourning, the fifth and last stage of the team development process, is the stage in which the team finishes its job and prepares to disband.

Affirmative action program is an organizational program whose basic purpose is to eliminate barriers against and increase employment opportunities for underutilized or disadvantaged individuals.

Alderfer's ERG theory is an explanation of human needs that divides them into three basic types: existence needs, relatedness needs, and growth needs.

Allocating skill is the ability to provide the organizational resources necessary to implement a strategy.

Angel investors are wealthy individuals who provide capital to new companies.

Appropriate human resources are the individuals within the organization who make valuable contributions to management system goal attainment.

Argyris's maturity-immaturity continuum is a concept that furnishes insights into human needs by focusing on an individual's natural progress from immaturity to maturity.

Assessment center is a program in which participants engage in, and are evaluated on, a number of individual and group exercises constructed to simulate important activities at the organizational levels to which they aspire.

Authentic leadership is leadership conducted by leaders who are deeply aware of their own and others' moral perspectives and who are confident, hopeful, optimistic, resilient, and of high moral character.

Authority is the right to perform or command.

Automation is the replacement of human effort by electromechanical devices.

Avoiding is a conflict management technique whereby managers simply ignore the conflict.

Bank financing occurs when an entrepreneur obtains financing from a financial institution in the form of a loan.

Behavior modification is a program that focuses on encouraging appropriate behavior by controlling the consequences of that behavior.

Behavioral approach to management is a management approach that emphasizes increasing production through an understanding of people.

Bias refers to departures from rational theory that produce suboptimal decisions.

Bicultural stress is stress resulting from having to cope with membership in two cultures simultaneously.

Bounded rationality refers to the fact that managers are bounded in terms of time, computational power, and knowledge when making decisions.

Brainstorming is a group decision-making process in which negative feedback on any suggested alternative to any group member is forbidden until all group members have presented alternatives that they perceive as valuable.

Break-even analysis is the process of generating information that summarizes various levels of profit or loss associated with various levels of production.

Break-even point is that level of production where the total revenue of an organization equals its total costs.

Budget is a control tool that outlines how funds in a given period will be spent, as well as how they will be obtained.

Bureaucracy is the term Max Weber used to describe a management system characterized by detailed procedures and rules, a clearly outlined organizational hierarchy, and impersonal relationships among organization members.

Business portfolio analysis is an organizational strategy formulation technique that is based on the philosophy that organizations should develop strategy much as they handle investment portfolios.

Buyer power refers to the power that customers have over the firms operating in an industry; as buyer power increases, the attractiveness of the industry decreases.

Capacity strategy is an operational plan of action aimed at providing an organization with the right facilities to produce the needed output at the right time.

Career is a sequence of work-related positions occupied by a person over the course of a lifetime.

Career plateauing is a period of little or no apparent progress in the growth of a career.

Cash cow is an SBU that has a large share of a market that is growing only slightly.

Centralization refers to the situation in which a minimal number of job activities and a minimal amount of authority are delegated to subordinates.

Change agent is an individual inside or outside the organization who tries to modify the existing organizational situation.

Change-related activities are management efforts aimed at modifying organizational components.

Changing an organization is the process of modifying an existing organization to increase organizational effectiveness.

Clan culture is an organization culture characterized by a strong internal focus with a high degree of flexibility and discretion.

Classical approach to management is a management approach that emphasizes organizational efficiency to increase organizational success.

Closed system is one that is not influenced by, and does not interact with, its environment.

Coaching is leadership that instructs followers on how to meet the special organizational challenges they face.

Code of conduct is a document that reflects the core values of an organization and suggests how organization members should act in relation to those values.

Code of ethics is a formal statement that acts as a guide for making decisions and acting within an organization.

Collaboration is the ability to work with others in accomplishing a task.

Command group is a formal group that is outlined in the chain of command on an organization chart. Command groups typically handle routine activities.

Commercial entrepreneurship involves individuals or corporations that pursue entrepreneurial opportunities for the purposes of generating sales and profits.

Commitment principle is a management guideline that advises managers to commit funds for planning only if they can anticipate, in the foreseeable future, a return on planning expenses as a result of long-range planning analysis.

Committee is a task group that is charged with performing some type of specific activity.

Communication is the process of sharing information with other individuals.

Communication macrobarriers are factors hindering successful communication that relate primarily to the communication environment and to the larger world in which communication takes place.

Communication microbarrier is a factor hindering successful communication that relates primarily to such variables as the communication message, the source, and the destination.

Competitive dynamics refers to the process by which firms undertake strategic and tactical actions and how competitors respond to these actions.

Competitor awareness refers to how mindful a company is of its competitor's actions.

Competitor capability refers to a firm's ability to undertake an action.

Competitor motivation refers to the incentives that an organization has to take action.

Compromise means the parties to the conflict settle on a solution that gives both of them part of what they wanted.

Computer-aided design (CAD) is a computerized technique for designing new products or modifying existing ones.

Computer-aided manufacturing (CAM) is a technique that employs computers to plan and program equipment used in the production and inspection of manufactured items.

Conceptual skills are skills involving the ability to see the organization as a whole.

Conflict is defined as a struggle that results from opposing needs or feelings between two or more people.

Consensus is an agreement on a decision by all the individuals involved in making that decision.

Consideration behavior is leadership behavior that reflects friendship, mutual trust, respect, and warmth in the relationship between leader and followers.

Content theory of motivation is an explanation of motivation that emphasizes people's internal characteristics.

Contingency approach to management is a management approach emphasizing that what managers do in practice depends on a given set of circumstances—a situation.

Contingency theory of leadership is a leadership concept that hypothesizes that, in any given leadership situation, success is determined primarily by (1) the degree to which the task being performed by the followers is structured, (2) the degree of position power possessed by the leader, and (3) the type of relationship that exists between the leader and the followers.

Control entails ensuring that an event occurs as it was planned to occur.

Control tool is a specific procedure or technique that presents pertinent organizational information in a way that helps managers to develop and implement an appropriate control strategy.

Controlling is the process managers go through to control. It is "a systematic effort . . . to compare performance to predetermined standards, plans, or objectives to determine whether performance is in line with these standards" or needs to be corrected.

Coordination is the orderly arrangement of group effort to provide unity of action in the pursuit of a common purpose. It involves encouraging the completion of individual portions of a task in an appropriate, synchronized order.

Corporate entrepreneurship is the process in which an individual or group of individuals in an existing corporation creates a new organization or instigates renewal or innovation within that corporation.

Corrective action is managerial activity aimed at bringing organizational performance up to the level of performance standards.

Cost leadership is a strategy that focuses on making an organization more competitive by its producing products more cheaply than competitors can.

Creativity is the ability to generate original ideas or new perspectives on existing ideas.

Critical path is the sequence of events and activities within a program evaluation and review technique (PERT) network that requires the longest period of time to complete.

Critical question analysis is a strategy development tool that consists of answering basic questions about the present purposes and objectives of the organization, its present direction and environment, and actions that can be taken to achieve organizational objectives in the future.

Cross-cultural experience refers to experience living in a foreign country.

Cross-functional team is an organizational team composed of people from different functional areas of the organization who are all focused on a specified objective.

Cultural artifact is a dimension of an organization that helps to describe and reinforce the culture—or the beliefs, values, and norms—in which an artifact exists.

Culture is the set of characteristics of a given group of people and their environment.

Customer dimension of organization culture is a facet of organization culture that focuses on catering to the needs of those individuals who buy goods or services the organization produces.

Data are facts or statistics.

Decentralization refers to the situation in which a significant number of job activities and a maximum amount of authority are delegated to subordinates.

Decision is a choice made between two or more available alternatives.

Decision tree is a graphic decision-making tool typically used to evaluate decisions involving a series of steps.

Decision tree analysis is a statistical and graphical, multiphased decision-making technique that contains a series of steps showing the sequence and interdependence of decisions.

Decline stage is the fourth and last stage in career evolution; it occurs near retirement age, when individuals of about 65 years of age show declining productivity.

Decoder/destination is the person or persons in the interpersonal communication situation with whom the source is attempting to share information.

Delegation is the process of assigning job activities and related authority to specific individuals within the organization.

Delphi technique is a group decision-making process that involves circulating questionnaires on a specific problem among group members, sharing the questionnaire results with them, and then continuing to recirculate and refine individual responses until a consensus regarding the problem is reached.

Demographics are statistical characteristics of a population.

Department is a unique group of resources established by management to perform some organizational task.

Departmentalizing is the process of establishing departments within the management system.

Developing is that step of the innovation process that makes a new idea practical.

Differentiation is a strategy that focuses on making an organization more competitive by its developing a product or products that customers perceive as being different from products offered by competitors.

Diffusing is that step of the innovation process that puts a new idea to use by end users or customers.

Direct investing is using the assets of one company to purchase the operating assets of another company.

Directive behavior is aimed at telling followers what to do and how to do it.

Discrimination is the act of treating an issue, person, or behavior unjustly or inequitably on the basis of stereotypes or prejudices.

Diversity refers to characteristics of individuals that shape their identities and the experiences they have in society. Major areas of diversity are gender, race, ethnicity, religion, social class, physical ability, sexual orientation, and age.

Diversity dimension of organization culture is a component of organization culture that encourages the existence of basic human differences among organization members.

Diversity training is a learning process designed to raise managers' awareness and develop their competencies to deal with the issues endemic to managing a diverse workforce.

Divestiture is a strategy adopted to eliminate a strategic business unit that is not generating a satisfactory amount of business and has little hope of doing so in the near future.

Division of labor is the assignment of various portions of a particular task among a number of organization members. Division of labor calls for specialization.

Dog is an SBU that has a relatively small share of a low-growth market.

Domain definition occurs when a firm proactively seeks to create a new product market position that competitors have not recognized.

Domestic organization is an organization that essentially operates within a single country.

Dominant organization culture is the shared values about organizational functioning held by the majority of organization members.

Downside loss refers to the resources (i.e., money, relationships, etc.) that the entrepreneur could lose if the opportunity does not succeed.

Economics is the science that focuses on understanding how people of a particular community or nation produce, distribute, and use various goods and services.

Effectiveness is the degree to which managers attain organizational objectives; it is "doing the right things."

Efficiency is the degree to which organizational resources contribute to production; it is "doing things right."

Emotional intelligence is the capacity of people to recognize their own feelings and the feelings of others, to motivate themselves, and to manage their own emotions as well as their emotions in relationships with others.

Employee-centered behavior is leader behavior that focuses primarily on subordinates as people.

Entrepreneur is an individual who identifies, evaluates, and exploits opportunities.

Entrepreneurial alertness refers to an individual's ability to notice and be sensitive to new information about objects, incidents, and patterns of behavior in the environment.

Entrepreneurial opportunity is an occasion to bring into existence new products and services that allow outputs to be sold at a price greater than their cost of production.

Entrepreneurial risk is the likelihood and magnitude of the opportunity's downside loss.

Entrepreneurship refers to the identification, evaluation, and exploitation of opportunities.

Environmental analysis is the study of the organizational environment to pinpoint environmental factors that can significantly influence organizational operations.

Environmental footprint is a measure of the usage of environmental resources. The greater the amount of resources consumed by an organization, the greater the organization's footprint.

Equal Employment Opportunity Commission (EEOC) is an agency established to enforce federal laws prohibiting discrimination on the basis of race, color, religion, gender, disability, sexual orientation, national origin, and genetic information in recruitment, hiring, firing, layoffs, and all other employment practices.

Equity theory is an explanation of motivation that emphasizes the individual's perceived fairness of an employment situation and how perceived inequities can cause certain behaviors.

Establishment stage is the second stage in career evolution; individuals of about 25 to 45 years of age typically start to become more productive, or higher performers.

Esteem need is Maslow's fourth set of human needs, which includes the desires for self-respect and respect from others.

Ethics is the capacity to reflect on values in the corporate decision-making process, to determine how these values and decisions affect various stakeholder groups, and to establish how managers can use these observations in day-to-day company management.

Ethics dimension of organization culture is a facet of organization culture that focuses on making sure that an organization emphasizes not only what is good for the organization but also what is good for other human beings.

Ethnocentric attitude reflects the belief that multinational corporations should regard home-country management practices as superior to foreign-country management practices.

Ethnocentrism is the belief that one's own group, culture, country, or customs are superior to those of others.

European Union (EU) is an international market agreement established in 1994 dedicated to facilitating trade among member nations.

Event is a completion of major project tasks.

Exclusion occurs when individuals exclude the least desirable alternatives from a larger set of alternatives.

Existence need is the need for physical well-being.

Expatriate is an organization member who lives and works in a country where he or she does not have citizenship.

Expected value (EV) is the measurement of the anticipated value of some event, determined by multiplying the income an event would produce by its probability of producing that income (EV = $I \times P$).

Exploitation refers to the activities and investments that are committed to gain returns from the new product or service arising from an opportunity.

Exploration stage is the first stage in career evolution; it occurs at the beginning of a career, when the individual is typically 15 to 25 years of age, and it is characterized by self-analysis and the exploration of different types of available jobs.

Exporting is selling goods or services to another country.

Extrinsic reward is a reward that is extraneous to the task accomplished.

Feasibility analysis is analysis that helps entrepreneurs understand whether an idea is practical.

Feedback is, in the interpersonal communication situation, the destination's reaction to a message.

Five Forces Model outlines the primary forces that determine competitiveness within an industry and illustrates how those forces are related; perhaps the best-known tool for industry analysis, it was developed by internationally acclaimed strategic management expert Michael E. Porter.

Fixed cost is an expense incurred by the organization regardless of the number of products produced.

Fixed-position layout is a layout plan in which the product is stationary while resources flow. It is appropriate for organizations involved in a large number of different tasks that require low volumes, multipurpose equipment, and broad employee skills.

Flextime is a program that allows workers to complete their jobs within a workweek of a normal number of hours that they schedule themselves.

Focus is a strategy that emphasizes making an organization more competitive by targeting a particular customer.

Forcing is a technique for managing conflict in which managers use their authority to declare that conflict is ended.

Forecasting is a planning tool used to predict future environmental happenings that will influence the operation of the organization.

Formal group is a group that exists within an organization by virtue of management decree to perform tasks that enhance the attainment of organizational objectives.

Formal organizational communication is organizational communication that follows the lines of the organization chart.

Formal structure is defined as the relationships among organizational resources as outlined by management.

Forming is the first stage of the team development process, during which members of the newly formed team become oriented to the team and acquainted with one another as they explore issues related to their new job situation.

Friendship group is an informal group that forms in organizations because of the personal affiliation members have with one another.

Functional authority consists of the right to give orders within a segment of the management system in which this right is normally nonexistent.

Functional similarity method is a method for dividing job activities in an organization.

Gantt chart is a scheduling tool composed of a bar chart with time on the horizontal axis and the resource to be scheduled on the vertical axis. It is used for scheduling resources.

Gender-role stereotypes are perceptions about people based on what our society believes are appropriate behaviors for men and women.

General environment is the level of an organization's external environment that contains components normally having broad, long-term implications for managing the organization; its components are economic, social, political, legal, and technological.

Geocentric attitude reflects the belief that the overall quality of management recommendations, rather than the location of managers, should determine the acceptability of management practices used to guide multinational corporations.

Good corporate citizen is a manager who is committed to building an organization's local community and environment as a vital part of managing.

Graicunas's formula is a formula that makes the span-of-management point that as the number of a manager's subordinates increases arithmetically, the number of possible relationships between the manager and the subordinates increases geometrically.

Grapevine is the network of informal organizational communication.

Grid organization development (grid OD) is a commonly used organization development technique based on a theoretical model called the managerial grid.

Group is "any number of people who (1) interact with one another, (2) are psychologically aware of one another, and (3) perceive themselves to be a group."

Groupthink is the mode of thinking that group members engage in when the desire for agreement so dominates the group that it overrides the need to realistically appraise alternative solutions.

Growth is a strategy adopted by management to increase the amount of business that a strategic business unit is currently generating.

Growth need is the need for continuing personal growth and development.

Healthy organization culture is an organization culture that facilitates the achievement of the organization's mission and objectives.

Heuristics are simple rules of thumb used to make decisions.

Hierarchy culture is an organization culture characterized by an internal focus along with an emphasis on stability and control.

Horizontal dimensioning of an organization refers to the extent to which firms use lateral subdivisions or specialties within the organization.

Host country is the country in which an investment is made by a foreign company.

Host-country national is an organization member who is a citizen of the country in which the facility of a foreign-based organization is located.

Human relations movement is a people-oriented approach to management in which the interaction of people in organizations is studied to judge its impact on organizational success.

Human relations skill is the ability to work with people in a way that enhances organizational success.

Human resource inventory is information about the characteristics of organization members; the focus is on past performance and future potential, and the objective is to keep management up to date about the possibilities for filling a position from within.

Human resource strategy is an operational plan to use an organization's human resources effectively and efficiently while maintaining or improving the quality of work life.

Human skills are skills involving the ability to build cooperation within the team being led.

Hygiene, or maintenance, factors are items that influence the degree of job dissatisfaction.

Illusion of control exists when entrepreneurs overestimate the extent to which they can control the outcome of an opportunity.

Importing is buying goods or services from another country.

Inclusion occurs when individuals choose a smaller set of the most desirable alternatives from a larger set of alternatives.

Industry environment is the level of an organization's external environment that contains components normally having relatively specific and immediate implications for managing the organization.

Influencing is the process of guiding the activities of organization members in appropriate directions.

Informal group is a collection of individuals whose common work experiences result in the development of a system of interpersonal relations that extend beyond those established by management.

Informal organizational communication is organizational communication that does not follow the lines of the organization chart.

Informal structure is defined as the patterns of relationships that develop because of the informal activities of organization members.

Information is the set of conclusions derived from data analysis.

Information appropriateness is the degree to which information is relevant to the decision-making situation the manager faces.

Information asymmetry refers to the fact that individuals vary in terms of the information to which they have access.

Information quality is the degree to which information represents reality.

Information quantity is the amount of decision-related information a manager possesses.

Information system (IS) is a network of applications established within an organization to provide managers with the information that will assist them in decision making. An IS gets information to where it is needed.

Information technology (IT) is technology that focuses on the use of information in the performance of work.

Information timeliness is the extent to which the receipt of information allows decisions to be made and action to be taken so that the organization can gain some benefit from possessing the information.

Innovation is the process of applying a new idea to the improvement of organizational processes, products, or services.

Innovation dimension of organization culture is an aspect of organization culture that encourages the application of new ideas to improve organization processes, products, or services.

Innovation process is defined as the steps managers take to implement creative ideas.

Integrating is that step of the innovation process that establishes an invention as a permanent part of the organization.

Intensity of rivalry refers to the intensity of competition among the organizations in an industry; as the intensity of rivalry increases, the attractiveness of the industry decreases.

Interacting skill is the ability to manage people during implementation.

Interest group is an informal group that gains and maintains membership primarily because of a common concern members have about a specific issue.

Internal environment is the level of an organization's environment that exists inside the organization and normally has immediate and specific implications for managing the organization.

International joint venture is a partnership formed between a company in one country and a company in another country for the purpose of pursuing some mutually desirable business undertaking.

International management is the performance of management activities across national borders.

International market agreement is an arrangement among a cluster of countries that facilitates a high level of trade among these countries.

International organization is an organization based primarily within a single country but having continuing, meaningful transactions in other countries.

Intrinsic reward is a reward that comes directly from performing a task.

Intuition refers to an individual's inborn ability to synthesize information quickly and effectively.

Inventing is that step of the innovation process that establishes a new idea that could help the organization be more successful.

Job analysis is a technique commonly used to gain an understanding of what a task entails and the type of individual who should be hired to perform that task.

Job-centered behavior is leader behavior that focuses primarily on the work a subordinate is doing.

Job description is a list of specific activities that must be performed to accomplish some task or job.

Job design is an operational plan that determines who will do a specific job and how and where the job will be done.

Job enlargement is the process of increasing the number of operations an individual performs in order to enhance the individual's satisfaction with work.

Job enrichment is the process of incorporating motivators into a job situation.

Job rotation is the process of moving workers from one job to another rather than requiring them to perform only one simple and specialized job over the long term.

Job specification is the characteristics of the individual who should be hired to perform a specific task or job.

Jury of executive opinion method is a method of predicting future sales levels primarily by asking appropriate managers to give their opinions on what will happen to sales in the future.

Just-in-time (JIT) inventory control is a technique for reducing inventories to a minimum by arranging for production components to be delivered to the production facility "just in time" for them to be used.

Labor force planning is an operational plan for hiring the right employees for a job and training them to be productive.

Law of small numbers refers to individuals relying on small samples of information to guide their decisions.

Layout is the overall arrangement of equipment, work areas, service areas, and storage areas within a facility that produces goods or provides services.

Layout strategy is an operational plan that determines the location and flow of organizational resources around, into, and within production and service facilities.

Leader flexibility is the idea that successful leaders must change their leadership styles as they encounter different situations.

Leader-member relations is the degree to which the leader feels accepted by the followers.

Leadership is the process of directing the behavior of others toward the accomplishment of objectives.

Leadership style is the behavior a leader exhibits while guiding organization members in appropriate directions.

Learning organization is an organization that does well in creating, acquiring, and transferring knowledge and in modifying its behavior to reflect new knowledge.

Lecture is primarily a one-way communication situation in which an instructor trains an individual or group by orally presenting information.

LEED (Leadership in Energy and Environmental Design) is an ecology-oriented certification program that rates the ecology impact of buildings of all types.

Level 5 leadership is an approach to leadership that blends personal humility with an intense will to build long-range organizational success.

License agreement is a right granted by one company to another to use its brand name, technology, product specifications, and so on in the manufacture or sale of goods and services.

Life cycle theory of leadership is a leadership concept that hypothesizes that leadership styles should reflect primarily the maturity level of the followers.

Line authority consists of the right to make decisions and to give orders concerning the production-, sales-, or finance-related behavior of subordinates.

Location strategy is an operational plan of action that provides an organization with a competitive location for its headquarters, manufacturing, services, and distribution activities.

Loss is the amount of the total costs of producing a product that exceeds the total revenue gained from selling the product.

Maintenance stage is the third stage in career evolution; individuals of about 45 to 65 years of age show either increased performance (career growth), stabilized performance (career maintenance), or decreased performance (career stagnation).

Majority group refers to that group of people in the organization who hold most of the positions that command decision-making power, control of resources and information, and access to system rewards.

Management is the process of reaching organizational goals by working with and through people and other organizational resources.

Management by exception is a control tool that allows only significant deviations between planned and actual performance to be brought to a manager's attention.

Management employability skills refer to a person's ability to gain and maintain a career as a manager.

Management functions are activities that make up the management process. The four basic management activities are planning, organizing, influencing, and controlling.

Management inventory card is a form used in compiling a human resource inventory. It contains the organizational history of an individual and indicates how that individual might be used in the organization in the future.

Management manpower replacement chart is a form used in compiling a human resource inventory. It is people oriented and presents a composite view of the individuals management considers significant to human resource planning.

Management responsibility guide is a tool that is used to clarify the responsibilities of various managers in the organization.

Management science approach is a management approach that emphasizes the use of the scientific method and mathematical techniques to solve operational problems.

Management skill is the ability to carry out the process of reaching organizational goals by working with and through people and other organizational resources.

Management system is composed of a number of parts that function interdependently to achieve a purpose; its main parts are organizational input, organizational process, and organizational output.

Managerial effectiveness refers to management's use of organizational resources in meeting organizational goals.

Managerial efficiency is the proportion of total organizational resources used during the production process.

Managerial grid is a theoretical model based on the premise that concern for people and concern for production are the two primary attitudes that influence management style.

Market culture is an organization culture that reflects values that emphasize stability and control along with an external focus.

Materials control is an operational activity that determines the flow of materials from vendors through an operations system to customers.

McClelland's acquired needs theory is an explanation of human needs that focuses on the desires for achievement, power, and affiliation that people develop as a result of their life experiences.

Mechanistic structure is a formal organizational structure.

Message is encoded information that the source intends to share with others.

Message interference refers to stimuli that compete with the communication message for the attention of the destination.

Minority group refers to that group of people in the organization who are fewer in number than the majority group or who lack critical power, resources, acceptance, or social status.

Mission statement is a written document developed by management, normally based on input by managers as well as nonmanagers, that describes and explains what the mission of an organization actually is.

Monitoring is that step of the innovation process in which a newly implemented idea is tracked to determine if and when the idea should be improved or terminated.

Monitoring skill is the ability to use information to determine whether a problem has arisen that is blocking strategy implementation.

Moral courage is the strength to take actions that are consistent with moral beliefs despite pressures, either inside or outside of the organization, to do otherwise.

Motion study finds the best way to accomplish a task by reducing each job to the most basic movements possible.

Motion-study techniques are operational tools that are used to improve productivity.

Motivating factors (or motivators) are items that influence the degree of job satisfaction.

Motivation is the inner state that causes an individual to behave in a way that ensures the accomplishment of some goal.

Motivation strength is an individual's degree of desire to perform a behavior.

Moving average method utilizes historical data to predict future sales levels.

Multinational corporation is a company that has significant operations in more than one country.

Need for achievement (nAch) is the desire to do something better or more efficiently than it has ever been done before.

Need for affiliation (nAff) is the desire to maintain close, friendly, personal relationships.

Need for power (nPower) is the desire to control, influence, or be responsible for others.

Needs-goal theory is a motivation model that hypothesizes that felt needs cause human behavior.

Negative reinforcement is a reward that consists of the elimination of an undesirable consequence of behavior.

Nominal group technique is a group decision-making process in which every group member is assured of equal participation in making the group decision. After each member writes down individual ideas and presents them orally to the group, the entire group discusses all the ideas and then votes for the best idea in a secret ballot.

Nonprogrammed decision is typically a one-shot decision that is usually less structured than programmed decisions.

Nonverbal communication is the sharing of information without using words.

Norming, the third stage of the team development process, is characterized by agreement among team members on roles, rules, and acceptable behavior while working on the team.

North American Free Trade Agreement (NAFTA) is an international market agreement aimed at facilitating trade among member nations.

On-the-job training is a training technique that blends job-related knowledge with experience in using that knowledge on the job.

Open system is one that is influenced by, and is continually interacting with, its environment.

Operations control is making sure that operations activities are carried out as planned.

Operations management is performance of managerial activities entailed in selecting, designing, operating, controlling, and updating production systems.

Organic structure is a less formal organizational structure and represents loosely coupled networks of workers.

Organization chart is a graphic illustration of organizational structure.

Organization culture is a set of values that organization members share regarding the functioning and existence of their organization.

Organization development (OD) is the process that emphasizes changing an organization by changing organization members and bases these changes on an overview of structure, technology, and all other organizational components.

Organization subculture is a mini-culture within an organization that can reflect the values and beliefs of a specific segment of the organization that is formed along lines such as established departments or geographic regions.

Organizational ceremony is a formal activity conducted on important organizational occasions.

Organizational commitment can be defined as the dedication of organization members to uphold the values of the organization and to make worthwhile contributions to fulfilling the organizational purpose.

Organizational communication is interpersonal communication within organizations that directly relates to the goals, functions, and structure of human organizations.

Organizational mission is the purpose for which, or the reason why, an organization exists.

Organizational myth is a popular belief or story that has become associated with a person or institution and is considered to illustrate an organization culture ideal.

Organizational objective is the target toward which the open management system is directed. It flows from the organization's mission.

Organizational purpose is what the organization exists to do, given a particular group of customers and customer needs.

Organizational rejuvenation involves improving a firm's ability to execute strategies and focuses on new processes instead of new products.

Organizational resources are all assets available for activation during the production process; they include human resources, monetary resources, raw materials resources, and capital resources.

Organizational saga is a narrative describing the adventures of a heroic individual or family significantly linked to an organization's past or present.

Organizational socialization is the process by which management can appropriately integrate new employees into the organization's culture.

Organizational storytelling is the act of passing along organizational myths and sagas to other organization members.

Organizational symbol is an object that has meaning beyond its intrinsic content.

Organizing is the process of establishing orderly uses for resources within the management system.

Organizing skill is the ability to create throughout the organization a network of people who can help solve implementation problems as they occur.

Overlapping responsibility refers to a situation in which more than one individual is responsible for the same activity.

Paradox of choice is having too many alternatives, which may actually demotivate decision makers, which harms decision making.

Parent company is the company investing in international operations.

Participative behavior is aimed at seeking suggestions from followers regarding business operations to the extent that followers are involved in making important organizational decisions.

Path-goal theory of leadership is a theory of leadership that suggests that the primary activities of a leader are to make desirable and achievable rewards available to organization members who attain organizational goals and to clarify the kinds of behavior that must be performed to earn those rewards.

People change emphasizes increasing organizational effectiveness by changing certain characteristics of organization members such as their attitudes and leadership skills.

People factors are attitudes, leadership skills, communication skills, and all other characteristics of the organization's employees.

People-related activities are management efforts aimed at managing people in organizations.

Perception is an individual's interpretation of a message.

Performance appraisal is the process of reviewing individuals' past productive activities to evaluate the contributions they have made toward attaining management system objectives.

Performing, the fourth stage of the team development process, is characterized by a focus on solving organizational problems and meeting assigned challenges.

Personal humility means being modest or unassuming when it comes to citing personal accomplishments.

Personal power is power derived from a manager's relationships with others.

Philanthropy   promotes the welfare of others through generous monetary donations to social causes.

Physiological need   is Maslow's first set of human needs for the normal functioning of the body, including the desires for water, food, rest, sex, and air.

Planning   is the process of determining how the organization can get where it wants to go and what it will do to accomplish its objectives.

Planning tools   are techniques managers can use to help develop plans.

Pluralism   refers to an environment in which differences are acknowledged, accepted, and viewed as significant contributors to the entirety.

Policy   is a standing plan that furnishes broad guidelines for taking action consistent with reaching organizational objectives.

Polycentric attitude   reflects the belief that because foreign managers are closer to foreign organizational units, they probably understand them better, and therefore foreign management practices should generally be viewed as more insightful than home-country management practices.

Porter-Lawler theory   is a motivation theory that hypothesizes that felt needs cause human behavior and that motivation strength is determined primarily by the perceived value of the result of performing the behavior and the perceived probability that the behavior performed will cause the result to materialize.

Position power   is determined by the extent to which the leader has control over the rewards and punishments followers receive; is power derived from the organizational position a manager holds.

Position replacement form   is used in compiling a human resource inventory. It summarizes information about organization members who could fill a position should it open up.

Positive reinforcement   is a reward that consists of a desirable consequence of behavior.

Power   is the extent to which an individual is able to influence others so that they respond to orders.

Prejudice   is a preconceived judgment, opinion, or assumption about an issue, behavior, or group of people.

Probability theory   is a decision-making tool used in risk situations—situations in which decision makers are not completely sure of the outcome of an implemented alternative.

Problem   is any factor within an organization that is a barrier to organizational goal attainment.

Problem-solving team   is an organizational team set up to help eliminate a specified problem within the organization.

Procedure   is a standing plan that outlines a series of related actions that must be taken to accomplish a particular task.

Process control   is a technique that assists in monitoring production processes.

Process (functional) layout   is a layout pattern based primarily on grouping together similar types of equipment.

Process strategy   is an operational plan of action outlining the means and methods an organization will use to transform resources into goods and services.

Process theory of motivation   is an explanation of motivation that emphasizes how individuals are motivated.

Product layout   is a layout designed to accommodate a limited number of different products that require high volumes, highly specialized equipment, and narrow employee skills.

Product life cycle   is made up of the five stages through which most products and services pass: introduction, growth, maturity, saturation, and decline.

Product stages method   predicts future sales by using the product life cycle to better understand the history and future of a product.

Product strategy   is an operational plan of action outlining which goods and services an organization will produce and market.

Production   is the transformation of organizational resources into products.

Productivity   is the relationship between the total amount of goods or services being produced (output) and the organizational resources needed to produce them (input).

Professional will   is a strong and unwavering commitment to do whatever is necessary to build long-term company success.

Profit   is the amount of total revenue that exceeds the total costs of producing the products sold.

Program   is a single-use plan that is designed to carry out a special project within an organization that, if accomplished, will contribute to the organization's long-term success.

Program evaluation and review technique (PERT)   is a scheduling tool that is essentially a network of project activities showing estimates of time necessary to complete each activity and the sequence of activities that must be followed to complete the project.

Programmed decision   is a decision that is routine and repetitive and that typically requires specific handling methods.

Programmed learning   is a technique for instructing without the presence or intervention of a human instructor. Small amounts of information requiring responses are presented to individual trainees, and the trainees determine from comparing their responses to provided answers whether their understanding of the information is accurate.

Punishment   is the presentation of an undesirable behavior consequence or the removal of a desirable behavior consequence that decreases the likelihood that the behavior will continue.

Pure-breakdown (repair) policy   is a maintenance control policy that decrees that machine adjustments, lubrication, cleaning, parts replacement, painting, and needed repairs and overhaul will be performed only after facilities or machines malfunction.

Pure-preventive maintenance policy   is a maintenance control policy that tries to ensure that machine adjustments, lubrication, cleaning, parts replacement, painting, and needed repairs and overhauls will be performed before facilities or machines malfunction.

Quality   is the extent to which a product reliably does what it is intended to do.

Quality assurance   is an operations process involving a broad group of activities aimed at achieving an organization's quality objectives.

Quality circle   is a small group of workers that meets to discuss quality-related problems in a particular project and to communicate their solutions to these problems to management at a formal presentation session.

Quality dimension of organization culture   is an element of organization culture that focuses on making sure that a product, in the opinion of the customer, does what it is supposed to do.

Question mark   is an SBU that has a small share of a high-growth market.

Ratio analysis   is a control tool that summarizes the financial position of an organization by calculating ratios based on various financial measures that appear on the organization's balance sheet and income statements.

Rational decision-making process   comprises the steps the decision maker takes to arrive at a choice.

Recruitment   is the initial attraction and screening of the supply of prospective human resources available to fill a position.

Regression method predicts future sales by analyzing the historical relationship between sales and time.

Relatedness need is the need for satisfying interpersonal relationships.

Relevant alternative is an alternative that is considered feasible for solving an existing problem and for implementation.

Repatriation is the process of bringing individuals who have been working abroad back to their home country and reintegrating them into the organization's home-country operations.

Resolving is a technique for managing conflict by working out the differences between managers and employees.

Responsibility is the obligation to perform assigned activities.

Responsibility gap exists when certain organizational tasks are not included in the responsibility area of any individual organization member.

Retrenchment is a strategy adopted by management to strengthen or protect the amount of business a strategic business unit is currently generating.

Reverse discrimination is the term used to describe inequities affecting members of the majority group as an outcome of programs designed to help underrepresented groups.

Reverse mentoring is a process that pairs a senior employee with a junior employee for the purpose of transferring work skills, such as Internet skills, from the junior employee to the more senior employee.

The Rights Standard is a guideline that says that behavior is generally considered ethical if it respects and promotes the rights of others.

Risk refers to situations in which statistical probabilities can be attributed to alternative potential outcomes.

Robotics is the study of the development and use of robots.

Role conflict is the conflict that results when a person has to fill competing roles because of membership in two cultures.

Role overload refers to having too many expectations to comfortably fulfill.

Rule is a standing plan that designates specific required actions.

Salesforce estimation method predicts future sales levels primarily by asking appropriate salespeople for their opinions of what will happen to sales in the future.

Satisfice occurs when an individual makes a decision that is not optimal but is "good enough."

Scalar relationship refers to the chain-of-command positioning of individuals on an organization chart.

Scheduling is the process of formulating a detailed listing of activities that must be accomplished to attain an objective, allocating the resources necessary to attain the objective, and setting up and following time tables for completing the objective.

Scientific management emphasizes the "one best way" to perform a task.

Scope of the decision is the proportion of the total management system that a particular decision will affect. The broader the scope of a decision, the higher the level of the manager responsible for making that decision.

Security or safety need is Maslow's second set of human needs, which reflects the human desire to be free from physical harm.

Selection is choosing an individual to hire from all those who have been recruited.

Self-actualization need is Maslow's fifth, and final, set of human needs, which reflects the human desire to maximize personal potential.

Self-managed team is an organizational team that plans, organizes, influences, and controls its own work situation with only minimal intervention and direction from management.

Serial transmission involves passing information from one individual to another in a series.

Servant leadership is an approach to leading in which leaders view their primary role as helping followers in their quests to satisfy personal needs, aspirations, and interests.

Signal is a message that has been transmitted from one person to another.

Single-use plan is a plan used only once—or, at most, several times—because it focuses on unique or rare situations within the organization.

Situational approach to leadership is a relatively modern view of leadership that suggests that successful leadership requires a unique combination of leaders, followers, and leadership situations.

Social audit is the process of measuring the present social responsibility activities of an organization. It monitors, measures, and appraises all aspects of an organization's social responsibility performance.

Social entrepreneurship involves the recognition, evaluation, and exploitation of opportunities that create social value as opposed to personal or shareholder wealth.

Social need is Maslow's third set of human needs, which reflects the human desire to belong, including longings for friendship, companionship, and love.

Social networks represent individuals' patterns of social relationships.

Social responsibility is an approach to meeting social obligations that considers business as having both economic and societal goals.

Social responsiveness is the degree of effectiveness and efficiency an organization displays in pursuing its social responsibilities.

Social value refers to the basic, long-standing needs of society and has little to do with profits.

Social values are the relative degrees of worth a society places on the manner in which it exists and functions.

Sociogram is a sociometric diagram that summarizes the personal feelings of organization members about the people in the organization with whom they like to spend free time.

Sociometry is an analytical tool that can be used to determine what informal groups exist in an organization and who the leaders and members of those groups are.

Source/encoder is the person in the interpersonal communication situation who originates and encodes information to be shared with others.

Span of management is the number of individuals a manager supervises.

Spirituality dimension of organization culture is an aspect of organization culture that encourages organization members to integrate spiritual life and work life.

Stability is a strategy adopted by management to maintain or slightly improve the amount of business that a strategic business unit is generating.

Staff authority consists of the right to advise or assist those who possess line authority as well as other staff personnel.

Stakeholder is an individual or group that is directly or indirectly affected by an organization's decisions.

Standard is the level of activity established to serve as a model for evaluating organizational performance.

Standing plans are plans that are used over and over because they focus on organizational situations that occur repeatedly.

Star is an SBU that has a large share of a high-growth market and typically needs large amounts of cash to support rapid and significant growth.

Statistical quality control is the process used to determine how many products should be inspected to calculate a probability that the total number of products will meet organizational quality standards.

Stereotype is a positive or negative assessment of members of a group or their perceived attributes.

Storming, the second stage of the team development process, is characterized by conflict and disagreement as team members try to clarify their individual roles and challenge the way the team functions.

Strategic business unit (SBU) is, in business portfolio analysis, a significant organizational segment that is analyzed to develop organizational strategy aimed at generating future business or revenue. SBUs vary in form, but all are a single business (or collection of businesses), have their own competitors and a manager accountable for operations, and can be independently planned for.

Strategic control is the last step of the strategy management process and consists of monitoring and evaluating the strategy management process as a whole to ensure that it is operating properly.

Strategic management is the process of ensuring that an organization possesses and benefits from the use of an appropriate organizational strategy.

Strategic planning is long-range planning that focuses on the organization as a whole.

Strategic renewal occurs when a firm attempts to alter its own competitive strategy.

Strategy is a broad and general plan developed to reach long-term objectives; it is the end result of strategic planning.

Strategy formulation is the process of determining appropriate courses of action for achieving organizational objectives and thereby accomplishing the organizational purpose. Strategy development tools include critical question analysis, SWOT analysis, business portfolio analysis, and Porter's Model for Industry Analysis.

Strategy implementation is the fourth step of the strategy management process and involves putting formulated strategy into action.

Stress is the bodily strain that an individual experiences as a result of coping with some environmental factor.

Stressor is an environmental demand that causes people to feel stress.

Structural change is a change aimed at increasing organizational effectiveness through modifications to the existing organizational structure.

Structural factors are organizational controls, such as policies and procedures.

Structure refers to the designated relationships among resources of the management system.

Structure behavior is leadership activity that (1) delineates the relationship between the leader and the leader's followers or (2) establishes well-defined procedures that the followers should adhere to in performing their jobs.

Successful communication refers to an interpersonal communication situation in which the information the source intends to share with the destination and the meaning the destination derives from the transmitted message are the same.

Succession planning is the process of determining who will follow whom in various organizational positions.

Supplier power denotes the power that suppliers have over the firms operating in an industry; as supplier power increases, industry attractiveness decreases.

Supportive behavior is aimed at being friendly with followers and showing interest in them as human beings.

Sustainability is the degree to which a person or entity can meet its present needs without compromising the ability of other people or entities to meet their needs in the future.

Sustainable organization is an organization that has the ability to meet its present needs without compromising the ability of future generations to meet their needs.

Sustained regeneration occurs when firms develop new cultures, processes, or structures to support new product innovations in current markets as well as introduce existing products into new markets.

SWOT analysis is a strategic development tool that matches internal organizational strengths and weaknesses with external opportunities and threats.

Symptom is a sign that a problem exists.

System is a number of interdependent parts functioning as a whole for some purpose.

System approach to management is a management approach based on general system theory—the theory that to understand fully the operation of an entity, the entity must be viewed as a system.

Tactical planning is short-range planning that emphasizes the current operations of various parts of an organization.

Task group is a formal group of organization members who interact with one another to accomplish nonroutine organizational tasks. Members of any one task group can come from various levels in the organizational hierarchy.

Task-related activities are management efforts aimed at carrying out critical management-related duties in organizations.

Task structure is the degree to which the goals—the work to be done—and other situational factors are outlined clearly.

Team is a group whose members influence one another toward the accomplishment of an organizational objective(s).

Technical skills are skills involving the ability to apply specialized knowledge and expertise to work-related techniques and procedures.

Technological change is a type of organizational change that emphasizes modifying the level of technology in the management system.

Technological factors are any types of equipment or processes that assist organization members in the performance of their jobs.

Technology consists of any type of equipment or process that organization members use in the performance of their work.

Testing is examining human resources for qualities relevant to performing available jobs.

Theory X is a set of essentially negative assumptions about human nature.

Theory Y is a set of essentially positive assumptions about human nature.

Theory Z is an effectiveness dimension that implies that managers who use either Theory X or Theory Y assumptions when dealing with people can be successful, depending on their situation.

Third-country national is an organization member who is a citizen of one country and who works in another country for an organization headquartered in still another country.

Threat of new entrants refers to the ability of new firms to enter an industry; as the threat of new entrants increases, the attractiveness of the industry decreases.

Threat of substitute products refers to the extent to which customers use products or services from another industry instead of the focal industry. As the threat of substitutes increases, which implies that customers have more choices, the attractiveness of the industry decreases.

Tokenism refers to being one of the few members of your group in the organization.

Total cost is the sum of fixed costs and variable costs.

Total power is the entire amount of power an individual in an organization possesses. It is made up of position power and personal power.

Total quality management (TQM) is the continuous process of involving all organization members in ensuring that every activity related to the production of goods or services has an appropriate role in establishing product quality.

Total revenue is all sales dollars accumulated from selling manufactured products or services.

Training is the process of developing qualities in human resources that will enable them to be more productive and thus to contribute more to organizational goal attainment.

Training needs are the information or skill areas of an individual or group that require further development to increase the productivity of that individual or group.

Trait approach to leadership is an outdated view of leadership that sees the personal characteristics of an individual as the main determinants of how successful that individual could be as a leader.

Transformational leadership is leadership that inspires organizational success by profoundly affecting followers' beliefs in what an organization should be as well as their values, such as justice and integrity.

Transnational organization, also called a global organization, views the entire world as its business arena.

Triangular management is a management approach that emphasizes using information from the classical, behavioral, and management science schools of thought to manage the open management system.

Triple bottom-line emphasizes that managers should focus on building organizations that are sustainable in economic, environmental, and societal activities.

Uncertainty refers to situations where the probability that a particular outcome will occur is not known in advance.

Unhealthy organization culture is an organization culture that does not facilitate the achievement of the organization's mission and objectives.

Unity of command is the management principle that recommends that an individual have only one boss.

Unsuccessful communication refers to an interpersonal communication situation in which the information the source intends to share with the destination and the meaning the destination derives from the transmitted message are different.

The Utilitarian Standard is a guideline that indicates that behavior can generally be considered ethical if it provides the most good for or does the least harm to the greatest number of people.

Value is a person's or social group's belief in which they have an emotional investment.

Value analysis is a cost control and cost reduction technique that examines all the parts, materials, and functions of an operation to help managers control operations.

Values statement is a formally drafted document that summarizes the primary values within the culture of a specific organization.

Variable budget (also known as a flexible budget) is one that outlines the levels of resources to be allocated for each organizational activity according to the level of production within the organization.

Variable cost is an expense that fluctuates with the number of products produced.

Venture capitalists are firms that raise money from investors and then use this money to make investments in new firms.

Verbal communication is the sharing of information through words, either written or spoken.

Vertical dimensioning refers to the extent to which an organization uses vertical levels to separate job responsibilities.

Virtual corporation is an organization that extends significantly beyond the boundaries and structure of a traditional organization by comprehensively "tying together" its stakeholders—employees, suppliers, and customers—via an elaborate system of e-mail and other Internet-related vehicles such as videoconferencing.

Virtual office is a work arrangement that extends beyond the structure and boundaries of the traditional office arrangement.

Virtual organization is an organization having the essence of a traditional organization but lacks some aspect of traditional boundaries and structure.

Virtual teams are groups of employees formed by managers that extend beyond the boundaries and structure of traditional teams in that members in geographically dispersed locations "meet" via realtime messaging on an intranet or the Internet to discuss special or unanticipated organizational problems.

Virtual training is a training process that extends beyond the boundaries and structure of traditional training.

The Virtue Standard is a guideline that determines behavior to be ethical if it reflects high moral values.

Vroom expectancy theory is a motivation theory that hypothesizes that felt needs cause human behavior and that motivation strength depends on an individual's degree of desire to perform a behavior.

Vroom-Yetton-Jago (VYJ) model of leadership is a modern view of leadership that suggests that successful leadership requires determining, through a decision tree, what style of leadership will produce decisions that are beneficial to the organization and will be accepted and committed to by subordinates.

Whistle-blower is the employee who reports the alleged activities of suspected misconduct or corruption within an organization.

Whistle-blowing is the act of an employee reporting suspected misconduct or corruption believed to exist within an organization.

Work measurement methods are operational tools that are used to establish labor standards.

Work methods analysis is an operational tool used to improve productivity and ensure the safety of workers.

Work team is a task group used in organizations to achieve greater organizational flexibility or to cope with rapid growth.

Workplace bullying refers to individuals being isolated or excluded socially and having their work efforts devalued.

Zero-base budgeting requires managers to justify their entire budget request in detail rather than simply refer to budget amounts established in previous years.

Author Index

Figures are indicated by "*f*" and tables by "*t*."

Subject Index